Prepare with The Power of Classroom Practice

Register for **MyEducationLab**
today at www.myeducationlab.com

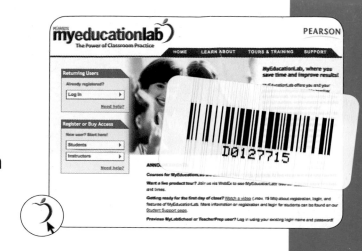

What is MyEducationLab?

MyEducationLab is easy to use and integrate into this book. Wherever you see the MyEducationLab logo in the margins or elsewhere in the text, follow the simple instructions to access the videos, strategies, cases, and artifacts associated with these assignments, activities, and learning units on MyEducationLab. MyEducationLab is organized topically to enhance the coverage of the core concepts discussed in the chapters of your book. For each topic on the course you will find most or all of the following resources:

Students:

• Take **Practice Tests** for each chapter of your text.
  – Completion of each practice test generates a **study plan** that is unique to you.
  – The study plan links to text excerpts, activities with feedback, and videos and other media that can help you master concepts covered in your text.

• Complete **Assignments and Activities** to apply text content to real classroom situations.

• Explore the **Building Teaching Skills and Dispositions** exercises to practice and strengthen the skills that are essential to teaching.

MyEducationLab offers:

• Authentic **classroom video** shows real teachers and students interacting, and helps prepare you for the classroom.

• **Case studies** offer real-life perspectives on common issues and challenges faced in the classroom.

• Authentic student and teacher **classroom artifacts** provide you with the actual types of materials encountered every day by teachers.

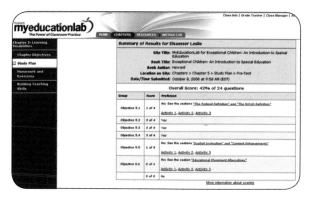

CONNECTION TO NATIONAL STANDARDS: Now it is easier than ever to see how coursework is connected to national standards. Each topic on MyEducationLab lists intended learning outcomes connected to the appropriate national standards. And all of the Assignments and Activities and all of the Building Teaching Skills and Dispositions in MyEducationLab are mapped to the appropriate national standards and learning outcomes.

ASSIGNMENTS AND ACTIVITIES: Designed to save instructors preparation time and enhance student understanding, these assignable exercises show concepts in action (through video, cases, and/or student and teacher artifacts). They help students synthesize and apply concepts and strategies they read about in the book.

BUILDING TEACHING SKILLS AND DISPOSITIONS

These learning units help students practice and strengthen skills that are essential to quality teaching. Students are presented with the core skill or concept and then given an opportunity to practice their understanding of this concept multiple times by watching video footage (or interacting with other media) and then critically analyzing the strategy or skill presented.

STUDY PLAN

A MyEducationLab Study Plan is a multiple choice assessment tied to chapter objectives and supported by study material. A well-designed Study Plan offers multiple opportunities to fully master required course content as identified by the objectives in each chapter:

- **Chapter Objectives** identify the learning outcomes for the chapter and give students targets to shoot for as they read and study.
- **Multiple Choice Assessments** assess mastery of the content. These assessments are mapped to chapter objectives, and students can take the multiple choice quiz as many times as they want. Not only do these quizzes provide overall scores for each objective, but they also explain why responses to particular items are correct or incorrect.
- **Study Material: Review, Practice and Enrichment** give students a deeper understanding of what they do and do not know related to chapter content. This material includes text excerpts, activities that include hints and feedback, and interactive multi-media exercises built around videos, simulations, cases, or classroom artifacts.
- **Flashcards** help students study the definitions of the key terms within each chapter.

GENERAL RESOURCES ON YOUR MYEDUCATIONLAB COURSE

The Resources section on MyEducationLab is designed to help students pass their licensure exams, put together effective portfolios and lesson plans, prepare for and navigate the first year of their teaching careers, and understand key educational standards, policies, and laws. This section includes:

- **Licensure Exams:** Contains guidelines for passing the Praxis exam. **The Practice Test Exam** includes practice multiple-choice questions, case study questions, and video case studies with sample questions.
- **Lesson Plan Builder:** Helps students create and share lesson plans.
- **Licensure and Standards:** Provides links to state licensure standards and national standards.
- **Beginning Your Career:** Educate Offers tips, advice, and valuable information on:

   o Resume Writing and Interviewing: Expert advice on how to write impressive resumes and prepare for job interviews.
   o Your First Year of Teaching: Practical tips on setting up a classroom, managing student behavior, and planning for instruction and assessment.
   o Law and Public Policies: Includes specific directives and requirements educators need to understand under the No Child Left Behind Act and the Individuals with Disabilities Education Improvement Act of 2004.

What if I need help?

We've got you covered 24/7.
There is a wealth of helpful information on the site, under "Tours and Training "and" Support."
Technical support is available 24 hours a day, seven days a week, at http://247pearsoned.custhelp.com.

Visit **www.myeducationlab.com** for a demonstration of this exciting new online teaching resource.

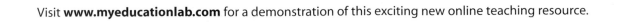

Becoming a
PROFESSIONAL
in the 21st Century

Like their students, teachers need knowledge and skills to succeed. Readers of this text will develop 21st century teaching skills through these interactive features and topics:

- **Understanding how technology influences learning** – "Teaching and Technology" (Sections integrated throughout the text)

- **Using technology to develop professionally** – MyEducationLab (Integrated throughout the text)

- **Understanding student diversity** – "Exploring Diversity" (Integrated throughout the text, plus three chapters on student diversity)

- **Becoming self-directed professionals** – "Decision Making" (Integrated throughout the text)

- **Examining their own beliefs** – "This I Believe" (Interactive feature frames every chapter)

- **Becoming knowledgeable about current issues** – "Taking a Stand in an Era of Reform" (Interactive feature in every chapter)

■ ■ TECHNOLOGY AND TEACHING Cyber-Bullying

The growing presence of the Internet in students' lives has resulted in **cyber-bullying**, a new form of bullying that occurs when students use electronic media to harass or intimidate other students. Concerns about cyber-bullying peaked in 2006, when a 13-year-old Missouri teenager committed suicide after receiving harassing messages on the Internet. Since then, both school officials and parents have become aware of this growing problem (Stobbe, 2007).

Research suggests that cyber-bullying follows the same patterns as traditional forms of bullying; students who are bullies and victims on the playground play similar roles in cyberspace (Raskauskas & Stoltz, 2007). The anonymity of the Internet distinguishes cyber-bullying from other types, and this anonymity can make bullies more insensitive to the hurtful nature of the bullying incid...

Exploring Diversity

Integration

Laws shape our lives and the ways we educate our students. They also shape the ways we approach diversity in our schools. As educators, one of our goals is to teach students to work with and get along with different kinds of people. In addition, we want to ensure that all students have access to a quality education. **Segregation**, or the separation of students on racial or socioeconomic criteria, creates one obsta...

governments. Mandated busing became the most controversial aspect of this struggle, and was based on the belief that integration was important enough to justify transporting students from their neighborhoods to schools across town. However, parents were upset about both the loss of neighborhood schools and the possibility that their children would be exposed to the drugs, crime, and poverty found in inner-city schools.

Bending to political pressure, federal courts slowly backed away from mandatory busing (Pulliam & Van Patten, 2007). Instead, districts employed a variety of strategies, including magnet schools and transfer programs, to encourage parents to voluntarily send their children to integrated schools.

This approach to integration seemed to work until 2007. In response to parents' objections to busing, school districts in Seattle and Louisville, Kentucky, had designed school desegregation plans based on parental choice. In these plans, more than 90 percent of all students were assigned to their first- or second-choice schools (Wells & Frankenberg, 2007). Some parents objected, however, to the race-based intent of these programs, and the case went all the way to the Supreme Court. The Court ruled that districts cannot take individual students' race into account when assigning them to schools unless the program is specifically designed to remedy the harms of past segregation. Chief Justice Roberts, in defending the 5–4 decision, stated, "The way to stop discrimination on the basis of race is to stop discriminating on the basis of race."

The status of future federal efforts to promote racial integration is unclear. Although the Supreme Court did ban assignment to schools on the basis of race, other districts are successfully de-

signing programs to integrate students on the basis of income or poverty (Kahlenberg, 2006). Because poverty and race frequently occur together (Macionis, 2009), the legal status of these programs is uncertain.

Diversity in Your Classroom

Integration has two goals: to provide all students with access to quality learning environments, and to provide opportunities for people to learn about different cultures and segments of our society.

You can help reach these goals with the decisions you make in your classroom. For example, you can promote a genuine form of integration in your classroom by treating all your students as equitably as possible. This means seating them so they aren't grouped by race or culture, calling on all of them in learning activities, and designing activities and group projects that require students from different racial and ethnic backgrounds to work together. In doing so, students will realize that they're much more alike than they're different, and the barriers that exist among them will gradually break down. In many cases, friendships across racial and cultural lines result from these experiences.

QUESTIONS TO CONSIDER

1. Why is integration important in our society, and why are schools so important in this effort?

2. Why are seemingly simple teacher efforts, such as calling on all students as equitably as possible, effective for promoting integration in classrooms?

myeducationlab To respond to these questions online, explore this topic further, and receive feedback, go to the *Book Specific Resources* section in the MyEducationLab for your course, select your text, and then select *Exploring Diversity* for Chapter 10.

ISSUES IN EDUCATION

Taking a Stand in an Era of Reform

Zero Tolerance

The era of zero tolerance began in 1994 when Congress passed the Gun-Free Schools Act, which required states receiving federal funds to expel for 1 year any student who brought a firearm to school. The Safe and Drug Free Schools and Communities Act broadened the focus from firearms to all weapons and also included expelling students for possessing drugs or drug paraphernalia. This act became part of the No Child Left Behind Act of 2001 and continues to have a powerful effect on school policies.

THE ISSUE

The need for safe schools is obvious, and the premise of zero-tolerance policies—that students who endanger or disrupt the learning environment for the majority of the school population should be removed—is intuitively sensible. Students can't learn if they don't feel both physically and emotionally safe. Parents and other taxpayers rank school safety and drug use as critical problems facing U.S. schools (Bushaw & Gallup, 2008), and zero-tolerance policies are popular. Both teachers (70 percent) and parents (68 percent) judged zero-tolerance policies to be effective deterrents to serious infractions in schools (Public Agenda, 2004).

On the other hand, critics have identified several problems with zero-tolerance policies. First, largely because of zero-tolerance policies, the suspension rate of students has increased dramatically.

A Florida study found a 14 percent increase in school suspensions between 2000 and 2004, almost twice as high as the student population growth (Gewertz, 2006a). One middle school in Dade County, Florida, had an expulsion rate of 34 percent, whereas another—serving essentially the same student population—had a rate of only 2.8 percent (Morgan, 2001). Explanations for these uneven percentages range from higher rates of poverty and misbehavior to inexperienced teachers, crowded classrooms, and academically sterile learning environments.

When they suspend you, you get in more trouble, 'cause you're out in the street. . . . And that's what happened to me once. I got into trouble one day 'cause there was a party, and they arrested everybody in that party. . . . I got in trouble more than I get in trouble at school, because I got arrested and everything. (Skiba & Peterson, 1999, p. 376)

Expelled students typically fall further behind academically, experience sometimes never return to complete school (Reyes, 2006).

Third, the implementation of the policies is inconsistent. Critics point to these disproportionate effect on members of cultural minorities. For example, although African American students in San Francisco made up less than 20 percent of all students, they accounted for more than half of students suspended (Gordon, Della Piana, & Keleher, 2001). A Florida study found a similar pattern: African American students made up nearly more than 20 percent of the student population, but they received nearly half of

out-of-school suspensions (Gewertz, 2006a).

YOU TAKE A STAND

Now it's your turn to take a position on the issue. Do zero-tolerance programs make schools safer and better places to learn, or do the related negative side effects outweigh the benefits?

myeducationlab To explore both sides of this issue and take a stand, select the *Book Specific Resources* section in the MyEducationLab for your course, select your text, and then select *Taking a Stand in an Era of Reform* for Chapter 3.

ISSUES IN EDUCATION

Segregation The separation of students based on racial or socioeconomic criteria.

Knowledge Covered in the PRAXIS™ Principles of Learning and Teaching Tests	Chapter Topic Aligned with Knowledge Covered in the PRAXIS™ Principles of Learning and Teaching Tests
I. STUDENTS AS LEARNERS (APPROXIMATELY 33% OF TOTAL TEST)	
A. Student development and the learning process	**Ch. 1** Creating productive learning environments **Ch. 5** Developmental differences in the classroom **Ch. 8** Early childhood programs, elementary schools, junior highs, middle schools, and high schools What is an effective school? **Ch. 11** Curriculum in elementary, middle, junior high, and high schools **Ch. 12** Developing learner responsibility Developmental differences in students **Ch. 13** Instructional strategies
B. Students as diverse learners	**Ch. 3** Changes in American families The influence of socioeconomic factors on students Changes in our students At-risk students **Ch. 4** Cultural diversity Language diversity Gender **Ch. 5** Developmental differences in the classroom Ability differences Learning styles Students with exceptionalities **Each Chapter** Exploring Diversity
C. Student motivation and the learning environment	**Ch. 1** Creating productive learning environments **Ch. 3** Effective teachers for at-risk students **Ch. 4** Culturally responsive teaching Language diversity in the classroom Gender and classrooms **Ch. 5** Learning styles: Implications for teachers Students with exceptionalities: Implications for teachers **Ch. 12** Creating communities of learners Caring: An essential element in teaching Creating a positive classroom climate **Ch. 13** Student motivation and effective teaching High expectations Modeling and enthusiasm Questioning Effective feedback
II. INSTRUCTION AND ASSESSMENT (APPROXIMATELY 33% OF TOTAL TEST)	
A. Instructional strategies	**Ch. 3** Effective teachers for at-risk students Effective instruction and support **Ch. 4** Culturally responsive teaching Language diversity in the classroom Gender and classrooms **Ch. 5** Learning styles: Implications for teachers Students with exceptionalities: Implications for teachers **Ch. 13** Specifying learning objectives Questioning Direct instruction Lecture discussion Guided discovery Cooperative learning Capitalizing on technology in instruction
B. Planning instruction	**Ch. 1** Creating productive learning environments **Ch. 3** Effective teachers for at-risk students **Ch. 4** Culturally responsive teaching Language diversity in the classroom Gender and classrooms **Ch. 5** Learning styles: Implications for teachers Students with exceptionalities: Implications for teachers **Ch. 11** Curriculum in the elementary schools Curriculum in middle schools Curriculum in junior high and high schools Standards and accountability

The Correlation Matrix for the Praxis Principles of Teaching and Learning Exam continues on page 517. In addition, the Correlation Matrix for the INTASC Standards for Beginning Teachers begins on page 518.

introduction to teaching
BECOMING A PROFESSIONAL

fourth edition

Don Kauchak
University of Utah

Paul Eggen
University of North Florida

Boston   Columbus   Indianapolis   New York   San Francisco   Upper Saddle River
Amsterdam   Cape Town   Dubai   London   Madrid   Milan   Munich   Paris   Montreal   Toronto
Delhi   Mexico City   Sao Paulo   Sydney   Hong Kong   Seoul   Singapore   Taipei   Tokyo

Vice President and Editor in Chief: Jeffery W. Johnston

Acquisitions Editor: Meredith D. Fossel

Development Editor: Amy J. Nelson

Editorial Assistant: Nancy Holstein

Vice President, Director of Marketing: Quinn Perkson

Senior Marketing Manager: Darcy Betts Prybella

Senior Managing Editor: Pamela D. Bennett

Senior Project Manager: Mary M. Irvin

Senior Operations Supervisor: Matt Ottenweller

Senior Art Director: Diane Lorenzo

Text Designer: Candace Rowley

Cover Designer: Diane Lorenzo

Cover Art: Shutterstock

Media Project Manager: Rebecca Norsic

Composition: S4Carlisle Publishing Services

Printer/Binder: Courier Kendallville, Inc.

Cover Printer: Leheigh-Phoenix Color Corp.

Text Font: Times New Roman

Credits and acknowledgments borrowed from other sources and reproduced, with permission, in this textbook appear on appropriate page within text. Photo credits can be found on p. 520.

Every effort has been made to provide accurate and current Internet information in this book. However, the Internet and information posted on it are constantly changing, so it is inevitable that some of the Internet addresses listed in this textbook will change.

Library of Congress Cataloging-in-Publication Data

Kauchak, Donald P.
   Introduction to teaching : becoming a professional / Donald Kauchak, Paul Eggen. — 4th ed.
      p. cm.
   Includes bibliographical references and index.
   ISBN-13: 978-0-13-701232-9
   ISBN-10: 0-13-701232-2
   1. Teachers. 2. Teaching—Vocational guidance. 3. Education—United States. I. Eggen, Paul D.
II. Title.
   LB1775.K37 2011
   371.10023'73—dc22

                                                    2009034122

10 9 8 7 6 5 4 3 2 1

www.pearsonhighered.com

ISBN 13: 978-0-13-701232-9
ISBN 10:   0-13-701232-2

Welcome to the 4th Edition!

This fourth edition of *Introduction to Teaching: Becoming a Professional* continues to introduce beginning education students to the real world of teachers, students, classrooms, and schools through *integrated cases*. This case-based approach maximizes student understanding of new concepts by providing concrete frames of reference throughout each chapter. As in the first three editions, this text continues to highlight the importance of *diversity* and adapting teaching to meet the needs of diverse students. This fourth edition also emphasizes the challenges and rewards of *teaching in urban settings*. This emphasis on understanding the realities of today's students, teachers, classrooms, and schools helps readers answer two fundamental questions:

- Do I want to become a teacher?
- What kind of teacher do I want to become?

A Case-Based Approach

The book introduces readers to the real world of teaching through the use of case studies woven throughout the book. These compelling classroom snapshots help the reader understand new educational concepts by connecting them to the real world of classrooms and schools. Each chapter begins with a case that provides the framework for the discussion that follows. Cases and vignettes are integrated throughout every chapter to provide concrete frames of reference for educational concepts.

New to This Edition!

To help students make critical, personal decisions about becoming professional educators, the fourth edition actively involves students in the decision-making process, helping them to develop their professional teaching identities. With strong coverage of diversity and other hot topics and issues in education today, the fourth edition introduces the following:

- *Chapter 5, Student Diversity: Development, Ability, and Exceptionalities*—This new chapter explains how developmental differences affect teachers as well as students. It also connects developmental differences to ability differences and exceptionalities.

- *Chapter 14, Assessment, Standards, and Accountability*—Students explore a comprehensive and current overview of the issues surrounding these important topics.

- *Teaching in Urban Environments*—Expanded to provide more coverage on this important topic, this integrated discussion introduces students to the challenges and rewards of teaching in urban settings and how effective teachers adapt their teaching to meet the needs of students in urban classrooms.

- *Integrated discussion of technology in every chapter*—Students can now view technology as an integrated piece of the instructional and learning process rather than as a separate entity.

- *Five new ABC News videos*—Linked to MyEducationLab, a total of ten videos allows students to explore current issues in education today such as bilingual education, NCLB, diversity, zero tolerance policies and more! (Chapters 1–6, 9, and 10).

- *Coverage of current topics*—The fourth edition discusses current topics that affect education today, including 21st century skills, merit/performance pay, cyber bullying, the middle school grade dilemma, urban mayoral takeovers, technology access issues, President Obama's plans for education, and more!

- *MyEducationLab*—This online resource offers ready-made assignments and activities set in the context of real classrooms. Fully integrated within the text, it provides opportunities for reflection and practice in an easy-to-assign format. MyEducationLab for this text includes:

  - *Learning Outcomes*—Each topic of MyEducationLab connects intended learning outcomes to INTASC standards.

  - *Building Teaching Skills and Dispositions*—Students can practice and strengthen skills that are essential to teaching. Students are first presented with a core skill, given an opportunity to practice the skill multiple times, and then critically analyze the skill.

  - *Assignments and Activities*—These assignable exercises present content in an active format and provide questions that probe student understanding of a concept or strategy.

  - *Teacher Talk*—Each chapter begins with a Teacher of the Year feature that invites students to go to MyEducationLab to watch these exemplary teachers in their classrooms as they describe their personal reasons for why they teach and what teaching means to them.

  - *Book Specific Resources*—These resources are unique to this book and include:

    - **Study Plan Quiz with Review, Practice and Enrichment**—Includes multiple-choice assessments tied to chapter objectives. Chapter-specific study plans offer multiple opportunities to master course content fully.

    - **Exploring Diversity**—An extension of the book, this feature provides assignable questions to promote student reflection on important diversity issues and their implications for today's classrooms.

    - **Taking a Stand in an Era of Reform**—This popular text feature introduces and explores current reform issues. Through MyEducationLab assignments, the student is encouraged to develop a personal stance on important reform issues and consider their impact on future practice. These reflections can be submitted as assignments or printed for use in a professional portfolio.

    - **Online Portfolio Activites**—Located on MyEducationLab, these activities are connected to INTASC Standards and encourage readers to evaluate their own professional growth. Activities include visiting the websites of professional organizations, beginning work on their philosophy of education, as well as connecting with local districts and state offices of education.

Text Themes

The fourth edition highlights the following themes: Professionalism, Diversity, and Decision Making. You will find the themes integrated into every chapter to provide students with a comprehensive guide to teaching in today's classrooms.

PROFESSIONALISM

Professionalism strongly emphasizes the importance of understanding classroom contexts in the process of becoming a professional. It also emphasizes the ability to use this knowledge to make decisions in complex and ill-defined situations. Students explore what it means to be a professional teacher and apply this understanding to their own careers through the following chapter features:

- *This I Believe*—Students are encouraged to assess their personal beliefs about critical issues in education.

- *Taking a Stand in an Era of Reform*—Students learn about current reform issues and determine their stance on these important topics through assignments available on this text's online resource—MyEducationLab.

- *Decision-Making: Defining Yourself as a Professional*—This feature allows students to decide how to handle a situation related to chapter content and consider its implications for their development as professional educators.

- *Exploring Diversity*—This feature promotes student reflection on important diversity issues and how those issues affect classrooms, and is accompanied by MyEducationLab assignments.

- *NEW! MyEducation-Lab*—Applying content to exercises and activities on this text's online resource gives students the opportunity to develop as a professional educator and experience the situations that teachers experience in today's classrooms.

DIVERSITY

Culture, language, ability differences, gender, development, and exceptionalities are just some of the areas of diversity that require understanding and the ability to adapt classroom practices to maximize student learning. Readers explore today's diverse classrooms and their implications for classroom teaching through:

- *Three Chapters on Diversity:*
  - *Chapter 3, Changes in American Society: Their Influences on Today's Students*
  - *Chapter 4, Student Diversity: Culture, Language, and Gender*
  - NEW! *Chapter 5, Student Diversity: Development, Ability, and Exceptionalities.*
- *Teaching in Urban Environments* chapter discussions
- *Exploring Diversity* features found in every chapter

5
CHAPTER

Student Diversity
Development, Ability, and Exceptionalities

CHAPTER OUTLINE

Developmental Differences in the Classroom
- Dimensions of Development
- Technology and Teaching: Cheating and Plagiarism
- Learner Development: Implications for Teachers
- Taking a Stand in an Era of Reform: Grade Retention

Differences in Ability
- What Is Intelligence?
- Ability Grouping and Tracking: Schools' Responses to Differences in Ability
- Learning Styles

Learners With Exceptionalities
- Federal Laws Change the Way Schools and Teachers Help Students With Exceptionalities
- Dimensions of Exceptionalities
- Students With Exceptionalities: Implications for Teachers
- Exploring Diversity: Employing Technology to Support Learners with Disabilities
- Diversity: The Big Picture

LEARNING OBJECTIVES
After you have completed your study of this chapter, you should be able to:

1. Explain how developmental differences influence students as well as learners. INTASC Standard 2, Knowledge of Human Development and Learning

2. Explain differences in current definitions of intelligence, and describe how schools respond to ability differences. INTASC Standard 3, Adapting Instruction to Learner Needs

3. Explain how schools have changed the ways they help students with exceptionalities. INTASC Standard 3, Adapting Instruction to Learner Needs

What will you encounter when you teach your first class? How will your experience compare to this teacher's?

Malaria Parker, an intern from a nearby university, is ready to teach her first lesson in Mrs. Jenkins's math class. The topic is the decimal system, including a number of place value, such as identifying 3,154 as comprised of 3 "thousands," 1 "hundred," 5 "tens," and 4 "ones." Though she's nervous at the beginning, everything goes smoothly as she illustrates and explains the concept. As Malaria passes out practice worksheets, Mrs. Jenkins walks over to her and whispers, "You're doing great. I need to run down to the office. I'll be right back." The students quickly begin to work, and Malaria's nervousness calms as she circulates among the students, periodically making brief comments and offering suggestions. She notices that some are galloping through the assignment, others need only a hint, and a few seem totally confused. As she works with students, she notices that the quiet of the classroom is turning into a low buzz.

125

"I teach because I love working with people—adults, children, and especially those in the middle. Life is hard for middle schoolers living in that in-between space, and I believe my job, as a teacher, is to guide them through that transition from child to young adult. Middle school students need to feel special and deserve to be surrounded by adults who care about them and understand their needs."

BETH OSWALD, 2008 Teacher of the Year, Wisconsin

myeducationlab To view a video clip of Beth, the 2008 Wisconsin Teacher of the Year, go to Topic 2: Diversity in the MyEducationLab for your course and select Teacher Talk, then Be...

DECISION MAKING

Becoming a professional requires teachers continually to examine their beliefs about themselves as well as their students and make decisions based on those beliefs. The fourth edition provides students with opportunities to construct their own personal, professional identities through interactive activities focused on decision making. The following features, found in every chapter, immerse students in professional decision making:

- *This I Believe*
- *Taking a Stand in an Era of Reform*
- *Exploring Diversity*
- *Decision Making: Defining Yourself as a Professional*

Understand and Learn About Current Issues in Education Today

- **NEW!** *Chapter 14, Assessment, Standards, and Accountability*
- **NEW!** Integrated discussion of technology in every chapter
- **NEW!** *Coverage of current topics:* 21st century skills, merit/performance pay, cyber bullying, middle school grade dilemma, urban mayoral takeovers, technology access issues, President Barack Obama's plan for education, and more!
- *Taking a Stand in an Era of Reform*
- *Teaching in Urban Environments* chapter discussions
- *ABC News videos*

MyEducationLab

THE POWER OF CLASSROOM PRACTICE

"Teacher educators who are developing pedagogies for the analysis of teaching and learning contend that analyzing teaching artifacts has three advantages: it enables new teachers time for reflection while still using the real materials of practice; it provides new teachers with experience thinking about and approaching the complexity of the classroom; and in some cases, it can help new teachers and teacher educators develop a shared understanding and common language about teaching. . . ."[1] As Linda Darling-Hammond and her colleagues point out, grounding teacher education in real classrooms—among real teachers and students and among actual examples of students' and teachers' work—is an important, and perhaps even essential, part of preparing teachers for the complexities of teaching in today's classrooms. For this reason, we have created a valuable, time-saving website—MyEducationLab—that provides you with glimpses of real classrooms that research on teacher education tells us is so important for professional development. The authentic in-class video footage, interactive skill-building exercises and other resources available on MyEducationLab offer you a uniquely valuable teacher education tool.

Instructors will find MyEducationLab easy to use and integrate into courses and assignments. Wherever you see the MyEducationLab logo in the margins or elsewhere in the text, follow the simple instructions to access videos, strategies, cases, and artifacts connected to assignments, activities, and learning units on MyEducationLab. MyEducationLab is organized topically to enhance the coverage of core concepts discussed in the chapters of your book. For each topic on the course you will find the following resources:

Connection to National Standards

Now it is easier than ever to see how your coursework is connected to national standards. In each topic of MyEducationLab you will find intended learning outcomes connected to the appropriate national standards for your course. All of the Assignments and Activities and all of the Building Teaching Skills and Dispositions in MyEducationLab are mapped to corresponding national standards and learning outcomes.

Assignments and Activities

Designed to save instructors preparation time, these assignable exercises show concepts in action through video, cases, and student and teacher artifacts and then provide thought-provoking questions that probe student understanding of these concepts or strategies. (Feedback for these assignments is available to instructors.)

Building Teaching Skills and Dispositions

These learning units help students practice and strengthen skills that are essential to quality teaching. Students are first presented with the core skill or concept and then given an opportunity to develop their understanding of this concept by watching video footage or interacting with other media and then critically analyzing the strategy or skill in classroom contexts.

IRIS Center Resources

The IRIS Center at Vanderbilt University (http://iris.peabody.vanderbilt.edu)—funded by the U.S. Department of Education's Office of Special Education Programs OSEP—develops training enhancement materials for pre-service and in-service teachers. The Center works with experts from across the country to create challenge-based interactive modules, case study units, and podcasts that provide research-validated information about working with students in inclusive settings. This text's MyEducationLab course integrates this information to enhance the content coverage in your book.

---

[1] Darling-Hammond, l., & Bransford, J., Eds.(2005). *Preparing Teachers for a Changing World.* San Francisco: John Wiley & Sons

Teacher Talk

Each chapter in the fourth edition introduces a Teacher of the Year on the first page. Students can go to MyEducationLab to watch exceptional teachers from across the country discussing their classrooms as well as their personal stories of why they teach. This National Teacher of the Year Program is sponsored by the Council of Chief State School Officers (CCSSO) and focuses public attention on teaching excellence.

General Resources on Your MyEducationLab Course

The *Resources* section on your MyEducationLab course is designed to help your students pass their licensure exam, put together an effective portfolio, develop lesson plans, prepare for and navigate their first year of teaching, and understand key educational standards, policies, and laws. This section includes:

- *Licensure Exams*: Students can access guidelines for passing the Praxis exam, as well as state-specific tests. The *Practice Test Exam* includes practice questions, *Case Histories*, and *Video Case Studies*.
- *Portfolio Builder and Lesson Plan Builder*: Students can create, update, and share portfolios and lesson plans.
- *Preparing a Portfolio*: Students can access guidelines for creating a high-quality teaching portfolio that will allow them to document their growth as professional educators.
- *Licensure and Standards*: Links to state licensure standards and national standards provide a helpful reference resource.
- *Beginning Your Career*: Students can explore valuable information, advice and access tips on the following:
  - Resume Writing and Interviewing: Expert advice on how to write effective resumes and prepare for job interviews.
  - Your First Year of Teaching: Practical tips on how to set up a classroom, manage student behavior, and learn to organize for instruction and assessment.
  - Law and Public Policies: Specific directives and requirements students need to understand the No Child Left Behind Act and the Individuals with Disabilities Education Improvement Act of 2004.
  - Professional Organizations: Students can explore a list of web links that take them to 40 professional organizations for educators.
  - Teaching Job Web Sites: Students can visit the state departments of education web site for all 50 states.

Book-Specific Resources

TAKING A STAND IN AN ERA OF REFORM

Students learn about current reforms within this text feature and then go to MyEducationLab to explore different perspectives on the issue and determine their personal stance on these important changes in education. Students receive structured hints to help them analyze both sides of an issue to help decide how the issue will affect their professional lives. Students receive immediate feedback once they submit their response.

EXPLORING DIVERSITY

Through this feature, students examine and consider diversity issues and their implications for today's classrooms. Students apply these issues to their own teaching through assignable activities on MyEducationLab where they receive hints and feedback.

STUDY PLAN

The MyEducationLab Study Plan provides multiple choice assessments tied to chapter objectives and are supported by study materials. A well-designed Study Plan offers multiple opportunities to fully master required course content targeted by objectives in each chapter:

- *Learning Outcomes* identify important learning outcomes for each chapter and provide focus for students as they read and study.
- *Multiple Choice Assessment*s, tied to each chapter's objectives, assess mastery of content through exercises that students can take as many times as needed. These quizzes provide overall scores for each objective and also explain why responses to particular items are correct or incorrect.
- *Study Material: Review, Practice and Enrichment* resources provide students with a deeper understanding of chapter content. After taking the Multiple Choice Assessment Quiz, students receive information regarding the chapter content on which they still need work. This review material includes text excerpts, activities with hints and feedback, and media assets (video, simulations, and additional cases).
- *Flashcards* help students study the definitions of the key terms within each chapter.

Visit www.myeducationlab.com for a demonstration of this exciting new online teaching resource.

INSTRUCTOR SUPPLEMENTS

The text has the following ancillary materials to assist instructors in their attempts to maximize learning for all students. These instructor supplements are located on the Instructor Resource Center at www.pearsonhighered.com.

- **Instructor's Manual and Test Bank** provides concrete chapter-by-chapter instructional and media resources with full integration of MyEducationLab.
- **PowerPoint Slides** are available to download for each chapter. Presentations include key concept summaries and other aids to help students understand, organize, and remember core concepts and ideas.
- **Pearson MyTest** is a powerful assessment generation program that helps instructors easily create and print quizzes and exams. Questions and tests are authored online, allowing ultimate flexibility and the ability to efficiently create and print assessments anytime, anywhere! Instructors can access Pearson MyTest and their test bank files by going to www.pearsonmytest.com to log in, register, or request access.
- **Online Course Management.** Contact your local Pearson representative to learn how the online and instructor resources available with this book can be customized for delivery through today's popular learning management systems, including BlackBoard, WebCT, and more.

Acknowledgments

A project such as this text is the result of the collective efforts of many people that we would like to both thank and acknowledge. First, special thanks to our editor, Meredith Fossel, who helped us turn our ideas into a viable project. Amy Nelson, our developmental editor, brought energy and dedication to the project and has always been a supportive advocate for this book. Melissa Grusz, our copy editor, made this the cleanest and clearest edition yet. Mary Irvin, our production editor, conscientiously steered the final project to completion, ensuring the highest level of text quality. Darcy Betts, our link to instructors, helped us craft our thoughts into a text that will hopefully help teachers develop to their fullest potential. We are deeply grateful for all their efforts.

In addition we would like to acknowledge all the reviewers who helped us understand what students and instructors need and want: Allan F. Cook, University of Illinois at Springfield; Elizabeth DeGiorgio, Mercer County Community College; Cindi H. Fries, Northeastern State University; Carol Higy, University of North Carolina, Pembroke; Doris G. Johnson, Wright State University; Mike Kelly, Dominican College; Thomas Kopp, Miami University; Janice Elaine Lupton, Texas Tech University; Cahndice Matthews, Clarion University of Pennsylvania; and Debra Pratt, Purdue University, North Central.

Finally, we would appreciate your feedback about the text, as well as any of the supplements that accompany it. Please feel free to contact either of us at don.kauchak@gmail.com or peggen@comcast.net. We promise to respond to you.

About the Authors

DON KAUCHAK   Don has taught and worked in schools in nine different states and in higher education for 35 years. He has published in a number of scholarly journals, including the *Journal of Educational Research, Journal of Teacher Education, Teaching and Teacher Education, Phi Delta Kappan,* and *Educational Leadership.* In addition to this text, he has co-authored or co-edited six other books on education. He has also been a principal investigator on federal and state grants examining teacher development and evaluation practices, and presents regularly at the American Educational Research Association.

Don strongly believes in the contribution that public schools make to our democracy, and his two children benefited greatly from their experiences in state-supported K–12 schools and public institutions of higher education.

PAUL EGGEN   Paul has worked in higher education for 35 years. He is a consultant to public schools in his university's service area and has provided support to teachers in 12 different states. Paul has also worked with teachers in international schools in 23 countries, including ones in Africa, South Asia, the Middle East, Central America, South America, and Europe. He has published several articles in national journals, is the co-author or co-editor of six other books, and presents regularly at national and international conferences.

Paul is strongly committed to public education. His wife is a middle school teacher in a public school; his two children are graduates of public schools and state-supported universities.

PART 2 **STUDENTS 67**

CHAPTER 7

Educational Philosophy: The Intellectual Foundations of American Education 194

CHAPTER 8

The Organization of American Schools 222

PART 4 TEACHING 317

11

CHAPTER 11

The School Curriculum in an Era of Standards and Accountability 318

CHAPTER 14

Assessment, Standards, and Accountability 410

14

1  Do I Want to Be a Teacher?

2  Developing as a Professional

"If you're watching this and you're thinking of teaching, join us. We need the best and the brightest in our profession. And I guarantee, at the end of the day, you'll feel like you made a difference. Of course, I'm a little biased. I'm a teacher."

ERIC LANGHORST, 2008 Teacher of the Year, Missouri

To view a video clip of Eric, the 2008 Missouri Teacher of the Year, go to Topic 1: *The Teaching Profession*, in the MyEducationLab for your course and select *Teacher Talk* then, *Eric Langhorst*.

Do I Want to Be a Teacher?

LEARNING OBJECTIVES

After you have completed your study of this chapter, you should be able to:

1. **Describe major rewards and challenges of teaching.** INTASC Standard 9, Teacher Professionalism

2. **Describe the essential characteristics of professionalism, and explain how they relate to teaching.** INTASC Standard 9, Teacher Professionalism

3. **Identify different dimensions of diversity and explain how diversity affects the lives of teachers.** INTASC Standard 3, Adapting Instruction to Learner Needs

4. **Explain how the current reform movement in education is changing the teaching profession.** INTASC Standard 9, Teacher Professionalism

"Do I want to be a teacher?" This question is probably on your mind as you begin your study of this book. In this chapter, we'll help you begin answering this question by providing you with information about the teaching profession and what your life might be like as a teacher. As you read the following case studies, think about each teacher's experiences and how they compare to your own.

I always liked working with kids. I enjoyed watching my little brother when my mom ran errands, and I often helped out with summer youth programs.
In high school I started thinking about being a music teacher, since I enjoyed playing the piano and singing in choral groups.

Then, I went to college and one of my courses required us to be a high school teacher's aide. I worked with a music teacher but never felt like I really fit in. Luckily, in a second course I had a chance to work in an elementary school. I went home after the first day and thought, "Yes, this is it."

There have been ups and downs, of course. My first job was in an urban second-grade classroom with 26 kids. Fortunately, I had an aide who spoke Spanish, and she was a huge help, since several of my students were still struggling to learn English.

Now here I am, 10 years later, married with a family of my own, and I still love teaching. The first few years were a struggle at times, but I learned so much. Now I've got my own student teacher, and I'm eager to help her figure it all out. (Amy Carson, first-grade teacher in an urban elementary school)

Before I became a teacher, I worked for 20 years in the pharmaceutical industry, first in a research lab and then as a project manager. It was challenging, and I made a good salary, but I began to feel that there was more to life than making money for some big company.

A couple years ago I read a book in which the author described the difference between a person's "job" and a person's "work." Your job is how you make money; your work is how you contribute to the world. It began to crystallize everything for me. Business, for me, was a job, but I didn't really have any "work."

Then, I thought about my high school chemistry teacher, and I remembered how much he loved that stuff. I began to think about teaching, and, to make a long story short, I went back to school, and this time I did what I've always wanted to do. Of course it's tough some days. The kids can be "off the wall," and I periodically feel like I'm drowning in paperwork. But, when you see the light bulb go on for someone, it's all worth it. Now, my job and my work are the same thing. (Matt Shepard, high school science teacher in a suburban high school and recent entry into teaching)

Some of you probably are similar to Amy or Matt. You're intelligent and introspective, and you've had a number of life experiences. You've thought about teaching but aren't sure if it's for you or where you might fit in it. Others are less certain, because you're still in the process of deciding what you want to do with your life. You enjoyed your school experiences, and most of your ideas about teaching are based on them. The idea of working with young people is attractive, but you're still not sure.

To begin answering the question "Do I want to be a teacher?" we invite you to consider some reasons people go into teaching by responding to the accompanying questionnaire in the *This I Believe* feature on page 5.

We gave this survey to other prospective teachers, averaged their responses, and ranked them from most (1) to least (7) important reasons for becoming a teacher. Table 1.1 summarizes the results. Let's see how yours compare.

You see from Table 1.1 that the desire to work with young people (Item 3) and wanting to contribute to society (Item 4) were survey participants' two most important reasons for considering teaching. These reasons are consistent with Amy's and Matt's thinking as well as polls of teachers over nearly 25 years, as well as polls of teachers in other countries (Watt & Richardson, 2007).

A Public Agenda poll of new teachers found similar results, with nearly 9 of 10 viewing teaching as "a true sense of calling," 3 of 4 considering teaching a lifelong choice, and nearly 70 percent reporting teaching as very satisfying. In addition, an amazing 96 percent of beginning teachers reported that teaching is work they love to do (Wadsworth, 2001).

REWARDS AND CHALLENGES IN TEACHING

As these polls suggest, people go into teaching because they find it rewarding. As with any occupation, however, it can also be challenging. Let's look at some of the rewards and challenges in teaching.

For each item, circle the number that best represents your thinking. Use the following scale as a guide.

4 = I strongly believe the statement is true.
3 = I believe the statement is true.
2 = I believe the statement is false.
1 = I strongly believe the statement is false.

1. Job security is a major reason I'm considering becoming a teacher.

    1   2   3   4

2. Long summer vacations are important to me as I consider teaching as a career.

    1   2   3   4

3. My desire to work with young people is an important reason I'm considering becoming a teacher.

    1   2   3   4

4. I'm thinking of teaching because I'd like to contribute to our society.

    1   2   3   4

5. My interest in a subject matter field is a major reason I'm thinking about becoming a teacher.

    1   2   3   4

6. I'm considering entering teaching because of the influence of a former elementary or secondary teacher.

    1   2   3   4

7. I'm considering teaching because of the opportunity for a lifetime of self-growth.

    1   2   3   4

myeducationlab To download and complete this form, go to the *Book Specific Resources* section in the MyEducationLab for your course, select your text, and then select *This I Believe* for Chapter 1.

This I BELIEVE!

Table 1.1   Responses to *This I Believe* Survey

Survey Rank	Item Focus	Average Response of Students	Item Number
1	Work with youth	3.7	3
2	Value to society	3.6	4
3	Self-growth	3.1	7
4	Content interest	3.0	5
5	Influence of teachers	2.9	6
6	Job security	2.5	1
7	Summer vacations	2.3	2

Rewards in Teaching

The rewards in teaching can be either **intrinsic**, existing within oneself and satisfying for emotional or intellectual reasons, or **extrinsic**, coming from the outside, such as job security and vacations.

INTRINSIC REWARDS   Many people enter teaching because of intrinsic rewards. A national survey suggests that teachers as a group are satisfied with the profession, and their level of satisfaction has increased in the last 25 years (MetLife, 2009). For example, more than 60 percent of the teachers in the survey reported being very satisfied with their careers, compared to 40 percent in 1984. Other comparisons with teachers in 1984 are also positive. Teachers in the 2009 survey felt better prepared (67% vs. 46%), more respected by society (66% vs. 47%), and more likely to advise young people to pursue a career in

Intrinsic rewards Rewards that come from within oneself and are personally satisfying for emotional or intellectual reasons.

Extrinsic rewards Rewards that come from the outside, such as job security and vacations.

Teachers' interactions with their students provide a major source of intrinsic rewards.

teaching (75% vs. 45%). In addition, more than 8 of 10 teachers in the survey reported that they "love to teach." Many of these perceptions are related to intrinsic rewards, which fall into two broad categories—emotional and intellectual.

Emotional Rewards.   People often go into teaching because they want to interact with young people and help them learn and develop. To illustrate these ideas, let's look at some true stories teachers have shared with us.

Kasia, 23, calls her boyfriend, Jeff. It's "Teacher Appreciation Week" at her middle school, and she has just received a dozen roses from a group of her seventh-grade science students.

"I was always on them about whispering too," she excitedly tells Jeff. "I maybe would have expected something from my fifth-period class, but never from this bunch."

"Let me read the note I got from them," she continues. She reads,

"Thank you for all that you've done for us and for all the wonderful things that you've teached [sic] us. You are truly an amazing teacher. Thank you again."

Happy Teacher Appreciation Week,

Sincerely, Alicia, Rosa, Shannon, Tina, Stephanie, Melissa, Jessica, and Becca

"That's wonderful," Jeff laughs. "Good thing you're not their English teacher."

"I know. I showed Isabel [the students' English teacher] the note, and she broke up. 'So much for grammar,' she said."

Miguel Rodriguez, 42, another middle school teacher, received the following note from one of his students.

Mr. Rodriguez,

I wanted to think of some creative way to thank you for being the best teacher I ever had. (But I couldn't).

Even though all the geography skills I'll ever use in my life I learned in second grade, I just wanted to say thanks for teaching me how to really prepare for life in the years to come.

Every day I looked forward to coming to your class (and not just because of Mike [a boy in the class]). I always enjoyed your class, because there was a hidden message about life in there somewhere.

Your [sic] my very favorite teacher and you've taught me some of the best lessons in life I could ever learn. Thank you so much.

A grateful student,

Erica Jacobs

P.S. No, I didn't write this to raise my grade.

These notes and the flowers Kasia received symbolize some of the emotional rewards you'll encounter in teaching. "They're what keep you going," Miguel commented matter-of-factly while discussing his enjoyment of his work.

Sharon, a veteran first-grade teacher, also describes emotional rewards in her work. "The beginning of the day gets me going," she said, smiling when she described her continued commitment to her career. "I stand at the door, and the kids give me a hug, a high five, or a handshake when they come in the room. Even if the previous day was a bad one, all those little faces are enough to get me started all over again."

Sometimes students show their affection in strange ways, as this teacher experienced:

Joanne, a first-year teacher, entered her classroom first thing in the morning on her birthday. Her students had arranged with the custodian to gain access to her room and had moved all the desks to the center of the room and had wrapped them with tape and toilet paper. How would you react?

Joanne was delighted. "I called [the perpetrators] out of class and had them come down and [another teacher] took a picture of them standing out in the middle of it all. I left it here all day. I made them sit on the floor. It was really fun. It was really a fun day." (Bullough, 1989, p. 86)

It helps to have a sense of humor when you teach. All teachers reap emotional rewards from their work with students, whether they are wide-eyed first graders, middle school students like Erica Jacobs, or high school seniors struggling to become adults.

Intellectual Rewards.   Although emotional rewards motivate them as well, many people choose to teach because they're interested in a certain content area and want to share their interest with others (Liston, 2004).

David Ling, a high school physics teacher, enthusiastically begins his class: "Think about these questions and try to figure out what they have in common," and he then writes the following on the board:

Why do we have seatbelts in our cars?

Why does an automatic washer have holes in the drum?

How does a dog shake the water off itself when it comes out of a pond?

The students look at the list, and after several seconds David continues, "Now, what have we been studying?"

"Inertia," Taneka responds after hesitating briefly.

"Exactly," David says, smiling. "So let's review for a minute. What is inertia? . . . Go ahead, Dana."

"The tendency . . . of something moving to keep on moving . . . straight."

"Or something not moving to remain still," Jamal adds.

"Excellent," David responds with a nod. "Now, let's answer the questions on the board using the idea of inertia."

With David's guidance, students conclude that if cars suddenly stop, their bodies tend to keep moving because of inertia, and seatbelts stop them, so they don't get hurt. They also decide that inertia separates water from clothes in the washer because the water goes straight out through the holes in the drum, but the clothes are kept in it. Finally, they determine that as the dog shakes one way, and then stops, the water keeps moving, and the same thing happens when it shakes the other way. So the dog uses the principle of inertia to shake the water from itself.

"Neat," Rebecca says. "Where'd you get that stuff, Mr. Ling?"

"I just thought up the questions," David replies. "The more I study, the more examples I find. . . . That's what we're here for. We study science so we can learn how the world around us works."

Our survey, discussed earlier (Table 1.1), found that "the opportunity for a lifetime of self-growth" (Item 7) and "interest in a subject matter field" (Item 5) were major reasons for considering teaching, ranking 3 and 4 out of 7. Learning more about the world and seeing students get excited about the same things we do are two of the intellectual rewards of teaching. One teacher candidate commented, "I would like to think that contact with me would . . . deepen their confidence in their own thinking and make them more curious about the world" (P. Richardson & Watt, 2005, p. 485). Not surprisingly, these intellectual rewards also help keep veteran teachers in the field. One researcher

This I BELIEVE

studying exemplary veteran teachers concluded, "Without exception, intellectual stimulation is a burning need of the teachers I interviewed" (Williams, 2003, p. 72).

EXTRINSIC REWARDS   Extrinsic rewards also attract people to teaching. For example, job security and summer vacations ranked sixth and seventh, respectively, in the survey.

The job security found in teaching is greater than in most other occupations. For example, after a short probation period—usually 3 years—teachers are typically awarded tenure. Designed to attract good people and protect them from political pressures, tenure provides teachers with job security.

For some, working in a profession with long vacations is also rewarding. According to an old joke, a student asked to identify three reasons for going into teaching responded, "June, July, and August." In addition, teachers have vacations throughout the year at times when vacations are most attractive—the Friday after Thanksgiving, the winter holiday season, and spring break, for example.

Besides job security and desirable vacations, teachers' work schedules have positive features, and they enjoy high occupational status. For instance, teachers' schedules are similar to those of students, so their own children don't go home to empty houses after school. Additionally, despite perceptions to the contrary, the teaching profession enjoys considerable occupational status (National Education Association, 2002). If you have doubts, consider how parents feel as they approach their first parent–teacher conference: They want nothing more than to hear that everything is okay in school and that their child is growing academically and socially. Into no other profession's hands is so much care of young people placed.

Whether teachers' salaries can be considered an extrinsic reward is often debated (American Federation of Teachers, 2008). They are low compared to other professions, and are often cited as a reason that teachers leave the profession after a few years (Ingersoll & Smith, 2003). Salaries are improving, however. The average teacher salary in the United States for 2006–2007 was $51,009, ranging from a high of $63,640 in California to a low of $35,378 in South Dakota. In the same year, the average beginning salary was slightly more than $35,000. Significantly, one survey indicated that although less than half of teachers were satisfied with their salaries, more than 9 of 10 were satisfied with being a teacher (American Federation of Teachers, 2008).

Your beginning salary will depend on a number of factors, including the location of the school district and the cost of living in your area. Local property taxes are a major funding source for schools, so your salary will depend on property values in your district. Also, urban districts typically have higher salaries than their rural counterparts because of a higher cost of living.

Other economic factors also influence the attractiveness of teaching. For example, annual salary increases are virtually guaranteed, and, as you saw earlier in the chapter, vacation periods are ideal. Medical, dental, and retirement benefits are usually provided, and job security is high. In addition, teachers are often paid supplements for extra duties, such as club sponsorships, coaching, chairing academic departments (e.g., chairing the English department in a middle school), and mentoring beginning teachers. In schools with year-round schedules, teachers work 11 months of the year versus 9 or 10 and are paid accordingly.

Table 1.2 lists the average and beginning teacher salaries for each state in 2006–2007. Take a look at your state and any others that you are considering teaching in. Would you consider these salaries to be a reward or a challenge if you entered the teaching profession?

Challenges in Teaching

Teaching can be rewarding, but it's also challenging. The complexities of classrooms and the multiple roles that teachers perform contribute to those challenges.

Table 1.2   Average and Beginning Teacher Salaries for U.S., 2006–2007

State	Average Salary (Rank)	Beginning Salary (Rank)
Alabama	$43,389 (36)	$35,517 (17)
Alaska	54,678 (11)	42,006 (2)
Arizona	44,700 (31)	35,127 (20)
Arkansas	44,493 (32)	30,510 (37)
California	63,640 (1)	38,875 (9)
Colorado	45,832 (28)	36,211 (15)
Connecticut	61,039 (2)	41,497 (3)
Delaware	54,537 (12)	39,941 (6)
Florida	47,219 (24)	37,600 (12)
Georgia	49,836 (17)	31,659 (29)
Hawaii	51,916 (14)	39,361 (8)
Idaho	45,094 (30)	30,000 (41)
Illinois	58,275 (6)	38,363 (11)
Indiana	47,832 (22)	32,076 (28)
Iowa	42,922 (38)	30,331 (39)
Kansas	43,318 (37)	30,408 (38)
Kentucky	43,787 (35)	31,304 (34)
Louisiana	42,816 (39)	34,410 (22)
Maine	42,103 (42)	28,517 (44)
Maryland	56,927 (8)	40,849 (4)
Massachusetts	58,178 (7)	*
Michigan	55,541 (9)	34,100 (23)
Minnesota	49,719 (18)	33,018 (25)
Mississippi	40,182 (47)	32,141 (26)
Missouri	40,384 (46)	31,285 (35)
Montana	41,146 (44)	27,134 (45)
Nebraska	42,044 (43)	29,215 (42)
Nevada	49,426 (19)	35,480 (18)
New Hampshire	46,797 (25)	30,185 (40)
New Jersey	59,730 (3)	44,523 (1)
New Mexico	42,780 (40)	32,081 (27)
New York	59,557 (4)	39,500 (7)
North Carolina	46,137 (27)	31,478 (31)
North Dakota	38,586 (48)	27,064 (46)
Ohio	53,536 (13)	35,676 (16)
Oklahoma	42,379 (41)	36,278 (14)
Oregon	51,080 (15)	35,400 (19)
Pennsylvania	54,977 (10)	36,599 (13)
Rhode Island	58,420 (5)	34,838 (21)
South Carolina	44,355 (33)	31,336 (33)
South Dakota	35,378 (50)	26,988 (47)
Tennessee	43,815 (34)	33,459 (24)
Texas	45,392 (29)	38,522 (10)
Utah	37,775 (49)	28,653 (43)
Vermont	47,645 (23)	*
Virginia	49,130 (20)	*
Washington	47,880 (21)	31,442 (32)
West Virginia	40,534 (45)	30,626 (36)
Wisconsin	46,707 (26)	31,588 (30)
Wyoming	50,771 (16)	40,084 (5)
U.S. AVERAGE	$51,009	$35,284

Source: American Federation of Teachers (2008).

*Not available

Classrooms are complex learning environments in which many events occur simultaneously.

COMPLEXITIES OF CLASSROOMS "Classrooms are complex" is an understatement; teachers make literally hundreds of decisions every day, and many must be made with nearly split-second timing (Kennedy, 2006). What does it feel like to make these decisions every day? Let's look at several teachers' experiences.

Ken, an elementary teacher, shares the following incident in his teaching journal:

March 3: My class is sitting in a circle. I look up and notice one of the girls, Sylvia, is crying. Joey, she claims, has called her a fat jerk. The rest of the students all look at me to watch my response. I consider the alternatives: send Joey to hallway and talk to him in a few minutes; have Joey sit next to me; ask Joey to apologize; direct Sylvia to get a thick skin; ask Sylvia, "How can you solve this problem?"; send Joey to principal; have Joey write an apology letter; ask Joey, "Why did you do this?"; ignore the situation completely; keep Sylvia and Joey in for recess for dialogue; put Joey's name on the board; yell at Joey; send Sylvia and Joey to hallway to work out problem; tell them to return to their seats and write in journals about problem.

It took me about 10 seconds to run through these alternatives, and after each one I thought of reasons why it wasn't a good idea. By the time I look up at Sylvia after this brief introspection, she had stopped crying and was chattering away with a friend about something else. On surface, the problem had gone away. (Winograd, 1998, p. 296)

Joanne, a first-year middle school English teacher, has the following experience the first day back after a 4-day holiday. The students are excited and difficult to settle down. They talk about their weekends, some wander in late, and others are listless as she tries to get class started.

Finally, she can begin, but keeping them on task is a struggle. They don't listen to her directions, and their questions, complaints, and requests for help seem never-ending.

Joanne limps through the day, and as the end appears in sight, she nearly explodes. While her back is turned, one student throws a sponge ball across the room, another jumps up to catch it and knocks his desk over with a clatter. The rest of the class erupts into laughter, and Joanne says loudly, "Everyone settle down this instant, or there will be after-school detention." This seems to work. "If every day was like this, I'm not sure I would make it," she sighs after her students have finally left for the day.

Two high school student teachers, Cheryl and Dani, discuss their frustrations in taking attendance on the day of a special school dance held during regular class hours:

Cheryl: *One boy comes in, he's dressed up. He says, "I have to go to the dance." Comes In early and tells me. Good kid. I'm like, "OK, that's fine Aaron." Then, Kent comes in five minutes late. This is tall Kent, has his own band and never lets me mark him tardy even though he's always tardy, "I'm going to the dance!" After I've already started class! "Ahem. Thank you, Kent. Please sit down." So he's wanting to leave but I can't let him go because he just interrupted my class and . . . I was so mad at him. So I say, "Do you have a ticket?" And he's like, "Well, yeah," and pulls out a ticket that goes to the movie he went to on Friday night and I say, "No, that's not the right ticket."*

Dani: *What color was it?*

Cheryl: *Pink.*

Dani:	What was the color for the . . . ?
Cheryl:	The other guy who was legit had a gray one. But then, then, I don't know. And I mean WHO KNOWS! I said, "You're not on my excused list" but neither was the other guy and I'm like . . .
Dani:	I didn't even get an excused list! I didn't even know this dance was—I kind of heard something over the intercom. (Dulude-Lay, 2000, p. 4)

Each of these vignettes illustrates the challenging and sometimes frustrating world of teaching. Researchers have identified several characteristics of classrooms that make them complex and demanding (W. Doyle, 2006):

- *Multidimensional:* Large numbers of events and tasks take place because so many people live in a classroom.
- *Simultaneous:* Classroom events and tasks happen at the same time.
- *Immediate:* Events occur rapidly; sometimes too rapidly.
- *Unpredictable:* Classrooms often take unexpected turns.
- *Public:* Teachers perform in "fishbowls" with people constantly observing their actions.

These characteristics are outlined in Figure 1.1 and discussed in the following sections.

Classrooms Are Multidimensional.   Think about the different roles you'll perform today: You're a student, a friend, a coworker, and perhaps even a parent. Your life is multidimensional; a classroom is as well. For instance, while working with one group of students, you'll need to monitor other groups working on assignments; students will request permission for routine activities, such as going to the bathroom; and learners with special needs may be pulled out of your classroom for extra help. Some students will be attentive and involved in your learning activities, whereas others will drift off and may even be disruptive. Ken found this out when he tried to begin his lesson.

Announcements, assemblies, and other school functions add to the complexity. For example, Cheryl and Dani had to adjust their plans because of the dance. "If I only had time to teach," is a common teacher lament.

Classroom Events Are Simultaneous.   Many classroom events occur at the same time. For example, Ken and Joanne had management problems at the same time they were trying to teach. And, as Cheryl and Dani were trying to take roll and begin class, students came in needing immediate attention, asking questions, showing hall passes, and presenting admission slips. Knowing which problem to attend to first can be challenging, if not bewildering.

Classroom Events Are Immediate.   Experts estimate that teachers make somewhere between 800 and 1,500 decisions every day (Jackson, 1968; Murray, 1986). Beyond the sheer numbers, the need to make decisions *right now* adds to the demands on a teacher. Sylvia was crying; Ken needed to decide whether to intervene. Kent came in with a bogus hall pass; Cheryl needed to decide whether to honor it. And they needed to decide "right now." The immediacy of classroom life requires challenging, split-second decision making.

Figure 1.1 Characteristics of Classrooms

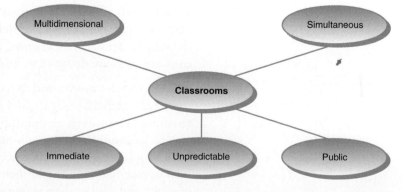

Classrooms Are Unpredictable.

> One first-grade teacher brought a shoe into class, attempting to involve students in a lesson about a story they had read about shoes. Pulling it out of a bag, she began, "What can you tell me about this shoe?"
> "It's red," Mike responded.
> The shoe was black—there was no sign of red on it anywhere!

Effective teachers plan carefully, but even this may not be enough: Planning for this child's response, for example, was impossible. Similarly, Ken couldn't anticipate the incident between Joey and Sylvia, and the same is true for many of the events in Joanne's, Cheryl's, and Dani's classrooms. Often, teachers have little time for thoughtful analysis and consideration of alternatives. After the fact, it's often easy to see what should have been done, but in the heat of the moment, a teacher must respond immediately to unanticipated events. Classrooms are exciting, unpredictable places—one reason people find teaching both exhilarating and challenging.

Classrooms Are Public. The fact that we teach in front of people is obvious. In a sense, we're on stage, and our triumphs and mistakes occur in public for all to see. As we work with students, we are bound to make mistakes, and our actions can have unintended consequences. Ken ignored Joey's (allegedly) calling Sylvia a "fat jerk"; did he unintentionally communicate that verbal abuse is acceptable? Cheryl considered allowing one student to slip out of her class with a bogus pass; if she had, would other students try the same thing? A "fishbowl" is an apt metaphor for teaching: As we swim through our day, both students and other teachers watch us and form judgments about our actions.

Will your first year of teaching necessarily consist of a series of unpredictable situations? Probably. Learning to teach is a journey filled with unanticipated events, and your first year will be exhausting, at times overwhelming, and frequently exhilarating. It may help to remember, however, that thousands of other beginning teachers have not only survived but flourished.

THE MULTIPLE ROLES OF TEACHING   The multiple professional roles that teachers perform is a second factor that makes teaching so challenging. Following are three of the most important roles:

- Creating productive learning environments
- Working with parents and other caregivers
- Collaborating with colleagues

Creating Productive Learning Environments. Creating a productive learning environment is a teacher's most important role. A productive learning environment is one that is safe and inviting, focuses on learning, and provides opportunities for social and personal growth (Watson & Battistich, 2006). In productive learning environments, students feel safe, both physically and emotionally, and the day-to-day routines—including the values, expectations, learning experiences, and both spoken and unspoken rules and conventions—are designed to help students learn and grow (Weinstein, 2007).

Working With Parents and Other Caregivers. Learning should be a cooperative venture, with teachers, students, and parents/caregivers working together. Because the home environment has such a powerful influence on learning, teachers need to develop strategies to increase parental involvement in their children's academic life. These strategies should go beyond traditional once-a-year parent–teacher conferences and should actively involve parents, encouraging them to monitor and help with homework, limit television viewing, and read to their young children (Allen, 2007).

Students benefit from home–school cooperation in several ways:

- Higher long-term achievement
- Greater willingness to do homework
- More positive attitudes and behaviors
- Better attendance and graduation rates
- Higher levels of responsibility and self-regulation
- Increased enrollment in postsecondary education (C. L. Green, Walker, Hoover-Dempsey, & Sandler, 2007; Sheldon, 2007)

These outcomes result from parents' increased participation in school activities, higher expectations for their children's achievement, and teachers' increased understanding of learners' home environments. Deciding how to respond to a student's disruptive behavior, for example, is easier when his teachers know that his mother or father has lost a job, his parents are going through a divorce, or there's an illness in the family.

Parent–teacher collaboration can also have long-term benefits for teachers. Teachers who encourage parental involvement have more positive feelings about teaching and about their school, and they have higher expectations for parents and rate them higher in helpfulness and follow-through (C. Weinstein & Mignano, 2007). Virtually all schools have formal communication channels, such as open houses (usually occurring within the first 2 weeks of the school year when teachers introduce themselves and describe their plans for the school year); interim progress reports, which tell parents about their youngsters' achievements at the midpoint of each grading period; parent–teacher conferences; and, of course, report cards.

Collaborating With Colleagues.   Collaborating with colleagues is a third essential teacher role. Teachers collaborate in decisions about curriculum, assessment, and teaching strategies, and administrators assess teachers' ability and inclination to work with colleagues in the initial job interview. Many principals view collaboration as one of the most essential characteristics of effective teachers.

We said earlier that one goal of this text was to help you decide whether you want to be a teacher. Understanding the rewards and challenges in teaching and the multiple roles you'll play if you choose to teach can help you make this decision.

PEARSON
myeducationlab

To examine the multiple professional roles that teachers perform, go to the *Assignments and Activities* section of Topic 1, *The Teaching Profession*, in the MyEducationLab for your course and complete the activity titled *The Multiple Roles of Teachers*.

■ ■ ■ ■ CHECK YOUR UNDERSTANDING

1.1   What are the major rewards in teaching?

1.2   What are the major challenges in teaching?

1.3   Identify the four most commonly cited reasons people give for entering teaching.

For feedback, go to the appendix, *Check Your Understanding*, located in the back of this text.

THE TEACHING PROFESSION

What does it mean to be a professional, and are teachers professionals? Attempts to answer these questions have increased during the past several years (Labaree, 2005; Neville, Sherman, & Cohen, 2005). Advocates contend that developing teaching into a profession comparable to medicine and law would benefit teachers, students, and their parents; it would mean better preparation programs for teachers, higher standards for performance and ethics, and greater trust in teachers by parents. We believe in the potential of professionalism to transform teaching in many positive ways, and have made it the subtitle and a major theme of this text. Let's examine the issue further.

Characteristics of Professionalism

Researchers, examining established professions such as medicine and law, have concluded that **professionalism** has the following characteristics:

- A specialized body of knowledge
- Autonomy
- Emphasis on decision making and reflection
- Ethical standards for conduct (Labaree, 2004; Neville et al., 2005)

Let's look at them.

Figure 1.2 Professionalism Requires a Specialized Body of Knowledge

A SPECIALIZED BODY OF KNOWLEDGE Professionals understand and utilize a specialized body of knowledge in serving their clients (see Figure 1.2). A physician, for example, understands and recognizes symptoms of diseases and prescribes medications, surgical procedures, or other forms of therapy to eliminate both the symptoms and their causes. People seek the advice and help of physicians because of their specialized knowledge.

Do teachers possess specialized knowledge? Researchers believe the answer is *yes*, and suggest this knowledge exists in four forms (Putnam & Borko, 2000):

- *Knowledge of content:* Research indicates that the more teachers know about a content area, such as algebra, American history, or chemistry, the more effective they are in teaching it (Krauss et al., 2008; T. Smith, Desimone, & Ueno, 2005). Acquiring a deep understanding of the content they teach is one of beginning teachers' biggest challenges. In addition, the No Child Left Behind Act of 2001 requires states to ascertain that teachers demonstrate their knowledge of content in areas they teach.

- *Pedagogical content knowledge:* Knowing a content area well enough to pass a test and being able to teach it require different kinds of knowledge (E. Davis, Petish, & Smithey, 2006). The ability to illustrate abstract concepts, such as equivalent fractions in math or nationalism in history, in ways that are understandable to students reflects **pedagogical content knowledge**.

- *General pedagogical knowledge:* General principles of teaching and learning, such as the ability to maintain an orderly and learning-focused classroom and guide student learning using skilled questioning, constitute general pedagogical knowledge.

- *Knowledge of learners and learning:* Understanding the way people learn and develop, such as that students' powers of attention and memory are sometimes very limited, illustrates knowledge of learners and learning.

Professionalism Trait of an occupation characterized by a specialized body of knowledge with emphasis on autonomy, decision making, reflection, and ethical standards for conduct.

Pedagogical content knowledge A part of teachers' professional knowledge that includes the ability to represent abstract concepts in ways that students understand.

To these we add knowledge of the profession, which includes understanding the social, historical, philosophical, organizational, and legal aspects of teaching. These different forms of knowledge allow teachers to make professional decisions in complex and ill-defined situations (Krull, Oras, & Sisask, 2007).

The inclination to continue learning is also essential for professionals. Just as physicians must continually upgrade their knowledge of medications, surgical procedures, and therapies, teachers must stay abreast of research in their field. For instance, intuition suggests that we encourage students who aren't successful to work harder, but research indicates that this can be counterproductive. Young children generally believe they are already working hard, so they're bewildered by the suggestion, and older students often believe that an admonition to work hard indicates low ability in the student (Schunk, Pintrich, & Meece, 2008). Teachers who are aware of this research encourage students to change the *way* they study instead of the *amount* they study. Professional knowledge allows teachers to adapt their instruction to best meet students' needs. A major goal of this text is to help develop your knowledge of the profession.

Extended Training for Licensure. Extended training for licensure is required to develop these different dimensions of professional knowledge. As with physicians, lawyers, and engineers, teachers must earn a license that allows them to practice their profession. The license is intended to certify that the teacher is competent, and, as with other professions, teachers must periodically renew their license to confirm that they are staying current in their fields. Teachers need at least a bachelor's degree before licensure, and in many states they must complete the degree in a content area, such as math or English, before they begin teacher preparation experiences (Darling-Hammond & Bransford, 2005). Licensure also requires clinical experiences, such as internships, which are designed to ensure that teachers can apply the professional knowledge they have acquired in the real world of schools.

AUTONOMY   With knowledge comes **autonomy**, the capacity to control one's own professional life. Professionals have the authority to make decisions based on their specialized knowledge (see Figure 1.3). When a person sees a physician because of stomach problems, for example, no set of standards mandates specific treatments or medications; doctors have the authority to treat patients as they see fit. Some researchers suggest that teaching isn't a profession because states and districts, instead of teachers, prescribe what teachers teach (the **curriculum**) as well as how student understanding is measured (**assessment**) (van den Berg, 2002).

Indeed, states and districts prescribe **standards**, statements specifying what students should know and be able to do upon completing an area of study, and districts often require students to meet these standards before moving from one grade to another or graduating from high school (McCombs, 2005). In spite of these mandates, teachers have a great deal of autonomy. They have control over what is taught, how they teach it, and—even though yearly standardized assessments are mandated—how students are assessed. Although some argue that teachers lack the autonomy to be called true professionals, we disagree: They, in fact, have considerable autonomy to determine what goes on in their classrooms.

Figure 1.3 Professionalism Requires Autonomy

Autonomy The capacity to control one's own professional life.

Curriculum What teachers teach and students learn in schools.

Assessment The process teachers use to gather data and make decisions about progress in student learning and development.

Standards Statements specifying what students should know or be able to do upon completing an area of study.

Teacher autonomy to design and implement instruction comes with teacher professionalism.

Figure 1.4 Professionalism Requires Decision Making and Reflection

EMPHASIS ON DECISION MAKING AND REFLECTION As you saw earlier in the chapter, classrooms are complex, and teachers make many decisions in ill-defined situations. For example, Ken had to decide whether to ignore the incident when Sylvia accused Joey of calling her a fat jerk or to intervene. And if he decided to intervene, what should this intervention be? Should he take Joey out of the classroom and talk to him? make him apologize or write a note to Sylvia? call his parents? And, what if Sylvia wasn't telling the truth, or misunderstood what Joey said? David Ling, in his lesson on inertia, had to decide how to begin his lesson, what examples to use, what students to call on and in what order, how long he would give them to answer, what kind of follow-up question he would ask if they were unable to answer, and a host of other decisions.

These situations were ill-defined for both Ken and David, yet decisions had to be made. This is why professional knowledge is so essential: Without it, wise decision making is virtually impossible. This text attempts to help you develop your professional decision-making abilities by providing a "Decision Making: Defining Yourself as a Professional" exercise at the end of each chapter.

But how do teachers know they have made good decisions? Unfortunately, they receive little formal feedback about the effectiveness of their work. Typically, they are observed by administrators a few times a year at most, and they receive only vague, sketchy, and uncertain feedback from students and parents; they get virtually no feedback from their colleagues, unless the school has a peer coaching or mentoring program (Gilbert, 2005). To develop as a professional, teachers must be able to assess their own decisions.

Professional ethics guide teachers in their interactions with students, parents and caregivers, and colleagues.

The ability to conduct this self-assessment requires that teachers develop a disposition for continually and critically examining their work; this is the essence of a simple, yet powerful idea called **reflection** (Clarke, 2006), the act of thinking about and analyzing your actions. Reflective teachers are thoughtful and critical about their teaching. They plan lessons carefully and take the time to analyze them afterward.

Reflection is important because it improves our teaching and helps us develop as professionals (Bransford, Darling-Hammond, & LePage, 2005; Hammerness, Darling-Hammond, & Bransford, 2005). As we analyze our work, we gradually develop a coherent philosophy of education that helps us integrate theory and application and continually refine our practice (Gimbel, 2008) (see Figure 1.4).

PROFESSIONAL ETHICS Professionals also have ethical standards for conduct. To understand what this means, consider the following scenarios:

An ardent advocate of gun control, you believe that access to guns should be strictly regulated, and you have said so in class. Eric, one of your students, brings a newspaper editorial to school that makes a compelling argument against gun control. Because of your beliefs, you don't allow him to share the editorial with the class.

Reflection The act of thinking about and analyzing your actions.

Greg is a difficult student in one of your classes. He is disruptive and periodically shouts insults at other students and sometimes even at you. You've tried everything you know to control his behavior, but you've been unsuccessful. Finally, in exasperation one day, you walk up to him while he is talking, clap your hands together, and say angrily, "Greg, I've had it with you! You can't keep your mouth closed for more than 1 minute, and you're an embarrassment to yourself and the other students in this class. I don't want to hear another sound out of you the rest of the period." Surprisingly, Greg sits quietly for the remainder of the period. Now, finding that anger seems to be the only way to keep Greg from being disruptive, you sometimes use it to manage his behavior.

Have you behaved "ethically" in these examples? How do you know? **Ethics** are sets of moral standards for acceptable professional behavior, and all professions have codes of ethics intended to guide professionals as they make decisions about how to act (see Figure 1.5). In its code of ethics, the National Education Association (NEA), the largest professional organization in education, addresses the behavior of teachers working with their students (see Figure 1.6).

Figure 1.5 Professionalism Requires Ethical Standards for Conduct

Let's evaluate your actions based on the information in the NEA Code of Ethics. Item 2 of Principle I, *Commitment to the Student*, states that a teacher "shall not unreasonably deny the student access to varying points of view." In the first example, you didn't let Eric share the editorial with other students, so you have denied them access to a view that differs from your own. Whether your denial was "unreasonable" is open to interpretation, as is the case with ethical standards in any profession.

In the second example, you were desperately searching for a way to manage Greg's behavior, and by chance you found that anger (and possibly intimidation) was the only thing that seemed to work. However, Item 5 of Principle I says a teacher "shall not intentionally expose the student to embarrassment or disparagement." This case is clear: In your desperation and frustration, you intentionally used anger and disparagement as a strategy with Greg, so you are in violation of the ethical code.

Other examples of ethical lapses sometimes seen in teaching include retaliating against students for alleged slights or offenses by grading unfairly or making unfair placement decisions, accepting fees for tutoring one's own students, and cheating on state tests by giving students more than the prescribed time or by giving them clues and/or answers (Raths & Lynman, 2003). Ethical standards are so important to professionals that they are often written into employment contracts; they are also important because they can provide a basis for your own professional decision making.

Are Teachers Professionals?

Not everyone believes that teachers are professionals. Critics' arguments most commonly include lack of rigorous training and lack of autonomy (Labaree, 2004, 2005). Let's examine these arguments.

LACK OF RIGOROUS TRAINING   The academic rigor of teachers' professional training has historically been criticized (Neville, Sherman, & Cohen, 2005). Entrance into teaching isn't as competitive as entrance into professions such as medicine or law, and many proposed reforms suggest that pedagogical content knowledge, general pedagogical knowledge, and knowledge of learners and learning be de-emphasized in favor of knowledge of content (Berry, Hoke, & Hirsch, 2004). Although this position is not

Ethics Sets of moral standards for acceptable professional behavior.

Figure 1.6 National Education Association Code of Ethics

Preamble

The educator, believing in the worth and dignity of each human being, recognizes the supreme importance of the pursuit of truth, devotion to excellence, and the nurture of democratic princi- ple. Essential to these goals is the protection of freedom to learn and to teach and the guaran- tee of equal educational opportunity for all. The educator accepts the responsibility to adhere to the highest ethical standards.

The educator recognizes the magnitude of the responsibility inherent in the teaching process. The desire for the respect and confidence of one's colleagues, of students, of parents, and the members of the community provides the incentive to attain and maintain the highest possible degree of ethical conduct. The Code of Ethics of the Education Profession indicates the aspiration of all educators and provides standards by which to judge conduct.

The remedies specified by the NEA and/or its affiliates for the violation of any provision of this Code shall be exclusive and no such provision shall be enforceable in any form other than one specifically designated by the NEA or its affiliates.

Principle I—Commitment to the Student

The educator strives to help each student realize his or her potential as a worthy and effective member of society. The educator therefore works to stimulate the spirit of inquiry, the acquisition of knowledge and understanding, and the thoughtful formulation of worthy goals.

In fulfillment of the obligation to the student, the educator—

1. Shall not unreasonably restrain the student from independent action in the pursuit of learning.
2. Shall not unreasonably deny the student access to varying points of view.
3. Shall not deliberately suppress or distort subject matter relevant to the student's progress.
4. Shall make reasonable effort to protect the student from conditions harmful to learning or to health and safety.
5. Shall not intentionally expose the student to embarrassment or disparagement.
6. Shall not on the basis of race, color, creed, sex, national origin, marital status, political or re- ligious beliefs, family, social or cultural background, or sexual orientation unfairly:
   a. Exclude any student from participation in any program;
   b. Deny benefits to any student;
   c. Grant any advantage to any student.
7. Shall not use professional relationships with students for private advantage.
8. Shall not disclose information about students obtained in the course of professional service, unless disclosure serves a compelling professional purpose or is required by law.

Principle II—Commitment to the Profession

The education profession is vested by the public with a trust and responsibility requiring the highest ideals of professional service.

In the belief that the quality of the services of the education profession directly influences the nation and its citizens, the educator shall exert every effort to raise professional standards, to promote a climate that encourages the exercise of professional judgment, to achieve condi- tions which attract persons worthy of the trust to careers in education, and to assist in prevent- ing the practice of the profession by unqualified persons.

In fulfillment of the obligation to the profession, the educator—

1. Shall not in an application for a professional position deliberately make a false statement or fail to disclose a material fact related to competency and qualifications.
2. Shall not misrepresent his/her professional qualifications.
3. Shall not assist entry into the profession of a person known to be unqualified in respect to character, education, or other relevant attribute.
4. Shall not knowingly make a false statement concerning the qualifications of a candidate for a professional position.
5. Shall not assist a noneducator in the unauthorized practice of teaching.
6. Shall not disclose information about colleagues obtained in the course of professional service unless disclosure serves a compelling professional purpose or is required by law.
7. Shall not knowingly make a false or malicious statement about a colleague.
8. Shall not accept any gratuity, gift, or favor that might impair or appear to influence profes- sional decisions or actions.

Source: National Education Association. (2008). Code of Ethics of the Education Profession, NEA Representative Assembly. Reprinted by permission.

supported by research, critics of teacher preparation programs often argue that the only thing teachers need is knowledge of the subjects they teach (Darling-Hammond & Bransford, 2005). The complexities of teaching, the decision making that's required, and the awesome responsibility of guiding the lives of young people suggest that teaching is a demanding profession requiring a great deal of professional knowledge. Training in all professions can always be more rigorous, but suggesting that teaching doesn't require deep, extensive, and varied knowledge reflects a lack of understanding of the profession (Darling-Hammond & Bransford, 2005).

LACK OF AUTONOMY   In the previous section, we argued that teachers have a great deal of autonomy. We maintain this position, but we acknowledge that teachers have less autonomy than other professionals. For example, unlike physicians and lawyers, teachers are supervised and evaluated by their principals, and states and districts mandate a portion of the curriculum. Teachers have little to say about the standards for licensure, and some teachers even have to sign in at the beginning of the day and sign out at the end. The extent to which this detracts from their being true professionals continues to be debated.

Putting Teacher Professionalism Into Perspective

The issue of teaching as a profession is controversial and won't be resolved anytime soon. Without question, the training required for professions such as medicine and law is more rigorous than the training required for teaching, although rigor in teacher education is on the rise (Darling-Hammond & Bransford, 2005). Prospective teachers are expected to know and do more, and their professional knowledge is now more commonly assessed with tests that measure their understanding of the content they teach as well as their understanding of how to help students learn. We discuss these tests later in the chapter.

With respect to autonomy, a battle is currently being fought on both sides of the issue (Whitcomb, Borko, & Liston, 2007). Some would curtail teachers' autonomy by mandating what and how to teach and how to assess student learning. Others argue that this technical view of teaching isn't feasible, because teaching requires too many split-second decisions to be reduced to mandates, and attempts to do so discourage creative people from considering teaching as a career (Kohn, 2000).

It is clear that teachers share many characteristics that describe members of established professions: They possess a specialized body of knowledge; they make an enormous number of decisions as they work; and they have a significant amount of autonomy. Effective teachers also take time to reflect on their actions and are careful to follow the ethical standards established by educational leaders. Are teachers professionals? At this time, many educational commentators seem to be saying "not quite" (Labaree, 2004, 2005; Neville et al., 2005). Researchers believe that to truly "professionalize" teaching, a number of reforms are necessary. We discuss these in the next section.

PEARSON
myeducationlab

To see how school principals describe the professional knowledge that teachers need, go to the *Assignments and Activities* section of Topic 1, *The Teaching Profession,* in the MyEducationLab for your course and complete the activity titled *Teachers as Professionals: Two Principals' Views.*

■ ■ ■ ■ ■ CHECK YOUR UNDERSTANDING

2.1   What are the essential characteristics of professionalism?

2.2   What are the primary arguments that teaching is a profession?

2.3   What are the major arguments that teaching is not a profession?

2.4   How do the arguments for and against teacher professionalism balance each other?

For feedback, go to the appendix, *Check Your Understanding*, located in the back of this text.

DIVERSITY: THE CHANGING FACE OF AMERICAN CLASSROOMS

myeducationlab

Go to the *IRIS Center Resources* section of Topic 2: *Student Diversity* in the MyEducationLab for your course and watch and listen to the podcast titled *Leonard Baca on the Use of Native Languages in the Classroom.*

When you walk into your first classroom, one fact will likely strike you: Our students have become remarkably diverse. For example, experts in California predict that by 2014, half of the children in that state's public schools will be Hispanic, and many will have limited English language skills. By 2020, only a third will be white, more than 40 percent of the state's residents will be Latino, close to another 15 percent will be Asian, and the remaining approximately 10 percent will be African American or Native American (Coleman, 2005). Although perhaps extreme, California is not unique; every state in our country is becoming more culturally and ethnically diverse. Nationwide, more than 4 of 10 students in P–12 schools are students of color, and in our 25 largest cities, these students make up more than half the student population (Ladson-Billings, 2005; U.S. Bureau of Census, 2006b). Combined with this cultural and ethnic diversity, you will likely teach students who speak a native language other than English.

Your students' **socioeconomic status**—the combination of their parents' income, level of education, and jobs they have—will also differ, and these differences will strongly affect learning (Macionis, 2009). Some parents can afford trips to other states and even countries, for example, whereas others are barely able to provide a place to live and enough to eat. Some students will have trips to zoos, museums, and other places that provide the school-related experiences that make learning easy, but others' experiences will be limited. These differences can result in dramatic differences in their success in school.

In a single grade you will also have learners who are mature for their age and others who are slower in developing. Some will be poised and self-confident; others, shy and hesitant. You will certainly have a mix of boys and girls, and you're likely to have students with learning problems who will require extra help.

Each of these forms of diversity can affect students' success in the classroom, and how you respond to these differences will influence how much students learn, how they feel about school, and your own enjoyment of teaching. In addition, the No Child Left Behind Act, which requires states to report student progress in terms of specific ethnic, cultural, and socioeconomic groups, emphasizes the importance of success for all students. Because learner diversity is so important to your teaching success, we devote Chapters 3, 4, and 5 to the topic and include a special section called "Exploring Diversity" in every chapter.

■ ■ ■ ■ ■ CHECK YOUR UNDERSTANDING

3.1 Identify the different dimensions of student diversity. Explain how these dimensions will influence your work as a teacher.

3.2 Why is an understanding of different teaching and learning environments important for beginning teachers?

For feedback, go to the appendix, *Check Your Understanding*, located in the back of this text.

Socioeconomic status The combination of parents' income, level of education, and jobs they have.

Teaching in Rural, Suburban, and Urban Environments

Because of its influence on teaching, we have made diversity a second major theme of this text, together with professionalism—our first theme. The "Exploring Diversity" feature in each chapter examines an issue related to the topic, and in this chapter, we examine teaching in rural, suburban, and urban contexts. Understanding different learning and teaching contexts is important for beginning teachers because these environments present different opportunities and challenges. Teaching in a rural school, for example, can be very different from teaching in one located in the suburbs or in the inner city, influenced both by the social context and by the students themselves (Gardner, 2008). We begin with rural schools.

TEACHING IN RURAL SCHOOLS

In 1900, 60 percent of the population in our country lived in rural areas; today that figure is slightly more than 20 percent (U.S. Bureau of Census, 2006b). More than 1 of 5 students attends a rural school, and enrollments in these schools have increased in recent years (R. Tompkins, 2008). As would be expected, rural schools are much smaller than their urban and suburban counterparts; in fact, approximately 350 one-teacher, one-room schools remain in rural areas of our country (Swidler, 2004). The smallest rural districts had an average of 126 students in the 2001–2002 school year, compared to more than 4,000 in suburban and urban districts (U.S. Government Accounting

URBAN EDUCATION

Office, 2006). The schools in these small districts are also small, enrolling an average of 77 students, compared to an average of more than 550 in nonrural schools. Their small size results in low student–teacher ratios, with the smallest rural schools averaging 11 students per class versus 17 for their counterparts in larger districts (U.S. Government Accounting Office, 2006).

Students in rural districts tend to be less culturally diverse than those in urban and suburban districts, although this is rapidly changing (Lichter & Johnson, 2006). Immigrants from Latin America and Asia are finding their way into rural America, seeking jobs in construction, meatpacking, and other food-processing industries, slowing an earlier trend of general population declines in rural areas (Macionis, 2009). Twenty-three percent of rural students are members of minority groups, and these populations grew 55 percent between 1996 and 2005; many of these are English language learners (R. Tompkins, 2008).

Poverty is also an issue in rural districts, particularly in the South and Southwest (Hardy, 2005). For example, more than 40 percent of students in rural districts qualify for free or reduced-price lunch programs, and many rural students come to school with inadequate health care (U.S. Government Accounting Office, 2006).

Teaching in rural districts has both advantages and disadvantages. Because they are small, they have a strong sense of community, with schools often serving as the social center for the community (Brooke, 2003). Because of small class sizes, communication with parents is often easier. And, rural districts' small size can make innovation and change easier to accomplish than in larger dis-

tricts (E. Reeves & Bylund, 2005). As you'll see in the next sections, however, rural districts may not offer all of the services found in larger school districts.

TEACHING IN SUBURBAN SCHOOLS

The last half of the 20th century resulted in unprecedented growth in the suburbs of our major cities. By the turn of the 21st century, many people had moved to suburbs from both rural and urban areas, and now the majority of our population lives there (Macionis, 2009). The exodus to the suburbs brought with it a growing tax base, which resulted in more money for suburban schools (Macionis & Parillo, 2010; Spring, 2006). More money then translates into smaller class sizes and greater access to resources such as science labs and technology.

Suburban schools are also culturally diverse, but much of the diversity comes from well-educated professionals working in high-tech industries (Macionis, 2009). They are less diverse than urban schools, however, and average household incomes tend to be higher than in rural or urban areas.

Most of the highest achieving school districts in our country are found in suburban areas, and many suburban families select neighborhoods based on the reputation of the school district (Brimley & Garfield, 2008; Spring, 2006). Because teaching in suburban schools is considered to be highly desirable, competition for jobs in them is stiff, and, as a beginning teacher, it will be challenging for you to secure a job in one of these schools.

TEACHING IN URBAN SCHOOLS

With respect to jobs, urban schools are "where the action is." Consider the fol-

Urban schools provide job openings and opportunities for personal and professional growth.

lowing statistics (Dalton, Sable, & Hoffman, 2006):

- The nation's 100 largest school districts represent less than 1 percent of all districts but are responsible for educating nearly one fourth of our students. For example, the New York City Public Schools and the Los Angeles Unified School District, the two largest in the nation, each have enrollments greater than the total enrollments of 27 states.
- The 100 largest districts employ more than a fifth of the nation's teachers.

Nearly 70 percent of urban students are cultural minorities, and some urban schools have enrollments that are more than 95 percent minority (Macionis & Parillo, 2010). More than half of all urban students are eligible for free or reduced-price lunches, and more than 10 percent are enrolled in English language programs (Dalton et al., 2006).

Unquestionably, teaching in urban schools differs from teaching in other settings. Urban schools are large, and most of their students come from culturally diverse backgrounds. Research also indicates that in urban schools,

> Children are often taught by teachers who are the least prepared; children are less likely to be enrolled in academically challenging courses; they are too often treated differently in what they are expected to do and the kinds of assignments they are given and teachers often lack the resources they need to teach well. (Armour-Thomas, 2004, p. 113)

Teaching in urban schools is considered to be more challenging than in either rural or suburban environments. In a national survey of urban teachers, low academic standards, few resources, lack of parental support, and poverty were all identified as obstacles to successful teaching and learning in urban schools (MetLife, 2009).

A number of negative stereotypes about urban students also exist, ranging from "All urban kids are in gangs" to "Urban children are mostly from poor, dysfunctional homes, homeless shelters, or foster homes and come to school 'just to grow up' and then drop out" (R. Goldstein, 2004, pp. 43–44). These stereotypes tend to create fear in people not familiar with the situation; this fear can then lead to actions that are damaging to everyone. One urban student reported,

> When I was in high school, we had the chance to host a group of students from the suburbs. . . . So, this girl comes with her friends, and they pair us up. Later on I find that they [the students from the suburbs] were told not to wear any jewelry or nice clothes or bring any money with them so they wouldn't get robbed. . . . All they saw when they visited us were people who might rob them. (R. Goldstein, 2004, p. 47)

Diversity in Your Classroom

How is this information relevant to you as a prospective teacher, and how might it help you answer the question "Do I want to be a teacher?" First, urban student stereotypes are untrue; these students want to succeed and learn and grow just as other students do. In many cases, their access to educational experiences has been lacking, so they come to schools with greater needs than do more advantaged students (Armour-Thomas, 2004; Rubinson, 2004). Second, many job opportunities exist in urban environments, so your first job offer likely will be in an urban setting. Many school districts now offer special incentives, such as salary bonuses, support for housing, and moving expenses, to encourage highly qualified professionals to work in urban settings (Herszenhorn, 2006). Finally, although urban environments pose special challenges, they can also be immensely rewarding, providing opportunities for you to grow in a number of dimensions (Weiner, 2006). Now is the time to begin thinking about the opportunities that working in an urban environment might afford.

QUESTIONS TO CONSIDER

1. How might the size of a district influence a teacher's private life and, ultimately, his or her satisfaction with a teaching position?

2. What are the advantages and disadvantages of teaching in schools similar to the ones you attended as a student? For example, if you grew up in a rural town, what would be the pros and cons of teaching in a similar setting?

myeducationlab To respond to these questions online, explore this topic further, and receive feedback, go to the *Book Specific Resources* section in the MyEducationLab for your course, select your text, and then select *Exploring Diversity* for Chapter 1.

THE MODERN REFORM MOVEMENT IN EDUCATION

You're considering teaching in one of the most tumultuous periods in the history of American education. Critics, both inside and outside the profession, are calling for **reforms**, suggested changes in teaching and teacher preparation intended to increase student learning. To implement these reforms, teachers must be well prepared, and states and districts often hold teachers accountable for their performance in classrooms. The current reform movement has already changed teaching and will continue to do so as you enter the profession. To prepare you for these changes, we have made reform the third theme for this text (together with professionalism and learner diversity).

The modern reform movement began in 1983, when the National Commission on Excellence in Education published *A Nation at Risk: The Imperative for Educational Reform.* This widely read document suggested that America was "at risk" of being unable to compete in the world economic marketplace because our system of education was inadequate. The term "at-risk students" grew out of this report, and educators use it to refer to students who are unlikely to acquire the knowledge and skills needed for success in our modern technological society. Since 1983, many additional reforms have been suggested for improving our nation's schools and the teachers who work in them.

Some of the more prominent of these current reform efforts include the following:

- *Standards:* Designed to clearly define what all students should know and be able to do

- *Test-based accountability:* Using tests to determine whether students have mastered essential knowledge and skills, and basing promotion and graduation on test performance

- *Choice:* Attempts to provide parents with alternatives to regular public schools through charter schools and vouchers

We discuss these reforms and the implications they will have for your life as a new teacher in later chapters. Reforms that focus on changes in teacher preparation, however, will have an immediate impact on you, and we examine them in the next section.

Changes in Teacher Preparation

Increased emphasis on professionalism combined with criticism suggesting that too many underqualified teachers enter the field has resulted in a number of reforms in teacher education, most enacted at the state level (Raths & Lynman, 2003). These reforms include the following:

- Raising standards for admission into teacher training programs

- Requiring teachers to take more rigorous courses than in the past

Reforms Suggested changes in teaching and teacher preparation intended to increase student learning.

- Requiring higher standards for licensure, including teacher competency tests
- Expanding teacher preparation programs from 4 to 5 years
- Requiring experienced teachers to take more rigorous professional-development courses (Cochran-Smith, 2005)

No Child Left Behind

To see a video of the controversies surrounding No Child Left Behind, go to the *Assignments and Activities* section of Topic 9: *Assessment, Standards, and Accountability* in the MyEducationLab for your course and complete the activity titled *NCLB*.

ISSUES IN EDUCATION

The emphasis on increased professionalism was reinforced by the **No Child Left Behind (NCLB)** Act of 2001, a federal law that included improved teacher quality as a major provision. NCLB required that by 2005–2006, all teachers were to be fully qualified, and paraprofessionals working in schools should have 2 years of college or demonstrate equivalent knowledge on a competency test (S. Dillon, 2006). This provision resulted from research indicating that teachers have a powerful effect on student learning (Milanowski & Kimball, 2005) and that many poor, minority, and urban children are often taught by underqualified teachers (Rhee & Levin, 2006).

NCLB also changed teachers' responsibilities by mandating that students acquire proficiency in basic skills in the elementary grades. To meet this mandate, every state was required to design an accountability system to test students' growth in reading and math. Schools that didn't produce **adequate yearly progress (AYP)** in these academic areas would be subject to a variety of sanctions, including providing students with transportation to alternate schools, supplementary tutoring services, and even takeovers of the school.

This complex and comprehensive (670 pages) reform effort is controversial, with both backers and critics. On the plus side, NCLB has focused the nation's attention on the importance of education, especially on basic skills that are essential for success both in school and later life. In addition, by requiring states to report academic progress by specific subgroups such as cultural minorities, it has highlighted the problem of uneven achievement in U.S. students. Finally, its emphasis on standards and accountability has made these part of every current discussion of educational reform.

Critics of NCLB concentrate not so much on the idea itself—that all children need to succeed in school—as on implementation details. One major criticism of NCLB was the stipulation that allowed each state to design its own standards and evaluation system to document students' attainment of those standards; this has resulted in a patchwork of standards and accountability systems that are haphazard at best, and often inaccurate and misleading (Isaacson, 2009). States, faced with the possibility of later federal sanctions for not meeting their standards, have gamed the system by creating lax accountability programs that reward mediocre and even poor performance. Part of this problem was due to a key component of the act that required all of the different student groups in a state to become proficient in basic skills by the year 2014. Critics point out that this is as unrealistic as asking the country to do away with crime, poverty, or cancer by a certain date. It just can't be done.

The future of NCLB is unclear, especially with a new president and Congress elected in 2008. There is no doubt that major provisions of the law will be revised and modified, but its long-term effects on reform in general and standards and accountability in particular will persist long into the future.

Educational Reform: Future Direction

So what is the future of educational reform for new teachers entering the profession? Although it's always difficult and risky to gaze into the future—especially in the area of education, when presidential elections can dramatically change the landscape—there are some hints about the future of educational reform.

The first is the American Recovery and Reinvestment Act, which pumped $81 billion into education. Most of the funds were intended to provide short-term help to beleaguered states and districts feeling the financial effects of a major recession, but

No Child Left Behind (NCLB) A reauthorization of the Elementary and Secondary Education Act that mandates statewide testing in reading and math for grades 3–8, and holds individual schools accountable for student achievement in these areas.

Adequate Yearly Progress (AYP) A provision of No Child Left Behind that requires students to show demonstrated progress in statewide tests toward meeting state standards.

provisions in the bill suggested that teachers are central to President Obama's educational vision. To ensure that poor and minority students are taught by qualified teachers, it asked states to develop teacher enhancement efforts for hard-to-staff schools that included induction programs for new teachers, improvement in working conditions in these schools, and differentiated pay and other recruitment incentives.

Additional hints about future directions for reform came from President Obama's first major speech on education (Associated Press, 2009). In it, the president called for rewarding good teachers, encouraging charter schools, and lengthening both the school day and the school year. He also connected education to our country's future: "The relative decline of American education is untenable for our economy, unsustainable for our democracy, and unacceptable for our children. We cannot afford to let it continue. What is at stake is nothing less than the American dream" (Associated Press, 2009, p. 14). This link between education and economic success is a reform theme that has resonated for the last 30 years and is likely to become stronger in the future.

A third, and perhaps most telling, hint about future directions of educational reform comes from President Obama's first major budget proposal (Klein, 2009). In it were substantial increases for these areas:

- School improvement programs targeting underperforming schools, and especially middle schools and high schools
- Teacher improvement grants to school districts to develop performance-pay programs
- Federal matching funds to encourage districts to develop prekindergarten programs

The pace of educational reform is likely to quicken under a risk-taking president and a friendly Congress. The good news is that many of his proposals specifically target teachers and are intended to enhance the quality of teachers and their working conditions.

Teaching in an Era of Reform

Because reform is one of the themes for this book, we ask you to examine important current reforms with a feature in each chapter, "Taking a Stand in an Era of Reform." We introduce the feature in this chapter and illustrate how you can use it to increase your understanding of educational reforms in the United States.

The feature incorporates the following elements:

- A discussion of a reform issue such as merit pay (Chapter 2) or teacher tenure (Chapter 9)
- Positions taken by both proponents and critics of the reform
- An opportunity for you to take a position with respect to the issue in a MyEducationLab exercise

We illustrate this process in the *Taking a Stand* box on the next page, using teacher testing as the reform issue. If you haven't already encountered teacher tests as an entrance requirement for admission into a teacher education program, you likely will as you move through your program and apply for licensure in your state.

Praxis: Comprehensive Teacher Testing

The most widely used form of teacher testing is the Praxis Series™, published by Educational Testing Service. The Praxis Series (*praxis* refers to putting theory into practice) is currently being used in 44 states and exists at three levels (Educational Testing Service, 2008):

- *Praxis I: Academic Skills Assessments.* These tests are designed to measure basic skills in reading, writing, and math that all teachers need.

Testing Teachers

Currently, most states require some form of testing for prospective teachers, but the exact form that this testing takes varies from state to state (Swanson, 2008). Some states require tests of basic skills before admission to a teacher education program, and others test professional knowledge after program completion. In addition, some states require tests of your knowledge of the subjects you'll be teaching, especially if you're a middle or high school teacher. Virtually all of these tests are paper-and-pencil, though most new teachers will also be evaluated on their classroom performance during their first year.

Testing teachers is not new; for example, teachers were tested all the way back in the 1840s using oral exams that focused primarily on candidates' moral qualifications (S. Wilson & Youngs, 2005). The current emphasis on testing teachers is part of a larger accountability movement in education in which students, teachers, and even principals are being tested, and the results are being used to evaluate the effectiveness of educational efforts.

THE ISSUE

Critics of teacher testing argue that the tests aren't valid and that they fail to differentiate between good and bad prospective teachers. They make the following arguments:

- It's difficult, if not impossible, for a paper-and-pencil test to measure something as complex as teacher competency.
- In an attempt to capture the complexities of teaching, test developers include items that are ambiguous, making them unreliable and consequently invalid (Berliner, 2005b).
- Performance on a test does not guarantee performance in the

Prospective teachers are being asked to demonstrate their professional knowledge on state and national tests.

classroom, which further detracts from their validity (S. Wilson & Youngs, 2005).

- Cutoff scores established by different states are arbitrary, based more on the demand for new teachers than on any objective measure of minimal teacher competency.
- The tests penalize cultural minorities and nonnative speakers because they rely on verbal skills that may or may not influence teaching effectiveness (Bennett, McWhorter, & Kuykendall, 2006; Guarino, Santibañez, & Daley, 2006).

On the other hand, advocates of teacher testing argue that standardized tests are valid because they keep unqualified teachers out of classrooms, and they further assert that the tests are necessary because of the uneven quality of teacher education programs (Education Leaders Council, 2001). Advocates further claim that these tests are fair and that they minimize or even eliminate evaluator bias; a test doesn't know if the test taker is male or female, or if he or

she is a member of a cultural minority. Further, research indicates that teachers' verbal ability is strongly correlated with student learning (Good & Brophy, 2008).

The tests are also economical and cost-effective, and the public at large supports teacher testing, with 77 percent indicating that teachers should have to pass a national test in the subjects they teach (Bushaw & Gallup, 2008).

YOU TAKE A STAND

Now it's your turn to take a position on the issue. Are teacher tests an effective way to ensure teacher quality, or are there better ways to guarantee competency?

PEARSON myeducationlab To explore both sides of this issue and take a stand, go to the *Book Specific Resources* section in the MyEducationLab for your course, select your text, and then select *Taking a Stand in an Era of Reform* for Chapter 1.

ISSUES IN EDUCATION

- *Praxis II: Subject Assessments.* The subject assessments are intended to measure teachers' knowledge of the subjects they will teach. In addition to 70 content-specific tests, Praxis II includes the Principles of Learning and Teaching (PLT) tests, which measure professional knowledge.

- *Praxis III: Classroom Performance Assessments.* These tests use classroom observations and work samples to assess beginning teachers' ability to plan, instruct, manage, and understand professional responsibilities. In addition, Praxis III assesses the teacher's sensitivity to learners' developmental and cultural differences.

You are most likely to encounter Praxis I before being admitted to a teacher licensure program, Praxis II after its completion, and Praxis III during your first years of teaching.

The four Principles of Learning and Teaching (PLT) tests, designed for teachers seeking licensure in Early Childhood or in grades K–6, 5–9, and 7–12, are an important part of the Praxis Series; the topics these tests cover are outlined in the Praxis Correlation Matrix at the beginning of this text. Each of the grade-level tests has two parts (Educational Testing Service, 2008): The first consists of 24 multiple-choice questions similar to items in the test bank that accompanies this text, and the second part presents case histories with three short-answer questions to read and analyze.

Analyzing One Statewide Reform: The Kentucky Education Reform Act

Will reform efforts produce the hoped-for results? One of the most ambitious and well-known state reform efforts, the Kentucky Education Reform Act (KERA), was precipitated by a 1989 Kentucky Supreme Court ruling that declared the state's system of funding public schools was unconstitutional (A. Flanagan & Murray, 2004). Funding disparities between rich and poor school districts had resulted in a system that was inequitable and inefficient. The state legislature responded with a comprehensive educational reform bill that addressed several of the issues. The major components of the effort, and the changes that resulted, are found in Table 1.3.

As you can see from Table 1.3, KERA affected every student and every teacher in the state. To fund these reforms, the Kentucky legislature approved a $1.3 billion tax increase, and public school expenditures increased 50 percent over the first 5 years of implementation ("Will KERA?", 2003).

Table 1.3 Major Provisions of Kentucky Education Reform Act	
Reform Component	**Result**
Curriculum guides established	Clearly defined student learning goals for key areas such as math, reading, and social studies.
Assessment and accountability systems	Created a statewide testing system that held schools accountable for student learning.
Ungraded primary program for K–3	Eliminated grade levels and used multiage grouping to educate primary students.
Extended school services for students placed at risk	Provided extra instruction after school and in the summer for students placed at risk.
School-based decision making	Created school-level councils consisting of parents and teachers to provide input on how schools were run.
Preschool program for children placed at risk	Students who were eligible for free or reduced lunches or those who were developmentally delayed received developmentally appropriate preschool programs.
Family and youth resource centers	Provided links between schools and families and offered information on other government agencies.

How successful was this "most sweeping statewide education reform plan ever enacted" (Rothman, 1997)? Evaluations range from "success beyond all expectations" to "dismal failure" (Petroska, Lindle, & Pankratz, 2000). Research suggests that this reform did improve student performance: Between 1992 and 1996, 92 percent of Kentucky's schools showed improvements in achievement (Rothman, 1997). These increases were especially evident at the elementary level in math, reading, and social studies (Petroska et al., 2000). In addition, the preschool programs for at-risk students appeared to have long-lasting benefits for young students. Other measures, however, such as high school graduation and college attendance rates, failed to show significant improvements, and some researchers wonder if gains were due to easier tests and were not true achievement gains (Cech, 2008a, 2008b; Hoyt, 2005).

As with all reforms, the Kentucky plan was not without its critics. Conservatives argued that it cost too much, and as often happens with education reforms, funding for the program significantly decreased over time (D. Hoff, 2003). In addition, teachers questioned whether the emphasis on accountability narrowed the curriculum and forced teachers to "teach to the test," a common complaint about accountability through testing.

In many respects, the Kentucky Education Reform Act, with its emphasis on systemic reform and accountability, was a precursor to the No Child Left Behind Act, the federal reform effort. But KERA differed from No Child Left Behind in several important respects. First, it is a state versus a federal effort, which gives the people in the state more control over it. Second, it didn't rely solely on testing and accountability to improve education; instead, it provided extra funding for the reform, something that critics of No Child Left Behind believe hampered federal efforts to improve student performance (Archer, 2005). This extra money provided additional services to both students and their families, something experts believe is necessary for long-term change in the education of at-risk students (Mathis, 2005).

■ ■ ■ ■ CHECK YOUR UNDERSTANDING

4.1   How is the current reform movement in education changing the teaching profession?

4.2   Describe the major changes in teacher preparation that have resulted from the reform movement in education.

4.3   What are the major arguments for and against testing teachers?

4.4   What is the Praxis Series, and how does praxis relate to the reform movement?

4.5   What is the Kentucky Education Reform Act, and how is it similar to and different from No Child Left Behind?

For feedback, go to the appendix, *Check Your Understanding*, located in the back of this text.

Now it's your turn to apply the information in this chapter to a problem or dilemma facing many prospective teachers. Read the following case and answer the question that follows.

Rewards and Challenges in Teaching

You're a sophomore in college taking your first education course, and you're trying to decide whether you want to be an elementary or a secondary teacher. Fortunately, your class provides clinical experiences at both levels, so you can observe teachers working with both younger and older students.

Your first experience is with a third-grade teacher. At times, the classroom seems bewildering, with small groups of students working on a number of different projects at the same time. After a while, you start to make sense of the schedule Mrs. Ortiz puts on the board each morning, and you're beginning to learn students' names.

Then you move to a high school math classroom. The students seem really old, and they are, compared to the third graders and even you: Some are only 2 or 3 years younger than you are. At first, you're intimidated, but then after you start working with students one-on-one, you realize they share many of the characteristics of the third graders: They come to school to learn, but having friends and being respected by others are really important to them. You also become aware that you know more math than you realized and that it's fun helping others understand how to solve problems.

At the end of the term, you find that you still haven't firmly decided on a grade level but that you know a lot more than you did before the term started. To help you decide, you reread the section "Rewards and Challenges in Teaching."

What level would you choose?

1 MEETING YOUR LEARNING OBJECTIVES

1. Describe major rewards and challenges of teaching.
   - Rewards in teaching include both intrinsic and extrinsic benefits. Intrinsic rewards include both helping young people grow emotionally, socially, and academically and opportunities for a lifetime of intellectual growth. Examples of extrinsic rewards are desirable vacation times, convenient work schedules, and occupational status.
   - Challenges in teaching include the complexities of classrooms as well as the multiple roles that teachers perform. Classrooms are multidimensional, and the events that occur in classrooms are simultaneous, immediate, unpredictable, and public. Teachers' roles include creating productive learning environments, serving as ambassadors to the public, and working with other professionals as collaborative colleagues.

2. Describe the essential characteristics of professionalism, and explain how they relate to teaching.
   - Characteristics of professionalism include a specialized body of knowledge, autonomy, the ability to make decisions in ill-defined situations and reflect on one's own performance, and ethical standards that guide professional conduct.
   - Some argue that teachers aren't professionals, suggesting their training isn't rigorous and they lack autonomy. Others contend that teaching is a developing profession that is still evolving.
   - The future status of teaching will be largely determined by current reform efforts.

3. Identify different dimensions of diversity and explain how diversity affects the lives of teachers.

   • The following are all dimensions of diversity that influence student learning: culture and ethnicity; religion; socioeconomic status; academic ability; cognitive, physical, and emotional maturity; gender; and learner exceptionalities.

   • Understanding different learning and teaching environments is important for beginning teachers because these environments present different opportunities and challenges.

   • Rural districts tend to be smaller and more homogeneous in terms of diversity. Suburban districts are intermediate in size and funded better than other districts, but competition for teaching jobs is greater there. Urban districts are more culturally diverse and also offer the most teaching opportunities for first-year teachers. Urban environments also present unique challenges and opportunities, and school districts often offer incentives to encourage teachers to take jobs in urban classrooms.

4. Explain how the current reform movement in education is changing the teaching profession.

   • Prospective teachers will encounter reforms calling for higher standards, more rigorous training, and increased teacher testing. In addition to increased use of licensure exams, beginning teachers will be asked to demonstrate their competence through professional portfolios.

   • The No Child Left Behind Act of 2001 focused attention on the academic performance of different groups of U.S. students. This act has resulted in increased emphasis on standards and accountability and will continue to influence both teachers' and students' lives in the future.

   • Testing teachers has been proposed as a major way to improve education in the United States. Advocates claim that teacher tests are a valid and reliable way to ensure teacher quality, and that these tests are practical and economical. The public supports the testing of teachers.

   • Critics counter that these tests are neither valid nor reliable, that they fail to capture the complexities of successful performance in the classroom, and that they punish minority candidates and those whose first language is not English, because they are language based.

   • The Praxis Series is the most widely used teacher test; four versions test teachers at the pre-K and elementary, middle, and high school levels. The Praxis tests are designed to assess teachers' basic skills, subject matter mastery, and classroom performance. The Principles of Learning and Teaching test assesses teacher knowledge.

   • The Kentucky change to alsdkf;alkdf Reform Act created a statewide system of comprehensive reform; it addresses curriculum standards, accountability systems, extended school services for at-risk students, school-based decision making, and school-based resource centers. Because of its scope, many compare this state's act to the federal No Child Left Behind Act.

IMPORTANT CONCEPTS

adequate yearly progress (AYP) (p. 24)
assessment (p. 15)
autonomy (p. 15)
curriculum (p. 15)
ethics (p. 17)
extrinsic rewards (p. 5)
intrinsic rewards (p. 5)

No Child Left Behind (NCLB) (p. 24)
pedagogical content knowledge (p. 14)
professionalism (p. 14)
reflection (p. 16)
reforms (p. 23)
socioeconomic status (p. 20)
standards (p. 15)

DISCUSSION QUESTIONS

1. Do the reasons cited in the chapter for becoming a teacher change with the grade level or content area targeted by teachers? Why or why not?

2. Do you believe teaching is more or less rewarding than it was in the past? Is it more or less difficult? Why do you think so?

3. Which of the intrinsic and extrinsic rewards in teaching are likely to become more important in the future? less important?

4. For which group of teachers—teachers of elementary students (grades K–5), middle school students (grades 6–8), or high school students (grades 9–12)— are emotional rewards likely to be the greatest? Why?

5. For which group of teachers—elementary, middle, or high school teachers— are intellectual rewards likely to be the greatest? Why?

6. Is teaching a profession? If not, what would be necessary to make it one?

7. Will the move toward teacher professionalism be beneficial for teachers? Why or why not?

PEARSON
myeducationlab

Now go to Topic 1, *The Teaching Profession,* in the MyEducationLab at www.myeducationlab.com for your course, where you can:

- Find learning outcomes for *The Teaching Profession* along with the national standards that connect to these outcomes.

- Complete *Assignments and Activities* that can help you more deeply understand the chapter content.

- Apply and practice your understanding of the core teaching skills identified in the chapter with the *Building Teaching Skills and Dispositions* learning units.

- Check your comprehension of the content covered in the chapter by going to the *Study Plan* in the *Book Specific Resources* for your text. Here you will be able to take a chapter quiz, receive feedback on your answers, and then access *Review, Practice, and Enrichment* activities to enhance your understanding of chapter content.

- To learn more about the Praxis exam, review test-taking strategies, and see sample questions, go to MyEducationLab for your course, select *Resources* and then *Licensure Exams.*

Develop Your Professional Portfolio

To further apply your understanding of chapter content, and address the INTASC standards, go to the *Book Specific Resources* section in the MyEducationLab for your course, select your text, then select this chapter's *Portfolio Activities.*

"*I want to be the one who makes children believe that they can be anything they want. I teach because long after I'm gone, I want my life to count for something. I want it to matter.*"

DENISE CANNON, 2008 Teacher of the Year, New Mexico

To view a video clip of Denise, the 2008 New Mexico Teacher of the Year, go to Topic 14: *Professional Development* in the MyEducationLab for your course and select *Teacher Talk,* then *Denise Cannon.*

2

Developing as a Professional

CHAPTER OUTLINE

Beliefs of Preservice and Beginning Teachers

Entering the Profession

- Traditional and Alternative Licensure
- Making Yourself Marketable
- Finding a Job

  Exploring Diversity: The Competition for Minority Teachers

Your First Year of Teaching

- Survival Skills for the First Year
- Induction and Mentoring Programs
- Teacher Evaluation

  Taking a Stand in an Era of Reform: Merit Pay

Career-Long Professional Development

- INTASC: A Beginning Point for Professional Development
- Membership in Professional Organizations
- Becoming a Teacher-Leader
- Attaining Certification: The National Board for Professional Teaching Standards

LEARNING OBJECTIVES

After you have completed your study of this chapter, you should be able to:

1. **Describe the beliefs of beginning teachers, and explain how they could influence your success in your first years of teaching.** INTASC Standard 9, Teacher Professionalism

2. **Explain differences between traditional and alternative licensure and identify the factors involved in finding a desirable job.** INTASC Standard 9, Teacher Professionalism

3. **Identify factors that contribute to a successful first year of teaching.** INTASC Standard 9, Teacher Professionalism

4. **Describe career-long professional-development opportunities available to teachers.** INTASC Standard 9, Teacher Professionalism

Chapter 1 was designed to help you begin thinking about whether teaching is for you. In this chapter, we continue this process by looking at how you, as a beginning teacher, will enter the profession, find a job, succeed in your first year of teaching, and develop as a professional. Let's begin by looking at one new teacher's experience.

My first faculty meeting. Very interesting. Mrs. Zellner [the principal] seems ■ ■ ■ really nice. She went on and on about what a great job the teachers did last year and how test scores were way up compared to the year before. She also extended a special welcome to those of us who are new.

Speaking of new teachers, there sure are a lot of us. I wonder if they're all as scared as I am. I'm not sure what I would have done if Mrs. Landsdorp [the teacher in the room next door] hadn't taken me under her wing. She made me feel much better about starting in an urban school. So many of the kids come from low-income homes, and English isn't the first language for several of them. She said that some of the teachers tend to "write them off" and assume that they can't learn, but that isn't true at all. In fact, many of them are quite bright. They just need a lot of help and support. She's wonderful. She's sort of gruff, but Andrea [a new friend and second-year teacher] says she's a softy underneath, and she really loves the kids.

I can't believe how much there is to do—IEPs, progress reports, CPR training, being responsible for spotting signs of abuse. When do I teach? I hope I can cut it. (Shelley, a beginning third-grade teacher, reflecting on her first faculty meeting)

When you finish your program, and if you choose to teach, you'll be joining others like Shelley. What challenges do beginning teachers face, and what can you do to meet them? We address these questions in this chapter, but before you begin your study, please respond to the items in the *This I Believe* feature on page 35. You will see how your responses compare to other beginning teachers as you go through the chapter.

BELIEFS OF PRESERVICE AND BEGINNING TEACHERS

Teachers' beliefs have a strong influence on how they teach and develop as professionals (V. Richardson, 2003). Our goal in this section is to help you examine your own beliefs and the impact they can have on your professional growth.

Let's begin by looking at your responses to the *This I Believe* survey on the next page. If you either agree or strongly agree with each statement, your beliefs are consistent with those held by other students in teacher preparation programs. Let's see what research tells us about these beliefs.

Item 1: *When I begin teaching, I will be a better teacher than most of the teachers now in the field.* Preservice teachers are optimistic and idealistic: "Prospective teachers report being confident and self-assured in their teaching ability," but they "may be unrealistically optimistic about their future teaching performance" (Borko & Putnam, 1996, p. 678). The danger occurs when the realities of classrooms shock beginning teachers, who then feel as though "nobody prepared me for this" (Feiman-Nemser, 2001). Optimism wanes, and they may question their career choice; about 1 of 4 quits by the end of the second year, and 4 of 10 leave the profession within the first 5 years (Grant, 2006). This isn't good either for the teachers or for the profession, because it is continually losing teachers who are hitting their prime as professionals.

Item 2: *As I gain experience in teaching, I expect to become more confident in my ability to help children learn.* As with Item 1, most preservice teachers expect to become increasingly confident in their ability to help children learn. However, the opposite often occurs: When they struggle, many become less confident in their ability to overcome the limitations of students' home environments and family backgrounds (Bransford, Darling-Hammond, & LePage, 2005).

However, after the initial decline, the confidence of successful compared to less successful teachers diverges dramatically (see Figure 2.1). A significant increase in confidence occurs for successful teachers: As they become more experienced and knowledgeable, their confidence increases. One teacher reflecting on her professional growth commented, "I kind of like it better every year. I think part of that is becoming a better

For each item, circle the number that best represents your thinking. Use the following scale as a guide.

4 = I strongly believe the statement is true.
3 = I believe the statement is true.
2 = I believe the statement is false.
1 = I strongly believe the statement is false.

1. When I begin teaching, I will be a better teacher than most of the teachers now in the field.

   1   2   3   4

2. As I gain experience in teaching, I expect to become more confident in my ability to help children learn.

   1   2   3   4

3. The most effective teachers are those best able to clearly explain the content they teach their students.

   1   2   3   4

4. I will learn about most of the important aspects of teaching when I get into a classroom.

   1   2   3   4

5. If I thoroughly understand the content I'm teaching, I'll be able to figure out a way of getting it across to students.

   1   2   3   4

PEARSON myeducationlab To download and complete this form, go to the *Book Specific Resources* section in the MyEducationLab for your course, select your text, and then select *This I Believe* for Chapter 2.

This I BELIEVE!

Figure 2.1 Confidence Levels of More and Less Successful Teachers

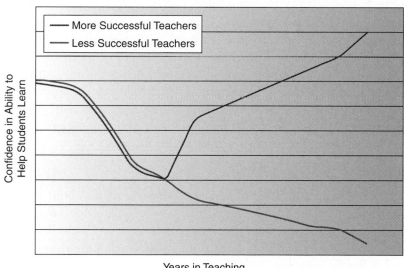

teacher" (Keller, 2007, p. 27). Many who leave the profession do so because they're unable to survive the challenges of teaching in complex and often bewildering classrooms. They fail to become more confident because they fail to become more competent. A major goal of this chapter is to help you avoid this trap.

Item 3: *The most effective teachers are those best able to clearly explain the content they teach their students.* Many preservice teachers believe that teaching is essentially a process of "telling" or explaining content to students, probably because this is what most of their own teachers did (van den Berg, 2002; J. Wang & Odell, 2002). Research suggests, however, that lecturing to students, especially those who are young or unmotivated, is quite ineffective (Bransford, Derry, Berliner, Hammerness, & Beckett, 2005; Eggen & Kauchak, 2010).

Let's look at one intern's experience.

> My first lesson with the kids. Chris [her supervising teacher] said I was on my own, sink or swim. I hardly slept last night, but today I feel like celebrating.
>
> The kids were so into it. I brought my Styrofoam ball and had the kids compare the latitude and longitude lines I had drawn on it and then look at the globe. I thought the first period was supposed to be Chris's lowest, but they did the best. He was impressed.
>
> Now I understand the stuff Dr. Martinez [one of her professors] stressed so much when he was always after us to use concrete examples and question, question, question. I know I have a lot to learn. I thought I could just explain everything to them, but they got confused and drifted off so fast I couldn't believe it. As soon as I started asking questions about the lines on the Styrofoam ball, though, they perked right up. I think I can do this. It was actually a heady experience. (Gabriela, an intern in a seventh-grade geography class)

As Gabriela quickly discovered, teaching is much more complex than simply explaining.

Item 4: *I will learn about most of the important aspects of teaching when I get into a classroom.* This is another common belief of preservice teachers. Many believe that experience is the only way they will learn to teach, and that their teacher education classes are little more than hoops they must jump through before getting into their own classrooms (Faject, Bello, & Leftwich, 2005).

Experience in classrooms is essential in learning to teach, but it isn't sufficient by itself. Unfortunately, in many cases, experience results in using the same techniques year after year, even when they're ineffective. Research consistently indicates that students who go through traditional teacher preparation programs (such as the one you're in) are more successful and satisfied in their work than those who go into classrooms with little training (Darling-Hammond, 2000). Research and theory, combined with experience, help beginning teachers make sense of the often bewildering classrooms and students they'll encounter. This is one of the reasons you're studying this text.

Item 5: *If I thoroughly understand the content I'm teaching, I'll be able to figure out a way of getting it across to students.* One of the most pervasive myths about teaching is that knowledge of subject matter is all that is necessary to teach effectively. Knowledge of content is essential, of course, but learning to teach requires a great deal of additional knowledge—knowledge you'll acquire in your teacher preparation program (Darling-Hammond & Baratz-Snowdon, 2005).

■ ■ ■ ■ CHECK YOUR UNDERSTANDING

1.1. Describe the beliefs of beginning teachers.

1.2. How could the beliefs of beginning teachers influence your success in your first years of teaching?

1.3. How does teachers' confidence change as they acquire experience?

For feedback, go to the appendix, *Check Your Understanding*, located in the back of this text.

ENTERING THE PROFESSION

Having examined the beliefs of beginning teachers, let's now look at how teachers enter the profession and how this influences their future success.

Traditional and Alternative Licensure

All professionals—physicians, lawyers, and engineers, for example—must be "licensed" in order to work in their occupations, and this applies to teachers as well. The process of licensure is designed to protect the public and ensure competence in each profession. In this section, we examine the processes involved in earning a license and what you can do to make yourself marketable.

TRADITIONAL LICENSURE   Teachers are required by law in all 50 states and the District of Columbia to be licensed by a state department of education before they can teach in public schools. **Licensure** is the process by which a state evaluates the credentials of prospective teachers. By awarding a license, the state certifies that a teacher is competent in subject-area content, possesses professional skills, and is morally fit to work with young people.

During the process of licensure, teachers are increasingly being asked to demonstrate their competence through portfolios, interviews, tests, and on-the-job performance.

You're likely taking this course in a traditional licensure program through which you'll earn a bachelor's degree. Most programs consist of a general education component that includes courses in history, English, math, and science, as well as education courses designed to help you develop your professional knowledge—the pedagogical content knowledge, general pedagogical knowledge, and knowledge of learners and learning described in Chapter 1. If you're planning to become a secondary teacher, you are also required to earn a specified number of hours in the subject area, such as math, in which you plan to teach, and pass a content-area exam in your major.

Increasingly, teachers are also being asked to pass competency tests that measure their basic skills in reading, writing, and mathematics. High school teachers' understanding of an academic area, such as chemistry or English, and their understanding of learning and teaching will also be tested (McCabe, 2006). The Praxis Series™, which consists of all three of these components, is currently being used in 44 states (Educational Testing Service, 2008).

The specific requirements for licensure vary from state to state, and the student-advising office in your college or university can help you access them. If you're planning to move to another state, you can visit that state's website, which will describe its specific licensure requirements. You can also write or call the state certification office directly. To find the addresses and phone numbers of these offices, go to MyEducationLab and click on the Resources tab.

ALTERNATIVE LICENSURE   To meet the growing demand for teachers, many states are developing alternative routes to licensure, and some of you taking this course may be involved in one. **Alternative licensure** provides a shorter route to teaching for those who already possess a bachelor's degree. Currently, 45 states have alternative-route programs, and more than 75 percent of college or university teacher education programs run one or

Licensure The process by which a state evaluates the credentials of prospective teachers.

Alternative licensure A shorter route to licensure for those who already possess a bachelor's degree.

collaborate with them. Nationally, 1 of 4 new teachers enters through an alternative certification program (Humphrey, Wechsler, & Hough, 2008).

A person seeking alternative licensure must hold a bachelor's degree in the content area to be taught, such as math or English; pass a licensure exam; complete a brief, intensive teacher training experience; and complete a supervised teaching internship.

Teach for America is the best known alternative licensure program. Founded in 1989 and claiming more than 14,000 alumni, the organization has an annual budget of $120 million and has more than 6,000 teachers working nationwide, mostly in hard-to-staff urban and rural schools. Candidates must possess a bachelor's degree and commit to 2 years of teaching; while teaching, they receive modest federal grants and college loan deferments in addition to their salaries (N. Dillon, 2007a).

Alternative licensure is controversial. Proponents argue that—partially because they are shorter than traditional licensure programs—they tend to attract members of cultural minorities as well as talented and experienced people in areas of critical need, such as math and science (Sawchuk, 2008). Also, most candidates for alternative licensure are older than students in undergraduate education programs, so they've had more life experiences. And, because they've already earned bachelor's degrees, they are more focused on learning to teach than undergraduates who must combine classes in their content areas with courses in professional education (Ng & Thomas, 2007). Proponents also argue that students in these programs are more academically talented than those in traditional programs (N. Dillon, 2007a).

Critics, however, argue that because of the brief training in pedagogy they receive, alternative licensure candidates lack a great deal of professional knowledge, such as the pedagogical content knowledge, general pedagogical knowledge, and knowledge of learners and learning discussed in Chapter 1. Critics maintain that this limited training results in instruction that is not responsive to students' needs (Darling-Hammond, Chung, & Frelow, 2002). Further, the intensive mentoring and supervision during the first few months of full-time teaching, which is supposed to compensate for the new teachers' lack of formal course work, often doesn't exist (Fowler, 2008); consequently, the first year of teaching becomes sink-or-swim, with many teachers (and their students) failing (Darling-Hammond et al., 2002).

Finally, critics cite statistics indicating that the dropout rate for alternative licensure candidates is considerably greater than the national average for new teachers (Fowler, 2008). This statistic may be skewed, however, because alternative licensure teachers are disproportionately assigned to the most demanding teaching situations, such as urban schools with high numbers of cultural minorities from low-income households. Paradoxically, students who need experienced teachers the most are often least likely to have them (Archer, 2003; Blair, 2003).

Conclusive assessments of alternative licensure are difficult to make because so much variation exists among programs (Baines, 2006; S. Johnson & Birkeland, 2006). High-quality alternative licensure programs are both time-consuming and costly. Research examining the performance of students taught by teachers from alternative licensure programs is mixed. Some data suggest students fare as well as those taught by traditionally prepared teachers; however, other data do not (Darling-Hammond et al., 2001; Laczko-Kerr & Berliner, 2003).

Making Yourself Marketable

Earning a license is an essential part of getting a teaching job, but there's more to it. In this section, we examine factors that can make you marketable.

DEVELOPING A PROFESSIONAL REPUTATION   Because you're at the beginning of your teacher preparation program, it might appear that preparing for a job is well into the

Teach for America An alternative licensure program that enables recent college graduates without state licensure to teach in hard-to-staff schools following a short period of training and supervision.

future. This isn't true. The time to begin developing a professional reputation is now. Let's look at one student's experience.

> I really wish someone had reminded me of these things sooner. When I started, like a lot of others, I didn't take it all too seriously. I'd blow class off now and then, and I didn't always get there on time. I actually did study, but I guess not as hard as I should have.
>
> When I asked Dr. Laslow for a letter of recommendation, he refused. Actually, he said he didn't know me well enough to write a good one. I couldn't believe it. He was nice about it, but he wouldn't write one, advising me to find someone who knew me better and was more familiar with my work. And a couple others were sort of lukewarm, especially in my major. I guess the classes were just too large for them to get to know me. Now it's too late. My record is a little spotty and I feel bad about it now, but I can't go back. I used to wonder why Brad and Kelly always seemed to get all the breaks. Now I get it. (Jeremy, a recent graduate without a job)

Do you know people who seem to get a lot of breaks? Do you get your share? Do your instructors know you, and do they respect and value your work? Students who get breaks do so for a reason. They attend all their classes, turn their work in on time, and attempt to learn as much as possible from their experiences. The quality of their work is consistently high. In other words, they behave professionally. Just as teachers in the field are expected to be professional, students are expected to as well. Professors value conscientiousness, and students like Jeremy trouble them. It's easy to understand why Brad and Kelly got breaks but Jeremy didn't.

What can you do to develop a professional reputation? Here are some suggestions:

- Attend all classes, and be on time. If you must miss, see your professor in advance or explain afterward. (Don't ever miss class and then ask your professor, "Did I miss anything really important?")
- Turn in required assignments on time, and follow established guidelines or criteria.
- Study conscientiously, and try to learn as much as possible in all your classes.
- Participate in class: Offer comments and ask questions. You will enjoy your classes more and also learn more from them.
- Extend your classroom behavior to your life. Take every opportunity to learn something new. For example, travel, especially to other countries, provides opportunities to learn about other cultures and the ways they approach education. Trips like these also make valuable entries on your résumé (which we'll discuss shortly).
- Read and try to be well informed. Learn for the sake of learning.
- Set the goal for yourself to be the best student you can.

If you sincerely attempt to learn and grow, your professional reputation will take care of itself. But you must begin now.

BROADENING YOUR PROFESSIONAL EXPERIENCES   One way to make yourself marketable is to acquire as much professional knowledge and experience as possible. The knowledge component will be addressed in the courses you'll take in your program; your professional experiences will complement this knowledge by applying it in varied contexts. Some suggestions for potential professional experiences are listed in Table 2.1. If you pursue any of these experiences, you can write about them in your portfolio and include them in the résumé you construct to summarize your qualifications.

Table 2.1 Broadening Your Professional Experiences		
Suggested Experience	**Example**	**Professional Benefits**
Develop a minor area of study in a high-need area.	If you're a French major, consider a minor in Spanish. If you're a biology major, consider a minor in chemistry.	You'll have more versatility in the jobs you apply for.
Target clinical work in diverse schools and classrooms.	Request to do your clinical work in schools with high concentrations of low SES, cultural minorities, and English language learners.	You'll establish background and expertise to work in high-demand schools.
Tutor a child.	Become a reading tutor at a local school. Most schools welcome volunteer tutors and may also share your name with parents interested in a private tutor.	You'll gain direct experience working with children and may earn some extra money.
Seek leadership positions.	Run for a student government office.	Leadership experience on a résumé tells potential employers that you have effective human relations skills and the desire to be a lifelong learner.
Do volunteer work.	Spend a few hours each weekend helping out at the local food pantry.	Volunteer work can be enriching, and it indicates your desire to contribute to society.
Become an aide.	Ask your local school district about job openings for part-time classroom aides.	Working as an aide will give you valuable classroom experience and a part-time job.
Join professional organizations.	Join your university's chapter of the National Education Association or a student chapter of another professional organization. (Professional organizations are listed in Table 2.4.)	You'll stay up-to-date on issues in your field and expand your network of professional contacts.

BUILDING A PORTFOLIO AND A RÉSUMÉ

The interview was going okay, but I was uneasy. The principal I was interviewing with was cordial, but she certainly wasn't enthusiastic. "I've had it," I thought to myself. She even quit asking me questions after about 20 minutes. I really wanted the job, too.

As I was about to leave, I happened to mention, "Would you like to see my portfolio?" She looked at it for a couple minutes, and then she started asking some probing questions. When she stuck my DVD in her computer and saw me teaching, she really lit up. I got the job! (Shelley, the new teacher at the beginning of the chapter)

A **professional portfolio**, a collection of materials representative of one's work, provides an effective way to document your competence and qualifications (Devlin-Scherer, Burroughs, Daly, & McCarten, 2007). Just as an artist prepares a portfolio of artwork, prospective teachers produce a professional portfolio to document their developing knowledge and skills. A **digital portfolio** allows you to compress large amounts of information into a computer file, making it easy to edit and burn to a CD that can be shared with prospective employers (Zuger, 2008a).

As you move through your teacher preparation program, you will likely be required to prepare a portfolio to document your developing professional competence, and it will be a tool you can use during job interviews to demonstrate your capabilities as a teacher. We provide *Online Portfolio Activities* at the end of each chapter of this text, and *Guidelines for Beginning a Professional Portfolio* can be found on the text's website at myeducationlab.com.

The first item that appears in your portfolio should be a résumé summarizing your strengths and accomplishments as a teacher. A **résumé** is a document that provides a clear and concise overview of an individual's job qualifications and work experience. It typically is the first thing a prospective employer sees, and it should make a clear and persuasive statement about your qualifications.

Professional portfolio A collection of materials representative of one's work that provides an effective way to document your competence and qualifications.

Digital portfolio A collection of materials contained in an electronic file that makes the information accessible to potential viewers.

Résumé A document that provides a clear and concise overview of an individual's job qualifications and work experience.

When constructing your résumé, clarity and simplicity should be guiding principles. People reading your résumé want to be able to easily find personal information, such as your address and phone number, as well as information about your education, work experience, and interests. They'll expect you to list references or be willing to provide them later. An effective résumé has the following components:

- Personal data
- Professional objectives
- Education
- Teaching experience
- Work experience
- Extracurricular activities
- Honors and awards
- References

The office of career planning and placement at your college or university will be able to help you prepare your own résumé. A sample résumé containing these components is shown in Figure 2.2.

CREATING A CREDENTIALS FILE   Your college or university has a placement center designed to help graduates find jobs. In addition to providing information about job openings, serving as a repository for your credentials file is an essential service of this center. A **credentials file** is a collection of important personal documents teachers submit when they apply for teaching positions. It typically includes background information about you, your résumé, type of position sought, courses taken, performance evaluations by your directing teacher and college or university supervisor during internship, and letters of recommendation (usually three or more). When you apply for a job, you notify the placement center, which then sends your credentials file to the prospective employer. If, after reviewing this file, the district believes there is a potential match, you'll be contacted for an interview.

WRITING A SUCCESSFUL LETTER OF APPLICATION   You have written a résumé and constructed a portfolio showcasing your skills and experiences; now it's time to actually apply for a teaching position. School districts typically have a number of positions open before the start of the school year, so your letter of application, which will serve as a cover letter for your résumé, should clearly state the kind of position you are applying for. In addition, it should highlight the key elements of your résumé that you'd like to emphasize to a potential employer. And, finally, it should close with a statement detailing your availability for an interview, the topic of the next section.

Using correct grammar, punctuation, and spelling is an absolute must in a letter of application. The letter is the first thing people evaluating you see, and even minor errors create a negative impression. Be sure to read your letter carefully before sending it, and, if possible, have a friend read it with a critical eye. (See Figure 2.3 for a sample letter of application.)

Finding a Job

To this point, we have discussed factors that will make you marketable. But when and how do you get started in the process of finding a specific teaching position? The answer to *when* is *now*. We address the question of how in this section.

WHERE ARE THE JOBS?   Your goal is to locate a teaching position that will allow you to utilize your skills and develop as a professional, but the ideal position can be hard to

Credentials file A collection of important personal documents teachers submit when they apply for teaching positions.

Figure 2.2   A Sample Résumé

Melinda Garcia

Personal Data
Address:
2647 Bay Meadows Road
Jacksonville, FL 32224

Home phone: 904-267-5943
Work phone: 904-620-6743
E-mail: mgarcia@msn.com

Professional Objectives:
Elementary Teaching Position, K–6
Elementary Title I Reading Teacher, K–6

Education:
B.A. Elementary Education, University of North Florida, June 2010
Major Area: Elementary Education, K–8
Endorsements: Reading, K–8

Teaching Experience:
Student Teaching: Paxon Elementary, Duval County School District
      Cooperating Teacher: Mrs. Nola Wright
      Worked in a first-grade urban classroom with seven students who were English Language Learners; assumed
      full control of classroom for one eight-week grading period. Also worked with Mrs. Althea Walkman,
      First Grade Title I Coordinator. Administered reading diagnostic tests and developed specialized reading
      programs for groups of students.

Math and Reading Clinical Experience: Matthew Gilbert Elementary, Duval County School District
      Cooperating Teacher: Ms. Linda Gonzalez
      Served as a teacher aide in a fifth-grade, self-contained classroom. Taught both small-group and whole-class
      lessons in reading and math.

Elementary Tutoring: Sandalwood Elementary, Duval County School District
      Cooperating Teacher: Mrs. Alice Watkins
      Observed and tutored third-grade students in all subject matter areas. Tutored students in reading and math
      one-on-one and in small groups.

Work Experience:
Counselor and Tutor: YWCA After-school Activities Program. June 2009 to present. Worked with elementary students
in both academic and recreation areas.

Lifeguard, Duval County Recreation Program. Summers, 2008, 2009. Full-time summer lifeguard; also provided
swimming lessons for young students (4–6 years old).

Extracurricular Activities and Interests:
Vice President, University of North Florida, Student International Reading Association
Senator, University of North Florida, Student Government Association
Member, University of North Florida Swim Team

Honors and Awards:
B. A. with Honors, University of North Florida
Florida UTEACH Scholarship Recipient, 2008–2010

References:
References and credentials file available upon request.

Figure 2.3   Letter of Application

Melinda Garcia
2647 Bay Meadows Road
Jacksonville, FL 32224

June 20, 2010

Dr. Robert Allington
Personnel Director
Duval County School District
2341 Prudential Drive
Jacksonville, FL 32215

Dear Dr. Allington,

I am writing this letter to apply for an elementary teaching position in your district beginning this fall. I recently graduated with honors from the University of North Florida, with a degree in elementary education and an endorsement in reading.

As my enclosed résumé indicates, I have had a number of rewarding experiences working with students in your district. Early in my elementary education program, I observed and tutored students in a third-grade classroom at Sandalwood Elementary School. I then did extensive clinical experiences in fifth-grade math and reading classes at Matthew Gilbert Elementary. During my internship at Paxon Elementary School, I was assigned to a first-grade classroom with significant numbers of Title I students and English Language Learners. During this experience, I learned a great deal about helping culturally diverse first-graders become skilled readers.

As I worked toward my degree, I focused on reading as my major area of endorsement. Reading is the key to success in all other subjects, and I believe I have the knowledge and skills to help young children become successful readers. Through my extensive experiences in classrooms at different levels, I have seen how effective reading programs build on the background knowledge and skills of developing readers. Please note that I have had formal course work in reading diagnosis as well as hands-on experiences implementing different diagnostic tests. I would like to utilize this expertise in a teaching position in your district.

I have arranged for my credentials file to be sent to you from the Placement Office at the University of North Florida. Please feel free to contact me at the telephone numbers listed on my résumé for any additional information. I am available for an interview at any time this summer.

Thank you for considering my application.

Sincerely,

Melinda Garcia

Melinda Garcia

find. Several factors influence the availability of positions; student demographics is one. The P–12 student population increased 14 percent between 1992 and 2005, and public school enrollments are projected to increase an additional 18 percent between 2005 and 2017. The number of public school teachers is also projected to rise 18 percent from 2005 to 2017, with additional job openings resulting from teacher retirements and career changes (National Center for Education Statistics, 2008b). A recent study predicted that more than a third of the nation's teachers could retire between 2010 and 2014, opening up over a million new teaching positions (S. Dillon, 2009b). In addition, the "highly qualified" provision of NCLB, which requires that teachers possess an academic major in the field they are teaching in, will increase the demand for high-quality teachers.

Geography is another factor influencing the availability of positions. Student growth patterns vary by geographic area and grade level, mirroring demographic trends in the country. The greatest enrollment increases are occurring in the South (19 percent) and the West (15 percent). Experts predict that public school enrollments will increase by more than 40 percent in Arizona and Nevada, with substantial increases (more than 25 percent) in Texas, Florida, and Utah (National Center for Education Statistics, 2008b).

Within geographic areas, specific locations also influence job availability. Opportunities are greater in rural and urban schools than in the suburbs, and these districts employ a number of recruiting strategies to attract teachers, such as signing bonuses, financial help for professional-development courses, and even housing incentives (Rubenstein, 2007). For example, New York City recently offered housing subsidies of up to $14,600 to attract math, science, and special education teachers (Herszenhorn, 2006). Shelley, our new teacher at the beginning of the chapter, experienced these patterns:

> *At first I looked for jobs in two suburban schools, but there were no openings. However, I received offers from three different urban schools. I was a little hesitant at first because I had read about the challenges of working in urban settings, especially for first-year teachers. But one of the assistant principals was great. She talked to me about the job, what it entailed, and the kind of help I'd receive in an induction program at that school. I was paired with a wonderful mentor (Mrs. Landsdorp), and I'm having a challenging but great year. I love these kids and think I'm going to make it.*

The specific teaching position you seek will also affect your chances of finding a job. The greatest areas of need are in special education, English language learning (including bilingual education and English as a second language), foreign languages (especially Spanish), math, physics, chemistry, and technology. Lower areas of teacher need include English, history, and physical education (P. Murphy, DeArmond, & Guin, 2003).

What implications do these job patterns have for you? First, if you haven't already decided on a major, don't select one based on job availability alone: To be effective (and happy), you need to be interested in and want to teach in the area you select. Don't major in chemistry, for example, if you dislike chemistry. But if you like chemistry and want to teach it, you now know that there is a high probability of getting a job in that area. Second, learn where teaching jobs exist; the career placement center at your college or university can help. You'll increase your chances of finding a job if you're flexible about where you'll teach. Your first teaching position may not be in an ideal location, but you can use it to gain experience, which can lead to other positions.

INTERVIEWING EFFECTIVELY

> *You're interviewing for your first job, and the principal at the school where you'd like to work asks, "You've got a classroom full of unmotivated fourth graders. What would you do to increase their motivation?"*
>   *How would you respond?*

Your interview is your best opportunity to show a prospective employer that you are a knowledgeable and committed professional. This is the setting that will probably determine whether you get a job. Some guidelines for interviewing effectively are outlined in Table 2.2.

Schools look for the following in new teachers:

Interviews provide opportunities for teaching candidates not only to explain their qualifications but also to find out about the positions they're applying for.

- Knowledge of a content area, or areas, as well as an understanding of how students learn

- An understanding of how to organize and manage a classroom—beginning teachers' number one concern

- An ability to convert state standards into meaningful learning experiences for your students

- A sincere interest in making a difference in students' lives

- A variety of life experiences that can contribute to your classroom

- The ability to work with others

- Adaptability and flexibility (Clement, 2008)

If you are genuinely interested in working with young people, and if you've been conscientious in your teacher preparation program, the interview will largely take care of itself. Nothing communicates more effectively than a sincere desire to do the job you're interviewing for.

Additional preparation can increase the positive impression you make, however. For example, how would you respond to the following questions, all of which are frequently asked in teacher interviews?

- Why do you want to teach?

- Why do you want to work in this school?

- What is your philosophy of education?

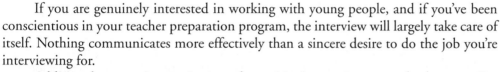

Table 2.2 Guidelines for Interviewing Effectively

Guideline	Rationale
Be on time.	Nothing creates a worse impression than being late for an interview.
Dress appropriately.	Wear an outfit appropriate for an interview, and be well groomed. Shorts, jeans, and T-shirts are inappropriate, as is an eyebrow ring. You have the right to dress and groom yourself in any way you choose, but if you are serious about getting a job, you won't demonstrate your freedom of expression during a job interview.
Speak clearly, and use Standard English grammar.	Clear language is correlated with effective teaching, and your verbal ability creates an impression of professional ability.
Cell phone should be turned off.	You want to show the interviewer that this is important enough to warrant your undivided attention.
Sit comfortably and calmly.	Fidgeting—or worse, glancing at your watch—suggests either that you're nervous or that you'd rather be somewhere else.
Communicate empathy for children and a desire to work with them.	Communicating an understanding of learning, learner development, and instruction demonstrates that you have a professional knowledge base.

- How would you plan for classroom management?
- How would you handle an incident of misbehavior?
- How would you organize a unit on a topic in your area?
- How would you design your classroom for students of varying ability levels?
- How would you involve parents or caregivers in their children's education?

We suggest you keep these questions in mind and begin to form answers to them as you go through your teacher preparation program. If you're prepared, you will also be more at ease during the interview.

The more specific and concrete your responses to questions, the more positive an impression you will make. During your interview, be specific, and use concrete examples from your own experience to illustrate your answers (Clement, 2008). For example, here is a specific response to the question about teaching philosophy:

"I believe that all children can learn, and I would try my best to make that happen by ensuring that all students are involved in the lessons I teach. Research suggests that active involvement is essential for learning. During my student teaching, I try to get my students involved by calling on each of them as often as possible and use group work to develop content knowledge and social skills."

The answer communicates that you're clear about what you would try to do and why. Also, citing research suggests that you are knowledgeable, something all school districts value (Strong & Hindman, 2003). In contrast, a vague response, such as "I am a humanistic and learner-centered teacher," leaves the interviewer with the impression that you're just saying words you learned in a class, which is much less persuasive.

ASSESSING PROSPECTIVE SCHOOLS   Your interview is a two-way street: You are being interviewed, but at the same time you're interviewing the school. You want a job, but you also want to determine if this is the kind of place in which you want to work. Research suggests that both the upkeep and the condition of the school and its professional culture have a powerful influence on teachers' satisfaction on the job (Buckley, Schneider, & Shang, 2005). When you interview, you should ask specific questions of the principal and other people you will work with; doing so helps you learn about the position and communicates that you are thoughtful and serious about the job.

Factors to consider when evaluating a school as a potential workplace include the following:

- *Teacher morale and efficacy:* Is teacher morale high, and do they believe that they make a difference in students' lives? Teaching is stressful, and school morale can make a big difference in how you feel about your job (Ware & Kitsantas, 2007).
- *Commitment and leadership of the principal:* The principal's leadership sets the tone for the school (Ubben, Hughes, & Norris, 2006). Does the principal communicate caring for students and support for teachers? Lack of support from administrators is an important reason teachers leave a school (Luekens, Lyter, & Fox, 2004).
- *School mission:* Does the principal communicate a clear school mission, and do teachers feel as if they're a team, all working for the benefit of students? Teachers have a strong positive effect on both teacher morale and student achievement when they collectively believe they can positively influence students' lives (Goddard, Hoy, & Hoy, 2004).
- *School climate:* Does the emotional climate of the school seem positive, and do people communicate a positive and upbeat attitude? How do office personnel

treat students? Do the support staff, such as custodians and cafeteria workers, feel like they're part of the team? Emotional and physical workplace conditions strongly influence whether teachers remain in a school (Luekens et al., 2004).

- *The physical plant:* Are student work products, such as art and woodshop projects, displayed in cases and on the walls? Do posters and signs suggest that the school is a positive environment for learning? Are the classrooms, halls, and restrooms clean and free of debris and graffiti?

- *Student behavior:* Are students orderly and polite to one another and to teachers? Do they seem happy to be at school?

- *Community support:* Do people in the community value education and support teachers? How does the school involve parents in their children's education, and do parents support school functions? The support of parents and the community has an important influence on students' attitudes, behaviors, and work habits (Marzano, 2003; MetLife Survey of the American Teacher, 2006).

- *An induction program for teachers:* Does the school have a mentoring program for beginning teachers? First-year teachers who participate in mentoring programs are more likely to succeed and stay in teaching than those who don't (Darling-Hammond & Baratz-Snowdon, 2005). (We examine induction and mentoring programs in more detail later in the chapter.)

These questions are difficult to answer in one visit, but they are important for your future development and satisfaction with the job. Working conditions in schools vary dramatically, and they can make the difference between a rewarding first year and one that makes you reconsider your decision to teach.

PRIVATE SCHOOL EMPLOYMENT   Teaching in a private school is another potential source of employment; approximately 12 percent of P–12 students attend private schools (Kober, 2006). There were 6.1 million private P–12 students in the United States in 2001, a figure that is projected to increase by 5 percent over the next 10 years (National Center for Education Statistics, 2008b). More than three fourths of private schools are religiously oriented, with Catholic schools being the most common. Because of the cost of tuition, private schools attract more affluent students, and these schools generally have fewer learners with exceptionalities, members of cultural minorities, and English language learners than public schools (Bracey, 2008). You are most likely to find private school employment in urban areas and in the South.

Starting salaries for private school teachers are about 30 percent lower than those in public schools, however, and the difference increases to more than 40 percent for maximum salaries. In addition, private schools typically don't provide the same insurance benefits offered in public schools. Because of these financial issues, private school teachers are almost twice as likely to leave teaching as are their public school counterparts (Luekens et al., 2004). When they leave private schools, more than half transfer to public schools.

Private schools sometimes waive the licensing requirements that public school teachers are required by law to meet, which can make them attractive to someone who doesn't want to spend the time and money to earn a traditional license. In addition, teachers sometimes choose private school employment because the school is dedicated to religious or intellectual principles consistent with their beliefs. Communication between administrators and teachers also is easier because these schools are often smaller, and parents whose children attend private schools tend to be more involved in school activities than those with children in public schools. Deciding to teach in a public or a private school will ultimately be a decision that only you can make.

In the next section, we examine the role of minority teachers in meeting the needs of a diverse student population.

The Competition for Minority Teachers

Four of 10 school-age children in the United States are members of cultural minorities, and in the 25 largest cities in our country, students of color compose at least half of the student population (U.S. Bureau of Census, 2006a). Projections indicate that before the mid-21st century, more than half of the nation's students will be members of cultural minorities (U.S. Bureau of Census, 2003). At the same time, the percentage of teachers who are members of minority groups remains fixed at about 12 percent, and in some areas is as low as 1 percent (Ladson-Billings, 2005; U.S. Bureau of Census, 2006a).

Concern over these changing demographics has resulted in increased efforts to recruit minority teachers. Although nonminority teachers can work effectively with minority students, many educators believe that minority teachers bring valuable perspectives to classrooms (Michie, 2004). Students need role models who share their cultural backgrounds, and minority role models may motivate more effectively because students can identify more closely with them (Schunk, Pintrich, & Meese, 2008).

Minority teachers can also provide culturally relevant instruction by helping bridge differences between schools and minority students' homes and cultures. Also, they can enrich a school's faculty by providing additional perspectives on effective teaching and learning practices for minority students (Ladson-Billings, 2005; Yan & Gong, 2003).

To attract minority candidates to teaching, recruiters in many states have developed scholarships and loan-forgiveness programs. And, alternative licensure is a promising recruitment tool. For example, in both Texas and California, more than 40 percent of the people who went through their alternative licensure program in the late 1990s were members of cultural minorities (National Center for Education Information, 2000).

Difficulties with these programs exist, however. For example, the recruitment strategies sometimes conflict with reforms in education. Recruiters want to attract teachers, whereas reformers are calling for higher academic standards, usually measured by standardized tests. And, standardized testing has a history of negatively and disproportionately affecting minorities (Guar-

ino, Santibañez, & Daley, 2006). Also, as you saw earlier in the chapter, a higher proportion of teachers who go through alternative licensure programs leave teaching than those who complete traditional programs.

Some trends are beginning to emerge. The enrollment of African American students in colleges of education increased from 6 to 9 percent in the 1990s (Archer, 2000a). Surveys indicate that African American, Native American, and Hispanic college graduates are more likely to become teachers than are White graduates. But because minority students are less likely than White students to graduate from high school, a bottleneck in K–12 schools exists (Barton, 2006; Swanson, 2004). Leaders suggest that a nation wanting the teaching force to more nearly reflect the composition of society must first focus its educational efforts on today's K–12 students.

Diversity in Your Classroom

So where does this leave you as a beginning teacher? If you're not a member of a cultural minority, it doesn't mean that you can't effectively teach minority students. On the other hand, if you are a member of a cultural minority, you can bring some unique qualities to your classroom. And, you—members and nonmembers of minorities—will be on the same faculty; this will give you the opportunity to work together, which can result in increased learning for all students.

Increased learning begins with sensitivity to and awareness of the cultural attitudes and values as well as the knowledge your students bring to the classroom. Make a special effort at the beginning of the year to get to know each of your students as individuals; simply asking them about their interests, and making an effort to include all students in learning activities, will communicate with your actions that you're committed to them and their learning.

Minority teachers act as role models for minority students and help bridge gaps between homes and schools.

(We discuss strategies for getting to know your students in the next section.)

The bottom line is that students need to believe that you care about them and will do everything in your power to help them learn. With this foundation, effective teachers create classroom management systems that are fair and inviting, design learning activities that are challenging and that lead to success, and use assessment systems that encourage effort and achievement. These aren't easy tasks, but the rest of this text, as well as the teacher education program you're now in, will prepare you for these challenges.

QUESTIONS TO CONSIDER

1. What can a nonminority teacher do to prepare for teaching in a culturally diverse setting?
2. Should nonminority teachers imitate or try to act more like their minority teacher counterparts? What are the advantages and disadvantages of this approach?

myeducationlab To respond to these questions online, explore this topic further, and receive feedback, go to the *Book Specific Resources* section in the MyEducationLab for your course, select your text, and then select *Exploring Diversity* for Chapter 2.

CHECK YOUR UNDERSTANDING

2.1. What are the two primary differences between traditional and alternative licensure?

2.2. What are the two most essential factors involved in finding a desirable job?

2.3. In which areas are teaching jobs most plentiful?

For feedback, go to the appendix, *Check Your Understanding*, located in the back of this text.

YOUR FIRST YEAR OF TEACHING

What will your first year of teaching be like? Let's see what one first-year teacher has to say.

> Wow! Was I naive. I was tired of sitting in classes, and I wanted so badly to be finished and get out into the "real world." What I never realized was just how cushy being a student was. If I was a little tired or didn't study enough, I would just coast through class. Now, no coasting. You have to be ready every minute of every day. I've never been so tired in my life. You're in front of kids all day, and then you go home and work late into the night to get ready for the next day. They have us filling out reports, doing surveys, and everything other than teaching, so I don't get a chance to plan during the day. I can't even make a phone call unless it's during my lunch break or planning period.
>
> And then there's my fourth period. They come in from lunch just wired. It takes me half the period to get them settled down, and that's on a good day.
>
> Sometimes I just need someone to talk to, but we're all so busy. Everybody thinks they're an expert on teaching, because they've been a student. They don't have a clue. Let them try it for 2 days, and they'd be singing a different tune. (Antonio, a first-year middle school math teacher)

About 6 percent of all public school teachers leave the profession each year, but the number of new teachers who leave is much higher—about 15 percent after their first year, another 15 percent after their second, and an additional 10 percent after their third year (Ingersoll & Smith, 2004). After the fifth year, more than 45 percent of new teachers have left the profession (Kober, 2006).

New teachers face the following challenges:

- Unruly students and a disorderly teaching environment
- Loneliness and alienation

- Working conditions that require teachers to spend too much time on non-teaching duties, offer them too little time for planning, and provide no time for themselves (S. Johnson & Birkeland, 2003)

The first year can also be rewarding, even exhilarating. Let's look at another of Antonio's experiences:

> Wow, what a day. We've been working so hard on solving equations, and all of a sudden Jeremy [one of Antonio's weaker students] bursts out right in the middle of our discussion, "Hey, I get this. It ain't all that bad." What a rush. When you see the lightbulb finally come on in a kid's head, it keeps you going for another month. And, yesterday, Natalia [another struggling student] came up and said, "Mr. Martinez, I used to really, really hate math, but now I actually look forward to coming to algebra." I didn't drive home after school yesterday; I flew.

In Chapter 1, we talked about rewards in teaching, and Antonio experienced some of them. It is, indeed, a heady experience to see students understand something new and know that you helped make it happen.

Survival Skills for the First Year

You can prepare for your first year of teaching by developing the following "survival skills":

- *Organization:* Using your time efficiently
- *Classroom management:* Creating an orderly classroom environment
- *Teaching effectively:* Involving students in meaningful learning activities
- *Knowing your students:* Connecting with students at a personal level

Let's see how these skills can help you survive—and even thrive—in your first year of teaching.

ORGANIZATION   Lack of time will be one of the first and most significant challenges you'll face as a beginning teacher (Kyriacou & Kunc, 2006). You'll feel as though you don't have a second to yourself. As Antonio commented, "I've never been so tired in my life. You're in front of kids all day, and then you go home and work late into the night to get ready for the next day." And, at the beginning of the chapter, Shelley commented, "I can't believe how much there is to do—IEPs, progress reports, CPR training, responsibility to look for signs of abuse. When do I teach?"

Although a simple solution to this problem doesn't exist, careful organization can make a difference (Mandel, 2006). A large body of research, dating back to the 1970s, indicates that effective teachers are well organized—both in their classrooms and in their lives (Good & Brophy, 2008, Rutter et al., 1979). A student in one of our classes observed the following in a first-year teacher he visited:

> His desk was a mess. Books and papers piled everywhere. He couldn't find anything, and he was always shuffling through papers looking for something. He always acted like he wasn't quite ready for what was coming next.

Organization can help teachers maximize the time they have for the numerous professional roles they perform.

If he couldn't find "anything," you can bet he wasted time looking for lesson plans and student papers. If you frequently or even occasionally lament that "I must get organized," now is a good time to start changing your habits. Thoroughly planning your lessons, having your instructional materials stored and readily accessible, creating procedures for routine tasks (e.g., turning in, scoring, and returning papers), and establishing policies for absences and making up missed work are all essential for using time effectively. For expert teachers, these skills have become automatic; for beginning teachers, they must be learned (Weinstein, 2007).

CLASSROOM MANAGEMENT Classroom management has historically been the primary concern of beginning teachers, and disruptive students are an important source of stress for beginners and veterans alike (Public Agenda, 2004; M. Romano, 2006). It is a major reason that teachers leave the profession during their first years of teaching (Liu & Meyer, 2005). New teachers often feel ill-equipped to deal with management, and this dimension of effective teaching is one of the most important and demanding skills you'll learn in your teacher education program.

TEACHING EFFECTIVELY Even though classroom management is the primary concern of beginning teachers, it's virtually impossible to have a well-managed classroom without effective instruction (Good & Brophy, 2008). If instruction is boring or if students don't understand what they're supposed to be learning and why, the likelihood of having classroom management problems increases dramatically.

KNOWING YOUR STUDENTS Knowing your students is essential. It communicates that you care about students as people, and it allows you to adjust your instruction to the interests and needs of your students. Commit yourself to learning all your students' names within the first week of school. Again, watch your professors and teachers out in the field. See how they use students' names in their instruction: You will notice a striking difference between teachers who know and address students by name and those who do not.

Knowing students' names is important, but it's only a first step. Experienced teachers often begin the school year by having students fill out a questionnaire addressing questions such as these:

- Describe three important things about yourself as a person.
- What do you want to learn from this class?
- What are your favorite topics?
- How do you like to learn?
- What kinds of learning activities do you enjoy?

More important than the actual questions is the fact that you care enough to ask them. It makes students feel as if you and they are working cooperatively together, which is important for your relationship with them.

Being well organized, developing an effective classroom management system, teaching effectively, and knowing your students are essential for a successful first year; this is why we call them *survival skills*. But what else can beginning teachers do to make their first year of teaching productive? Induction and mentoring programs connect beginning teachers to experts for advice (and comfort).

Induction and Mentoring Programs

Mrs. Landsdorp is wonderful. She is so supportive, and she is the person I always go to when I want a straight answer about what's really going on in the school and the district. She's also been very helpful in giving suggestions about how to deal with difficult parents and how I should handle myself in situations where I'm uncertain. She hasn't helped me a whole lot with nitty-gritty stuff, like planning lessons or watching me teach, but that's not her fault. She has a full teaching load too, so she really doesn't have time. I guess what it really amounts to is that she's been a real source of emotional support, and this year is going better than I could have hoped for. (Shelley, first-year third-grade teacher, talking about her mentor)

The transition to teaching is rarely as smooth as Shelley experienced. Teachers are sometimes hired at the last moment, left isolated in their classrooms, and given little help—the sink-or-swim experience of many beginning teachers. As you saw earlier, nearly a third of new teachers leave the profession within the first 2 years (Ingersoll & Smith, 2004), and isolation and lack of support are major reasons why.

The stress of the first year is reduced, however, when teachers have someone to turn to for help. Beginning teachers without mentors and support are nearly twice as likely to leave as those with programs designed to help them make the transition from the university to the K–12 classroom (Horn, 2005).

To address this problem, many schools offer induction and mentoring programs for new teachers. **Induction programs** are professional experiences for beginning teachers that offer assistance to ease the transition into teaching. These programs include structured staff development activities (e.g., workshops focusing on problems commonly experienced by first-year teachers), systematic efforts to provide new teachers with crucial information, and mentors. **Mentors** are experienced teachers who provide guidance and support for beginning teachers (Bartell, 2005). Ideally, mentors are sources of both emotional support, as Shelley reported, and technical support in planning and conducting lessons and assessing student learning. The most effective mentors match a new teacher's specific teaching assignment, so they can provide information that is both grade-level and content-area specific (Moir, 2008/2009). Effective induction and mentoring programs not only provide technical and psychological assistance and support, they also significantly reduce the failure rate for beginning teachers (Ingersoll & Smith, 2004).

Successful induction programs have the following elements (Gilbert, 2005; Wong, Britton, & Ganser, 2005):

- A systematic attempt to help beginning teachers with both classes and opportunities to observe and dialogue with experienced teachers
- Feedback to new teachers based on classroom observation
- Special help in the beginning years of their career to help them link their instruction to state and district standards
- Mentor support with everyday problems and encouragement for developing a reflective professional attitude
- Professional-development activities designed to increase mentors' effectiveness and compensation for mentors

Actual classroom observations with feedback are essential; beginning teachers provided with this help significantly improve in organizing and managing instruction, and their students are better behaved and more engaged during lessons (Evertson & Smithey, 2000).

Many beginning teachers, however, don't participate in anything more than perfunctory school orientations, and many of the mentoring programs that exist are like the one Shelley described: They provide emotional support but little specific help in the process of learning to teach (Olson, 2003). Ask the principal and talk to teachers—and especially those who are new—about the availability of induction and mentoring programs. Whether a school has a well-organized mentoring program is something you should seriously consider in evaluating a prospective school.

**PEARSON
myeducationlab**

To hear one principal's advice to preservice teachers, go to the *Assignments and Activities* section of Topic 14: *Professional Development* in the MyEducationLab for your course and complete the activity titled *Preparing to Teach: Advice from Two Professionals.*

Induction programs Professional experiences for beginning teachers that provide assistance to ease the transition into teaching.

Mentors Experienced teachers who offer guidance and support for beginning teachers.

Teacher Evaluation

Teacher testing and accountability have become facts of professional life, and you will be required to pass competency tests before you're licensed. You'll also be evaluated during your first years of teaching as you progress from provisional status to regular teacher, and most states require regular evaluations of all teachers (Olson, 2008).

Teacher evaluation has two primary purposes: **formative**, which is the process of gathering information and providing feedback that teachers can use to improve their practice, and **summative**, which is the process of gathering information about a teacher's competence for the purpose of making decisions about retention and promotion (Ubben et al., 2006). You will encounter both in your first years of teaching.

Evaluation processes vary, so you should check to see how they are handled in your state and district. Typically, they are based on theory and research that examine the relationships between teacher actions and student learning (Borman & Kimball, 2005; Odden, Borman, & Fermanich, 2004); observation instruments are then created based on the literature (Pecheone & Chung, 2006). For example, research indicates that effective teachers have well-established classroom routines, use instructional strategies that produce high levels of student involvement, and quickly identify and eliminate sources of disruption (Emmer, Evertson, & Worsham, 2009; Evertson, Emmer, & Worsham, 2009). Observation instruments would then have observers assess elements such as the following:

- Whether routines are in place and used effectively
- The extent to which students are attentive and involved in the lesson
- Whether the teacher can correctly identify sources of misbehavior and deal with them quickly

Observers use the same process to evaluate skills in other domains.

Before being observed, you should ask to see the instrument that will be used. If you're uncertain about the meaning of any of the categories, ask an administrator or an experienced teacher to explain them. It always helps to know how you'll be evaluated, and knowing this also helps reduce the stress and anxiety that are always there when someone observes your teaching.

Some states use existing standards, such as the INTASC (Interstate New Teacher Assessment and Support Consortium) principles you'll study later in the chapter, as frameworks for designing evaluation systems. Teachers compile portfolios of lesson plans, videotapes, student artifacts, and reflections that address each of the principles, and trained experts then evaluate these portfolios (Lashley, 2001). Portfolio-based teacher evaluation systems are becoming more prominent, which makes developing an effective portfolio early in your program an important strategy for finding a job.

In the next section, we discuss merit pay and how it will influence your life as a beginning teacher.

■ ■ ■ ■ ■ CHECK YOUR UNDERSTANDING

3.1. Identify four factors that contribute to a successful first year of teaching.

3.2. What are the characteristics of successful induction programs?

3.3. How are teacher evaluation systems created and used?

For feedback, go to the appendix, *Check Your Understanding*, located in the back of this text.

Formative evaluation The process of gathering information and providing feedback that teachers can use to improve their practice.

Summative evaluation The process of gathering information about a teacher's competence, usually for the purpose of making decisions about retention and promotion. Can also apply to students' academic progress.

Merit Pay

As a beginning teacher, you will certainly want to know how much you'll be paid and how pay increases over the years will be determined. Historically, most salary increases have been based on years of experience and the number of graduate and in-service credit hours that teachers have earned (Figure 2.4). However, **merit pay**, a supplement to a teacher's base salary used to reward exemplary performance, is one reform movement receiving increased attention.

As you see in Figure 2.4, merit pay is one type of *pay for performance*, which—in addition to merit pay—includes teaching in high-need areas, such as math, science or special education, and increased teacher responsibilities, such as mentoring a new teacher or being a team leader (Odden, 2003).

Because many policy makers want some form of pay for performance for teachers, and because many school districts are considering performance-pay experiments, it's likely that you will encounter the issue early in your career (Drevitch, 2006). For example, in 2006,

Merit pay A supplement to a teacher's base salary used to reward exemplary performance.

at least 30 states were offering incentives, such as housing benefits or loan forgiveness, to address teacher shortages in certain content and geographical areas (Jacobson, 2006).

Merit pay differs from other pay-for-performance plans in two ways. First, it is available to all teachers, not just those who take on extra responsibilities, such as being a team leader. Second, it is based entirely on exemplary performance, which is measured in different ways, such as through student test scores or observations by a school administrator. The interest in merit pay increased when the Obama administration supported research and development examining its effectiveness and allocated $200 million in additional funding to support efforts to develop merit pay plans (Sawchuk, 2009c).

True merit pay, sometimes referred to as "differentiated pay" or "cash incentives," exists in different forms (S. Dillon, 2007). Some merit systems reward individual teachers based on their students' performance on tests; others reward them based on administrators' observations or on teaching artifacts such as exemplary lessons or student work. A third type rewards entire

schools for student test performance (Keller, 2002; Odden, 2003). Rewarding exemplary or meritorious performance is the common factor in these plans.

THE ISSUE

Merit pay is highly controversial. Proponents argue that exemplary teaching performance should be rewarded and that money can provide incentives for teacher excellence (Honawar & Olson, 2008). The superintendent of the Houston, Texas, district, the largest to experiment with merit pay, commented, "It simply doesn't make sense any more. The system that pays the worst teacher the same that it pays the best teacher is not working" (Cook, 2006, p. 4). Advocates of merit pay also claim that effective merit pay systems would attract brighter, more competent people into the profession and prove to be a way of retaining the best and brightest teachers.

The general public is also in favor of most incentive proposals. In a 2008 poll, 76 percent of the general public supported incentive pay for teachers; for those who had children in school, this figure rose to 79 percent (Bushaw & Gallup, 2008). Further, in a 2007 poll, 81 percent of parents favored basing

Figure 2.4 Different Teacher Compensation Plans

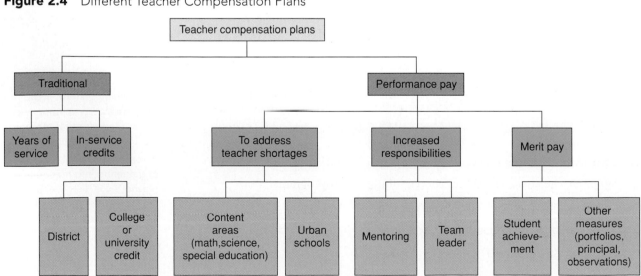

teacher rewards on student test scores (Rose & Gallup, 2007).

Teachers, however, are more skeptical of these plans. The majority (more than 60 percent) of teachers are in favor of higher pay for teachers who work in tough neighborhoods with low-performing students, for those who work harder and put in longer hours, or for those who consistently receive high evaluations from their principals (Public Agenda, 2003). But teachers' support for incentive pay drops to 42 percent for paying teachers in high-demand areas, and to 38 percent when the system is based primarily on student test scores.

Critics contend that merit pay is divisive, damages morale, and makes teachers less likely to cooperate with each other (Ramirez, 2001). They also question the assumption that teachers will work harder for more pay.

> To believe that teachers will try harder if offered a financial incentive is to assume that they aren't trying hard now, that they know what to do, but simply aren't doing it, and that they are motivated more by money than by their students' needs. These are unlikely and unsupported conclusions, which teachers find insulting rather than motivating. (Gratz, 2009, pp. 40, 32)

Another criticism is that merit systems often are too complex and fail to address the need for higher base salaries for all teachers (Cook, 2006). In addition, some critics contend that many merit-pay systems are put into place without clear guidelines, agreed-upon and objective measures of teacher performance, or effective processes for identifying high-performing teachers (Guthrie & Schuermann, 2008). They say that teachers won't buy into a system if they don't understand it or believe it's fair, or if it doesn't reward the best teachers (S. Dillon, 2007).

Finally, research has so far failed to find a link between merit-pay systems and increased student achievement, the ultimate criterion for any educational reform (Honawar, 2008). Experts also identify several important, unanswered questions about merit pay:

- Does it work? Will merit pay encourage teachers to work harder or differently?
- Will merit pay based on student achievement encourage teachers to focus on some aspects of student learning (i.e., that which is tested and rewarded) while neglecting others?
- Are individual or group awards, such as rewarding an entire school for achievement gains, more effective?

- What are the long-term effects on student achievement, teacher morale, and teacher recruitment?

Obviously, increased research is needed to accompany development efforts in this area.

YOU TAKE A STAND

Now it's your turn to take a position on the issue. Is merit pay an effective way to increase the quality of our teachers and their instruction?

myeducationlab To explore both sides of this issue and take a stand, go to the *Book Specific Resources* section in the MyEducationLab for your course, select your text, and then select *Taking a Stand in an Era of Reform* for Chapter 2.

myeducationlab To hear one superintendent's views on the pros and cons of performance pay, go to the *Assignments and Activities* section of Topic 5: *Governance and Finance* in the MyEducationLab for your course and complete the activity titled *Performance Pay: A Superintendent's Perspective.*

ISSUES IN EDUCATION

CAREER-LONG PROFESSIONAL DEVELOPMENT

To this point, we have discussed finding your first job and how to succeed in your first year of teaching. Now is also the time to begin thinking about your career 3 to 5 or more years down the road, because long-term professional goals can guide you during your teacher preparation program. In this section, we examine four aspects of career-long professional development:

- The Interstate New Teacher and Support Consortium (INTASC)
- Membership in professional organizations
- Becoming a teacher-leader
- Attaining certification through the National Board for Professional Teaching Standards

INTASC: A Beginning Point for Professional Development

A rapidly expanding body of research consistently demonstrates that teaching now requires professionals who are highly knowledgeable and skilled (Berliner, 2005a; Darling-Hammond & Bransford, 2005), and the profession is responding. Created in 1987, the Interstate New Teacher Assessment and Support Consortium (INTASC) was designed to help states develop better teachers through coordinated efforts of support and assessment. INTASC (1993) has raised the bar by setting rigorous standards for new teachers in important areas such as planning, instruction, and increasing student motivation. These standards describe what you should know and be able to do when you first walk into a classroom and provide a concrete starting point for your own professional development.

To date, INTASC has prepared general, or "core," standards organized around 10 principles (see Table 2.3) and is preparing standards for various subject-matter areas and specific student populations. INTASC is also developing a Test for Teaching Knowledge (TTK) linked to the core principles. The Assignments and Activities and Building Teaching Skills and Dispositions sections found on MyEducationLab are keyed to INTASC standards; in addition, each of the Online Portfolio Activities found at the end of the chapters is linked to the INTASC core standards, and a matrix correlating INTASC standards to this text's content can be found on the inside cover.

PEARSON
myeducationlab

Go to the *Building Teaching Skills and Dispositions* section of Topic 1: *The Teaching Profession* in the MyEducationLab for your course and complete the activity titled *INTASC Standards and Teaching Practice*.

Table 2.3 The INTASC Principles

Principle	Description
1. Knowledge of subject	The teacher understands the central concepts, tools of inquiry, and structures of the discipline(s) he or she teaches and can create learning experiences that make these aspects of subject matter meaningful for students.
2. Learning and human development	The teacher understands how children learn and develop, and can provide learning opportunities that support their intellectual, social, and personal development.
3. Adapting instruction	The teacher understands how students differ in their approaches to learning and creates instructional opportunities that are adapted to diverse learners.
4. Strategies	The teacher understands and uses a variety of instructional strategies to encourage students' development of critical thinking, problem solving, and performance skills.
5. Motivation and management	The teacher uses an understanding of individual and group motivation and behavior to create a learning environment that encourages positive social interaction, active engagement in learning, and self-motivation.
6. Communication skills	The teacher uses knowledge of effective verbal, nonverbal, and media communication techniques to foster active inquiry, collaboration, and supportive interaction in the classroom.
7. Planning	The teacher plans instruction based upon knowledge of subject matter, students, the community, and curriculum goals.
8. Assessment	The teacher understands and uses formal and informal assessment strategies to evaluate and ensure the continuous intellectual, social, and physical development of the learner.
9. Commitment	The teacher is a reflective practitioner who continually evaluates the effects of his/her choices and actions on others (students, parents, and other professionals in the learning community) and who actively seeks out opportunities to grow professionally.
10. Partnership	The teacher fosters relationships with school colleagues, parents, and agencies in the larger community to support students' learning and well-being.

Source: Interstate New Teacher Assessment and Support Consortium (1993). *Model standards for beginning teacher licensing and development: A resource for state dialogues.* Washington, DC.: Council of Chief State School Officers. Reprinted by permission.

The INTASC standards are demanding, but this is as it should be. If you expect to be treated as a professional, you should have the knowledge and skills that allow you to make the decisions expected of a professional. Being able to meet the INTASC standards is a good beginning.

Membership in Professional Organizations

One of the first steps in your professional growth should be involvement in the professional organizations in education. These organizations support a variety of activities designed to improve teaching and schools:

- Providing professional-development activities for teachers

- Disseminating up-to-date research and information on trends in the profession through professional publications

- Holding yearly conferences that present research about recent professional advances

- Providing resources where teachers can find answers to questions about professional issues and problems

- Providing politicians and policy makers with information about important issues facing education

Table 2.4 presents a list of prominent professional organizations, their websites, and descriptions of their missions or goals. We recommend that you join a professional organization as an integral part of your professional growth; many organizations have student memberships that allow you to become involved while still in school.

Two of the largest professional organizations are the **National Education Association (NEA)** and the **American Federation of Teachers (AFT)**. Founded in 1857, NEA is the largest professional organization, enrolling approximately two thirds of the teachers in this country (National Education Association, 2006a). Most (78 percent) of the members are teachers, but NEA also includes guidance counselors, librarians, and administrators. AFT was founded in 1916 and has more than 1.3 million members who primarily teach in urban areas (American Federation of Teachers, 2006). AFT doesn't allow administrators to join and has gained notoriety for its emphasis on better pay and better working conditions. You are likely to encounter representatives from one or both of these organizations in your first year on the job. Talk with experienced teachers in your school about the pros and cons of each.

Becoming a Teacher-Leader

At this point in your career, you may react to becoming a teacher-leader with "Teacher-leader! I'm just trying to become a teacher!" Expectations for teachers have risen significantly since the beginning of the 1990s, and teachers' roles are also changing. For example, teachers now have much more input into decisions about teacher preparation, certification, and staff development than in the past; this change has thrust teachers into new leadership roles, and the term *teacher-leader* has become part of the language of educational reform (Williams, 2007). Becoming a teacher-leader also creates a tangible goal for your growth as a professional educator.

Teachers can develop leadership skills in a number of ways:

- Serving on school-level or district-wide curriculum committees

- Helping establish school-level or district-wide policies on issues such as grading, dress codes, and attendance

- Writing grant proposals for student development or teacher development projects

- Proposing and facilitating staff development projects

PEARSON
myeducationlab

To hear advice for beginning teachers from a superintendent, go to the *Assignments and Activities* section of Topic 14: *Professional Development* in the MyEducationLab for your course and complete the activity titled *A Principal's Advice for Preservice Teachers*.

PEARSON
myeducationlab

Go to the *Building Teaching Skills and Dispositions* section of Topic 14: *Professional Development* in the MyEducationLab for your course and complete the activity titled *Characteristics of Professionalism*.

National Education Association (NEA) The nation's oldest and largest teacher professional organization, founded in 1857.

American Federation of Teachers (AFT) The nation's second-largest teacher professional organization, founded in 1916 and affiliated with the AFL-CIO, a major national labor union.

Table 2.4 Professional Organizations for Educators

Organization and Website	Organization Mission or Goal
American Council on the Teaching of Foreign Languages http://www.actfl.org	To promote and foster the study of languages and cultures as an integral component of American education and society
American Federation of Teachers http://www.aft.org	To improve the lives of our members and their families, to give voice to their legitimate professional, economic, and social aspirations
Association for Supervision and Curriculum Development http://www.ascd.org	To enhance all aspects of effective teaching and learning, including professional development, educational leadership, and capacity building
Council for Exceptional Children http://www.cec.sped.org	To improve educational outcomes for individuals with exceptionalities, students with disabilities, and/or the gifted
International Reading Association http://www.reading.org	To promote high levels of literacy for all by improving reading instruction, disseminating research and information about reading, and encouraging the lifetime reading habit
Music Teachers National Association http://www.mtna.org/flash.html	To advance the value of music study and music making to society and to support the professionalism of music teachers
National Art Education Association http://www.naea-reston.org	To promote art education through professional development, service, advancement of knowledge, and leadership
National Education Association http://www.nea.org	To fulfill the promise of a democratic society, NEA shall promote the cause of quality public education and advance the profession of education
National Science Teachers Association http://www.nsta.org	To promote excellence and innovation in science teaching and learning for all
National Council for the Social Studies http://www.ncss.org	To provide leadership, service, and support for all social studies educators
National Council of Teachers of English http://www.ncte.org	To promote the development of literacy, the use of language to construct personal and public worlds and to achieve full participation in society, through the learning and teaching of English and the related arts and sciences of language
National Council of Teachers of Mathematics http://www.nctm.org	To provide broad national leadership in matters related to mathematics education
National Association for Bilingual Education http://www.nabe.org	To recognize, promote, and publicize bilingual education
Phi Delta Kappa http://www.pdkintl.org	To promote quality education as essential to the development and maintenance of a democratic way of life by providing innovative programs, relevant research, visionary leadership, and dedicated service
Teachers of English to Speakers of Other Languages http://www.tesol.org	To improve the teaching of English as a second language by promoting research, disseminating information, developing guidelines and promoting certification, and serving as a clearinghouse for the field

- Arranging school–business partnerships
- Initiating and facilitating school-to-work activities
- Conducting action research

Often these professional-development options are organized into a **career ladder system**, a series of professional steps that involve teachers in leadership responsibilities. Career ladder options are receiving increased attention in various performance-pay plans that pay teachers more for increased professional responsibilities.

Because of its emphasis on research and professional knowledge and its potential for developing teachers as professionals, we examine action research in more detail next.

DESIGNING AND CONDUCTING ACTION RESEARCH   Understanding and critically examining others' research are ways for teachers to increase their professional knowledge; another is for teachers to conduct research in their own classrooms. **Action research** is a form of applied research designed to answer a specific school- or classroom-related question (Meier & Henderson, 2007; Wiersma & Jurs, 2005). The primary intent in action research is to improve practice within a specific classroom or school (McMillan, 2004). In one sense, all expert teachers are action researchers, continually seeking answers about

Career ladder system A professional-development system that provides teachers with opportunities to assume different leadership responsibilities in a school or district.

Action research A form of applied research designed to answer a specific school- or classroom-related question.

their teaching effectiveness. Action research formalizes the process, providing structure for teachers trying to improve their practice.

Four steps guide teachers as they plan and conduct action research studies (B. Johnson & Christensen, 2004):

1. Identify a problem.
2. Plan and conduct a research study.
3. Implement the findings.
4. Use the results to generate additional research.

Let's see how Tyra Forcine, an eighth-grade English teacher, implemented these steps in her classroom.

Action research provides opportunities for teachers to build on their professional knowledge by dialoguing with other teachers about important issues.

Tyra and a group of her colleagues 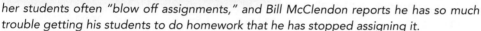 are discussing the problems they are having with homework. Kim Brown complains that her students often "blow off assignments," and Bill McClendon reports he has so much trouble getting his students to do homework that he has stopped assigning it.

"I've heard teachers say that homework doesn't help that much in terms of learning, anyway," Selena Cross adds.

"That doesn't make sense to me," Tyra counters, shaking her head. "It has to help. The more kids work on something, the better they have to get at it."

Tyra consistently gives her students homework and checks to see if they have done it, but because of the conversation, she decides to take a more systematic look at its effects. She can't find a satisfactory answer on the Internet or in any of her college textbooks, so she decides to find out for herself.

Tyra begins her study at the start of the third grading period. She collects homework every day and gives the students 2 points for having done it fully, 1 point for partial completion, and 0 points for minimal effort or not turning it in. Each day, she discusses some of the most troublesome items on the homework. On Fridays, she quizzes students on the content covered Monday through Thursday, and she also gives a midterm test and a final exam. She then tries to see if a relationship exists between students' homework averages and their performance on the quizzes and tests.

At the end of the grading period, each student has a homework score, a quiz average, and an average on the two tests. Tyra calls the district office to ask for help in summarizing the information, and together they find a positive but fairly low correlation between homework and test averages.

"Why isn't the correlation higher?" she wonders in another lounge conversation.

"Well," Kim responds. "You're only giving the kids a 2, 1, or 0 on the homework—you're still not actually grading it. So I suspect that some of the kids are simply doing the work to finish it, and they aren't really thinking about it."

"On the other hand," Bill acknowledges, "homework and tests are correlated, so maybe I'd better rethink my stand on no homework. . . . Maybe I'll change what I do next grading period."

"Good points," Tyra responds. "I'm going to keep on giving homework, but I think I need to change what I'm doing, too. . . . It's going to be a ton of work, but I'm going to do two things. . . . I'm going to repeat my study next grading period to see if I get similar results, and then, starting in the fall, I'm going to redesign my homework, so it's easier to grade. I'll grade every assignment, and we'll see if the correlation goes up."

"Great idea," Kim replies. "If the kids see how important it is for their learning, maybe they'll take their homework more seriously, and some of the not-doing-it problem will also get better. . . . I'm going to look at that in the fall." (Adapted from Eggen & Kauchak, 2010)

Figure 2.5 Conducting Action Research Enhances Professionalism

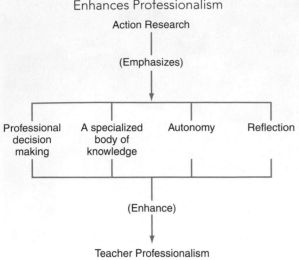

Let's see how Tyra applied the four action research steps in her classroom. First, she identified a problem central to her teaching: To what extent does homework contribute to my students' performance on quizzes and tests? This personalized approach increases teachers' motivation to do action research, because it answers questions that are important to them.

Second, she systematically designed and conducted her study, and third, Tyra and her colleagues immediately implemented the results of her project. Bill, for example, planned to give homework during the next grading period. Action research is rewarding because it can address issues and problems that teachers really care about.

Finally, like most research, Tyra's project led to reflection about her teaching and to further studies (Hyland & Noffke, 2005). She planned another study to see if scoring the homework more carefully would increase the correlation between homework and tests, and Kim planned to investigate the question of whether more careful scoring would lead to students' more conscientiously doing their homework.

In addition to answering questions about real classroom issues, conducting action research increases teachers' feelings of professionalism (Zeichner, 2007). Contributing to a body of knowledge and making decisions based on research help teachers grow both personally and professionally (Darling-Hammond & Hammerness, 2005). Engaging in action research projects also contributes to teachers' perceptions of their own efficacy and autonomy. These factors are outlined in Figure 2.5.

The results of well-designed studies can often be presented at professional conferences and published in professional journals. This allows the knowledge gained to be made public and integrated with other research, two important steps in the development of a professional body of knowledge (Hiebert, Gallimore, & Stigler, 2002).

Attaining Certification: The National Board for Professional Teaching Standards

Earlier, we saw that licensure is the process states use to ensure that teachers meet professional standards. In comparison, **certification** is special recognition by a professional organization indicating that an individual has met rigorous requirements specified by the organization.

One important form of certification is offered by the **National Board for Professional Teaching Standards (NBPTS)**. Created in 1987 as an outgrowth of the Carnegie Forum report *A Nation Prepared: Teachers for the 21st Century* (Carnegie Forum on Education and the Economy, 1986), the board is composed mostly of K–12 teachers but also includes union and business leaders and university faculty (NBPTS, 2006). NBPTS seeks to strengthen teaching as a profession and raise the quality of education by recognizing the contributions of exemplary teachers, compensating them financially, giving them increased responsibility, and increasing their role in decision making.

National Board certification is based on standards that grew out of the board's policy statement, *What Teachers Should Know and Be Able to Do* (1994). The NBPTS summarized the professional standards contained in this report into five core propositions about professional teacher competencies; these propositions and how they play out in practice are outlined in Table 2.5.

National Board certification has five important components:

- It is designed for experienced teachers. Applicants must have graduated from an accredited college or university and must have taught at least 3 years.

- Applying for National Board certification is strictly voluntary and independent of any state's licensure. The certification is intended to indicate a high level of skill and professionalism.

Certification Special recognition by a professional organization indicating that an individual has met rigorous requirements specified by the organization.

National Board for Professional Teaching Standards (NBPTS) A professional board that sets voluntary professional standards for experienced teachers to recognize those who possess extensive professional knowledge.

Table 2.5 Propositions of the National Board for Professional Teaching Standards

Proposition	Description
1. Teachers are committed to students and their learning.	• Accomplished teachers believe that all students can learn, and they treat students equitably. • Accomplished teachers understand how students develop, and they use accepted learning theory as the basis for their teaching. • Accomplished teachers are aware of the influence of context and culture on behavior, and they foster students' self-esteem, motivation, and character.
2. Teachers know the subjects they teach and how to teach those subjects to students.	• Accomplished teachers have a rich understanding of the subject(s) they teach, and they appreciate how knowledge in their subject is linked to other disciplines and applied to real-world settings. • Accomplished teachers know how to make subject matter understandable to students, and they are able to modify their instruction when difficulties arise. • Accomplished teachers demonstrate critical and analytic capacities in their teaching, and they develop those capacities in their students.
3. Teachers are responsible for managing and monitoring student learning.	• Accomplished teachers capture and sustain the interest of their students and use their time effectively. • Accomplished teachers are able to use a variety of effective instructional techniques, and they use the techniques appropriately. • Accomplished teachers can use multiple methods to assess the progress of students, and they effectively communicate this progress to parents.
4. Teachers think systematically about their practice and learn from experience.	• Accomplished teachers are models for intellectual curiosity, and they display virtues—honesty, fairness, and respect for diversity—that they seek to inspire in their students. • Accomplished teachers use their understanding of students, learning, and instruction to make principled judgments about sound practice, and they are lifelong learners. • Accomplished teachers critically examine their practice, and they seek continual professional growth.
5. Teachers are members of learning communities.	• Accomplished teachers contribute to the effectiveness of the school, and they work collaboratively with their colleagues. • Accomplished teachers evaluate school progress, and they utilize community resources. • Accomplished teachers work collaboratively with parents, and they involve parents in school activities.

- Acquiring National Board certification requires that teachers pass content exams in their area of specialty, such as math, science, early childhood, or physical education and health.

- Additional evidence, such as videotapes of teaching and a personal portfolio, is used in the assessment process.

- The primary control of the NBPTS is in the hands of practicing teachers, which increases the professionalism of teaching.

Certification by the NBPTS is for veterans, so you may be wondering why we provide information about it to preservice teachers early in their programs. We believe three reasons exist. First, professionalism is a theme of this book, and the NBPTS is a national effort to professionalize teaching. The propositions in Table 2.5 emphasize the pedagogical content knowledge, general pedagogical knowledge, and knowledge of learners and learning discussed in Chapter 1. The NBPTS recognizes that increasing professionalism requires teachers who are both highly knowledgeable and skilled in their areas of specialization.

Second, National Board certification can be a long-term career goal for which there is also a financial incentive. As of 2003, an estimated $316 million had been spent on this venture at the national level, including $100 million of federal funds (Viadero & Honawar, 2008). As of 2006, 42 states and nearly 200 school districts spent millions of additional dollars to reward teachers who successfully completed the process, and more than 63,000 teachers were board certified between 2003 and 2007 (Honawar, 2008). For example, the state of Florida appropriated $69 million during 2003–2004 to provide a

Finding a Job

You're interviewing for a position in a large urban middle school. The leadership team of the school is composed of the school principal, a vice principal, and two assistant principals. Both the principal and the vice principal are involved in the interview, which is scheduled for 1 hour.

You've been asked a number of probing questions, such as "What is the biggest problem you faced in your internship?" "How would you motivate a class of unmotivated learners?" and "How would you enforce rules with students who are disruptive in your class?"

As you respond, the vice principal appears to listen attentively, but the principal appears distracted. He nods and responds in general terms to your answers but doesn't follow up on any of the questions.

After 45 minutes, the interview seems to be winding down, so you attempt to ask some questions about the school. The principal cuts you off, saying he has a meeting he must attend. He cordially thanks you for coming and quickly leaves the office, 10 minutes before the scheduled end of the interview. The vice principal, on the other hand,

asks you to come into his office and says he is willing to try to answer any questions you have. You spend another half hour with him, and he takes you on a tour of the school, during which your discussion of the school and the students continues. The principal's name doesn't come up in the discussion, but the physical plant is clean and attractive, the students are orderly as they move between classes, and one who accidentally bumps you says, "Oh, excuse me."

If offered, would you take a job at this school? Why or why not?

10-percent salary raise to board-certified teachers and mentors for future board-certified teachers (Thirunarayanan, 2004). In addition, in 2003–2004, the state of Washington rewarded board-certified teachers with a $3,500 bonus (Margolis, 2004).

Finally, some evidence indicates that National Board certification makes a difference in teacher quality. In a study comparing teachers who had completed the process to those who had failed to achieve certification, the nationally certified teachers scored higher on nearly all measures of teaching expertise. The study involved at least 75 hours of observation of each teacher, along with interviews and samples of student work (Blair, 2000). A more recent study, however, found no achievement gains for students taught by National Board–certified teachers (Keller, 2006). But another study found that the certification process encouraged teachers to become more reflective about their work and their relationships with other professionals (Park, Oliver, Johnson, Graham, & Oppong, 2007). National Board certification is well worth pursuing, and we encourage you to keep it in mind as you begin your career.

■ ■ ■ ■ ■ CHECK YOUR UNDERSTANDING

4.1. Describe three career-long professional-development opportunities available to you as a teacher.

4.2. What is INTASC? How has it influenced teacher preparation?

4.3. What are five activities professional organizations support that are designed to improve teaching and schools?

4.4. What are the two primary assessment processes involved in attaining National Board certification?

For feedback, go to the appendix, *Check Your Understanding*, located in the back of this text.

Now it's your turn to apply the information in this chapter to a problem or dilemma facing many prospective teachers. Read the case at the top of the page and answer the question at the end of the case.

2 MEETING YOUR LEARNING OBJECTIVES

1. Describe the beliefs of beginning teachers, and explain how these could influence your success in your first years of teaching.

   - Beginning teachers are idealistic and optimistic. They generally believe that they will be effective, and they often believe that they'll be more effective than teachers now in the field.

   - Beginning teachers expect to become more confident about their ability to promote learning as they acquire experience. Unfortunately, the opposite often occurs.

   - Beginning teachers believe that effective teachers are those who are best able to clearly explain content to students, and if they understand their content, they will be able to teach it effectively.

   - Beginning teachers tend to believe that they'll learn most of what they need to know to be an effective teacher from their experiences in classrooms.

   - The beliefs of beginning teachers are often naive and frequently run counter to research about good teaching. Understanding these beliefs can help beginning teachers avoid potential pitfalls.

2. Explain differences between traditional and alternative licensure and identify the factors involved in finding a desirable job.

   - Traditional licensure consists of a general education component, as well as education courses designed to develop teachers' professional knowledge. Secondary majors are also required to take a specified number of course hours in the subject area (e.g., math) in which they plan to teach.

   - In alternative licensure programs, people who have bachelor's degrees in areas other than education complete a short, intensive training program with a clinical component.

   - Finding a desirable job requires developing a professional reputation, building a portfolio and a résumé, and creating a credentials file. The sooner students in preservice programs begin to develop a professional portfolio, gathering experiences that make them marketable and building their professional reputation, the better equipped they will be to find a job when they graduate.

3. Identify factors that contribute to a successful first year of teaching.

   - Lack of time and classroom management are the most common problems beginning teachers face. Getting organized, becoming well informed about effective management strategies, getting to know their students, and developing effective instructional strategies are the most effective ways to prepare for both an internship and the first year of teaching.

   - Induction and mentoring programs help beginning teachers make the transition from being students to being effective teachers. The best mentoring programs provide systematic help for beginning teachers, help teachers link their instruction to state and district standards, provide teachers with support in dealing with everyday problems, encourage teachers to develop a reflective professional attitude, and provide feedback based on classroom observation.

• Evaluation is also a part of every beginning teacher's experience. Formative evaluation is designed to provide helpful feedback to teachers; summative evaluation is designed to ensure adequate performance by teachers. Research-based and standards-based teacher evaluation are two approaches that schools commonly use throughout the United States.

4. Describe career-long professional-development opportunities available to teachers.

• INTASC, the Interstate New Teacher Assessment and Support Consortium, was designed to help states develop better teachers. It outlines 10 basic principles that guide the preparation of new teachers. The Online Portfolio Activities at the end of each chapter are linked to these principles.

• Professional organizations provide a variety of services for teachers throughout their careers. These include publications detailing current research, professional-development activities, annual conferences, and resources for teachers' questions and concerns.

• Teachers can develop professionally by becoming teacher-leaders, such as by serving on district- and state-level committees; writing grants; designing and facilitating staff development activities; and conducting action research, research designed to address an immediate school-level problem.

• To professionalize teaching, the National Board for Professional Teaching Standards (NBPTS) has established rigorous standards and assessments for teachers who have completed at least 3 years of successful service. Substantial financial rewards are available in many states for teachers who have completed National Board certification.

IMPORTANT CONCEPTS

action research (p. 58)
alternative licensure (p. 37)
American Federation of Teachers (AFT) (p. 57)
career ladder system (p. 58)
certification (p. 60)
credentials file (p. 41)
digital portfolio (p. 40)
formative evaluation (p. 53)
induction programs (p. 52)
licensure (p. 37)

mentors (p. 52)
merit pay (p. 54)
National Board for Professional Teaching Standards (NBPTS) (p. 60)
National Education Association (NEA) (p. 57)
professional portfolio (p. 40)
résumé (p. 40)
summative evaluation (p. 53)
Teach for America (p. 38)

DISCUSSION QUESTIONS

1. What can preservice teachers do to decrease the likelihood that they will leave the profession? What can school leaders do?

2. The National Board for Professional Teaching Standards is attempting to increase the professionalism of teaching. How successful is it likely to be? Explain your thinking.

3. What are the advantages and disadvantages of alternative licensure?

4. In this chapter, we suggested that you begin to establish a professional reputation by being conscientious in your classes. What are some other ways students can develop a professional reputation?

5. We offered several suggestions in this chapter for making yourself marketable. Is it reasonable to expect that preservice teachers involve themselves in these activities? Explain your thinking.

6. What are some professional qualities beginning teachers should look for in a mentor? What are some personal qualities?

PEARSON
myeducationlab

Now go to Topic 14: *Professional Development* in the MyEducationLab (www.myeducationlab.com) for your course, where you can:

- Find learning outcomes for *Professional Development* along with the national standards that connect to these outcomes.

- Complete *Assignments and Activities* that can help you more deeply understand the chapter content.

- Apply and practice your understanding of the core teaching skills identified in the chapter with the *Building Teaching Skills and Dispositions* learning units.

- Check your comprehension on the content covered in the chapter by going to the *Study Plan* in the *Book Specific Resources* section for your text. Here you will be able to take a chapter quiz, receive feedback on your answers, and then access *Review, Practice, and Enrichment* activities to enhance your understanding of chapter content.

Develop Your Professional Portfolio

To further apply your understanding of chapter content and address the INTASC standards, go to the *Book Specific Resources* section in the MyEducationLab for your course, select your text, then select this chapter's *Portfolio Activities*.

3

Changes in American Society:
Their Influences
on Today's Students

4

Student Diversity: Culture,
Language, and Gender

5

Student Diversity:
Development, Ability,
and Exceptionalities

PART 2 Students

"Many of the students I teach are not only at risk of failing, but they don't believe in themselves. I teach because I believe our most at-risk students need advocates. They need people to influence them to believe they can succeed."

EMILY JENNETTE, 2008 Teacher of the Year, Georgia

To view a video clip of Emily, the 2008 Georgia Teacher of the Year, go to Topic 3: *Schools and Society* in the MyEducationLab for your course and select *Teacher Talk*, and then *Emily Jennette*.

Changes in American Society
Their Influences on Today's Students

LEARNING OBJECTIVES

After you have completed your study of this chapter, you should be able to:

1. **Describe changes that have occurred in the American family over the last 50 years.** INTASC Standard 3, Adapting Instruction to Learner Needs

2. **Define** *socioeconomic status*, **and explain how different socioeconomic patterns influence school success.** INTASC Standard 3, Adapting Instruction to Learner Needs

3. **Describe societal changes and the implications of these changes for education.** INTASC Standard 3, Adapting Instruction to Learner Needs

4. **Describe the characteristics of at-risk students and how schools and teachers can help at-risk students be successful.** INTASC Standard 3, Adapting Instruction to Learner Needs

Teaching today is more challenging than at any point in our history, in large part because our society is changing. As you read the following case study, think about the changes in our society and how these changes will affect your life as a teacher.

It is the end of August, and Carla Torres, a second-year first-grade teacher, is excited about the new school year. Relocating to the Midwest because of her husband's job, she has been assigned a first-grade classroom in a large city. Looking forward to her new position, she has spent the summer planning for the year.

Two weeks into the school year, Carla shuffles into the faculty lounge on her lunch break.

"You look tired. Been getting enough sleep?" her hall mate, 20-year veteran Rae Anne Johnson, asks.

"No, I'm not tired," Carla responds, collapsing in a chair. "Just discouraged."

"Anything you want to talk about?" Rae Anne asks.

"It's my class," Carla replies. "I had such high hopes. . . . I had my room all set up with learning centers and neat stuff. I knew what I was going to teach, and I was really looking forward to it. But these kids . . . I don't know. I'm really struggling, and now I'm beginning to wonder if it's me."

Rae Anne shrugs. "Maybe, but you're so conscientious. . . . I doubt it's you. What's got you so down?"

"I can't quite figure it out. Some of the kids are really squirrelly. It's hard to get them to sit down at all. Others literally fall asleep in the middle of lessons. I've got four thumb-suckers and, frankly, some of them just don't seem ready for first-grade work. I hand out a worksheet, and they look at it like I wrote it in Greek or something."

"You might be right. . . . I know it's tough. I have some of the same problems. One of my kids was upset yesterday, so I sat her down at recess, and she told me that her parents had had a big fight the night before. And then there's Johnny . . . He's always so droopy, so I asked him if he'd had breakfast this morning. He said he never eats it, so I called his home and told his mother about the school's free breakfast program. I had to call three times to get her—I didn't want to just leave a message on the machine. She was apologetic about sending him to school without it, but she works weird hours, and she's a single mom, so I know it's tough for her too. It's hard for a lot of kids."

"I guess you're right, but they didn't prepare me for this. I was so eager, and, I guess, idealistic about making a difference. Now, I'm not so sure."

Today's students are indeed different from those who came to school in the years past. Fewer come from homes where the father is the breadwinner and the mother is the primary caregiver; and more come to school hungry, tired, or emotionally drained because of conditions in their homes and communities. Consider another first-grade teacher's lament.

I just don't know what I'm going to do. Every year, my first grade class has more and more of these kids. They don't seem to care about right or wrong, they don't care about adult approval, they are disruptive, they can't read and they arrive at school absolutely unprepared to learn. Who are these kids? Where do they come from? Why are there more and more of them? I used to think that I was a good teacher. I really prided myself on doing an outstanding job. But I find I'm working harder and harder, and being less and less effective. A good teacher? Today I really don't know. I do know that my classroom is being overwhelmed by society's problems and I don't understand it. What's happening to our schools? What's happening to society? I don't understand all of this and I sure don't know what we're going to do about it. (Barr & Parrett, 2001, p. 1)

The issues continue as students get older. For example, students are more sexually active, and they use alcohol and other drugs more often than students did in the past. Many come to school with "baggage" that students didn't have in the past, and these problems are often linked to societal issues. How do these changes in society affect our students? And, how will these changes affect your life as a teacher? One superintendent of a large urban district in the Southeast commented that teaching is tougher now than it has ever been, and he attributed the challenges primarily to changes in our society (Ed Pratt Dannals. Personal communication, January 30, 2009).

In this chapter, we examine the implications these changes will have for you, but before you begin your study, please respond to the items that follow.

For each of the following statements, circle your choice using the following options:

4 = I strongly believe the statement is true.
3 = I believe the statement is true.
2 = I believe the statement is false.
1 = I strongly believe the statement is false.

1. The most common family pattern for the students you'll teach is for the father to work and the mother to stay at home to take care of the children.

   1   2   3   4

2. The level of education attained by parents strongly influences their children's school success.

   1   2   3   4

3. Most parents don't want schools to provide sex education, preferring to provide this education themselves.

   1   2   3   4

4. In recent years, student use of drugs and alcohol has declined.

   1   2   3   4

5. Teachers are required by law to report instances of child abuse.

   1   2   3   4

myeducationlab To download and complete this form, go to the *Book Specific Resources* section in the MyEducationLab for your course, select your text, and then select *This I Believe* for Chapter 3.

CHANGES IN AMERICAN FAMILIES

As teachers, we want to provide a quality education for all our students, and for many this is possible; they come from stable, supportive families, and they have experiences that prepare them to learn. Unfortunately, for other students, this isn't the case.

> With head resting on his hands, Brad looks puzzled when he is asked how many brothers and sisters he has—a seemingly simple question, but not so easy for Brad to answer. He scrunches his face, pauses, pushes back in his chair, purses his lips, rolls his dark eyes, and begins counting on his fingers slowly, deliberately, then says, "Let's see, hmmm, six." "Six?" "Wait, seven." "Seven?" "Wait, eight." "That's a hard question." It wasn't meant to be. Brad explains: "I didn't count my sister Mary or my sister Kerrie." "Oh?" "My dad was married to four different ladies and has had quite a few kids." Brad has a hard time remembering when he last saw two of his siblings, who are older and live in other states. Even with his best effort, he is off one child. (Bullough, 1999, p. 10)

Brad's story, although extreme, illustrates some of the ways the American family has changed. The "traditional" family—a husband who is the primary breadwinner, a mother who doesn't work outside the home, and two school-age children—made up only slightly more than 1 of 20 households in the United States in 2000. Census data from that year also reveal some additional facts about families and households with children:

- Families headed by married couples made up slightly more than two thirds of all households, compared to close to 80 percent in 1980.
- Seven of 10 women with children were in the workforce.

- The divorce rate quadrupled from 1978 to 2000.

- Nearly 1 of 4 children live only with their mothers, 5 percent live only with their fathers, and 4 percent live with neither.

- The incidence of poverty among single-parent families was nearly 10 times higher than in families headed by married couples. (Federal Interagency Forum on Child and Family Statistics, 2008; U.S. Bureau of Census, 2007a)

Poverty, divorce, families where both parents work, and single parents pose challenges to parents, their children, and teachers. Parents, in general, spend less time with their children than did the parents of previous generations. And even when they have time, many parents are uncertain about how to help their children with schoolwork. The combination of less time and less support means that children often come to school less prepared to learn.

What does this information suggest for you when you begin teaching? First, be aware of changing family patterns. Teachers often think and talk about families in traditional ways, with the father as breadwinner and the mother staying at home, but this is no longer the prevailing pattern (Graue, 2005). As with other examples, when you talk with students, communicate that different family configurations exist and are acceptable, and attempt to be flexible with meeting times for parent–teacher conferences. These actions communicate that you care about the children, that you're committed to their education, and that you're aware of the pressures that today's parents are experiencing.

This section addresses the first item in this chapter's *This I Believe* feature, "The most common family pattern for the students you'll teach is for the father to work and the mother to stay home to take care of the children." This statement is not true. Today, 7 of 10 mothers work outside the home, which raises questions about both child care and "latchkey" children, the topics of the next two sections.

Child Care

Quality child care is an important issue for the more than 60 percent of working mothers with a child under 2 (U.S. Bureau of Census, 2003). When a working parent is single or when both parents work outside the home, young children spend a great deal of time in child care, and questions about its impact on the emotional and intellectual development of children have been asked for years. Critics contend that young children need the presence of a mother in the home, and that child care isn't an adequate substitute. Supporters counter that children readily adapt to different care patterns and learn valuable lessons from interacting with other children.

Researchers examining this issue focus on the quality of the child care instead of the larger issue of working parents. Their research indicates that high-quality child care is positively correlated with children's long-term cognitive and emotional development, higher earnings later in life, and greater marital stability. It also reduces delinquency, teenage pregnancy, drug use, and dropout rates (Berk, 2008, 2009; A. Lewis, 2005). We want to emphasize the term *high-quality:* Poor-quality child care can have the exact opposite effect.

Although quality child care is important for all children, it is essential for the children of poverty. Unfortunately, research suggests that children from low-income families are the least likely to have early childhood education programs such as nursery school and prekindergarten available to them (Bracey, 2005b; National Center for Education Statistics, 2005e). In 2005, for example, 6 of 10 middle-class families participated in preschool activities compared to less than half of poor families. And the rate of participation for poor families has decreased since 1999. The reasons are uncertain, but our country is clearly losing an important opportunity to invest in its children. Experts estimate that an economic return of $13 results from every dollar spent on quality child care (Jacobson, 2004).

Latchkey Children

Ana Rosa opens the door to her apartment, goes inside, and quickly relocks it, remembering what her mother has said about strangers. She drops her school pack on the sofa, deciding to do her homework later. The house is quiet, too quiet. She goes in the living room, turns on the TV, and surfs through the menu of talk shows, cartoons, and soap operas. Then, she heads to the kitchen and checks out snacks. A soft drink and chips look good. She returns to the living room and settles in with the TV. Her mom will be home from work in 3 hours.

Latchkey children, children who return to empty houses after school and who are left alone until parents arrive from work, are another problem many parents face: Between 4 and 5 million children return to an empty house or apartment after school (Federal Interagency Forum on Child and Family Statistics, 2008). This raises issues ranging from concerns about children's safety to questions of supervision, excessive time spent watching television, and lack of help with homework. Teachers can address the last issue by ensuring that students understand exactly what is expected of them on their homework assignments and can do the work before sending children home (H. Cooper, Robinson, & Patall, 2006).

Some schools respond with after-hours offerings, but a more common solution is for schools to cooperate with community agencies, such as YMCAs or youth clubs, to offer after-school programs. In addition to providing safe, supervised environments, these programs teach children how to respond to home emergencies, use the phone to seek help, make healthful snacks, and spend time wisely.

■ ■ ■ ■ CHECK YOUR UNDERSTANDING

1.1 Describe changes that have occurred in the American family over the last 50 years.

1.2 Describe the implications of the changes in American families for child care in this country.

1.3 Who are latchkey children? What problems do they encounter in their homes?

For feedback, go to the appendix, *Check Your Understanding*, located in the back of this text.

THE INFLUENCE OF SOCIOECONOMIC FACTORS ON STUDENTS

As you begin this section, think about the amount of time kids spend in school. It's actually quite limited; experts estimate that school-age children spend five times as many hours in their homes and neighborhoods as they do in school (Berliner, 2005a). During this out-of-school time, students learn a great deal about the world, and they develop attitudes and values that they bring into your classroom.

Interest in the influence that families, neighborhoods, and peers have on learning peaked in 1966 when the famous and controversial Coleman Report suggested that family background was the primary factor influencing student achievement (Coleman et al., 1966; Viadero, 2006). **Socioeconomic status (SES)**, the combination of family income, parents' occupations, and level of parental education, is one way to describe differences in family background. Researchers describe socioeconomic status using four

Latchkey children Children who return to empty houses after school and who are left alone until parents arrive from work.

Socioeconomic status (SES) The combination of family income, parents' occupations, and level of parental education.

Table 3.1	Characteristics of Different Socioeconomic Classes			
	Upper Class	**Middle Class**	**Working Class**	**Lower Class**
Income	$170,000+	$80,000–170,000 (½) $40,000–80,000 (½)	$25,000–$40,000	Below $25,000
Occupation	Corporate or professional (e.g., doctor, lawyer).	White collar, skilled blue collar.	Blue collar.	Minimum-wage unskilled labor.
Education	Attended college and professional schools and expect children to do the same.	High school, college, or professional schools. Strive to help their children do the same or higher.	High school; may or may not encourage college.	High school or less; cost a major factor in education.
Housing	Own home in prestigious neighborhood	Usually own home.	About half own a home.	Rent.

Source: Macionis (2009); U.S. Census Bureau (2007b).

classes—upper, middle, working, and lower—with finer distinctions within each (Macionis, 2009). Table 3.1 outlines characteristics of these different socioeconomic classes. Before you continue, look at Table 3.1, see where you are, and think about how your family background influenced your attitudes and values related to school. We'll share ours later in this section.

The **upper class**, composed of highly educated, highly paid professionals (people who usually have a bachelor's degree or higher and make more than $170,000 per year), is at the top of the SES pyramid. Though only a small part of the total population (about 5 percent), the upper class controls a disproportionate amount of the wealth (some estimate that the top 5 percent own almost 60 percent of the wealth in this country), and the gap between the upper and other classes is growing (Macionis, 2009; Mishel, Berstein, & Allegretto, 2006).

The **middle class** is composed of managers, administrators, and white-collar workers. Teachers are in this category; they hold bachelor's or higher degrees, work in professional organizations, and, as you saw in Chapter 1, earn an average of $51,009 per year (American Federation of Teachers, 2008). Middle-class incomes typically range between $40,000 and $170,000, and about 4 of 10 families fall into this category (Macionis, 2009).

Working-class families, also called *lower middle class,* earn between $25,000 and $40,000 per year and compose about a third of the population. Most have a high school education and hold steady blue-collar jobs involving manual labor, such as construction or factory work. About half of this group owns a home. College is a reality for only about a third of working-class children.

Families in the **lower class** typically make less than $25,000 per year, have a high school education or less, and work in low-paying, entry-level jobs. About 1 of 5 families in our country falls into this category, and the percentage is increasing. Only half of lower-class family members complete high school, and only 1 of 4 reaches college. People in the lowest-earning segment of this category often depend on public assistance to supplement their incomes and are often the third or fourth generation to live in poverty.

The term **underclass** is often used to describe people with low incomes who continually struggle with economic problems. Research indicates that escaping from the underclass is very difficult, and that poverty poses special challenges to these families and their children, a topic we examine in the next section (Macionis, 2009).

Poverty

Upper class The socioeconomic class composed of highly educated (usually a college degree), highly paid (usually above $170,000) professionals who make up about 5 percent of the population.

Middle class The socioeconomic level composed of managers, administrators, and white-collar workers who perform nonmanual work.

Working class (also called *lower middle class*). The socioeconomic level composed of blue-collar workers who perform manual labor.

Lower class The socioeconomic level composed of people who typically make less than $25,000 per year, have a high school education or less, and work in low-paying, entry-level jobs.

Underclass People with low incomes who continually struggle with economic problems.

When Sally gets a spare moment (and there are precious few of them), she loves to draw, mostly fantasy creatures. "What is your favorite thing to draw?" "A mermaid thing, cuz it's not real—there's no such thing as a mermaid—but I like to draw things that aren't real. Fairy tales. Fairies, monsters." She lights up talking about her creations. But Sally's life is not a fairy tale. With her brother she hurries home from school, immediately does her homework, and "I mean right after my homework I have to clean up my room and do the dishes for dinner and cook dinner." "You cook dinner? Every day?" Staring straight across the table separating us, and without blinking her blue eyes, Sally responded slightly defensively, "I'm a good cook." For all the talk about food, Sally's greatest fear, she said, was that she will not get enough to eat and will get sick. Who would take care of the family, then? "I worry . . . [will] end up getting too skinny and die cuz I'm really skinny." (Bullough, 1999, p. 13)

Poverty can exert a powerful negative influence on school success.

Sally has to do all this work because her mother, who has severe diabetes, works 10 hours a day as a waitress. When her mother returns home from work, she collapses on the sofa exhausted. When Sally gets home from school, this is how she usually finds her. Life is not easy for Sally.

Poverty exerts a toll on both families and children. To assist families, the federal government establishes **poverty thresholds**, household income levels that represent the lowest earnings required to meet basic living needs. In 2007, the poverty level for a family of four was $20,650 (U.S. Department of Health and Human Services, 2007). These levels are determined primarily by food costs and largely ignore other factors such as the cost of housing, transportation, and energy.

Some disturbing patterns exist in our country with respect to poverty. As we move toward the second decade of the 21st century, the number of children living in poverty continues to increase, with minorities and single-parent families overrepresented (U.S. Bureau of Census, 2006a). And, the percentage of U.S. families below the poverty level in 2004 was 5 times greater than in other industrialized countries (Education Vital Signs, 2005). In 2006, nearly 1 of 5 U.S. students lived in poverty, and more than a third were eligible for free or reduced-price federal lunch programs (Kober, 2006; Wolf, 2007).

The federal government addresses the problems of poverty through the National School Lunch Program. In 2008, children from a family of four with income below $27,650 a year were eligible for free breakfasts and lunches; families earning below $39,220 qualified for 30-cent breakfasts and 40-cent lunches (S. Dillon, 2008a). Although virtually all schools participate in the program, fewer than 6 of 10 families that qualify for free or reduced meals participate, being either too proud or unaware that the programs are available (Brimley & Garfield, 2008). What are the implications of this poverty for teachers?

> What this means is that at least one-fifth of all children who come through the schoolhouse door in America today are likely to be experiencing poverty-associated problems such as substandard housing, an inadequate diet, threadbare or hand-me-down clothes, lack of health insurance, chronic dental or health problems, deprivation and violence in their communities, little or no funds for school supplies, and whose overburdened parents subsist on welfare or work long hours at miserably paid jobs. These facts pose enormous problems for America's schools. (Biddle, 2001, p. 5)

Teachers also respond in a variety of ways, such as keeping boxes of crackers, granola bars, and other snacks in their desks for students who come to school hungry.

The powerful effect that poverty can have on learning is reflected in integration-by-income programs implemented by a number of districts in the country, including Louisville, Kentucky, Omaha, Nebraska, and San Francisco (Bazelon, 2008; Kahlenberg,

Poverty thresholds Household income levels that represent the lowest earnings required to meet basic living needs.

2006). These programs integrate students from different SES levels in a variety of ways, such as creating magnet schools, using vouchers, and even busing. All are based on the belief that high concentrations of students from impoverished backgrounds limit a school's ability to meet students' learning needs. Initial results of these integration programs are promising; in North Carolina, more than 60 percent of integrated-by-income students passed state-mandated end-of-course exams compared to less than 50 percent in comparable surrounding areas (Kahlenberg, 2006).

Homelessness

Homelessness is a direct result of poverty. An accurate count of homeless students is difficult, but experts estimate that between 500,000 and 1 million children are homeless sometime during any given year; in 2007, families with children accounted for 30 percent of the homeless population (National Law Center on Homelessness and Poverty, 2006; Swarns, 2008). Homeless children often come from unstable families, suffer from inadequate diets, and lack medical care. At least one fifth of homeless children fail to attend school regularly (U.S. Department of Education, 2005a). Homeless children are three times more likely to repeat a grade and four times more likely to drop out of school than other children (Macionis & Parillo, 2010).

Schools respond to the problem of homelessness in several ways. Recognizing that students' home situations are difficult, they attempt to make school admission, attendance, and course requirements flexible; they provide outreach services such as counselors, after-school programs, and financial aid for transportation; and school officials coordinate with other community agencies to ensure that basic needs, such as food and shelter, are met.

One elementary school in Phoenix, Arizona, targets homeless children as its primary clients (Sandham, 2000). It sends school buses around the city to pick up the children and maintains a room that students can visit to get clean underwear and changes of clothes. Volunteer pediatricians staff an on-site clinic that provides free medical care and immunizations. The school even hands out alarm clocks (old-fashioned windups because many of the children don't have access to electricity) to help them get to school on time. Teacher dedication and effort make the school work. One teacher commented, "There's something about watching the buses roll out of here, with all the kids' faces pressed against the windows. I get this feeling it's what I should be doing" (Sandham, 2000, p. 29).

The whole problem of homelessness has been exacerbated by the recent economic downturn that hit the U.S. economy, and experts estimate that home foreclosures will affect an additional 2 million students nationwide (Gewertz, 2008b). Families that used to own homes or were renting now find shelter in one-room motel rooms, forced there by an inability to pay the upfront costs of renting, such as security and utility deposits (Eckholm, 2009). Often as many as six members of a family share one room, which serves as living room, kitchen, and bedroom. Homework is a challenge when the TV is on and there is no quiet place to work.

When you begin teaching, what can you do to help homeless children? First, talk with experienced teachers about community resources for these students and their families, and pass this information on to parents. Second, care and flexibility are essential. Demonstrating that you genuinely care about students and their learning is important for all children; for those who are homeless, it's critical.

Socioeconomic Status and School Success

Socioeconomic status consistently predicts a number of indicators of school success, including achievement test scores, grades, truancy, and dropout and suspension rates (Macionis, 2009; Votruba-Drzal, 2006). How does SES influence school success? A researcher went to the house of a struggling fifth grader named Socorro to find out why she struggled. While interviewing Socorro's mother, here is what he found.

Nick [Socorro's uncle] passed through the apartment apparently returning to work after taking a brief break. The phone rang. Socorro's 5-year-old step-brother curled up in his mother's lap and began talking into her ear. The television was on. There is a television in every room; one is Socorro's. The apartment is spotlessly clean. Life is busy, very busy. Once off the phone, the mother exclaims, proudly, "I let her do whatever she wants . . . she does whatever she wants." Working two jobs, one in housekeeping at a nearby hospital and another, an evening job as a parking lot attendant to obtain money . . . leaves her no option: She is not home often. . . ."I want to support my kids," the mother says, and this requires that she is "never home for them." She works very hard.

Socorro's problem in school, her mother asserts, is that "her mind wanders." Her teachers tell another tale: Socorro cannot read and is struggling. Her mother seems unconcerned that Socorro frequently misses school. As her teacher said, "She is out of school more than she is in it." Attending school irregularly, Socorro is slipping further and further behind her classmates. Concerned, teachers made arrangements to place Socorro for part of the day with the special education teacher. They didn't know what else to do, having failed to gain the mother's help in getting Socorro to school regularly. (Bullough, 2001, p. 33)

Socioeconomic status influences school success in a number of ways but has its most powerful influence at the lower income levels (Macionis, 2009). For example, low-SES elementary students are more than twice as likely as their higher SES peers to fall below basic levels of reading, and they are only one third as likely to achieve at a proficient level. Dropout rates for the poorest families exceed 50 percent (Allington & McGill-Franzen, 2003). About 1 of 4 high school graduates from lower SES classes goes to college and earns a degree, compared to nearly 8 of 10 graduates from the highest SES classes (Macionis, 2009).

This section addresses the second question in this chapter's *This I Believe* feature, "The level of education attained by parents strongly influences their children's school success." This statement is true; but what accounts for these dramatic differences in achievement? Experts identify the following factors:

- Fulfillment of basic needs
- Family stability
- School-related experiences
- Interaction patterns in the home
- Parental attitudes and values

Most families in our country take for granted fulfillment of basic needs, such as food, shelter, and medical care. Many low-SES families lack adequate medical care, however, and an increasing number of children come to school without proper nourishment (Rothstein, 2004a, 2004b). In 2006, more than 35 million people in the United States reported going hungry, and almost 13 million of them were children (Children's Alliance, 2007). Research also indicates that poor nutrition can affect attention and memory and even lead to lower scores on intelligence tests (Berk, 2009).

In high-poverty schools, the school nurse often serves as a substitute for the family doctor because families in poverty don't have medical insurance and can't afford to seek medical help. One school nurse reported,

> Mondays we are hit hard. It's not like in the suburbs, where families call the pediatrician. When our kids get sick on the weekends, they go to the emergency room, or they wait. Monday morning, they are lined up, and they have to see the nurse. (F. Smith, 2005, p. 49)

It is hard to learn when you're sick or hurting.

Children of poverty also relocate frequently; in some low-income schools, mobility rates are above 100 percent, which means they can have a complete turnover in students during an academic year (Rothstein, 2004a). Researchers have found that nearly a third of the poorest students attend at least three schools by third grade, compared to only 1 of 10 for middle-class students. These frequent moves are stressful for students and a challenge for teachers attempting to develop caring relationships with them (Barton, 2004).

Family stability also influences learning and school success. In some low-SES families, daily struggles and economic problems result in parental frustration and anger, which can lead to marital conflicts and unstable home environments (Rainwater & Smeeding, 2003). Children then come to school lacking the sense of safety and security that would equip them to tackle school-related challenges. Students from poor families also have a greater incidence of depression and other emotional problems than their more advantaged peers (G. Evans & English, 2002).

School-related experiences in the home influence students' learning as well (Pomerantz, Moorman, & Litwack, 2007). For example, high-SES parents are more likely than their low-SES counterparts to provide their children with educational activities outside school, such as visits to museums, concerts, and libraries, to have materials at home that support learning (e.g., newspapers and computers with Internet access), and to arrange for formal out-of-school learning experiences, such as music or dance lessons, participation in tennis and soccer camps, and computer classes. These experiences provide a foundation that helps students succeed in school activities. Low-SES students are also less likely to participate in enriching activities in the community and extracurricular activities provided by schools, often because of parents' work demands, transportation problems, or simply being unaware that the opportunities exist.

Interaction patterns in the home also influence learning. In general, high-SES parents talk with their children more than do lower SES caregivers, and this verbal give-and-take provides students with practice in developing their language skills. These discussions also prepare children for the kind of verbal interaction found in the schools. Sometimes called "the curriculum of the home," these rich interaction patterns, together with the enrichment experiences described in the previous paragraph, provide a solid foundation for reading and vocabulary development (Bardige, 2005; Holloway, 2004).

Experts estimate that by the age of 3, children of professional parents have heard 30 million words and children with working-class parents 20 million, but children with parents on welfare have heard only 10 million (Chance, 1997). High-SES parents are also more likely to treat their children as conversational partners, explain ideas and the causes of events, encourage independent thinking, and emphasize individual responsibility (Berk, 2008; Tomasello, 2006). Low-SES parents, by contrast, are more likely to "tell" rather than explain, their language is less elaborate, their directions are less clear, and they are less likely to encourage problem solving.

Finally, parental attitudes and values shape the way students think about schools and learning (Pomerantz et al., 2007). Because reading materials are more common in high-SES homes, children learn that reading is an important part of people's lives. Parents who enjoy books, newspapers, and magazines communicate that the information they contain is valuable and that reading is a useful activity for its own sake. When children see their parents read, they imitate the behavior, which influences their learning at school (G. Tompkins, 2009).

Parents also communicate their attitudes about education through the expectations they hold for their children and through their involvement in their children's activities (Benner & Mistry, 2007). High-SES parents are more likely to encourage their children to graduate from high school and attend college (K. Brown, Anfara, & Roney, 2004). They also support their children's education by attending curricular and extracurricular activities. One mother commented, "When she sees me at her games, when she sees me going to open house, when I attend her Interscholastic League contests, she knows I am interested in her activities. Plus, we have more to talk about" (Young & Scribner, 1997, p. 12).

SES: Some Cautions and Implications for Teachers

It's important to remember that the research findings reported in this section describe group differences; individuals within groups will vary widely. For example, many low-SES parents read and talk to their children, encourage their involvement in extracurricular activities, and attend school events. Both of your authors come from low-SES families, and we were given the enriching experiences associated with high-SES parents. Conversely, belonging to a high-SES family does not guarantee that a child will have enriching experiences and caring, involved parents. When you work with your students, be careful to avoid stereotypes; remember that your students are individuals, and treat them as such. Keep your expectations appropriately high for all students.

One popular staff development program that targets the children of poverty has been criticized for stereotyping these children. Based on Ruby Payne's *A Framework for Understanding Poverty* (2005), these workshops help teachers understand how the values and beliefs of low-SES children are different from those of middle-class students and adversely affect school success. Critics contend that the book oversimplifies issues related to poverty and encourages teachers to treat these children as having collective deficits rather than as individuals with potential (Gorski, 2008). Despite these criticisms, the book has sold more than 800,000 copies, and the author has been called the "dominant voice on class and poverty" in education (Gorski, 2008, p. 130).

A second, related, caution: We know that certain home conditions make it more difficult for students to succeed in school, but we also know that schools and teachers can do much to overcome these problems (Barton, 2004; Darling-Hammond & Bransford, 2005). As you'll see later in the chapter, schools that are safe, nurturing, and demanding, and teachers who hold high expectations for their students' success and use effective instructional strategies can make a significant difference in all students' lives.

■ ■ ■ ■ CHECK YOUR UNDERSTANDING

2.1   Define *socioeconomic status*.

2.2   Explain how different socioeconomic patterns influence school success.

2.3   How does the government define *poverty?* How does poverty influence learning?

2.4   How does homelessness influence learning?

For feedback, go to the appendix, *Check Your Understanding*, located in the back of this text.

CHANGES IN OUR STUDENTS

We've seen that families and socioeconomic patterns have changed over time. As a result of these changes and other societal influences, our students have also changed, and they present special challenges to teachers. Consider these 2007 statistics from a survey of high school students (Centers for Disease Control and Prevention, 2008):

- Forty-five percent consumed alcohol within 30 days before the survey, 10 percent drove after drinking, and nearly 3 of 10 rode in a car when a driver had been drinking.

- Nearly 40 percent had used marijuana; 7 percent had used cocaine, and 20 percent had smoked tobacco in the previous month.

Figure 3.1 Changes in Our Students

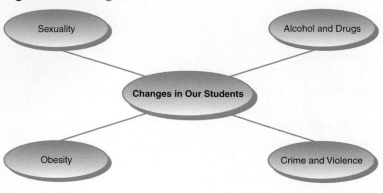

- Sexuality
- Alcohol and Drugs
- Changes in Our Students
- Obesity
- Crime and Violence

- Nearly 1 of 5 reported carrying a weapon to school on one or more days during the preceding month.

- Seven percent attempted suicide within the last 12 months, and 14 percent had seriously contemplated it.

Our students are engaging in risky and sometimes downright dangerous activities. In this section, we examine students' sexuality, use of alcohol and other drugs, obesity, school violence, suicide, and child abuse, all risk factors for their safety and health. These factors are outlined in Figure 3.1 and discussed in the sections that follow.

Sexuality

In the past, we tacitly thought of our teenagers as either asexual or restrained. We knew they were going through puberty but assumed that they weren't sexually active—or we chose not to think about it.

The facts suggest otherwise. In 2007, nearly half of teens reported being sexually active by the end of high school, nearly 1 of 10 said they had sex before age 13, and more than 10 percent of 10th graders said they had four or more sex partners (Centers for Disease Control and Prevention, 2008; Grunbaum et al., 2002). In addition, the average age at first intercourse dropped from 19 to 15 between 1943 and 1999 (Tonn, 2005b). This level of sexual activity poses a number of risks, including teenage pregnancy and sexually transmitted diseases.

TEENAGE PREGNANCY Although the annual teenage birthrate declined steadily from a high of 89 births per 1,000 students in 1960 to 42 per 1,000 in 2003, it rose in 2006, and the United States still has the highest rates of teenage pregnancy and births in the Western industrialized world (National Campaign to Prevent Teen Pregnancy, 2006; Orr, 2009). Experts attribute the decline to both decreased sexual activity and increased use of contraceptives. Eighty percent of teenage pregnancies are to unmarried teens, and slightly more than half of teenage mothers (57 percent) keep their babies (Alan Guttmacher Institute, 2004). These pregnancies take a terrible toll on both the mothers and the children.

Teen pregnancies force children to mature too rapidly, diverting attention from their own personal development.

Becoming teenage parents forces students to mature too quickly, diverting energy from their own development to the care of a baby. Economics is also a problem; more than half of the households headed by teen mothers live in poverty (Macionis, 2009). Juggling child rearing with work and school, teenage mothers are more likely to drop out, develop poor work skills, and have limited employment opportunities. Their babies also fare poorly: Because of inadequate prenatal care, they are often born prematurely or with health problems.

Efforts to deal with the problem of teenage pregnancy focus on programs that encourage mothers to complete their educations through home instruction, or programs in which mothers bring their babies to school and attend child-care and regular classes. Despite these efforts, the majority of teen mothers drop out of school.

SEXUALLY TRANSMITTED DISEASES (STDS) Many teens have sex without protecting themselves from sexually transmitted diseases such as herpes, human papillomavirus, chlamydia, genital warts, syphilis, and gonorrhea. One survey found that 1 of 4, or more than 3 million, teenage girls was infected with at least one form of STD (Altman, 2008). AIDS (acquired immune deficiency syndrome), which can be transmitted through sexual activity, has made the problem more urgent and deadly (U.S. Department of Health and Human Services, 2006). Although it was first believed that the AIDS virus was transmitted primarily through sexual contact between male homosexuals or through intravenous drug use, we now know HIV is also spread through heterosexual sex.

Almost half of teenagers report being sexually active, and some have several partners. Nevertheless, only about half of sexually active teenage girls and about two thirds of teenage boys report using condoms, the only reliable defense—other than abstinence—against sexually transmitted diseases (Grunbaum et al., 2002).

SEX EDUCATION   In response to teenagers' increasing sexual activity, many school districts have implemented sex education, but because sex education is controversial, the form and content of instruction vary widely. Polls suggest that the vast majority of parents (more than 90 percent) favor sex education (T. Hoff, 2002; Kaiser Family Foundation, 2004b), and courts have historically upheld districts' rights to offer sex education courses (Fischer, Schimmel, & Stellman, 2006). Parents who object are free to take their children out of the programs.

This section addresses the third question in this chapter's *This I Believe* feature, "Most parents don't want schools to provide sex education, preferring to provide this education themselves." This statement is not true: Polls suggest that most parents want schools to provide sex education for their children.

This I BELIEVE

SEXUAL ORIENTATION AND IDENTITY   Experts estimate that between 3 and 10 percent of U.S. students differ in their sexual orientation, but accurate figures are hard to obtain because of the social stigma involved (Berk, 2009). The labels *lesbian, gay, bisexual,* and *straight* refer to a person's sexual orientation; *transgender* refers to sexual identity. Lesbian, gay, bisexual, and transgender (LGBT) students are often rejected by both peers and society, leading to feelings of alienation and depression, to drug use, and to suicide rates considerably higher than in the heterosexual population (Berk, 2009; Macionis, 2009).

Discussions about sexual orientation and identity are controversial, with some believing that they're genetic and others attributing them to learning and choice (Gollnick & Chinn, 2009). Those arguing that the causes are genetic ask why someone would voluntarily choose an orientation or identity that would result in discrimination and rejection, and their position has considerable research support. For example, if one identical twin is homosexual, the other twin is much more likely also to be homosexual than is the case with fraternal twins (Berk, 2008, 2009).

Research also suggests that LGBT students go through a three-phase sequence in their attempts to understand who they are sexually. The first is feeling different, a slowly developing awareness that they aren't like other children. One gay student described his experience:

> As long as I can remember, I always felt a little different when it came to having crushes on other people. When I was in elementary school I never had crushes on girls, and when I look back on that time now, I was probably most attracted to my male friends. I participated in some of the typical "boy" activities, like trading baseball cards and playing video games, but I was never very interested in rough sports. (McDevitt & Ormrod, 2007, p. 545)

The second phase is a feeling of confusion, which occurs during adolescence. In this phase, LGBT students attempt to understand their developing sexuality, looking for both social support and role models. The same gay male described his feelings during this phase:

> To my dismay, middle school and the onset of puberty only brought more attention to my lack of interest in girls. The first time I thought about being gay was

when I was in the 6th grade, so I was probably 11 or 12 years old at the time. But in my mind, being gay was not an option and I began to expend an incredible amount of energy repressing my developing homosexual urges. (McDevitt & Ormrod, 2007, p. 545)

Finally, in the third phase, the majority of gay and lesbian teenagers reach a point where they accept their homosexuality and share it with those who are close to them. Unfortunately, rather than understanding, LGBT students are often subjected to harassment. Let's look at this topic in more detail.

SEXUAL HARASSMENT

Hey, babe. Lookin' good in that sweater!
Hey, sugar. Want to make me happy tonight?

Comments like these, heard in many classrooms and hallways in our nation's schools, may constitute **sexual harassment**, unwanted and/or unwelcome sexually-oriented behavior that interferes with a student's life (American Association of University Women, 2001). A problem that affects both males and females, it can also interfere with a student's learning and development. In one survey, 4 of 5 teenagers in grades 8–11 reported some type of sexual harassment in schools (American Association of University Women, 2001). Sexual comments, gestures, and looks, as well as touching and grabbing, were most commonly cited. Figure 3.2 shows the percentages of boys and girls who were subjected to various forms of sexual harassment. Equally disturbing is a recent college survey indicating that two thirds of college students experience sexual harassment at some point, including nearly one third of first-year students (American Association of University Women, 2006).

A sea change has occurred in awareness of school policies toward sexual harassment: In contrast to a 1992 study indicating that only about 25 percent of students were aware of sexual harassment policies, a 2001 study found that awareness had increased to nearly 70 percent (American Association of University Women, 2001). This is a positive trend, but more needs to be done to make schools safe for all students, and particularly for those who are lesbian, gay, bisexual, or transgender. One national survey found that 90 percent of homosexual students frequently hear expressions such as, "That's so gay" or "You're so gay"; 75 percent frequently encountered terms such as "faggot" or "dyke"; and more than 60 percent reported other forms of verbal harassment (Kosciw & Diaz, 2006). One teenage boy commented, "To call someone gay or fag is like the lowest thing you can call someone. Because that's like saying that you're nothing" (Warner, 2009, p. 2). And, the

Figure 3.2 Sexual Harassment in U.S. Schools

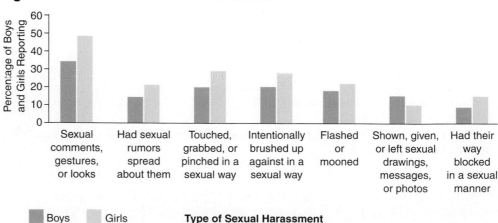

Boys Girls   **Type of Sexual Harassment**

Source: American Association of University Women Educational Foundation. (2001). *Hostile hallways: Bullying, teasing, and sexual harassment in school.* New York: Harris Interactive. Reprinted by permission.

Sexual harassment Unwanted and/or unwelcome sexual-oriented behavior that interferes with a student's sense of well-being.

abuse often goes beyond verbal: More than 4 of 10 homosexual students reported physical harassment, and 6 of 10 said they didn't feel safe at school (Maxwell, 2008). One student described this experience:

> When I was changing classes, I had all the books in my hands. . . . I'd hear someone mutter "faggot" and have my books knocked down. People are walking over me as I'm trying to gather my books. I don't have time to turn around to see who said it. (Sears, 1993, p. 129)

Students report that harassment makes them feel "sad," "worthless," and "powerless" (Shakeshaft et al., 1997). Harassment such as this contributes to the higher rates of depression, drug abuse, and suicide for LGBT students that we discussed in the previous section. Unfortunately, many school counselors and teachers feel unprepared to deal with these issues (M. Wood, 2005).

Schools and teachers need to do a better job of making classrooms and hallways safe for all students. A Supreme Court ruling that holds school districts legally responsible in cases where sexual harassment is reported but not corrected is likely to make both teachers and administrators more sensitive to this issue (Fischer et al., 2006).

All students—boys and girls and those that are LGBT—have a right to harassment-free schools, and teachers play an essential role in ensuring that this happens. Talk with your students about the problem, and emphasize that no form of harassment, sexual or otherwise, will be tolerated.

Use of Alcohol and Other Drugs

Student use of alcohol and other drugs has declined in recent years, but substance abuse still poses a serious problem for our teenagers. Consider these statistics from a 2005 national survey (Monitoring the Future, 2006):

- More than half of all students tried an illegal drug by the time they finished high school.
- Seventy-five percent of high school seniors reported drinking alcohol, with nearly half drinking in the last 30 days.
- Forty-five percent of seniors experimented with marijuana or hashish.
- Half of high school seniors, nearly 40 percent of 10th graders, and more than 25 percent of 8th graders reported smoking cigarettes.

This pattern of drug use starts early: More than 20 percent of 8th graders and a third of 10th graders reported drug or alcohol use in the past year (L. Johnson, Bachman, & O'Malley, 2001). Schools, which ought to be drug-free havens for students, also are part of the problem: Sixty percent of high school students and 30 percent of middle schoolers reported that drugs are kept, used, or sold in their schools (Center on Addiction and Substance Abuse, 2001).

What leads teenagers to alcohol and other drug use? Some blame the mixed messages teens receive from our culture as well as the media. In 2001, the tobacco industry spent more than $11 billion on advertising, and one study found that students who were exposed to smoking in movies were more than two and a half times as likely to smoke as their peers who hadn't seen them (Bowman, 2004; Honawar, 2005). Although educators and parents talk about the dangers of these substances, the media, and particularly teenage pop culture, often glorify alcohol, tobacco, and other drugs, implying not only that they're acceptable but that they are the preferred ways of dealing with problems such as stress, loneliness, or depression.

As teenagers become drug dependent, they place themselves at risk for other problems, such as poor health, car accidents, and even suicide. They also fail to develop healthy mechanisms for coping with life's problems (Berk, 2009; Crosnoe, 2006). Drug dependence can also reinforce feelings of alienation and encourage students to drop out of school. As is intuitively sensible, students who have little attachment to school and devalue its importance are those most likely to use drugs during school hours (K. Finn, Willert, & Marable, 2003).

Efforts to curtail drug use include programs that teach students facts about drugs while helping them learn to make their own decisions and understand and avoid peer pressure. They also work to develop students' self-esteem. Probably best known is the Drug Abuse Resistance Education (DARE) program, which started in California and spread across the country. In 2005, the federal government distributed $346 million to states to combat student drug use, but in 2006, the Bush administration recommended eliminating the funds, calling the grants ineffective (M. Davis, 2006). Research on these programs is mixed, and experts agree that delivering the "Just Say No" message without further intervention efforts is rarely effective (Viadero, 2005b).

This I BELIEVE

This section addresses the fourth item in our *This I Believe* feature at the beginning of the chapter, "In recent years student use of drugs and alcohol has declined." This statement is true, but research suggests that large numbers of students are still abusing different forms of drugs, and that this abuse interferes with healthy development.

Obesity

A health-care worker at the Obesity Center of Children's Hospital, Los Angeles, encountered the following:

> *One of my patients, 16-year-old Max, who weighed close to 300 pounds, told me that he drank a six-pack of sweetened soda every day. I was appalled: he was consuming more than a thousand empty calories every day just in soda. And I was puzzled, too. Max was on his high school's junior varsity football team, which meant he arrived at school early in the morning and left late in the afternoon, after practice. How, I asked, did he manage to drink six cans of soda in the remaining hours of the day?*
>
> *The answer floored me: Max explained that he bought five cans of sugared soda from school vending machines every day, one each before his first class, his second class, and lunch. Before football practice he downed a fourth can, and he topped it off with a fifth can of soda when practice was over. That left one for home. I asked why he didn't drink water. He told me the water that came out of the fountains was brown and smelly and the vending machines didn't sell it. The rest of his diet was equally bad. In the mid-morning he bought a candy bar at the student store, at lunch he had high-calorie, high-fat burrito and fries or cheese nachos, and after football practice there were boxes of doughnuts. . . . there was literally nothing in his daily environment that was both nutritious and appealing. (Kaufman, 2005, p. 243)*

Student obesity has emerged as a major health issue facing our youth. Nationwide, 1 of 6 children ages 6 to 19—more than 9 million students—is overweight, triple the proportion in 1980 (Education Vital Signs, 2006; Schibsted, 2006). This figure increases to 1 in 5 for 4-year-olds, with higher rates for Native Americans (31%), Hispanics (22%), and Blacks (21%) (L. Tanner, 2009). In addition to immediate health risks such as high blood pressure and joint problems, overweight youth face rejection from their peers and the risk of developing into heavy adults with additional health problems, such as heart disease and Type II diabetes (DeAngelis, 2004). In response to these problems, the American Academy of Pediatrics recently approved the use of cholesterol-fighting drugs for children as young as 8 years old (L. Tanner, 2008). The problem is especially acute for low-SES children living in poverty who often do not have access to affordable healthful foods (Kaufman, 2005).

The causes of this epidemic are multifaceted and range from lack of exercise to just plain unhealthy diets. One poll found that the average 8- to 18-year-old spends more than 44 hours a week in front of either a television or a computer screen and spends less than 2 hours a day in outdoor play (Education Vital Signs, 2005; Lafee, 2005).

Television ads are also a source of concern. Children 8 to 12 years old watch an average of 21 food ads a day—more than 7,600 a year (Hellmech, 2007). Advertisers spend more than $10 billion a year marketing food and beverages to children, mostly for products not considered nutritious. Food is the major product targeted to children, and more than a third of the food ads push candy and snacks, with none promoting fresh fruits and vegetables.

Schools also contribute to the problem. Elementary school recess has largely been eliminated, and the number of high school students taking P.E. declined from 41 to 28 percent between 1991 and 2003 (Greifner, 2006; Schibsted, 2006). Sugar-laden soft drinks sold in schools are also a problem: A number of school districts, strapped for cash, signed lucrative contracts with corporations to place soft-drink machines in school hallways (Lafee, 2005). (An average can of nondiet soda has 10 teaspoons of sugar and 150 calories; students drinking three or four cans a day can add 5 or 6 pounds to their weight in a month.)

State legislatures have responded with both stricter nutritional guidelines for school lunches and bans on soft-drink sales during school hours (Christie, 2005; Schibsted, 2006). In addition, beverage companies such as Coca-Cola and PepsiCo, under pressure from a number of advocacy groups, agreed to limit sales of sugar-laden soft drinks in schools (Samuels, 2006b). Under the agreement, the companies would sell only water, unsweetened juice, and low-fat milk to elementary and middle schools, and only diet sodas to high schools. Research suggests these efforts may be paying off: One report found that after a 25-year increase, the percentage of U.S. children who were overweight or obese leveled off (Parker-Pope, 2008). This is a start, but other dimensions of the problem such as exercise and healthful diets still need to be addressed.

Crime and Violence

For the past few months, Juan and his mother have been in hiding, the entire time he has attended Lafayette Elementary. His 29-year-old mother has been in gangs since she was twelve, and her sons, including Juan, grew up believing that at some point they would gain membership for themselves, and in gaining membership would enjoy status and achieve a measure of safety for themselves and their families. One bloody evening, however, crushed her and Juan's world-view, leaving behind a fearful, small boy and a mother overwhelmed with regret. (Bullough, 1999, p. 22)

Juan's uncle was shot and killed in a drive-by shooting; his uncle's girlfriend still wears a metal brace on her leg from the incident. Juan not only witnessed the shooting but had the presence of mind to pull the uncle's two children to the ground to protect them from danger. Juan's school principal, unaware of this and similar incidents, wonders why Juan is so angry in school.

Unfortunately, crime and violence sometimes enter school doors. The problem of school violence came to national attention in 1999 with the tragedy at Columbine High School in Littleton, Colorado, in which 2 students went on a rampage, gunning down 13 students before killing themselves. It was then amplified in 2005 when a high school student in Red Lake, Minnesota, killed seven people, including a teacher and a security guard, and wounded seven others.

Consider these statistics from the 2002–2003 school year:

- Thirty-three percent of high school students reported being in a fight in the previous 12 months, with 13 percent reporting that the fight took place on school property.

- Twenty-three students died in schools, 15 from homicides and 8 from suicide.
- Students aged 12–18 were victims of 1.9 million nonfatal crimes, including 1.2 million thefts and 740,000 violent crimes.
- At the high school level, both males (12 percent) and females (6 percent) reported being threatened or injured with a weapon on school property (National Center for Education Statistics, 2005e).

Despite these statistics, three trends are clear: First, the incidence of violence in schools is declining; second, students are safer in schools than on the streets where they live (National Center for Education Statistics, 2005c); and third, school violence is more common in some school contexts than in others. For example, incidents of violence are highest at the middle school level and decline as students get older (National Center for Education Statistics, 2007b). Also, violence is more common in urban than in suburban or rural schools, and concerns about violence are greatest in high-poverty areas. School violence is often associated with gangs, and more than 1 of 5 secondary students reported that street gangs were present at their school (National Center for Education Statistics, 2005e).

BULLYING   How would you react to the following incidents?

You are monitoring students on the playground when you overhear one student say to another, "No, way. Absolutely not! I already told you that you can't play with us." The student leaves and is isolated, playing alone for the remaining time with tears in her eyes. This is not the first time this individual has kept someone from joining her group of playmates.

You have assigned the students in your class to work in groups of 4 on their projects. While the students are getting in their groups you see one student push another with enough force that he falls to the ground. The push was clearly intentional and was not provoked. The child that fell yells, "Stop pushing me around! You always do this, just leave me alone." (Adapted from Bauman & Del Rio, 2006)

Bullying, a more subtle form of school violence, is receiving increased attention, as educators are realizing its damaging effects on students and its possible links to suicide and school shootings. **Bullying** involves a systematic or repetitious abuse of power between students (Berger, 2007).

All of us remember teasing and taunting in the halls and on school playgrounds, and many parents and educators considered this to be a normal rite of passage. Research, however, links bullying to a number of antisocial and aggressive behaviors that can have negative consequences for both bullies and victims (Raskauskas & Stoltz, 2007). Research suggests that bullying is a major factor in many school shooting incidents such as the Columbine tragedy (Fast, 2008). Another study found that both bullies and victims were more likely to carry a weapon, bring it to school, and become involved in serious fights (Viadero, 2003b).

People who bully take advantage of imbalances in power, such as greater size or strength, higher status, or the support of a peer group. The bullying itself can be a face-to-face attack, threats, teasing about perceived sexual orientation, or refusing to let someone participate or play. It can also include behind-the-back behaviors, such as spreading malicious rumors, writing harmful graffiti, or encouraging others to exclude a child (D. Cooper & Snell, 2003; Siris & Osterman, 2004). Though physical bullying declines with age, more subtle forms persist, such as the example at the beginning of this section where a student said, "No, way. Absolutely not! I already told you that you can't play with us" (Berger, 2007).

PEARSON myeducationlab

To see a video of the destructive effects of school bullying, go to the *Assignments and Activities* section of Topic 3: *Schools and Society* in the MyEducationLab for your course and complete the activity titled *The In Crowd and Social Cruelty*.

ISSUES IN EDUCATION

Bullying A systematic or repetitious abuse of power between students.

Bullying is more common than many adults realize. Surveys indicate that nearly 75 percent of 8- to 11-year-olds and more than 85 percent of 12- to 15-year-olds reported bullying in their schools (W. Roberts, 2006). In other studies, nearly one third of students reported that they had bullied, been a victim of bullying, or both within the last month (Viadero, 2003b). As with other forms of violence, bullying is most prevalent at the middle school level, with more than 40 percent of students reporting at least one incident of bullying a week, compared to slightly more than 20 percent at both the elementary and high school levels (National Center for Educational Statistics, 2007b). Experts think the incidence of bullying is actually higher than reported because it most commonly occurs in areas where students interact informally, such as playgrounds, hallways, cafeterias, and school buses, and where they have little adult supervision (Siris & Osterman, 2004).

Teachers often fail to take steps to address the problem because they perceive bullying incidents as part of the normal rough-and-tumble give-and-take that amounts to a rite of passage for young people (D. Cooper & Snell, 2003). And, students are often hesitant to report bullying because they fear reprisals or don't want to appear weak or unable to solve their own social problems (R. Newman, 2008). Research indicates that beginning teachers are less likely than veterans to respond to incidents of bullying (Bauman & Del Rio, 2006). It is an important issue, however, and one you need to be aware of when you begin your first teaching job.

SCHOOLWIDE SAFETY PROGRAMS   Schoolwide safety programs are designed to make schools safe havens for teaching and learning through comprehensive antiviolence and antibullying programs (Colgan, 2005; Conoley & Goldstein, 2004). In successful programs, school leaders establish policies that violence and bullying will not be tolerated, and parents, administrators, and teachers then monitor playgrounds, lunchrooms, and hallways, areas where these incidents are most common. When an incident occurs, it's quickly identified and defused, and consequences are administered to perpetrators.

In other attempts to increase school safety, many schools are adopting comprehensive security measures, such as having visitors sign in, closing campuses during lunch, and controlling access to school buildings (Colgan, 2005; Conoley & Goldstein, 2004). Schools are also adding prevention policies that include use of hallway police, student photo ID badges, transparent book bags, handheld metal detectors, and breathalyzers to check for alcohol consumption. In many districts, visitors are screened through an electronic system that matches drivers' licenses to a database of convicted sex offenders (Maxwell, 2006). Students are being warned to avoid jokes about violence and are given hotline numbers to anonymously report any indications that a classmate could turn violent. Schools are also creating peer buddy systems and adult mentorship programs, and are teaching conflict-resolution skills as alternatives to violence (Conoley & Goldstein, 2004; D. Johnson & Johnson, 2006).

Schoolwide security programs are designed to make schools safe places to learn.

The enormous publicity generated by school shooting incidents has led many schools around the country to experiment with new approaches to making schools safe. One of the most controversial involves the issue of **zero-tolerance policies**, which call for students to receive automatic suspensions or expulsions as punishment for certain offenses, primarily those involving weapons, threats, or drugs. Such policies have become increasingly popular across the nation. We examine controversies surrounding zero-tolerance policies in our *Taking a Stand in an Era of Reform* feature that follows this section.

Zero-tolerance policies Policies that call for students to receive automatic suspensions or expulsions as punishment for certain offenses, primarily those involving weapons, threats, or drugs.

■ ■ TECHNOLOGY AND TEACHING Cyber-Bullying

The growing presence of the Internet in students' lives has resulted in **cyber-bullying**, a new form of bullying that occurs when students use electronic media to harass or intimidate other students. Concerns about cyber-bullying peaked in 2006, when a 13-year-old Missouri teenager committed suicide after receiving harassing messages on the Internet. Since then, both school officials and parents have become aware of this growing problem (Stobbe, 2007).

Research suggests that cyber-bullying follows the same patterns as traditional forms of bullying; students who are bullies and victims on the playground play similar roles in cyberspace (Raskauskas & Stoltz, 2007). The anonymity of the Internet distinguishes cyber-bullying from other types, and this anonymity can make bullies even more insensitive to the hurtful nature of the bullying incidents (Willard, 2006).

Cyber-bullying is hard to measure, but experts estimate that between 10 and 30 percent of students are victims of online harassment (Stobbe, 2007). Given the popularity of Internet use among teenagers (estimates indicate that most teenagers use it every day) cyber-bullying is likely to remain a persistent problem (Raskauskas & Stoltz, 2007).

Bullying is most commonly learned, with modeling and reinforcement by parents and peers playing major roles (W. Roberts, 2006). For example, bullies tend to come from homes where parents are authoritarian, hostile, and rejecting. The parents may have poor problem-solving skills and use fighting as a solution to conflicts; their children then imitate these behaviors. Bullies are often emotionally underdeveloped, and they're unable to understand or empathize with others' perspectives or regulate their own behavior (Berk, 2008, 2009).

Attempts to prevent bullying focus on both specific individuals and the entire school. Efforts to eliminate bullying at the individual level attempt to help students understand the consequences of their negative behaviors and teach alternative prosocial behaviors (W. Roberts, 2006). One of the unfortunate outcomes of bullying is suicide, which we discuss in the next section.

SUICIDE   Think about this statistic: Suicide is the third-leading cause of teen death, surpassed only by car accidents and homicide (Kids Health for Parents, 2006)! About a half million young people attempt suicide each year, and between 2,000 and 5,000 succeed; accurate figures are hard to obtain because of the social stigma attached to suicide (Fisher, 2006; J. Moore, 2007). The suicide rate among adolescents has quadrupled in the last 50 years. Girls are twice as likely as boys to attempt suicide, but boys are 4 times more likely to succeed. Boys tend to employ more lethal means, such as shooting themselves, whereas girls choose more survivable methods, such as overdosing on drugs.

Causes of teen suicide vary, but most are related to the stresses of adolescence; they include family conflicts, parental unemployment and divorce, drug use, failed peer relationships, and peer harassment, especially for lesbian, gay, bisexual, and transgender youngsters (Berk, 2008, 2009).

Indicators of potential suicide include the following:

- An abrupt decline in the quality of schoolwork

- Withdrawal from friends or classroom and school activities

- Neglect of personal appearance or radical changes in personality

- Changes in eating or sleeping habits

- Depression, as evidenced by persistent boredom or lack of interest in school activities

- Student comments about suicide as a solution to problems (Fisher, 2006; Kids Health for Parents, 2006)

Cyber-bullying The use of electronic media to harass or intimidate other students.

If you observe any of these indicators in a student, contact a school counselor or psychologist immediately; early intervention is essential.

Zero Tolerance

The era of zero tolerance began in 1994 when Congress passed the Gun-Free Schools Act, which required states receiving federal funds to expel for 1 year any student who brought a firearm to school. The Safe and Drug Free Schools and Communities Act broadened the focus from firearms to all weapons and also included expelling students for possessing drugs or drug paraphernalia. This act became part of the No Child Left Behind Act of 2001 and continues to have a powerful effect on school policies.

THE ISSUE

The need for safe schools is obvious, and the premise of zero-tolerance policies—that students who endanger or disrupt the learning environment for the majority of the school population should be removed—is intuitively sensible. Students can't learn if they don't feel both physically and emotionally safe. Parents and other taxpayers rank school safety and drug use as critical problems facing U.S. schools (Bushaw & Gallup, 2008), and zero-tolerance policies are popular. Both teachers (70 percent) and parents (68 percent) judged zero-tolerance policies to be effective deterrents to serious infractions in schools (Public Agenda, 2004).

On the other hand, critics have identified several problems with these policies. First, largely because of zero-tolerance policies, the suspension rate of students has increased dramatically.

A Florida study found a 14 percent increase in school suspensions between 2000 and 2004, almost twice as high as the student population growth (Gewertz, 2006a). Second, when expulsions occur, fewer than 6 of 10 students are sent to an alternative placement; the rest are sent home to fend for themselves, making the likelihood of truancy and crime even greater. One student described the problem in this way:

> When they suspend you, you get in more trouble, 'cause you're out in the street. . . . And that's what happened to me once. I got into trouble one day 'cause there was a party, and they arrested everybody in that party. . . . I got in trouble more than I get in trouble at school, because I got arrested and everything. (Skiba & Peterson, 1999, p. 376)

Expelled students typically fall further behind academically, experience increased social difficulties, and sometimes never return to complete school (Reyes, 2006).

Third, the implementation of the policies is inconsistent. Critics point to their disproportionate effect on members of cultural minorities. For example, although African American students in San Francisco made up less than 20 percent of all students, they accounted for more than half of students suspended (Gordon, Della Piana, & Keleher, 2001). A Florida study found a similar pattern: African American students made up slightly more than 20 percent of the student population, but they received nearly half of

out-of-school suspensions (Gewertz, 2006a). One middle school in Dade County, Florida, had an expulsion rate of 34 percent, whereas another—serving essentially the same student population—had a rate of only 2.8 percent (Vergon, 2001). Explanations for these uneven percentages range from higher rates of poverty and misbehavior to inexperienced teachers, crowded classrooms, and academically sterile learning environments.

Finally, because these policies don't discriminate between major and minor disruptions, schools sometimes punish students for trivial and innocent transgressions. For example, one fifth grader was suspended for bringing a miniature plastic gun to school with his G.I. Joe action figure, and in another case, a 6-year-old was suspended for kissing one of his classmates (Cornelius, 2002).

YOU TAKE A STAND

Now it's your turn to take a position on the issue. Do zero-tolerance programs make schools safer and better places to learn, or do the related negative side effects outweigh the benefits?

myeducationlab To explore both sides of this issue and take a stand, go to the *Book Specific Resources* section in the MyEducationLab for your course, select your text, and then select *Taking a Stand in an Era of Reform* for Chapter 3.

ISSUES IN EDUCATION

CHILD ABUSE   Child abuse is another serious problem facing today's youth. In 2003, child protective services agencies received 2.9 million reports of child abuse; investigation of these cases confirmed that more than 900,000 children had been victims of abuse or mistreatment (U.S. Department of Health and Human Services, 2006). Because abuse and neglect are often hidden or not reported, reliable figures are difficult to obtain. More than 60 percent of abuse victims suffer from neglect, about one fifth experience physical abuse, and about 10 percent are sexually abused (Centers for Disease Control and Prevention, 2007). When sexual abuse occurs, it most commonly involves a family member or friend. Although child abuse can occur at any level of society, it tends to be associated with poverty and is often linked to parental substance abuse.

myeducationlab

To see a video of the controversies surrounding zero tolerance policies, go to the *Assignments and Activities* section of Topic 3: *Schools and Society* in the MyEducationLab for your course and complete the activity titled *Action, Reaction, Zero Tolerance*.

ISSUES IN EDUCATION

Teachers are in a unique position to identify child abuse because they work with children every day. Here are some symptoms of abuse:

- Neglected appearance
- Sudden changes in either academic or social behavior
- Disruptive or overcompliant behavior
- Repeated injuries such as bruises, welts, or burns

Teachers in all 50 states are legally bound to report suspected child abuse, and teachers and schools are protected from civil and criminal liability if the report is made honestly and includes behavioral data, such as observations of the symptoms just listed (Fischer et al., 2006).

This section addresses the fifth item in this chapter's *This I Believe* feature, "Teachers are required by law to report instances of child abuse." This statement is true. Every state and the District of Columbia require that teachers report instances of child abuse either to school authorities or to the police. The intent of the laws is to encourage teachers to report these problems and to protect them if they do.

This I BELIEVE

■ ■ ■ ■ CHECK YOUR UNDERSTANDING

3.1 What changes have occurred in student sexuality over time? What are the implications of these changes for education?

3.2 Explain the trends in student use of alcohol and other drugs over the last several years, and describe the implications of these changes for education.

3.3 How has the rate of student obesity changed over the years? How are schools responding to this problem?

3.4 How have crime and violence changed in U.S. schools? What are the implications for education?

For feedback, go to the appendix, *Check Your Understanding*, located in the back of this text.

AT-RISK STUDENTS

Failing students can be found in any school. Many reasons exist, but some students share characteristics that decrease their chances for success. **At-risk students** are in danger of failing to complete their education with the skills necessary to function effectively in modern society. The term *at risk* is derived from medicine, which uses the term "risk factors," such as high cholesterol and obesity, in describing dangers to health. *At risk* became widely used after 1983, when the National Commission on Excellence in Education proclaimed the United States a "nation at risk," emphasizing the growing link between education and economic well-being in today's technological society (National Commission on Excellence in Education, 1983).

Since 1983, researchers have focused considerable attention on problems involving at-risk students. Table 3.2 outlines some of the academic, social, and emotional problems these students experience. You will almost certainly have these students in your classes.

The Dropout Problem

Because it has an enormous impact on subsequent employment and income, dropping out of school is one of the most pernicious outcomes of being at risk. High school graduates earn 34 percent more than high school dropouts; over a lifetime, a high school

URBAN EDUCATION

At-risk students Students in danger of failing to complete their education with the skills necessary to survive in modern society.

Table 3.2   Characteristics of At-Risk Students

Background Factors	Educational Problems
Low SES/Poverty	High dropout rates
Transient/Homeless	Low grades
Divorced Families	Retention in grade
Inner City	Low achievement
Minority	Low participation in extracurricular activities
Nonnative English Speaker	Low motivation
Environments With Alcohol and Drug Abuse	Poor attendance
High Neighborhood Criminal Activity Rates	Misbehavior in classes
	Low self-esteem
	Low standardized test scores
	Lack of interest in school
	High suspension rates

dropout earns $260,000 less than someone with a high school diploma (Economic Policy Institute, 2005). In addition, dropping out of high school closes the door to college and well-paying jobs (Sykes, 2006).

Experts disagree about the number of students who drop out of school (Bracey, 2005a; Mishel, 2006), but they agree that dropout rates vary dramatically by ethnicity. For example, one study indicated that 71 percent of students graduate from high school, but Hispanic (58 percent), African American (55 percent), and Native American (51 percent) students had much lower graduation rates (see Figure 3.3) (U.S. Department of Education, 2008a.) Think about this: Nearly one third of the students who enter ninth grade won't graduate in 4 years, and the dropout rate increases to about half for cultural minorities!

Dropout rates are strongly affected by poverty; students from low-income families are 6 times more likely to drop out than those from high-income families (Olson, 2006b). Other factors contributing to high dropout rates include unstable families, high rates of student mobility, previous retention in a grade, as well as higher graduation standards and high school exit exams (Barton, 2006).

What can schools do to address this problem? Research suggests that motivation is a major factor in dropping out. One study indicated that nearly 70 percent of dropouts said they weren't motivated or inspired to work hard, almost half said their classes weren't interesting, and two thirds identified a lack of challenge as a major factor in dropping out

PEARSON
myeducationlab

To hear one superintendent's experiences with and advice about teaching urban, at-risk students, go to the *Assignments and Activities* section of Topic 3: *Schools and Society* in the MyEducationLab for your course and complete the activity titled *Urban, At-Risk Students: A Superintendent's Perspective.*

Figure 3.3 Public School Graduation Rates in the United States (2005)

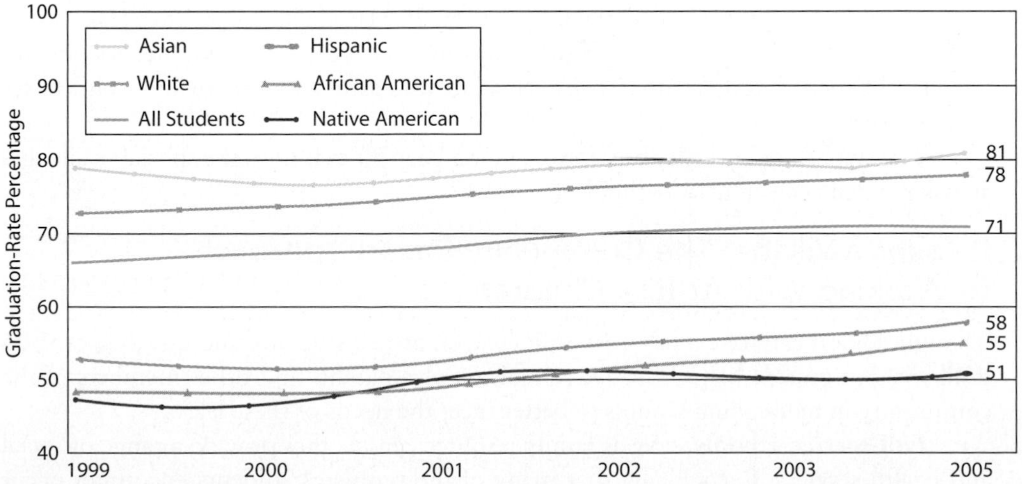

Source: U.S. Department of Education (2008a).

Urban Schools and At-Risk Students

At-risk students face special challenges in urban schools, which tend to be large and located in high-poverty areas. As a result, they are less well funded than their suburban counterparts, and because they are large, they can become impersonal (Kincheloe, 2004). Urban high schools can be "tough, confusing places where students can easily get lost" (Ilg & Massucci, 2003, p. 69).

The diversity of urban neighborhoods, the distances students often must travel over public transportation, and the fact that teachers in urban schools typically don't live in the same neighborhoods make it difficult for teachers to connect with students and empathize with their lives outside school (Charner-Laird et al., 2004). Extracurricular activities, which can serve as a meet-

ing point for students, are often inaccessible (R. Brown & Evans, 2002), compounding the problem of establishing supportive interpersonal relationships with students (Kincheloe, 2004). One study found that only 20 percent of urban African American males and less than 30 percent of African American females believed that their teachers supported them and cared about their success (Noguera, 2003). It is difficult for teachers to influence their students' development when mutual trust and caring are absent.

As you saw earlier in the chapter, poverty often has an adverse effect on student achievement, and

Meaningful relationships with students make urban schools and classrooms more inviting places to learn.

(Gewertz, 2006b). Each of these issues can be addressed with effective instruction, a crucial topic that will be addressed in your teacher preparation program.

Additional research suggests that the human factor is essential: Students thinking about dropping out need to believe that they belong in school and that someone cares about them as people and about their success (Barton, 2006). This is where your work is crucial, because you and your colleagues are the only people in the school who interact with students every day (Doll, Zucher, & Brehm, 2004). Make it a point to learn about your students and their families, and share information about your own life. You are not trying to be their "buddy"; rather, you're an adult who cares about them and wants to see them succeed.

The Exploring Diversity box above and on page 93 examines the special challenges at-risk students face in urban schools.

It Takes a Village: The Community-Based Approach to Working With At-Risk Children

Though schools can have a powerful influence on at-risk students' success, they can't do it all without outside help. Effective schools involve parents and other members of the community in redesigning schools to better meet the needs of these learners.

Full-service schools Schools that serve as family resource centers to provide a range of social and health services.

Full-service schools serve as family resource centers that provide a range of social and health services. Recognizing that many of the problems students encounter occur

research indicates that urban environments have higher rates of poverty (nearly 20 percent) than areas outside central cities (less than 10 percent) (U.S. Bureau of Census, 2004). In addition, incomes in urban areas are about two thirds of those in the suburbs (U.S. Bureau of Census, 2005).

Lower incomes and the lower residential property values that go with them mean less money for schools. Less money often means that class sizes are larger and schools have fewer resources, such as computers and science lab equipment (Archer, 2003; Blair, 2003).

Finally, because working in urban areas is viewed as very challenging and with few rewards, veteran teachers often choose jobs in the suburbs instead of in urban settings. As a result, urban students, who most need experienced professionals, are unlikely to get them. This can present opportunities for you: If you consider working in an urban environment, the likelihood of getting a job is high. In addition, schools are increasingly offering incentive pay for teachers willing to work in urban schools, and working with urban students can be rewarding as you help them develop, both personally and intellectually.

Diversity in Your Classroom

The challenge for urban educators is to create contexts in which students can interact meaningfully with both teachers and other students. One proposed solution is to create smaller schools, or schools within a school, that allow for the creation of more personal learning communities. Students in smaller schools "behave better, are more likely to be involved in extra-curricular activities, . . . fight less, feel safe, and feel more attached to their schools" (Ilg & Massucci, 2003, p. 69).

Although teachers alone can't create smaller schools, urban teachers can make a special effort to create learning communities within their classrooms that nurture both the social and the cognitive development of their students. Let's see what an urban seventh grader has to say about one of her teachers.

> She's probably the strictest teacher I've ever had because she doesn't let you slide by if you've made a mistake. . . . If you've made a mistake she's going to let you know it. And if you're getting bad marks, she's going to let you know it. She's one of my strictest teachers and that's what makes me think she cares about us the most. (Alder, 2002, pp. 251–252)

Effective urban teachers combine high expectations for academic success with clear messages about the need for student effort and responsibility.

QUESTIONS TO CONSIDER

1. Why do you think this student believes that her teacher's strictness and demands on students are a sign of caring?
2. In addition to being strict and demanding, how can teachers communicate that they care about students?

myeducationlab To respond to these questions online, explore this topic further, and receive feedback, go to the *Book Specific Resources* section in the MyEducationLab for your course, select your text, and then select *Exploring Diversity* for Chapter 3.

---

outside school walls, and that supporting families also strengthens children, full-service schools attempt to create a safety net of services to students and their families. Some of these services are listed in Table 3.3.

The School Development Program, created by Yale psychiatrist James Comer, is one example of a full-service model (Comer, Joyner, & Ben-Avie, 2004); it integrates schools and the community by bringing principals, teachers, and parents together in

Table 3.3 Services Provided by Full-Service Schools

Child care
Medical and dental screening
Immunizations
Nutrition/weight management
Employment and housing assistance
Legal and immigration advice
Individual counseling/mental health services
Substance abuse treatment
Recreation, sports, and culture
Parent education
After-school teacher assistance with homework

school planning and management teams. School services, such as counseling and support for students with learning problems, are coordinated through teams of psychologists, counselors, and special educators. This coordination is important because services for students are often fragmented. For example, one depressed, pregnant, drug-using teenager saw three counselors each week: one for suicide prevention, another for parenting, and a third for drug abuse. Unfortunately, none of these people talked to each other (Tyson, 1999). Comprehensive school programs address this problem by coordinating services and focusing on the child's physical, social, emotional, and academic growth in integrated efforts.

From its start in New Haven, Connecticut, the School Development Program has spread to more than 500 schools across the country. Evaluations indicate that the program is effective; researchers report increases in achievement and student self-concepts and declines in absences, suspensions, and management problems in schools where the program is fully implemented (Comer et al., 2004). Research on other comprehensive school programs shows similar positive effects (Whalen, 2002).

The teacher's role in a full-service school changes from one of instructor to partner with the community. If you work in one of these schools, you'll be asked to serve on community councils that attempt to link schools with their surrounding communities, and you'll also be asked to be proactive in making contacts with parents and other caregivers (M. Ginsberg, 2007). Your workload will be greater, but the rewards that come from seeing your students succeed because of your outreach efforts will be substantial.

Promoting Student Resilience

Despite the obstacles they encounter, many students succeed against the odds and graduate from school with the skills necessary to succeed in life. **Resilient students** are at-risk students who have been able to rise above adverse conditions to succeed in school and in other aspects of life (Borman & Overman, 2004; Doll et al., 2004).

Resilient children have well-developed "self systems," including high self-esteem and feelings that they are in control of their destinies. They set personal goals, possess good interpersonal skills, and have positive expectations for success. They are motivated to learn and are satisfied with school (Borman & Overman, 2004).

How do these adaptive skills develop? First, resilient children have relationships with caring adults who hold high moral and academic expectations for them (Reis, Colbert, & Hébert, 2005). Second, they come from schools that are both demanding and supportive; in many instances, schools serve as homes away from home. Let's look more closely at how schools and teachers foster resilience in students.

EFFECTIVE SCHOOLS FOR AT-RISK STUDENTS   Effective schools for at-risk students focus on personal responsibility, cooperation, and mutual respect between teachers and students (Barr & Parrett, 2001; Griffith, 2002). Effective schools emphasize these factors:

- A safe, orderly school climate in which students understand the meaning behind and the purpose of school and classroom rules
- Academic objectives focusing on mastery of content
- Cooperation, a sense of community, and prosocial values
- Student responsibility and self-regulation with decreased emphasis on external controls
- Strong parental involvement
- Caring and demanding teachers who hold high expectations for all students (Ilg & Massucci, 2003; Pressley, Raphael, & Gallagher, 2004)

The next section examines these teachers in more detail.

PEARSON
myeducationlab

Go to the *Building Teaching Skills and Dispositions* section of Topic 3: *Schools and Society* in the MyEducationLab for your course and complete the activity entitled *Keeping Students in School*.

Resilient students At-risk students who have been able to rise above adverse conditions to succeed in school and in other aspects of life.

EFFECTIVE TEACHERS FOR AT-RISK STUDENTS

Well-run and academically focused schools are important, but they aren't sufficient in themselves. Teachers in these schools are simultaneously caring and demanding (Doll et al., 2004). In many cases, they are the caring adults who hold high moral and academic expectations for students. In essence, they refuse to let students fail. One high school teacher reported the following:

> A graduate whom I had not seen for many years stopped by after school when he saw me working late. His eyes were thick with tears as he spoke: "You never gave up on me. You never ignored me. You always encouraged me to get my work in and pass all of my classes, even when I wasn't nice to you. Thank you." (Barnoski, 2005, p. 37)

Caring teachers with high expectations for success help at-risk students achieve in school.

This kind of teacher commitment is essential because the needs and personal sensitivities of at-risk students make them vulnerable to failure, personal slights, hints of favoritism, and questions about the relevance of school.

Teachers who are ineffective with at-risk students are more authoritarian and less accessible. They distance themselves from students and place primary responsibility for learning on them. They view being emotionally supportive as "babying students" or "holding students' hands." Lecture is a common teaching strategy, and motivation is the students' responsibility. Students perceive these teachers as adversaries, to be avoided if possible, tolerated if not.

In addition to being caring and demanding, what do effective teachers of at-risk students need to do? We answer that question in the next section.

EFFECTIVE INSTRUCTION AND SUPPORT

Teachers of at-risk students don't need to teach in fundamentally different ways; instead, they systematically apply the strategies that are effective with all students (Eggen & Kauchak, 2010). They provide enough instructional support to ensure success while teaching students active learning strategies that allow them to take control of their own learning. Effective practices for teaching at-risk students include the following:

- High classroom structure with predictable routines
- Clear learning objectives
- High levels of interaction between the teacher and students
- Frequent and thorough assessment
- Informative feedback to promote student success
- Emphasis on student responsibility (Borman & Overman, 2004; Brophy, 2004)

Let's see how one teacher does this.

When students enter Dena Hine's second-grade classroom after recess, they see a review assignment on the chalkboard. As Dena takes roll, students get out their books and start on the assignment. Five minutes later, Dena begins with a brief review of the previous day's lesson. Because the students answer her questions quickly and correctly, she believes that her class knows the content and is ready to move on.

PEARSON
myeducationlab

To read a case study illustrating a teacher attempting to provide effective instruction for the students in her class who are at risk, go to the *Assignments and Activities* section in Topic 3: *Schools and Society* in the MyEducationLab for your course and complete the activity titled *Effective Instruction for At-Risk Students*.

As she introduces two-column subtraction, she comments that this is an important skill that everyone will be able to learn. Then she presents the following problem and discusses how two-column subtraction will help them solve it:

Teresa was saving her money to buy a toy for her little sister. The toy cost $.99, and she has already saved $.67. How much more money did she need to buy the toy?

Next, she gives each student bundles of 10 craft sticks bound together with rubber bands. She guides students through the subtraction steps by having them take apart the bundles to illustrate the process, asking many questions as she proceeds. She also uses questioning to help them link the craft sticks to the numbers she writes on the board. Then she has students solve problems on their own mini-chalkboards and hold them up to allow her to check their solutions. Whenever mistakes occur, she stops, explains the errors, and helps students correct them.

When most of the class is correctly solving the problems, Dena starts the students on additional practice problems, which they check in pairs. As they work, she helps those still having difficulty, moving around the room to respond to pairs who disagreed with each other or who have questions.

Effective teachers actively involve their students in learning activities, and they provide instruction that is challenging, motivating, and connected to students' lives.

■ ■ TECHNOLOGY AND TEACHING Access Issues for Students

Technology is changing the way we live and learn, and access to it has become an important issue. If teachers and students don't have access to technology, they obviously can't use it to increase learning.

One survey of educational technology use across the country found that in 2003, nearly 100 percent of public schools and 93 percent of classrooms had Internet access (National Center for Education Statistics, 2006a). Between 2003 and 2005, the ratio of students per Internet-connected computer dropped from 4.4 to 3.8 (Swanson, 2006b). So, in a class of 30 students, the "average" teacher might have about seven Internet-connected computers available. This statistic is misleading, however, because many schools cluster computers in labs where they are accessible only once or twice a week. This ratio is a significant improvement from one Internet-connected computer per 12 students in 1998, but it still requires instructional juggling to provide computer access to all students when they need it. When asked to identify barriers to effective use of technology, teachers targeted insufficient number of computers as a major problem (Rother, 2005).

Significant disparities in educational funding exist between "rich" and "poor" school districts, which result in differences in teachers' salaries, the kinds of buildings and classrooms teachers and students work in, and the resources available to promote learning. They also affect students' access to technology, suggesting a possible "digital divide" between different groups of students (Corporation for Public Broadcasting, 2003; Trotter, 2006a).

Considerable variation exists among different ethnic groups and families with differing levels of parents' education and income. For example, as you see in Figure 3.4, 80 percent of White households with school-age children had a computer in the home versus only 61 percent of African American and 67 percent of Hispanic households (Kaiser Family Foundation, 2004b). And whereas 67 percent of White students were likely to use the

Internet, just 47 percent of African American students and 44 percent of Hispanic students were likely to do so (Trotter, 2006a). Also, 82 percent of students whose parents had a college degree had access to the Internet at home versus 74 percent and 68 percent for households with some or no college, respectively.

Family income also influences access to technology. As you see in Figure 3.5, in 2002, 65 percent of low-income families owned computers versus 98 percent of high-income families (Corporation for Public Broadcasting, 2003). When asked about their ability to access the Internet from any location (home, school, or library), 55 percent of low-income students reported access versus 77 percent of high-income students. The biggest difference between the groups was seen in home online use of computers: Less than half as many low-income as high-income students said they used the Internet at home. The cost of buying, installing, and maintaining computers is the probable reason for this disparity. When students are expected to work on computers at home to complete assignments, access can be a serious problem.

These differences are troubling for several reasons. Research suggests that the number and quality of computers influence teachers' use of technology (Roblyer & Doering, 2010). When obstacles are too great, teachers tend not to use it, which deprives their students of valuable learning opportunities. From a student perspective, these statistics raise the question of whether all students have equal opportunities to learn, not only about technology, but in other content areas as well. In the long term, access to computers can also influence the career options available to students: Students are less likely to pursue high-tech careers in areas such as science and engineering if they have inadequate technology backgrounds or haven't been introduced to ways that technology is used in these areas. The challenge for educators is to prepare all students to compete in such an environment.

Figure 3.4 Ethnicity, Parental Education, and Home Internet Access for Children (Ages 8–18)

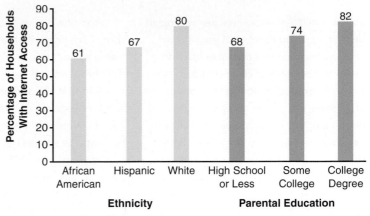

Source: Adapted from Kaiser Family Foundation (2004b). *Survey Snapshot: The Digital Divide.*

Figure 3.5 Household Income and Technology Access

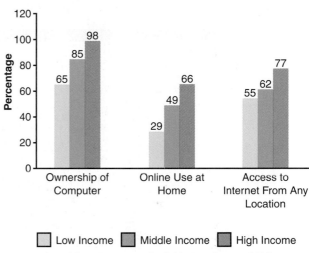

Source: Adapted from Corporation for Public Broadcasting (2003).

■ ■ ■ ■ CHECK YOUR UNDERSTANDING

4.1 What are the characteristics of at-risk students?

4.2 What unique challenges do urban schools present to at-risk students?

4.3 What can schools and teachers do to help at-risk students achieve success?

For feedback, go to the appendix, *Check Your Understanding*, located in the back of this text.

Now it's your turn to apply the information in this chapter to a problem or dilemma facing many prospective teachers. Read the following case and answer the question that follows.

Child Abuse

You're a middle school teacher in a rural district, and you meet with your homeroom students every day. You use homeroom to take care of daily routines and get to know your students as individuals. Janine has always been a bright, happy student who gets along well with her classmates. Lately she seems withdrawn, and her personal appearance is disheveled. As you periodically look at her, you see that she seems hesitant to make eye contact. You ask her to come in after school to talk. She says she has to go right home to help care for her younger brothers and sisters, so you suggest her lunch break instead. She reluctantly agrees.

When she comes in she appears nervous, fidgeting with her hands and refusing to look at you. You ask her how she feels, and she replies, "Fine." You mention that she seems to be different lately, preoccupied. She only shrugs. You ask if there is anything bothering her, and she shakes her head no. You reaffirm your availability if she ever wants to talk, and she smiles briefly. As she gathers her book to get up and leave, her sweater slides off her shoulder, revealing bruises.

"Janine, what happened to your arm?"

"Oh, I fell the other day."

"But how did you hurt the inside of your arm?"

Janine's pained and embarrassed expression suggests that a fall wasn't the cause.

"Did someone try to hurt you, Janine? You can tell me."

"Only if you promise not to tell," she blurts out.

Without thinking, you agree. She proceeds to tearfully tell you about an angry father who has been out of work for months and who becomes violent when he drinks. As she leaves, she makes you promise that you won't tell anyone.

What would you do in this situation?

3 MEETING YOUR LEARNING OBJECTIVES

1. Describe changes that have occurred in the American family over the last 50 years.

   - The traditional family, which historically has been described as a father who is the breadwinner and a mother who works in the home and cares for two children, has become a minority in this country.

   - The majority of mothers now work outside the home, raising concerns about child care. Quality child care can provide an environment where children learn both cognitive and interpersonal skills; these skills then provide a foundation when students enter school. In addition, the benefits of quality early child care extend into adulthood.

   - Latchkey children present another problem for working parents. Unsupervised children not only pose safety risks to themselves but also spend large amounts of unsupervised time in front of televisions and computers.

2. Define *socioeconomic status*, and explain how different socioeconomic patterns influence school success.

   - Socioeconomic status (SES) describes the combined effects of income, occupation, and educational level on people's attitudes, values, and behaviors. SES can also have powerful influences on how children respond to schools.

   - Poverty presents a number of challenges, ranging from lack of basic needs to unstable home environment. Recently, the rate of childhood poverty has increased, creating challenges for both teachers and students.

- SES influences educational success in several ways, including whether students' basic needs, such as nutrition and medical care, are met. It also influences the language skills and school-related experiences students bring to the classroom. Finally, SES shapes parents' and students' attitudes and values about the importance of education and school.

- Homelessness affects large numbers of children, influencing their ability to succeed in school. High percentages of homeless children don't attend school regularly, and when they do, they suffer from inadequate diets and substandard medical care as well as unstable families.

3. Describe societal changes and the implications of these changes for education.

- Students are becoming sexually active at an earlier age, placing themselves at risk for pregnancy and sexually transmitted disease. Schools attempt to deal with these problems through sex education programs. Other aspects of student sexuality include homosexuality and sexual harassment. Teachers play an essential role in communicating that sexual harassment won't be tolerated in schools or classrooms.

- The use of alcohol and other drugs, violence, suicide, and child abuse all present challenges to youth as well as the teachers who work with them. Although the use of alcohol and drugs is declining, significant numbers of students experiment with and use these at an early age.

- Obesity has become another health issue threatening students. Although it's increasingly common in all students, its negative effects are seen more often in low-SES and some cultural minority youths.

- Crime and violence are on the decline in schools as well as society as a whole, but still pose a problem to educators. Bullying has also been identified as a major school safety issue because of its potential not only to damage individuals but also to lead to more serious forms of violence. In response to these issues, schools have implemented schoolwide safety programs.

- A major response to crime and violence in the schools has been the implementation of zero-tolerance policies that expel students from school for any infraction involving drugs or weapons. Although adopted by a number of school districts, zero-tolerance policies have some problems, ranging from increased student dropout rates to punishing students for minor offenses and differential treatment of minority students.

4. Describe the characteristics of at-risk students and how schools and teachers can help at-risk students be successful.

- At-risk students face a number of challenges to school success, ranging from poverty to transience and unstable families. These conditions result in several educational problems that create barriers to school success.

- Urban schools present many challenges to at-risk students. Urban schools are often in high-poverty areas and have less experienced teachers. They are also less well funded than their suburban counterparts and tend to be larger and more impersonal.

- Community-based approaches to working with at-risk students actively involve parents and the community in designing and implementing comprehensive educational programs. Community-based programs attempt to integrate the services available to students by linking various support agencies.

- Effective schools for at-risk students create a safe, orderly learning environment that emphasizes academic goals. Studies of successful or resilient children suggest that caring home and school environments with supportive, understanding adults can help these students withstand societal challenges (Reis et al., 2005). Effective teachers for at-risk students combine supportive interpersonal contacts with instructional structure and support.

IMPORTANT CONCEPTS

at-risk students (p. 90)

bullying (p. 86)

cyber-bullying (p. 88)

full-service schools (p. 92)

latchkey children (p. 73)

lower class (p. 74)

middle class (p. 74)

poverty thresholds (p. 75)

resilient students (p. 94)

sexual harassment (p. 82)

socioeconomic status (SES) (p. 73)

underclass (p. 74)

upper class (p. 74)

working class (p. 74)

zero-tolerance policies (p. 87)

DISCUSSION QUESTIONS

1. How can family structure influence school success? What can schools and teachers do to accommodate different family structures?

2. How would your role as a teacher change if you worked in an upper SES suburb? in a lower SES part of a city?

3. How would your actual instruction change if you worked in an upper SES suburb? in a lower SES part of a city?

4. What role should schools play in dealing with teenage sexuality? What specifically could teachers do in this area?

5. What role should schools play in dealing with drug and alcohol abuse? What specifically could teachers do to assist in dealing with this problem?

6. Why is bullying more common at the middle school level than at others? Why is it more common in males than in females? What can teachers do in their own classrooms to address this problem?

7. What strengths do at-risk students bring to the classroom? How can teachers take advantage of these strengths?

8. What will be your biggest challenges in working with the parents of at-risk students?

PEARSON
myeducationlab)

Now go to Topic 3: *Schools and Society* in the MyEducationLab
(www.myeducationlab.com) for your course, where you can:

- Find learning outcomes for *Schools and Society* along with the national standards that connect to these outcomes.

- Complete *Assignments and Activities* that can help you more deeply understand the chapter content.

- Apply and practice your understanding of the core teaching skills identified in the chapter with the *Building Teaching Skills* and *Dispositions* learning units.

- Check your comprehension on the content covered in the chapter by going to the *Study Plan* in the *Book Specific Resources* section for your text. Here you will be able to take a chapter quiz, receive feedback on your answers, and then access *Review, Practice, and Enrichment* activities to enhance your understanding of chapter content.

Develop your Professional Portfolio

To further apply your understanding of chapter content and address the INTASC standards, go to the *Book Specific Resources* section in the MyEducationLab for your course, select your text, then select this chapter's *Portfolio Activities*.

"I teach so that my students know that there's at least one adult in their lives that cares about them."

PAMELA HARMAN, 2008 Teacher of the Year, Alabama

To view a video clip of Pamela, the 2008 Alabama Teacher of the Year, go to Topic 2: *Student Diversity* in the MyEducationLab for your course and select *Teacher Talk*, then *Pamela Harman*.

4

Student Diversity
Culture, Language, and Gender

CHAPTER OUTLINE

Cultural Diversity

- Cultural Attitudes and Values
- Cultural Interaction Patterns
- Educational Responses to Cultural Diversity
- Urban Schools and Cultural Diversity

Language Diversity

- Language Diversity: The Government's Response
- Language Diversity: Schools' Responses

  Taking a Stand in an Era of Reform: Bilingual Education

  Exploring Diversity: Language Diversity in the Classroom

Gender

- Gender and Society
- Gender and Classrooms

LEARNING OBJECTIVES

After you have completed your study of this chapter, you should be able to:

1. **Explain how cultural diversity influences learning and how effective teachers respond to this diversity.** INTASC Standard 3, Adapting Instruction to Learner Needs go to the *Book Specific Resources* section for the MyEducationLab for your course, select your text, and then select *This I Believe* for Chapter 4.

2. **Describe the major approaches to working with ELL students.** INTASC Standard 4, Multiple Instructional Strategies

3. **Explain how gender differences influence school success and how effective teachers respond to these differences.** INTASC Standard 3, Adapting Instruction to Learner Needs

Teachers often begin their careers expecting to find classrooms like the ones they experienced when they were students, and in many ways they are the same. Students go to school to study and learn, but they also want to have fun and be with their friends. They expect to work, but often need a push from their teachers. They're typical kids.

Classrooms are changing, however, because our students are coming from increasingly diverse backgrounds. As you read the following case study, think about this diversity and how it will influence your life as a teacher.

Carla Jackson, a first-grade teacher in an urban elementary school, watches as her students stream into her room on the first day of school. She has 14 girls and 12 boys in her class, and the names. Wow. In addition to a Smith and a Jones, there is Lee, Wong, Hassad, Trang, and Jamal, among others. Carla is in a large urban school, and she knew in advance that her students would come from a variety of backgrounds, but she wasn't quite prepared for this—11 different cultures and nearly as many different languages. She jokingly refers to her class as her "Little United Nations."

URBAN EDUCATION

When you begin teaching, your students are likely to come from backgrounds that are more varied than those of your classmates when you went through school, primarily because the diversity of today's students is rapidly increasing and also because new teachers are likely to find jobs in schools that serve diverse populations (Olson, 2003). *Culture* and *language* are two of the most important dimensions of this diversity. In addition, we have both boys and girls in our classes, and this dimension of diversity can have a powerful influence on learning.

How do effective teachers capitalize on the cultural and linguistic diversity in their classrooms? And how should you adapt your instruction to meet the needs of both boys and girls? We address these questions in this chapter. But before you begin your study, please respond to the questions in the *This I Believe* box above.

CULTURAL DIVERSITY

Think about the clothes you wear, the kind of music you like, and even the food you eat: Your clothing, music, and foods, along with other dimensions such as language and religion, are all part of your **culture**, the knowledge, attitudes, values, customs, and behavior patterns that characterize a social group (Banks, 2008). **Cultural diversity** refers to the different cultures you'll encounter in classrooms and how these cultural differences influence learning.

Culture influences many aspects of our lives, and something as simple as eating is an example. For instance, do you sit down for dinner at 6:00 in the evening, or do you often wait until 8:00 P.M. or later? Does your family sit down together, or do you "eat on the run"? Do you eat with a knife and fork or perhaps chopsticks—and if you use a knife and fork, do you cut a piece of meat and then transfer the fork back to your right hand or leave it in your left hand? These patterns are all influenced by culture, and it, of course, influences what we eat as well, as evidenced by the many ethnic restaurants around the country.

Ethnicity, which refers to a person's ancestry—the way people identify themselves with the nation they or their ancestors came from—is an important component of cul-

Culture The knowledge, attitudes, values, customs, and behavior patterns that characterize a social group.

Cultural diversity The different cultures encountered in classrooms and how these cultural differences influence learning.

Ethnicity A person's ancestry; the way individuals identify themselves with the nation they or their ancestors came from.

ture. Members of an ethnic group share an identity defined by their history, language (although sometimes not spoken), customs, and traditions. Experts estimate that nearly 300 distinct ethnic groups currently reside in the United States (Gollnick & Chinn, 2009).

Immigration and other demographic shifts have resulted in dramatic changes in our country's school population. The Immigration Act of 1965, which ended quotas based on national origin, resulted in more immigrants coming to the United States and also in changes in their point of origin. More than 1 of 10 people in our country is now foreign born, the highest percentage in more than 100 years (U.S. Bureau of Census, 2004).

Although most immigrants during the early 1900s came from Europe, more recently they have come from Central America (nearly 40%), Asia (25%), and the Caribbean (10%), with only 14 percent having Europe as their point of origin (U.S. Bureau of Census, 2004). Significantly, *Garcia* and *Rodriguez* recently replaced *Moore* and *Taylor* in the 10 most common last names in the United States (S. Roberts, 2007). This demographic shift has resulted in a dramatic increase in the proportion of students who are members of cultural minorities (U.S. Department of Education, 2005b), and it helps us understand why the backgrounds of Carla's students are so diverse. Currently, 4 of 10 public school students are children of color, with Hispanic and African American students topping the list (See Figure 4.1).

By the year 2020, the school-age population will see many more changes (see Figure 4.2). Experts predict considerable increases in the percentages of all groups of students except White, non-Hispanic. During this time, the percentage of White students will decrease from more than 60 percent to a little more than half of the total school population (U.S. Bureau of Census, 2003). By 2050, no single group will be a majority among adults.

Figure 4.1 Percentages of Public-School Students by Race/Ethnicity

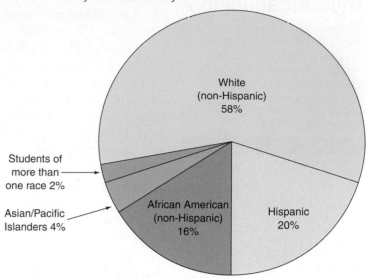

Source: National Center for Education Statistics (2007a). *The condition of education 2007.* Washington, DC: Author.

Figure 4.2 Changes in School-Age Population, 2000–2020

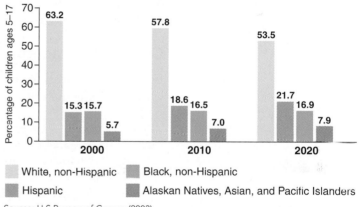

Source: U.S Bureau of Census (2003).

Cultural Attitudes and Values

Our students come to school with a history of learning influenced by the cultures of their homes and neighborhoods. Some of these attitudes and values complement school learning; others do not (D. Hughes et al., 2006). Let's see why.

Language is one example. Students are sometimes hesitant to drop the use of nonstandard English dialects in favor of "school English" because doing so might alienate their peers (Ogbu, 1999). The same problem occurs in classrooms where students are asked to learn English and to quit using the languages of their homes. Programs encouraging students to drop their native languages can distance them from their parents, many of whom can't speak English (Qin, 2006).

Even school success can be an issue. Members of minorities sometimes interpret succeeding in school as rejecting their native culture; to become a good student is to become "White"—to embrace and uphold only White cultural values. Members of minorities who study and succeed academically risk losing the friendship of their peers. John Ogbu, an anthropologist who studied the achievement of minority students, found that

PEARSON
myeducationlab

Go to the *IRIS Center Resources* section of Topic 2: Student Diversity in the MyEducationLab for your course and listen to the podcast titled *Episode 1: Donna Ford on Cultural* and *Linguistic Differences.*

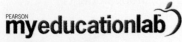

in many schools, peer values either don't support school learning or actually oppose it; students form what he called "resistance cultures" (Ogbu & Simons, 1998). Low grades, management and motivation problems, truancy, and high dropout rates are symptoms of this conflict (Carter, 2006).

In other cases, students' attitudes and values can complement learning. For instance, researchers studying the amazing academic success of Vietnamese and other Asian American students found that hard work, perseverance, and pride were heavily emphasized in the home (Kristoff, 2006). In 2005, Asian American students scored highest (an average 1091) on the math and verbal parts of the Scholastic Aptitude Test (SAT), outscoring Whites by 23 points and other cultural minorities by an average of 168 points. Willingness to take challenging courses was also a factor: 4 of 10 Asian American students took calculus in high school, compared to fewer than 3 of 10 in the general population. One Vietnamese student who became the valedictorian at her high school after only 7 years in the United States commented, "Anybody can be smart, can do great on standardized tests. But unless you work hard, you're not going to do well" (Kristoff, 2006, p. 13).

Research on Indian students' success in U.S. national spelling bees found a similar emphasis on hard work and study (Bracey, 2005b). Children of Indian descent consistently place high in these academic contests, winning much more often than other ethnic groups. Experts joke about an Indian "spelling gene," but emphasize instead the hard work and determination instilled by cultural attitudes and values.

This section addresses the first item in this chapter's *This I Believe* feature, "Although students from different cultures have varying attitudes and values, these variations have little impact on student learning." This statement is most definitely not true: Students' attitudes and values have a powerful effect on student learning.

Cultural Interaction Patterns

Because our students learn to interact with others at home, cultural conflict can occur when they enter our classrooms. Let's look at an example:

> *Cynthia Edwards, a second-grade teacher in an elementary school in the Southwest, is reading a story. "What do you think is going to happen next? . . .Tony?" Cynthia asks in response to his eagerly waving hand.*
>
> *"I think the boy is going to meet his friend."*
>
> *"How do you think the boy feels about meeting his friend?" she continues.*
>
> *After Tony responds, Cynthia calls on Sharon Nighthawk, one of the Native Americans in her class, even though Sharon has not raised her hand. When Sharon doesn't answer, Cynthia prompts her by rephrasing the question, but Sharon continues to look at her in silence.*
>
> *Slightly exasperated, Cynthia wonders if Sharon understands her questions, or if she is asking the right kind of questions, because Sharon seems to be enjoying the story and also understands it. Why won't she answer?*
>
> *Thinking about the lesson after school, Cynthia realizes that this has happened before, and that, in fact, her Native American students rarely answer questions in class. She can't get them to talk.*

How might we explain this incident? Some experts suggest that Native American children aren't used to the fast-paced, give-and-take patterns that characterize many American classrooms (Starnes, 2006). When involved in discussions, such as the one in Cynthia's class, they are uncomfortable and reluctant to participate (Banks, 2008). Similar issues can exist with students who are members of other cultures.

So, how should teachers respond? We address this question when we discuss *culturally responsive teaching* later in the chapter.

Educational Responses to Cultural Diversity

Historically, social commentators have used different metaphors to describe the relationships among the diverse cultures in the United States; a "melting pot" was one of the first. Those who saw the United States as a melting pot emphasized **assimilation**, a process of socializing people so that they adopt dominant social norms and patterns of behavior. Assimilation attempted to make members of minority cultural groups "similar" to those belonging to the dominant cultural group, typically Whites of northern European descent.

The melting pot metaphor was especially popular in the early 1900s, when large numbers of immigrants from southern and eastern Europe came to the United States. Society assigned schools the task of teaching immigrants how "Americans" were supposed to think, talk, and behave. Immigrants, eager to become "American" and share in this country's economic wealth, generally accepted assimilation efforts.

About the middle of the 20th century, a shift in thinking occurred: People realized that assimilation had never totally worked and that there was no "melting pot," as indicated by neighborhoods and groups that continued to speak their home languages, celebrate their unique cultural holidays, and maintain their cultural habits, such as eating ethnic foods. The contributions of different cultural and ethnic groups were increasingly recognized, and leaders began to realize that some educational practices aimed at assimilation were actually counterproductive. For example, in an effort to encourage English language acquisition, schools in the Southwest didn't allow students to speak Spanish, even on playgrounds. Schools became hostile places where students had to choose between family, friends, and school. The policy probably did as much to alienate Hispanic youth as it did to encourage English language development (Spring, 2006).

MULTICULTURAL EDUCATION   To remedy these problems, educators began developing new approaches to addressing cultural diversity. **Multicultural education** is a term that describes a variety of strategies schools use to accommodate cultural differences in teaching and learning. Instead of trying to create a melting pot, these approaches align with new metaphors that describe the United States as a "mosaic" or a "tossed salad," in which society recognizes and values each culture's unique contributions.

Multicultural education is controversial. Critics contend that it's divisive because it emphasizes differences between cultural groups instead of what we have in common (Zirkel, 2008b). Textbooks have also been scrutinized; for example, a spokesperson for the American Textbook Council criticized modern history textbooks as emphasizing multicultural themes at the expense of basic information about American history (Sewall, 2000). As another example, a controversy erupted over singing the national anthem in Spanish (D. Goldstein, 2006). Critics claimed that the national anthem is a symbol of unity for a diverse people united by common values and our country's Constitution. Criticism became so widespread that bills were submitted in Congress mandating that the anthem never be recited or sung in a language other than English, even though the national anthem has historically been translated and sung in a number of languages, including French, Polish, and Italian.

Proponents of multicultural education assert that building on students' cultures is nothing more than sound teaching; by recognizing, valuing, and utilizing students' cultures and languages in their instruction, teachers help them link the topics they study to what they already know, a process consistent with effective teaching (Eggen & Kauchak, 2010; Ormrod, 2008). Proponents also assert that the United States has always been a nation of immigrants and that diversity has long been recognized. For example, our society embraces holidays, such as St. Patrick's Day, Cinco De Mayo, Hanukkah, and the Chinese New Year, as well as the music and foods of many cultures. Multicultural education continues this tradition by recognizing and building on students' cultural heritages, proponents argue.

Assimilation A process of socializing people so that they adopt dominant social norms and patterns of behavior.

Multicultural education A general term that describes a variety of strategies schools use to accommodate cultural differences in teaching and learning.

Multicultural education will evolve as educators discover what works and what doesn't. *Culturally responsive teaching* is one approach to working with students from diverse backgrounds that appears to have promise.

CULTURALLY RESPONSIVE TEACHING

Shannon Wilson, a fifth-grade teacher in a large urban elementary school, walks around her classroom, helping students as they work on a social studies project. A number of hands are raised, and she feels relieved that she has Maria Arguelas, her special education resource teacher, to help her. Shannon has 27 students, 7 of whom are not native English speakers. Five are Hispanic, and fortunately, Maria can help them with language-related problems. Shannon often spends extra time with Kwan and Abdul, the other two non-English speakers.

Shannon's class is preparing for Parents' Day, an afternoon when parents and other caregivers join the class in celebrating the students' ancestral countries. The students present information about the countries' history, geography, and cultures in their projects. The class has already prepared a large world map with pins marking the students' countries of origin. Although several of the pins are clustered in Mexico and Central and South America, the map shows that students also come from many other parts of the world. Each student is encouraged to invite a family member to come and share a part of the family's native culture. The parents can bring food, music, and native dress from their different homelands.

Culturally responsive teaching builds on students' cultural backgrounds, accepts and values differences, and accommodates different cultural learning styles.

Culturally responsive teaching is instruction that acknowledges and capitalizes on cultural diversity (Gay, 2005; Leonard, 2008). It attempts to do this in three ways:

- Accepting and valuing cultural differences
- Accommodating different patterns of cultural interaction
- Building on students' cultural backgrounds

Accepting and Valuing Cultural Differences. By recognizing and accepting student diversity, teachers communicate that all students are welcome and valued. This is particularly important for members of cultural minorities, who sometimes feel alienated from school. As a simple example, Shannon had her students identify their ethnic homelands on the map; this showed an interest in each student and helped him or her feel accepted and valued.

Genuine caring is essential in making students feel welcome in classrooms. Teachers communicate caring in several ways, including these:

- Devoting time to students—for example, being available before and after school to help with schoolwork and to discuss students' personal concerns
- Demonstrating interest in students' lives—for example, asking about Jewish, Muslim, Latin American, and African American holidays and festivals
- Involving all students in learning activities—for example, calling on all students as equally as possible

Culturally responsive teaching
Instruction that acknowledges and accommodates cultural diversity.

Each of these suggestions communicates that the teacher welcomes and values all students.

Accommodating Cultural Interaction Patterns.   Teachers who are sensitive to possible differences between interaction patterns of home and school adapt their instruction to best meet their students' needs. For example, you saw earlier that the communication patterns of Native Americans may clash with typical classroom practices (Starnes, 2006). Recognizing that some of your students may not be comfortable in question-and-answer activities that require one specific answer, you can use more open-ended questions, such as "What do you notice?" and "How do these items compare?" that allow a variety of acceptable responses. This type of questioning involves students and encourages them to respond while removing the pressure to give "the" right answer. Effective teachers also use different cooperative-learning activities to complement their question-and-answer sessions and involve all students.

As another example, when a teacher realized that her routines may be clashing with her students' cultures, she made a simple adaptation.

> I traditionally end every day with the students lining up and receiving a hug before they leave. My Vietnamese kids were always the stiff huggers until October. Through my understanding of their cultures, I now give all students the choice of a hug, handshake, or high five. This simple act may make children feel more comfortable interacting with me. (McAllister & Irvine, 2002, p. 440)

Accommodating different interaction patterns can help students with diverse backgrounds adapt to the dominant culture, including that of schools, without losing their native identities, a process called "accommodation without assimilation" (Ogbu, 1999, 2003). Accommodation without assimilation helps students function comfortably in both cultures, including using different language patterns in school than in the home or other social environments (DeMeulenaere, 2001). The challenge for teachers is to help students learn about the "culture of schooling," the norms, procedures, and expectations necessary for success in school, while honoring and valuing their home cultures.

Building on Students' Backgrounds.   Effective teachers also learn about their students' cultures and use this information to promote personal pride and motivation, as we saw in Shannon's class and as we see in the following example:

> *Jack Seltzer, a high school biology teacher on the Navajo Nation Reservation,*  *uses his students' background experiences to illustrate hard-to-understand science concepts. He uses Churro sheep, a local breed that Navajos use for food and wool, to illustrate genetic principles. When they study plants, he focuses on local varieties of squash and corn that have been grown by students' ancestors for centuries. He uses geologic formations in nearby Monument Valley to illustrate igneous, sedimentary and metamorphic rocks. (D. Baker, 2006)*

Both students and their parents benefit from building on students' cultural backgrounds (Leonard, 2008): Student achievement increases, and parents become more positive about school, both of which enhance student motivation. Shannon recognized this when she invited parents and other caregivers to share their cultural heritages with her class. Jack also capitalized on this idea by providing examples the students could personally identify with.

Urban Schools and Cultural Diversity

The term *cultural minority* is often used to refer to various non-White cultural groups. Based on sheer numbers, this term may soon be obsolete and is already a misnomer in many parts of the country, especially in urban areas. For example, Hispanics, African Americans, and Asians—when combined—now make up the majority of the population in almost half of the 100 largest U.S. cities (Macionis, 2009). In addition, children of color make up the

URBAN EDUCATION

The cultural diversity in urban schools provides teachers with both opportunities and challenges.

majority of public school enrollments in six states and more than 90 percent of the students in Detroit, the District of Columbia, Chicago, Houston, and Los Angeles (Kober, 2006).

The growth of minority student populations in urban areas is the result of immigration coupled with higher birth rates. For example, between 1990 and 2000, Hispanic populations increased 43 percent and Asian populations surged 40 percent in urban areas (Lichter & Johnson, 2006). Experts estimate that almost 1 of 5 students is a child of immigrants (Kober, 2006). Urban centers are often called "gateway cities" for recently arriving immigrants (Lichter & Johnson, 2006), and these population increases are reflected in urban schools. In Adlai Stevenson High School in New York City, for example, African Americans and Hispanics make up 97 percent of the student population; only one half of 1 percent of students are White (Kozol, 2005). Many of these recent immigrants don't speak English as their first language, which poses challenges for schools and teachers. Teachers skilled in helping students simultaneously learn English and the content of their classes are sorely needed.

Knowledge of the cultural attitudes and values these students bring to school is also essential. Teaching students whose first language isn't English is the topic of the next section.

This section addresses the second item in our *This I Believe* feature, "Culturally sensitive teachers treat all students the same way." This statement isn't true and, in fact, is the opposite of culturally responsive teaching. Effective teachers adapt their instruction in response to students' cultural backgrounds.

This I BELIEVE

▪ ▪ ▪ ▪ CHECK YOUR UNDERSTANDING

1.1 Explain how cultural diversity influences learning.

1.2 Describe three ways in which effective teachers respond to cultural diversity in their classrooms.

1.3 Describe the relationship between urban schools and cultural diversity.

For feedback, go to the appendix, *Check Your Understanding*, located in the back of this text.

LANGUAGE DIVERSITY

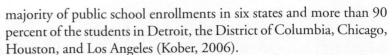

myeducationlab

To see a video of the controversies involved with bilingual education, go to the *Assignments and Activities* section of Topic 2: *Student Diversity* in the MyEducationLab for your course and complete the activity titled *Controversy Over Bilingual Education.*

ISSUES IN EDUCATION

Imagine trying to help students make sense of a topic you're teaching if they don't understand the words you're saying. And, what if you can't understand what they're trying to say to you? This is the task many teachers in today's schools face.

Language is one of the most important parts of any culture, and language influences learning more than any other single factor. For this reason, we focus on language diversity in this section. Let's see how one school responds.

Ellie Barton, a language arts teacher at Northeast Middle School, is the *school's English Language Learner (ELL) Coordinator. She teaches ELL classes and is also in charge of the school's testing and placement program.*

Her job is challenging, as her students vary considerably in their knowledge of English. For instance, one group of Somali-Bantu children just arrived from a refugee camp in Kenya. They cannot read or write, because there is no written language for their native tongue, Mai-Mai. Language isn't their only challenge; many had never been in a building with more than one floor, and others found urinals and other aspects of indoor plumbing a mystery. At the other end of the continuum is a young girl from India who can read and write in four languages: Hindi, the national language of India; Urdu, the language of her Persian ancestors; Telegu, a regional language in India; and Arabic.

To sort out this language diversity, the district uses a placement test that categorizes students into three levels: newcomer classrooms for students who have little or no expertise with English; self-contained ELL classrooms, where a primary emphasis is on learning to read and write English; and sheltered English, where students receive structured help in learning academic subjects such as science and social studies. However, the placement process is not foolproof, since English skills are sometimes nonexistent, and some parents don't know the exact ages of their children. Ellie's principal deals with this information void in creative ways; he recently asked a dentist friend to look at a student's teeth to estimate the child's age. (Adapted from Romboy & Kinkead, 2005)

As you saw earlier in the chapter, immigration has brought increasing numbers of students with limited backgrounds in English to our country's classrooms. The number of **English language learners (ELLs)**, students whose first language is not English and who need help in learning to speak, read, and write in English, increased by more than 60 percent between 1995 and 2005, totaling more than 5 million students, or 10 percent of the student population (Gollnick & Chinn, 2009). There were more than 1.5 million ELL students in California alone in 2006, and the Los Angeles Unified School District had close to 300,000 English language learners (California Department of Education, 2007; Los Angeles Board of Education, 2006). Currently, 440 languages are spoken in the United States, the most common of which are Spanish, Vietnamese, Hmong, Chinese, and Korean (McCardle & Chhabra, 2006; OELA, 2004). Public interest in educating ELLs has increased with the passage of the No Child Left Behind (NCLB) Act of 2001, which requires states to document the educational progress of these students.

Go to the *IRIS Center Resources* section of Topic 2: *Student Diversity* in the MyEducationLab for your course and watch and listen to the podcast titled *Episode 2: Diane Torres-Velasquez on Diverse Learners.*

Language Diversity: The Government's Response

The federal government, through legislation and court rulings, initially attempted to address the needs of ELL students through bilingual approaches, strategies intended to maintain the first language while students learn English. In 1968, Congress passed the Bilingual Education Act, which provided federal funds for educating nonnative English speakers. In the controversial 1974 *Lau v. Nichols* case, the Supreme Court ruled unanimously that the San Francisco School District unlawfully discriminated against minority students by failing to address non-English-speaking children's language problems (Bennett, 2007). More recently, the English Acquisition component of NCLB mandated that the primary objective of schools should be teaching English without any attempt to preserve minority languages. Accordingly, the previous Office of Bilingual Education became the Office of English Language Acquisition (OELA). In 2006, during a debate on immigration reform, the U.S. Senate voted to designate English as the national language (Hulse, 2006). Each of these government actions has changed both schools and classrooms, as we see in the next section.

Language Diversity: Schools' Responses

Schools across the country have responded to the challenge of language diversity in very different ways, outlined in Table 4.1. Although all of the programs are designed ultimately to teach English, they differ in how fast English is introduced and to what extent the first language is encouraged and maintained.

Bilingual maintenance language programs place the greatest emphasis on using and sustaining the first language while teaching English. In these programs, students initially receive most or all of their instruction in their first language, which is usually

English language learners (ELLs) Students whose first language is not English and who need help in learning to speak, read, and write in English.

Bilingual maintenance language programs Language programs that place the greatest emphasis on using and sustaining the first language.

Table 4.1 Different Programs for ELL Students

Type of Program	Description	Advantages	Disadvantages
Bilingual Maintenance	First language maintained through reading and writing activities in first language while English introduced.	Students become literate in two languages.	Requires teachers trained in first language. Acquisition of English may not be as fast.
Transition	Students learn to read in first language and are given supplementary instruction in English as a Second Language. Once English is mastered, students are placed in regular classrooms and first language discontinued.	Maintains first language. Transition to English is eased by gradual approach.	Requires teachers trained in first language. Acquisition of English may not be as fast. First language is dropped.
Immersion	Students learn English by being "immersed" in classrooms where English is the only language spoken.	When effective, quick transition to English. Does not require teachers trained in second language.	Loss of native language. Sink-or-swim approach hard on students.
English as a Second Language (ESL) Programs	Pull-out programs where students receive supplementary English instruction or modified instruction in content areas (also called Sheltered English programs).	Easier to administer when dealing with diverse language backgrounds.	Students may not be ready to benefit from content instruction in English. Pull-out programs segregate students.

Educational responses to language diversity differ in the degree to which they build on and attempt to maintain students' first language.

Immersion programs Language programs that emphasize a rapid transition to English.

English as a second language (ESL) programs Language programs that emphasize rapid transition to English through structured help with English.

Transition programs Language programs that maintain the first language until students acquire sufficient English to succeed in English-only classrooms.

Spanish, and a corresponding small percentage in English (Tong, Lara-Alecio, Irby, Mathes, & Kwok, 2008). The emphasis on English then increases in each subsequent grade. The future of maintenance programs is uncertain given the English Acquisition component of NCLB, which discourages such programs.

At the opposite end of the continuum, **immersion** and **English as a second language (ESL) programs** emphasize rapid transition to English. ESL programs, the most common educational response to linguistic diversity, vary across the country, with some focusing on content-based ESL, others on pull-out ESL instruction, and still others on sheltered or structured English instruction (Viadero, 2009b). Halfway between the two ends of the continuum, **transition programs** maintain the first language until students acquire sufficient English to succeed in English-only classrooms; the primary goal is to help students reach English proficiency.

Logistics are often a factor when schools consider which type of program to use. For example, transition programs can be effective when classes are composed of large numbers of ELL students who speak the same language, such as Spanish-speaking students in Los Angeles, because a teacher who speaks the students' native language can be hired. This isn't possible when several first languages exist. For example, in 2001, nearly 8 of 10 ELL students spoke Spanish, but the remaining 20 percent spoke a wide variety of other languages, making it impossible to find teachers who spoke all the different languages in one classroom (Girard, 2005). This happened at Northeast Middle School and is a primary reason why Ellie Barton teaches in an ELL program that places minimal emphasis on students' first language.

In the *Taking a Stand* box that starts on the next page. we examine controversies surrounding bilingual education.

A major challenge facing teachers is how to adapt their instruction to meet the needs of English language learners. We discuss different ways to do this in the *Exploring Diversity* box on page 114.

2.1 What has been the government's response to language diversity in our nation's schools?

2.2 What are the primary differences in the two major approaches schools use in working with English language learners?

2.3 What are the major ways that teachers can adapt their instruction to meet the needs of students with varying language backgrounds?

For feedback, go to the appendix, *Check Your Understanding,* located in the back of this text.

PEARSON
myeducationlab

To see an example of one teacher's attempts to make her instruction effective for culturally and linguistically diverse students, go to the *Assignments and Activities* section of Topic 2: *Student Diversity,* in the MyEducationLab for your course and complete the activity titled *Effective Teaching for English Language Learners.*

Taking a Stand in an Era of Reform

Bilingual Education

Bilingual education has been the focus of several reform efforts. Through the Bilingual Education Act of 1968 and guidelines drafted as a result of *Lau v. Nichols* in 1974, the federal government signaled its commitment to providing services for nonnative English speakers.

A counterreform occurred in California in 1998, when voters passed Proposition 227, a ballot initiative that sharply reduced bilingual education programs, replacing them with English-only immersion programs for ELL students. Similar measures were passed in Arizona and 25 other states (R. Garcia, 2006). These initiatives have sharply curtailed the use of bilingual education in the United States. For example, before the initiatives occurred in Arizona and California, about one third of ELL students were taking bilingual education classes; after the initiatives, the numbers plummeted to 11 percent in both states (Zehr, 2002). In addition, 29 states have passed laws making English the official language (U.S. English, 2008). (See Figure 4.3.) Although these laws are mostly symbolic, they influence state government publications, and they illustrate

Figure 4.3 States With Official Language Legislation

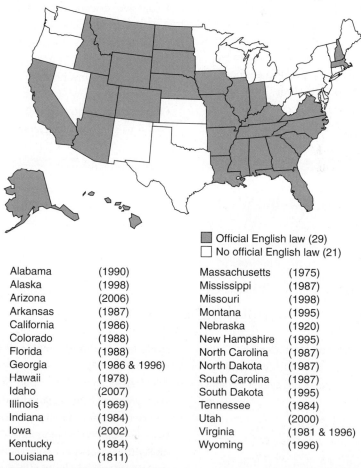

Official English law (29)
No official English law (21)

Alabama	(1990)	Massachusetts	(1975)
Alaska	(1998)	Mississippi	(1987)
Arizona	(2006)	Missouri	(1998)
Arkansas	(1987)	Montana	(1995)
California	(1986)	Nebraska	(1920)
Colorado	(1988)	New Hampshire	(1995)
Florida	(1988)	North Carolina	(1987)
Georgia	(1986 & 1996)	North Dakota	(1987)
Hawaii	(1978)	South Carolina	(1987)
Idaho	(2007)	South Dakota	(1995)
Illinois	(1969)	Tennessee	(1984)
Indiana	(1984)	Utah	(2000)
Iowa	(2002)	Virginia	(1981 & 1996)
Kentucky	(1984)	Wyoming	(1996)
Louisiana	(1811)		

Source: U.S English, Inc. (2008). Washington, DC.

growing public sentiment in favor of English as well as fears about losing English as a common cultural bond.

In addition, Congress failed in 2002 to renew the Bilingual Education Act, instead packaging funds for English language learners into NCLB, which requires students to attain "English fluency" in 3 years and requires schools to teach students in English after that time period (Viadero, 2009b).

THE ISSUE

The essence of bilingual programs is an attempt to maintain and build on students' native languages while they learn English. Proponents make several arguments in support of bilingual education (Crawford, 2007; Tong et al., 2008). First, they contend the programs make sense with respect to learning because they provide a smooth and humane transition to English by building on students' first languages. They also argue that being able to speak two languages has practical benefits: A bilingual person can live and communicate in two worlds, which can increase economic and career opportunities. They also cite research. One review concluded that evidence favors bilingual approaches over English immersion approaches in helping students learn to read (Slavin & Cheung, 2005). Further research indicates that knowledge and skills acquired in a native language are "transferable" to the second language, providing students with a better understanding of the role of language in communication and how language works (Guglielmi, 2008).

Proponents of bilingual education also contend that immersion programs place unrealistic language demands on learners. They note that conversational English, such as that spoken in the lunchroom and on the playground, is learned quite quickly, but the cognitively demanding language needed for academic success is learned much more slowly (Peregoy & Boyle, 2008).

Critics of bilingual education attack it on several grounds. They contend that it is

- divisive, encouraging groups of non-native English speakers to remain separate from mainstream American culture;
- ineffective, slowing the process of acquiring English for ELL students; and
- inefficient, requiring expenditures for the training of bilingual teachers and

materials that could be better spent on quality monolingual programs (U.S. English, 2008).

Critics also cite their own research. For instance, one California school district reported that standardized test scores for students in the early grades—those most affected by the move from bilingual to immersion programs—improved from the 35th to the 45th percentile after students spent just 1 year in an immersion program, and additional research found similar positive results across California (Barone, 2000).

YOU TAKE A STAND

Now it's your turn to take a position on the issue. Should schools make efforts to retain students' native languages, or should they move students into English as quickly as possible?

myeducationlab To explore both sides of this issue and take a stand, go to the *Books Specific Resources* section in the MyEducationLab for your course, select your text, and then select *Taking a Stand in an Era of Reform* for Chapter 4.

ISSUES IN EDUCATION

Language Diversity in the Classroom

As you work with ELL students, it's easy to fall into the trap of tacitly assuming that all ELL students are similar in their understanding of their native languages. This isn't true (Zehr, 2009). As with

URBAN EDUCATION

students in general, some come from homes where books, newspapers, and the Internet are a regular part of their lives, whereas others come from families whose members can barely read and write in their native language. Also, the ability to converse in English doesn't mean students can learn effectively in English (Tong et al., 2008; Zweirs, 2007). ELL students usually pick up enough English

to communicate with peers and teachers after 3 or 4 years, but it can take up to 8 years to learn enough English to function effectively in academic content areas.

How will language diversity affect you as a teacher? First, although bilingual programs have been reduced, the need for teachers with ELL expertise will only increase. Experts estimate that in the next 5 years, U.S. schools will need an additional 56,000 teachers with ESL certification to meet the demands of these students, and 11 states have incentive policies to encourage teachers to pursue education in this area (Honawar, 2009). In addition, more than 7 of 10 urban school districts identify bilingual teachers as a critical hiring need (Recruiting New Teachers, 2006). Teacher candidates who speak two languages, and especially Spanish, are in high demand across the country.

Second, the likelihood is high that you'll have students in your classroom whose first language is not English. Your ability to make informed professional decisions will be essential to help them learn. In working with students from diverse cultural and language backgrounds, your professional knowledge will be tested, perhaps more than in any other area of your work.

Diversity in Your Classroom

Research offers a number of suggestions for working with students from varying language backgrounds:

- Create a warm and supportive classroom environment by taking a personal interest in all students and involving everyone in learning activities. Get to know students, and strive to personalize the content you're teaching.

- Mix whole-class instruction with group work and cooperative learning to allow students to interact informally and practice their developing language skills with the topics they study.
- Use question-and-answer sessions to involve all students in classroom activities and concrete examples to provide reference points for new ideas and vocabulary (Echevarria & Graves, 2007; Peregoy & Boyle, 2008).
- Continually check for understanding through questions, assignments, and quizzes. Misunderstandings are a normal part of teaching, and are even more common with students who are members of cultural minorities. Use these checks to adjust instruction.
- Avoid situations that draw attention to students' lack of English skills, such as making students read aloud in front of the whole class.

These strategies represent good instructional practice for all students; for ELL students, they're essential.

This section addresses the third question in our *This I Believe* feature, "Students who aren't native English speakers learn English most effectively by hearing the teacher use correct English." This statement isn't true: The only truly effective way for students to learn English is to practice it in language-related activities.

QUESTIONS TO CONSIDER

1. The preceding suggestions encouraged you to personalize content, use question-and-answer sessions to involve all students in classroom activities, and provide concrete examples as reference points for new ideas and vocabulary. Suppose you're teaching a concept such as *bilateral symmetry*; how would you apply these suggestions to this concept?

2. Should teachers encourage the use of English by banning students from using their first language in the classroom? What should a teacher do if an ELL student responds to a question with words or phrases from his or her native language?

myeducationlab To respond to these questions online, explore this topic further, and receive feedback, go to the *Book Specific Resources* section in the MyEducationLab for your course, select your text, and then select *Exploring Diversity* for Chapter 4.

GENDER

What Geri Peterson saw on her first day of teaching advanced-placement calculus was both surprising and disturbing: Of the 26 students watching her, only 4 were girls, and they sat quietly in class, responding only when she asked them direct questions. One reason that Geri had gone into teaching was to share her interest in math with other females, but this situation gave her little chance to do so.

Lori Anderson, the school counselor at an urban middle school, looked up from the desk where she was working on her annual report to the faculty. From her course work at the university and her internship, she knew that boys traditionally outnumber girls with respect to behavioral problems, but the numbers she was seeing were disturbing. In every category—referrals by teachers, absenteeism, tardies, and fights—boys outnumbered girls by more than 2 to 1. In addition, the number of boys referred to her for special education testing far exceeded referrals for girls.

URBAN EDUCATION

Gender and Society

The fact that males and females are different is so obvious that we often don't think about it, but research has uncovered some important differences. For example, females generally are more extroverted, anxious, and trusting; they're less assertive and have slightly lower self-esteem than males of the same age and background; and their verbal and motor skills tend to develop faster than boys' (Berk, 2008, 2010). In addition, the play habits of boys and girls differ, with boys typically preferring more "rough and tumble" play. Gender differences also make a significant contribution to diversity in the classroom.

Why do these differences exist? As with most other individual differences, research suggests the influence of both genetics and environment (Berk, 2008, 2010). Genetics results in physical differences such as size and growth rate and may also influence temperament, aggressiveness, and early verbal and exploratory behaviors. And some researchers now believe that boys' and girls' brains are wired differently for learning. For example, components of the brain that focus on words and fine-motor skills are developmentally a year ahead in girls, which gives them an advantage in reading, small-motor tasks, such as using pencils and scissors, and printing and cursive writing. Emotional centers in the brain are also more advanced for girls, making them calmer and more able to sit still for the long periods that classrooms often require. These researchers argue that schools, as they currently exist, may be more compatible with girls' genetic makeup (Gurian & Stevens, 2007).

The environment also influences gender differences. From the day they're born, boys and girls are treated differently (Berk, 2008, 2010). Girls are given pink blankets, are called *cute* and *pretty*, and are handled delicately. Boys are dressed in blue, are regarded as handsome, and are seen as tougher, better coordinated, and hardier. Fathers are rougher with their sons and involve them in more physical stimulation and play; they tend to be gentler with their daughters and offer more sex-stereotyped toys, such as dolls and stuffed animals. Not surprisingly, boys and girls grow up looking and acting differently.

This section addresses the fourth item on our *This I Believe* feature, "Most differences between boys and girls are due to heredity." This statement isn't true. Although both heredity and environment play a role in shaping boys' and girls' behavior, it's difficult to say which is more powerful. Genetics predisposes each sex to certain types of behaviors, but the environment is important in determining how these predispositions are shaped.

This I BELIEVE

Gender and Classrooms

Differences between boys and girls should generally be celebrated, but **gender bias** becomes a problem when forces in schools and the larger society limit the growth and academic potential of either boys or girls, as appeared to be the case in Geri Peterson's AP calculus class. For example, in high school, girls score lower than boys on the math sections of the SAT and the ACT, two tests that are essential for college admission, and women score lower on all sections of the Graduate Record Exam, the Medical College Admissions Test, and admissions tests for law, dental, and optometry schools (Alperstein, 2005). These tests are important because they serve as gatekeepers to high-paying professions.

As you saw in Lori Anderson's school, boys have their own problems. They're retained or held back in grade more often, they're more than twice as likely to be placed in special education classes, and they far outnumber girls in remedial English and math classes. Boys receive both lower grades and the majority of failing grades, and they drop out of school 4 times more often than girls. They are also cited for disciplinary infractions as much as 10 times more often than girls (Gurian & Stevens, 2005; Hunsader, 2002).

So, we have an uneven picture of male and female strengths and weaknesses, but historically, concerns about girls received the most attention. For instance, in 1992's *How Schools Shortchange Girls*, the American Association of University Women (AAUW)

Gender bias Discrimination based on gender that limits the growth possibilities of either boys or girls.

argued that differential treatment of boys and girls by both teachers and society seriously hampered the educational progress, self-esteem, and career choices of girls. In the 1998 *Gender Gaps: Where Schools Still Fail Our Children*, the AAUW reiterated many of its earlier claims.

These assertions have been controversial. For example, Christina Sommers (2000), author of *The War Against Boys: How Misguided Feminism Is Harming Our Young Men*, outlined many of the problems boys encounter in school that we describe here. Yet it's the myth of the fragile girl that continues to receive the lion's share of attention, Sommers argued. As time has passed, however, the problems of boys have received more attention. For example, the January 30, 2006, issue of *Newsweek* focused on "The Trouble With Boys" as their lead story.

These educational problems extend into college. A *New York Times* article on the subject proclaimed, "At college women are leaving men in the dust" (Lewin, 2006, p. A1). Women are more likely to attend college, earn a degree (57 to 43%), get higher grades, and earn a master's degree (59 to 41%): and 2006 was the 5th year in a row in which the majority of research PhDs awarded to U.S. citizens went to women (Sommers, 2008).

As with gender differences in general, a combination of genetics and the environment probably explains the relative strengths and weaknesses of boys and girls in school. Because little can be done about genetics, more attention has been given to the environment, particularly the part gender-role identity differences play in shaping student behaviors.

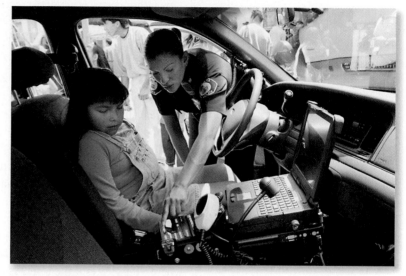

Role models are effective in preventing students from forming gender-stereotypic views about appropriate careers.

Gender-role identity describes societal differences in expectations and beliefs about appropriate roles and behaviors of the two sexes. Society treats boys and girls differently and expects them to develop different gender-role identities. These identity differences aren't a problem unless they perpetuate stereotypes or negatively influence behavior, learning, or expectations for school success. A **stereotype** is a rigid, simplistic caricature of a particular group of people. For example, "Women aren't good at math" and "Men don't make good nurses or teachers" are both inaccurate and damaging stereotypes because they limit career choices.

This section addresses the fifth item on our *This I Believe* feature, "Boys generally get better grades in school than girls." This statement is not true, and, in fact, quite the opposite is the case: Girls generally do better than boys on a number of academic measures, with grades being one of the most obvious.

GENDER AND CAREER CHOICES   Look around your classroom for this course; if it's a typical education course, the vast majority of the students are women. The same would be true for classes in nursing, but you would find the opposite in math, science, engineering, and computer-related fields (Cavanagh, 2008a).

Where do stereotypes of "appropriate" careers for boys and girls come from? Society perpetuates some stereotypes, but ironically, parents—and particularly mothers—are among the most powerful sources. For instance, one study found that mothers who held negative gender-stereotyped attitudes about girls' ability in math adversely influenced their daughters' achievement in, and their attitudes toward, math. When mothers believed that math was a male domain, their daughters took fewer math classes, got lower grades in them, and were less likely to pursue math-related fields such as computer science and statistics.

This I BELIEVE

Gender-role identity Differences in expectations and beliefs about appropriate roles and behaviors of the two sexes.

Stereotype A rigid, simplistic caricature of a particular group of people.

Parents can also have powerful positive influences on their children. Here is what one female software developer reported:

> My mother always engendered in me the attitude that I could do absolutely anything I ever want to do. So she really gave me the confidence that is a big part of success in academics and maybe in other things—sometimes you get to a point where you don't have that much either skill or knowledge, and you have to just go on your guts or your confidence. You have to just kind of push your way through something until you have the time to accumulate the knowledge. And I think that that's something she engendered in me just by always being herself so confident of my abilities, rightly or wrongly. And my father certainly never detracted from that. He always portrayed her as being the smarter of the two. So I was raised in an environment where women were not only capable but were even potentially very well and highly regarded. (Zeldin & Pajares, 2000, p. 229)

Gender-stereotypic views can also negatively influence career decisions (Francis & Skelton, 2005; Wessel, 2005). Girls are less than half as likely as boys to pursue careers in engineering and physical and computer sciences. At the high school level, only 11 percent of students taking the College Board advanced placement test in computer science in 2001 were women (Stabiner, 2003). The percentages of female physicians (26 percent), lawyers (27 percent), and engineers (8 percent), as well as new doctorates in science-related fields (38 percent), remain low as well (Wessel, 2005). The problem of gender-stereotypic views of math, science, and computer science careers is especially acute for minority females (Dance, 2002; A. Ginsberg, Shapiro, & Brown, 2004).

Similar problems exist for men. Go to any elementary school, and you'll see that the faculty is overwhelmingly female. This is especially true at the kindergarten and preschool levels, where 98 percent of the teachers are women (U.S. Bureau of Census, 2006a). And although more men are choosing nursing as a career, they remain a distinct minority (less than 10%).

Single-sex classrooms attempt to build on students' strengths and remove the distractions from the other sex.

Single-sex classes and schools
Classes and schools where boys and girls are segregated for part or all of the day.

SINGLE-SEX CLASSROOMS AND SCHOOLS

How would you respond to a class of fifth graders who weren't working hard enough? Here is how one urban teacher responded, "You—let me see you trying! Come on, faster!" Another, right across the hall, said this, "This is so sloppy, honey. Remember what I spoke to you about? About being the bright shining star that you are?" (Medina, 2009b, p. A24). Can you guess which teacher was talking to an all-girls class and which was addressing a room full of boys?

One response to gender-related problems has been the creation of **single-sex classes and schools**, where boys and girls are segregated for part or all of the day (Anfara & Mertens, 2008). One argument for single-sex classrooms is that they minimize distractions from the other sex. One director of a single-sex school notes, "The boys don't feel like they need to put on a big show for the girls, and the girls feel like they can strive academically without having to dumb down their ability" (Standen, 2007, p. 47). The number of single-sex classrooms in the United States has increased dramatically, from less than a dozen in 2000 to 455 in 2009 (Medina, 2009b; Thiers, 2006). In 2009, there were also 95 completely single-sex schools in the United States. (Standen, 2007). Interestingly, England, with a long history of private, single-sex schools, is moving away from them and toward coeducational classrooms (Younger & Warrington, 2006).

Some research indicates that both girls and boys benefit from single-sex schools. Girls in these schools are more apt to assume leadership roles, take more math and science courses, have higher self-esteem, and have firmer beliefs that they're in control of their destinies (Datnow, Hubbard, & Conchas, 2001; Shapka & Keating, 2003). Advocates of all-male schools claim that they promote male character development and are especially effective with males from low-income and minority families.

Research raises other issues, however. For example, because boys and girls are isolated from one another, single-sex schools and classes can exacerbate stereotypic views of the opposite sex and fail to prepare students for the "real world" in which males and females must work together (Standen, 2007). One critic observed, "a boy who has never been beaten by a girl on an algebra test could have some major problems having a female supervisor" (Medina, 2009b, p. A24). Some critics also question the legality of single-sex schools and classrooms based on Title IX, the federal law that prohibits discrimination on the basis of sex (Fischer, Schimmel, & Stellman, 2006; Thiers, 2006). But a recent legal directive by the Bush administration cleared these legal objections—if enrollments are voluntary (Schemo, 2006). More research is needed to determine whether these experiments are effective for helping students learn and develop. At this point, the research is inconclusive (Anfara & Mertens, 2008).

GENDER AND CLASSROOMS: IMPLICATIONS FOR TEACHERS   What can you do to promote gender equality in your classroom? The following suggestions offer some help:

- Communicate openly with students about gender issues and concerns. Simply telling your students that teachers often treat boys and girls differently and that you're going to work to treat them equally is a positive first step.

- Encourage equal participation in all classes. One demanding but extremely effective technique is to call on everyone in your classes individually and by name, regardless of whether their hands are raised (Kauchak & Eggen, 2007).

- Make an effort to present cases of men and women in nonstereotypical roles, such as women who are engineers and men who are first-grade teachers.

- Encourage girls to pursue science-related careers and boys to consider careers in nontraditional male fields, such as nursing and teaching (Francis & Skelton, 2005; A. Ginsberg et al., 2004).

Effective teachers are sensitive to gender differences in the classroom and make a conscious effort to involve all students.

The powerful influence that teachers can have on students is captured in the following remembrance from a 42-year-old female math professor:

It was the first time I had algebra, and I loved it. And then, all of a sudden, I excelled in it. And the teacher said, "Oh no, you should be in the honors course," or something like that. So, there's somebody who definitely influenced me because I don't think I ever even noticed. I mean, I didn't care one way or the other about mathematics. It was just something you had to do. I remember she used to run up and down the aisle. She was real excited. . . . She said, "Oh, you gotta go in this other class. You gotta." And she kind of pushed a little bit, and I was willing to be pushed. (Zeldin & Pajares, 2000, p. 232)

myeducationlab

To see how one teacher explores a gender-laden topic in a gender-neutral way, go to the *Assignments and Activities* section of Topic 2: *Student Diversity*, in the MyEducationLab for your course and complete the activity titled *Gender-Bias-Free Instruction*.

The student ended up majoring in math and ultimately became a math professor. When teachers believe in their students, students start believing in themselves. No one is suggesting that boys and girls are, or should be, the same. Nevertheless, teachers should strive to provide the same academic opportunities and encouragement for all students.

Cultural Diversity

You've been invited to a community awards ceremony at a local church of Pacific Island immigrants to honor students from your school. (This invitation and the events that followed actually happened to one educator.) You gladly accept, arrive a few minutes early, and are ushered to a seat of honor on the stage. After an uncomfortable (to you) wait of over an hour, the ceremony begins, and the students proudly file to the stage to receive their awards. Each is acknowledged, given an award, and applauded. After this part of the ceremony, you have an eye-opening experience.

The children all go back and sit down in the audience again, and the meeting continues with several more items on the agenda. The kids are fine for a while, but get bored and start to fidget. Fidgeting and whispering turn into poking, prodding, and open chatting. You become a little anxious at the disruption, but none of the other adults appear to even notice, so you ignore it, too. Soon, several of the children are up and out of their seats, strolling about the back and sides of the auditorium. All adult faces continue looking serenely up at the speaker on the stage. Then the kids start playing tag, running circles around the seating area, and yelling gleefully. No adult response—you are amazed, and struggle to resist the urge to quiet the children. Then some of the kids get up onto the stage, run around the speaker, flick the lights on and off, and open and close the curtain! Still nothing from the Islander parents who seem either unaware or unconcerned about the children's behavior! You are caught in the middle of a conflict of cultures—yours and the Pacific Islanders'. You don't know what to do. (Adapted from Winitzky, 1994.)

What insights does research provide in this situation?

■ ■ ■ ■ ■ CHECK YOUR UNDERSTANDING

3.1. Explain how society influences gender differences in our students.

3.2. How should teachers respond to gender differences?

For feedback, go to the appendix, *Check Your Understanding*, located in the back of this text.

Now it's your turn to apply the information in this chapter to a problem or dilemma facing many prospective teachers. Read the case above and answer the question that follows.

4 MEETING YOUR LEARNING OBJECTIVES

1. Explain how cultural diversity influences learning and how effective teachers respond to this diversity.

   • As students from diverse cultural backgrounds enter our classrooms, they bring with them unique attitudes and values. Sometimes these cultural attitudes and values complement school learning; at other times, they don't.

   • Diversity also results in differences in the cultural interaction patterns students bring to our classrooms. Often the interaction patterns of the classroom conflict with those of the home. Teachers who recognize this problem can adapt their instruction to meet the needs of students and also teach them how to adapt to the interaction patterns of the classroom.

- Educational responses to cultural diversity have changed over time. Initially, the emphasis was on assimilation, or socializing students to adopt the dominant social norms and patterns of behavior. Multicultural education, and especially culturally responsive teaching, recognizes, accommodates, and builds on student cultural differences.

- Urban areas are often called "gateway cities," because many of the immigrants to the United States first settle there. Consequently, the number of cultural minorities attending urban schools is large. In addition, many of these recent immigrants don't speak English as their first language.

2. Describe the major approaches to working with ELL students.

- Language diversity is increasing in U.S. classrooms. During the 1960s and 1970s, the federal response to this diversity was to encourage bilingual programs. Currently, the federal emphasis is on the rapid acquisition of English with little or no emphasis on preserving students' home languages.

- Educational responses to language diversity range from recognizing and building on the home language to teaching English as quickly as possible. Currently, despite research that suggests advantages for maintaining the first language, political sentiment favors teaching English as quickly as possible.

- Teachers who have ELL students in the classroom can do several important things to help them learn. In addition to creating a warm and inviting classroom, they can provide multiple opportunities for students to practice their developing language skills with their peers. Teachers also should use a variety of concrete examples and graphics to illustrate abstract ideas and concepts.

3. Explain how gender differences influence school success and how effective teachers respond to these differences.

- Males and females are different, and these differences reflect genetic influences as well as differences in the way society treats boys and girls. Parents also exert powerful influences on gender differences.

- Evidence suggests that both boys and girls encounter problems in today's schools. For girls, these problems focus more on achievement and career choices, especially in math, science, and computer science, whereas for boys, the problems are more behavioral and connected to learning problems. Suspected causes of these problems range from societal and parental expectations to differential treatment in classrooms. Teachers play a major role in ensuring that gender differences don't become gender inequalities.

IMPORTANT CONCEPTS

assimilation (p. 107)
bilingual maintenance language programs (p. 111)
cultural diversity (p. 104)
culturally responsive teaching (p. 108)
culture (p. 104)
English as a second language (ESL) programs (p. 112)
English language learners (ELLs) (p. 111)

ethnicity (p. 104)
gender bias (p. 116)
gender-role identity (p. 117)
immersion programs (p. 112)
multicultural education (p. 107)
single-sex classes and schools (p. 118)
stereotype (p. 117)
transition programs (p. 112)

DISCUSSION QUESTIONS

1. Is multicultural education more important at some grade levels than at others? Why or why not? Is multicultural education more important in some content areas than in others? Why or why not?

2. Which approach to teaching English to ELL students makes the most sense in the teaching setting where you hope to find your first job? Why?

3. What kinds of instructional strategies are effective for helping ELL students learn English? Which are ineffective?

4. What are the advantages and disadvantages of bilingual education? Should it play a larger role in ELL instruction?

5. Are "English-only" laws a good idea? What advantages and disadvantages exist for this type of legislation?

6. Should teachers have boys and girls line up by sex or compete in games by sex? Why or why not?

7. Are single-sex classrooms a good idea? Why or why not?

PEARSON
myeducationlab

Now go to Topic 2: *Student Diversity* in the My EducationLab (www.myeducationlab.com) for your course, where you can:

- Find learning outcomes for *Student Diversity* along with the national standards that connect to these outcomes.

- Complete *Assignments and Activities* that can help you more deeply understand the chapter content.

- Apply and practice your understanding of the core teaching skills identified in the chpater with the *Building Teaching Skills and Dispositions* learning units.

- Check your comprehension on the content covered in the chapter by going to the *Study Plan* in the *Book Specific Resources* section for your text. Here you will be able to take a chapter quiz, receive feedback on your answers, and then access *Review, Practice, and Enrichment* activities to enhance your understanding of chapter content.

Develop Your Professional Portfolio

To further apply your understanding of chapter content and address the INTASC standards, go to the *Book Specific Resources* section in the MyEducationLab for your course, select your text, then select this chapter's *Portfolio Activities*.

"I teach because I love working with people—adults, children, and especially those in the middle. Life is hard for middle schoolers living in that in-between space, and I believe my job, as a teacher, is to guide them through that transition from child to young adult. Middle school students need to feel special and deserve to be surrounded by adults who care about them and understand their needs."

BETH OSWALD, 2008 Teacher of the Year, Wisconsin

To view a video clip of Beth, the 2008 Wisconsin Teacher of the Year, go to Topic 2: *Student Diversity* in the MyEducationLab for your course and select *Teacher Talk*, then *Beth Oswald*.

5

Student Diversity
Development, Ability, and Exceptionalities

CHAPTER OUTLINE

Developmental Differences in the Classroom

- Dimensions of Development
- Technology and Teaching: Cheating and Plagiarism
- Learner Development: Implications for Teachers

  Taking a Stand in an Era of Reform: Grade Retention

Differences in Ability

- What Is Intelligence?
- Ability Grouping and Tracking: Schools' Responses to Differences in Ability
- Learning Styles

Learners With Exceptionalities

- Federal Laws Change the Way Schools and Teachers Help Students With Exceptionalities
- Dimensions of Exceptionalities
- Students With Exceptionalities: Implications for Teachers

  Exploring Diversity: Employing Technology to Support Learners with Disabilities

- Diversity: The Big Picture

LEARNING OBJECTIVES

After you have completed your study of this chapter, you should be able to:

1. **Explain how developmental differences influence students as well as teachers.** INTASC Standard 2, Knowledge of Human Development and Learning

2. **Explain differences in current definitions of intelligence, and describe how schools respond to ability differences.** INTASC Standard 3, Adapting Instruction to Learner Needs

3. **Explain how schools have changed the ways they help students with exceptionalities.** INTASC Standard 3, Adapting Instruction to Learner Needs

What will you encounter when you teach your first class? How will your experience compare to this teacher's?

Melanie Parker, an intern from a nearby university, is ready to teach her first lesson in Mrs. Jenkins's math class. The topic is the decimal system, including a review of place value, such as identifying 3,154 as composed of 3 "thousands," 1 "hundred," 5 "tens," and 4 "ones." Though she's nervous at the beginning, everything goes smoothly as she illustrates and explains the concept. As Melanie passes out practice worksheets, Mrs. Jenkins walks over to her and whispers, "You're doing great. I need to run down to the office. I'll be right back." The students quickly begin to work, and Melanie's nervousness calms as she circulates among the students, periodically making brief comments and offering suggestions . She notices that some are galloping through the assignment, others need only a hint, and a few seem totally confused. As she works with students, she notices that the quiet of the classroom is turning into a low buzz.

"Joel, why aren't you working?" Melanie asks as she turns to a student near her.

"I'm done."

"Hmm?" she thinks as she looks around the room.

"Beth, finish your assignment and stop talking," Melanie says, turning to another student visiting with her neighbor.

"I can't do this stuff!"

Melanie looks at the clock and sees that there are still 10 minutes to the bell, and, from the fidgeting and talking, it appears that several of the students have completed their assignment, while others have barely begun. Now what? (Adapted from Kauchak & Eggen, 2007)

As experienced teachers know, and as Melanie discovered, some students simply learn faster than others, and this fact of classroom life makes instruction much more challenging. The reasons for these differences in students are complex and multifaceted. Development results in profound differences between younger and older students, as well as significant variation within a given classroom. In addition, students vary considerably in ability, which influences both teachers' and students' lives in classrooms. Some of these differences are so great they require extra help in the form of special education services.

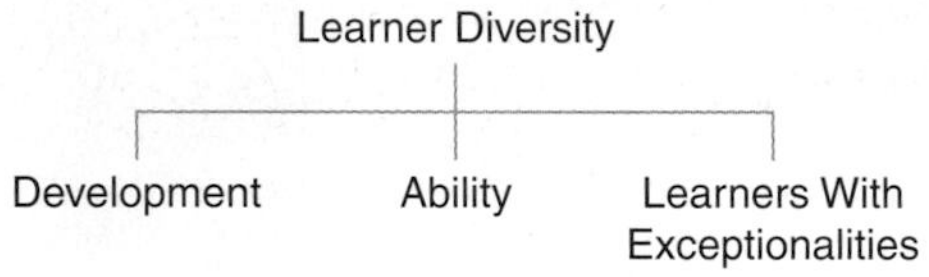

Whatever the causes, these dimensions of diversity are found in all classrooms, and today's teachers are asked to deal with them (see Figure 5.1). What does research tell us about these students? And how do expert teachers deal with this diversity to promote learning for all students? These questions are the focus of this chapter.

Before you begin your study, please respond to the items in the *This I Believe* box on the next page.

Figure 5.1 Diversity: Development, Ability, and Exceptionalities

Learner Diversity

Development   Ability   Learners With Exceptionalities

DEVELOPMENTAL DIFFERENCES IN THE CLASSROOM

A volunteer tutor is working on sight word vocabulary with two first graders, and the word "under" comes up. The tutor asks what under means. After he shows several examples of classroom items that are "under" other objects, Tran, the boy, pulls up his shirt to show his Disney-character underwear, proudly proclaiming, "Underwear!" The girl giggles. The tutor, nervous about the prospect of others seeing this display of underwear, says, "Tran, pull down your shirt. What would the principal do if he saw you showing your underwear?" After a moment's pause, Tran replies, "Give me a wedgie?"

Anyone who has spent time in classrooms knows that young children look, act, and think differently than older students, and they respond differently to teachers as well. These differences reflect their **development**, the physical, intellectual, moral, emotional, and social changes that occur in students as a result of maturation and experience. These differences offer both challenges and opportunities for teachers.

Why should you be interested in student development at this point in your program? Three reasons exist. First, understanding student development will help you decide whether you want to be a teacher. Not everyone will be happy working with young kids—or big ones, for that matter—and an understanding of development will help you decide whether teaching is right for you. Second, if you believe teaching is right for you, understanding student development can help you decide at what level you want to teach. We know first-grade teachers who love their jobs but who would hate to teach at the high school level, and we know high school teachers who feel exactly the opposite. An understanding of development will help you find the grade level that is the best fit for you. Finally, understanding your students will help you adapt your instruction to their developmental differences, which will make you a more effective teacher.

Development The physical, intellectual, moral, emotional, and social changes that occur in students as a result of their maturation and experience.

Dimensions of Development

Development refers to the systematic changes that occur as people progress through life. In the following sections, we consider four dimensions of development that influence both teachers and their students: cognitive, moral, personal, and social development (See Figure 5.2).

Figure 5.2 Dimensions of Development

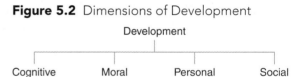

COGNITIVE DEVELOPMENT **Cognitive development** refers to changes in students' thinking as they mature and acquire experiences. As you saw with Tran, little people think differently about the world than do older students, and these differences can have a profound influence on your teaching. To illustrate these differences consider the following lesson involving a first-grade class.

Jenny Newhall, a first-grade teacher, wants her students to understand the properties of air, and she designs a lesson focusing on the idea that air takes up space. To illustrate this idea, she pushes a paper towel into the bottom of a tall drinking glass, inverts the glass, and pushes it into a fishbowl of water as shown here.

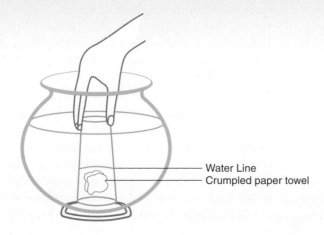

Water Line
Crumpled paper towel

Cognitive development Changes in students' thinking as they mature and acquire experiences.

127

Concrete experiences provide opportunities for students to learn abstract concepts.

She pulls the glass out of the water and says, "Marisse, come up here and check the paper towel and tell us whether it's wet or dry."

Marisse feels the towel, thinks for a moment, and says, "Dry."

"Why did it stay dry? . . . Raise your hand if you can tell us why it stayed dry. What do you think, Jessica?" Jenny asks.

" 'Cause it's inside and the water is outside?"

"Because it's way, way down in the glass," Andrea adds.

"But why didn't the water go into the glass? What kept the water out? . . . Anthony?"

"A water seal."

"A water seal," Jenny repeats, forcing herself not to smile. Hmm. . . . There's all that water on the outside. How come it didn't go inside? . . . How can the towel stay dry?"

Samantha volunteers, "Because there's air in there."

"Can you explain that for us?" Jenny asks.

"Well, when I was in a swimming pool with my dad and we put a glass under the water, it stayed dry, but when we tipped it, air bubbles came out, and water went in. The air was keeping the water out."

Even though all the students in this episode were first graders, their thinking reflects differences in development. Let's look again at the explanations the students offered for why the towel stayed dry.

Jessica:	It's inside and the water is outside?	
Andrea:	Because it's way, way down in the glass.	
Anthony:	A water seal.	
Samantha:	Because there's air in there.	

The thinking of young children tends to be dominated by their perception—what they can see—and they tend to focus on the most perceptually obvious aspect of an object or event. This tendency was illustrated in Jessica's, Andrea's, and Anthony's thinking: The glass, paper, and water were more perceptually obvious than the air in the glass, so they didn't consider air in their explanation. Samantha, on the other hand, had the experience of playing in the swimming pool with her dad, and because of this experience, her thinking was more fully developed than the thinking of her classmates.

This example addresses the first question in the *This I Believe* feature, "Because students are grouped by age, students in a class will be similar with respect to their development." This statement is far from true. In fact, striking developmental differences often exist in students of the same age.

As children mature and acquire experiences, they gradually overcome tendencies to focus on the here and now, and begin to think logically and systematically. For example, because most middle school students have had experiences with air, they're likely to quickly conclude that the towel stayed dry because air was trapped in the glass.

Jean Piaget (1896–1980), the famous Swiss psychologist, explored children's thinking by listening as they tried to solve different types of problems, and he systematically described the patterns in their reasoning. He found that older children don't simply know more than their younger counterparts; they think in fundamentally different ways.

This I BELIEVE

Piaget's Cognitive Developmental Theory describes how students' thinking changes over time and how experiences contribute to development.

In addition to documenting that younger students think differently from older ones, researchers found that development occurs in an orderly fashion and is dependent on the experiences that students have. This last point is important because teachers play a major role in students' development through the kinds of activities they provide. The quality of those experiences will have a major impact on students' development.

MORAL DEVELOPMENT **Moral development**, students' changing conceptions of right and wrong, is a second dimension of student development. As an example of differences in this dimension, look at the following classroom incident.

> "I need to go to the office for a moment," Adam Kellinger announces as his 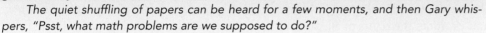 students work on a seatwork assignment. "Work quietly until I get back. I'll be gone for only a few minutes."
>
> The quiet shuffling of papers can be heard for a few moments, and then Gary whispers, "Psst, what math problems are we supposed to do?"
>
> "Shh! No talking," Talitha says, pointing to the rules posted on the bulletin board.
>
> "But he needs to know so he can do his work," Krystal replies. "It's the evens on page 79."
>
> "Who cares?" Duane growls. "He's not here. He won't catch us."

Piaget (1965) also investigated students' moral development and found that responses to moral problems such as this occur in two broad stages. In the first, **external morality**, children view rules as fixed, permanent, and enforced by authority figures. When Talitha said "Shh! No talking" and pointed to the rules, she was operating at this stage. It didn't matter that Gary was only asking about the assignment; rules are rules. In responding "Who cares? He's not here. He won't catch us," Duane also functioned at this stage, focusing on the fact that no authority figure was there to enforce the rule. External morality typically lasts to about age 10. Piaget believed that parents and teachers who stress unquestioned adherence to adult authority retard moral development and unintentionally encourage students to remain at this level.

When students advance to what Piaget labeled **autonomous morality**, they develop rational ideas of fairness and see justice as a reciprocal process of treating others as they would want to be treated (Turiel, 2006). Children at this stage begin to rely on themselves instead of others to regulate their behavior. Krystal's comment, "But he needs to know so he can do his work," demonstrates autonomous morality: She viewed Gary's whispering as an honest request for assistance rather than an infraction of rules.

Lawrence Kohlberg (1929–1987) built on Piaget's work and found that the way children think about moral issues could be divided into three broad levels that also develop over time (see Table 5.1). In the first, called *preconventional ethics*, students think about right and wrong in terms of the consequences of an act for them. Duane's comment, "Who cares? He's not here. He won't catch us," illustrates this level: He was concerned only about whether they would get caught. This response, similar to Piaget's external morality, is characteristic of the moral reasoning of young children. For example, because

Piaget's Cognitive Developmental Theory A theory that describes how students' thinking about the world changes over time and how experiences contribute to development.

Moral development Students' conceptions of right and wrong that change with experience and maturity.

External morality A stage of moral reasoning in which children view rules as fixed, permanent, and enforced by authority figures.

Autonomous morality A stage of moral reasoning in which children develop rational ideas of fairness and see justice as a reciprocal process of treating others as they would want to be treated.

Table 5.1 Kohlberg's Levels of Moral Development	
Level	**Description**
Preconventional Ethics	Right and wrong determined by consequences of action
Conventional Ethics	Morality determined by rules
Postconventional Ethics	Moral decisions based on basic principles of right and wrong

they focus on consequences for themselves, children who are punished conclude that they must have been bad; they don't consider the act and the consequence independent of themselves.

When students advance to conventional ethics, the next level, their thinking focuses on obeying rules, following the thinking of the majority, and concern for others. People who obey rules because rules are rules and ought to be followed are reasoning at this level. Talitha illustrated this level of moral reasoning when she pointed to the rule that said no talking; the rule said no talking, so talking was wrong. A student working diligently on a group project because he doesn't think it's right to let his group-mates down is reasoning at this level as well. On the other hand, a student who thinks it's okay to cheat because other people in the class are cheating is also reasoning at this level.

At the third level, postconventional ethics, students make moral decisions based on basic principles of right and wrong. For example, students who treat others the way they would want to be treated are considering "the Golden Rule" and are operating at this level. Students who obey rules because the class agreed, on principle, that the rules are fair and promote the rights of all students in the class are also reasoning at this level.

We examine the implications of differences in both cognitive and moral development later in this section.

Cheating. American students cheat! That's not news to teachers, and it isn't anything new; students have always cheated. But the magnitude of the current problem is unsettling: A study conducted by Duke University found that 75 percent of high school students admitted to cheating, and if copying another student's homework is included, the number climbs to 90 percent (McMahon, 2007). And, the problem isn't limited to students simply trying to pass: 80 percent of honors and AP students cheat on a regular basis.

The most common ways that students cheat include the following:

- Copying from other students
- Plagiarizing by downloading information from the Internet
- Using cell phone capabilities, such as text messaging, photographing and sharing test information, and downloading information from the Internet
- Getting test questions or papers from a previous grading period
- Bringing illegal information on a permitted graphing calculator (McMahon, 2007)

As you see, many of these problems are connected to technology, a topic we discuss in the next section.

So, is the problem students' moral development, or do other causes exist? Although moral development does influence students' honesty, there are other factors at work. One is our society and the pressures students feel to get good grades, get into the right college, and launch a successful career. Experts also believe that teachers can contribute to the problem, both in how they structure their classes and in how they confront incidents of cheating (M. Casey, 2008). Students are also more likely to cheat in classrooms that emphasize competition and high grades versus understanding and mastering content (Anderman & Midgley, 2004). In addition, a teacher's forthright discussion of the topic combined with structural safeguards, such as seating students apart from each other, can do much to discourage cheating.

■ ■ TECHNOLOGY AND TEACHING
Cheating and Plagiarism

Technology can be a valuable learning tool, but it can also be used to cheat, as you just saw. Students often use technology, such as cell phones and graphing calculators, to bring disallowed information into testing situations. Many schools combat this problem by

myeducationlab

To examine developmental differences in students' moral reasoning, go to the *Assignments and Activities* section of Topic 2: *Student Diversity* in the MyEducationLab for your course and complete the activity titled *Moral Reasoning.*

banning all electronic devices in testing rooms. In fact, some schools require students to turn their cell phones off when they enter school each day and turn them on again only at the end of the day. A de-emphasis on grades combined with frequent assessment using a variety of forms, such as traditional tests and quizzes, homework, and observations, can also do much to relieve the grading pressures students experience (Kohn, 2007).

Plagiarism is also a major issue in many classrooms. The easy access to information, and even complete papers, on the Internet has become a temptation for students and a problem for teachers: Students download papers or sections of papers and hand them in as their own. In addition to ethical problems, plagiarism robs students of valuable experiences in analyzing, organizing, and expressing their own ideas. Suggestions for addressing this problem range from instructional approaches to high-tech solutions that analyze student work and compare it to databases containing hundreds of thousands of papers.

The writing assignment itself is a place to start (D. Johnson, 2004). For example, assignments that require students to react personally to content and think at higher levels both increase learner motivation and discourage plagiarism (Freedman, 2004). Effective teachers also hold honest discussions about problems involved with plagiarism, and they work closely with students from the initial draft stages to the final product. If all else fails, websites exist (e.g., TurnItIn.com) that can help teachers detect copying and wholesale borrowing of intact passages.

PERSONAL AND SOCIAL DEVELOPMENT

"Ahh," Melissa Anderson, an eighth-grade English teacher, sighs as she slumps into a chair in the faculty lounge.

"Tough day?" her friend Beth asks.

"Yes, it's Sean again," Melissa nods. "I can't seem to get through to him. He won't do his work, and he has a bad attitude about school in general. I talked with his mother, and she said he's been a handful since birth. He doesn't get along with the other students, and when I talk with him about it, he says they're picking on him for no reason. I don't know what's going to become of him. The funny thing is, I get the feeling that he knows he's out of line, but he just can't seem to change."

"I know what you mean," Beth responds. "I had him for English last year. He was a tough one, very distant. At times he would almost open up to me, but then the wall would go up again."

"Sean's a bright boy, too," Melissa continues, "but he seems to prefer avoiding work to doing it. I know that I can help him . . . if I can just figure out how."

Personal development refers to changes in our personalities and our ability to manage our feelings, and it influences the way we interact with our physical and social environments. For instance, Sean's refusal to do his work, his inability to get along with his classmates, and his conclusion that they're picking on him for no reason suggest problems with his personal development. Personal development is important because students like Sean tend to be unhappy in school and achieve less than their peers (Zins, Bloodworth, Weissberg, & Walberg, 2004). In addition, they're less able to make friends and work productively with others, important dimensions of social development.

Social Development

Octavio, Mindy, Sarah, and Bill are studying American westward expansion in social studies. They've been working as a group for 3 days and are preparing a report to be delivered to the class. There is some disagreement about who should present which topics.

"So what should we do?" Mindy asks, looking at the others. "Octavio, Sarah, and Bill all want to report on the Pony Express."

"I thought of it first," Octavio argues.

"But everyone knows I like horses," Sarah counters.

Personal development Changes in our personalities and our ability to manage our feelings.

Social interaction provides opportunities for students to develop perspective-taking and social problem-solving skills, important dimensions of social development.

"Why don't we compromise?" Mindy suggests. "Octavio, didn't you say that you were kind of interested in railroads because your grandfather worked on them? Couldn't you talk to him and get some information for the report? And Sarah, I know you like horses. Couldn't you report on horses and the Plains Indians?. . . And Bill, what about you?"

"I don't care . . . whatever," Bill replies, folding his arms and peering belligerently at the group.

Social development, another major dimension of development, refers to the changes over time in the ways we relate to others. Social development is important for teachers for two reasons. First, research shows that students who are more socially skilled have advantages, both in school and in life: They are happier, achieve more, and get along better with their classmates (Viadero, 2008d; Zins et al., 2004). Second, teachers who understand the benefits of healthy social development can design classrooms where students can learn to work on and develop their social skills.

Two important dimensions of social development are perspective taking and social problem solving. We saw these at work in the case at the beginning of this section: Mindy was able to understand the motives and feelings of others in the group and used this knowledge to come up with a solution that satisfied everyone except Bill. Young children such as Tran, who was concerned about a "wedgie" from his principal, tend to see the world from their own perspective and are unable to understand how others think and feel. Mindy was also good at social problem solving, the ability to understand a situation involving social conflict, and come up with a solution that moved the group forward.

Social development is becoming increasingly important in classrooms because of the widespread use of cooperative learning, peer tutoring, and other small-group instructional strategies. To participate effectively in these activities, students need to be able to apply these skills:

- Take turns participating and not dominate a discussion
- Listen to others' ideas and build on them
- Involve everyone in the group in the activity
- Disagree in a positive way

Social interaction skills such as these develop over time and with practice (D. Johnson & Johnson, 2006). As we see later in the chapter, teachers promote social development in their classrooms through teaching, modeling, and providing opportunities for students to interact with and learn from their classmates.

INFLUENCES ON PERSONAL AND SOCIAL DEVELOPMENT. Parents and peers both play important roles in children's personal and social development. Initially, parents are more influential; later, during the school years, peers start to play a more powerful role (H. Wilson, Pianta, & Stuhlman, 2007).

Parents and Other Adults. Parents and other caregivers provide love and support, and are the most powerful influences on children's personal and social development (Landry, Smith, & Swank, 2006; Soenens et al., 2007). This makes sense, given the amount of

Social development Changes over time in the ways we relate to others.

Table 5.2 Parenting Styles and Healthy Development

Interaction Style	Parental Characteristics	Child Characteristics
Authoritative	Firm but caring. Consistent. Explain reasons for rules. High expectations.	High self-esteem. Confident and secure. Willing to take risks. Successful in school.
Authoritarian	Stress conformity. Detached. Don't explain rules. Don't encourage verbal give-and-take.	Withdrawn. Worry more about pleasing parents than solving problems. Defiant. Lack social skills.
Permissive	Give children total freedom. Hold few expectations. Make few demands on children.	Immature. Lack self-control. Impulsive. Lack motivation.
Uninvolved	Have little interest in children's lives. Hold few expectations.	Lack self-control. Lack long-term goals. Easily frustrated. Disobedient.

time children—and especially young children—spend with their parents. Experts estimate that children up to age 18 spend nearly 90 percent of their waking hours outside of school under the guidance of their parents (Kamil & Walberg, 2005).

Research indicates that certain **parenting styles**, general patterns of interacting with and disciplining children, promote more healthy personal and social development than others (Baumrind, 1991), and the effects of these styles can last into the college years, influencing motivation, achievement, and relationships with teachers (Berk, 2010). Researchers have identified four parenting styles and the patterns of development associated with them; these are summarized in Table 5.2.

As you see in Table 5.2, an authoritative parenting style is most effective for promoting healthy personal development. Authoritative parents set high expectations for their children and provide the structure and support that help children meet them. At the same time, authoritative parents encourage their children to develop values and goals to guide their actions (Soenens et al., 2007).

The other styles are less effective. Authoritarian parents, for example, are rigid and unresponsive, and in extreme cases, their children have low self-esteem and behave aggressively in attempts to cope with problems (Maughan & Cicchetti, 2002). Also, if parents set high expectations but fail to provide the support needed to meet them, children may view the expectations as unfair, and rebel. Permissive parents set few expectations, and uninvolved parents have little interest in child raising and exert little influence on their children's lives.

Healthy parent–child relationships promote personal development by helping children acquire a sense of autonomy, competence, and belonging (Christenson & Havsy, 2004). Such relationships also support the development of personal responsibility, which is essential for success both in school and in later life.

Understanding parenting styles is valuable for teachers because the effective classroom management practices of teachers strongly parallel effective parenting styles (Emmer, Evertson, & Worsham, 2009; Evertson, Emmer, & Worsham, 2009). Teachers who adopt an authoritative approach to classroom management and their interactions with students are more effective than teachers who are too rigid or too permissive.

Peers. Think back to the friends you had in middle and high school: How did they influence who you are today? Next to parents, peers exert the most powerful influence on personal and social development, especially for adolescents. Peers influence development through the attitudes and values they communicate and the emotional support they provide (Rubin, Bukowski, & Parker, 2006; Eisenberg, Fabes, & Spinrod, 2006). For example, when students have academically oriented friends, their grades improve; but when their friends don't value studying and learning, their grades are lower and behavior problems increase (Benson, Scales, Hamilton, & Sesma, 2006; Rubin et al., 2006). Friends also provide the emotional support that contributes to personal development, and interactions with peers enable students to develop their social skills. Teachers can promote

Parenting style General patterns of interacting with and disciplining children.

healthy personal and social development by providing opportunities for students to work together in productive ways.

Learner Development: Implications for Teachers

Expert teachers understand the powerful influence of development on classroom learning. They also realize that within the same classroom there will be significant differences in students' developmental levels, and these differences will affect their instruction. Developmentally appropriate practice adapts instruction to meet the development needs of all students. Let's see how teachers do this at different grade levels.

ELEMENTARY   Experience is essential for all forms of development, and expert teachers design learning activities for students that promote that development. To see this idea illustrated in the area of cognitive development, let's return to Jenny Newhall's work with her first graders. As you saw, she demonstrated that air takes up space by putting a paper towel in the bottom of a glass, inverting the glass, and pushing it into a fishbowl of water. She wanted students to understand that the towel stayed dry because air kept the water out of the glass, but most of her students didn't consider air in their attempts to explain why the towel stayed dry. Let's see what she does next.

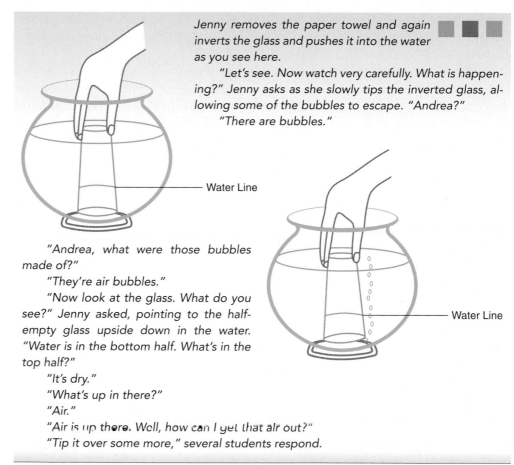

Jenny removes the paper towel and again inverts the glass and pushes it into the water as you see here.

"Let's see. Now watch very carefully. What is happening?" Jenny asks as she slowly tips the inverted glass, allowing some of the bubbles to escape. "Andrea?"

"There are bubbles."

Water Line

"Andrea, what were those bubbles made of?"

"They're air bubbles."

"Now look at the glass. What do you see?" Jenny asked, pointing to the half-empty glass upside down in the water. "Water is in the bottom half. What's in the top half?"

"It's dry."

"What's up in there?"

"Air."

"Air is up there. Well, how can I get that air out?"

"Tip it over some more," several students respond.

Water Line

In this brief episode, Jenny provided her students with concrete experiences they could use to understand their world. Because they didn't consider air in their initial explanations, she demonstrated that air was in the glass in a perceptually obvious way: They could see the air bubbles rising from the inverted glass. Providing concrete experiences in this way is invaluable for promoting cognitive development.

Effective elementary teachers use concrete experiences in all content areas. For instance, they use squares of candy bars to illustrate equivalent fractions, real crabs and lobsters to demonstrate exoskeletons in animals, experiences in the classroom and school as topics for teaching how to write effective paragraphs, and students' neighborhoods to teach about *communities*. Role playing, in which students assume the roles of different people or characters, not only provides concrete experiences for students but also can encourage perspective taking, an important element of social development.

Effective elementary teachers also use classroom management to promote student moral development, and rules and procedures are the foundation of their classroom management systems (Evertson et al., 2009; J. Murphy, 2007). Moral development occurs when students understand how their actions influence others and take personal responsibility for their actions.

Rules and procedures help students understand how they should act and interact in classrooms, and they provide structure for guiding student development. For example, researchers found that implementing a rule that prohibited kindergarteners from excluding classmates promoted social acceptance to a greater extent than did individual efforts to help excluded or isolated children (Harriet & Bradley, 2003). Figure 5.3 contains an example of rules from one elementary classroom.

Figure 5.3 Rules From One Elementary Classroom

- We raise our hands before speaking.
- We leave our seats only when given permission by the teacher.
- We stand politely in line at all times.
- We keep our hands to ourselves.
- We listen when someone else is talking.

In introducing classroom rules at the elementary level, effective teachers describe them clearly, explain why they're important, and teach how they should be followed. Elementary students, especially younger ones, are often unaware of rules and may not understand how they contribute to a healthy classroom environment that promotes learning. Because their cognitive development often focuses on the concrete and tangible, special efforts to demonstrate what the rules mean, the reasons for their existence, and their connection to personal responsibility and learning are important.

The elementary grades also lay the foundation for the development of social responsibility and self-control. Teachers who help students understand the impact of their actions on others help them make the transition from egocentric morality, with its emphasis on rewards and punishment, to an understanding of why rules are important for both classrooms and the world outside of school.

Elementary students also need opportunities to practice perspective taking and social problem solving. Discussions and group work, where students can interact with others and practice these skills, are effective learning experiences.

MIDDLE SCHOOL

A middle school science teacher wants his students to understand how pendulums work. He also wants them to be able to design effective experiments in which only one variable is changed while the others are controlled, or kept the same. After introducing his class to the general idea of pendulums, he displays a simple one at the front of the room and asks, "What determines how fast a pendulum swings?"

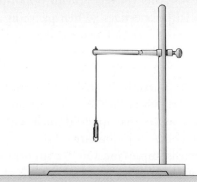

Students offer several hypotheses, including the length of the string, the weight of the pendulum, and the height from which the pendulum is launched. The teacher then breaks the class into groups of four and asks each group to design a series of experiments to determine which, if any, of the variables—length, weight, and height—influence how fast the pendulum swings. The class agrees to count the number of swings per half minute, and the teacher asks each group to share their results at the end of the class period. The groups design different experiments that are haphazard at best and come up with radically different conclusions about the workings of pendulums. The teacher uses the different conclusions to illustrate in concrete ways both the working of pendulums and how to properly design experiments.

Although middle school students are beginning to learn how to deal with abstract ideas, they still need the concrete experiences that make abstract concepts meaningful. They continue to need a great deal of scaffolding when working with content that is becoming more abstract, such as in pre-algebra and science. The middle school teacher in the example provided both concrete experiences and scaffolding to help his students understand abstract and potentially difficult concepts. And, the more practice these students get putting their developing ideas into words, the more effective their learning will be.

Middle school students also need firm, caring teachers who empathize with them and their sometimes capricious actions, while providing the security of clear limits for acceptable behavior (Mawhinney & Sagan, 2007). Classroom management provides opportunities to advance moral reasoning from preconventional to conventional thinking through effective classroom management systems that emphasize personal responsibility.

Clear rules that are carefully explained and consistently enforced continue to be the foundation of classroom management at the middle school level. Effective middle school teachers adapt these rules to create classrooms that address the developmental needs of adolescents. For example, personal appearance is foremost in middle schoolers' minds, and classrooms can become mini beauty salons, with students endlessly combing and recombing their hair. There is nothing wrong with good grooming per se, but it can distract young learners when you're trying to teach something. Specific rules about not grooming in class help to focus classrooms on learning rather than on preening.

As middle schoolers develop socially and emotionally, effective teachers help them understand that they are also responsible for helping to create a productive learning environment. Making the transition from external to internal authority, they obey rules because the rules make sense instead of obeying rules because of the threat of punishment for breaking them. Teachers promote this orientation by explicitly teaching responsibility and emphasizing the reasons for rules and procedures. Students understand that order is important for learning and the need for rules to create a classroom that allows everyone to learn.

Developing student responsibility is both sensible and practical. Learners are more likely to obey rules that make sense and when they recognize that rules exist to protect their rights and the rights of others (Good & Brophy, 2008). This responsibility orientation can also contribute to ethical thinking and character development (Nucci, 2006). Children don't call their classmates nasty names, for example, because they recognize that name calling hurts other people's feelings, a dimension of perspective taking. By promoting student responsibility and understanding, teachers promote both moral and social development, and make their own jobs easier.

The increasing importance of peers can present both challenges and opportunities in middle schools. Whispering, note passing, and general attempts to socialize can be problems, and clear, consistently applied rules become essential. Well-organized group work can effectively provide opportunities to experience different cognitive, moral, and social perspectives. When planning small-group work, effective teachers create groups that are developmentally and culturally diverse, providing rich opportunities for students to learn from each other.

HIGH SCHOOL   High school students are beginning to wrestle with who they are and what they want to become. Developing personal responsibility is important, and private conferences that appeal to their sense of responsibility are effective. Peers continue to exert a powerful influence on behavior, so avoiding embarrassing students in front of their peers is important. Often a simple request to turn around or get busy is all the intervention that is necessary.

Linking content to students' lives is particularly valuable at this age. For example, examining ideas about gender and occupational trends in social studies and showing how math and science will influence their futures are important for these students. Discussions,

Grade Retention

Our schools are organized to expose students to increasingly complex ideas as they develop, so children progress from grade to grade as they grow older. But what happens when a student isn't ready for or doesn't master course content at a specific grade level?

Recently, schools have shown an increased interest in **grade retention**, the practice of requiring students to repeat a grade if they don't meet certain criteria (Van Horn, 2008). An important plank in many reform efforts is the elimination of "social promotion," promoting low-achieving students to the next grade so they can be with their age-similar peers.

Grade retention is not new, but its popularity as a reform tool has grown recently; in the 2000–2001 school year, for example, more than 1 of 10 Texas third graders were retained (Bali, Anagnostopoulos, & Roberts, 2005). In 2005, seven other states linked retention to test scores, typically in grades 3, 5, and 8, and Florida considered grade retention policies based on test scores for all grade levels (Richard, 2005).

A variation on grade retention involves delaying kindergarten entry for children whose birthdays are near the cutoff date or who are developmentally immature. Advocates suggest that giving students, and especially boys, an extra year to develop increases chances for success and minimizes the risk of failure from developmental lags.

THE ISSUE

Proponents of grade retention argue that retaining students in a grade until they've acquired the knowledge and skills for that level makes sense (Greene & Winters, 2006). For example, allowing students to move from the fourth to the fifth grade when they haven't mastered the content and skills expected of typi-

Grade retention The practice of requiring students to repeat a grade if they don't meet certain criteria.

cal fourth graders is counterproductive, because students are less likely to succeed in the fifth grade. Spending a second year in a grade gives learners another chance to acquire the necessary understanding and skills and sends the message that schoolwork is important.

Opponents of grade retention argue that holding students back doesn't improve their academic performance, and they further argue that the costs outweigh any benefits that might result (Eide & Goldhaber, 2005). Critics point to studies indicating that students retained in grade perform lower on subsequent achievement tests than their nonretained classmates, and they are also more likely to later drop out of school (Holmes, 2006; Jimerson, Pletcher, & Graydon, 2006). Opponents note that school dropouts are 5 times more likely to have repeated a grade than students who complete high school and that the probability of dropping out for students who repeat two grades is nearly 100 percent. In addition, minorities and students from low-income families are much more likely to be retained than are their White, wealthier counterparts (Anagnostopoulos, 2006).

Similar reservations apply to holding children back for kindergarten. Research indicates that this practice results in few advantages and even some disadvantages (Berk, 2010). Delayed students perform no better academically, and they actually experience more behavioral problems than students who aren't held back.

Opponents also argue that grade retention causes emotional problems. In one study, children reported that the prospect of repeating a grade was more stressful than "wetting in class" or being caught stealing. Going blind and losing a parent were the only two life events that children felt were more stressful than being retained (Shepard & Smith, 1990). Opponents note that the psychological effects of grade retention are es-

pecially acute in adolescence, where physical size differences and peer awareness exacerbate the problem (Jimerson et al., 2006).

Finally, opponents suggest that better alternatives to social promotion are available (Van Horn, 2008). For example, before- and after-school tutoring, summer school programs with reduced class sizes, instructional aides who work with low-achieving children, and peer tutoring are all possibilities. Each is less expensive than the thousands of dollars spent on having children repeat what they have already experienced, and students in these alternative programs are more likely to meet standards than those who have repeated grades (Jimerson et al., 2006).

This discussion addresses the second item on our *This I Believe* feature, "Retaining students in a grade is the most effective intervention for those who fail to master the content in a particular grade level." As you see, experts disagree, and you now have the opportunity to weigh in on the issue.

YOU TAKE A STAND

It's your turn to take a position on the issue. Given the information you've studied here and any experience you've had with grade retention, decide whether grade retention is beneficial to students or whether other alternatives would be more effective.

myeducationlab To explore both sides of this issue and take a stand, go to *Book Specific Resources* section in the MyEducationLab for your course, select your text, and then select *Taking a Stand in an Era of Reform* for Chapter 5.

small-group work, and focused writing assignments provide valuable opportunities for students to integrate new ideas into their developing self-identities.

Though high school students are cognitively more advanced than their younger counterparts, the ability to think in the abstract depends on their prior knowledge and experiences. When new concepts are introduced, high school students still need concrete examples. Lectures, though widely used at the high school level, are less effective than instruction that promotes discussion and interaction. As you move through your program, seize every opportunity to learn to guide your students through questioning instead of simply lecturing to them; it will pay major dividends in both learning and motivation.

One solution to developmental differences in students is grade retention. In the *Taking a Stand* feature on page 137, we examine the pros and cons of this practice.

■ ■ ■ ■ CHECK YOUR UNDERSTANDING

1.1 Describe the major dimensions of development. How are they similar and different?

1.2 How is the thinking of young children different from the thinking of older students?

1.3 How is the moral thinking of young children different from that of older students?

1.4 What is *social development*, and why is it important for classroom teachers?

For feedback on these exercises, go to the appendix, *Check Your Understanding*, located in the back of this text.

DIFFERENCES IN ABILITY

When you were in grade school, what reading group did you belong to? ■ ■ ■
Were you a Robin, a Bluebird, or a Sparrow? In middle school, did you take biology and pre-algebra or general science and basic math? In high school, were you in the college preparatory program or a general and vocational track?

Most of us experienced some form of ability grouping as we went through school, but we might not have thought much about it at the time. When one of your authors made the transition from a K–8 elementary school to high school, he seldom saw some of his old friends in classes and wondered why. Only later, when people started talking about college, did he notice that most of the other students in his classes were headed to college, but some of his old friends were not. Most of these assignments to different classes were based on perceptions of differences in ability. Differences in ability are also important to teachers: A recent national survey found that 43 percent of teachers identified these differences as a major challenge in teaching (MetLife, 2009). In this section, we examine ability differences and discuss how teachers and schools attempt to deal with this form of diversity.

What Is Intelligence?

One of the most popular ways to think about differences in ability is in terms of intelligence. But, what exactly is intelligence? To begin to answer this question, examine the following questions, and think about what they have in common.

1. A coat priced $45 is marked one third off. When it still doesn't sell, the sale price is reduced by half. What is the price after the second discount?

2. Who was Albert Einstein?

3. What are the largest and smallest states in the United States in land area?

4. How are a mountain and a plateau alike?

The common feature of these questions may surprise you: Each is similar to an item found on the Wechsler Intelligence Scale for Children—Fourth Edition (Wechsler, 2003), one of the most widely used intelligence tests in the United States. In other words, experts believe that the ability to answer questions such as these is an indicator of a person's intelligence.

We all have intuitive notions of intelligence; it's how "sharp" people are, how much they know, how quickly and easily they learn, and how perceptive and sensitive they are. Researchers, however, more precisely define **intelligence** as the capacity to acquire and use knowledge, solve problems, and reason in the abstract (Ackerman & Lohman, 2006; Eggen & Kauchak, 2010). It is these three dimensions that intelligence tests attempt to measure, and they play a powerful role in influencing learning ability and school success.

CHANGES IN VIEWS OF INTELLIGENCE Historically, researchers believed that intelligence was a single trait and that all people could be classified along a single continuum of "general" intelligence (Waterhouse, 2006). Thinking has changed, however, and many researchers now believe that intelligence is composed of several distinct dimensions that may occur alone or in various combinations in different individuals.

Howard Gardner, a psychologist who did groundbreaking work in this area, is one of the best known proponents of this idea (Gardner, 1983; Gardner & Moran, 2006). He proposed a theory of **multiple intelligences**, which suggests that overall intelligence is composed of eight relatively independent dimensions (Table 5.3).

Gardner's theory makes intuitive sense. For example, we all know people who don't seem particularly "sharp" analytically but who excel in getting along with others; this ability serves them well in jobs requiring "people" skills such as sales and even teaching, and in some instances they're more successful than their "brighter" peers. Other people seem very self-aware and can capitalize on their personal strengths and minimize their weaknesses. Gardner would describe these people as high in *interpersonal* and *intrapersonal* intelligence, respectively.

Gardner's Theory of Multiple Intelligences reminds us that intelligence and ability are multifaceted and require a broad range of learning activities to develop fully.

Despite the theory's popularity with teachers, most classrooms focus heavily on the linguistic and logical-mathematical dimensions and virtually ignore the others (Seider, 2009). If the other dimensions are to develop, however, students need experiences with them. For example, cooperative-learning activities can help students develop interpersonal intelligence, participation in sports or dance can improve bodily-kinesthetic abilities, and playing in a band or singing in choral groups can improve musical intelligence.

This section addresses the third item in our *This I Believe* feature, "Experts believe that intelligence is unidimensional and that students who are smart in one area will also be smart in others." Although experts used to believe that intelligence is unidimensional, today most think it has many facets that schools can help develop through different types of experiences.

This I BELIEVE

Intelligence The capacity to acquire and use knowledge, solve problems, and reason in the abstract.

Multiple intelligences Theory that suggests that overall intelligence is composed of eight relatively independent dimensions.

Table 5.3 Gardner's Dimensions of Intelligence

Dimension	Description	Individuals Who Might Be High in This Dimension
Linguistic intelligence	Sensitivity to the meaning and order of words and the varied uses of language	Poet, journalist
Logical-mathematical intelligence	The ability to handle long chains of reasoning and to recognize patterns and order in the world	Scientist, mathematician
Musical intelligence	Sensitivity to pitch, melody, and tone	Composer, violinist
Spatial intelligence	The ability to perceive the visual world accurately and to re-create, transform, or modify aspects of the world on the basis of one's perceptions	Sculptor, navigator
Bodily-kinesthetic intelligence	A fine-tuned ability to use the body and to handle objects	Dancer, athlete
Interpersonal intelligence	An understanding of interpersonal relations and the ability to make distinctions among others	Therapist, salesperson
Intrapersonal intelligence	Access to one's own "feeling life"	Self-aware individual
Naturalist intelligence	The ability to recognize similarities and differences in the physical world	Biologist, anthropologist

Source: Adapted from H. Gardner & Hatch (1989) and Chekles (1997).

Ability Grouping and Tracking: Schools' Responses to Differences in Ability

The most common response to differences in students' abilities is through **ability grouping**, the practice of placing students of similar abilities into groups and matching instruction to the needs of each group (Chorzempa & Graham, 2006; McCoach, O'Connell, & Levitt, 2006). Let's see why ability grouping is so popular in the elementary grades.

> Adrian Foster sat back and thought as he finished checking his third-grade students' math quiz. The scores were almost bimodal: Half of the class understood multiplication with carrying and half were still struggling. If he continued with multiplication, half the class would be bored; if he went ahead with division, the other half would be lost. What to do?
>
> The next day, Adrian began math class by explaining that some students were ready for division, and some needed some more work on multiplication. He gathered the students still working on multiplication around him in one corner of the room and gave them a sheet with additional problems on it. He told them that they would get back together as soon as he introduced division to the other group. As he worked with the division group, he kept one eye on them and the other on the group doing their multiplication. Some hands went up but Adrian had to tell them to wait a few minutes until he was done with the division group. It wasn't an easy juggling act but he didn't know what his alternatives were.

Ability grouping The practice of placing students of similar abilities into groups and matching instruction to the needs of each group.

Between-class ability grouping Dividing all students in a given grade level into groups, such as high, medium, and low.

Within-class ability grouping Dividing students within one classroom into ability groups.

Tracking Placing students in a series of classes or curricula on the basis of ability and career goals.

Ability grouping is most popular in elementary schools and typically exists in two forms: **Between-class ability grouping** divides all students in a given grade level into groups, such as high, medium, and low, whereas **within-class ability grouping** divides students within one classroom into ability groups, as Adrian did. Most elementary teachers endorse ability grouping, particularly in reading and math.

In middle, junior high, and high schools, ability grouping goes further, with high-ability students studying advanced and college preparatory courses and lower ability classmates receiving vocational or work-related instruction. In some schools, students are grouped only in certain areas, such as English or math. In others, the grouping exists across all content areas, a practice called **tracking**, which places students in a series of classes or curricula on the basis of ability and career goals. Some form of tracking exists in most middle, junior high, and high schools (Oakes, 2008).

Why is ability grouping so common? Advocates claim that it increases learning because it allows teachers to adjust methods, materials, and instructional pace to better meet students' needs (Chorzempa & Graham, 2006). Because lesson components and assessments are similar for students in a particular group, instruction is also easier for the teacher, they argue. Research, however, has uncovered several serious problems with both ability grouping and tracking:

- Homogeneously grouped low-ability students achieve less than heterogeneously grouped students of similar ability. Often this problem results from inferior instruction in lower classes (Burris, Heubert, & Levin, 2006; Chorzempa & Graham, 2006).

- Within-class grouping creates logistical problems for teachers, because different lessons and assignments are required, and monitoring students in different tasks is difficult (Good & Brophy, 2008). We saw this in Adrian's classroom.

- Improper placements occur, and placement tends to become permanent. Cultural minorities are underrepresented in high-ability classes and overrepresented in those with lower ability students (O'Conner & Fernandez, 2006).

- Low groups are stigmatized, and the self-esteem and motivation of students in these groups decrease (Oakes, 2008).

In addition, absentee rates, delinquency, truancy, and dropping out of school are much higher for students in low groups than for students in general (Slavin, 2009). Tracking also often results in racial or cultural segregation of students, which impedes social development and the ability to form friendships across cultural groups (Oakes & Wells, 2002).

You will undoubtedly experience some form of ability grouping when you start teaching. And, although teachers generally prefer to work with high-ability groups, you'll likely work with students placed in low-ability groups at some point in your career. Teachers can avoid many of the problems associated with ability grouping and tracking by having appropriately high expectations for all students and working with them in heterogeneous groups whenever possible. Instructional adaptations will be needed, however, to ensure the success of students of varying abilities. Some effective strategies include the following:

- Challenge students in all of your groups, and use instructional strategies that actively engage all students.

- Provide additional instructional support for those who need it. For example, while most of the class is doing seatwork, you might work with four or five students who need extra help.

- Give students extra time to complete assignments.

- Provide peer tutors for students requiring extra help.

- Use both whole-class and small-group instruction. Small-group work provides variety and can help students learn from each other.

- Provide options on some assignments, such as giving students the choice of presenting a report orally or in writing (Tomlinson, 2006; Vaughn & Bos, 2006).

You will continually need to adapt instruction to meet your students' needs, and these adaptations are even more important for those whose ability is lower.

Learning Styles

To understand something, do you need to "see" it? or hear it described? or touch it? People often describe themselves as *visual*, *verbal*, or *tactile* learners. These descriptions reflect your unique **learning style**, or your preferred way of learning and studying (Denig, 2003).

Learning style A preferred way of learning and studying.

Learning styles also influence classroom teaching, as Chris Burnette discovers.

> One thing Chris remembers from his methods classes is the need for variety. ▪ ▪ ▪
> He has been primarily using large-group discussions in his middle school so-
> cial studies classes, and most of the students seem to respond okay. But others seem un-
> interested, and their attention often drifts.
>
> Today, Chris decides to try a small-group activity involving problem solving. The class
> has been studying the growth of American cities, and he wants the students to think about
> solutions to some of the problems of big cities. As he watches the groups interact, he's sur-
> prised at what he sees: Some of the students who are most withdrawn in whole-class dis-
> cussions are leaders in the groups.
>
> "Great!" he thinks. But at the same time, he notes that some of his more active stu-
> dents are sitting back and not getting involved.

There is no doubt that each student approaches learning differently, but which of these differences are important? One approach to studying learning styles distinguishes between deep and surface approaches to processing information (C. Evans, Kirby, & Fabrigar, 2003). For instance, when you study a new idea, do you ask yourself how it relates to other ideas, what examples of the idea exist, and how it might apply in a different context? If so, you're using a deep-processing approach. On the other hand, if you simply memorize the definition, you're using a surface approach. As you might expect, deep-processing approaches result in higher achievement if subsequent tests focus on understanding and application, but surface approaches can be successful if tests emphasize learning and memorization of facts.

An alternative approach to applying learning styles in classrooms was created by Rita and Kenneth Dunn (1978, 1987). They identified a number of preferred learning style dimensions, including the following:

- *Modality:* Does the student learn better through listening or reading?
- *Structure/Support:* Does the learner need high structure, or is he or she an independent learner?
- *Individual/Group:* Does the learner work best independently or in groups?
- *Motivation:* Is the student self-motivated, or does he or she require external rewards?
- *Environment:* How do light, temperature, noise, and time of day influence learning? (Dunn & Dunn, 1978)

These preferences or "styles" make intuitive sense. We've all heard people say, "I'm a morning person" or "Don't try to talk to me until I've had my cup of coffee." And, as you already saw, many people describe themselves as visual, verbal, or tactile.

The work of Dunn and Dunn was popular with teachers in the 1970s and 1980s, and many consultants conducted in-service workshops for teachers on both the Dunns' and others' approaches to learning styles. These approaches are controversial, however. Advocates claim that matching learning environments to learner preferences results in increased achievement and improved attitudes (Farkas, 2003; Lovelace, 2005). Critics counter by questioning the validity of the tests used to identify learning styles (S. Stahl, 2002), and they also cite research indicating that attempts to match learning environments to learning preferences have resulted in no increases and, in some cases, even decreases in learning (Brophy, 2004; Kratzig & Arbuthnott, 2006).

This discussion addresses the fourth item in our *This I Believe* feature, "It is important for teachers to adapt their instruction to the individual learning styles of their students." As you saw earlier in the chapter, you should represent the topics you teach as concretely as possible. And, you should always represent them both visually and verbally,

This I BELIEVE

and even tactilely if possible, to meet the needs of visual, verbal, and tactile learners. Beyond this multisensory approach that attracts and holds student attention, research supports few of the contentions of advocates of learning styles (Good & Brophy, 2008); in fact, the vast majority of the research examining learning styles supports critics (S. Stahl, 1999; Yates, 2000). The following quote summarizes their position.

> We also do not see much validity in the claims made by those who urge teachers to assess their students with learning style inventories and follow with differentiated curriculum and instruction. First, the research bases supporting these urgings tend to be thin to nonexistent. Second, a single teacher working with twenty or more students does not have time to plan and implement much individualized instruction. With respect to student motivation, much more is to be gained by focusing on students' learning goals, values, and expectancies than on the variable emphasized in learning style inventories. (Good & Brophy, 2008, p. 268)

LEARNING STYLES: IMPLICATIONS FOR TEACHERS The concept of learning style has three implications for teachers. First, as Chris Burnette discovered when he tried to use a one-size-fits-all approach to his teaching, no single instructional approach will work with all students, so you should vary the way you teach. This notion is both intuitively sensible and is corroborated by research (Brophy, 2004).

Second, the idea of learning styles can increase your sensitivity to differences in your students, making it more likely that you will respond to your students as individuals. Third, it suggests that teachers should encourage students to think about their own learning, that is, to develop their metacognition.

Metacognition refers to students' awareness of the ways they learn most effectively and their ability to control these factors. For example, a student is demonstrating metacognition when she realizes that studying with music reduces her ability to concentrate, and then turns the radio off. Students who are metacognitive can adjust strategies to match learning tasks better than their less metacognitive peers can and, as a result, they learn more (Eggen & Kauchak, 2010). By encouraging students to think about how they learn best, teachers provide a powerful learning tool students can use throughout their lives.

PEARSON
myeducationlab

Go to the *Building Teaching Skills and Dispositions* section of Topic 2: *Student Diversity* in the MyEducationLab for your course and complete the activity titled *Modifying Instruction for Student Diversity.*

■ ■ ■ ■ ■ CHECK YOUR UNDERSTANDING

2.1 Explain the differences in current definitions of intelligence.

2.2 How do schools respond to differences in ability? What does research suggest about these responses?

2.3 What are *learning styles*? What are the implications of learning styles for teachers?

For feedback on these exercises, go to the appendix, *Check Your Understanding*, located in the back of this text.

LEARNERS WITH EXCEPTIONALITIES

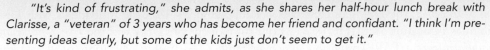

Celina Curtis, a beginning third-grade teacher in a large urban elementary school, has survived her hectic first weeks. She is starting to feel comfortable, but at the same time, some things are bothering her.

"It's kind of frustrating," she admits, as she shares her half-hour lunch break with Clarisse, a "veteran" of 3 years who has become her friend and confidant. "I think I'm presenting ideas clearly, but some of the kids just don't seem to get it."

Metacognition Students' awareness of the ways they learn most effectively and their ability to control these factors.

> *"Maybe you're being too hard on yourself,"* Clarisse responds. *"Students are different. Remember some of the stuff you studied in college? One thing the professors emphasized was that we should be trying our best to treat students as individuals."*
>
> *"Well, . . . yes, I understand that, but that seems too simple. I still have this feeling. For instance, there's Rodney. You've seen him on the playground. He's cute, but his engine is stuck on fast. I can barely get him to sit in his seat, much less work.*
>
> *"When he sits down to do a reading assignment, he really struggles. In math and science he's just fine, except when he has to read something. And he seems like a bright kid.*
>
> *"Then there's Amelia; she's so sweet, but she simply doesn't get it. I've tried everything under the sun with her. I explain it, and the next time, it's as if it's all brand new. I feel sorry for her, because I know she gets frustrated when she can't keep up with the other kids. When I work with her one-on-one, it seems to help, but I don't have enough time to spend with her. She's falling farther and farther behind."*
>
> *"Maybe it's not your fault. You're supposed to be bright and energetic and do your best, but you're going to burn yourself out if you keep this up,"* Clarisse cautions. *"Check with the Teacher Assistance Team. Maybe these students need some extra help."*

myeducationlab

To see a video of a student with a physical disability who refused to let this become a handicap, go to the *Assignments and Activities* section of Topic 2: *Student Diversity* in the MyEducationLab for your course and complete the activity titled *Jessica Parks Surmounts Her Obstacles.*

ISSUES IN EDUCATION

As Celina discovered, students differ in several important ways, and effective teachers consider these differences when they plan and teach. **Students with exceptionalities** are learners who need special help to reach their full potential. Exceptionalities include **disabilities**, functional limitations or an inability to perform a certain act, such as hear or walk, as well as **giftedness**, abilities at the upper end of the continuum that require support beyond regular classroom instruction to reach full potential. Extra help and resources can include special educators, special schools, self-contained classrooms designed especially for these students, resource rooms where students can go to receive supplemental instruction, and inclusion in regular classrooms with the support of specially trained professionals.

Special education refers to instruction designed to meet the unique needs of students with exceptionalities. The terms *children with exceptionalities, students with special needs,* and *individuals with disabilities* have all been used to describe students needing additional help to reach their full potential. Note that in all of these terms, children, students, and individuals come first. This "people-first" mind-set emphasizes that, foremost, these individuals are people like you and other students, and they deserve to be treated with the same care and respect.

Why should you be studying about learners with exceptionalities at this early point in your teacher preparation program? As with students who come from different cultural backgrounds, who vary with respect to development, or who differ in ability, you will undoubtedly have students with exceptionalities in your classroom. Developing an understanding of these students will allow you to begin thinking about how you can adjust your instruction to meet their needs.

Students with exceptionalities Learners who need special help to reach their full potential.

Disabilities Functional limitations or an inability to perform a certain act, such as hear or walk.

Giftedness Abilities at the upper end of the continuum that require support beyond regular classroom instruction to reach full potential.

Special education Instruction designed to meet the unique needs of students with exceptionalities.

Federal Laws Change the Way Schools and Teachers Help Students With Exceptionalities

In the past, students with exceptionalities were separated from their peers and placed in segregated classrooms or schools. Unfortunately, instruction in these settings was often inferior, achievement was no better than in regular education classrooms, and students didn't learn the social and life skills they needed to function well in the real world (Karten, 2005; T. Smith, Polloway, Patton, & Dowdy, 2004). Educators and lawmakers looked for other ways to help these students.

In 1975, the U.S. Congress passed Public Law 94–142, the Individuals with Disabilities Education Act (IDEA). A central component of IDEA was the *free appropriate public education* (FAPE) provision, which guarantees a free public education for all students with exceptionalities (Sack-Min, 2007b). This law helped ensure consistency in how different states addressed the needs of these students. IDEA, combined with later amendments, provides the following guidelines for working with students having exceptionalities:

- Guarantee an appropriate education for all students with exceptionalities.
- Identify the needs of students with exceptionalities through assessment that doesn't discriminate against any students.
- Involve parents in decisions about each child's educational program.
- Create an environment that doesn't restrict learning opportunities for students with exceptionalities.
- Develop an individualized education program (IEP) of study for each student.

Since 1975, Congress has amended IDEA three times in attempts to ensure that all children with disabilities are protected and provided with a free appropriate public education (Sack-Min, 2007b). For example, one amendment extended the provisions of IDEA to children aged 3 through 5 and held states accountable for locating young children who need special education services. A second helps ensure protection against discrimination in testing, and requires districts to keep confidential records of each child and share them with parents on request. Because students who are culturally and linguistically diverse are overrepresented in special education classes, the third requires that methods be established to reduce the number of students from culturally and linguistically diverse backgrounds who are inappropriately placed in special education. It also requires procedures that allow districts to remove students from the classroom who "inflict serious bodily injury" on others.

THE EVOLUTION TOWARD INCLUSION   As educators realized that segregated classes and services weren't meeting the needs of students with exceptionalities, they searched for alternatives. The first was **mainstreaming**, the practice of placing students with exceptionalities from segregated settings in regular education classrooms, often for selected activities only. Popular in the 1970s, mainstreaming began the move away from segregated services. Mainstreaming had problems, however, as one student's experience documents:

> When I got to sixth grade, they put me in regular ed. classes. The work was way too hard, and the teachers did not try to help me. They went way too fast, and I got confused. I got scared and angry. I needed the help, but none of the teachers seemed to care. They didn't pay attention to me. No one ever noticed that I couldn't keep up with the work they were giving me. They were too busy teaching. (Schrimpf, 2006, p. 87)

Students with exceptionalities were often mainstreamed into regular classrooms without adequate support and services, and the results were unsatisfactory (Hardman, Drew, & Egan, 2008).

To remedy the problems involved with mainstreaming, educators developed **inclusion**, a comprehensive approach to educating students with exceptionalities that incorporates a total, systematic, and coordinated web of services (Sapon-Shevin, 2007). Inclusion has three essential components:

- Include students with special needs in a regular school campus.
- Place students with special needs in age- and grade-appropriate classrooms.
- Provide special education support within the regular classroom.

Inclusion is broader than mainstreaming, and it means that as a regular classroom teacher, you will have students with exceptionalities in your classroom, and you will have the support of special education assistance.

INDIVIDUALIZED EDUCATION PROGRAM   To ensure that inclusion works and that learners with exceptionalities don't get lost in the regular classroom, a team of educators prepares an **individualized education program (IEP)**. Special education and general

Go to the *IRIS Center Resources* section of Topic 2: *Student Diversity* in the MyEducationLab for your course and explore the module titled *Accessing the General Education Curriculum: Inclusion Considerations for Students with Disabilities.*

Mainstreaming The practice of moving students with exceptionalities from segregated settings into regular education classrooms, often for selected activities only.

Inclusion A comprehensive approach to educating students with exceptionalities that incorporates a total, systematic, and coordinated web of services.

Individualized education program (IEP) An individually prescribed instructional plan collaboratively devised by special education and general education teachers, resource professionals, parents, and sometimes the student.

education teachers, resource professionals, parents, and sometimes the student collaborate to devise this individually prescribed instructional plan. An IEP specifies the following:

- An assessment of the student's current level of performance
- Long- and short-term objectives
- Services or strategies to ensure the student's academic progress
- Schedules for implementing the plan
- Criteria for evaluating the plan's success

Teachers and other professionals work with parents to design an IEP that meets each student's individual learning needs.

A sample IEP is illustrated in Figure 5.4. It has three important features. First, the initials of all participants indicate that its development is a cooperative effort. Second, the information in sections 3–7 provides sufficient detail to guide the classroom teacher and special education personnel as they implement the plan; classroom teachers play an integral role in creating and implementing IEPs. Third, the mother's signature indicates that a parent was involved in developing the plan and agrees with its provisions.

An **individualized family service plan (IFSP)** provides the same type of planned care as an IEP but targets developmentally delayed preschool children. A product of PL 99-457, an IFSP provides for early intervention and care for children from birth to age 2. It differs from an IEP in two important ways (Heward, 2009). First, it targets the child's family and provides supplemental services to the family as well as the child. Second, it includes interventions and services from a variety of health and human services agencies in addition to education; these could include physical therapy as well as family training and counseling.

myeducationlab

To see an illustration of the process of constructing an IEP, go to the *Assignments and Activities* section of Topic 10: *Creating Productive Learning Environments* in the MyEducationLab for your course and complete the activity titled *Involving Parents in the Educational Process.*

INCLUSION AND NO CHILD LEFT BEHIND   As you saw in Chapter 1, the No Child Left Behind (NCLB) Act had a major influence on education. It also affected the education of students with exceptionalities. To clarify how NCLB would influence these students, the U.S. Department of Education issued regulations requiring students with exceptionalities to be tested as part of NCLB's comprehensive testing program (U.S. Department of Education, 2003b). Although states are allowed to create alternative tests and standards for these students, the test scores are used in determining whether a school has made adequate yearly progress.

Advocates of this testing requirement claim that teachers will expect more of students and work harder at teaching students with exceptionalities if they know these students will be tested (Samuels, 2006a). Critics question whether testing procedures developed for the general population can provide an accurate picture of learning for students with exceptionalities (Meek, 2006). NCLB was the signature educational initiative of the Bush administration; with a new administration in power, its future has become somewhat uncertain, and how potential changes will affect you remains to be seen.

Dimensions of Exceptionalities

Individualized family service plan (IFSP) A comprehensive service plan, similar to an IEP, that targets the families of young children (birth to 2 years) who are developmentally delayed.

More than 6 million students in the United States are enrolled in special education programs, two thirds of them for relatively minor problems (Heward, 2009). Approximately 14 percent of students in a typical school receive special education services; 78 percent of these are in a regular classroom for a significant portion of the school day (Kober, 2006).

Figure 5.4 Individualized Education Program (IEP)

INDIVIDUALIZED EDUCATION PROGRAM

Date _____3-2-09_____

(1) Student	(2) Committee	
		Initial
Name: Joe S.	Mrs. Wrens — Principal	Ɖ.ɑ.W.
School: Adams	Mrs. Snow — Regular Teacher	AS
Grade: 5	Mr. LaJoie — Counselor	ſℓℐ
Current Placement: Regular Class/Resource Room	Mr. Thomas — Resource Teacher	M.T.
	Mr. Ryan — School Psychologist	H.R.R.
	Mrs. S. — Parent	J.ℐ.
Date of Birth: 10-1-97 Age: 11-5	Joe S. — Student	Joe L. EP from _3-16-09_ to _3-16-10_

(3) Present Level of Educational Functioning	(4) Annual Goal Statements	(5) Instructional Objectives	(6) Objective Criteria and Evaluation
MATH Strengths 1. Can successfully compute addition and subtraction problems to two places with regrouping and zeros. 2. Knows 100 basic multiplication facts. Weaknesses 1. Frequently makes computational errors on problems with which he has had experience. 2. Does not complete seatwork. Key Math total score of 2.1 Grade Equivalent.	Joe will apply knowledge of regrouping in addition and renaming in subtraction to four-digit numbers.	1. When presented with 20 addition problems of 3-digit numbers requiring two renamings, the student will compute answers at a rate of one problem per minute and an accuracy of 90%. 2. When presented with 20 subtraction problems of 3-digit numbers requiring two renamings, the student will compute answers at the rate of one problem per minute with 90% accuracy. 3. When presented with 20 addition problems of 4-digit numbers requiring three renamings, the student will compute answers at a rate of one problem per minute and an accuracy of 90%. 4. When presented with 20 subtraction problems of 4-digit numbers requiring three renamings, the student will compute answers at a rate of one problem per minute with 90% accuracy.	Teacher-made tests (weekly) Teacher-made tests (weekly) Teacher-made tests (weekly)

(7) Educational Services to be provided

Services Required	Date initiated	Duration of Service	Individual Responsible for the Service
Regular reading-adapted	3-16-09	3-16-10	Reading Improvement Specialist and Special Education Teacher
Resource room	3-16-09	3-16-10	Special Education Teacher
Counselor consultant	3-16-09	3-16-10	Counselor
Monitoring diet and general health	3-16-09	3-16-10	School Health Nurse

Extent of time in the regular education program: 60% increasing to 80%
Justification of the educational placement:
It is felt that the structure of the resource room can best meet the goals stated for Joe, especially when coordinated with the regular classroom.
It is also felt that Joe could profit enormously from talking with a counselor. He needs someone with whom to talk and with whom he can share his feelings.

(8) I have had the opportunity to participate in the development of the Individualized Education Program.
    I agree with the Individualized Education Program   (✓)
    I disagree with the Individualized Education Program   ( )
Parent's Signature ___*mrs S.*___

Source: Adapted from *Developing and Implementing Individualized Education Programs* (3rd ed., pp. 308, 316) by B. B. Strickland & A. P. Turnbull, 1990, Upper Saddle River, NJ: Merrill/Prentice Hall.

Table 5.4	Number of Students Ages 6–21 Who Received Special Education Services Under the Federal Government's Disability Categories	
Disability Category	**Number**	**Percentage of Total**
Specific learning disabilities	2,816,361	47.2
Speech or language impairments	1,118,543	18.8
Mental retardation	570,643	9.6
Emotional disturbance	482,597	8.1
Other health impairments	449,093	7.5
Autism	140,473	2.3
Multiple disabilities	131,225	2.2
Hearing impairments	71,188	1.2
Orthopedic impairments	67,772	1.1
Developmental delay	65,878	1.1
Visual impairments	25,294	0.4
Traumatic brain injury	22,459	0.4
Deaf-blindness	1,603	<0.1
All disabilities	5,963,129	100.0

Source: U.S. Department of Education. (2004a). Individuals with Disabilities Education Act (IDEA) data (Table AA3). Washington, DC: Author. Available at http://www.ideadata.org/PartBdata.asp.

Federal legislation has created categories to identify students eligible for special education services, which educators use in developing programs to meet students' specific needs. The use of categories is controversial, however. Advocates argue that categories provide a common language for professionals and encourage specialized instruction that meets the specific needs of students (Heward, 2009). On the other hand, opponents claim that categories are arbitrary, that many differences exist within them, and that categorizing encourages educators to treat students as labels rather than as people. Despite the controversy, these categories are widely used, so they should be part of your professional knowledge base.

IDEA, the federal law describing the educational rights of students with disabilities discussed earlier in this chapter, lists 13 categories of disability. These are listed by order of frequency in Table 5.4.

This section addresses the fifth item in the *This I Believe* feature, "Intellectual disabilities are the most common forms of exceptionality that you are likely to encounter as a classroom teacher." This statement is false; the most common form of exceptionality found in classrooms is a learning disability.

This I BELIEVE

STUDENTS WHO ARE GIFTED AND TALENTED As a classroom teacher, you'll also encounter students who are gifted and talented. What is it like to be gifted or talented in a regular classroom? Here are the thoughts of one 9-year-old:

> Oh what a bore to sit and listen,
> To stuff we already know.
> Do everything we've done and done again,
> But we still must sit and listen.
> Over and over read one more page
> Oh bore, oh bore, oh bore.
> Sometimes I feel if we do one more page
> My head will explode with boreness rage
> I wish I could get up right there and march right out the door.
> (Delisle, 1984, p. 72)

Although we don't typically think of gifted and talented students as having exceptionalities, they often have learning needs not met by the regular education cur-

Table 5.5 Acceleration and Enrichment Options for Students Who Are Gifted and Talented	
Enrichment Options	**Acceleration Options**
1. Independent study and independent projects	1. Early admission to kindergarten and first grade
2. Learning centers	2. Grade skipping
3. Field trips	3. Subject skipping
4. Saturday and summer programs	4. Credit by exam
5. Simulations and games	5. College courses in high school
6. Small-group inquiry and investigations	6. Correspondence courses
7. Academic competitions	7. Early admission to college

riculum. Students who are **gifted and talented** are at the upper end of the ability continuum and need special services to reach their full potential. The National Center for Education Statistics (2005a) reports approximately 3 million students who are gifted and talented, slightly more than 6 percent of the total student population. At one time, the term *gifted* was used to identify these students, but the category has been enlarged to include both students who do well on intelligence tests and those who demonstrate above-average talents in a variety of areas such as math, creative writing, and music (G. Davis & Rimm, 2004).

Meeting the needs of students who are gifted and talented requires both early identification and instructional modifications. Conventional procedures often miss students who are gifted and talented because they rely heavily on standardized test scores and teacher nominations; as a result, females, low-SES students, and students from cultural minorities are typically underrepresented in these programs (Gootman & Gebelof, 2008; J. Lewis, DeCamp-Fritson, Ramage, McFarland, & Archwamety, 2007). To address this problem, experts recommend more flexible and less culturally dependent methods, such as creativity measures, tests of spatial ability, and peer and parent nominations in addition to teacher recommendations (G. Davis & Rimm, 2004).

As a regular classroom teacher, you may be responsible for adapting instruction for students who are gifted and talented, or students may attend special programs. These programs are typically based either on **acceleration**, which keeps the curriculum the same but allows students to move through it more quickly, or on **enrichment**, which provides richer and varied content through strategies that supplement usual grade-level work (Schiever & Maker, 2003). Table 5.5 lists different acceleration and enrichment options. Failure to address the needs of these students can result in gifted underachievers, with social and emotional problems linked to boredom and lack of motivation (Cross, 2005).

Students With Exceptionalities: Implications for Teachers

Because of inclusion, the classroom teacher now plays a central role in helping students with exceptionalities learn and develop to their full potential. This process begins with identification, an important first step in understanding and diagnosing learning problems. Following identification, classroom teachers collaborate with special educators and other support personnel to design and implement the IEP. Finally, and perhaps most importantly, classroom teachers adapt instruction to meet the learning needs of students with exceptionalities. Let's see how identification is key to the whole process.

IDENTIFYING STUDENTS WITH EXCEPTIONALITIES Classroom teachers are involved in identifying students with exceptionalities. In the past, information from teacher-made assessments as well as teachers' direct observations were typically compared

Gifted and talented Students at the upper end of the ability continuum who need special services to reach their full potential.

Acceleration A gifted and talented program that keeps the curriculum the same but allows students to move through it more quickly.

Enrichment A gifted and talented program that provides richer and varied content through strategies that supplement usual grade-level work.

with standardized test scores. A **discrepancy model** looked for differences between these factors:

1. Performance in the classroom and scores on standardized tests
2. Scores on intelligence and achievement tests
3. Intelligence test scores and classroom achievement
4. Subtests on either intelligence or achievement tests

Performance in one area, such as an intelligence test, should predict performance in others; when the two are inconsistent, a learning problem may be the cause.

Many experts became dissatisfied with the discrepancy model, arguing that it identifies a disability only after a problem surfaces, sometimes after several years of failure and frustration (Brown-Chidsey, 2007). Instead, they argue, educators need early screening measures, so they can prevent failure before it occurs. Critics also contend that the discrepancy model doesn't provide specific information about the nature of the learning problem or what should be done to correct it (Lose, 2008).

The **response to intervention (RTI) model of identification** addresses both of these problems. RTI typically begins at the start of the school year with pretesting designed to identify any potential learning problems early (Samuels, 2008, 2009c). As soon as a learning problem surfaces, the classroom teacher adapts instruction to meet the student's needs; common adaptations include small-group work, working with students while other students do seatwork, or one-on-one tutoring outside of regular school hours. Developing both skills, such as highlighting important vocabulary, and study strategies, such as using a dictionary, reading assignments aloud, and finding a quiet place to study that is free of distractions, is also emphasized. If the adaptations are unsuccessful, a learning exceptionality is possible. As teachers adapt their instruction, they also specify what works and what doesn't; this provides valuable information for later interventions.

COLLABORATION   A second major role for classroom teachers working with students with exceptionalities is collaboration. Initially, inclusion meant additional services to help students with exceptionalities function in regular school settings (Turnbull, Turnbull, & Wehmeyer, 2010), but gradually, the concept of collaboration replaced this additive approach. **Collaboration** involves communication and decision making among educational professionals to create an optimal learning environment for students with exceptionalities (Karten, 2005). In collaboration, special and regular education teachers work closely to ensure that learning experiences are integrated into the regular classroom curriculum. For example, rather than pulling a student with special needs out of the classroom for supplementary instruction in math, a special education teacher coordinates instruction with the regular classroom teacher and then works with the student in the regular classroom on tasks linked to the standard math curriculum, as the following example illustrates:

> *Sharon Snow noticed that Joey Sanchez was having difficulties with three-digit addition problems. After checking the IEP she had helped design in collaboration with the special education team (see Figure 5.4), she found that mastering these math problems was one of Joey's goals. She met with Ken Thomas, the resource teacher, after school, and examined some recent work samples from Joey's math homework and quizzes. They discovered he was having trouble with problems that involved place value and carrying values over to the next column, such as the following:*
>
> $$345$$
> $$+296$$
>
> *During the next week, when Sharon's class was working on similar problems, Ken stopped by Joey's desk to help him. At first, they went to the back of the room, and Ken reviewed place values for him. When Ken thought Joey understood how place value af-*

Go to the *IRIS Center Resources* section of Topic 2: *Student Diversity* in the MyEducationLab for your course and explore the module titled *RTI (Part 1): An Overview.*

Discrepancy model of identification A method of identifying students with exceptionalities that focuses on differences between classroom performance and tests, achievement and intelligence tests, or subtests within tests.

Response to intervention (RTI) model of identification A method of identifying a learning disability that focuses on the specific classroom instructional adaptations and their success.

Collaboration Communication and decision making among educational professionals to create an optimal learning environment for students with exceptionalities.

fected the addition problems, he sent him back to his seat to work on the next few problems. Both Sharon and Ken monitored Joey's progress carefully so he wouldn't get discouraged. When the number of problems seemed overwhelming to Joey, Ken broke them down into smaller blocks of five, providing feedback and encouragement after each block. Slowly, Joey started to catch on and gained confidence. Collaboration had worked.

Through collaboration, the classroom teacher and the special educator combined their efforts to make sure that Joey succeeded in his classroom work.

How will collaboration change your role as a classroom teacher? You are virtually certain to have students with exceptionalities in your classroom, and you'll be expected to do the following:

- Aid in the process of identifying students with exceptionalities.
- Collaborate in the creation of IEPs that will help students with exceptionalities succeed in the classroom.
- Adapt your instruction to meet the needs of students with exceptionalities, actively seeking out the help of special educators in the process.
- Maintain communication with parents, school administrators, and special educators about the progress of students in your classroom who have special needs.

Unquestionably, having learners with exceptionalities in your classroom will make your teaching more demanding, but helping a student with a disability adapt and even thrive can be one of the most rewarding experiences you'll have as a teacher.

MODIFYING INSTRUCTION TO MEET STUDENTS' NEEDS   Research indicates that instruction that is effective with students in general is also effective with students having exceptionalities (Tomlinson, 2006; Vaughn & Bos, 2006). "In general, the classroom management and instruction approaches that are effective with special students tend to be the same ones that are effective with other students" (Good & Brophy, 2008, p. 223).

You will need to provide additional support, however, to help students overcome a history of failure and frustration and to convince them that renewed effort

Go to the *IRIS Center Resources* section of Topic 2: *Student Diversity* in the MyEducationLab for your course and explore the module titled *Collaborating with Families*.

Inclusive classrooms require that teachers assist in identifying students with exceptionalities and adapt instruction to meet students' needs.

Employing Technology to Support Learners With Disabilities

Julio is partially deaf, barely able to use a hearing aid to understand speech. Kerry Tanner, his seventh-grade science teacher, works closely with the special education instructor assigned to her classroom to help Julio. Seated near the front of the room to facilitate lipreading, Julio takes notes on a laptop computer during teacher presentations. Other students take turns sharing their notes with him so he can compare and fill in gaps. He especially likes to communicate with other students on the Internet, because this levels the communication playing field. When he views video clips on his computer, he uses a special device with earphones to increase the volume.

Jaleena is partially sighted, with a visual acuity of less than 20/80, even with corrective lenses. Despite this disability, she is doing well in her fourth-grade class. Terrence Banks, Jaleena's teacher, has placed her in the front of the room so that she can better see the chalkboard and overhead projector and has assigned students to work with her on her projects. Using a magnifying device, she can read most written material, but the computer is giving her special problems: The small letters and punctuation on websites and other information make it difficult for her to use the computer as an information source. Terrence works with the special education consultant in his district to get a monitor that magnifies the display. He knows it's a success when he sees Jaleena quietly working alone at her computer on the report due next Friday.*

Assistive technology, a set of adaptive tools that support students with disabilities in learning activities and daily life tasks, can be a powerful tool for students with exceptionalities. These assistive tools are required by federal law under the Individuals with Disabilities Education Act (IDEA) and include motorized chairs, remote control devices that turn machines on and off with the nod of the head or other muscle action, and machines that amplify sights and sounds (Heward, 2009; J. Hopkins, 2006).

Probably the most widespread use of assistive technology is in the area of computer adaptations. Let's look at them.

ADAPTATIONS TO COMPUTER INPUT DEVICES

To use computers, students must be able to input their words and ideas; however, this can be difficult for those with visual or other physical disabilities that impede standard keyboarding. Enhancing the keyboard, such as making it larger and easier to see, arranging the letters alphabetically to make them easier to find, or using pictures for nonreaders are adaptations that accommodate these disabilities. AlphaSmart, one

---

will work. For instance, while the majority of the class is completing a seatwork assignment, effective teachers work with an individual student or a small group; this is how Sharon and Ken helped Joey with his math skills. Peer tutoring has also been used effectively, providing benefit to both the tutor and the person receiving the tutoring; home-based tutoring programs that involve parents can also be effective (Vaughn & Bos, 2006).

Here are some additional instructional modifications (Turnbull et al., 2010):

- Teaching in small steps and providing detailed feedback on homework
- Involving students with exceptionalities by calling on them as often as other students in your classes
- Carefully modeling solutions to problems and other assignments
- Providing outlines, hierarchies, charts, and other forms of organization for the content you're teaching
- Increasing the amount of time available for tests and quizzes
- Utilizing available technology
- Teaching learning strategies

Assistive technology A set of adaptive tools that support students with disabilities in learning activities and daily life tasks.

The last item deserves further elaboration. Strategy training is one of the most promising approaches for helping students with learning problems. For example, in applying

widely used program, helps developing writers by providing spell-check and word-prediction scaffolding (Fine, 2002): When a student hesitates to finish a word, the computer, based on the first few letters, then either completes the word or offers a menu of suggestions, freeing students to concentrate on ideas and text organization.

Additional adaptations bypass the keyboard altogether. For example, speech/voice-recognition software translates speech into text on the computer screen (Silver-Pacuilla & Fleischman, 2006). These systems can be invaluable for students with physical disabilities that affect hand and finger movement. Other adaptations use switches activated by a body movement, such as a head nod, to interact with the computer. Touch screens also allow students to go directly to the monitor to make responses.

Research also indicates that students with learning disabilities encounter difficulties translating ideas into written words (Hasselbring & Bausch,

2005/2006; Quinlan, 2004). Speech-recognition technology eases this cognitive bottleneck by bypassing the keyboard, helping to produce initial drafts that are longer, with fewer errors.

ADAPTATIONS TO OUTPUT DEVICES

Adaptations to computer output devices also exist. For example, the size of the display can be increased with a special large-screen monitor, such as the one Jaleena used, or with a magnification device. For students who are blind, speech synthesizers read words and translate them into sounds. In addition, special printers can convert text into Braille and Braille into text.

Diversity in Your Classroom

These technologies are important because they prevent disabilities from becoming obstacles to learning. Their importance to students with exceptionalities is likely to increase as technology becomes a more integral part of classroom instruction.

Students will be naturally curious when you introduce any of these new technologies into your classroom. Use this as an opportunity to discuss the whole topic of exceptionalities: that everyone is different, with unique strengths and abilities, and that knowing these allows us to make the most out of what each of us possesses.

QUESTIONS TO CONSIDER

1. What is one potential downside to the use of assistive technology in the classroom? What can teachers do to minimize this potential problem?
2. Would students who are gifted and talented ever benefit from assistive technology? Why or why not?

myeducationlab To respond to these questions online, explore this topic further, and receive feedback, go to the *Book Specific Resources* section in the MyEducationLab for your course, select your text, and then select *Exploring Diversity* for Chapter 5.

---

a strategy to understand the content of a chapter, one middle school student with a learning disability in reading first looked at the chapter outline to see how the chapter was organized, and then he referred to the outline as he read the chapter. He then read the chapter to himself aloud, stopping every few paragraphs to summarize to himself what he had just read. When he was unable to summarize the information, he reread the section.

Students with learning difficulties often approach tasks passively or use the same strategy for all objectives (Vaughn & Bos, 2006). Because he was attempting to comprehend the content of the chapter, this student used a strategy different than one he might use for learning to spell a list of words, for example. Students with learning problems can learn to use strategies, but they need to be taught the strategies explicitly (Carnine, Silbert, Kame'enui, Tarver, & Jongjohann, 2006). Teacher modeling and explanation, together with opportunities for practice and feedback, are essential.

In the *Explore Diversity* feature that begins on page 152, we explore different ways to use technology to assist students with exceptionalities.

Diversity: The Big Picture

Chapters 3, 4, and 5 describe important dimensions of learner diversity that will influence your life as a teacher (see Figure 5.5, Dimensions of Diversity). Chapter 3 focuses on societal factors such as family structures, socioeconomic factors, and challenges to our

Figure 5.5 Dimensions of Diversity

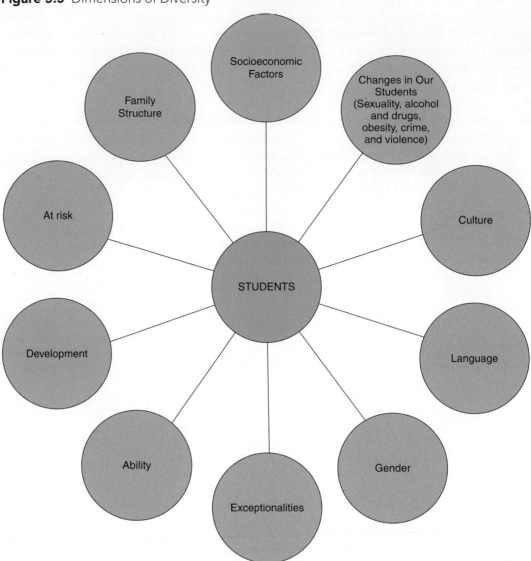

students, including early sexuality, alcohol and drugs, obesity, and crime and violence. At-risk students are targeted by many of these potentially damaging factors. Chapter 4 examines cultural and linguistic diversity and how gender influences school success. In this chapter, we look at developmental and ability differences and see how exceptionalities influence the lives of both students and teachers.

These different dimensions of diversity offer both opportunities and challenges for students and teachers. For students, diversity provides opportunities to learn about themselves as they interact with different students. Like all of us, students tend to think that the whole world is basically like them; learning to learn with and work with different kinds of students helps them understand not only their own uniqueness but also how other students are similar to and different from them. For teachers, diversity offers opportunities for professional and personal growth. Although more challenging than homogeneous classrooms, diverse settings challenge teachers to examine their own beliefs about effective teaching and learning practices. Dealing with diverse students on an individual level also helps teachers develop as human beings, broadening their understanding of themselves and what it means to be human.

■ ■ ■ ■ CHECK YOUR UNDERSTANDING

3.1 Explain the legal foundation of special education.

3.2 What are the major categories of exceptionalities found in classrooms?

3.3 What roles do classroom teachers play in helping students with exceptionalities succeed in their classrooms?

For feedback on these exercises, go to the appendix, *Check Your Understanding*, located in the back of this text.

Now it's your turn to apply the information in this chapter to a problem or dilemma facing many prospective teachers. Read the following case and answer the question that follows.

Decision Making • Defining Yourself as a Professional

Development Implications for Teachers

Several middle school teachers are discussing their classrooms during their lunch break. Beth Hansen, a first-year social studies teacher, puts down her sandwich and asks the other teachers, "I don't know how you do it. Where do you find time for everything? Sometimes I feel like there just aren't enough minutes in the day. Management-wise, we spend time talking about making our classrooms a better place to learn. Instructionally, I try to involve students in learning activities, but group work takes so much time. Then I try to save some extra time at the end of the class to work with struggling students, but I never seem to have enough time. What am I doing wrong?"

"I don't have that problem," Jim Clancy, a 15-year veteran, replies. "In terms of management, I lay down the rules on the first day of class. In essence, it's my way or the highway. Instructionally, I lecture to them. Time-wise, it's the most efficient way of teaching, and they've got to learn how to take lecture notes sooner or later. In my class, it's going to be sooner. We aren't here to baby our students. In fact, when we do, I believe we do them a disservice. They've got to learn sometime. The same applies to our special ed kids. Sometimes I think they don't need more help, just higher expectations and more responsibility."

How would you respond to Jim?

5 MEETING YOUR LEARNING OBJECTIVES

1. Explain how developmental differences influence students as well as teachers.

   • *Development* refers to the systematic changes that occur in people as they progress through life and consists of three major dimensions: cognitive, moral, and personal and social.

   • These dimensions of development are similar in that they all depend on experiences, particularly with parents, teachers, other adults, and peers. In addition, they all change over time, and each dimension of development influences achievement and satisfaction in school as well as success in later life.

- *Cognitive development* describes changes in the ways students think about the world; *moral development* deals with students' changing conceptions of right and wrong; *personal development* refers to developments in individuals' personalities and their ability to manage their emotions; *social development* refers to changes over time in the ways we relate to others.

2. Explain differences in current definitions of intelligence, and describe how schools respond to ability differences.

- Experts describe intelligence as having three components: the capacity to acquire knowledge, the ability to think and reason in the abstract, and the ability to solve problems.

- Experts at one time believed that intelligence was composed of a single trait. A differing view of intelligence, based on Howard Gardner's work, suggests that it is composed of eight relatively independent dimensions.

- Ability grouping and tracking, which place students of similar ability into homogeneous groups or academic tracks, are schools' most common response to differences in students' ability.

- Learning styles emphasize differences in the ways students prefer to learn in the classroom. The concept of learning styles reminds us that all students learn differently; effective teachers are sensitive to these differences, adapt their teaching accordingly, and help students become metacognitively aware of their own learning styles.

3. Explain how schools have changed the ways they help students with exceptionalities.

- The legal foundation for special education was established in 1975 with the passage of the Individuals with Disabilities Education Act. IDEA, combined with later amendments, mandates a free appropriate education, protection from discrimination in testing, parental involvement, a learning environment that doesn't restrict learners, and an individualized program of study for learners with exceptionalities.

- Students with exceptionalities require extra help to reach their full potential. The majority of students with exceptionalities fall into four major categories: learning disabilities, communication disorders, intellectual disabilities, and behavior disorders. A substantial number of students with exceptionalities are also gifted and talented.

- Regular classroom teachers collaborate with other professionals to provide individualized educational services to students with exceptionalities. This collaboration begins with helping to identify students with exceptionalities, continues during the creation of IEPs, and extends into the classroom, where teachers adapt their instruction to meet the learning needs of these students. Throughout this process, the teacher maintains continual communication with parents, school administrators, and other school professionals.

- Effective teachers use the same basic instructional strategies that work with all students, but they also provide additional support for students with exceptionalities. The emphasis is on helping students with exceptionalities succeed on their academic tasks. Effective teachers use modeling, provide peer and one-on-one tutoring, break large tasks into smaller ones, provide visual aids, use assistive technology, and teach students how to utilize learning strategies.

IMPORTANT CONCEPTS

ability grouping (p. 140)
acceleration (p. 149)
assistive technology (p. 152)
autonomous morality (p. 129)
between-class ability grouping (p. 140)
cognitive development (p. 127)
collaboration (p. 150)
development (p. 126)
disabilities (p. 144)
discrepancy model of identification
  (p. 150)
enrichment (p. 149)
external morality (p. 129)
gifted and talented (p. 149)
giftedness (p. 144)
grade retention (p. 137)
inclusion (p. 145)
individualized education program (IEP)
  (p. 145)

individualized family service plan (IFSP)
  (p. 146)
intelligence (p. 139)
learning style (p. 141)
mainstreaming (p. 145)
metacognition (p. 143)
moral development (p. 129)
multiple intelligences (p. 139)
parenting style (p. 133)
personal development (p. 131)
Piaget's Cognitive Developmental Theory
  (p. 129)
response to intervention (RTI) model of
  identification (p. 150)
social development (p. 132)
special education (p. 144)
students with exceptionalities (p. 144)
tracking (p. 140)
within-class ability grouping (p. 140)

DISCUSSION QUESTIONS

1. Which dimension of development—cognitive, moral, or personal and social—is most important for school success? For success in later life? For happiness in life?

2. Do you believe that moral development should be promoted in schools, or should morals be taught primarily in the home or in churches? Explain why you believe as you do.

3. Think about the dimensions of intelligence identified by experts: a) abstract thinking and reasoning, b) problem-solving ability, and c) capacity to acquire knowledge. Which is most important in today's world? least important? Why?

4. How do learning styles relate to Gardner's multiple intelligences? Do you think these differences are influenced primarily by genetics or by the environment? Explain.

5. What implications does Gardner's theory of multiple intelligences have for teachers at different grade levels and in different content areas? In answering this question, be sure to relate your answer to the grade level and content area(s) in which you plan to teach.

6. Experts debate whether teachers should adjust instruction to match student learning styles or teach students to broaden their learning repertoires. Which approach is more desirable?

7. What are the advantages and disadvantages of full-time inclusion in the regular education classroom? Should it be used with all students with exceptionalities?

myeducationlab

Now go to Topic 2: *Student Diversity* in the MyEducationLab (www.myeducationlab.com) for your course, where you can:

- Find learning outcomes for *Student Diversity* along with the national standards that connect to these outcomes.

- Complete *Assignments and Activities* that can help you more deeply understand the chapter content.

- Apply and practice your understanding of the core teaching skills identified in the chapter with the *Building Teaching Skills and Dispositions* learning units.

- Check your comprehension on the content covered in the chapter by going to the *Study Plan* in the *Book Specific Resources* section for your text. Here you will be able to take a chapter quiz, receive feedback on your answers, and then access *Review, Practice, and Enrichment* activities to enhance your understanding of chapter content.

Develop Your Professional Portfolio

To further apply your understanding of chapter content and address the INTASC standards, go to the *Book Specific Resources* section in the MyEducationLab for your course, select your text, then select this chapter's *Portfolio Activities*.

PART 3 Foundations

"I teach to greet children at the door each morning, to create those magical moments that bring childhood alive and joyous. I teach so that each child can have an experience of what the world should be like. I teach because I believe in their future; I believe in a future that's rich in promise. I teach because I believe in them."

EILEEN JOHNSON, 2008 Teacher of the Year, Wyoming

Education in the United States

Its Historical Roots

LEARNING OBJECTIVES

After you have completed your study of this chapter, you should be able to:

1. **Explain how the diversity of the original colonies shaped our educational system, and describe the role of religion in colonial schools.** INTASC Standard 9, Teacher Professionalism

2. **Explain how the early national period influenced education in this country.** INTASC Standard 9, Teacher Professionalism

3. **Explain how the common school movement influenced education in our country today.** INTASC Standard 9, Teacher Professionalism

4. **Describe the historical roots of contemporary secondary schools.** INTASC Standard 9, Teacher Professionalism

5. **Identify similarities and differences in minority groups' struggles for educational equality.** INTASC Standard 9, Teacher Professionalism

6. **Explain how schools became instruments for national purpose during the modern era.** INTASC Standard 9, Teacher Professionalism

Education in our country is unique. The way we organize schools, the content we teach, and our teaching methods differ from those in other countries. The reasons for these differences lie in the historical roots of our education system. As you read the following case study, think about the ways that history has affected the schools in which you'll teach.

"I've about had it," Dave Carlisle, a first-year teacher at Westmont Middle School, says as he drops into a chair in the teachers' lounge.

"Having a bad day?" Monica Henderson, one of Dave's colleagues, asks.

"Bad day. You could say that," Dave replies. "We had lunch money missing again today. And I'm pretty sure there was cheating on the test I gave last week. They think cheating is fine if they can get away with it. It's almost like these kids have no ideas about right and wrong. I sometimes think they could use some religion."

"We already tried that," Monica replies, looking up from the papers she is grading.

"When?" Dave asks.

"Back in our country's history, and often since then."

"Oh, no. Not more of that history stuff. . . . What's that class you're taking?"

"Actually, it's interesting. I understand much better why our schools are the way they are, and why some of the issues politicians fight about still exist. It's really good," Monica replies with a smile.

"Yeah, 'Those that don't know history are destined to repeat it,'" Dave says, rolling his eyes, "but how will it help me with my cheating and stealing problems?"

Studying our country's educational history may not give Dave a direct answer to his questions, but it can help you understand today's schools. For example, why is the issue of teaching creationism versus evolution in science classes such a political hot potato? Why does our country provide a free public education for all students? And why is education considered the responsibility of the states instead of the federal government? We address these and other questions in this chapter, but before you begin your study, please respond to the items in the *This I Believe* box on the next page.

The history of American education is often traced back to 1607, when the Jamestown Colony was founded. This is where we begin.

THE COLONIAL PERIOD (1607–1775)

Think again about Dave's lament: "We had lunch money missing again today. And I'm pretty sure there was cheating on the test I gave last week. They think cheating is fine if they can get away with it. It's almost like these kids have no ideas about right and wrong." His comment relates to the issue of teaching morals in today's schools. Educators generally agree that some education with respect to moral development is needed, but they disagree about the form it should take. Some advocate linking it to religious values that are normally taught in homes and churches, but others argue that this religious foundation is neither desirable nor possible, given the religious diversity in the United States (Gollnick & Chinn, 2009). The roots of this controversy can be traced back to the colonial period of education in America.

Parents who believe schools should teach values and emphasize student discipline often send their children to private, church-supported schools. Should these schools receive federal assistance—money supported by general tax revenues? Proponents argue that these schools have as much right to federal education monies as do other schools; opponents claim that federal support of parochial schools violates the Constitution. Controversies surrounding religious schools in our country are also rooted in the colonial period.

For each item, circle the number that best represents your thinking. Use the following scale as a guide.
4 = I strongly believe the statement is true.
3 = I believe the statement is true.
2 = I believe the statement is false.
1 = I strongly believe the statement is false.

1. The Constitution of the United States requires that religion and public schooling be kept separate from each other.

   1   2   3   4

2. A free public education for all students has historically been a cornerstone of education in the United States.

   1   2   3   4

3. The American high school has historically attempted to meet the needs of all students.

   1   2   3   4

4. With the end of slavery in this country, cultural and ethnic minorities were welcomed into U.S. schools.

   1   2   3   4

5. In recent times, the federal government has viewed the schools as an instrument to achieve national goals.

   1   2   3   4

PEARSON myeducationlab To download and complete this form, go to the *Book Specific Resources* section in the MyEducationLab for your course, select your text, and then select *This I Believe* for Chapter 6.

This I BELIEVE!

Religion and schools are closely linked in many states. Some public schools, for example, want to allow prayer in classrooms, hold religious assemblies, and give students Bibles (Fischer, Schimmel, & Stellman, 2006; LaMorte, 2005). As with support for religious schools, critics claim these practices violate the Constitution, but proponents counter that this emphasis promotes positive values. The issue is repeatedly debated in courts and reflects an ongoing controversy about the proper role of religion in public education (Fischer et al., 2006). This tension has its beginnings in the colonial period.

Now, let's look at the Jamestown Colony and how it's related to these issues. Jamestown was the first permanent English settlement in North America, and religion was an integral part of the colony from its conception. King James of England, after whom the colony was named, wanted to establish a

Religion was a major reason early settlers came to America and was a major force in shaping colonial schools.

foothold for Protestantism in the New World, for both spiritual and political reasons. The English believed it was their duty to spread the gospel and convert the Native Americans they encountered to Protestant Christianity, and King James also recognized the importance of establishing English colonies as a counter to the energetic colonizing efforts of the Spanish, who were zealously converting native people in their colonies to Roman Catholicism (Glasson, 2007). Colonial schools were formed in response to this felt need, and they laid the foundation for many of the controversies that exist today.

As would be expected, the schools the settlers created reflected the values and beliefs derived from their European roots. As a result, schooling in colonial America had the same class and gender distinctions common in Europe at the time. For example, formal education was usually reserved for wealthy White males and ignored females and those less wealthy. Differences in the colonies existed, however; we examine them next.

Differences in Colonies

After Jamestown was settled, large numbers of people from Europe came to the New World, and although the majority were English speaking, others came from a number of countries and settled in each of the 13 colonies. They had some similarities, such as being linked to Europe and having a desire for better lives, but geography, economics, and the reasons the colonists came to America resulted in regional differences. Let's look at them.

THE SOUTHERN COLONIES   Life in the Southern colonies—Maryland, Virginia, the Carolinas, and Georgia—revolved around agriculture, much of which occurred on large plantations where African slaves and indentured servants worked land owned by wealthy landlords. Poor White settlers worked small farms on the margins, barely scratching out an existence.

Life for most people in the colonial South was hard, and formal education was a luxury reserved for the wealthy (Pulliam & Van Patten, 2007). Private tutors often lived on plantations, or parents pooled their resources to hire a tutor to teach the children of several families. Private schools sponsored by the Church of England—the religion of the original Jamestown settlement—and boarding schools for the wealthy sprang up in larger Southern cities, such as Charleston and Williamsburg. The English tradition of education for the wealthy few made an easy leap over the Atlantic to the Southern colonies.

THE MIDDLE COLONIES   The middle colonies—New York, Rhode Island, New Jersey, Delaware, and Pennsylvania—were more diverse than the Southern colonies. For example, substantial pockets of Dutch in New York, Swedes in Delaware, and Germans in Pennsylvania brought their native cultures to the New World. As a result, middle colonists belonged to a number of religious groups, such as Dutch Reformists, Quakers, Lutherans, Baptists, Roman Catholics, and Jews (Pulliam & Van Patten, 2007). Because religious freedom was an important reason for coming to America, and because religion played a central role in people's lives, it was difficult to create schools that satisfied everyone.

In response to this diversity, families in the middle colonies created parochial schools, schools that included the study of religion in addition to the three R's. Students learned in their native languages, and local religious beliefs, such as the study of the Lutheran religion in German schools, were an integral part of the curriculum.

THE NEW ENGLAND COLONIES   We've all heard of maxims, such as "Idle minds are the Devil's workshop" and "Spare the rod and spoil the child," as well as the three R's—reading, 'riting, and 'rithmetic. Let's see where they came from.

The New England colonies—Massachusetts, Connecticut, and New Hampshire—differed from the other colonies in two important ways. First, they were culturally and religiously homogeneous, which made consensus about school goals easier to achieve. Second, industry and commerce encouraged the clustering of people into towns, which allowed the formation of common schools.

For example, in Massachusetts, where the Puritans, followers of John Calvin, settled, religion played a huge role in people's lives. The Puritans came to America because of conflicts with the Church of England, which they believed had grown too liberal and tolerant of "immoral practices." Puritans believed that humans were inherently evil, having fallen when Adam and Eve committed original sin. They advocated a "purity" of worship and doctrine, hence the name "Puritan," and education was viewed as the vehicle for helping people follow God's commandments and resist the devil's temptations (Morone, 2003). By learning to read and write, people gained access to God's word through the

Bible. Education was important because it made people more righteous, industrious, resourceful, and thrifty.

The Puritans' views shaped the schools they created. They saw children as savage and primitive, requiring education (and religion) to become civilized and God-fearing. Puritans viewed play as idleness and considered children's talk to be prattle, and they commonly used corporal punishment, such as beating students with switches or forcing them to kneel on hard pebbles, as punishment for unacceptable behavior. This is the source of ideas such as "Spare the rod and spoil the child."

Religion also influenced both what was taught (the curriculum) and how it was taught (instruction). For the Puritans, the curriculum was composed of four R's—reading, writing, arithmetic, and religion—and instruction focused on memorization and recitation. Teachers expected children to sit quietly for long periods of time and discouraged questions and opinions. They had no formal professional preparation, and curriculum materials were virtually nonexistent.

Paradoxically, a landmark piece of legislation, the Massachusetts Act of 1647, also known as the **Old Deluder Satan Act**, arose from this grim educational landscape. The law was designed to produce scripture-literate citizens who would thwart Satan's trickery, and it required every town of 50 or more households to hire a teacher of reading and writing. The historical significance of this act is enormous, because it provided the legal foundation for public support of education: It gave birth to the idea that the public good was enhanced by public education, and it became a cornerstone of education in our country.

European Crosscurrents

Schools in the colonies focused on religion and emphasized memorization and recitation, but change was occurring in Europe and gradually making its way across the Atlantic. Prominent European philosophers were changing the way people thought about schools, teachers, and children. Although their ideas came from different places, all involved a more humane, child-centered, and practical view of education. These philosophers are important because they planted the seeds of educational change that would fundamentally alter the education of students in the United States.

John Amos Comenius (1592–1670; Czech philosopher) questioned the effectiveness of memorization and recitation, emphasizing instead the importance of basing teaching on children's interests and needs.

John Locke (1632–1704; English philosopher) emphasized the importance of firsthand experiences in helping children learn about the world.

Jean-Jacques Rousseau (1712–1778; French philosopher) viewed children as innately good and argued that teachers should provide children with opportunities for exploration and experimentation.

Johann Pestalozzi (1746–1827; Swiss philosopher) criticized authoritarian educational practices that stifled students' playfulness and natural curiosity and recommended that teachers use concrete experiences to help children learn.

The Legacy of the Colonial Period

The colonial period shaped American education in three important ways. First, it was the source of inequality in American schools: With few exceptions, poor Whites, females, and minorities such as Native Americans and African Americans were excluded from schools (Spring, 2005). William Berkeley, the aristocratic governor of Virginia, supported this exclusion, and in 1671 railed against both free public education and access to books:

"I thank God, there are no free schools nor printing, and I hope we shall not have them these hundred years, for learning has brought disobedience, and heresy, and

Old Deluder Satan Act A landmark piece of legislation designed to produce scripture-literate citizens who would thwart Satan's trickery.

sects into the world, and printing has divulged them, and libels against the best government. God keep us from them both." (Pulliam & Van Patten, 2007, p. 88)

European ideas of class structure and privilege didn't die easily in the New World. Given attitudes such as these, it's easy to see why equality of educational opportunity wasn't a legal reality until the mid-20th century, and some critics argue that today's schools are still racist and sexist (Spring, 2005).

Second, although education was a privilege reserved for wealthy males, with the passage of the Old Deluder Satan Act, the colonial period also laid the foundation for public support of education and local control of schools, two principles shaping education in our country today.

Third, and perhaps most significantly, the relationship between religion and schooling, so dominant in the colonial period, helps us understand why religion continues to be an important and contentious issue in education today.

■ ■ ■ ■ CHECK YOUR UNDERSTANDING

1.1 How did the diversity of the original colonies shape the educational system in the United States?

1.2 What role did religion play in colonial schools? What are the implications of this role for contemporary schools?

1.3 Explain why the Old Deluder Satan Act of Massachusetts was important for the development of our American educational system.

For feedback, go to the appendix, *Check Your Understanding*, located in the back of this text.

THE EARLY NATIONAL PERIOD (1775–1820)

Teresa Sanchez moved with her family from a large urban center in the Northeast to a sprawling city in the South. Although the teenager encounters changes in climate and lifestyle, she finds her new high school surprisingly similar to the one she had previously attended. The buildings and their physical layout are similar, with long hallways lined with lockers and interspersed with classrooms. Even the central office seems the same, and the guidance counselor who works with her assures her that she won't lose credits because of the move.

But there are differences. Teresa rides a district school bus instead of using public transportation. The students, although friendly, talk differently, and their interests differ from those of her friends back home. And the textbooks she receives, although covering the same basic material, do so in different ways.

Her mother, an elementary teacher, also notices both similarities and differences. She is hired almost immediately, but is told that her teaching certificate is only temporary and that she'll have to take additional course work for it to become permanent. The textbooks she is given are different from the ones she had previously used, but the principal's emphasis on testing at the end of the year isn't. Some things never change.

At first glance, the United States appears homogeneous. A McDonald's in California looks much like one in Ohio, for example, and television programs, movies, and music across the country are similar. However, many regional and state differences exist (Gollnick & Chinn, 2009).

The same paradox occurs in education. Although schools across the country appear similar, a closer look reveals important regional and state differences. For example, students in Texas study Texas state history and take specially constructed tests to determine grade advancement and even graduation, and students in other states study their own history and take their own state-specific graduation tests (Feller, 2006). Education to assist English language learners (ELLs) exists in all states, but the form of this assistance varies considerably (Hinkel, 2005). Why do these differences exist? Some answers can be found in the early national period of our country.

Before 1775, the United States was a loose collection of separate colonies that looked mostly to Europe for trade and ideas. During the 45 years from 1775 to 1820, however, the separate colonies became the United States of America, and this country shaped its future through the Constitution and the Bill of Rights, as you see in the next section.

The Constitution Shapes Education

The U.S. Constitution, written in 1787 and adopted in 1789, played a major role in shaping the educational system we have today. It has had 27 amendments, the first 10 of which are known as our Bill of Rights. Because of the religious diversity that existed in the colonies, the "establishment clause" of the First Amendment prohibited the government from passing legislation to establish any one official religion over another. This created the principle widely known as *separation of church and state.*

Considering the importance of religion in the colonies, it's easy to see how the principle of separation of church and state has led to controversies about religion that continue to exist today. Questions such as the following are common:

- Should prayer be allowed in schools?
- Should federal money be used to provide instruction in religious schools?
- What role should religion play in character education?

Severing the federal government's ties between religion and education also raised another question: Who should be responsible for organizing and managing education in our new country? Establishing a national education system was one suggestion. Proponents argued that a national system would best meet the country's growing agricultural, industrial, and commercial needs. Opponents cited the monolithic and unresponsive systems in Europe. Opponents also argued that the beginnings of viable local and state systems, such as those in Massachusetts, already existed; why create another level of bureaucracy and control when it wasn't needed?

The Constitution's framers sidestepped the issue with the Tenth Amendment, which said that areas not explicitly assigned to the federal government would be the responsibility of each state. This amendment was important for two reasons: First, it implicitly removed the federal government from a central role in running and operating schools, and second, it passed this responsibility on to the individual states.

To support states' efforts, Congress passed the Land Ordinance of 1785 (Brimley & Garfield, 2008). At that time, the United States Congress didn't have the power to directly tax American citizens, so the Land Ordinance was designed to raise money through the sale of land in the territories west of the original colonies that were acquired from Britain at the end of the Revolutionary War. It specified that land was to be divided into townships consisting of 36 one-square-mile sections, with the income from one section reserved for support of public education. Although not directly involved in governing or operating schools, the federal government provided material support for schools and education, a tradition that persists to this day. With respect to education, the lines of responsibility between state and federal governments were already being blurred.

The Legacy of the Early National Period

The early national period shaped the schools of the future, and planted the seeds of controversies to come, in three important ways. First, it established the principle of separation of church and state. Second, legislators removed control of education from the federal government and gave it to the states. Third, with the passage of the Land Ordinance of 1785, the federal government established a role for itself in public education.

The influence of these actions is still felt today. For example, courts have repeatedly upheld the principle of separation of church and state, and individual states and local school districts make specific decisions about school and classroom policies. Nevertheless, the federal government plays an important role in education: Public schools receive federal funding and must adhere to federal laws, and the federal government continues to use our schools to achieve national goals. When the economy sputters, for example, or when significant portions of the school-age population underachieve, the federal government steps in. The No Child Left Behind (NCLB) Act of 2001 is one example: The law required each state to develop a comprehensive accountability plan to ensure that all students acquire basic skills in reading, math, and science.

This section addresses the first item in our *This I Believe* feature at the beginning of the chapter, "The Constitution of the United States requires that religion and public schooling be kept separate from each other." This statement is essentially true: The framers of our Constitution wanted to avoid problems associated with governments—federal, state, or local—caused by establishing an official religion. It's difficult to keep the two completely apart, however, as you'll see at different points in the text.

■■■■■ CHECK YOUR UNDERSTANDING

2.1   Explain how the early national period influenced education in this country.

2.2   What is the Tenth Amendment to the Constitution? Why is it important for education today?

2.3   What was the historical significance of the Land Ordinance of 1785?

For feedback, go to the appendix, *Check Your Understanding*, located in the back of this text.

THE COMMON SCHOOL MOVEMENT: THE RISE OF STATE SUPPORT FOR PUBLIC EDUCATION (1820–1865)

Many of you reading this text will become teachers of elementary students ■ ■ ■ and work in public schools. Others of you will work in middle or high schools.

Think about these schools for a moment. First, the students you'll teach won't be charged for their schooling and will be required by law to be there; virtually all states require students to attend school until they're 16. Your salary and the salaries of other teachers and administrators, the building itself, materials and supplies, buses that take kids to and from school, and even some of your students' lunches will be publicly supported, meaning a portion of federal, state, and local taxes will pay for them.

Typically, your school will be organized into grade levels. At the elementary level, 5-year-olds will be in kindergarten, 6-year-olds will be in the first grade, and so on; at the middle and high school levels, classes will focus on different content areas, such as ninth-grade English, chemistry, or geometry. You will have a designated grade level or content area to teach.

Getting a job will require you to be licensed. You'll have to complete a specified set of university courses, which is one reason you're in this class, and you'll complete clinical experiences in schools, including an internship. You'll probably also have to take a standardized test—the content of which will vary from state to state—to assess your competency.

The origins of all these structures and policies occurred during the period from approximately 1820 to 1865.

Although developing a literate citizenry was a goal before 1820, American education during the early national period was largely reserved for the wealthy; the vast majority of children received little or no formal education. The common school movement changed that.

Historians describe the period from 1820 to 1865 as the "Age of the Common Man." Andrew Jackson, a popular and down-to-earth person who gained fame as a general in the War of 1812, was elected president in 1828. Westward expansion provided opportunities for people and changed the social landscape; the poor and landless could start over by pulling up stakes and heading west. The land area of the United States nearly doubled between 1830 and 1865, and the population increased from 13 to 32 million, 4 million of whom were new immigrants (U.S. Government Printing Office, 1975).

This unprecedented growth presented both opportunities and challenges. Industrialization created jobs and contributed to the growth of cities such as New York and Boston, but it also resulted in pollution, crime, and urban slums. Many immigrants didn't speak English and weren't accustomed to the American way of life. The country needed an informed citizenry that could participate in politics and contribute to the nation's economy, but most people were functionally illiterate. America turned to its schools for help (Tyack, 2003).

The Common School Movement: Making Education Available to All

The American educational system at the beginning of the 19th century was a patchwork of private and quasi-public schools. Those defined as "public" often charged partial tuition, discouraging all but the wealthiest from attending. States didn't coordinate their efforts, and the quality of education was uneven at best (Pulliam & Van Patten, 2007).

Around 1820, changes began to occur that marked the beginning of the **common school movement**, a historic attempt to make education available to all children in the United States. Important events that occurred during this period include the following:

- States and local governments directly taxed citizens to support public schools. Educators attempted to increase the attendance of underrepresented groups such as the urban poor and freed slaves.

The common school movement made education accessible to the common person.

- States created state education departments and appointed state superintendents of instruction.

- Educators organized schools by grade level and standardized the curriculum.

- States improved teacher preparation.

Common school movement A historic attempt in the 1800s to make education available to all children in the United States.

THE CONTRIBUTIONS OF HORACE MANN   Horace Mann, a lawyer turned educator, was a key figure in the common school movement (Tyack, 2003). Secretary of the Massachusetts State Board of Education from 1837 to 1848, he was an outspoken advocate for public education, believing that it was the key to developing our country and improving the quality of life for all people.

Under Mann's influence, Massachusetts became the leader of education in the United States. It doubled state appropriations for education, built 50 new secondary schools, increased teacher salaries by 50 percent, and passed the nation's first compulsory school attendance law in 1852. (By 1900, 32 other states had passed similar laws.) Mann's most important legacy, however, was the idea that public education, in the form of tax-supported elementary schools (common schools), should be a right of all citizens.

EXPANSION OF THE COMMON SCHOOL MOVEMENT   The common school movement prospered despite obstacles, such as business interests that feared a loss of cheap child labor, citizens who objected to increased taxes and having to pay to educate other people's children, and competition from private and parochial schools. Following are reasons for its unprecedented growth:

- Parents began viewing education as a way of improving their children's lives.
- National and local leaders saw education as the vehicle for assimilating immigrants and improving national productivity.
- Industry and commerce were growing and required an increasingly educated populace.

Fifty percent of U.S. children were enrolled in public schools by the beginning of the Civil War, and by 1865, 28 of 35 states had established state boards of education. In contrast, only 2 percent of British 14-year-olds were enrolled during that same time period (Goldin & Katz, 2008). During the common school movement, tax-supported public elementary schools were firmly established as a cornerstone of the U.S. educational system. (New Jersey eliminated the requirement that parents pay for their children's elementary education in 1871; it was the last state to do so.)

Although free public elementary school slowly became available to all, the same didn't occur in secondary education until much later. For example, in 1906, 150,000 students entered first grade in Tennessee, 10,000 remained by the eighth grade, and only 575 graduated from high school (Tyack, 2003). By the 1930s, however, the majority of American children attended high school, a stark contrast with England, where less than 10 percent of 17-year-olds were enrolled in school. Economists believe this access to schooling played a major role in our country's economic growth during that period (Goldin & Katz, 2008).

ISSUES OF QUALITY IN EDUCATION   Although the common school movement dramatically increased access to education, quality was a problem. During the early to mid-1800s,

> Teachers' workloads were heavy, and only the fundamentals were taught. For the most part, school buildings and equipment were very poor, even in the private schools and academies. Textbooks, blackboards, and all working materials were in extremely short supply. Buildings were not kept up, lighting was not adequate, and quite often one poorly trained teacher was in charge not only of one school but also of an entire district. Teachers who possessed only an elementary school education were frequently hired. (Pulliam & Van Patten, 2007, p. 139)

But this was soon to change; then, as now, teachers were seen as keys to improving schools. The creation of **normal schools**, 2-year institutions developed in the early 1800s to prepare prospective elementary teachers, was the first significant attempt to solve this

Normal schools Two-year institutions developed in the early 1800s to prepare prospective elementary teachers.

problem (Fraser, 2006). Before the creation of normal schools, the typical teacher was a man, either preparing or waiting for a position in the ministry. Because these teachers had no training in education, they used primitive methods, such as memorization and recitation, and they maintained order with stern disciplinary measures, including corporal punishment. Normal schools, in contrast, targeted women as potential teachers and attempted to provide both content background and pedagogical training beyond the high school level.

Many of today's state colleges and universities began as normal schools, such as Eastern Michigan University (formerly Michigan State Normal School), Illinois State University (formerly Illinois State Normal University), Sam Houston State University (formerly Sam Houston Normal Institute), San Jose State University (formerly the California State Normal School), and, perhaps most famous, UCLA, the University of California at Los Angeles (formerly Los Angeles Normal School). The functions of normal schools are now performed by undergraduate and graduate schools of education in a college or university such as the one you're now attending.

School quality also increased when larger elementary schools began separating students into grade levels, which eliminated congested conditions and the overlapping curricula often found in one-room schools. Grade differentiation also resulted in more age-appropriate instruction and allowed content to be taught in greater depth for older students. Finally, as paper and printing presses became more common, more textbooks became available, and educational materials improved.

The Legacy of the Common School Movement

The common school movement was a turning point in American education (Tyack, 2003). The idea of universal access to a tax-supported education was planted and took root. The number of children who attended elementary schools increased steadily during this time, and public support for the idea grew. State governance and control of education were institutionalized with the creation of state departments of education, and teacher training and quality improved with the development of normal schools.

Despite these advances, the common school movement left two issues that remain today. One involves the inequitable funding of education from state to state and district to district, both of which affect quality. In his book *Savage Inequalities*, Jonathan Kozol (1991) addresses this issue:

> Americans abhor the notion of a social order in which economic privilege and political power are determined by hereditary class. Officially, we have a more enlightened goal in sight: namely, a society in which a family's wealth has no relation to the probability of future educational attainment and the wealth and station it affords. By this standard, education offered to poor children should be at least as good as that which is provided to the children of the upper-middle class. (p. 207)

This often doesn't occur, however (Berliner, 2005a; S. Gill, McLean, & Courville, 2004). Wide differences in funding exist among states and even districts within states. Nationally, wealthy districts spend an average of 23 percent more on their students than do poorer districts. In Alaska, wealthier districts spent more than double the amount per pupil spent in poorer districts in the state ($16,546 versus $7,379) (Biddle & Berliner, 2002).

Teacher quality is the second contentious issue that remains from the common school movement. The question of what constitutes a well-qualified teacher continues to be debated, as evidenced in two contradictory movements in education today. Alternative licensure, which attempts to increase access to teaching, is the first. In contrast, the effort to increase teacher professionalism by making entry into teaching more intellectually rigorous is the second movement—and a theme of this text (Darling-Hammond & Bransford, 2005). How the issue will be resolved in the future is unclear.

Table 6.1   A Summary of Historical Periods in American Education (1607–1865)

Period	Significant Features	Issues That Remain Today
Colonial period, 1607–1775	• Education reserved for wealthy White males • Seeds planted for public support of education • Religion at the core of education	• Whether prayer should be allowed in schools and in what circumstances • Tax support for religious schools • The relationship between religion and character education
Early national period 1775–1820	• The principle of separation of church and state established • Control of education given to the states, rather than to the federal government • Education viewed as crucial for furthering the national interest	• The role of the federal government in education • National testing of students • A national curriculum
Common school movement, 1820–1865	• Access to tax-supported education for all established • Grade levels introduced in elementary schools • Normal schools created to prepare teachers	• Inequities in funding among states and school districts • Teacher quality and alternative routes to teacher certification

This I BELIEVE

Table 6.1 outlines the important events in our country's early history, their influence on education, and the issues that remain today.

This section addresses the second item in our *This I Believe* feature, "A free public education for all students has historically been a cornerstone of education in the United States." This statement isn't true: Originally, access to education was reserved for the wealthy, and only slowly did this access spread to students from all walks of life.

■ ■ ■ ■ CHECK YOUR UNDERSTANDING

3.1   Explain how the common school movement influenced education in our country today.

3.2   How was the common school movement linked to the growing number of immigrants coming to the United States?

3.3   Who was Horace Mann, and what was his contribution to education in the United States?

For feedback, go to the appendix, *Check Your Understanding*, located in the back of this text.

THE EVOLUTION OF THE AMERICAN HIGH SCHOOL

Kareem and Antonio walk to high school together, have lockers that are side by side, and even have the same homeroom period. But that's where their contact ends. Kareem is in a college preparation track, along with about a third of the other students in his school. As he goes from class to class, he sees many of the same students. Antonio is in a vocational track, and many of his classes are designed to explore different career options. A technology class focuses on business applications of computers and introduces him to jobs in the computer field. A metalworking class includes welding and even allows him to work on his family's car as a class project. Once Kareem and Antonio leave homeroom, they often don't see each other until soccer practice at the end of the day.

Think about your experience in high school. Some of you took honors classes in English, chemistry, or math; others were in "standard" classes, designed for students of average ability. You may have enrolled in some vocational courses, such as word processing or woodworking, designed to provide you with skills that were marketable as soon as you graduated from high school. You may have even taken driver's training or other "life management" courses. These options existed because you attended a unique American invention, the **comprehensive high school**, a secondary school that attempts to meet the needs of all students by housing them together and providing curricular options geared toward a variety of ability levels and interests (Hammack, 2004). How did this uniquely American invention evolve?

Today, a high school education is seen as essential for success in life, but this wasn't always the case: Before the turn of the 20th century, less than 10 percent of students went beyond elementary school (U.S. Department of Education, 1995). In contrast, in the year 2000, 96 percent of all teenagers attended high school (National Center for Education Statistics, 2005c). A high school education has evolved from a luxury to a right, and now to a necessity.

Historical Roots of the Comprehensive High School

Our current high school is the result of a long evolutionary history. A time line illustrating this development appears in Figure 6.1 and is discussed in this section.

To understand the evolution of today's high schools, we need to go all the way back to 1635, when The *Boston Latin Grammar School* was established. It was the first American high school, but it had a decidedly European flavor, with its focus on the colonial elite. As the name suggests, it was a **Latin grammar school**, a college-preparatory school designed to help boys prepare for the ministry or a career in law. Girls didn't attend, because they could be neither ministers nor lawyers. The narrow curriculum and high cost made Latin grammar schools unattainable and irrelevant for the vast majority of Americans.

In reaction to this narrow academic orientation, Benjamin Franklin opened the *Academy of Philadelphia*, in 1751. Free of religious orientation and uniquely American, an **academy** was a secondary school that focused on the practical needs of colonial

Today's modern comprehensive high school can be traced back to academies, such as Franklin's Academy of Philadelphia, and English classical schools, such as the English High School in Boston.

Figure 6.1 The Evolution of the American High School

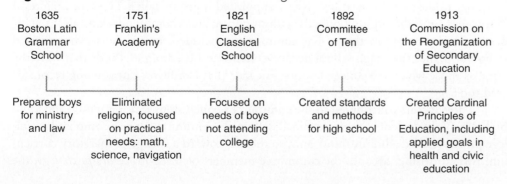

1635	1751	1821	1892	1913
Boston Latin Grammar School	Franklin's Academy	English Classical School	Committee of Ten	Commission on the Reorganization of Secondary Education
Prepared boys for ministry and law	Eliminated religion, focused on practical needs: math, science, navigation	Focused on needs of boys not attending college	Created standards and methods for high school	Created Cardinal Principles of Education, including applied goals in health and civic education

Comprehensive high school A secondary school that attempts to meet the needs of all students by housing them together and providing curricular options.

Latin grammar school A college-preparatory school designed to help boys prepare for the ministry or, later, for a career in law.

Academy An early secondary school that focused on the practical needs of colonial America as a growing nation.

America. Math, navigation, astronomy, bookkeeping, logic, and rhetoric were all taught, and both boys and girls attended. The students selected courses from this menu, which created the precedent for electives and alternative programs at the secondary level that exist today.

Merchants and craftsmen, who had questioned the emphasis on Latin and Greek in the Latin grammar schools, enthusiastically supported this curriculum. By 1860, a quarter of a million students were enrolled in 6,000 tuition-charging academies, and they were the most common type of high school until about 1890 (Reese, 2005).

The academies made three important contributions to American education. First, they emphasized a practical curriculum, suggesting that schools should continuously adapt to changes in society. Second, they eliminated religion from the curriculum, reinforcing the principle of separation of church and state. Third, they were partially supported by public funds, which established a trend that flourished during the common school movement. These characteristics—practical, secular, and public—are themes that remain in today's schools.

In addition to the academies, another uniquely American educational institution appeared: In 1821, Boston established the first **English classical school**, a free secondary school designed to meet the needs of boys not planning to attend college. The English Classical School offered studies in English, math, history, science, geography, bookkeeping, and surveying; to reflect this practical emphasis, the name was changed to the English High School in 1824.

Schools modeled after the English High School spread slowly because of competition from the academies and public opposition to being taxed to support the schools. Taxpayers disagreed with the idea that secondary schools should be free, natural extensions of elementary education. The schools were also unable to decide whether their mission was practical or college preparatory, so they responded by offering both types of classes. This uncertainty also affected students: In 1900, only 1 of 10 students expected to attend college, but the majority took a college-preparatory curriculum. As you see in the next section, this confusion about the American high school's mission continued into the 20th century and persists even today.

This section addresses the third item in our *This I Believe* feature, "The American high school has historically attempted to meet the needs of all students." This statement isn't true; initially, a high school education was a luxury, reserved only for the wealthy elite. Today, although all students have access to a high school education, many students (some estimate this figure to be as high as one fourth to one third) fail to graduate on time, and this figure is higher for cultural minorities (S. Dillon, 2008d).

This I BELIEVE

Redefining the High School

The American high school in the late 1800s was an institution in search of an identity. It began as an elitist, college-preparatory institution, but its curriculum evolved into a disorganized mix of college-preparatory, terminal, and vocational courses.

Educational leaders recognized that something needed to be done, so in 1892, the National Education Association (NEA) appointed a group called The Committee of Ten to examine the high school curriculum and make recommendations about standards, programs, and methods. The committee concluded that students who planned to go no further than high school needed content and teaching methods that were the same as those who were college bound—an idea that lost favor, but is being reconsidered today.

Three factors contributed to the committee's conclusions (Spring, 2005). First, no high school teachers or parents were included on the committee; it was composed of college professors and administrators only, so the bias toward a college-preparatory curriculum isn't surprising. Second, the committee members believed in *faculty psychology*, the

English classical school A free secondary school designed to meet the needs of boys not planning to attend college.

view that exercising the powers of the mind promoted intelligence. Proponents of this view held that everyone, regardless of where they were heading in life, should practice mental discipline to achieve a "stronger" mind. A third factor influencing the committee was the large number of non-English-speaking immigrants and a growing lower class that threatened to create divisions in American society. The committee felt that a different curriculum for college- and non-college-bound students might create a class-based system of education and damage national unity.

Educators recognized, however, that the college-preparatory curriculum wasn't providing prospective workers with the skills needed for increasingly complex jobs. To resolve this dilemma, NEA appointed a second committee, the Commission on the Reorganization of Secondary Education. Its 1918 report, *The Cardinal Principles of Secondary Education*, broadened the high school curriculum to include basic skills such as reading and math, vocational education, personal health, worthy home membership, civic education, effective use of leisure time, and ethical character (Kliebard, 2002). To accommodate these more applied goals, the commission proposed the idea of comprehensive high schools with different tracks for different students; the hope was that the diverse student body, separated into different tracks, would be integrated by sports and other extracurricular activities (Spring, 2005).

Efforts to solve the problems of intellectual and cultural diversity persist today. Although the idea of different tracks was designed to provide a customized education for all students, it also created two negative side effects (Oakes, 2008). First, the curriculum in the non-college-bound tracks frequently offers little intellectual challenge; teachers tend to have low expectations for students, and they often use primitive and ineffective teaching methods, such as lecture and seat work (Good & Brophy, 2008). Second, the move to make high schools comprehensive often made them very large, particularly in urban areas. We address this issue in the next section.

URBAN EDUCATION

THE CHALLENGE OF TEACHING IN LARGE URBAN HIGH SCHOOLS When high schools are very large, students often don't identify with their school, and teachers struggle to establish personal relationships with students (Kincheloe, 2004). More than 70 percent of U.S. high schools have 1,000 students or more, and a number of urban districts have high schools with more than 5,000 students. Large urban schools pose challenges to both teachers and students. Classrooms are often crowded, and teachers find it difficult to get to know their students on a personal basis. Students can get lost in the shuffle and are too often treated as numbers rather than as people.

How can teachers respond to this problem? One way is to create a classroom community in which students and the teacher believe that they're "in this together" and work together to adapt to the size of the school. Effective teachers in large urban high schools make a special effort to get to know students as people by quickly learning their names, learning about their hopes and fears, and spending out-of-class time with them (B. Wilson & Corbett, 2001). They model courtesy and respect for all students and expect similar courtesy in return. And they create clear standards for behavior that require students to treat each other the same way. This creates a sense of community in their classrooms that can help assuage the impersonal feel of large high schools. This is very challenging, but it's an ideal worth striving for.

Effective urban teachers create warm, caring learning communities in their classrooms.

Junior High and Middle Schools

While groups such as the Committee of Ten and the Commission on the Reorganization of Secondary Education wrestled with curricular issues, other educators questioned the effectiveness of the then-prevalent organizational pattern of 8 years of elementary and 4 years of high school. Critics argued that too much emphasis was being placed on basic skills in the upper elementary grades, time that should be spent learning content in depth. Developmental psychologists also noted that early adolescence is a time of intellectual, emotional, and physical transition, and students undergoing these transitions require a different kind of school. In response to these arguments, educators created **junior high schools** to provide a unique academic curriculum for early adolescents. The first junior high, for grades 7, 8, and 9, opened in Columbus, Ohio, in 1909. The concept spread quickly, and by 1926, junior highs had been set up in 800 school systems (Kliebard, 2002).

The 6–3–3 organizational pattern (6 years of elementary school, 3 of junior high, and 3 of high school) was more a change in form than substance, however. Most "junior" highs were exactly that—imitations of high schools with emphasis on academic disciplines and little attention to adolescent development.

In spite of these weaknesses, junior highs remained popular until the 1970s, when continued criticism caused fundamental change. The creation of **middle schools**, targeted at grades 6–8 and designed to meet the unique social, emotional, and intellectual needs of early adolescents, was a response to these criticisms (Kellough & Carjuzaa, 2009).

Middle schools provided opportunities for teachers to get to know students by creating student and teacher teams. For example, a science, English, math, and social studies teacher would form a team and would all have the same group of students for the school year; this organization allowed teachers to share information about learner progress and integrate topics they were teaching to make them more meaningful to students. For instance, the science teacher working on the acceleration of falling bodies might integrate the topic with the math teacher on the team, who would demonstrate how the acceleration could be represented graphically. And the social studies teacher, whose students are studying the Civil War, might work with the English teacher, who would have her students read *The Red Badge of Courage*, a novel that focuses on a young soldier's reactions to a Civil War battle. This integration promotes both intellectual and emotional development. In addition, educational psychologists encouraged teachers to move away from lecture-dominated instruction, so prominent in high schools, and focus more on interactive instruction guided by teacher questioning.

The middle school philosophy has grown in popularity. The number of junior highs decreased from more than 7,000 in 1968 to about a thousand in 1996 (Viadero, 1996), with an accompanying increase in middle schools.

AMERICAN SECONDARY SCHOOLS: FUTURE DIRECTIONS   The history of American secondary schools helps us understand some of the questions facing educators today. Begun as college-preparatory institutions, high schools became comprehensive in an effort to meet the needs of a diverse student body (Hammack, 2004). To help adolescents make the transition from elementary to high school, junior highs were created; when those schools failed to fulfill that mission, educators created middle schools. The academic pendulum has now swung back, however, and some leaders are calling for a redesign of middle schools to make them more academic and rigorous (Yecke, 2006).

Questions remain. For example, have American secondary schools been too trendy, quickly zigzagging in response to changes in society, or have they been too conservative, hanging on to outmoded academics that are no longer relevant? We examine these questions later in the chapter when we discuss the modern era in American education.

Junior high schools Schools designed for early adolescents that are similar in form and focus to high schools.

Middle schools Special schools targeting grades 6–8 and designed to meet the unique social, emotional, and intellectual needs of early adolescents.

■■■■ CHECK YOUR UNDERSTANDING

4.1   Describe the historical roots of contemporary secondary schools.

4.2   How have the goals of high school education changed over time?

4.3   How are junior highs and middle schools different from each other?

For feedback, go to the appendix, *Check Your Understanding*, located in the back of this text.

SEARCHING FOR EQUALITY: THE EDUCATION OF CULTURAL MINORITIES

To this point, the history of American education has been generally positive. Despite lurches and false starts, the quality of education improved, and it became more accessible. The story isn't so positive for cultural minorities, however. In this section, we outline the experiences of four minority groups: Native Americans, African Americans, Hispanic Americans, and Asian Americans. We begin with Native Americans.

Education of Native Americans

> The first thing to do was to clean them [Native Americans] thoroughly and to dress them in their new [military] attire . . . [Then] everything except swallowing, walking, and sleeping had to be taught; the care of person, clothing, furniture, the usages of the table, the carriage of the body, civility, all those things which white children usually learn from their childhood by mere imitation, had to be painfully inculcated and strenuously insisted on. In addition to this, they were to be taught the rudiments of an English school course and the practical use of tools. (U.S. Bureau of Indian Affairs, 1974, p. 1749)

The history of Native American education is a story of largely unsuccessful attempts to assimilate different tribes into the American mainstream (Fleming, 2006). **Assimilation** is the process of socializing people to adopt the dominant society's social norms and patterns of behavior. Historically, for example, educators sought to bring minorities, and particularly Native Americans, into the mainstream of American life by teaching basic skills and instilling White, middle-class values, and they asked minorities to reject important aspects of their own histories and cultures. This policy is illustrated in the quote that introduces this section.

As with American education in general, the education of Native Americans began with a religious orientation. During the 1700s and 1800s, mission schools run by various religious groups—primarily Catholic—provided a curriculum that focused on basic skills, agriculture, vocational education, and religion. Although instruction was in the native language, mission schools also attempted to assimilate Native Americans by helping them bridge the gap between tribal, communal life and one in which individuals owned land, had jobs, and followed the dominant culture (Spring, 2005).

Attempts at assimilation were formalized by the federal government, which was involved in the education of Native Americans from the beginning of our country (see Figure 6.2). From 1771 to 1870, it signed nearly 400 treaties with Native American tribes designed to provide federal assistance for agriculture, medical care, and education. From 1890 to 1930, the federal government established boarding schools run by the Bureau of Indian Affairs. The best way to "Americanize" the children, educators thought, was to remove them from tribal settings and provide them with a strict program of cultural transformation. Consequently, children were forced to live at the schools, English was spoken and taught, and native languages and customs were forbidden.

Assimilation The process of socializing people to adopt the dominant society's social norms and patterns of behavior.

Figure 6.2 Time Line of Native American Education

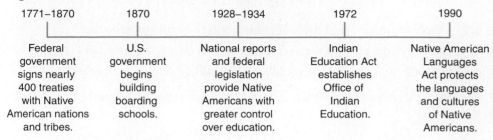

1771–1870	1870	1928–1934	1972	1990
Federal government signs nearly 400 treaties with Native American nations and tribes.	U.S. government begins building boarding schools.	National reports and federal legislation provide Native Americans with greater control over education.	Indian Education Act establishes Office of Indian Education.	Native American Languages Act protects the languages and cultures of Native Americans.

Source: N. Dillon, 2007b; Fleming, 2006.

The failure of the boarding schools was evidenced by low participation, high dropout rates, and a tendency for students to return to the reservation after graduation. For example, only 300 of 5,000 eligible Navajo children attended these schools in 1901, and many ran away and returned to the reservation because the curriculum didn't apply to their culture or their interests (Button & Provenzo, 1989).

Despite the failure of boarding schools, federal control of Native American education continued through the 1960s (Lomawaima & McCarty, 2006). Tribal schools, which added Native American culture to the curriculum, opened in 1965, but teachers were poorly paid, instructional materials were limited, and schools depended on the federal government for finances, all problems difficult to overcome.

Legislation during the 1970s gave Native Americans greater control over their schools (N. Dillon, 2007b), and more recently, the federal government shifted responsibility for Native American education from tribal schools to public schools. Currently, there are approximately 4.4 million American Indian and Alaska Natives in the United States; most are clustered in western states, with Alaska (27%), Oklahoma (19%), Montana (11%), and New Mexico (11%) having the highest percentages of Native American students (Zehr, 2008). Of these, only 540,000 live on reservations or trust lands, with nearly 60 percent living in metropolitan areas (Fleming, 2006). Despite this shift and increased involvement by tribal governments, problems with Native American education persist: Underachievement, high dropout rates, low rates of college attendance, and high rates of poverty indicate that current educational practices are still not working (K. Flanagan & Park, 2005).

There is an ongoing debate among Native American educators about the benefits of reservation schools versus nearby public schools (K. Johnson, 2008). Although acknowledging that public schools may offer better academic programs in areas such as advanced science and math, Native American educators fear their students may lose an important part of their cultural heritage, including their native languages (Fleming, 2006).

Education of African Americans: Up From Slavery to . . .

The first African Americans arrived in America shortly after the founding of Jamestown in 1607. Brought as slaves, they had few educational opportunities before the Civil War. In 1850, for example, about 4,000 Black students in slave states and 23,000 in free states attended schools—less than 2 percent of the African American population. And the literacy rate was low, somewhere between 5 and 10 percent (Reese, 2005).

The Civil War (1861–1865) ended legal slavery in the United States but was replaced by a policy of **separate but equal**, which formalized the segregation of African Americans in education, transportation, housing, and other aspects of public life (Bureau of International Information Programs, 2008). The policy justified segregation by claiming that African Americans were receiving different but equal treatment under the law. In education, the policy was implemented by creating separate schools with different curricula, teaching methods, teachers, and resources. Some historians believe that these efforts were well intentioned but misguided, whereas others argue that they were inherently

Separate but equal A policy of segregating African Americans in education, transportation, housing, and other areas of public life, although opportunities and facilities were considered equal to those of mainstream Americans.

Early efforts at educating African Americans were often substandard because of inadequate funding and resources.

racist (Spring, 2005). The policy remained in place until it was overturned by the Supreme Court in 1954 in the famous watershed case, *Brown v. Board of Education of Topeka* (1954).

Unfortunately, the *separate but equal* policy resulted in schools that could more accurately be described as *separate* and *unequal* (E. Gordon, 2007). Substandard schools were predominant, and funding for African American schools was consistently lower than for White schools. In 1877, for example, expenditures for African American students in the South were less than half those for Whites; by the 1940s, they had dropped to a fifth (J. Anderson, 1988). In 1907, White teachers in Alabama were paid 5 times more than African American ones. In Georgia in the late 1920s, 99 percent of the money budgeted for teaching equipment went to White schools, even though African Americans made up more than a third of the state's student population (E. Gordon, 2007). In 1952, Arkansas spent $102 to educate each White child but only $67 for each African American child. Separate but equal wasn't working.

PROPOSED SOLUTIONS TO THE PROBLEM The education of African Americans was clearly inferior to that of Whites, but a solution to the problem remained elusive. Finally, two leaders, with sharply different perspectives, emerged.

Booker T. Washington (1856–1915) was born a slave and taught himself to read. Educated at Hampton Institute, a vocational school for African Americans, he established the Tuskegee Institute in 1881. Short of supplies and resources, he had his students build the school themselves; this hands-on approach to learning illustrated his strategy for bettering the education and lives of African Americans in the South. He believed that hard work, practical training, and economic cooperation with Whites were the keys to success. His philosophy became popular, and he was often invited to address White audiences on the topic of African American education. Washington also encouraged his students to become teachers; he believed that attempting to enter other professions or politics was premature and would lead to conflict with the White power structure in the South.

Although Washington was accepted by many African Americans and was popular with Whites, his policy of accommodating segregation angered other African American leaders. W. E. B. Dubois (1868–1963) was an important opponent whose resistance to

PEARSON
myeducationlab

To see historical news footage of public reaction to education laws that shaped current educational practices, go to the *Assignments and Activities* section of Topic 7: *History of Education* in the MyEducationLab for your course and complete the activity titled *Brown v. Board of Education*.

Washington's stance was predictable, given the differences in their backgrounds. Dubois was born in Massachusetts and educated in integrated schools. He attended colleges and universities in the United States and Europe and was the first African American to receive a PhD in the United States (Watkins, 2001).

Dubois was committed to changing the status of African Americans and advocated a determined stand against segregation and racism. He focused his energies on students achieving in the top 10 percent, believing that they would provide leadership and create opportunities for the rest of the African American population. He also believed that this group could take its place among the business, professional, and intellectual leaders of the White population. Dubois believed that Washington's separatist approach implied inferiority and, although expedient in the short term, would retard the educational progress of African Americans in the long run. He advocated social activism and was a leader in establishing the National Association for the Advancement of Colored People (NAACP). This organization played a major role in the advancement of African Americans in the 20th century.

THE COURTS EXAMINE "SEPARATE BUT EQUAL"   Before the Civil War, African Americans lived apart from the White majority because of slavery and legal restrictions. Segregation continued after the Civil War because of the *separate but equal* policy. A federal challenge to the policy came in Louisiana in 1896 in a court case involving segregated railroads: In *Plessy v. Ferguson*, the Supreme Court ruled that separate but equal railroad facilities didn't violate the Constitution (Spring, 2005). This decision was also applied to education, and *separate but equal* remained for almost 50 years. (We examine the federal government's response to the "separate but equal" policy in education in the Exploring Diversity section later in the chapter.)

Education of Hispanic Americans

Hispanic is a label that refers to a diverse group of people who speak Spanish or are of Latin American or Caribbean heritage (Banks, 2006); Mexican Americans in the Southwest, Puerto Rican Americans in the Northeast, and Cuban Americans in Florida are all included in this group. The term *Hispanic* is more popular in the Northeast, with groups in the Southwest preferring *Latino* (*Latina*, female). The term *Chicano* (*Chicana*, female) refers to Hispanics of Mexican American heritage.

Hispanics are both the largest and the fastest-growing minority group in the United States, making up 15 percent of the nation's population (Gollnick & Chinn, 2009). By the year 2025, 1 of 4 children in our country's elementary schools is predicted to be of Hispanic heritage.

Hispanic education in America began with Catholic mission schools in the Southwest, but it shifted to public schools after the Mexican–American War in 1848. Initially, the education of Hispanics focused on assimilation; classes were taught in English, Spanish was forbidden, and students' own Hispanic heritage was either ignored or disparaged (Banks, 2006; Spring, 2005).

Apathy and resistance to school, as occurred with Native Americans, were pervasive, and dropping out was common. These educational problems persist today: In 2003, 44 percent of the Hispanic school-age population left school before graduation, compared to 24 percent of White students (Olson, 2006a). Also, only 12 percent of 22-year-old Hispanics have a bachelor's degree, compared to 30 percent of Whites and 15 percent of African Americans (Bowman, 2000c). When Hispanics go to college, they're much more likely than other groups to attend a 2-year institution (Pew Hispanic Foundation, 2003).

Language differences have been the source of many problems in the education of Hispanics. Language symbolizes differences between Hispanics and the dominant culture, and language differences often interfere with student learning. Some experts argue that language barriers explain why Hispanic students have historically scored lower on both intelligence and achievement tests, because they're largely language based (Abedi, Hofstetter, & Lord, 2004; Popham, 2004).

Education of Asian Americans

Like Hispanics, Asian Americans are a diverse group of people with varied histories (Banks, 2006). The first Asian Americans were Chinese who came to the United States to work in the California gold mines and on the first transcontinental railroad. Japanese immigrants came to California and Hawaii in the late 1800s as farm workers. More recently, Korean and Southeast Asian immigrants came to the United States seeking a better life and an escape from the Korean and Vietnam Wars.

Asian immigrants initially were welcomed because they relieved an acute labor shortage in the West. Then competition for jobs, together with racism, resulted in a series of changes in immigration laws that prevented further Chinese immigration in 1882 and then Japanese immigration in 1924 (Spring, 2005). A dark page in Asian American history came during World War II, when more than 100,000 Japanese Americans were forced out of their homes near the Pacific coast and into internment camps in barren areas of the West.

Like other minority groups, Asian Americans experienced discrimination. For example, in 1906, San Francisco established segregated schools for Asian Americans. Instruction was in English, which resulted in problems similar to those that Native Americans and Hispanics encountered. A federal court ruled in 1974 (*Lau v. Nichols*) that the San Francisco school system had violated the rights of Chinese American students and that students who find their educational experience "wholly incomprehensible" must be taught in the first language if that language is not English.

As a group, Asian Americans have fared better than other minority groups in the American educational system (Ngo & Lee, 2007). For example, Asian Americans typically score higher on achievement tests and have higher rates of college attendance and completion than other groups, including White students (National Center for Education Statistics, 2005e), and the proportion of Asian Americans in colleges and universities is higher than that of the general population. This success has led some educators to label this group "the model minority," a stereotypic term that can be misleading (Steele, Spencer, & Aronson, 2002): Many Asian American students have problems in school, and language and poverty remain obstacles for them (Lew, 2006; Ngo & Lee, 2007). In addition, research shows considerable differences between the educational experiences of different Asian American groups (Ngo & Lee, 2007). Chinese and Korean students, for example, enroll in colleges at much higher rates than Cambodians and Hmong. Focusing on group differences can result in inappropriate expectations for and unjust treatment of individual members of those groups. In short, you need to remember that your students are individuals and treat them that way.

The Search for Equality: Where Are We Now?

The United States has always had ambivalent attitudes toward ethnic and cultural diversity. While accepting and even valuing this diversity in the form of holidays (e.g., St. Patrick's Day, Chinese New Year), music, and food, our country has also placed significant value on assimilation and uniformity. Those who argue for greater cultural homogeneity emphasize the need for common values and a language to connect citizens from each of the 50 states. Conversely, advocates for greater cultural diversity argue that different ethnic and cultural groups contribute unique ideas and perspectives that make our country vibrant and culturally rich (Spring, 2005). As our country continues to attract immigrants from different countries and cultures, the debate is likely to continue.

Because of this country's ambivalence toward diversity, the federal government's role in the education of cultural minorities remains poorly defined. In the past, federal courts played a major role in desegregation. During the 1960s, the commendable goal of integration, which sought to provide opportunities for cultural minorities and White majority students to attend school together and learn about each other, often became synonymous with forced busing (Pulliam & Van Patten, 2007). Parents who wanted their children to attend neighborhood schools resisted busing; public support for integration waned, and a resegregation of cultural minorities in urban schools has resulted (Kozol, 2005). Because of the public's attitudes, the federal government has become reluctant to impose busing and other legal mechanisms to achieve integration (Caldas & Bankston, 2005).

As with the federal courts, the legislative branch also remains uncertain. Once an advocate for cultural diversity, the Senate voted 63 to 34 in 2006 to designate English as the national language (Hulse, 2006). We examine this changing federal role in education in the next section.

This section addresses the fourth item in our *This I Believe* feature, "With the end of slavery in this country, cultural and ethnic minorities were welcomed into U.S. schools." This statement isn't true: Even today, many cultural minorities fail to benefit from educational opportunities in our country.

■ ■ ■ ■ CHECK YOUR UNDERSTANDING

5.1. Identify similarities and differences in minority groups' struggles for educational equality.

5.2. How does the concept of *assimilation* relate to Native American boarding schools?

5.3. How does "separate but equal" relate to African Americans' educational experience in the United States?

5.4. How did the process of assimilation relate to Hispanic Americans and their native languages?

For feedback, go to the appendix, *Check Your Understanding*, located in the back of this text.

THE MODERN ERA: SCHOOLS AS INSTRUMENTS FOR NATIONAL PURPOSE AND SOCIAL CHANGE

The modern era in education began after World War II and continues to the present. It's characterized by an increased national emphasis on education, which is now viewed as the key to both individual success and the progress of the nation. Given this perspective, it isn't surprising to see the federal government more actively involved in education than it was in the past. This increased involvement occurred in four major areas:

- Education and the Cold War
- The War on Poverty
- The enlistment of schools in a worldwide economic battle
- The government's role in equity issues

We look at these areas next.

The Cold War: Enlisting America's Schools

After World War II, the United States became involved in a Cold War with communist countries, particularly the Soviet Union, with ever more powerful weapons being stockpiled on both sides. It was called a "Cold War" because no shots were fired, but a struggle for world leadership ensued. It also had a significant impact on education in our country.

The Russian launching of the satellite Sputnik in 1957 was a key event of the period (Bracey, 2007). Believing the United States was losing the technology war, our government authorized a fivefold increase in the funding of the National Science Foundation, which had been created in 1950 to support research and improve science education. Congress also passed the National Defense Education Act (NDEA) in 1958, which was designed to enhance "the security of the nation" by improving instruction in math, science, and foreign languages. The NDEA provided funds for teacher training, new equipment, and the establishment of centers for research and dissemination of new teaching methods. During this period, Admiral Hyman Rickover, the father of the American nuclear navy, called education the first line of defense against our enemies (Pulliam & Van Patten, 2007).

The War on Poverty and the Great Society

During the 1960s, leaders began to realize that despite the economic boom following World War II, many Americans were living in poverty. The United States was becoming a nation of "haves" and "have nots," and the problem was exacerbated by an economy that required ever-increasing skills from its workers.

For the unfortunate, a cycle of poverty began with inadequate education, which decreased employment opportunities, led to a poorer quality of life, and resulted in lowered achievement in the next generation (Macionis, 2009). To break this cycle and create a "Great Society" in which all could participate and benefit, President Lyndon Johnson stated in his 1964 State of the Union address that "this administration today, here and now, declares unconditional war on poverty in America."

Emphasis on education was a major thrust in the **War on Poverty**, a general term for federal programs designed to eradicate poverty during the 1960s. During this period, the federal government's involvement in education increased significantly. Initiatives included the following:

- Increased federal funding for K–12 education, which went from $900 million and about 4.4 percent of the total spent on education in 1964 (before Johnson's initiatives) to $3 billion and 8.8 percent of the total educational budget by 1968.

- The development of the Job Corps. Modeled after the Civilian Conservation Corps of the 1930s, the Job Corps created rural and urban vocational training centers, which helped young people learn marketable skills while working in government projects.

- The creation of the Department of Education in 1979. The department was originally part of the Department of Health, Education, and Welfare, but education was considered so important that it was elevated to its own cabinet-level position during President Carter's administration.

- Support for learners with exceptionalities. In Chapter 5, you learned that the federal government passed Public Law 94-142, the Individuals with Disabilities Education Act (IDEA), in 1975. In 1976–1977, the nation educated about 3.3 million children with exceptionalities; today, the schools serve more than 6 million, an increase of nearly 100 percent (Heward, 2009).

- The creation of national compensatory education programs.

Let's look at these compensatory programs in more detail.

War on Poverty A general term for federal programs designed to eradicate poverty during the 1960s.

COMPENSATORY EDUCATION PROGRAMS   **Compensatory education programs** are government attempts to create equal educational opportunities for disadvantaged youth. These programs provide supplementary instruction and attempt to prevent learning problems before they occur. The two best known are Title I and Head Start.

Title I: Improving the Academic Achievement of the Disadvantaged.   **Title I** is a federal compensatory education program that funds supplemental education services for low-income students in elementary and secondary schools. The program was part of President Johnson's War on Poverty; more than $185 billion was spent on Title I between 1965 and 2000, and these funds reach virtually all of our nation's school districts, serving 15 million low-income children in 47,600 schools (U.S. Department of Education, 2006a). Funded at $14 billion per year, Title I received an additional $13 billion in 2009 under the American Recovery and Reinvestment Act. Two thirds of the money goes to elementary schools, and this money is clustered, with 15 percent of the highest poverty schools receiving 46 percent of Title I funds. Title I currently serves 100,000 homeless and 2.5 million English language learners. Approximately 35 percent of the recipients are White, 31 percent are Hispanic American, and 27 percent are African American.

The outcomes of Title I programs have been uneven (Zigler, 2009). Part of Title I's ineffectiveness resulted from initial design problems (Borman, 2002/2003). Because the funds were initially restricted to only low-income students, "pull-out" programs—where students were taken out of their regular classrooms for supplementary instruction—prevailed. During the late 1990s, 60 percent of the instruction in these pull-out programs was conducted by unlicensed paraprofessionals, and more than 40 percent of these Title I aides spent half or more of their time without the supervision of a licensed teacher (U.S. Department of Education, 1999a). NCLB addressed this problem by specifying qualifications for Title I paraprofessionals, but unfortunately these were often not enforced or met (Honawar, 2006).

Pull-out Title I programs had other problems as well. Removing students from their classrooms caused logistical problems: Students who were pulled out missed regular instruction, and teachers had trouble helping them catch up. Also, pull-out instruction often focused on low-level skills having few links to the regular curriculum.

In response to these criticisms, Title I programs have been redesigned to focus on total school improvement, rather than instruction in pull-out programs. Newer programs aim to achieve schoolwide improvement in a variety of ways. For example, Comer's School Development Program, which you first studied in Chapter 3, focuses on involving parents and providing improved family services such as counseling and social services (Comer, Joyner, & Ben-Avie, 2004). Another program called Success for All® attempts to prevent school failure by emphasizing family involvement and by laying a strong foundation in reading, writing, and math during the early grades (Slavin & Cheung, 2004).

Head Start.   Another part of the federal war on poverty began in 1965. **Head Start** is a federal compensatory education program designed to help 3- to 5-year-old disadvantaged children enter school ready to learn. It has two goals: (1) to stimulate the academic achievement and development of low-income preschoolers, and (2) to educate and involve parents in the education of their children. Since its inception in 1965, Head Start has served more than 22 million children; in 2005, the program had a budget of $6.8 billion (Henry, Gordon, & Rickman, 2006).

The Head Start curriculum has undergone important changes in recent years, with a significant shift toward basic skills, such as counting and identifying numbers

---

Compensatory education programs Government attempts to create equal educational opportunities for disadvantaged youth.

Title I A federal compensatory education program that funds supplemental education services for low-income students in elementary and secondary schools.

Head Start A federal compensatory education program designed to help 3- to 5-year-old disadvantaged children enter school ready to learn.

and letters, combined with social skills, such as taking turns and following directions. The curriculum also develops parenting skills, such as reading and talking to children and providing experiences that increase readiness for school, including trips to zoos, libraries, and museums. To signal this change in emphasis, Head Start was moved in 2005 from the Department of Health and Human Services to the Department of Education.

In general, Head Start 4-year-olds perform better than comparable 4-year-olds who haven't participated in the program. In the more effective Head Start programs, such as the Perry Preschool Program in Ypsilanti, Michigan, researchers have found long-term benefits ranging from fewer special education placements to greater numbers of high school graduates and lower crime and teen pregnancy rates (Jacobson, 2004; A. Lewis, 2005).

Not all Head Start programs are effective, however, and some programs have had little impact on children's readiness to learn. Poor program quality and inadequate budgets are the most commonly cited reasons (Merrow, 2002).

Putting Compensatory Education Programs Into Perspective. Critics hope to do away with compensatory education programs, pointing to their uneven quality. This criticism underscores the general dilemma of federal aid to education: The aid is usually given with only broad guidelines that allow schools and districts to spend the money essentially as they see fit. This necessary flexibility also results in uneven quality.

Critics also argue that these programs have failed to eliminate differences in achievement between participants and other students. This criticism is more debatable: Expecting schools, alone, to solve the social problems associated with poverty, such as drug use, violence, unstable families, and unhealthy neighborhoods, is unrealistic (Berliner, 2005a). And a long history of research consistently demonstrates that these factors adversely affect learning (Macionis, 2009).

Schools and the Battle for Economic Survival

As you've seen in previous sections, schools in the 20th century were frequently asked to serve as agents in the nation's struggles. During the 1960s, the opponents were Russia in the Cold War and poverty; more recently, our country asked schools to aid in the battle for economic advantage in the global economy. This shift in focus was caused in large part by the revolution in technology, which resulted in fewer jobs in low-skilled areas. In short, if the United States was going to compete economically, it needed a highly educated and skilled workforce that could compete with workers in other countries.

The thinking of leaders resulted in what is commonly described as "the Standards Movement" in education. It began with the publication of the famous federal report *A Nation at Risk* (National Commission on Excellence in Education, 1983), which declared that our nation was at risk of losing its preeminence in technology, and continues to today with NCLB, passed in 2001. Recent research suggests that the United States has already lost its technology edge, that this loss can be attributed in large part to problems in our educational system, and that, as a result, our country has already lost more than $1 trillion to foreign competitors (Friedman, 2009). Standards, NCLB, and our standing in technology compared to other countries around the world continue to be debated today.

This section addresses the fifth item in our *This I Believe* feature, "In recent times, the federal government has viewed the schools as an instrument to achieve national goals." This statement is true: The federal government has increasingly used education as a tool to achieve national goals.

This I BELIEVE

The Federal Government's Role in Pursuing Equality

Consider the following statistics:

- The average 12th-grade low-income student of color reads at the same level as the average 8th-grade middle-class White student.
- As a group, African Americans have the lowest achievement test scores of any minority, and they're overrepresented in special education classes.
- Close to 30 percent of Hispanics live at or below the poverty line, and college attendance and graduation rates are substantially below those of the general population. (Fass & Cauthen, 2007; National Center for Education Statistics, 2006b)

The struggle for equality in education is an important area in which the federal government's role has increased. Civil rights and equity for women are two major areas where the federal role has made an important difference.

THE CIVIL RIGHTS MOVEMENT

Linda Brown was an 8-year-old African American student in Topeka, Kansas, in 1951. Instead of walking five blocks to an all-White elementary school, she was forced to cross unguarded and potentially dangerous railroad tracks to catch a bus to a school for African Americans 21 blocks away. In addition to objecting to the distance, her father believed that the African American school had substandard resources and programs. With the help of the NAACP, he went to court to change this.

Earlier in the chapter, you saw that the policy *separate but equal* was put into place after the Civil War. It remained a guiding principle until 1954, when Thurgood Marshall, who later became the first African American on the Supreme Court, represented the NAACP in arguing against the *separate but equal* doctrine that forced Linda Brown to attend a segregated school. In a unanimous decision, the Supreme Court ruled in the famous watershed case, *Brown v. Board of Education of Topeka* (1954), that separate educational facilities are inherently unequal and that racially segregated schools generated "a feeling of inferiority." The days of segregated education for African American students were supposed to be over.

In some school districts, however, Whites so strongly resisted integration that it had to be forced. For example, in 1957, President Eisenhower sent federal troops to an all-White high school in Little Rock, Arkansas, to enforce the Supreme Court's antisegregation decision and allow nine African American students to attend the school in safety. In spite of these efforts, discrimination remained widespread because the responsibility for desegregation was left to individual states and school districts, many of which resisted change.

Congress responded with the Civil Rights Act of 1964, which prohibited discrimination against students on the basis of race, color, or national origin in all institutions receiving federal funds. The federal government then had a mechanism to both encourage and enforce integration efforts.

To understand federal attempts to provide equality of education for all students, the distinction between *de jure* and *de facto* segregation is important. **De jure segregation** results from laws, such as those existing in many states that created schools that were supposedly "separate but equal." The Supreme Court decision *Brown v. Board of Education* put a legal end to de jure segregation in our country. **De facto segregation**, by contrast, results from individuals' private decisions, such as where to live and which friends to have. A major strategy to battle de facto segregation resulting from segregated housing was busing students, both Black and White, to integrated schools. This

De jure segregation Segregation resulting from laws, such as those existing in many states that created schools that were supposedly "separate but equal."

De facto segregation Segregation resulting from individuals' private choices, primarily about where to live.

Federal efforts through legislation such as Title IX have increased funding and participation in girls' athletics.

strategy was controversial and resisted by parents.

EQUITY FOR WOMEN

Earlier in the chapter, you saw that women were largely excluded from education in the early periods of American history, and they were historically underserved by our nation's schools. The federal government became involved in gender-equity issues by enacting Title IX of the Education Amendments of 1972:

> No person in the United States shall, on the basis of sex, be excluded from participation in, be denied benefits of, or be subjected to discrimination under any education program or activity receiving federal financial assistance.

Eliminating gender bias in the schools was the goal of this legislation. Title IX has had its largest impact on physical education and sports: The number of girls participating in high school athletics increased 875 percent from 1975 to 2005, and the number of female college athletes increased 435 percent in that same time span (World of Sports Science, 2008). Nevertheless, female participation in high school athletics is still well below that of boys, 3.02 million versus 4.37 million in 2007 (National Federation of State High School Associations, 2008). In addition, in most schools, women's teams don't receive comparable funding, facilities, equipment, publicity, travel budgets, or practice opportunities.

Title IX has become controversial at the college level. Critics of Title IX argue that to achieve an equal number of male and female athletes, schools have had to eliminate many of the "minor" men's sports, such as wrestling, swimming, gymnastics, and tennis (M. Davis, 2003). Supporters of Title IX argue that the extraordinary cost of college football skews the issue, and that a modest cut in football expenditures would allow for a greater investment in women's sports with no cuts to other men's sports.

PUTTING FEDERAL EQUALITY EFFORTS INTO PERSPECTIVE

So, how has federal intervention affected the struggle for equality in education? With respect to integration, progress is uncertain. For example, in the South in 1988, nearly 44 percent of African American students attended integrated schools, up from virtually none in 1954. By 1996, however, the figure had shrunk to about 35 percent (Hendrie, 1999). In the North, segregated housing patterns led to de facto segregated schools. This problem has been exacerbated in urban areas by "White flight" to the suburbs. Consider these statistics:

> In Chicago, by the academic year 2000–2001, 87 percent of public school enrollment was black or Hispanic; less than 10 percent of children in the schools were white. In Washington, D.C., 94 percent of children were black or Hispanic; less than 5 percent were white. In St. Louis, 82 percent of the student population was black or Hispanic by this point, in Philadelphia and Cleveland 78 percent, in Los Angeles 84 percent, in Detroit 95 percent, in Baltimore 88 percent. In New York City, nearly three quarters of the students were black or Hispanic in 2001. (Kozol, 2005, p. 8)

Currently, more than three fourths of Hispanic students attend schools populated predominantly by members of cultural minorities, and nearly 4 of 10 attend schools that are 90 to 100 percent minority (Borman, 2002/2003).

Various strategies have been proposed to achieve greater racial diversity, such as compensatory education, school boundary realignments, and mandatory busing. In the 1970s, **magnet schools**, public schools that provide innovative or specialized programs and accept enrollment from students in all parts of a district, were developed to aid in integrating White and minority students.

Magnet schools Public schools that provide innovative or specialized programs and accept enrollment from students in all parts of a district.

Magnet schools capitalize on school choice, avoiding the problems associated with mandatory busing to achieve racial integration (Jackson, 2007). These schools organize their curricula around high-interest or high-need areas such as math, science, and computer science, or around high-quality general programs designed to prepare students for college. They're most common in large cities, with about 4,000 schools that serve more than 2 million students, or about 3 percent of the K–12 student population (Kober, 2006). Six percent of the schools in the 100 largest districts are magnet schools, enrolling 9 percent of these districts' students (Dalton, Sable & Hoffman, 2006). The federal government encourages the growth of magnet schools by allocating federal funds to school districts (Magnet Schools of America, 2006; U.S. Department of Education, 2006b).

In spite of strong governmental support ($739 million for experimentation with magnet programs), magnet schools haven't always met their original goals. For instance, they tend to attract the highest-achieving minority students, robbing students from other schools of role models. When they succeed in attracting bright students from cultural minority groups, they sometimes can't attract high-performing White students into the same schools. Social class differences between wealthier and poorer students and cultural differences within magnet schools also thwart true integration and the development of cohesive learning communities (Dickinson, Holifield, Holifield, & Creer, 2000).

Civil rights and women's equity efforts also continue to be highly controversial. Some minority leaders and women's groups assert that progress for cultural minorities and women has been too slow, and the government should do more. On the other hand, conservative leaders contend that civil rights efforts have gone too far: They charge that women and minorities are receiving preferential treatment, which amounts to reverse discrimination. These debates are likely to continue in the future as critics on various sides become increasingly vocal and polar in their positions.

Diversity in Your Classroom

Although teachers may feel limited in what they can do about these issues at the national or state levels, there is much they can do in their own classrooms. Teachers play a major role in creating the classroom climate (Hallinan, 2008). They establish the rules and procedures, and they set a moral tone when they introduce them in the class-

room. They also act as role models in the way they treat students. Teachers also have frequent opportunities to teach about fairness and equity in their everyday interactions with students, including whom they call on in class and who receives extra teacher help and encouragement. Thoughtful teachers make their classrooms a microcosm of the kind of world they'd like their students to grow up in.

QUESTIONS TO CONSIDER

1. During learning activities, what is the most effective way to communicate

that all students are welcome in classrooms and are expected to learn?
2. Why are management rules and procedures so important for creating a positive emotional environment for students from diverse backgrounds?

myeducationlab To respond to the these questions online, explore this topic further, and receive feedback, go to the *Book Specific Resources* section in the MyEducationLab for your course, select your text and then select *Exploring Diversity* for Chapter 6.

Taking a Stand in an Era of Reform

Is the Federal Strategy for Educational Reform Working?

Reforms originate from various sources, such as professional organizations, states, local districts, and the federal government, with the federal government being one of the most powerful. The federal government expanded its efforts to influence education during the 20th century in three primary ways:

- Encouraging states to set standards
- Creating testing programs and encouraging states to create tests to address standards
- Offering financial incentives

SETTING STANDARDS

One way for the federal government to influence education is to encourage states to set standards, which provide common goals for educational efforts. NCLB, introduced in Chapter 1, requires each state to establish its own standards and create tests to assess the extent to which students meet them. NCLB was

the centerpiece of educational reform during the administration of George W. Bush. When the Obama administration came into power in 2009, and with Democrat majorities in Congress, the future of NCLB became cloudy. Standards are here to stay, however, regardless of which political party is in power.

TESTING PROGRAMS

Begun in 1969, the National Assessment of Educational Progress (NAEP) testing program, also known as "the Nation's Report Card," was designed to provide an objective, external measure of how students in the United States are performing (Popham, 2005b). The program conducts periodic assessments of students in 4th, 8th, and 12th grades in math, science, reading, writing, and the arts, and in the social studies areas of civics, geography, and U.S. history. Because of concerns about undue federal influence and the confidentiality of

scores, testing is voluntary, and only group scores are reported. In 2003, all 50 states participated in some aspect of the program. In addition to a nationwide snapshot of the competence of U.S. students, NAEP provides state profiles and comparisons of test scores.

FINANCIAL INCENTIVES

If national goals are worth pursuing, and if tests can measure progress toward these goals, then rewarding districts that make significant progress and punishing those that don't are logical next steps. This is what George W. Bush recommended during his presidential campaign and what Congress enacted in NCLB (DeBray, McDermott, & Wohlstetter, 2005). Low-performing schools that receive federal funds can be put on a 5-year schedule of remediation, and if scores don't improve, the schools can be taken over by the state or be reconstituted. In addition, states that fail to comply with NCLB provisions could lose federal educational funds. As we noted, with a shift in political power at the federal level, the future of these policies became uncertain.

THE ISSUE

Is the strategy of federal incentives to encourage states to set standards and create tests working? Setting standards and holding students accountable for meeting them seem sensible. Also, creating tests to measure how students in different states are doing and how states compare to one another is also sensible, and experts ask how we can improve our education systems if we don't know what our students are learning or how much they're learning (Ravitch, 2006)? Financial incentives also make sense intuitively: Why shouldn't teachers and schools be rewarded for increasing the amount their students learn (or punished when learning doesn't occur)?

Unfortunately, allowing each state to create its own standards results in dupli-cation of effort and a mishmash of confusing standards from state to state, but the alternative—national standards—has been criticized by both political conservatives and liberals, although for different reasons (R. Gordon, 2006). As Chester Finn, former assistant secretary of education under President Reagan, observed, "Republicans oppose any proposal with the word 'national' in it; Democrats oppose anything with the word 'standards' in it" (quoted in D. Doyle, 1999, p. 56).

Whether testing should be done at the state or national level is also controversial. Critics claim that state testing programs fail to provide an accurate picture of student achievement, because of both the variety of tests that are used and attempts by states to "dumb down" the tests to make their students' performance look good (Kahlenberg, 2008).

National testing is also controversial, however. Advocates claim that this is the only way to obtain an accurate picture of what American students are really learning. But critics contend it creates a national curriculum and causes teachers to "teach to the test," which narrows the curriculum and detracts from an overall education (Nichols & Berliner, 2005).

Critics charge that financial incentives will further encourage teachers to teach to tests. They also claim that states and districts will align their curricula with the content being tested—in essence, creating a de facto national curriculum (J. Newman, 2006).

YOU TAKE A STAND

Now it's your turn to take a position on the issue. Should the federal government play a greater role in educational reform, or should school reform be the major responsibility of states and local school districts?

myeducationlab To explore both sides of this issue and take a stand, go to the *Book Specific Resources* section in the MyEducationLab for your course, select your text and then select *Taking a Stand in an Era of Reform* for Chapter 6.

ISSUES IN EDUCATION

■ ■ ■ ■ ■ CHECK YOUR UNDERSTANDING

6.1 How did schools become instruments for national purpose during the modern era?

6.2 Identify one way each of the federal government's interventions were similar, and one way they were different.

6.3 What are magnet schools, and how do they relate to attempts to achieve equality in our schools?

6.4 What is Title IX, and how is it related to the concept of equality?

For feedback, go to the appendix, *Check Your Understanding*, located in the back of this text.

Now it's your turn to apply the information in this chapter to your own professional life. As you read the next section, think about how testing and reform will influence your teaching, then answer the question that follows.

myeducationlab

Go to the *Building Teaching Skills and Dispositions* section of Topic 7: *History in Education* in the MyEducationLab for your course and complete the activity entitled *Educational History in the Making*.

myeducationlab

To see a video of one successful integration effort, go to the *Assignments and Activities* section of Topic 7: *History of Education* in the MyEducationLab for your course and complete the activity titled *The Reunion*.

ISSUES IN EDUCATION

Testing and Reform

You're a first-year teacher in a large suburban district in the Midwest. When you interviewed for the job, the principal explained that the district was experiencing demographic changes, and parents were concerned about declining test scores. The fourth grade, where you have a self-contained classroom, is particularly important, because your students take the Stanford Achievement Test, a standardized test widely used to gauge individual student progress. In addition, they participate in the NAEP, the national test designed to assess the progress of students across the country.

During the weeks before school, the principal met with teams of teachers at each grade level to go over the district curriculum and explain how it has been aligned to cover content measured on the standardized tests. You design your unit and lesson plans around these goals and feel fairly confident as the school year begins.

After 2 or 3 weeks, you see that something is wrong. You have some classroom management problems, and a number of your students don't seem motivated. In addition, many of your students can't do the work you assign. Some have transferred from other districts where the curriculum was different, some are struggling with English as a second language, and others just don't seem to get it. After a number of troubled evenings, you approach one of your colleagues, an experienced teacher next door, and explain how you're considering dumping the planned curriculum, assessing your students, and starting over.

"You really think that would work?" your colleague asks after hearing your plan.

"I'm not sure, but I know what I'm doing now isn't."

"And what are you going to tell Mr. Livingston when he comes around to evaluate your teaching?"

What would you do in this situation?

6 MEETING YOUR LEARNING OBJECTIVES

1. Explain how the diversity of the original colonies shaped our educational system, and describe the role of religion in colonial schools.

   - Major geographic, economic, and cultural differences existed in the original 13 colonies. These differences spilled over into religious differences, which strongly influenced the decision to separate church and state.

   - Early colonial educational practices were largely negative and repressive. Over time, European philosophies that were more humane and child centered made their way across the Atlantic.

   - The colonial period resulted in three historical legacies. First, early schools were elitist, catering to wealthy White males. Second, the foundation of public support for education was established by the Old Deluder Satan Act. Finally, the tangled relationship between religion and education began.

2. Explain how the early national period influenced education in this country.

   - During the early national period, the framers of the Constitution used the First Amendment to separate religion from government control or influence.

   - The Tenth Amendment placed the primary responsibility for funding and governing education in the hands of state and local governments.

   - During this period, the federal government separated church and government, relegated educational responsibility to the states, and established the idea that schools were essential for improving the quality of life and helping the nation grow.

3. Explain how the common school movement influenced education in our country today.

- During the years leading up to the Civil War, states laid the foundations for universal access to tax-supported schools. States established state departments of education to govern schools and built normal schools to improve the professional training for teachers.

- The common school movement was a turning point in American education because it planted the idea of access to a tax-supported education for all. Though this ideal was not achieved in practice until later, establishing the principle was important.

4. Describe the historical roots of contemporary secondary schools.

- The history of the comprehensive American high school began with the Boston Latin School, the first secondary school in the colonies. This college-preparatory institution focused on the classics. Benjamin Franklin's Academy of Philadelphia introduced the idea of a practical curriculum. The English High School targeted non-college-bound students and was supported by public funds.

- The comprehensive American high school evolved as a compromise out of a tug-of-war between committee reports that advocated either academic or applied orientations. The goal of the comprehensive high school is to meet the needs of all students—general education, vocational, and college preparatory—under one roof.

- Current middle schools began as more traditional junior highs created in the early 1900s. Junior high schools were more academically oriented and were often "mini" versions of high schools. Middle schools were created to meet the unique developmental needs of young adolescents.

5. Identify similarities and differences in minority groups' struggles for educational equality.

- The education of cultural minorities in the United States aimed at assimilation. Although attempts were made to create schools that were separate but equal, they generally failed. Native American education efforts attempted to assimilate students through boarding schools.

- The education of African Americans in the United States had a long history of separate but unequal treatment that was finally challenged in the Supreme Court in 1954.

- Education for Hispanic Americans had a similar uneven history, with both segregation and unequal funding. Language was a central issue in the education of Hispanic students, and bilingual education, which is intended to preserve students' first language, has been a central controversy in the education of Hispanics.

- Asian Americans experienced educational problems similar to those of other cultural minorities. In attempts to assimilate them quickly, schools often ignored Asian Americans' native languages and cultures. Currently there is considerable diversity among Asian American groups and students.

- The federal government's proper role in pursuing equity in education is continually being debated. Other positions, such as local control, question whether equity efforts should come from states or the federal government.

6. Explain how schools became instruments for national purpose during the modern era.

- During the modern era, the federal government took a more active role in education, using it as an instrument of national purpose. During the Cold War with the Soviet Union, the federal government spent large amounts of money improving math, science, and foreign language education.

- During the War on Poverty and the Great Society, the federal government also used courts and federal spending to battle poverty and inequities in schools.

- The federal government also enlisted schools in its economic struggles with other countries. *A Nation at Risk* called for improved education to maintain U.S. "preeminence in commerce, industry, science, and technological innovation." No Child Left Behind, the latest attempt at federal reform, aimed to reform education through testing and accountability.

- Currently, consensus is lacking about the federal government's proper role in achieving education equity. Although most believe that reform is needed, whether the focal point of change should be federal or local is still undecided.

IMPORTANT CONCEPTS

academy (p. 173)
assimilation (p. 177)
common school movement (p. 169)
compensatory education programs (p. 184)
comprehensive high school (p. 173)
de jure segregation (p. 186)
de facto segregation (p. 186)
English classical school (p. 174)
Head Start (p. 184)

junior high schools (p. 176)
Latin grammar school (p. 173)
magnet schools (p. 187)
middle schools (p. 176)
normal schools (p. 170)
Old Deluder Satan Act (p. 165)
separate but equal (p. 178)
Title I (p. 184)
War on Poverty (p. 183)

DISCUSSION QUESTIONS

1. What is the proper relationship between education and religion? Is the connection between religion and education likely to become closer or more distant over the next 10 years? Why do you think so?

2. Will trends that emphasize choice, such as the use of school vouchers and enrollment in magnet schools, likely increase or decrease in the future? Why do you think so? Will choice positively or negatively influence education?

3. What is your position on bilingual education? Should it be generally banned, as it has been in some states, or was this a mistake? Explain your position.

4. How would you attempt to solve the problems with Native American education?

5. Do you believe that racial discrimination remains a major problem for society? What could or should schools do to alleviate this problem?

6. Would our educational system be better if control were at the national level instead of the local and state levels? Why or why not?

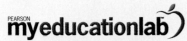

Now go to Topic 7: *History of Education* in the MyEducationLab (www.myeducationlab.com) for your course, where you can:

- Find learning outcomes for *History of Education* along with the national standards that connect to these outcomes.

- Complete *Assignments and Activities* that can help you more deeply understand the chapter content.

- Apply and practice your understanding of the core teaching skills identified in the chapter with the *Building Teaching Skills and Dispositions* learning units.

- Check your comprehension on the content covered in the chapter by going to the *Study Plan* in the *Book Specific Resources* section for your text. Here you will be able to take a chapter quiz, receive feedback on your answers, and then access *Review, Practice, and Enrichment* activities to enhance your understanding of chapter content.

Develop Your Professional Portfolio

To further apply your understading of chapter content and address the INTASC standards, go to the *Book Specific Resources* section in the MyEducationLab for your course, select your text, then select this chapter's *Portfolio Activities*.

"I teach children. I teach children to think on their own and to develop their own opinions and ideas. That is why I teach."

DANIEL KUZNIK, 2008 Teacher of the Year, Indiana

To view a video clip of Daniel, the 2008 Indiana Teacher of the Year, go to Topic 8: *Philosophy of Education* in the MyEducationLab for your course and select *Teacher Talk,* then *Daniel Kuznik.*

Educational Philosophy: The Intellectual Foundations of American Education

LEARNING OBJECTIVES

After you have completed your study of this chapter, you should be able to:

1. Define *philosophy* and explain the difference between *philosophy* and *theory.* INTASC Standard 9, Teacher Professionalism

2. Describe each of the branches of philosophy, and identify examples that illustrate each. INTASC Standard 9, Teacher Professionalism

3. Describe the major philosophies of education, and identify examples that illustrate each. INTASC Standard 9, Teacher Professionalism

4. Explain why a personal philosophy of education is important, and describe steps involved in forming one. INTASC Standard 9, Teacher Professionalism

P hilosophy often seems rather remote and disconnected from everyday life, but this isn't at all the case. We each have a "philosophy of life," for example, which is the set of principles we choose to live by.

As with individuals, professionals have philosophies that guide their practice. As you read the following case, think about the philosophical differences that guide the thinking of the two teachers in the conversation. Also, think about the kind of teacher you want to become and how you'll interact with your students. The answers to these questions will be influenced by your personal teaching philosophy

"What's happening?" Brad Norman, a middle school English teacher, asks Allie Skinner, a colleague who teaches science, as he walks into the teachers' lounge after school.

"Working on this quiz," Allie mumbles, glancing up at him.

"You sure do test the heck out of your kids, don't you? Every time I come in here, you're either writing a quiz or scoring one."

"Well, this is what I believe. . . . I've given all this a lot of thought, and this is the best I've been able to come up with so far. . . . Everything I read in the journals talks about how important background knowledge is for new learning. Everything we learn depends on what we already know. . . . And, there's real, practical stuff out there that kids need. They have to be good readers, they need to be able to write and do math, and they need to understand this stuff, the science I'm teaching. I'm not doing my job if I don't get them to learn as much as possible. And, practice, thorough assessment, and detailed feedback are some of the best ways we have of getting them to learn. That's reality."

"I like the idea of kids knowing stuff too, but school involves more than that. Where in your scheme do kids learn to solve problems and make choices and wise decisions? Everything I read says that kids need lots of experience in making decisions and solving problems. The only way they're going to get good at making decisions is to be put in situations where they're forced to make decisions. . . . That's how the world works, and I would be doing them, their parents, and ultimately our whole society a disservice if I didn't try to prepare them for life outside school.

"And," Brad continues, "exactly what is reality? You said, 'There's real, practical stuff out there that kids need.' I think being put in situations where they have to practice making decisions is 'real, practical, stuff.' Reality is, in fact, what you perceive it to be, and there's no objective source out there to decide which view is the 'right one.'"

"Aw, c'mon," Allie counters. "Sure, perception is important, but look at that oak tree outside the window. You can perceive it to be anything you want, but it's still an oak tree. And, it doesn't matter what anybody thinks: Two plus two is four—not three, not five, not anything else."

The bell rings cutting off their conversation. They laugh, agree to disagree, and promise to continue the discussion later.

We address the issues raised in Allie and Brad's conversation as the chapter unfolds, but before we begin, please respond to the items in the *This I Believe* feature on page 197, designed to encourage you to start thinking about your own philosophy of teaching. We address each of the items in this chapter.

PHILOSOPHY AND PHILOSOPHY OF EDUCATION

What is *philosophy*, and what does "philosophy of education" mean? At its most basic level, **philosophy** is a search for wisdom (Ozmon & Craver, 2007), but in a more formal sense, it's a study of theories of knowledge, truth, existence, and morality—matters of right and wrong (Gutek, 2005; M. Murphy, 2006).

We see evidence of this study in Allie and Brad's discussions in our opening case. Allie, for example, said, "I've given all this a lot of thought, and this is the best I've been able to come up with so far." She was describing her beliefs about knowledge and truth and what she believed was right. Although his beliefs and conclusions were different, Brad was pursuing the same goal. This is why philosophy is important for teachers, and it ad-

Philosophy The study of theories of knowledge, truth, existence, and morality.

This I BELIEVE!

dresses the first item in our *This I Believe* feature, "The function of philosophy is to help prospective teachers understand how past experts have thought about teaching." This statement is only partially true. A **philosophy of education** goes well beyond helping prospective teachers understand the thinking of past experts; it also guides what we do in the classroom and provides a framework for thinking about educational issues (Conroy, Davis, & Enslin, 2008).

Philosophy and Teacher Professionalism

In their conversation, Allie and Brad expressed different views, but their contrasting positions have common features, closely related to teacher professionalism (see Figure 7.1). Both decision making and reflection, critical elements of professionalism, are illustrated in their conversation. Allie and Brad reflected on their practice and made decisions about what topics were most important to study and how to best help students understand those topics. Allie, for example, said, "[T]here's real, practical stuff out there that kids need. They have to be good readers, they need to be able to write and do math, and they need to understand this stuff, the science I'm teaching." Based on her reflection, she decided to emphasize what she believed was essential knowledge, and she further decided to frequently assess her students to help them acquire this knowledge. Brad's reflection led him to different conclusions: He decided to directly involve students in decision-making and problem-solving activities, which, based on his reflection, he believed were more important.

A specialized body of knowledge is also a component of teacher professionalism, and both Allie and Brad based their decisions on research. For example, Allie said,

Figure 7.1 Elements of Professionalism in Allie's and Brad's Philosophies

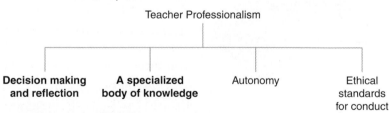

Philosophy of education A set of ideas and beliefs that guides teachers' actions and provides a framework for thinking about educational issues.

197

Teacher professionalism requires that teachers be able to explain why they teach the way they do.

"Everything I read in the journals talks about how important background knowledge is for new learning." She didn't base her decisions on intuition or whim; rather, they were grounded in professional knowledge. The same was true for Brad: "Everything I read says that kids need lots of experience in making decisions and solving problems." He disagreed with Allie, but his decisions were also based on knowledge.

The Relationship Between Philosophy and Theory

Philosophy and theory overlap in many ways, and the distinction between the two is often blurred (Ferrero, 2005). A philosophy and a theory are not identical, however. A **theory** is a set of related principles that are based on observation and are used to explain the world around us. The term "explain" in the definition is important: The primary function of theories is to help explain events we observe in our day-to-day lives.

Philosophies, by contrast, are based in part on theories, but go beyond them. For example, Allie's emphasis on knowledge is based on theories of learning that suggest "everything we learn depends on what we already know." Her philosophy goes beyond theory, however. Instead of explaining the way things *are*, philosophy suggests the way things *ought to be*, and also analyzes theories, ideas, and beliefs. Allie, for example, suggested that schools should emphasize knowledge and understanding, whereas Brad thought they should focus on decision making and problem solving. Allie also expressed the belief that kids need extensive background knowledge to learn new ideas, whereas Brad believed that experiences with decision making and problem solving were more important. In this regard, both Allie and Brad stepped beyond theory into the realm of philosophy.

Philosophies in other professions also suggest what ought to be. In medicine, for example, one school of thinking suggests that the medical profession should emphasize prevention through healthy lifestyles, whereas another focuses on healing through medication and other treatments. A description of the way something ought to be—such as the way educators, physicians, or other professionals ought to practice—is called a **normative philosophy** (Ferrero, 2005).

This discussion addresses the second item in our *This I Believe* feature, "Philosophy and theory are closely related, but not identical." This statement is true, and is true for all professions.

This I BELIEVE

Theory A set of related principles that are based on observation and are used to explain the world around us.

Normative philosophy A description of the way professionals ought to practice.

▪ ▪ ▪ ▪ CHECK YOUR UNDERSTANDING

1.1 Define *philosophy* and *normative philosophy*, and explain how they differ from *theory*.

1.2 To which part of teacher professionalism is philosophy most closely related? Explain.

1.3 What's the major difference between Allie's and Brad's normative philosophies?

For feedback on these exercises, go to the appendix, *Check Your Understanding*, located in the back of this text.

BRANCHES OF PHILOSOPHY

Like other areas of inquiry, such as biology, geography, and literature, philosophy has specific areas and topics of study. These areas include the following:

- Epistemology
- Metaphysics (ontology)
- Axiology
- Logic

We examine each in the sections that follow.

Epistemology

To understand epistemology, let's look again at Allie and Brad's discussion. Allie said, "And, there's real, practical stuff out there that kids need. . . . And, practice, thorough assessment, and detailed feedback are some of the best ways we have of getting them to learn. That's reality." She argued that practice and assessment with feedback are ways students come to know the ideas they learn.

Allie was making an epistemological argument. **Epistemology** is a branch of philosophy that examines questions of how we come to know what we know. A variety of ways of knowing exist. The scientific method, in which a problem is tested by collecting facts through observation and experiment, is one; intuition, authority, and even divine revelation are others.

Epistemology is important for teachers because our beliefs about how students gain knowledge and understanding affect our choices of teaching methods. For instance, many experts believe that students, and people in general, don't passively receive information from others; instead, they mentally process to make sense of it, and then create their own understanding. Teachers who adhere to this belief provide a variety of experiences for learners and lead discussions that help them make sense of their experiences. In contrast, teachers who believe that listening to an expert is the way people "come to know" are likely to lecture to students and expect them to reproduce what they've heard on tests. (We examine this issue again later in the chapter.)

Metaphysics

Whereas epistemology examines how we know, **metaphysics**—or ontology—is a branch of philosophy that considers what we know. Metaphysics considers questions of reality and ultimately attempts to answer the question "What is real?" (Jacobsen, 2003). With respect to metaphysics, Allie and Brad are far apart. Brad argued, "Reality is, in fact, what you perceive it to be, and there's no objective source out there to decide which view is the 'right one,'" to which Allie countered, "[L]ook at that oak tree outside the window. You can perceive it to be anything you want, but it's still an oak tree. And it doesn't matter what anybody thinks: Two plus two is four—not three, not five, not anything else." Allie believes in a reality independent of our perception, but Brad believes that perception and reality are inextricably intertwined.

Our metaphysical beliefs influence both the way we teach and the goals we establish. For instance, because Allie believes in a reality independent of people's perceptions, her goal is for students to understand that reality. In contrast, because Brad believes less strongly in an objective reality, his goals more strongly emphasize students' learning to critically examine their own thinking and make decisions based on that examination. The teaching methods they select will help their students best reach these goals.

Epistemology A branch of philosophy that examines questions of how we come to know what we know.

Metaphysics (*ontology*) The branch of philosophy that considers *what* we know.

Axiology

Axiology is a branch of philosophy that considers values and ethics, issues now prominent in American education. For example, surveys indicate that as many as three fourths of students admit to cheating on tests, and cheating appears to be on the rise from elementary school through college (Bracey, 2005a; Murdoch & Anderman, 2006). Also, large numbers of students in schools express concerns about being bullied (Raskauskas & Stoltz, 2007).

Outside of schools, corruption that led to the collapse of businesses such as Enron and WorldCom and the loan scandals that resulted in the financial crisis in the latter part of the last decade have sent shock waves through the financial community and American society in general. Rampant greed and a sense that "if you can get away with it, it's okay" seem to be the "moral" principles of the day. The American public is increasingly looking to education for solutions to problems such as these (Bushaw & Gallup, 2008).

How does axiology influence teachers? Let's look again at Allie and Brad's conversation. Allie argued, "I'm not doing my job if I don't get them to learn as much as possible"; Brad retorted, "I would be doing them, their parents, and ultimately our whole society a disservice if I didn't try to prepare them for life outside school." Both teachers argued that they wouldn't be behaving ethically if they weren't true to their beliefs about what's important in terms of their values. Axiology is involved when teachers examine their values to decide what's best for their students.

Logic

Logic is a branch of philosophy that examines the processes of deriving valid conclusions from basic principles. Allie's comments to Brad demonstrate a particular thinking process. Although these aren't Allie's exact words, the following statements represent her sequence of thoughts:

> *Practice, assessment, and feedback promote learning.*
> *I am providing my students with practice, and I'm assessing their learning and providing them with feedback.*
> *Therefore, I am promoting learning in my students.*

Allie was illustrating a form of logic called *deductive reasoning*, which begins with a proposition, called a *major premise;* this could be a principle or generalization such as "Practice, assessment, and feedback promote learning." The major premise is followed by a fact, called a *minor premise,* such as "I am providing my students with practice, and I'm assessing their learning and giving them feedback." Deductive reasoning then ends with a conclusion that follows from the two premises. In Allie's case, the conclusion was an explanation for why she believed she was promoting learning in her students.

Inductive reasoning, the counterpart to deductive reasoning, begins with particular facts or observations and ends with a conclusion that pulls these facts together. For instance, elementary students plant seeds under a variety of growing conditions and observe what happens to the plants. They find that warmth and moisture are important for germination and that sunlight is important for subsequent growth. On the basis of the specific instances, such as the seeds they planted, students make general conclusions about plant growth in general.

Logic helps both teachers and learners examine the validity of their thinking. For instance, in social studies, we help students see that if we stereotype a specific cultural group based on the behavior or appearance of a few members of the group, we're using faulty inductive reasoning. Similarly, many controversies in education and other aspects of life exist because proponents and critics disagree on the validity of conclusions that are derived from deductive reasoning. For example, many advocates of charter

Axiology The branch of philosophy that considers values and ethics.

Logic The branch of philosophy that examines the processes of deriving valid conclusions from basic principles.

schools conclude that they do a better job of educating students than traditional public schools (Nathan, 2005). They base this argument on the premise that any system with a large bureaucracy is ineffective (a major premise), and that our public schools, with their many layers of administration, are bureaucratic and inefficient (a minor premise). So, critics conclude that charter schools are more effective. Supporters of public schools disagree with both the major premise and the conclusion (Colgan, 2004; Hess, 2004b). Other controversies involve similar disagreements between premises and conclusions.

■ ■ ■ ■ CHECK YOUR UNDERSTANDING

2.1 Describe each of the major branches of philosophy.

2.2 Allie said, "I'm not doing my job if I don't get them to learn as much as possible." This comment best illustrates which branch of philosophy? Explain your answer.

2.3 Two teachers are in a discussion, and one says, "Everything we know depends on experience. So, the key is providing lots of experiences in the classroom. If we provide them with enough experiences, they'll learn." To which branch of philosophy is this person's statement most closely related? Explain your answer.

2.4 "That doesn't quite make sense," a teacher diplomatically comments to a colleague. "You said that your kids are so unmotivated, but last week you said that kids basically want to learn. . . . Those two don't fit." To which of the branches of philosophy is this person's comment most closely related? Explain your answer.

For feedback on these exercises, go to the appendix, *Check Your Understanding*, located in the back of this text.

PHILOSOPHIES OF EDUCATION

As you begin your study of this section, think about three basic and central questions:

1. What is the purpose of schooling?
2. What should schools be teaching? (the curriculum)
3. How should teachers teach? (instruction or teaching methods)

Philosophies of education help answer these and other questions about schooling, the curriculum, and instruction. We address these questions as we examine four philosophies of education:

- Perennialism
- Essentialism
- Progressivism
- Social reconstructionism

Perennialism

Think about the term *perennial*, which is an adjective meaning "perpetual" or "long-lasting." **Perennialism** is an educational philosophy suggesting that nature—including human nature—is constant. Consistent with beliefs in the constancy of nature, perennialists believe in a rigorous curriculum that is constant for all students. For them, education is preparation for future life, and the extent to which students find their studies relevant to their lives at the time they're in school, although valuable, isn't critical.

Perennialism An educational philosophy suggesting that nature—including human nature—is constant and that schools should teach classic knowledge.

Perennialists would answer our three framing questions in this way: "Developing individuals' intellect should be the purpose of schooling; math, science, and great literature should make up the curriculum, and teachers should be in charge of classes that include discussions of time-honored topics." Math, science, and literature are important in a perennialist curriculum because they expose learners to both the rigors of logical thought and the great ideas that have endured throughout history.

Historically, perennialism has been an important educational philosophy in our country; our founding fathers, for example, held perennialist views. It was prominent until the early 20th century, when the thinking of Thomas Dewey (1902, 1906, 1923, 1938) encouraged teachers to focus more on students' experiences, problem solving, and applications to everyday society. (We discuss Dewey's work later in this section.)

Perennialism experienced a brief renaissance in the early 1980s with the publication of Mortimer Adler's (1982) *The Paideia Proposal: An Educational Manifesto*. Adler advocated a general curriculum for all students that included math, science, history, geography, literature, and fine arts. Understanding the content of these subject areas was a means to an end, however, and not an end in itself: The goal in studying them was to develop intellectual skills, such as writing, speaking, computing, and problem solving. The content, together with these skills, would lead to higher-level thinking, reflection, and awareness.

Adler's ideas received considerable attention from the popular press, and William Bennett, who served as secretary of education in the Reagan administration from 1985 to 1988, gave Adler's thinking strong political support. Allan Bloom, an American philosopher and a faculty member at the University of Chicago, was also a strong supporter; he published his bestseller, *The Closing of the American Mind,* in 1987. Both Bennett and Bloom believed that American education had abandoned its historical ideals. Education at the time, they argued, was responsible for the lax social and sexual habits of modern students and for their focus on materialism as evidence of success.

Adler's suggestions were controversial. Critics argued that his proposals were elitist, aimed primarily at students with the highest ability (Ozmon & Craver, 2007). Critics also questioned the value of distant and abstract ideas for poorly motivated and intellectually unprepared students. Adler's efforts remain alive, however, with the reissue of his book (Adler, 1998) and renewed interest in student discussion and dialogue as a vehicle for learning (Billings & Fitzgerald, 2002).

PERENNIALISM IN THE CLASSROOM

Lane Wallace has his students involved in reading and analyzing Nathanial Hawthorne's The Scarlet Letter *(1850). This classic American novel set in Boston in the 1600s describes a tragic and illicit love affair between the heroine (Hester Prynne) and a minister (Arthur Dimmesdale). The novel's title refers to the letter A, meaning "adulterer," which the Puritan community makes Hester wear as punishment for her adultery.*

"Surprisingly, the kids love it," Lane comments. "Everyone has heard of the Puritans, and we use their intolerance and repressiveness as a metaphor for issues in today's society, such as gay and lesbian rights, cohabitation outside of marriage, and the counterculture of the 1960s. Then, we consider the concept of evil, and we ask which is more evil, Hester's and Dimmesdale's love affair, the Puritans' humiliating Hester by making her wear the 'A,' or her husband's attempted revenge directed toward her and Dimmesdale?...Then, as we discuss evil in a more general sense, the kids realize that it isn't as cut-and-dried as they previously thought. . . . They really get into it, and I've even had to stop them from yelling at each other and remind them that attempting to shout each other down is just another form of repression. . . . It's great."

Lane's efforts are consistent with perennialism. The concepts of *good* and *evil, sin* and *repression* are ideas that have been examined throughout history, and they're as timely today as at any point in history. The ideal perennialist curriculum would have students examine these and other important concepts through the study of classic literature, analyzing and evaluating the ideas presented in them, as Lane did with his students.

Essentialism

We've all heard of "back to the basics" movements, which recur in education on a cyclical basis. "Back to the basics" means that learning should focus on basic skills, such as reading, writing, mathematics, and, to a certain extent, science and social studies. And in the 21st century, technological literacy has also become a basic skill. People who support "back to the basics" movements periodically write newspaper editorials sounding the alarm about American students' ignorance of the world around them, their inability to communicate either orally or in writing, and their lack of ability to do rudimentary math (Ravitch, 2000). The recent No Child Left Behind (NCLB) Act, which emphasizes that every child in the United States should leave school with a grasp of basic skills, has a definite essentialist flavor.

Essentialism emphasizes knowledge and skills that are critical for success in school and life.

Essentialism, an educational philosophy, suggests that critical knowledge and skills exist that all people should possess. Essentialists would answer our three central questions by saying that the purpose of schooling is to advance society, the curriculum should include the skills needed to function effectively in society, and teachers should play a central role in directing classes to help students acquire these skills (Null, 2007). They also address the third item in our *This I Believe* feature, "Teachers' primary goals should be to help students master essential content rather than to help them develop emotionally and socially." People who have an essentialist philosophy would strongly argue that this statement is true.

Essentialism and perennialism share the view that knowledge and understanding are preeminent, and both are wary of educational trends, such as learner-centered education, integrated curricula, and a focus on learner self-esteem. Essentialists don't share perennialists' emphasis on universal truths through the study of classical literature, however; instead, they emphasize knowledge and skills that are useful in today's world.

Because of its emphasis on practical, usable knowledge, the essentialist curriculum is more likely to change than the perennialist curriculum. For instance, as our society becomes more diverse and as researchers better understand how diversity affects learning, teacher preparation programs place increasing emphasis on working effectively with learners from diverse backgrounds. This means you'll likely take a course in multicultural education, and topics in this area will be included in your other courses. Such an emphasis reflects the belief that understanding learner diversity is now an essential part of being an effective teacher. The same is true for technology: Most teacher education programs now have some type of technology component. These shifts in emphasis reflect essentialist thinking, and they wouldn't exist in a curriculum grounded in perennialist philosophy.

ESSENTIALISM IN THE CLASSROOM   Essentialism is prominent in American education today, and is reflected in Allie's comment, "There's real, practical stuff out there that kids need. They have to be good readers, they need to be able to write and do math, and they need to understand this stuff, the science I'm teaching." She believes a body of knowledge and skills exist that all students should master, and it's her job to be sure they do. Essentialists want to ensure that the educational system produces a literate and skilled workforce able to compete in a technological society. They're concerned about a general

Essentialism An educational philosophy suggesting that a critical core of knowledge and skills exists that all people should possess.

"dumbing down" of the curriculum, they decry social promotion of students, and they're wary of student-centered instruction.

Many of the reform efforts over the last 20 or 30 years have arisen from essentialist views. In the 1980s, reform was spurred by *A Nation at Risk* (National Commission on Excellence in Education, 1983), the widely publicized report that recommended that all high school students master core requirements in five "basics"—English, math, science, social studies, and computer science. NCLB (Christie, 2005; Popham, 2004) also drove many of the changes occurring in schools during the administration of George W. Bush: It emphasized the basic skills of reading and math and used extensive testing in an attempt to ensure that basic skills were mastered.

Essentialist philosophy is also found in teacher education programs. As a prospective teacher, you will be required to take a specified sequence of courses, and it's likely that you'll be expected to demonstrate mastery of essential teaching skills on a standardized test, either the Praxis Series™, which we discuss in Chapter 1, or a state-specific test. This emphasis is also reflected in the Important Concepts in the text are highlighted, defined in the margins, and listed at the end of each chapter. These requirements and features reflect the belief that an essential core of knowledge exists that all preservice teachers should master.

Progressivism

Should schools focus on filling students' heads with facts, or should they teach students how to think and solve problems? In our chapter's opening case, Brad made the following comment:

> *"Everything I read says that kids need lots of experience in making decisions and solving problems. The only way they're going to get good at making decisions is to be put in situations where they're forced to make decisions. That's how the world works, and I would be doing them, their parents, and ultimately our whole society a disservice if I didn't try to prepare them for life outside school."*

His view is consistent with **progressivism**, an educational philosophy emphasizing real-world problem solving and individual development. Progressivists would answer our three questions by saying that the purpose of schooling is to develop students as completely as possible—physically, intellectually, socially, and emotionally, (Hansen, 2007). The curriculum should be composed of experiences that reflect today's world, and instructionally, teachers should guide students in the process of development. People with a progressivist philosophy would agree with the fourth item in our *This I Believe* feature, "Schools ought to focus on teaching students to think and solve problems in the real world." They would argue that students need to see how content relates to and can be valuable in thinking about and understanding their own lives.

In our discussion of epistemology, we said that many experts believe that students and people in general don't passively receive information from others; instead, they mentally process it in an effort to make sense of it, thus creating their own understanding. This view is consistent with progressivism; it emphasizes concrete experiences, real-world tasks, and the central role of the individual in determining reality and promoting learning. Progressivism is grounded in the work of John Dewey (1923, 1938), which continues to be debated today. Because of its influence on American education, let's briefly look at the history of the progressive movement in this country.

THE PROGRESSIVE ERA IN AMERICAN HISTORY   From about 1890 to 1920, the American educational system experienced dramatic growth (Pulliam & Van Patten, 2007). School enrollments, fueled by accessibility and compulsory attendance laws, increased 70 percent, and the number of teachers grew by 80 percent.

Progressivism An educational philosophy emphasizing real-world problem solving and individual development.

During this period of growth, educators began to reexamine schooling practices. They questioned the value of teacher-centered instruction that asked students to sit passively and absorb information presented by teachers. At the center of this movement was John Dewey (1859–1952), an American philosopher, psychologist, and educational reformer. Dewey wrote extensively on education, and his work has had more impact on American education than that of any other philosopher. His ideas continue to be actively debated by educators today (e.g., Durst, 2005; J. Rogers & Oakes, 2005).

Dewey first encountered progressive teaching practices through his children, who attended an experimental lab school in Chicago. He became so fascinated with student-centered teaching that in 1896, he established his own lab school connected to the University of Chicago,

Progressivism focuses instruction on real-world problem solving and individual development.

where he worked. The school became the birthplace of progressive education, which gained prominence during the early to mid-20th century. Progressive education advocated a learner-centered curriculum and individual problem solving, and is reflected in Brad's views in his discussion with Allie. For Dewey, classrooms became microcosms of a democratic society: What students learn in school will help them in the real world. Goals such as personal growth and preparation for participation in a democracy are met through an activity-oriented curriculum. Content, which historically was an end in itself, now became a tool for solving problems.

Dewey's ideas created both excitement and criticism. To some, seeing learners actively involved in solving real-world problems was exciting. To others, progressive education seemed to de-emphasize content and cater to student whims.

Interest in progressive education as a general movement waned after the mid-20th century, caused in part by a well-intentioned but misguided attempt at fostering life-adjustment courses such as "Developing an Effective Personality" and "Marriage and Living," which were attacked by critics as devoid of content and lacking intellectual rigor (Norris, 2004). These criticisms were fueled by the furor caused by Russia's launching of the Sputnik satellite in 1957. The fact that Russia beat the United States into space symbolized a weak American educational system, critics asserted, and the progressive movement declined.

Nevertheless, aspects of progressive education, such as inquiry, problem-based instruction, and cooperative learning, are alive and well today. Dewey's defenders argue that critics either misrepresent Dewey or don't understand him (Engel & Martin, 2005; S. Weiss, DeFalco, & Weiss, 2005). Dewey didn't de-emphasize knowledge and understanding in favor of student interests, his defenders assert.

> He saw clearly that to ask, "Which is more important: the interests of the child or the knowledge of subject-matter?" was to ask a very dumb question indeed. The teacher's task, for Dewey, was to create an interaction between the child's interest and the funded knowledge of the adult world. (Proefriedt, 1999, p. 28)

Progressivism—when properly applied—suggests that effective education isn't a matter of process *or* content; it's a matter of process *and* content (J. Johnston, 2004; S. Weiss et al., 2005).

The progressive movement in education has recently experienced a boost with increased interest in **21st Century Skills**, a reform movement focusing on the development of cognitive skills that students will need to survive and succeed in a rapidly changing

PEARSON
myeducationlab

To see an elementary teacher using one of the educational philosophies to guide her instruction, go to the *Assignments and Activities* section of Topic 8: *Philosophy of Education* in the MyEducationLab for your course and complete the activity titled *Philosophy in an Elementary Classroom.*

21st Century Skills A recent reform movement that emphasizes the development of students' technological, analytical, and communication skills.

technological world. These skills emphasize technology as well as analytical and communication skills, and teachers are encouraged to use open-ended problem-based and project-based instruction that places students in small groups to work on real-world problems (Sawchuk, 2009a). Not surprisingly, perennialists criticize the movement for its lack of emphasis on content (Sawchuk, 2009b).

PROGRESSIVISM IN THE CLASSROOM   To see how progressivist philosophy can influence your teaching, let's join a group of urban middle school teachers as they talk over lunch.

"I'm having a heck of a time with my students," Kelly Erhardt, a first-year English teacher, confesses in the teachers' lounge after school. *"They simply couldn't care less about learning to write or studying To Kill a Mockingbird."*

"Welcome to middle school teaching," Dan Shafer, a geography teacher and "veteran" of 3 years, smiles. *"These kids have to see how the stuff they study applies to their lives. No magic solution exists, but here's what I did with my geography kids, and it went really well.*

"I told them we'd be working with maps all year, so understanding scale was important, both in class and in life outside of school. I showed them a map of our state and talked about scale. Then, I broke students into pairs, and each pair had to decide on a scale, construct a map of the room, and present it to the class. Some were a little disorganized, but gradually they did okay, and they're learning to work together. Tomorrow, we're going outside to make a map of the school grounds—to scale."

"That does sound like fun," Kelly responds. *"I wish we had done something like that when I studied maps. All we did was listen to the teacher talk."*

"Can't do that, or you'll lose them," Mary Burbank, the science teacher and a 10-year veteran, joins in. *"I'll offer another example that you might consider. . . . Yesterday, I started class by swinging a pair of athletic socks tied to a string around my head and then letting it go. I asked them what they observed and led them to notice that the socks traveled in a straight line after I let go of the string and they kept on going until the wall of the room stopped them. So, then I asked them what happens when they ride in a car and go around a curve. They said they were 'thrown' against the door of the car. So, then we got to the idea that being 'thrown' against the door was our bodies' tendencies to travel in a straight line as the car rounded the curve. We also talked about why we wear seatbelts, and they got the idea that when we slam on the brakes, our bodies tend to keep going, so we wear seatbelts to keep us from getting hurt. I finally described what we were discussing as the concept inertia, and not only did they get it, they liked it.*

"Like Dan just said, they have to see how ideas relate to their lives. If I started out lecturing about inertia, they'd drift off in five minutes. You have to figure out how to connect English to them right now. . . . You're a smart kid; you'll figure it out."

Think for a minute about the advice Kelly's colleagues gave her. None of the activities involved students' simply listening while teachers lectured; instead, the teachers involved students in learning activities that related to their personal lives. These activities reflect the emphasis placed on learner thinking and involvement that we see in many classrooms today and are examples of a progressivist philosophy (Bransford, Derry, Berliner, Hammerness, & Beckett, 2005; Eggen & Kauchak, 2010).

Social Reconstructionism

Think about our world today. Our students and the society they live in have changed. Too many students use drugs, engage in irresponsible sexual behavior, and bully other students. Many of them live in poverty, and some are homeless. In the world outside of school, maintaining a clean environment and having adequate supplies of water for growing populations are problems so huge that *Time* magazine focused on them in its De-

PEARSON
myeducationlab

To watch one fifth-grade teacher's attempts to help her students find the areas of irregular figures, go to the *Assignments and Activities* section of Topic 8: *Philosophy of Education* in the MyEducationLab for your course and complete the activity titled *Pledge of Allegiance*.

Social reconstructionism focuses students on critical problems in today's society.

cember 15, 2008 issue (B. Walsh, 2008). Each of these problems thrives in ignorance and is rooted in misinformation.

Social reconstructionists believe schools and teachers should be addressing these problems. **Social reconstructionism** is an educational philosophy asserting that schools, teachers, and students should take the lead in addressing social problems and improving society. Social reconstructionists answer the question "What is the purpose of schooling?" by saying that schooling should be used to eliminate social inequities by creating a new and more just society. The curriculum would include topics that reflect social issues, and discussion would be a primary teaching method.

The roots of social reconstructionism in the United States are traced to Theodore Brameld (1904–1987), an American philosopher and educator. Influenced by the thinking of John Dewey (1923, 1938) and affected by the horrors of World War II, Brameld believed that the human race possessed the potential either to annihilate itself through conflict and weapons such as the atomic bomb or to create a humane and just society through the use of technology and compassion. Teachers and schools, he believed, should serve as the agents for creating this just society.

Paulo Freire (1921–1997), a Brazilian philosopher and educator whose concerns for the poor and underprivileged were colored by his personal experiences with poverty and hunger during the Great Depression of the 1930s, also influenced social reconstructionist thinking in this country. He believed that schools are essentially institutions that dominant groups in specific cultures use to maintain social inequities (Freire, 1989). For example, many suburban schools in our country are modern, roomy, positive environments where teachers have access to adequate resources. Urban schools, by contrast—with students who are overwhelmingly members of cultural minorities—are often old, overcrowded environments where not even enough textbooks are available (Kozol, 1991, 2005). Social reconstructionists such as Friere would cite these facts as evidence for their position.

This section addresses the fifth item in our *This I Believe* feature, "Teachers should encourage their students to think about their personal responsibilities in making the world a better place." Social reconstructionists believe this statement is true; the next section describes some ways teachers can accomplish this.

Social reconstructionism An educational philosophy suggesting that schools, teachers, and students should lead in alleviating social inequities in our society.

SOCIAL RECONSTRUCTIONISM IN THE CLASSROOM   Let's look now at how the thinking of social reconstructionists can influence teachers.

> *Abby Wilkenson, an eighth-grade physical science teacher, shows her students a DVD recording of* Planet in Peril: Battle Lines, *a documentary about the ecological problems facing our planet. She also gives them copies of the article "Dying for a Drink," featured in the December 15 issue of* Time *magazine (B. Walsh, 2008), and assigns it for reading.*
>
> *The students examine the issues raised in both the video episode and the article, and Abby directs a discussion that leads to conclusions about what they personally, at this point in their lives, could do to help make our environment more livable.*
>
> *Jeremy Stevens, an American history teacher, has his students go to the Internet and watch Martin Luther King's famous "I Have a Dream" speech. In the speech, delivered on the steps of the Lincoln Memorial in Washington, DC, King describes his desire for a future where Blacks, Whites, and other races would coexist harmoniously as equals.*
>
> *"This speech was a defining moment of the American civil rights movement," he explains to his students.*
>
> *The next day, he displays the following paragraphs from the speech:*
>
>> I have a dream that one day on the red hills of Georgia, the sons of former slaves and the sons of former slave owners will be able to sit down together at the table of brotherhood.
>>
>> I have a dream that my four little children will one day live in a nation where they will not be judged by the color of their skin but by the content of their character.
>
> *He reminds students that the speech was given in 1963 and asks them why the speech in general, and the two paragraphs in particular, were so significant at the time. He then asks, "To what extent do you believe that racial injustice and inequality have been overcome in our country and in the world?" The question sparks hot debate among students, and Jerome reminds them that if they're practicing justice and equality in their classroom, all opinions are allowed and respected, no matter how strongly they disagree with each other.*
>
> *The class closes the discussion by creating a list of things they can do to promote justice and tolerance for dissenting opinions in their own school and how they can promote them in their lives outside of school.*

Abby and Jeremy both taught the traditional topics included in physical science and American history. In addition, however, they examined issues influencing the world both today and in the future, and they encouraged students to make commitments to make the world a better place in which to live. Abby's and Jeremy's efforts are applications of social reconstructionist philosophy.

Social reconstructionism can be politically controversial (Manzo, 2008). For example, conservative critics argue that social reconstructionists have abandoned intellectual pursuits in schools, and instead use schools for political purposes. Critics further contend that social reconstructionism is as controlling as more conservative philosophies, such as perennialism and essentialism; it merely establishes controls more to proponents' liking (Ozmon & Craver, 2007). Advocates respond that making and acting on pure moral decisions are an essential part of being a good citizen in our democracy. Filling students' heads with abstract ideas without encouraging them to develop a moral compass for their actions leaves them adrift in an amoral and even immoral world.

Classroom applications of the major educational philosophies are summarized in Table 7.1.

Table 7.1   Classroom Applications of the Educational Philosophies

Philosophy	Educational Goal	Curriculum	Teaching Methods	Learning Environment	Assessment
Perennialism	Train the intellect	Focus on enduring ideas	Lecture; questioning; discussion	High structure; strong focus on academic work	Frequent assessment and feedback
Essentialism	Acquire the basic skills needed to function in today's world	Essential knowledge and basic skills	Lecture; questioning; practice and feedback	High structure; strong focus on essential knowledge and skills	Frequent objective and performance assessments and feedback
Progressivism	Develop problem solving, decision making, and other life skills	Practice in problem solving and other life skills	Emphasizes applications in problem-based learning, cooperative learning, and guided discovery	Democratic; collaborative; emphasis on learner responsibility	Ongoing informal assessment
Social Reconstructionism	Contribute to the creation of a just society	Social issues	Discussion; collaboration; student projects	Model for equity and justice	Examination of written products; informal observation

How Psychology of Learning Influences Educational Philosophy

As you saw earlier, all professions have systems of beliefs that guide their professional practice, and that a *normative philosophy* guides professionals in their actions. In education, the way teachers ought to practice is influenced by our beliefs about the way students learn (Gibboney, 2006). Let's briefly look at three views of learning, each of which has influenced philosophical thinking.

BEHAVIORISM

During class, you offer a comment, and your instructor says, "Very insightful response. Excellent thinking." As a result, you're more likely to offer comments in the future.

This example illustrates a basic premise of *behaviorism*, which says that people's behavior is determined primarily by influences in the environment. Because you were praised, you're more likely to comment in the future; behaviorists would say you were *reinforced* for your comment. On the other hand, had your instructor frowned or made a sarcastic remark in response to your comment, you would have been *punished*, and consequently less likely to make comments in the future.

Behaviorism is a view of learning stating that people respond to influences in their environment. This view treats people as passive, responding to reinforcers and punishers that shape their behavior.

A normative philosophy influenced by behaviorism recommends that teachers provide appropriate reinforcers for desirable behaviors in their students as well as appropriate punishers for undesirable behaviors. For example, if teachers want their students to be able to multiply fractions, such as $\frac{1}{3} \times \frac{1}{4}$, they would present the rule saying, "To multiply fractions, you first multiply the numerators and then multiply the denominators." Students would then be reinforced for getting $\frac{1}{12}$ as an answer.

Behaviorism was the dominant view of learning until the middle of the 20th century. As you might expect, behaviorism is controversial with educators, but it continues to be commonly applied in classroom management systems.

Behaviorism A view of learning asserting that people respond primarily to influences in their environment.

CONSTRUCTIVISM   **Constructivism** is an alternative view of learners and learning that suggests that to make sense of their experiences, students actively construct their own understanding of the topics they study instead of having that understanding transmitted to them by someone else, such as a teacher. For example, language arts teachers have students read literature and then, through questioning, help them understand the meaning of what they've read. Science teachers involve students in experiments and then discuss them to help them understand the results. Social studies teachers have students analyze important historical events to help them understand their implications for us today. In each of these scenarios, students construct meaning with the help of the teacher. This is true for all learning, according to constructivists.

Constructivism has epistemological connections. For instance, in our earlier discussion of epistemology, we found that experts disagree about how we know about the world, with some believing that knowledge should come from the teacher and others believing that students actually construct their own understanding from the experiences teachers provide. Constructivism suggests that the way people come to know what they know is to construct the knowledge for themselves.

Constructivism is a part of a larger area called **cognitive psychology**, which views learners as thinking beings who are mentally active in attempts to gather information, organize it to make sense of it, and store it in memory for future use. Around the middle of the 20th century, cognitive psychology replaced behaviorism as the dominant view of learning, and it has been the most influential psychological theory in education since that time.

A normative philosophy influenced by constructivism recommends that teachers provide students with experiences, and then guide them in the process of constructing a valid understanding of those experiences. A teacher grounding her instruction in constructivism—rather than have students simply follow a rule for multiplying fractions—would demonstrate *why* $\frac{1}{3} \times \frac{1}{4} = \frac{1}{12}$ to help the operation make sense to the students. For example, the teacher might have them fold a piece of paper into thirds and then further divide the same piece into fourths—producing 12 equal parts. Through questioning, the teacher would help students see how what they did related to the math equation they were trying to understand. A normative philosophy based on constructivism results in very different instruction than one influenced by behaviorism.

HUMANISTIC PSYCHOLOGY   Also about the middle of the 20th century, an alternative view of learners began to emerge. This view, described as **humanistic psychology**, emphasizes the growth and needs of the "whole person," physical, social, emotional, thinking, and aesthetic. It has been strongly influenced by Carl Rogers (1967) and Abraham Maslow (1968, 1970), prominent American humanistic psychologists, who advocate a learner-centered and nondirective approach to education.

Humanistic psychology is grounded in the belief that all people instinctively attempt to be all they're capable of being—to be *self-actualized*. A normative philosophy influenced by humanistic psychology suggests that schools and teachers should strive to meet all of students' growth needs—physical, social, emotional, and intellectual; providing hot breakfasts for students who haven't eaten before they come to school and creating a safe and supportive learning environment are applications of this orientation. Teachers should be empathetic, and should care for their students unconditionally, helping them feel like worthy individuals. In the classroom, teachers should create *learning communities*, where the teacher and students work together to help everyone learn and grow as much as possible.

In the *Exploring Diversity* box, we examine how culture and philosophy interact, and classroom implications of these connections. Then, in the *Taking a Stand in an Era of Reform* feature box on page 212, we examine controversies surrounding essentialism in the classroom.

PEARSON
myeducationlab

To see two teachers with widely differing philosophies of education, go to the *Assignments and Activities* section of Topic 8: *Philosophy of Education* in the MyEducationLab for your course and complete the activity titled *Philosophy in the Social Studies Classroom*.

Constructivism A view of learning that asserts that to make sense of their experiences, students construct their own understanding of the topics they study instead of having that understanding transmitted to them by someone else.

Cognitive psychology A view of learners that suggests that they're thinking beings who are mentally active as they gather information, organize it to make sense of it, and store it in memory for future use.

Humanistic psychology A psychological view that emphasizes the "whole person's development," including physical, social, emotional, thinking, and aesthetic dimensions.

Philosophy and Cultural Minorities

To this point, the philosophies we've examined have been "Western," meaning their origins are European or American. Two principles undergird this Western orientation: The preeminence of the individual and the emphasis on rational thought. The first is seen in the emphasis on the individual's growth of knowledge in both perennialism and essentialism and the interaction of the individual with the environment in progressivism. The second is reflected in the emphasis on objectivity, science, and the scientific method. Essentialism and progressivism both emphasize clear, rational thinking and science as a way of knowing.

Some philosophers criticize this emphasis on science and objectivity and point to its undesirable consequences in American life. Americans are working more hours per week than they ever have in the past, technology dominates our lives, and we are chronically sleep deprived, for example. Critics of this Western orientation assert that valuable alternatives can be found in the philosophies of other cultures.

Some philosophies, such as those embedded in certain Native American cultures, use the shared folklore of elders and knowledge that comes from the heart as their sources of wisdom (Starnes, 2006). Because people in these cultures have a long history of living in harmony with the land, their philosophies emphasize ecological balance and interpersonal cooperation; this emphasis results in valuing individual achievement primarily as it contributes to a group's overall well-being. Competition and individual displays of achievement are frowned upon. Understanding these differences can help explain why Navajo students shun competitive classrooms

and are sometimes reluctant to participate in the competitive verbal give-and-take of fast-paced questioning sessions that require individuals to demonstrate how much they know (Starnes, 2006).

Similarly, for some African cultures, feelings and personal relationships, as ways of knowing, are as important as or more important than science and rational thought (Nieto, 2004). Further, in many African cultures, art and music are important means not only of expression but also of seeking knowledge. This philosophical view helps explain why music was such a prominent part of slaves' lives in America, why African Americans have made such a strong contribution to modern and impressionistic art, and why African influences can be seen in much of the contemporary music in Europe and the Americas.

Many Asians also value harmony. The desire to balance nature, life, family, and society leads to reverence for elders, respect for authority, and adherence to traditions. Because cooperation is so important, being polite is highly valued, and feelings and emotions tend to be controlled to maintain order and proper social relationships (Fong, 2007). Awareness of these perspectives helps teachers understand characteristics commonly attributed to Asian American students. For instance, they're often described as shy, reluctant to speak out in class, and restrained in their nonverbal behavior, which sometimes makes reading their nonverbal cues difficult.

Diversity in Your Classroom
Teachers should be sensitive to their students' beliefs, but they should also be cautious about drawing conclusions and making individual decisions about students on the basis of group descriptions alone. Critics argue that these de-

scriptions are little more than stereotypes that grossly oversimplify the complexities of alternative philosophies (Sternberg, 2007). For example, some Americans simplistically think of Africa as a country, not realizing that it's a vast continent more culturally and linguistically diverse than North or South America. In a similar way, the term *Asian* encompasses students from a number of diverse countries and cultures, including China, Japan, Vietnam, and Korea. To speak of a singular "African philosophy"—or Native American or Asian philosophy, for that matter—does an injustice to diverse groups of people and their philosophies (Ngo & Lee, 2007). Further, people are people, and categorizing them on the basis of sweeping and uncertain philosophical generalizations is questionable at best and perhaps even potentially damaging.

Rather than viewing students as Hispanic, Native American, or African American, or as representative of any other cultural or ethnic group, we should see students as individuals. Concluding that a boy named Ted Chang, for example, doesn't speak out in class solely because of the influence of his Chinese culture is unwise. Getting to know Ted as an individual will better help you understand why he's quiet and will help you find ways to involve him in learning activities, just as you would involve any student in your classes (Banks, 2008).

Respecting and valuing cultural differences are a good idea; making decisions that may detract from learning, based on overgeneralizations about these differences, is not. Realizing that not all people have the same philosophical orientations will help you be more sensitive to important individual differences in your students.

QUESTIONS TO CONSIDER

1. In terms of minority students' philosophies that are different from Western philosophies, should teachers attempt to change students' philosophies or adapt their classrooms to match students' attitudes and beliefs?

2. What are some ways that teachers can learn about the cultures and philosophies of their students?

myeducationlab To respond to these questions online, explore this topic further, and receive feedback, go to the *Book Specific Resources* section in the MyEducationLab for your course, select your text, and then select *Exploring Diversity* for Chapter 7.

Taking a Stand in an Era of Reform

The Essential Knowledge Debate

Americans in general, and American students in particular, are repeatedly criticized for their lack of knowledge and skills. For example, in a survey of 18- to 24-year-olds, 6 of 10 respondents couldn't locate Iraq on a map of the Middle East (Manzo, 2006b), and another study revealed that only about half of American fifth graders were able to solve the problem $45 \times 26 = ?$ (Stigler, Gonzales, Kawanaka, Knoll, & Serrano, 1999).

This issue has spawned books such as *The Dumbest Generation* (Bauerlein, 2008), and newspaper columnists' comments, such as "We are becoming the stupid giant of planet Earth: richer than Midas, mightier than Thor, dumber than rocks" (Pitts, 2008). The issues have even made their way into late-night comedy, such as *The Tonight Show's* segment "Jaywalking" in which former host Jay Leno asked people on the street basic questions such as, "Who are the people on Mount Rushmore?" which they could rarely answer.

In response to criticisms about American students' lack of knowledge, educators have written standards (introduced in Chapter 1 and examined in detail in Chapter 14) in virtually every content area. Experts call standards "essential questions: doorways to understanding" (Wiggins & McTighe, 2005, p. 105). Every state has specified standards, and to hold students and schools accountable, they have created tests to measure the extent to which the standards are being met. NCLB required that all states create standards for what every child should understand about different subjects (Christie, 2005; Popham, 2004). Standards apply to teachers as well: Virtually all states now require teachers to pass some type of exam in order to be licensed (Swanson, 2008).

THE ISSUE

Leaders who support standards believe that all people should master certain well-defined skills and bodies of knowledge, a view grounded in essentialist educational philosophy. Specifying standards and then testing students to ensure that they're being met are a way to ensure that students are acquiring essential knowledge and skills, they argue. E. D. Hirsch (1987), author of the controversial but widely read book *Cultural Literacy: What Every American Needs to Know*, illustrates this position. He identified a vast list of facts, concepts, and other information that he believed all citizens should know to function effectively in American society. For example, his alphabetized list of essential knowledge includes the following ideas or terms: Truman–Macarthur controversy, Nat Turner, Tutankhamen, Two China Policy, and Typhoid Mary. (When we shared this list with our students, many of them scratched their heads, and most weren't sure just how essential all of the items were.) Since then, he has produced a series of paperbacks that he describes as *the Core Knowledge curriculum*. Hirsch has written books such as *What Your Fourth Grader Needs to Know: Fundamentals of a Good Fourth-Grade Education* (Hirsch, 2005) and similar titles for each of the grade levels K–6. His *Core Knowledge* series is popular with both parents and teachers, because it provides concrete suggestions about what's important to learn and teach.

Research on learning also indicates that prior knowledge is essential for understanding new content (Bruning, Schraw, Norby, & Ronning, 2004; Eggen & Kauchak, 2010). For instance, to understand the civil unrest in the United States during the 1960s, students need to understand the relationships among the Vietnam War, the civil rights movement, and people's growing distrust of government and authority. Similarly, to understand the problems of sub-Saharan Africa, learners must also understand European colonialism as well as the geography and climate of this vast area. New knowledge builds on prior knowledge, and when this knowledge is lacking, learning suffers.

Critics argue, however, that Hirsch's series focuses on rote memory rather than on understanding, and they further assert that having students memorize more facts is an approach that has been proven unsuccessful (Kuhn, 2007). For example, K–12 students already are exposed to a great deal of American history (they take American history courses during both middle school and high school, plus smatterings during their elementary years). But, critics note, they apparently retain little of the content, as indicated by a number of surveys. So the issue is more complex than simply requiring more content and courses: Students apparently aren't learning from the courses they do take.

Critics of the essential knowledge position also cite research indicating that personal motivation and the ability to use strategies to acquire knowledge are better predictors of later success than the accumulation of facts (Berliner, 2004;

Kuhn, 2007). Rather than more facts, we need to teach students how to access information on the Internet and critically evaluate the overload of information they're already bombarded with daily.

Critics also question whether increased knowledge makes people happier and more productive workers, and they cite motivational research suggesting that increasing learner readiness and eagerness to learn should be the primary goals of schools (Schunk, Pintrich, & Meece, 2008). This position is more consistent with progressivism than with essentialism.

Finally, what knowledge is "essential" is hard to determine (Gutiérrez, 2002). For example, is it more important to remember that Christopher Columbus "discovered America" in 1492 or that his voyage precipitated huge social and cultural changes that are still being felt today? Such questions have been debated for years, and the debates will almost certainly continue. Further, the sheer amount of knowledge called for by standards is overwhelming. One testing ex-

pert commented, "Even if a modest number of super-general content standards are being used, beneath these standards there are still way too many curricular aims for teachers to successfully promote in a given year. Similarly, there are way too many curricular aims to assess in the hour or so available for the administration of any standards-based test" (Popham, 2004, pp. 77–78).

YOU TAKE A STAND

Now it's your turn to take a position on the issue. Is the emphasis on essential knowledge and standards a productive way to think about teaching, or do other philosophical positions offer a more promising perspective?

myeducationlab To explore both sides of this issue and take a stand, go to the *Book Specific Resources* section in the MyEducationLab for your course, select your text, and then select *Taking a Stand in an Era of Reform* for Chapter 7.

ISSUES IN EDUCATION

■ ■ ■ ■ ■ CHECK YOUR UNDERSTANDING

3.1 Describe the major philosophies of education.

3.2 Because students must be able to function effectively in, and adapt to, a changing world, a teacher emphasizes the "whole person"—physical, social, emotional, and intellectual—in her students. She stresses and models physical fitness, involves her students in discussions to help them practice social skills and perspective taking, and involves them in problem solving about modern-day topics. To which of the educational philosophies are the teacher's efforts most closely related? Explain.

3.3 You visit a school, and you overhear a conversation between two teachers. One says, "I love teaching Shakespeare. His work has been studied for hundreds of years, and it's as timely now as it was then." Which educational philosophy is best illustrated by the teacher's comment? Explain.

3.4 A teacher who wants her students to examine racism and injustice involves them in a unit on nonviolent noncooperation using a study of Gandhi's struggles against racism in India as an example. She further illustrates the ideas with a study of Martin Luther King Jr.'s nonviolent protests against American racism. To which of the educational philosophies is the teacher's efforts most closely related? Explain.

For feedback on these exercises, go to the appendix, *Check Your Understanding*, located in the back of this text.

DEVELOPING YOUR PHILOSOPHY OF EDUCATION

The philosophies you've studied in this chapter will help you make one of the most important decisions of your professional life: what kind of teacher you want to be by forming your own philosophy of education. This decision will influence the goals you emphasize in your classes, the teaching strategies you'll use as a teacher, and the criteria you use to reflect on and analyze your teaching (see Figure 7.1).

Professionals are able to articulate what they're doing and why. For instance, if you walk into a classroom, see students involved in basic skills activities, and ask the teacher why he or she selected these activities, a professional will give you clear and specific answers. A professional teacher holding an essentialist philosophy would answer that the activities will help the students acquire core knowledge and skills that learners need to function effectively in the world. Some teachers, however, do activities simply because the activities are next in their textbooks or curriculum guides or because they did the activities last year; these are inadequate and unprofessional reasons.

If teachers are clear about their philosophies, they can make systematic changes when they conclude that their instruction needs improvement. If their philosophies aren't clear, they're less likely to make needed changes, or they make changes at random. In either case, student learning suffers and professional growth doesn't occur. This is why philosophy is so important for beginning teachers.

As you begin to form your personal philosophy, keep three ideas in mind. First, any philosophy is evolving and dynamic, and will change and be refined as you gather experiences and learn. So don't be concerned if your own philosophy is initially uncertain; it will crystallize and become clearer as you think about and use it. Second, your personal philosophy is likely to include elements of more than one philosophy. Third, be open to other perspectives; changing your views as a professional is an indicator of the open-mindedness necessary for personal and professional growth.

The Role of Beliefs in a Philosophy of Education

To begin establishing your own philosophy of education, first try to identify your own beliefs, because these exert a powerful influence on how you'll teach (Speer, 2008). Allie and Brad both did a good job of describing their beliefs about teaching and learning. Here is a summary of Allie's beliefs:

> *"Everything we learn depends on what we already know."*
> *"There's real practical stuff out there that kids need. They have to be good readers, they need to be able to write and do math, and they need to understand this stuff, the science I'm teaching."*
> *"Practice, thorough assessment, and detailed feedback are some of the best ways we have of getting them to learn. That's reality."*

And here is a summary of Brad's beliefs:

> *"The only way [kids are] going to get good at making decisions is to be put in situations where they're forced to make decisions. . . . That's how the world works."*
> *"Being put in situations where they have to practice making decisions is 'real, practical, stuff.'"*
> *"Reality is, in fact, what you perceive it to be, and there's no objective source out there to decide which view is the 'right one.'"*

PEARSON
myeducationlab

Go to the *Building Teaching Skills and Dispositions* section of Topic 8: *Philosophy of Education* in the MyEducationLab for your course and complete the activity titled *Educational Philosophy and Teaching Practice*.

You can see that Allie's and Brad's beliefs are quite different, but both were sure about what they believed and were able to clearly state their positions.

The following questions can help you get started in identifying your own beliefs.

- What's the purpose of schooling? For example, should students focus on content, or is the development of self-concept, interpersonal skills, and other personal qualities more important?

- Is my role as a teacher to pass knowledge on to students, or should I guide students as they learn on their own?

- Is motivating students part of my job, or should motivation come from within students?

- How do students best learn? Should I push them, or should they be left largely on their own?

Examining Your Beliefs

Once you identify your beliefs, you should examine and analyze them. This is where knowledge and the educational philosophies you studied in the previous section become important. How does Allie, for example, know that her beliefs are valid? Do they "feel" right? Do they make sense intuitively? Is feeling or intuition adequate to justify the belief, or must she have research evidence to indicate that they're valid? If Allie is an essentialist or a progressivist, feelings and intuition are not adequate or trustworthy; she must have evidence.

From this discussion, we can see why understanding philosophy is important. For instance, if Allie describes herself as an essentialist but then accepts feelings and intuition as validation for her beliefs, her thinking is inconsistent, and she should reconsider what she really believes about knowing, learning, and teaching.

To assess your developing beliefs about education, respond to the following statements and then answer the questions that follow. Use this scale in making your responses:

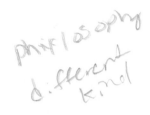

> 5 = strongly agree
> 4 = agree
> 3 = neither agree nor disagree
> 2 = disagree
> 1 = strongly disagree
>
> 1. Schools should emphasize important knowledge more than students' personal interests.   1   2   3   4   5
>
> 2. Teachers should emphasize interdisciplinary subject matter that encourages project-oriented, democratic classrooms.   1   2   3   4   5
>
> 3. Schools should emphasize each student's responsibility in making the world a better place.   1   2   3   4   5
>
> 4. The primary aim of education is to develop a person's intellectual capacity.   1   2   3   4   5
>
> 5. Schools should emphasize basic skills more than humanistic ideals.   1   2   3   4   5
>
> 6. Teachers should guide student's investigations about the physical and social world around them.   1   2   3   4   5
>
> 7. The best teachers lead students in discussions about important social issues.   1   2   3   4   5

8. The goals of education should be the same for everyone: All students should understand the important literature, mathematics, and science of Western civilization.

1 2 3 4 5

9. The purpose of schools is to ensure practical preparation for life and work more than personal development.

1 2 3 4 5

10. Curriculum should emerge from students' needs and interests; it *should not* be prescribed in advance.

1 2 3 4 5

11. The best education emphasizes the great works in the arts and humanities.

1 2 3 4 5

12. It is more important for teachers to involve students in activities that analyze and criticize society than to have them accumulate a lot of information.

1 2 3 4 5

13. Education should enhance personal growth through problem solving in the present rather than emphasizing preparation for a distant future.

1 2 3 4 5

14. Human nature's most distinctive quality is the ability to reason; therefore, the intellect should be the focus of education.

1 2 3 4 5

15. Schools should take the lead in combating racism and sexism camouflaged as traditional values.

1 2 3 4 5

16. Teachers should help students learn a common core of useful knowledge, *not* experiment with their own views about curricula.

1 2 3 4 5

Now add up your responses using the following scale:

Strongly Disagree = 1; Disagree = 2; Agree/Disagree = 3; Agree = 4; Strongly Agree = 5.

Perennialism:
Item #4 _____ + #8 _____ + #11 _____ + #14 _____ = _14_

Essentialism
Item #1 _____ + #5 _____ + #9 _____ + #16 _____ = _16_

Progressivism:
Item #2 _____ + #6 _____ + #10 _____ + #13 _____ = _19_

Social Reconstructionism
Item #3 _____ + #7 _____ + #12 _____ + #15 _____ = _15_

What do your responses tell you about your beliefs about education? How can these beliefs be formed into a comprehensive personal philosophy of education?

Forming a Philosophy

All new knowledge depends on what we already know. So, my job is to help kids learn as much as they can about the topics I teach, and that's what I try to do every day. I know that I can get them to learn. The best way to get kids to learn is to have them practice and then provide them with feedback. So, I'm going to give them lots

Table 7.2 An Analysis of Allie's Philosophy of Education

Belief Statement	Component of Her Philosophy
"Everything we learn depends on what we already know."	"My job is to help kids learn as much as they can about the topics I teach, and that's what I try to do every day."
"There's real practical stuff out there that kids need. They have to be good readers, they need to be able to write and do math, and they need to understand this stuff, the science I'm teaching."	"I'm going to be sure that the kids learn the real, practical stuff they need to function in today's world."
"Practice, thorough assessment, and detailed feedback are some of the best ways we have of getting them to learn. That's reality."	"I'm going to give them lots of practice; I'm going to quiz them thoroughly and often, and I'm going to give them detailed feedback about the quizzes."

of practice; I'm going to quiz them thoroughly and often, and I'm going to give them detailed feedback about the quizzes. If I do my job, they'll learn.

What you've just read is a succinct description of Allie's philosophy of education: It's clear, well articulated, and consistent with her beliefs. The relationships between her beliefs and components of her philosophy are outlined in Table 7.2

Because Allie's philosophy is well articulated, she can use it to guide her thinking as she defines her goals and designs learning activities and assessments. It helps ensure that all three—goals, learning activities, and assessments—are consistent with one another. You may or may not agree with Allie's goals or the rationale for them, but the fact that she's clear in her thinking increases the likelihood that her students will reach the goals, and she'll be more likely to make conscious choices to change and improve her teaching when she sees evidence that change is needed.

Armed with your analysis of your beliefs, and a description of Allie's philosophy, you should now be ready to create your personal philosophy that can guide your thinking and actions.

Dialoguing with other teachers can help beginning teachers shape their personal philosophy of education.

Philosophy of Education in Urban Environments

Forming a coherent philosophy of education is important for all teachers; for new teachers in urban classrooms, it's crucial. The philosophy that you develop will help you understand your role in urban classrooms and how you can best help urban students learn and develop (Szczesiul, 2004).

EXAMINING YOUR BELIEFS ABOUT URBAN LEARNERS   Understanding your own beliefs in forming your personal philosophy of education is particularly important when you work in urban environments. Answering the question "What do I believe about urban learners and working in urban settings?" is essential, and becoming aware of your beliefs will strongly influence how you approach your work with urban students. For instance, consider the following contrasting beliefs.

URBAN EDUCATION

- Urban students are much like all students: They want to learn, but they need some help and encouragement.

- Urban students don't want to learn, and they're in school only because they're required to be there.

- Urban students need caring and supportive teachers, as do all students.

- Working in an urban setting is much like working in any other school.

- Homework is as important a part of instruction when working with urban students as it is with all students.

- Urban students believe respecting and liking teachers are viewed as a sign of weakness.

- Working in an urban setting is dangerous, and teachers must be vigilant to prevent possible personal harm.

- There is little point to assigning homework to urban students, because they won't do it.

Though only examples, you can see how these different beliefs can influence the way you approach your work with urban students. For example, if you believe that—at a basic level—urban students want to learn and that their seeming reluctance is more a function of their life outside school than of a basic disinterest in learning, you will expend greater effort in helping them understand the importance of the topics you teach than if you believe that they genuinely don't want to learn. Similarly, if you believe that working in an urban setting is much like working in any other school, you will interact with students much differently than if you believe that urban environments are dangerous, where you must constantly "watch your back."

DEVELOPING A PHILOSOPHY FOR URBAN SETTINGS   As with forming a philosophy of education in general, constructing a philosophy that guides your actions in urban settings begins with a careful examination of your beliefs. However, the process of identifying and articulating your beliefs with respect to urban settings requires additional study, reflection, and perhaps some soul searching, because, as you've seen in our other discussions of teaching in urban environments, many negative stereotypes exist about urban schools and urban students. If you're uninformed, it's easy to slip into accepting a stereotype as true. When this happens, your negative beliefs will detract from your effectiveness in working with urban students.

Urban classrooms are challenging, and we're not suggesting that a set of positive beliefs will make your work with urban students simple and easy. However, a well-formed philosophy that you can reflect on can serve as a powerful foundation as you teach and interact with your urban students.

We hope that this chapter provides you with the professional knowledge needed to begin your journey toward developing a personal philosophy and that it encourages you to think about teaching in different ways. At this point, you won't have all the answers you'll need to decide what education should be and how you can help make it that way. But if you're now able to begin asking some important questions, then our goal for the chapter has been fulfilled. Good luck.

■ ■ ■ ■ ■ CHECK YOUR UNDERSTANDING

4.1 Why is a personal philosophy of education important?

4.2 What are the three essential steps involved in forming a philosophy of education?

4.3 Look again at Brad's thinking, as indicated by his conversation with Allie. Based on this information, what is his philosophy of education? Explain how his philosophy is based on his beliefs.

For feedback on these exercises, go to the appendix, *Check Your Understanding*, located in the back of this text.

As you read the next section on developing your own philosophy of education, think about how philosophy will influence what you do in the classroom. Then answer the question at the end of this feature.

Developing Your Philosophy of Education

You're an American History teacher, and you want your students to do more than simply memorize their way through the information you're teaching: You want them to develop their critical-thinking skills, learn to solve problems, make informed decisions, and get involved in lessons. This turns out to be a daunting task, however. The students seem to want you to describe every required detail in assignments, and when you call on students who don't have their hands raised, the most common response is "I didn't have my hand up" or "I don't know." In other cases, they say, "C'mon, just tell us what you want us to know," and "Why do we have to learn this stuff?"

How would you respond to these students?

7 MEETING YOUR LEARNING OBJECTIVES

1. Define *philosophy*, and explain the difference between *philosophy* and *theory*.
   - *Philosophy* is a search for wisdom. A normative philosophy describes the way something ought to be, such as the way educators ought to teach and treat their students. In forming a philosophy, a professional teacher searches for the wisdom to maximize learning for all students.
   - Philosophy provides a framework for thinking and guides professional practice. Philosophy and theory overlap but are not the same. Theories are used to explain events and behavior as they are, whereas philosophies go further to suggest the way events and behaviors ought to be.

2. Describe each of the branches of philosophy, and identify examples that illustrate each.
   - *Epistemology* is the branch of philosophy that describes how we know what we know. It's important for teachers because it influences how we teach and our choice of teaching methods.
   - *Metaphysics*, or *ontology*, considers what we know and addresses questions of reality and, ultimately, what is real. Our beliefs about reality influence our goals for our students, as we help them discover their own realities.
   - *Axiology* considers values and ethics and examines questions and issues involving decisions about right and wrong. Axiology is important because schools play an important role in shaping students' values and, ultimately, their moral behavior.
   - *Logic* is the process of deriving valid conclusions from basic principles. Effective teachers help students understand the logic of different arguments and also how to think clearly about ideas.

3. Describe the major philosophies of education, and identify examples that illustrate each.
   - *Perennialism* focuses on time-honored absolutes. Because truth doesn't change, a teacher's responsibility is to expose students to time-tested knowledge and truth. A teacher having students read *Moby Dick* because it focuses on the clash between good and evil is an example.
   - *Essentialism* suggests that a critical core of information exists that all people should possess, schools should emphasize basic skills and academic

subjects, and students should master these subjects. A curriculum that emphasizes reading, writing, and a deep understanding of math is consistent with essentialism.

- *Progressivism* views goals as dynamic and emphasizes that learning should be experience based and relevant to students' lives. A teacher involving students in problem-based learning activities would be applying progressivist philosophy.

- *Social reconstructionism* sees schools and other institutions in need of restructuring, with marginalized people and their works elevated to more prominent positions in the content of schooling.

4. Explain why a personal philosophy of education is important, and describe the steps involved in forming one.

- A personal philosophy of education is important because it guides your instructional decisions and specifies criteria you use to reflect on and analyze your teaching.

- A personal philosophy also helps you explain and defend your educational goals.

- Developing a personal philosophy begins with a description and an analysis of your beliefs and continues with an internally consistent articulation of your philosophy.

- Developing a personal philosophy of education increases your professionalism by providing a concrete frame of reference for both action and reflection.

IMPORTANT CONCEPTS

axiology (p. 200)
behaviorism (p. 209)
cognitive psychology (p. 210)
constructivism (p. 210)
epistemology (p. 199)
essentialism (p. 203)
humanistic psychology (p. 210)
logic (p. 200)
metaphysics (ontology) (p. 199)

normative philosophy (p. 198)
perennialism (p. 201)
philosophy (p. 196)
philosophy of education (p. 197)
progressivism (p. 204)
social reconstructionism (p. 207)
theory (p. 198)
21st Century Skills (p. 205)

DISCUSSION QUESTIONS

1. Four basic areas of philosophy are epistemology, metaphysics, axiology, and logic. Which of these is most useful for teachers? least useful?

2. Technology is becoming increasingly important in society as well as in education. Which of the four philosophies of education—perennialism, essentialism, progressivism, and social reconstructionism—is most compatible with applications of technology in education? least compatible?

3. Students are becoming increasingly diverse. How well do the different philosophies of education address issues of student diversity?

4. Which philosophy of education has the most current support in the geographic area in which you plan to teach? What evidence do you have for your conclusion?

5. Which of the different educational philosophies discussed in this chapter is most valuable in framing issues for preschool children? Middle school students? High school students? Does one particular philosophy fit with a content area that you'll be teaching?

6. Teachers in elementary schools commonly emphasize reading, language arts, and math much more strongly than other parts of the curriculum such as social studies, art, and music. What does this emphasis suggest about the teachers' philosophical positions?

myeducationlab

Now go to Topic 8: *Philosophy of Education* in the MyEducationLab (www.myeducationlab.com) for your course, where you can:

- Find learning outcomes for *Philosophy of Education* along with the national standards that connect to these outcomes.

- Complete *Assignments and Activities* that can help you more deeply understand the chapter content.

- Apply and practice your understanding of the core teaching skills identified in the chapter with the *Building Teaching Skills and Dispositions* learning units.

- Check your comprehension on the content covered in the chapter by going to the *Study Plan* in the *Book Specific Resources* section for your text. Here you will be able to take a chapter quiz, receive feedback on your answers, and then access *Review, Practice, and Enrichment* activities to enhance your understanding of chapter content.

Develop Your Professional Portfolio

To further apply your understanding of chapter content and address the INTASC standards, go to the *Book Specific Resources* section in the MyEducationLab for your course, select your text, then select this chapter's *Portfolio Activities*.

"I teach because it matters. But to be honest with you, I teach for selfish reasons, too. Working with students is fun. Being with teenagers all day is fun. They share their ideas, their stories, their energy. They are conflicted; they are complex; and they are fascinating."

DIANE BAHRENBURG, 2008 Teacher of the Year, Vermont

To view a video clip of Diane, the 2008 Vermont Teacher of the Year, go to Topic 6: *School Organization* in the MyEducationLab for your course and select *Teacher Talk*, then *Diane Bahrenburg.*

8

The Organization
of American Schools

CHAPTER OUTLINE

How Are Schools Organized?

- What Is a School?
- School Personnel
- The Physical Plant
- Organization of the Curriculum

School Levels

- Early Childhood Programs
- Elementary Schools
- Junior High and Middle Schools
- High Schools

  Taking a Stand in an Era of Reform:
  The Middle School Grade Dilemma

- Technology and Teaching: Distance Education Redefines
  Our Idea of a School

What Is an Effective School?

- Research on Effective Schools

  Exploring Diversity: School Organization and the Achievement of Cultural Minorities

LEARNING OBJECTIVES

After you have completed your study of this chapter, you should be able to:

1. **Describe different meanings of** *school,* **and identify components of a typical school organization.** INTASC Standard 9, Teacher Professionalism

2. **Describe important differences among schools at different levels.** INTASC Standard 2, Knowledge of Human Development and Learning

3. **Identify characteristics of an effective school.** INTASC Standard 9, Teacher Professionalism

Most of you are considering becoming teachers, but many of you may not have decided on the level best for you. Fortunately, we've all attended schools and experienced them as students, so we're familiar with the basic ways in which they're organized. But what do schools at different levels look like from a teacher's perspective? The answer to this question could help you decide whether to become an elementary, middle school, or high school teacher. Let's take a look at one teacher's experience.

"Wow, noon. I need to get going," Chris Lucio says to his colleague April Jackson as he finishes the last bite of his lunch and jumps up from the couch in the teacher's lounge. "My kids will be chomping at the bit trying to get into the room."

Chris hurriedly leaves the lounge, stops by the main office to check his box, and then walks across the courtyard to his building.

The courtyard sits at the center of the campus of Lakeside Junior High. Created 30 years earlier as a middle school for grades 6–9, Lakeside is now one of three junior high schools housing seventh and eighth graders in Orange Park, a suburb of a large eastern city. Four main buildings surround the courtyard: one for administration and three for classrooms. The administration building houses the principal's and other administrators' offices, a cafeteria—with a stage at one end—that doubles as an auditorium, and a media center and computer lab holding 30 computers. Positioned outside the main buildings are a gymnasium, a fine arts building, built 10 years ago when Lakeside was converted from a middle school to a junior high, and athletic facilities (tennis courts and baseball, softball, and soccer fields).

Chris walks briskly to the room where he teaches seventh-grade geography.

"Okay, everyone, the bell is going to ring in a couple minutes. Find your seats quickly," Chris calls out, unlocking the door to his room.

"Mr. Lucio, can I go to the bathroom?" Armondo asks as he heads through the open door.

"Hurry—you don't want to be tardy," Chris answers as he smiles at him.

"Are you going to come to our track meet this afternoon?" Devon, another of Chris's students asks as he enters the room. "We're going to kick butt on Ridgeview."

"Wouldn't miss it," Chris replies and thinks to himself, "Yikes, I almost forgot. . . . I promised Joe and Karen [the boys' and girls' track coaches] that I'd be a timer for the 100- and 200-meter races."

"What time does it start?" Chris asks Devon.

"Right after school—4 o'clock, I think."

As the bell signals the start of the period, Chris moves to the front of the room and starts taking roll as students begin working on a warm-up exercise that he has displayed on the overhead.

If you're in your mid-20's or younger, you've spent more than half of your life in school. But exactly what is a school, and what does it mean to teach and learn in one? And, how can beginning teachers find a good school as they begin their careers? We consider these questions in this chapter, but before you begin your study, please respond to the items in the *This I Believe* feature on the next page.

HOW ARE SCHOOLS ORGANIZED?

Think about the schools you attended before going to college. If you're typical, you first went to an elementary school, which began with kindergarten or prekindergarten, then to a middle or junior high school, and finally to a high school. This is the way schools are typically organized in our country. In this chapter, we look at why American schools are organized this way as we discuss each of the following:

- What is a school?
- School personnel
- The physical plant
- Organization of the curriculum

What Is a School?

There are many ways to think about schools. At the simplest level, it's a place where teachers teach and students learn. Schools have also been compared to factories, shopping malls, and even prisons, and each of these metaphors captures some aspects of schools. The factory metaphor considers students as raw material and turns them into finished

This I BELIEVE!

For each item, circle the number that best represents your thinking. Use the following scale as a guide.

4 = I strongly believe the statement is true.
3 = I believe the statement is true.
2 = I believe the statement is false.
1 = I strongly believe the statement is false.

1. Principals are the people who have the ultimate responsibility for the successful operation of the school.

   1   2   3   4

2. A major conflict in the organization of elementary schools is between the dual goals of meeting the developmental needs of students and content acquisition.

   1   2   3   4

3. Middle and junior high schools are essentially the same but are given different labels.

   1   2   3   4

4. In general, larger schools provide students with a better education, because they have better facilities and a wider variety of programs.

   1   2   3   4

5. Teachers' beliefs in their ability to affect learning can actually influence how much students learn.

   1   2   3   4

myeducationlab To download and complete this form, go to the *Book Specific Resources* section in the MyEducationLab for your course, select your text, and then select *This I Believe* for Chapter 8.

---

products, whose quality can be measured by standardized test scores (Cuban, 2003). Thinking of schools as shopping malls focuses on the broad array of offerings that exist in many schools, with choice and personal preference predominant. Some of schools' harshest critics even compare them to prisons: Students are required to attend until the age of 16, and student freedoms are severely limited while they are "incarcerated" in school.

Teachers and educational leaders like to think of schools as extended families, places where young people can learn and develop personally, socially, and intellectually. This often happens in the best schools, but it can be lost in others. (We examine the characteristics of effective schools later in the chapter.)

Finally, schools can be described as **social institutions**, organizations with established structures and rules designed to promote certain goals, and this is the way we think about schools in this chapter. As social institutions, schools have multiple, and sometimes competing, goals. One comprehensive study of schools identified the following major goals (Goodlad, 1984):

- *Academic:* Schools help students acquire the knowledge and skills that are essential for functioning in our culture.
- *Social and Civic:* Schools guide young people to become productive members of society.
- *Vocational:* Schools prepare students for the world of work.
- *Personal:* Schools help students develop as healthy, happy individuals.

Three factors related to these goals are significant. First, both parents and students believe each goal is important (Goodlad, 1984). Second, the goals sometimes compete, and conflicts can occur; for example, academics are strongly emphasized in today's schools, as evidenced by the focus on standards and testing. Critics argue that this emphasis shortchanges and sometimes ignores the personal and social growth of students

Social institution An organization with established structures and rules designed to promote certain goals.

(Amrein & Berliner, 2003; Van Horn, 2008). Third, the relative emphasis placed on each goal varies with grade level. Elementary schools, for example, typically place more emphasis on personal and social goals than do high schools, where the focus is more on academic and vocational goals.

In our definition, *social institutions* are described as having "established structures." These structures represent the ways schools are organized, and some ways of organizing schools are better than others. The differences influence how much students learn and how they develop, and they will also influence your life as a teacher.

Let's look now at how school personnel influence how schools operate.

School Personnel

No school is better than the people who work there. School personnel include all the people—the administrators, the support staff, and the teachers—who help make a school an effective social institution.

The central office is the school's nerve center; the office staff plays an important role in greeting guests and assisting teachers as well as students.

ADMINISTRATORS AND SUPPORT STAFF Elementary, middle, junior high, and high schools all have **administrators**, people responsible for the day-to-day operation of a school. The most important administrator is the **principal**, the person given ultimate administrative responsibility for the school's operation. As with expert teachers, the most effective principals possess a great deal of professional knowledge that helps them in their decision making (Saha & Biddle, 2006).

If the school is large, a vice principal, assistant principal, or both support the principal in his or her work, and they are part of the administration. Lakeside Junior High, the school in the case study at the beginning of the chapter, is large and has a principal, a vice principal, and two assistant principals. The vice principal's responsibilities include scheduling, collecting student records (e.g., grade reports) from teachers, keeping master records for the school, and maintaining communication with district-level administrators and parents. One of the assistant principals manages the physical plant, arranging the assignment of lockers to students, ordering and distributing textbooks to department heads, maintaining in-service records for teachers, coordinating the duties of the custodial staff, and overseeing all maintenance and construction. The other assistant principal is in charge of discipline—including referrals made by teachers and both in-school and out-of-school suspension of students.

Depending on the size of the school and the financial health and organization of the school district, some schools also have guidance counselors, school psychologists, and health-care providers, such as school nurses. Lakeside Junior High also has two full-time guidance counselors and a school psychologist it shares with other schools. The guidance counselors schedule and coordinate the statewide assessment tests and provide information to students about course offerings and career options. The school psychologist administers individualized intelligence tests and other tests used in making decisions about whether students qualify for special education or programs for the gifted and talented. The school psychologist also provides individual counseling for students having emotional problems and makes recommendations for further mental health assistance.

Lakeside also has a full-time licensed practical nurse; she maintains all student health records, supervises medical evacuations, dispenses all medications to students, and is trained in CPR. Students at Lakeside aren't allowed to take even an over-the-counter painkiller, such as aspirin, on their own, and teachers may not give students any form of medication. Nationally, 33 percent of schools have nurses (Kober, 2006).

Administrators People responsible for the day-to-day operation of a school.

Principal The person given ultimate administrative responsibility for a school's operation.

In addition, all schools have support staff, such as the following:

- Secretaries and receptionists, who greet visitors to the school
- Administrative and instructional support staff, who complete paperwork for the principal and other administrators, duplicate tests and handouts for teachers, maintain payroll records, and generally keep the school running
- Media center specialists, who manage different forms of technology as well as books
- Physical plant staff, such as custodians, who clean the rooms and buildings, and cafeteria workers, who prepare school lunches

Schools vary in the way they assign duties. As a result, the duties of the administrators and support staff in schools that you visit, or the school in which you take your first job, may differ from those described here.

Why do you need to understand school personnel and their roles? A school is a complex social institution, and all the people working in a school contribute to making it run smoothly. For example, if you have a chronically unruly student in your classroom, you'll need the support of the assistant principal and perhaps the advice of the school psychologist to help you address the problem.

As another example, experienced teachers know that school secretaries are the ones who really "run" a school. They know where things are and how to get things done. The way you treat support staff helps set the tone for a positive school climate and will also influence how much help they give you. For example, requesting—instead of demanding—services, such as having a test duplicated, communicates to support staff that you value their contributions to the overall functioning of the school.

The most effective schools are those in which all personnel work together for the benefit of students. As a professional, your ability to work with the other personnel will influence how effective you and the school will be. School leaders often describe the ability to work with others as one of the most important characteristics they look for in new teachers (S. Phillips, elementary principal, personal communication, January 21, 2009; E. P. Dannals, district superintendent, personal communication, January 30, 2009).

This section addresses the first item in our *This I Believe* feature, "Principals are the people who have the ultimate responsibility for the successful operation of the school." This statement is true: Principals are given the legal responsibility for running a school and have a major influence on its effectiveness.

TEACHERS Although school principals have ultimate administrative responsibility for the school's operation, teachers are at the heart of any effective school. A huge body of research consistently indicates that students taught by expert teachers learn more than those taught by teachers with less expertise (Bransford, Darling-Hammond, & LePage, 2005; Darling-Hammond & Baratz-Snowdon, 2005). "Supportive teachers and clear and high expectations are key to ensuring that students feel in control and confident about their ability to learn" (A. Lewis, 2006, p. 565). Helping you develop into an expert teacher who can support student learning is a major goal of this text.

The Physical Plant

In addition to people working together toward common goals, a school is a physical place. Schools have classrooms, hallways that allow students to move from one room to another, a central administrative office, and one or more large rooms, such as auditoriums, gymnasiums, music rooms, and cafeterias. Most schools have a simple boxlike structure, with hall upon hall of separate cells, which critics argue isolates teachers and fragments the curriculum. Separate classrooms also offer teacher privacy and sanctuary from the hectic pace of school life. When teachers retreat into their classrooms and close their doors, they control what goes on in there. Open classrooms with large, movable walls have gone in and out of popularity and are usually resisted by teachers because of noise and lack of privacy (Bolkan, Roland, & Smith, 2006).

An elementary school usually includes a staff parking area, playground, and driveway used for dropping off and picking up students. Middle, junior high, and high schools also have athletic facilities, such as playing fields, stadiums, and sometimes swimming pools. In some middle schools, however, the design intentionally omits gyms or other facilities that support competitive activities. High schools also have parking spaces available for students who drive to school.

School enrollments often increase so rapidly that physical plants can't keep up (Ortiz, 2004). As a result, many schools have "temporaries" or "modulars," individual buildings on the perimeter of school campuses that provide additional classroom space.

What will the physical arrangement of schools mean for you as a teacher? On the positive side, your classroom will be your own domain where you can define yourself as a teacher. But it can also separate you from other teachers: When you're in your classroom and you shut the door, as many teachers do, you'll be on your own. You'll be responsible for 20 to 30 second graders, for example, all day, every day. If you teach in middle or high school, you'll spend most of your workday in the confines of your classroom, where you'll be responsible for the education and safety of five or six classes of students.

However, although your primary responsibility will be to teach the students in your classroom, you'll also be expected to carry out noninstructional activities in other areas of the school. Teachers in an elementary school, for example, typically escort their students to and from the cafeteria or the media center. If you're a middle or secondary teacher, you'll be expected to monitor students as they move through the corridors and attend nonacademic events, such as assemblies and pep rallies. You may also be asked to sell tickets at football games, attend track meets, and go to band concerts. These different responsibilities are the result, in part, of the way schools are physically organized.

Organization of the Curriculum

Schools are social institutions designed to help young people acquire the knowledge and skills that will enable them to function effectively in today's world, and in this age of rapid change, they must be capable of learning throughout their lives. Our task as educators is to organize the curriculum so that schools can reach these goals. Different definitions of *curriculum* exist (Connelly, 2008), but in this book, we define **curriculum** simply as everything that teachers teach and students learn in schools.

The formal curriculum is typically organized around standards, such as the following:

- Students will recognize the letters of the alphabet.
- Students will write short paragraphs using correct structure.
- Students will use the correct order of operations to simplify expressions such as $9 + 4(7 - 3)/2$
- Students will understand the concepts *mass* and *inertia*.

Historically, educators have decided that the most efficient way of helping students reach goals such as these is to organize instruction according to grade levels and subject matter areas. For instance, children in kindergarten are expected to reach the first goal, third graders the second, pre-algebra students the third, and physics students the fourth. Standards for different grade levels and subject matter areas are part of a school's general curriculum, and these goals provide teachers with direction as they make decisions about what to teach.

SCHOOL ORGANIZATION AND THE CURRICULUM How should teachers and students be grouped to help students most effectively learn the curriculum? For example, does it make sense to have 6-year-olds in the same building with 17- and 18-year-olds?

Curriculum Everything that teachers teach and students learn in schools.

Table 8.1 Common Ways to Organize Schools	
School Level	**Grade Ranges**
Elementary school	K–2
	K–3
	K–5
	K–6
	K–8
Middle/Junior high school	5–8
	6–8
	7–8
	7–9
	8–9
High school	9–12
	10–12

Developmental differences in students, safety, and even seemingly minor concerns, such as the height of drinking fountains and toilets, suggest no.

As a result, school systems are organized into three levels: elementary schools for young children, middle or junior high schools for beginning adolescents, and high schools for later adolescents. The grades included at each level vary from place to place, however. Some of the most common are outlined in Table 8.1.

What factors do educators consider when making decisions about organizing schools? For example, why do middle schools typically include grades 6–8 or grades 7 and 8? Two factors are most powerful: (1) the developmental characteristics of students and (2) economics and politics.

DEVELOPMENTAL CHARACTERISTICS OF STUDENTS **Development** refers to the physical changes in children as well as changes in the way they think and relate to their peers that result from maturation and experience. For example, fifth graders are bigger, stronger, and more coordinated than first graders; they're physically more developed. Similarly, fifth graders think differently from first graders. When shown the drawing here, for example, typical first graders conclude that block A is heavier than block B, because their thinking tends to focus on size—the most obvious aspect of the balance and the blocks. Fifth graders, on the other hand, are more likely to conclude that the blocks weigh the same, because they recognize that the beam is balanced (level); their thinking is more developed (Eggen & Kauchak, 2010).

Differences in social development also exist. For example, when faced with a disagreement about who in a group gets to report on a topic, a fifth grader is more likely than a first grader to compromise because he or she is more capable of considering where classmates are "coming from"; a first grader's thinking in such a situation is more likely to be self-centered (Berk, 2010). Advances in social development allow teachers to use instructional strategies, such as cooperative learning, that are more effective with older children than with those who are younger or less developed socially (Brophy, 2006).

Such differences can also be found between fifth graders and high school students. Many older students are physically young men and women, some think quite abstractly, and they can be socially skilled.

These developmental differences influence how schools are organized. For example, students in elementary schools, and particularly in kindergarten and first grade, are typically assigned to one teacher who monitors the cognitive, social, and emotional growth of students in that classroom. In some schools, **looping**, the practice of keeping a teacher with one group of students for more than a year, is used to help teachers better nurture the development of individual students. Older students are more capable of learning on

Development The physical changes in children as well as changes in the way they think and relate to their peers that result from maturation and experience.

Looping The practice of keeping a teacher with one group of students for more than a year.

their own and fending for themselves, so they are assigned to a number of teachers who also serve as subject matter specialists.

This section addresses the second item in our *This I Believe* feature, "A major conflict in the organization of elementary schools is between the dual goals of meeting the developmental needs of students and content acquisition." This statement is true: Self-contained elementary classrooms attempt to meet the developmental needs of students but may not address content acquisition in some areas, such as science, social studies, music, or art.

ECONOMICS AND POLITICS "Why school districts house certain grades together under one roof is often a matter of practical necessity rather than instructional intent" (Burkam, Michaels, & Lee, 2007, p. 288). For example, both economics and politics influenced the development of Lakeside, Chris Lucio's school, first in its creation as a middle school and later in its conversion to a junior high.

> At the time Lakeside was developed, the elementary schools in the district had become overcrowded because of rapid population increases, and the process of building additional elementary schools couldn't keep up with demand. Creating middle schools temporarily solved the problem, because sixth graders could be moved into these schools. This was a decision based on economics.
>
> Also, the middle school movement was gathering momentum at this same time, and Mary Zellner, Lakeside's first principal, was an outspoken proponent of middle schools. She was a respected leader in district politics, and because of her influence, Lakeside was built according to middle school philosophy. This philosophy de-emphasized competition among students, and as a result, the school didn't have competitive athletics, which was the reason the school originally didn't have a gymnasium.
>
> Issues then became complicated. Coaches at the local high school complained that potential athletes came to them from middle schools without the athletic experiences students from competing schools enjoyed. (These pressures aren't unusual: Many middle-level schools in the United States offer organized competitive sports.) The fact that the high school, the only high school in the district, had become overcrowded presented an additional problem. District officials solved both problems by converting the middle schools into junior highs, moving ninth graders from the high school to the junior highs and sending sixth graders back to elementary schools. By this time, the elementary schools were able to handle the additional students, because a number of new elementary schools had been built in the city. The decision to convert the middle school to a junior high was based on both economics and politics; it had little to do with the developmental needs of students.

Organizational changes such as these, driven by economics and politics, are common in education. As another example, to accommodate exploding enrollments, a small district in Utah decided to change its grade-level alignments to elementary (K–4), intermediate school (5–6), junior high (7–8), and high school (9–12) (Smart, 2008). District officials estimated that these realignments would save tens of millions of dollars in new construction costs. Keep these factors—developmental, economic, and political—in mind as you look at schools at different levels in more depth in the next section.

■ ■ ■ ■ ■ CHECK YOUR UNDERSTANDING

1.1 What are three meanings of the concept *school?*

1.2 What are the major components of a typical school organization?

1.3 Most school systems are organized into three levels; describe each.

1.4 What are three factors that influence the way schools are organized?

For feedback, go to the appendix, *Check Your Understanding*, located in the back of this text.

SCHOOL LEVELS

In the previous section, we saw that schools are typically organized into elementary, middle or junior high, and high school levels to meet the developmental needs of students. In this section, we take a closer look at the various ways schools meet students' needs and how these differences influence teachers' lives. We begin with early childhood programs.

Early Childhood Programs

Visitors to Sharon Broderick's preschool classroom at first are struck by the apparent chaos. Students around her classroom are working on a number of seemingly unconnected tasks. Sharon and her aide, Carmen Sanchez, circulate among the groups, asking questions and offering suggestions.

Closer examination of the room reveals several clusters of activity organized around centers. One center has a tub of water where students measure water in different-sized cups and also determine which kinds of objects sink and float. Another has a table with an assortment of plastic geometric blocks and shapes that children are using to construct things. A third has different costumes and clothing along with two telephones that students use for pretend conversations and dialogues. A fourth contains a variety of picture books that require different amounts of expertise with letters and words. Children circulate among these centers, and the teacher and her aide keep track of who has been to which center and completed different tasks.

Most of you attended kindergarten, and some may have even attended a prekindergarten program. However, one of your authors, educated in a small town in a rural area, attended neither, because they weren't offered there at the time. In 2004, more than 7 of 10 students in this country attended kindergarten, most for a full day (National Center for Education Statistics, 2008a).

Early childhood education is a general term describing a range of educational programs for young children. It includes infant intervention and enrichment programs, nursery schools, public and private prekindergartens and kindergartens, and federally funded Head Start programs. Early childhood education in the United States is a mid-20th-century development, although its philosophical roots go back two and a half centuries. The French philosopher Rousseau, for example, gave this advice about educating young children:

> Do not treat the child to discourses which he cannot understand. No descriptions, no eloquence, no figures of speech. . . . In general, let us never substitute the sign for the thing, except when it is impossible for us to show the thing. . . . Things! Things! I shall never tire of saying that we ascribe too much importance to words. (Rousseau, quoted in Compayre, 1888)

Rousseau was arguing that young children need to play and work with concrete objects ("Things! Things!") rather than being taught with abstract words. This idea is consistent with the need for concrete experiences that the famous developmental psychologist Jean Piaget (1952, 1970) emphasized, and it's at the core of developmentally appropriate early childhood programs.

Developmental programs accommodate differences in children's development by allowing them to acquire skills and abilities at their own pace through direct experiences. Developmental programs are heavily influenced by the **Montessori method**, an approach to early childhood education inspired by Maria Montessori (1870–1952), an innovative Italian early childhood educator. Montessori believed that children develop discipline and self-confidence by exploring a classroom environment that provides options and choices. Visitors in a developmental classroom are likely to see learning centers

Early childhood education A general term describing a range of educational programs for young children, including infant intervention and enrichment programs, nursery schools, public and private prekindergartens and kindergartens, and federally funded Head Start programs.

Developmental programs Programs that accommodate differences in children's development by allowing them to acquire skills and abilities at their own pace through direct experiences.

Montessori method An approach to early childhood education that emphasizes individual exploration and initiative through learning centers.

around the room such as those in Sharon Broderick's class. Unlike traditional teacher-centered instruction, where the teacher spends most of the time talking or asking questions, the teacher's role is to provide experiences for children and encourage exploration (Schulz & Bonawitz, 2007).

The need for learning-related experiences early in life is well recognized (Berk, 2010), and the benefits of early intervention programs are long-lasting. For example, one long-term study compared the experiences of 123 economically deprived African American children attending 3 years of preschool to other students who did not (the program didn't have room for all applicants) (Bracey, 2003a). Dramatic differences were found between the preschool students and the students in the control group. By the time these students turned 27, more than 7 of 10 in the preschool group had attained a high school diploma or GED, compared to only a little more than half of the control group. More than 40 percent of the males in the preschool group reported making more than $24,000 a year, compared to only 6 percent of the males in the control group. More than a third of the preschool group, but only about 1 of 10 from the control group, owned homes. Control-group members had twice as many arrests as those who attended the preschool, and 5 times as many of the control group had been arrested five or more times. Clearly, the preschool program had long-lasting beneficial effects on the children it served.

A more ambitious program in North Carolina provided nutritional help and social services from birth, as well as parenting lessons and a language-oriented preschool program (Bracey, 2003a; Jacobsen, 2003). Follow-up studies revealed that compared to nonparticipants, participants scored higher on intelligence and achievement tests, were twice as likely to attend postsecondary education, and delayed having children by 2 years. Early childhood education programs pay off, both in school achievement and also later in life. David Broder, a prominent *Washington Post* columnist, observed: "The evidence that high-quality education beginning at age 3 or 4 will pay lifetime dividends is overwhelming. The only question is whether we will make the needed investment" (quoted in Bracey, 2003a, p. 32).

In the early 1970s, slightly more than one fifth of 4-year-olds were enrolled in early childhood programs; by 2001, this figure had increased to two thirds (Magnuson, Meyers, Ruhm, & Waldfogel, 2004). Much greater emphasis is now being placed on high-quality early intervention programs in all settings. Early childhood programs received a major boost in the $787-billion American Recovery and Reinvestment Act of 2009, which allocated an additional $4.1 billion from federal funds to child care and Head Start programs (D. Hoff, 2009a). And as full-time early childhood programs become increasingly common, job opportunities in these areas will continue to grow.

Elementary Schools

Elementary classrooms are typically self-contained, providing teachers with considerable amounts of autonomy. To see how this plays out in teachers' lives, let's look at the schedules of two elementary teachers. Examine the schedules in Table 8.2, and see what you notice. Your observations might include the following:

- Both teachers are responsible for all the content areas, such as reading, language arts, math, science, and social studies.
- The teachers' schedules are quite different. Although both teachers teach young children, Sharon begins with language arts, for example, and Susie begins by having the children practice their previous day's math and language arts.
- The amount of time each teacher allocates to the content areas varies considerably and is a personal decision. Sharon, for example, devotes 50 minutes to math, whereas Susie teaches math for 75 minutes a day.

Table 8.2 Schedules for Two Elementary School Teachers

Sharon's First-Grade Schedule		Susie's Third-Grade Schedule	
8:30 AM	School begins	8:30 AM	School begins
8:30–8:45	Morning announcements	8:30–9:15	Independent work (pratice previous day's language arts and math)
8:45–10:30	Language arts (including reading and writing)	9:15–10:20	Language arts (including reading and writing)
10:30–11:20	Math	10:20–10:45	Snack/Independent reading
11:20–11:50	Lunch	10:45–11:15	Physical education
11:50–12:20	Read story	11:15–12:15	Language arts/social studies/science
12:20–1:15	Center time (practice on language arts and math)	12:15–12:45	Lunch
1:15–1:45	Physical education	12:45–2:00	Math
1:45–2:30	Social studies/science	2:00–2:30	Spelling/catch up on material not covered earlier
2:30–2:45	Class meeting	2:30–2:45	Read story
2:45–3:00	Call buses/dismissal	2:45–3:00	Clean up/prepare for dismissal

In conversations, both teachers noted that the schedules in Table 8.2 were approximate and often changed, depending on their perception of students' needs and the day of the week. For example, if students were having trouble with a math topic, they might devote more time to math on a given day (S. Mittelstadt, personal communication, August 15, 2006; S. Van Horn, personal communication, August 16, 2006).

If you observe in elementary classrooms, you're likely to see a schedule that varies from those in Table 8.2. This level of individual teacher freedom and autonomy is characteristic of elementary school organization and is a major reason many people become elementary teachers.

Why are elementary schools organized this way? History and precedent are part of the answer. Until about the mid-1800s, elementary teachers

Self-contained elementary classrooms are designed to meet young students' developmental needs.

taught all grade levels and all subjects; schools weren't even organized into grade levels. In some rural areas, one-room schools still exist today (Swidler, 2004). This organizational pattern was born out of necessity rather than philosophy: Most small towns could afford only one teacher who was expected to teach all the subjects (Pulliam & Van Patten, 2007). So, history has influenced the way elementary schools are organized.

The developmental characteristics of students also influence the organization of elementary schools. We saw earlier that young children look, think, and interact with their peers differently from older students. Educators have historically believed that young children need the stability of one teacher and a single classroom to function most effectively in school; schools can be frightening places for little children, and self-contained classrooms provide emotional security. Further, simply moving from room to room, as middle and secondary students do, can be challenging for young children (S. Black, 2008a); imagine, for example, a first grader going to Room 101 for math, 108 for language arts, and so on. Rotating schedules, which are becoming increasingly popular under block scheduling, would be even more confusing.

Some educators question the efficacy of a single classroom and teacher; expecting one teacher to be sufficiently knowledgeable to effectively teach reading, language arts, math, science, and social studies is asking the impossible, they say (D. Tanner & Tanner,

PEARSON
myeducationlab

To view a grade-level meeting at an elementary school, go to the *Assignments and Activities* section of Topic 6: *School Organization* in the MyEducationLab for your course and complete the activity titled *Grade Level Meeting.*

2007). As a result, teachers commonly de-emphasize some content areas, such as science, social studies, art, and music. Both Sharon and Susie acknowledged that they strongly emphasized reading, language arts, and math and de-emphasized other areas, even though these other content areas appear on their schedules (see Table 8.2).

In response to these issues, beginning in grade 3 or 4, many elementary schools do a form of departmentalization (S. Phillips, personal communication, January 21, 2009). For example, two teachers work as a team, with one teaching reading and writing and the other focusing on math and science. The reading/writing teacher teaches one class in the morning while the math/science teacher teaches the other; then in the afternoon, they switch classes.

So educators, teachers, and parents face a dilemma: Are social and emotional well-being more important than content for elementary students? Historically, the answer has been yes. But tensions between these two positions will continue to increase as efforts to document student academic growth through testing continue to grow.

Junior High and Middle Schools

To see differences between elementary schools and middle, junior high, and high schools, you need only compare Chris's experiences (in the chapter's opening case) to Susie's and Sharon's (in Table 8.2). Elementary teachers often teach all the content areas and set their own schedules. In contrast, as a middle school teacher, Chris teaches only one subject (geography), and he (along with all the other teachers in his school) follows a predetermined schedule. The lengths of class periods are uniform for all content areas, and the beginnings and endings are signaled by a bell. Because of these schedules, junior high and middle school teachers have less control over their daily schedules.

Why are upper-level schools organized in this way? The answer to this question centers on the same tensions between content acquisition and the developmental needs of children. Historically, views about goals have shifted over time. In colonial times, the goal was for students to be able to read and understand the Bible. Much later—near the end of the 19th century—promoting mental discipline and assimilating a large influx of immigrants into American society were the goals. To help reach those goals, educators believed that college-bound and non-college-bound students should take the same curriculum.

As educational thinking evolved, leaders believed that society needed citizens well schooled in a variety of academic subjects, such as math, science, and history. This emphasis resulted in the departmentalization found in the middle schools or junior highs and high schools that you most likely attended. But a conflict exists between this emphasis on content and meeting the development needs of students. Let's see how this conflict affected the organization of middle and junior high schools.

Schools in the early 20th century were organized into eight elementary and four high school grades. But the 8–4 organization changed when emphasis shifted away from basic skills, such as reading and math, and toward the more intensive study of specific content areas, such as science, history, and literature. This intensive study required teachers who were subject matter experts. In addition, educators began to recognize the unique needs of early adolescents, the result was the development of the "junior" high school.

Most **junior high schools** today have a variety of offerings, although not as comprehensive as those in high schools, and they include competitive athletics and other extracurricular activities. Although initially designed to help students make the transition between elementary and high schools, they are in every sense of the word "junior" high schools.

This emphasis on content, however, failed to address the developmental needs of early adolescents, who vary considerably in their rates of development. Think back to your friends from sixth, seventh, or eighth grade: Some of the girls were young women, fully developed physically, whereas others were still little girls. Some boys needed to shave, but others looked like fifth graders. Boys and girls were becoming physically attracted to

Junior high schools Schools designed for early adolescents that are similar in form and focus to high schools.

each other, and in many cases they didn't know why. This was the transitional period of early adolescence (Berk, 2010).

Because of these rapid physical, emotional, and intellectual changes, early adolescence is a unique period in a child's development. At no other time in a person's life, except infancy, is change so rapid or profound. As a result, many educators believe that schools for young adolescents should be organized to meet their unique needs (Wiles & Bondi, 2007).

This thinking, along with the inability of junior highs to address early adolescents' developmental needs, led to the formation of **middle schools**. Typically encompassing grades 6–8, middle schools are specifically designed to help students through the rapid social, emotional, and intellectual changes characteristic of early adolescence.

What is teaching in a middle school like? Let's look at one teacher's experience.

Robin West is an eighth-grade science teacher in an urban middle school. She and her team members have a common planning period. They teach the same group of students and often spend their planning period discussing the students and the topics they're teaching. Many of their students aren't native English speakers, and their discussions often center on what can be done to help those who struggle with language. In addition, Robin has four students with learning disabilities in her classroom. Whenever possible, the teachers integrate topics across as many of the four areas as they can.

"Can you help me out with anything on graphing?" Maria, the math teacher, asks the others one Monday. "The kids just see graphs as some meaningless lines. I explain the heck out of them, but it doesn't seem to help all that much."

"I know what I can do," Robin offers, after thinking for a few seconds. "We've been talking about global warming and climate change for the last few weeks. We've looked at some temperature trends in our country as well as around the world—especially in the Arctic and Antarctica. We've looked only at raw data but haven't graphed any of it. How about I give you some of the figures—you know, dates and temperatures—and you can graph them in math. Let me know when you do, and I'll talk about the graphs the next day in science.

"By the way, how is Lorraine Williams doing in math?"

"Not so good," Mary responds. "In fact, I was going to ask you all about her. She hasn't been turning in her homework, and she seems only 'half there' in class."

"Same thing in history," Keith, the history teacher and Lorraine's homeroom teacher, adds. "We'd better see what's going on. . . . I'll call her parents tonight."

The first middle school was created in Bay City, Michigan, in 1950. From their inception, as this episode suggests, middle schools have tried to do things differently than junior highs (Wiles & Bondi, 2007). Effective middle schools make the following adaptations (C. Weiss & Kipnes, 2006):

- *They organize teachers and students into interdisciplinary teams:* For example, a team composed of a math, science, English, and social studies teacher instructs the same group of students and works together to coordinate topics.

- *They strive to create and maintain long-term teacher–student relationships with attention to emotional development:* In many middle schools, a period is set aside to allow teachers to carefully track their students' academic progress and discuss nonacademic topics. One new teacher, commenting on the success of a new student-advising system, noted "a dramatic shift in the climate of the building." (Keller, 2007, p. 29).

- *They use interactive teaching strategies:* Teachers are encouraged to move away from the lecture-dominated instruction so common in high schools and toward instruction based on student involvement. In addition, teachers place greater emphasis on study strategies, such as note taking and time management.

Middle schools Special schools targeting grades 6–8 and designed to meet the unique social, emotional, and intellectual needs of early adolescents.

- *They eliminate activities that emphasize developmental differences, such as competitive sports:* In middle schools, everyone is invited to participate in intramural sports and clubs.

When done well, these adaptations have a positive influence on students (C. Weiss & Kipnes, 2006). For instance, interdisciplinary teams allow teachers to efficiently plan for the integration of topics across different content areas, as Robin and Mary did with math and science. Also, when teachers have the same students, they can more carefully monitor their progress, as the team did with Lorraine. Forming relationships with students helps them adjust to an atmosphere less personal than in their elementary schools. And eliminating competitive sports encourages greater participation in athletic activities and minimizes the advantages early-maturing students have over their later-developing classmates.

Interactive teaching strategies, such as developing lessons with questioning and involving students in cooperative learning activities, are particularly important in middle school. These strategies actively involve students in learning activities that can also develop their thinking and social interaction skills. Research indicates that motivation often drops during the early adolescent years; some researchers believe this drop is due to increased use of lecture as a teaching strategy, because it places students in passive roles (Schunk, Pintrich & Meese, 2008).

The number of middle schools continues to increase: By the start of the 21st century, middle schools outnumbered junior highs by a ratio of 4 to 1 (National Center for Education Statistics, 2002). However, middle schools are currently being criticized by advocates of rigorous academics who question the emphasis on personal development. They recommend a return to basics, with greater attention given to reading and math. Defenders of the middle school concept claim that the problem isn't the idea itself but that it never has been effectively implemented (Swaim, 2004). The current emphasis on testing, accountability, and subject matter mastery is likely to fuel this controversy.

This section addresses the third item in our *This I Believe* feature, "Middle and junior high schools are essentially the same but are given different labels." This statement is false: These two types of schools have different philosophies and view students differently.

In the *Taking a Stand* feature that follows, we examine controversies surrounding the ideal grade configurations for developing adolescents, and also invite you to take a personal stand on this issue.

This I BELIEVE

High Schools

Each of you attended high school, and some of you have graduated only within the last year or two. Most of you probably graduated from a **comprehensive high school**, a secondary school that aims to meet the needs of all students. Let's examine the comprehensive high school more closely.

THE COMPREHENSIVE HIGH SCHOOL   In *The American High School,* James Conant (1959) argued persuasively that the most effective high schools are those large enough to offer diverse academic courses and facilities for all students (Hammack, 2004). In attempting to do this, most high schools organize students into tracks (Oakes, 2008). For example, students in the college-preparatory track take courses designed to prepare them for college-level work. A college-prep track might include honors or advanced placement classes in core subject areas. **Advanced placement classes** are courses taken in high school that allow students to earn college credit, making college less time-consuming and expensive. A general track composed of "standard" classes is designed for students of average ability who may or may not go on to college. Students in this track may take some vocational courses, such as word processing, designed to provide practical skills they can use immediately after graduating. A vocational track specifically targets students not going to college, preparing them for careers in such areas as automobile repair or technology.

Comprehensive high school A secondary school that attempts to meet the needs of all students.

Advanced placement classes Courses taken in high school that allow students to earn college credit, making college less time-consuming and expensive.

The Middle School Grade Dilemma

When John Smith, a swaggering sixth grader at one of New York City's growing collection of kindergarten- through eighth-grade schools, feels lost, he heads downstairs to the colorful classroom of his former third-grade teacher, Randi Silverman, for what she calls a "Silverman hug."

"When I get mad I go to her. . . . When I feel frustrated I'll go to her. When I feel like I can't do it no more I go to her, and she tells me I have to do it." (Gootman, 2007, p. 1)

What kind of middle school/junior high did you attend? How did it help you navigate through the perils of adolescence? What grade configuration is best for students as they journey through the developmental turmoil of adolescence? Controversies exist not only about the academic focus of classrooms, but also about the optimal grade configurations to help students as they develop into young adults. Research consistently reveals that early adolescence is a difficult period for students. Grades, motivation, and behavior all suffer during this period of transition, and experts are looking to alternative grade configurations to deal with the problem (Berk, 2010; Viadero, 2008b). Proposals range from retaining these students in extended K–8 elementary schools to incorporating them into 6–12 high schools.

A number of large city school districts, including Baltimore, Cleveland, Philadelphia, and Salt Lake City, Utah, are currently experimenting with K–8 schools (Fulton, 2008; Viadero, 2008b). Advocates for this configuration claim several advantages:

- Elementary schools tend to be smaller and more personal, thus providing a more nurturant and support-ive learning environment. We see this in the experiences of John Smith, the sixth grader in our introductory case.

- Early adolescents are protected from distractions such as sex and drugs, frequently found in high school environments.

- Transitions to high school are easier because there is only one to make, and this is delayed until students are more mature.

Critics, however, question whether K–8 classrooms provide sufficient academic rigor, and they believe that adolescents need, and are ready for, greater responsibility and freedom.

An alternative proposal merges the middle school years into 6–12 or 7–12 high schools; several large school districts, including New York City, are experimenting with this configuration (Gootman, 2007). Advocates claim that 11-, 12-, and 13-year-olds are ready for the enriched academic menu that comes with well-trained subject matter specialists, something that doesn't occur in current middle or K–8 schools (Juvonen, Le, Kaganoff, Augustine, & Constant, 2004). In addition, they say, these students would benefit from older role models and concrete goals, such as preparing for and getting into college (Gootman, 2007). Some middle school teachers suggest that treating middle school credits as part of high school graduation requirements would motivate students, making them more accountable for their class work (Berlin, 2008). Critics respond that children this young aren't ready for the impersonal atmosphere of a large high school and will get lost in the shuffle of making transitions to different classes (S. Black, 2008a; Hall, 2008).

So what does research tell us about these alternative proposals to reform middle schools? Unfortunately, current research is unclear about which approach is best. Some studies suggest that students learn more in K–8 schools, but others do not (Viadero, 2008b). Unfortunately, comparable research on 6–12 configurations is equally unclear about the relative benefits of that alternative organizational scheme. One major problem with all of this research is the criterion measures used: Should we look primarily at scores on standardized achievement tests, or should we also consider other measures such as emotional adjustment and satisfaction with school, success in high school, or the prevalence of disciplinary problems?

YOU TAKE A STAND

Now it's your turn to take a position on the issue. Which configuration, K–8 or 6–12, makes the most sense for education of early adolescents? Or, do separate middle schools provide the best education for these students? Because the research on this topic isn't clear, you may have to rely on your own experiences from those years: What grade configuration would have been best for you?

PEARSON myeducationlab *To explore* both sides of this issue and take a stand, go to the *Book Specific Resources* section in the MyEducationLab for your course, select your text, and then select *Taking a Stand in an Era of Reform* for Chapter 8.

ISSUES IN EDUCATION

A comprehensive high school also offers extracurricular activities (e.g., band, chorus, and theater) and athletics (e.g., football, swimming, soccer, and tennis). These options are intended to integrate students from different tracks, allowing them to mix and learn about each other, and to help all students develop personally, socially, and intellectually.

Extracurricular activities provide valuable learning opportunities not typically tapped by traditional classrooms.

Criticisms of the Comprehensive High School. Can a comprehensive high school be all things to all students? Critics say no and focus on four issues: tracking, size, departmentalization, and lack of academic rigor.

A paradox of the comprehensive high school is that different tracks, designed to present quality alternatives, often produce exactly the opposite. Instead of providing freedom and choice, tracking limits choices and segregates students, often leaving many with substandard educational experiences (Oakes, 2008). Lower-ability, minority, and low-socioeconomic status (SES) students are often steered into vocational or lower-level tracks, where the curriculum is less challenging and instruction is often poor. Instead of effectively preparing students for the world of work, lower tracks often segregate students from their college-bound peers and communicate that challenge and deep understanding are not for them. Some critics charge that tracking should be eliminated and that all students should be prepared, to the extent possible, for college work (Vander Ark, 2003).

A second criticism of comprehensive high schools relates to school size, which exceeds 1,000 students in many U.S. high schools (Feldman, López, & Simon, 2006; C. Howley & Howley, 2004). As schools become larger, they also tend to become more impersonal and bureaucratic. They virtually become shopping malls in which students mill around looking for entertainment and educational bargains. Like smart shoppers, the brighter students (or their parents) know what they want and quickly find the more challenging college-preparatory courses. Lower achievers get lost in the shuffle, spending time but not receiving a quality education (C. Howley & Howley, 2004). One critic remarked that because of their unwieldy size, "our high schools are the least effective part of the American education system" (Vander Ark, 2003, p. 52).

Departmentalization, or the organization of teachers and classes into separate academic areas, is a third problem facing comprehensive high schools, critics contend. Departmentalization fragments the curriculum and interferes with learning:

> While the adults organize as separate departmental entities isolated from one another, however, their teenage students seek interconnectedness and relevancy in their school experience. What they get instead is math with no relationship to social studies, science without any connection to literature, and so forth. This relevancy-starved approach continues year in, year out with no alternatives, and any "reforms" seen in public education are invariably found at the elementary or middle school level. (Cooperman, 2003, p. 30)

Some suggest that to prevent such fragmentation, schools cluster teachers and classes into interdisciplinary teams, as in effective middle schools, where connections between disciplines are emphasized.

Fragmentation in the curriculum also comes from the schedule itself, which breaks the day into 50-minute periods that many think are too short to pursue topics in depth. One solution to this problem is **block scheduling**, in which students spend more time in classes but meet less frequently during the week. One common variation is for classes to meet for 100 minutes every other day. Science teachers often prefer this scheduling arrangement because it allows more time for labs and problem-based learning. Music and foreign language teachers aren't so enthusiastic because block scheduling doesn't provide for the daily practice they believe produces learning gains. Teachers who have tried block scheduling are unanimous on one point—that teachers need to adapt their instruction to longer periods: It's much more difficult to engage students in whole-class, teacher-centered instruction for these longer periods.

Block scheduling A high school scheduling option in which classes are longer but meet less frequently.

A fourth criticism of comprehensive high schools relates to academic rigor: In attempting to be all things to all students, high schools fail to challenge students and provide them with the job skills needed for a technologically oriented modern society (Botstein, 2006; Perkins-Gough, 2005a). Bill Gates, founder of Microsoft, claimed U.S. high schools are "obsolete" and ruin the lives of millions of Americans every year because they fail to prepare students for the modern world of work (Hammack, 2005). Others decry the lack of academic challenge and the failure of high schools to engage the minds of teenage youth (Botstein, 2006). Solutions to these problems range from more rigorous graduation requirements, especially in core areas such as math, science, and English, to high school exit exams (Perkins-Gough, 2005b).

Alternatives to Comprehensive High Schools. One concrete solution to the problem of large high schools is to create "smaller learning communities" within large schools, allowing students to keep the same guidance counselor throughout high school and offering specific opportunities for students and teachers to get to know one another. These ideas are discussed further in the section on school size later in the chapter.

A second alternative to large, comprehensive high schools is **career technical schools** designed to provide students with education and job skills to enable them to get a job immediately after high school (Bottoms, Presson, & Han, 2004; Lynch, 2000). In more than 1,000 vocational centers nationwide, students attend part of the day or evening in specialized programs. They then attend their "home" high school for academic or general education courses during the other part of the day. In addition, about 250 career or specialty high schools in the United States focus on preparing students for work in a particular occupation or industry but also offer the academic and general courses at that school. Students attend these career technical schools full-time (Lynch, 2000).

Career technical, or vocational education, as it was called earlier, got its beginning in the early 1900s to better meet the needs of working-class children, who for the first time, were attending high schools in large numbers but weren't headed for professional careers. Early vocational programs were designed to prepare students with practical skills for the nation's farms, factories, and homes. Currently, programs have evolved, with more emphasis on technology-related careers.

Career academies, an innovative approach that combines both career education and the school-within-a-school movement, show promise. **Career academies** are small learning communities (typically 200 or fewer students) working with the same groups of teachers in career-oriented areas such as health and bioscience, business and finance, architecture and construction, education and child development, and information technology (Hoye & Stern, 2008). Applied classes are supplemented with field trips, job shadowing, and internships that provide realistic experiences for students. Research on these academies is promising: Students are more likely to stay in school, attend more classes, and receive more credits toward graduation (Viadero, 2008a). In addition, graduates earn 11 percent more than nonacademy students after graduation, comparable to the benefits of attending a community college for 1 or 2 years. The benefits are especially strong for students considered to be at high risk for dropping out of school.

As with many other aspects of education, career technical education is going through a process of reform. Most of the reforms are aimed at increasing academic standards and related general educational knowledge, together with teaching students all aspects of an industry rather than focusing on a specific job skill. The federal government currently contributes an annual $1.3 billion to these programs to encourage modernizing and focusing academic programs on essential job skills (Cavanagh, 2006a). However, interest in these programs continues to decline as more and more students opt for college-prep programs (J. Newman, 2006).

Career technical schools Schools designed to provide students with education and job skills that will enable them to get a job immediately after high school.

Career academies Small learning communities (typically 200 or fewer students) working with the same groups of teachers in career-oriented areas such as health and bioscience, business and finance, architecture and construction, education and child development, and information technology.

■ ■ TECHNOLOGY AND TEACHING Distance Education Redefines Our Idea of a School

When most people think of a school, they imagine a building with teachers and students. **Distance education**, a catchall term used to describe organized instructional programs in which teachers and learners, though physically separated, are connected through technology, is changing that view (Newby, Stepich, Lehman, & Russell, 2006). Distance learning meets student learning needs in three ways (Simonson, Smaldino, Albright, & Zvacek, 2009). First, it offers students in rural communities courses in specialized areas, such as advanced physics or Japanese, for which a local teacher is unavailable. Second, it provides instruction for nontraditional students, such as adults who can't attend classes during the day or those who are homebound. Third, it can deliver a class to students over a broad geographic area where driving to a central location isn't possible.

The earliest efforts at distance education were correspondence courses in which students read books, answered questions, and received feedback from instructors through the mail. Currently, distance education includes a number of options:

- Videoconferencing, which allows learners and teachers from various sites to ask and answer questions via two-way video and audio transmissions.

- Computer conferencing, which allows students and teachers to interact via the Internet. Like bulletin boards and chat rooms, these interactions can provide either simultaneous or a synchronous interaction.

- Web-based systems that allow learners not only to watch instructional programs on television but also to access information for research. For example, in one program, students across the country viewed Gettysburg battlefields, heard profiles of individual soldiers, and were directed to websites where they could find additional information for study.

Research suggests that the type of distance learning employed isn't as important as the quality and organization of the course and the availability of the instructor for answering questions and providing feedback (Roblyer & Doering, 2010). In addition, the most effective online courses provide students with choices for when and how to work on assignments and opportunities to interact with other students (Tallent-Runnels et al., 2006).

Higher and postsecondary education have shown the greatest interest in distance education; most American colleges and universities presently offer some type of distance learning program, and these numbers are growing (Roblyer & Doering, 2010). In 2008, more than one million K–12 students took online courses, a 47-percent increase over 2006 enrollments (M. Davis, 2009). Distance education has also entered the teacher education arena, offering courses and degrees at both the prelicensure and the master's levels (Sawchuk, 2009d). Flexibility and convenience are major attractions, but experts warn that teachers should investigate thoroughly before enrolling, because the courses can be expensive and their quality varies widely (Cavanagh, 2004).

Virtual schools are also appearing around the country, providing alternatives to standard attendance at school. These schools offer comprehensive K–12 courses that connect teachers and students over the Internet. In the 2005–2006 school year, 22 states had statewide virtual schools, and 16 states allowed for the creation of cyber charter schools (Swanson, 2006b). The Virtual High School, which first offered courses in 1997, currently offers more than 200 courses to more than 5,000 students; choices range from basic courses to 15 AP courses (Virtual High School, 2009). Although most common at the high school level, virtual courses are also appearing in elementary and middle schools (Galley, 2003). Most popular with homeschooled students, virtual courses also provide students in rural areas with access to education and students in all areas with courses in hard-to-teach areas such as advanced mathematics and some languages. Experts caution that when students are introduced to online instruction, they may need assistance in

Distance education Organized educational programs that connect teachers and students over the Internet.

Virtual schools Schools offering comprehensive K–12 courses that connect teachers and students over the Internet.

learning how to learn from these courses (J. Richardson & Newby, 2005). Critics warn against relying too heavily on this technology and argue that the lack of social interaction may result in less learning and decreased social development (Maeroff, 2003; Monke, 2005/2006).

■ ■ ■ ■ CHECK YOUR UNDERSTANDING

2.1 What are two ways in which teaching in an elementary school differs from teaching in a middle school, junior high, or high school?

2.2 What are four differences between effective middle schools and junior highs?

2.3 Describe a comprehensive high school. How does a comprehensive high school differ from a vocational high school?

For feedback, go to the appendix, *Check Your Understanding*, located in the back of this text.

WHAT IS AN EFFECTIVE SCHOOL?

A major factor that will influence your satisfaction in teaching is the quality of your first school. But what is an effective school, and what is it like to teach in one? We offer answers to these questions in this section.

Although the public commonly refers to schools as good or not so good, as in "Woodrow Wilson is a very good elementary school," researchers use the term *effective* instead. An **effective school** is one in which learning for all students is maximized. But how does a school maximize learning for all students? Researchers attempting to answer this question identified schools that, despite challenging circumstances, produced more learning than comparable ones that weren't as successful (Marzano, 2003). They also looked at poor-performing schools as counterexamples. Let's see what these researchers found.

Research on Effective Schools

Research has identified several essential characteristics of effective schools (Marzano, Waters, & McNulty, 2005; Taylor, Pressley, & Pearson, 2002). They are shown in Figure 8.1 and discussed in the sections that follow.

Figure 8.1 Characteristics of Effective Schools

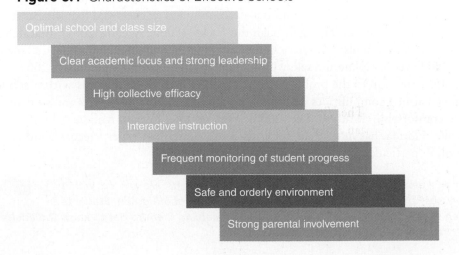

Optimal school and class size

Clear academic focus and strong leadership

High collective efficacy

Interactive instruction

Frequent monitoring of student progress

Safe and orderly environment

Strong parental involvement

Effective school A school in which learning for all students is maximized.

OPTIMAL SCHOOL AND CLASS SIZE   Size—both the size of the school and the size of classes—is an important dimension of school organization, and it can strongly affect students' learning experiences.

School Size.   Are small schools better than big ones, or is the reverse true? As it turns out, the relationship between size and quality isn't that simple. Schools must be large enough to provide the varied curricular offerings needed to help students learn in different content areas, but not so large that students get lost (Ready & Lee, 2008).

How big is too big? The largest high school on record, DeWitt Clinton High School in the Bronx, boasted 12,000 students in 1934 (R. Allen, 2002). (Can you imagine what it must have been like to be a ninth grader walking into that school on the first day of the school year?) One-room elementary schools are at the other end of the spectrum; for example, one elementary school in Nevada had one teacher and six students (one fifth grader, four fourth graders, and a first grader) in 2009 (Friess, 2009). Planning must be a real challenge for that teacher!

School size also relates to level, with elementary schools being the smallest and high schools the largest. More than 70 percent of U.S. high school students attend schools of 1,000 students or more, and a number of urban districts have high schools of more than 5,000 students (Allen, 2002).

Research suggests that the ideal size for a high school is somewhere between 600 and 900 students (V. Lee, 2000). Schools must be large enough to provide adequate facilities and resources, but not so large that they lose the personal dimension (Wainer & Zwerling, 2006).

School size affects low- and high-SES students differently: The decrease in learning in very large or very small high schools is greater for low-SES than it is for high-SES students (C. Howley & Howley, 2004). The only schools not fitting this pattern are elite private schools that enroll students with similar backgrounds and provide extensive resources, such as well-equipped science and computer labs. Unfortunately, a disproportionate number of low-SES students attend either very small or very large high schools. Examples include small rural schools in sparsely populated states, such as Wyoming or Montana, and large urban schools in major cities such as New York or Los Angeles.

How does school size influence student learning? Researchers suggest that school size, in itself, doesn't cause students to learn less. Rather, size influences other factors; as schools become larger, for example, it's more difficult to create learning environments that promote a sense of physical and emotional safety in students (J. Feldman et al., 2006). In large schools, education is less personal; it's harder for teachers and students to get to know one another and to work together, and individual teachers within classrooms are still the major factor influencing student learning (Wyse, Keesler, & Schneider, 2008).

Both parents and teachers want smaller schools, but the cost of building them deters taxpayers. In a national survey, parents said they believed their children received a more rigorous and personalized education in smaller schools, and teachers said that smaller schools prevented students from "falling through the cracks" (Public Agenda, 2002). Research also supports smaller schools: They have significantly higher graduation and college attendance rates and fewer discipline and safety issues than do large schools (Vander Ark, 2002).

One solution to the problem of large schools is to create **schools within schools**, smaller learning communities within larger schools where both teachers and students feel more comfortable (Ready & Lee, 2008). For example, Kernan Middle School in Jacksonville, Florida, has more than 1,200 students, more than experts recommend for any school, in particular for a middle school.

Schools within schools Smaller learning communities within larger schools where both teachers and students feel more comfortable.

To address the issue of school size, Kernan students are placed within "houses" of approximately 400 students at the start of 6th grade. Students then stay in their houses through 8th grade, enabling them to get to know the adults in their building. They deal with a small front office managed by an assistant principal, who, for all intents and purposes, is the principal of this mini school. The students get to know all the teachers in the hallway as well as other students who are part of their houses. The goal is for each student to be well known by at least one adult. Students are at ease in making the transition to the next grade level because of the feeling of familiarity with the house and all its components (people, rules, procedures). Typically, when asked, a student will identify himself or herself as a "house B student." At the end of the middle school experience, this student will hopefully have formed meaningful, personal relationships with more people than they would if they were in a school of 1,200 students with less of an identity. (D. DiFabio, personal communication, September 11, 2006)

Class Size.   Class size also influences a school's effectiveness. Classes of 20 or fewer students are considered optimal, but many classes are much larger, especially in middle, junior high, and high schools. One of your authors recently taught a high school health teacher who had 47 students assigned to her class. If all her students showed up for class, there weren't enough desks. One commonly used measure of class size is the **teacher–student ratio**, which expresses the number of students taught by one teacher. This ratio can be misleading, however, because districts typically include administrators and other district-level personnel in the computation, giving an inflated gauge of the class sizes teachers actually work with. Although critics argue either that class size doesn't matter or that reducing class size isn't worth the cost, research suggests that reducing class size does, indeed, increase learning for all students, and the effects are particularly pronounced in the lower grades and for at-risk students (Viadero, 2008c; Peevely, Hedges, & Nye, 2005).

Reductions in class size can have both short- and long-term positive effects (J. Finn, Gerber, & Boyd-Zaharias, 2005; Konstantopoulos, 2008). In Tennessee, where average class sizes were reduced from 25 to 15 students, researchers found immediate gains in reading and math scores. Follow-up studies revealed that the positive effects lasted through 12th grade; low-SES students who participated in the program for 4 years were twice as likely to graduate from high school as their counterparts in larger classes. Students in the smaller classes also took more challenging courses later on in school, and were more likely to attend college than those in larger classes. These positive effects were especially strong for low-SES and African American students.

Smaller class sizes also positively affect teachers' lives: When class sizes are reduced, teachers' morale and job satisfaction increase (Muñoz & Portes, 2002). In smaller classes, teachers spend less time on discipline and more time on small-group work and diagnostic assessment. Researchers caution, however, that these positive changes don't occur automatically: Teachers need to learn how to adjust their instruction to take advantage of the smaller numbers of students in their classrooms (Hess & Squire, 2008; Peevely, Hedges, & Nye, 2005).

This section addresses the fourth item in our *This I Believe* feature, "In general, larger schools provide students with a better education, because they have better facilities and a wider variety of programs." This statement is true up to a point: Although schools need to be large enough to offer a full menu of offerings, when they're too large, students can become lost and the human dimension suffers.

This I BELIEVE

CLEAR ACADEMIC FOCUS AND STRONG LEADERSHIP   In effective schools, a clearly stated academic mission exists, and it remains at the forefront of the thinking of the entire school staff (Marzano, Waters, & McNulty, 2005). For example, if developing literacy is emphasized in the mission of an elementary school, this theme appears in teachers' instruction. Teachers focus on reading comprehension in all classes, not simply when they're explicitly teaching reading, and children are given extensive practice in putting their understanding of math, science, and other content into words.

Teacher–student ratio A measure of class size found by dividing the average number of students in classes by the number of classroom teachers.

Promoting learning is the central mission of effective schools; this mission is clear to the teachers in the school, and the school principal sets the tone (Grady, 2007). In academically focused schools, teachers have high expectations, and they maximize the time available for instruction. Students are directly involved in learning activities, and instruction remains focused on essential content and skills. An array of clubs, sports, and other extracurricular offerings exist and are important, but they don't take precedence over learning. In effective schools, for example, classes aren't canceled so students can attend sporting events, and class time isn't used for club meetings.

Strong leadership is essential to the success of a school. In effective schools, the principal understands learning and teaching and acts as an instructional leader who can advise staff and serve as a resource to parents and students (Mosenthal, Lipson, Torncello, Russ, & Mekkelson, 2004; Sergiovanni, 2009a, 2009b). Faculty meetings focus on instructional issues, and learning and effective teaching are continually discussed topics.

Schools with an academic focus are more positive places in which to work because both students and teachers believe that learning is occurring. You will want to look for signs that an academic focus is present in the schools in which you're considering working.

HIGH COLLECTIVE EFFICACY   Contributing to a school's academic focus is **high collective efficacy**, the belief by teachers that their school can make a difference in students' lives (Goddard, Hoy, & Hoy, 2004). High collective efficacy begins with **personal teaching efficacy**, each teacher's belief that he or she can promote learning in all students, regardless of their backgrounds. High-efficacy teachers take responsibility for the success of their own instruction (Bruning, Schraw, Norby, & Ronning, 2004). In other words, if students aren't learning, rather than blaming students' lack of intelligence, poor home environments, uncooperative administrators, or some other cause, high-efficacy teachers conclude that they could be doing a better job and look for ways to increase student learning.

Two aspects of high-collective-efficacy schools are important. First, students from all socioeconomic levels learn more there than in schools where collective efficacy is lower (Goddard et al., 2004). This, in itself, isn't surprising; it makes sense that the more teachers strive for student learning, the more students learn. Second, low-SES students in high-collective-efficacy schools have achievement levels nearly equal to those of high-SES students in low-collective-efficacy schools. High-collective-efficacy schools help reduce achievement differences between groups of students who typically benefit quite differently from schooling.

This section addresses the fifth item in our *This I Believe* feature, "Teachers' beliefs in their ability to affect learning can actually influence how much students learn." This statement is true: Teachers who believe they can make a difference in students' lives are more likely to actually do so.

How do high-efficacy teachers and high-collective-efficacy schools accomplish these results? A number of factors contribute, but two are essential: (1) interactive instruction and (2) frequent monitoring of student progress.

INTERACTIVE INSTRUCTION   Imagine walking through the hallways of a school; the doors of classrooms are open so you can glance inside. Can you determine anything about the effectiveness of the school with a simple glance? The answer is yes, as this principal found.

Cassie Jones walks through the halls of the inner-city middle school where she is the principal and listens to the sounds coming from the different classrooms. As she walks by Ben Carlson's social studies class, she hears him say, "Yesterday we talked about the strengths and weaknesses of the North and South at the outbreak of the Civil War. Who remembers one of these?"

---

myeducationlab

To view a team of teachers who meet regularly to discuss curriculum and issues, as well as the team leader, go to the *Assignments and Activities section* of Topic 6: *School Organization* in the MyEducationLab for your course and complete the activity titled *Being a Team Leader*.

This I BELIEVE

High collective efficacy The belief by teachers that their school can make a difference in students' lives.

Personal teaching efficacy Each teacher's belief that he or she can promote learning in all students, regardless of their backgrounds.

As Cassie proceeds down the hall, she stops in front of Sarah McCarthy's science class. Sarah is at the front of the room swinging a set of keys from a piece of string. "Hmmm," Cassie thinks, "no wonder her class is so quiet—she's got them hypnotized." As she listens further, she hears Sarah ask, "Class, this is a simple pendulum, just like the one we find in grandfather clocks. Who can tell me what factors influence the rate at which a pendulum swings?"

"Good question," thinks Cassie. "Maybe that's why her kids are so quiet."

When Cassie turns the corner, she is greeted by a steady stream of student voices arguing about something.

"I don't care what you say, stealing is wrong."

"But his family didn't have enough to eat. They were hungry—he couldn't let them starve!"

"What's Hector up to today?" Cassie thinks as she listens more closely to Hector Sanchez's English class.

"Class," Hector breaks in with a booming voice, "it's not enough just to disagree with your partners. You have to explain why. Remember, one of the reasons we read books like Sounder is to help us understand our own lives. So, you have three more minutes in your discussion groups to explain why the father was right or wrong to steal food for his family."

Cassie chuckles as she hears Hector's class rejoin the battle. "He's sure got them stirred up today. I guess I'm lucky to have such a talented teaching staff that has so many different strengths." (Adapted from Jacobsen, Eggen, & Kauchak, 2009, pp. 223–224)

An effective school has teachers who actively involve students in learning activities. If the prevailing pattern is one in which teachers are asking large numbers of questions and students are involved in discussions, the likelihood that the school is effective increases. In contrast, if you see teachers primarily lecturing or students spending most of their time passively listening or working alone and doing seat work, the school is less likely to be effective. Evaluating schools in this way is admittedly simplistic, and many additional factors influence how much students learn. Nevertheless, interaction between teacher and students and students with one another is an essential ingredient for learning (Eggen & Kauchak, 2010).

Not only is interactive teaching essential for learning, it's also important for motivation (Schunk, Pintrich, & Meece, 2008). Students at all levels prefer challenging and interactive activities to ones that require them to sit passively, listening to teacher lectures (Brophy, 2004). Effective schools provide opportunities for students to become actively involved in their learning.

FREQUENT MONITORING OF STUDENT PROGRESS   The extent to which teachers frequently assess learning and provide students with feedback is another essential factor differentiating more effective and less effective schools. Experts suggest that effective learning environments are assessment centered (Stiggins, 2008b). In other words, assessment isn't tacked on at the end of an instructional period, such as giving a test once a month or at the end of a unit; rather, it's an integral part of the entire teaching–learning process. Teachers in effective schools continually collect information about students' learning progress. They regularly gather and grade work samples and give frequent quizzes and tests, and the assessments measure more than recall of facts. Teachers return assessments, such as quizzes and assignments, shortly after they're given, and they thoroughly discuss test items to provide students with feedback about their responses (Marzano, 2003; Stiggins, 2008b). The need for assessment-centered classrooms also helps us understand why interactive instruction is so essential: Teachers gather a great deal of information about students' understanding by listening to their responses to questions as they attempt to describe their developing thinking.

SAFE AND ORDERLY ENVIRONMENT   Students at all grade levels are concerned about school safety issues, such as fighting, bullying, and classmates who are disruptive. Schools, which should be sheltered communities for learning, often mirror the problems

PEARSON myeducationlab

To see how one teacher uses interactive instruction to involve her students in learning, go to the *Assignments and Activities* section of Topic 6: *School Organization* in the MyEducationLab for your course and complete the activity titled *Interactive Instruction*.

PEARSON myeducationlab

Go to the *IRIS Center Resources* section of Topic 6: *School Organization* in the MyEducationLab for your course and explore the module titled *Effective School Practices: Promoting Collaboration and Monitoring Student's Academic Achievement*.

One essential characteristic of an effective school is hallways that are safe and orderly.

of society. "If teachers and students do not feel safe, they will not have the necessary psychological energy for teaching and learning" (Marzano, 2003, p. 53).

The need for safe and orderly schools is supported by both research and theory. Researchers found effective schools to be places of trust, order, cooperation, and high morale (Marzano, 2003; Koth, Bradshaw, & Leaf, 2008). Students need to feel emotionally safe in school for healthy learning and development to occur.

Theories of learner development suggest that people prefer to live in an orderly rather than a chaotic world (Piaget 1952, 1970). In addition, the psychologist Abraham Maslow (1968), who described a hierarchy of human needs, argued that only the need for survival is more basic than the need for safety. Studies of classroom management also confirm the need for order: Orderly classrooms are important for both learning and student motivation (Emmer, Evertson, & Worsham, 2009; Evertson, Emmer, & Worsham, 2009).

Effective schools develop mechanisms to allow parents and teachers to work together.

STRONG PARENTAL INVOLVEMENT   Schools, no matter how well they're organized, can't be effective if parents aren't involved in their children's education (Marzano, 2003). Learning is a cooperative venture, in which teachers, students, and parents are in it together.

Research indicates that students benefit from home–school cooperation in a number of ways:

- Students achieve more, regardless of SES, ethnic/racial background, or the parents' levels of education. The more extensive the parental involvement, the higher the student achievement.

- Students earn higher grades and test scores, attend school more regularly, and complete homework more consistently.

- Students exhibit more positive attitudes and behavior.

- Student alcohol use, violence, and antisocial behaviors decrease as parental involvement increases.

- Educators hold higher expectations for students whose parents collaborate with teachers. They also have higher opinions of those parents (C. Green, Walker, Hoover-Dempsey, & Sandler, 2007; Sheldon, 2007).

School Organization and the Achievement of Cultural Minorities

Emphasis on higher standards and increased accountability is the most prominent reform in education today. Change, however, can have unintended outcomes, and one outcome of this reform has been a widening gap between the achievement of cultural minorities—particularly African American and Hispanic students—and that of their White and Asian counterparts. Between 1970, when the National Assessment of Educational Progress began systematically measuring students' achievement, and 1980, African American and Hispanic students made great progress in narrowing the achievement gap separating them from their White peers. This progress stopped abruptly in the late 1980s, however, and since then, the gap has either remained constant or widened (Fairchild, 2006; Viadero, 2009a). Dropout rates for minority students have followed a similar pattern, flattening out or even increasing (Olson, 2006b). Similarly, recent data on schools found lacking under No Child Left Behind rules found a preponderance of failing schools with high proportions of minority and high-poverty students (Archer, 2006a).

Researchers have identified several factors to explain differences in achievement between White and minority students, including poverty, peer pressure, and parental values (Byrnes, 2003; Ogbu, 2003). These are all likely candidates, but research has also identified two aspects of school organization that can influence the achievement of minority students: tracking and class size.

CULTURAL MINORITIES AND TRACKING

Earlier in the chapter, we saw that comprehensive high schools have been criticized for the practice of tracking, because evidence indicates that educational experiences in lower-level tracks are often substandard (Oakes, 2005, 2008). This evidence is particularly relevant for cultural minorities, because they tend to be underrepresented in higher-level tracks and overrepresented in lower-level ones. The problem is exacerbated by the fact that minority students tend not to enroll in more demanding classes. As shown in Table 8.3, the students least likely to enroll in such classes are also least likely to graduate from college (Viadero, 2000).

Tracking and minority achievement have a form of negative synergy: Student achievement in low-level classes is reduced compared to the achievement of students of comparable ability in high-level classes. Because decisions about tracking are based on records of students' past achievement, minority students continue to be placed in lower-level tracks, and the negative relationship between achievement and tracking is magnified. Unfortunately, school leaders haven't identified a satisfactory solution to this problem.

Tracking can result in the segregation of cultural minorities into low-level classes where instruction tends to be less challenging.

CULTURAL MINORITIES AND CLASS SIZE

The relationship between class size and minority achievement is more encouraging. Earlier we saw that research supports the contention that student achievement is higher in smaller classes. This research is important, because the beneficial effects of reducing class size are greater for cultural minorities than for nonminorities (P. Smith, Molnar, & Zahorik, 2003).

Two studies are particularly significant. First, assessments of a major Tennessee project for reducing class size (J. Finn et al., 2005; Illig, 1996) found the following:

- Children in small classes (about 15 students per class) consistently

	1992 High School Graduates Who Completed Algebra 2 and Geometry (%)	Freshmen at 4-Year Colleges Who Graduate Within 6 Years (%)
Race/Ethnicity		
Asian American	55.5	65
White	53.1	59
Hispanic American	41.9	46
Native American	35.7	37
African American	35	40

Table 8.3 Percentages of Students Taking Advanced Math Courses and Graduating From 4-Year Colleges

Source: Adapted from R. Johnston & Viadero (2000).

outperformed children in larger classes.

- Inner-city children (about 97 percent of whom were minorities) in small classes closed some of the achievement gap between themselves and nonminority children in large classes.
- Children in small classes outperformed children in larger classes, even when teachers in the large classes had support from aides.

In the second study, a 4-year experiment with reduction in class size in Wisconsin, researchers found the achievement gap between minorities and nonminorities shrank by 19 percent in smaller classes, whereas in comparable regular classrooms, it grew by 58 percent (Molnar, Percy, Smith, & Zahorik, 1998; P. Smith et al., 2003). In addition to narrowing the achievement gap between minority and nonminority students in first grade, the program also prevented it from widening when students in the smaller classes progressed to second and third grades. When class sizes are reduced, teachers have more personal contacts with individual students and can design more effective learning activities to engage students (Blatchford, Bassett, & Brown, 2005). The results of the class-size-reduction experiment were so compelling that the Wisconsin legislature appropriated $59 million to expand the program to 400 additional schools (Gewertz, 2000).

Diversity in Your Classroom

Teachers can't change the number of students they have in their classrooms, but they can and do influence the students they have in their class. The instructional decisions they make influence how their classrooms feel and what students learn about themselves. Teachers can examine their grouping practices to ensure that every student in the class has an opportunity to learn and succeed. They can also make their classrooms feel smaller by learning each student's name quickly and by including all students in learning activities. Even a teacher's choice of teaching strategies influences how a classroom feels: Interactive strategies such as questioning and group work provide opportunities for teachers to learn about their students.

QUESTIONS TO CONSIDER

1. What can teachers do to minimize the negative effects of tracking if they are assigned a basic class with low-performing students?
2. What should teachers do when they have cultural minority students in their upper-end, high-ability, college-prep classes?

myeducationlab To respond to these questions online, explore this topic further, and receive feedback, go to the *Book Specific Resources* section *in* the MyEducationLab for your course, select your text, and then select *Exploring Diversity* for Chapter 8.

ISSUES IN EDUCATION

These outcomes likely result from parents' increased participation in school activities, their more positive attitudes about schooling, and teachers' increased understanding of students' home environments.

In the *Exploring Diversity* box above, we describe how school organization influences the academic success of cultural minorities.

■ ■ ■ ■ CHECK YOUR UNDERSTANDING

3.1 Describe characteristics of an effective school.

3.2 What is the most distinguishing characteristic of effective instruction in effective schools?

3.3 Why is frequent monitoring of student progress essential for an effective school?

For feedback, go to the appendix, *Check Your Understanding*, located in the back of this text.

Now it's your turn to apply the information in this chapter to your own professional life. The *Decision Making* feature that follows asks you to think about how the research on effective schools will influence your own teaching.

Effective Schools and Classrooms

You're sitting in the teacher workroom about a month into a new school year, and one of your colleagues comes in and comments, "I just don't know what's wrong with these kids. I explained everything so carefully yesterday, and when they came in today it was as if they hadn't heard a word I said.

"On the other hand, these kids come from the worst backgrounds, so there isn't all that much we can do about them anyway. They won't pay attention, they don't give a rip about what we're studying, and they won't take a lick of responsibility for their own learning.

"Their parents, if they even are living with their parents, don't care either, so what's the use. If I can gut it out until the end of this year, I'm going to try for all I'm worth to get a transfer at the end the year."

What would you say to your colleague?

8 MEETING YOUR LEARNING OBJECTIVES

1. Describe different meanings of *school*, and identify components of a typical school organization.
   - One definition describes schools as places where young people go to learn and develop intellectually, personally, and socially. Another describes a school as a place—a building or set of buildings.
   - Schools are also social institutions, organized to promote student growth and development as well as the welfare of society. This is the definition used in this text.
   - Personnel—the school principal and other administrators, support staff, such as custodians and cafeteria workers, and teachers—are one important component of school organization.
   - The physical plant—buildings that house classrooms, the library, the cafeteria, and other support functions—make up a second component. In addition, junior highs and high schools usually have gymnasiums, playing fields, and sometimes swimming pools.
   - The curriculum, what is taught in school, is a third component, and it is typically organized into grade levels, with content intended to be taught to students of different ages.

2. Describe important differences among schools at different levels.
   - Elementary schools are organized so that a single teacher is often responsible for all of the instruction in the different content areas. Elementary teachers arrange their own schedules, and often emphasize reading, language arts, and math in their instruction while de-emphasizing content areas such as science, social studies, and the arts.
   - Middle schools, junior highs, and high schools differ from elementary schools in that they're organized into different content areas and have specified periods of time devoted to each.

- Effective middle schools differ from junior highs in four ways. First, unlike junior highs, middle schools organize teachers and students into interdisciplinary teams, where all teachers on a team have the same group of students. Second, middle schools place greater attention on students' emotional development than do junior highs. Third, teachers in effective middle schools more strongly emphasize interactive teaching strategies than teachers in junior highs. Finally, middle schools eliminate activities in which developmental differences among students become apparent, such as competitive athletics.

- A comprehensive high school aims to meet the needs of all students through differentiated offerings, which means it provides offerings for students who are likely to attend college, but at the same time it attempts to meet the needs of students who will be entering the job market after graduation.

3. Identify characteristics of an effective school.

- Size is one component of an effective school. Effective elementary schools keep class sizes below 20 students per class, and effective high schools have enrollments in the 600–900 range.

- Effective schools are safe and orderly, they're academically focused, they involve parents, and they have strong leadership from the principal. Teachers in effective schools take responsibility for student learning, maintain high levels of interaction with students, and continually monitor student progress.

IMPORTANT CONCEPTS

administrators (p. 226)
advanced placement classes (p. 236)
block scheduling (p. 238)
career academies (p. 239)
career technical schools (p. 239)
comprehensive high school (p. 236)
curriculum (p. 228)
development (p. 229)
developmental programs (p. 231)
distance education (p. 240)
early childhood education (p. 231)
effective school (p. 241)

high collective efficacy (p. 244)
junior high schools (p. 234)
looping (p. 229)
middle schools (p. 235)
Montessori method (p. 231)
personal teaching efficacy (p. 244)
principal (p. 226)
schools within schools (p. 242)
social institution (p. 225)
teacher–student ratio (p. 243)
virtual schools (p. 240)

DISCUSSION QUESTIONS

1. Based on the organization of typical elementary schools, what are the primary advantages and disadvantages of teaching in an elementary school? How could elementary schools be organized differently to improve the education of all students?

2. Based on the organization of typical middle schools, what are the primary advantages and disadvantages of teaching in a middle school? How could middle schools be organized differently to improve the education of all students?

3. Based on the organization of typical high schools, what are the primary advantages and disadvantages of teaching in a high school? How could high schools be organized differently to improve the education of all students?

4. In which kind of school—elementary, middle, junior high, or high school—do teachers have the most autonomy? the least autonomy? What implications does this have for you as a prospective teacher?

5. Consider what you know about the organization of elementary, middle, junior high, and high schools. Which type of school is best suited to your academic and personal characteristics? Why do you think so?

6. What should a prospective teacher look for when trying to decide whether to work in a school?

PEARSON
myeducationlab

Now go to Topic 6: *School Organization* in the MyEducationLab (*www.myeducationlab.com*) for your course, where you can:

- Find learning outcomes for *School Organization* along with the national standards that connect to these outcomes.

- Complete *Assignments and Activities* that can help you more deeply understand the chapter content.

- Apply and practice your understanding of the core teaching skills identified in the chapter with the *Building Teaching Skills and Dispositions* learning units.

- Check your comprehension on the content covered in the chapter by going to the *Study Plan* in the *Book Specific Resources* section for your text. Here you will be able to take a chapter quiz, receive feedback on your answers, and then access *Review, Practice, and Enrichment* activities to enhance your understanding of chapter content.

Develop Your Professional Portfolio

To further apply your understanding of chapter content and address the INTASC standards, go to the *Book Specific Resources* section in the MyEducationLab for your course, select your text, then select this chapter's *Portfolio Activities*.

"I teach because of the awesome pay, the perks, and the low-stress work environment that comes with being a teacher. Okay, I'm just kidding on that one. That's not why I teach. I teach because somewhere deep inside me, I'd like to think that sometimes, just sometimes, we make a difference."

MICHAEL SMART,   2008 Teacher of the Year, Minnesota

To view a video clip of Michael, the 2008 Minnesota Teacher of the Year, go to Topic 5: *Governance and Finance* in the MyEducationLab for your course and select *Teacher Talk*, then *Michael Smart.*.

9

Governance and Finance
Regulating and Funding Schools

CHAPTER OUTLINE

Governance: How Are Schools Regulated and Run?

■ Governance: A Legal Overview

■ State Governance Structures

■ School Districts

School Finance: How Are Schools Funded?

■ School Funding Sources

■ Educational Revenues: Where Do They Go?

Emerging Issues in School Governance and Finance

■ Savage Inequalities: The Struggle for Funding Equity

■ Urban Takeovers: Alternatives to Local Control

■ School Choice

Taking a Stand in an Era of Reform: The Privatization Issue

Exploring Diversity: School Choice and Cultural Minorities

LEARNING OBJECTIVES

After you have completed your study of this chapter, you should be able to:

1. **Describe the major educational governance structures at state and local levels.** INTASC Standard 9, Teacher Professionalism

2. **Explain the different sources and targets of educational funding.** INTASC Standard 9, Teacher Professionalism

3. **Describe major current issues in school governance and finance.** INTASC Standard 9, Teacher Professionalism

School governance and school finance may seem irrelevant to beginning teachers, but veterans know better. The way schools are run and the way school districts use money make a big difference in the quality of teachers' professional lives. And, reform efforts aimed at addressing funding inequities and providing more educational choices to parents are changing the teaching profession today. As you read the following case study, think about how governance and finance will influence your job satisfaction as a teacher.

Carla Buendia sits at her desk, looking at the pile of books and papers covering it. "I better get this one right, as it'll be our only chance," she thinks to herself. Carla is a member of Unified Metropolitan School District's Elementary Math Steering Committee. Unified Metropolitan is a large district in the Midwest, and the Steering Committee has been meeting regularly over the last 2 years to study the elementary math curriculum in the district. Test scores have been declining, especially in the areas of applications and problem solving, and the committee has been asked to make a recommendation to the district's school board. Tonight is the night.

"Don't be nervous," Carla tells herself, but her advice isn't working. She has been to school board meetings as a spectator when teacher salaries and contracts were being discussed, and she's clearly uneasy about being in front of the hundred or more people who will be in attendance. "Why did I ever say I'd do this?" she thinks. "Too late for that. I just better have my act together when it's my turn to speak."

It can be unsettling to go into two schools within a few miles of each other and see striking differences in how they look and feel: One is bright, cheerful, and clean, with student projects and works of art prominently displayed; the other is dark, depressing, and dirty, and the hallways are cluttered with trash. Many of these differences can be traced to the ways the schools are governed and financed.

School governance and finance also influence the resources available to teachers. As an example, drive across the state line from New Mexico, where the average spending per pupil in 2005 was $8,236, to Utah, where it was $5,245 (National Education Association, 2006b). Some politicians argue that money doesn't influence the quality of education, but evidence suggests otherwise (Biddle & Berliner, 2002). Money buys paper, supplies, and equipment, for example, and allows students to do science experiments instead of reading about them.

How do school governance and finance affect the lives of teachers and students? We address this question in this chapter, but before continuing, take a few minutes to respond to the survey in the *This I Believe* Feature on page 255. We discuss each of the items as the chapter unfolds.

GOVERNANCE: HOW ARE SCHOOLS REGULATED AND RUN?

In a few short years, you will walk into your own classroom, look around, and think, "At last, it's all mine." That's a good feeling, and it *will* be all yours—sort of. Although teachers have considerable autonomy in implementing their own vision of good teaching, they also operate within a specified governance framework.

Governance: A Legal Overview

Unlike many other countries, where the national government is responsible for schools, in the United States, the Tenth Amendment to the Constitution clearly assigns legal responsibility for education to the 50 states. Because the states differ significantly in geography, history, economics, and politics, you might think that they would also differ in their approaches to governing education, but they don't. Each of the states has a surprisingly similar organizational structure. These structures are outlined in Figure 9.1 and described in the next section.

State Governance Structures

In every state, a constitution outlines the roles and responsibilities of state education officers. Governors focus public attention on educational issues and solicit public support for educational funding. State legislatures meet annually to debate school finance and other issues. These legislative sessions are important to teachers because states supply almost half of a district's education budget, and legislative actions (or inactions) influence teacher salaries, class sizes, supplies, and equipment (Brimley & Garfield, 2008).

The information in this section answers the first item on our *This I Believe* feature, "Different states govern education in basically the same way." This statement is essentially true. Despite some variation in views about the ways schools should educate children, most states govern education in basically the same way.

This I BELIEVE

STATE BOARD OF EDUCATION   Because the governor and legislators have an entire state to run, they turn most of the responsibility for steering their state's schools to the

state board of education, the legal governing body that exercises general control and supervision of the schools in a state. State boards are similar in purpose to district school boards and perform both regulatory and advisory functions. State boards regulate education in these ways:

- Issuing and revoking teaching licenses
- Establishing the length of the school year
- Publishing curriculum standards to guide teachers' instruction
- Developing and implementing uniform systems for gathering education data, such as standardized achievement test scores, enrollment trends, and demographics

State boards set long- and short-term goals for their states and help create an educational agenda for the governor and the state legislature. For example, responding to the federal No Child Left Behind (NCLB) Act of 2001 was a pressing issue in all states during the administration of George W. Bush, and state boards assisted governors and legislatures in shaping responses to this initiative.

State board members are people outside professional education, meaning most haven't worked in or studied education formally. They are usually appointed by the governor, but about a fourth of the states elect these officials, who typically serve without pay (National Association of State Boards of Education, 2007).

STATE OFFICE OF EDUCATION   A state board of education makes policy; the **state office of education** is responsible for implementing policy within a state on a day-to-day basis. In contrast with state boards, which are composed of lay members who meet periodically to discharge their duties, state offices of education are staffed by full-time education professionals, virtually all of whom have been teachers and most of whom have advanced degrees in education.

State board of education The legal governing body that exercises general control and supervision of the schools in a state.

State office of education Office responsible for implementing educational policy within a state on a day-to-day basis.

Figure 9.1 State Administrative Organizational Structure

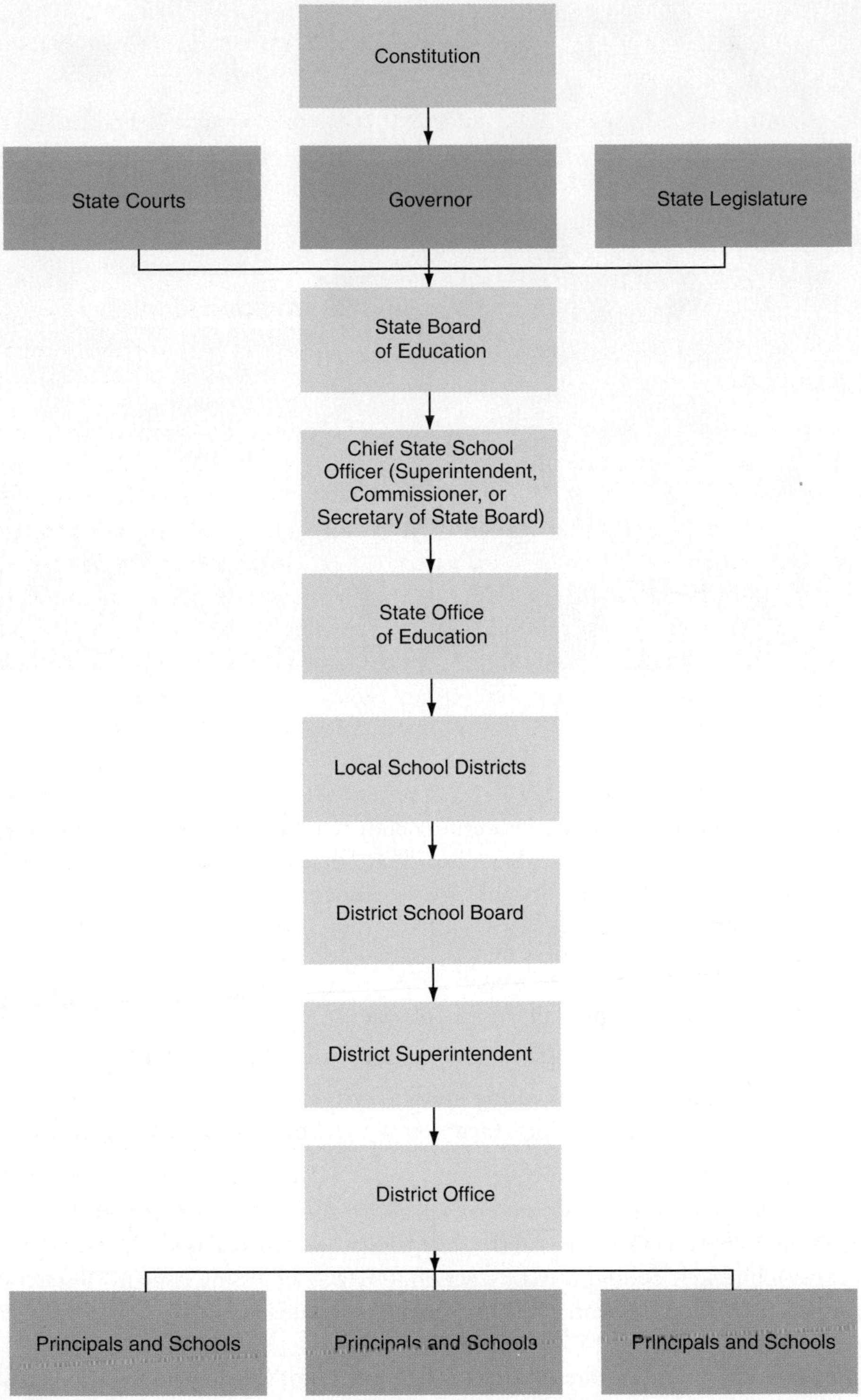

```
                        ┌─────────────────┐
                        │   Constitution  │
                        └────────┬────────┘
                                 │
                                 ▼
┌──────────────┐        ┌─────────────────┐        ┌──────────────────┐
│ State Courts │        │    Governor     │        │ State Legislature│
└───────┬──────┘        └────────┬────────┘        └────────┬─────────┘
        └────────────────────────┼──────────────────────────┘
                                 ▼
                        ┌─────────────────┐
                        │   State Board   │
                        │  of Education   │
                        └────────┬────────┘
                                 ▼
                        ┌─────────────────────┐
                        │ Chief State School  │
                        │ Officer (Superinten-│
                        │ dent, Commissioner, │
                        │ or Secretary of     │
                        │ State Board)        │
                        └────────┬────────────┘
                                 ▼
                        ┌─────────────────┐
                        │   State Office  │
                        │  of Education   │
                        └────────┬────────┘
                                 ▼
                        ┌─────────────────┐
                        │ Local School    │
                        │ Districts       │
                        └────────┬────────┘
                                 ▼
                        ┌─────────────────┐
                        │ District School │
                        │ Board           │
                        └────────┬────────┘
                                 ▼
                        ┌─────────────────┐
                        │ District        │
                        │ Superintendent  │
                        └────────┬────────┘
                                 ▼
                        ┌─────────────────┐
                        │ District Office │
                        └────────┬────────┘
        ┌────────────────────────┼──────────────────────────┐
        ▼                        ▼                           ▼
┌──────────────┐        ┌─────────────────┐        ┌──────────────────┐
│ Principals   │        │ Principals and  │        │ Principals and   │
│ and Schools  │        │ Schools         │        │ Schools          │
└──────────────┘        └─────────────────┘        └──────────────────┘
```

Each state office of education is headed by a chief state officer, with a title such as *superintendent, commissioner,* or *secretary of the state board.* Chief state officers are appointed by the state board of education or another board in 23 states, elected in 14 states, and appointed by the governor in 13 (McNeil, 2008a). The state office implements teacher and administrator licensing, supervises curriculum, approves school sites and buildings, and collects statistical data. As a new teacher, you will apply to the office of education in your state for an initial teaching license, the form and requirements of which are determined by the state board.

A state office of education influences the curriculum (what is taught) in a state in two important ways: state standards and textbook approval. Let's look at them.

State Standards.   State standards, statements specifying what students should know and what skills they should have upon completing an area of study, is one of the most important ways state offices of education influence curricula. Currently, all 50 states have written standards, most commonly in reading and math, but often in other areas such as science and social studies as well (Archer, 2006b).

State offices of education are also responsible for administering statewide testing programs based on standards, and initial research suggests that establishing standards and holding students and teachers responsible for reaching them have a modest effect on student achievement (Olson, 2006a).

Textbook Approval.   Textbook approval is a second way state offices of education influence curriculum. The textbooks individual schools use must be on a state-approved list; states usually offer districts a choice of several acceptable text series for a given grade level. The textbook selection process can be highly politicized when controversial topics are involved, such as evolution in science, phonics versus whole language in reading, or problem-based versus computationally oriented approaches to math. In this chapter's opening case, Carla's steering committee began its search for a math series by looking at the state-approved list. The committee then conferred with the state's math specialist to evaluate the options.

This section addresses the second item on the chapter's *This I Believe* feature, "The state office of education in each state is responsible for setting rules and regulations." The statement is technically false, because the state board of education is legally responsible for general control and supervision of the schools in a state. But many decisions about implementing the rules are left to the state office of education, so, in practice, the statement is true in some cases.

This I BELIEVE

Although state boards and state offices of education influence teaching and learning, for the most part they do so at arm's length; the day-to-day responsibility for educating students falls to the districts. This is why Carla's experience at a district school board meeting is relevant. Let's look at districts' roles in governing education.

School Districts

A **school district** is an administrative unit within a state that is defined by geographical boundaries and is legally responsible for the public education of children within those boundaries. With respect to educational governance, it's where the action is: School districts hire and fire teachers, and they determine the content that students learn (the curriculum) and, to a certain extent, the kinds of learning experiences (instruction) students will have in schools. That's why Carla was making her presentation to the district school board. She was involved in decisions about the district's elementary math curriculum. Decisions such as these are usually made at the district level; school districts also determine what books will be used and make them available to students at the beginning of the school year.

School districts differ dramatically in size. For example, in 2005, there were nearly 15,000 school districts in the United States, and if they were divided equally among the states, each state would have about 300 (Brimley & Garfield, 2008). However, the states differ dramatically in the number and size of their school districts. For example, the whole state of Hawaii constitutes one school district, whereas Texas has more than 1,000 districts. In 2004, the New York City School District had more than 1 million students, but close to 5,000 U.S. school districts had 600 or fewer students. Almost half of the districts

School district An administrative unit within a state that is defined by geographical boundaries and is legally responsible for the public education of children within those boundaries.

enroll fewer than 1,000 students per year. The largest 4 percent—districts enrolling more than 10,000 students each—educate more than half the students in this country (National Center for Education Statistics, 2005d).

Historically, the trend has been toward consolidating schools into fewer, larger districts. For instance, in 1930, the United States had more than 130,000 school districts, but 75 years later, it had fewer than 15,000 (Brimley & Garfield, 2008). Efficiency is the primary reason for consolidation: Larger districts can offer broader services and minimize duplication of administrative staff. For example, one medium-sized district with a superintendent and a district staff of 10 people is more efficient than two small districts that require a superintendent and a staff of 6 to 8 people each. However, parents often resist consolidation because of loyalty to high school athletic teams and longer bus rides for their children (Richard, 2004).

Small and large districts have both advantages and disadvantages. Small districts are less bureaucratic and easier to influence, but they often lack resources and instructional support staff. For example, Carla's committee functioned in a large district. As committee members did their work, they were assisted by a district math coordinator, a testing specialist, and technology experts who helped them evaluate the claims of different commercial math programs. This type of assistance doesn't exist in small districts.

Large districts also have problems. They tend to be hierarchical and bureaucratic, and getting things done takes time. Teachers sometimes feel like nameless and faceless cogs in large, impersonal organizations. In smaller districts, teachers can often rely on face-to-face contacts to make things happen quickly; decision making in larger districts is placed in the hands of sometimes contentious committees. The ideal district has an administrative structure that is supportive and responsive to teachers but also leaves them alone to do what they love most—work with their students.

Every school district has a local school board, a superintendent, and central staff. These are the people who make the district-level decisions about teaching and learning in their district's schools. Let's see how they will influence your life as a teacher.

Teachers often appear in front of local school boards to explain existing programs and seek funding for new ones.

Local school board A group of elected lay citizens responsible for setting policies that determine how a school district operates.

THE LOCAL SCHOOL BOARD A **local school board** is a group of elected lay citizens responsible for setting policies that determine how a school district operates. With respect to governance, what kinds of rules and regulations do school boards pass? Who are the members of these boards? How are school board members selected? Because they will influence your life as a teacher, you should know the answers to these questions.

What Do School Boards Do? School boards serve five important functions. They are outlined in Figure 9.2 and discussed in the paragraphs that follow.

Working with the district budget is the most important, and often most contentious, school board function. School boards are responsible for raising money through taxes and for disbursing funds to the schools within the district. They also make decisions about various district services, such as providing buses and maintaining lunch programs. School boards directly influence teachers by making decisions about salary increases and benefits, such as health care and retirement pay. They also affect teachers indirectly by making budget decisions that affect class size and the amount of instructional materials that are available. Wrestling with each year's budget occupies more than a quarter of a school board's time and energy; it's a continual process that begins in the fall and ends in the spring.

Personnel responsibilities are closely aligned with financial decisions. School boards are legally responsible for hiring and firing all school personnel, including teachers, principals, custodians, and school bus drivers. Your teaching contract will be offered by a district school board that has the legal authority to hire and fire teachers.

The curriculum—what teachers teach—is a third area of school board jurisdiction. School boards, assisted by district administrators, are responsible for defining the curriculum and implementing the general guidelines or standards developed by states. In virtually all districts, teachers are consulted about the curriculum; in the better ones, teachers are directly involved in curriculum decisions. For example, in the opening case, Carla's committee helped decide what math curriculum the district would adopt.

Decisions that affect students are also made by school boards. They set attendance, dress, grooming, conduct, and discipline standards for their districts. For example, the issue of school uniforms has been debated at district, state, and national levels, but the decision—sometimes after contentious debate—is ultimately made by local school boards.

School boards also determine extracurricular policies—from the mundane to the controversial. For example, some districts require students to maintain a certain grade-point average to participate in sports, a policy critics contend doubly punishes struggling student athletes by first failing them in the classroom and then preventing them from participating in sports. Supporters of no-pass/no-play policies argue that they improve motivation to learn by providing incentives for academic success (Camerino, 2003). The question of whether to grant gay and lesbian clubs equal status with other school-sponsored organizations is another topic that has generated controversy at school board meetings. As you would expect, attendance at these meetings increases when controversial issues are on their agendas.

Finally, school boards make decisions about district infrastructure. For example, they ensure that school buildings and school buses are maintained and safe, and they approve plans and hire contractors when new schools are built.

In recent years, meeting state standards and federal mandates, such as NCLB, combined with issues involving budgets and decisions about curriculum and instruction, has become the primary concerns of school board members (New York State School Board Association, 2006). Interestingly, as recently as the late 1980s, student achievement wasn't even listed in school board members' top 10 concerns. Reform efforts and the national trend toward greater school accountability have strongly affected the ways school boards operate.

Members of School Boards and Their Selection.   Who serves on school boards, and how do they get there? More than 95 percent of school boards consist of members who are elected for 3- or 4-year terms; the remainder have members appointed by large-city mayors or city councils (Land, 2002). School board elections can be controversial for two reasons. First, the voter turnout for most school board elections is embarrassingly low: As few as 5 to 10 percent of eligible voters often decide school board membership. Critics contend that this fact results in boards that don't represent the citizens in the district. The second controversy involves whether school board elections should be at-large or limited to specific areas within a city. At-large elections tend to favor wealthy, White-majority candidates who have more money to run an election campaign or who benefit from White-majority voting pools. In a limited-area election, only citizens who live in a specific part of the city are allowed to vote for candidates representing that area. Area-specific elections provide greater opportunities for minority candidates to represent local, ethnic-minority neighborhoods (Howell, 2005).

Figure 9.2 Functions of Local School Boards

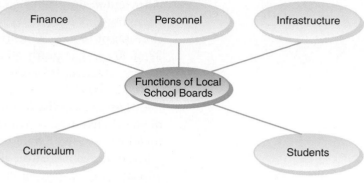

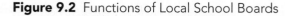

Go to the *Building Teaching Skills and Dispositions* section of Topic 5: *Governance and Finance* in the MyEducationLab for your course and complete the activity titled *The Impact of NCLB on School Governance and Financing.*

Who serves on school boards? The typical school board member is male, White, older, and wealthy, although membership is slowly becoming more diverse in some areas. For example, a 2004 survey found that more than 6 of 10 board members were male and close to 9 of 10 were White (Hess, 2004a). In addition, nearly 60 percent make more than $75,000 per year, nearly 40 percent have graduate degrees, and another 30 percent have undergraduate degrees. Only 7 percent have a high school degree or less (Carr, 2003; Hess, 2004a).

Disparities exist in the characteristics of school board members and the people they're elected to serve. For example, slightly more than 1 of 10 board members is a cultural minority, but a third of the nation's students are minorities, and that figure is projected to rise to more than 40 percent by the year 2010 (U.S. Department of Education, 2003a). Also, 45 percent of school board members are businesspeople or professionals, and 85 percent make more money than the average teacher (Carr, 2003). Critics contend that wealthy school board members can't empathize with the financial hardships that teachers and community members often experience. Critics also question the ability of male-dominated school boards to effectively represent the teaching force, which is almost three fourths female.

THE SUPERINTENDENT   The school board makes policy, and the **superintendent**, the school district's head administrative officer, along with his or her staff, implements that policy in the district's schools. The division of labor between the board and the superintendent isn't simple and well defined, however (Darden, 2008a). Because most board members have little or no background in professional education, the superintendent often plays a central role in leading the board and helping set agendas.

Historically, superintendents have been hired by school boards and have held an advanced degree in education. Although this is still true in many cases, events have changed, and some districts now look outside the field of education to find superintendents. For example, Joel Klein, the chancellor of the massive New York City school system, is a lawyer and politician who worked in the Justice Department in the Clinton administration (Fertig, 2009). And Arne Duncan, the former superintendent of the Chicago school system and President Barak Obama's secretary of education, graduated from Harvard with a degree in sociology (S. Dillon, 2008c).

As with school boards, women and minorities are underrepresented as superintendents (Gewertz, 2006c). Three quarters of the teaching force and slightly more than half of the general population are women, but they make up only 15 percent of superintendents. Similarly, members of cultural minorities make up a third of the student population and more than 10 percent of teachers, but they account for only 5 percent of superintendents.

When power and authority are shared, as is the case with school boards and superintendents, conflicts are inevitable, and when they occur, the superintendent usually loses. Nationally, the average tenure for superintendents is just under 6 years; in urban districts, it's less than 3 years (Snider, 2006). Accountability, in the form of student test scores, is a major reason that superintendents' tenure is so short, especially in urban districts.

Disputes with school boards, politics, and bureaucracy are major obstacles that superintendents face. When controversy flares over issues such as student drug use, school violence, desegregation, and lagging student achievement, a community looks to the superintendent for answers. Superintendents often get caught in the crossfire of politics and public opinion and, unable to quickly solve these problems, are either terminated or feel obliged to resign (Cuban, 2008).

What are superintendents paid for this frustrating and insecure job? Pay varies considerably with both location and district size; the average 2005–2006 salary was $116,244, but competition for superintendents in larger districts has resulted in salaries that are considerably higher (Swanson, 2006a). For example, superintendents in large urban districts average $172,387, and in 2005, the Miami-Dade school district in Florida

Superintendent The district's head administrative officer who, along with his or her staff, is responsible for implementing policy in the district's schools.

paid its new superintendent $480,000 plus benefits—more than the governor of the state (Bohman, 2006; Swanson, 2006a).

THE DISTRICT OFFICE   The district office assists the superintendent in translating school board policies into action (see Figure 9.1). It also coordinates the myriad curricular and instructional efforts within the district. The district office is responsible for these tasks:

- Ordering textbooks and supplies
- Developing programs of study
- Ordering, distributing, and analyzing standardized tests
- Evaluating teachers and assisting those with difficulties

The district office is instrumental in translating abstract state and school board mandates into reality. How it does this can give teachers a sense of empowerment or make them feel like hired hands.

The district office also plays an important role in helping new teachers. It typically provides new-teacher orientations, which may include an overview of the district's curriculum, any district-wide instructional initiatives, and district assessment programs. These policies and procedures are important because they frame the district's work expectations for new teachers. In addition, the central office coordinates mentoring and assessment programs for new teachers, helping them make the transition from university students to working professionals.

THE SCHOOL PRINCIPAL   The school **principal**, the person given the ultimate administrative responsibility for a school's operation, is the district administrator who has the greatest impact on teachers' lives. The principal is the person who hires and sometimes fires teachers, and who plays a major role in establishing both the academic and the work climates of a school.

A demographic profile of principals (see Table 9.1) mirrors that of school board members: Most are White, and males are still in the majority in secondary schools. Principals almost always have classroom experience, and most have at least a master's degree.

As the person who oversees the everyday operation of the school, the principal has wide-ranging responsibilities; two of the most important of these are teacher selection and evaluation (Sergiovanni, 2009a, 2009b). The school principal's interview with you will be a crucial factor in whether you get the job, and it will also give you an opportunity to learn about the person you'll be working for and the kind of school you'll be working in. During an interview, you should try to determine the principal's views about your role as a teacher and how the administrator runs the school.

The principal is also responsible for school-level curricular and instructional leadership, community relations, and the coordination of pupil services provided by school counselors, psychologists, nurses, and others. Principals also implement and monitor the school budget and ensure that the school's physical facilities are maintained. It's not easy being a principal; the job is both challenging and stressful, and many teachers resist becoming principals because the problems outweigh the benefits (A. Howley, Andrianaivo, & Perry, 2005).

Experienced teachers want principals who see themselves as instructional leaders and who take a hands-on approach to the teaching–learning process (Harris & Lowery, 2002). This leadership is especially important for beginning teachers, who need support,

Principals are crucial in creating well-run, learning-oriented schools.

Principal The person given the ultimate administrative responsibility for a school's operation.

Table 9.1 Profile of School Principals

	High School Principals	Middle School Principals	Elementary School Principals
Sex			
Male	78.8%	66.8%	44.8%
Female	21.2	33.2	55.2
Ethnic Background			
White	85.9	83.0	80.8
African American	8.4	10.5	12.0
Hispanic American	3.8	5.1	5.8
Asian American	0.9	0.7	0.7
Native American	1.1	0.8	0.7
Other	0.7	–	0.6
Highest Degree Earned			
Bachelor's	1.4	1.8	1.8
Master's	54.8	55.5	53.9
Professional diploma	31.6	33.6	34.6
Doctorate	12.1	9.1	9.7
Salary (12-month) (2006–2007)	$92,965	$87,866	$82,414

Sources: Bureau of Labor Statistics (2009); U.S. Department of Education (2008a).

To hear one superintendent's perspective on effective principals, go to the *Assignments and Activities* section of Topic 5: *Governance and Finance* in the MyEducationLab for your course and complete the activity titled *Effective Principals: A Superintendent's Perspective.*

mentoring, and feedback. Because of their busy schedules, however, many principals become managers who focus primarily on the day-to-day operation of the school and forget that their most important role is to support teaching and learning (M. Ginsberg & Murphy, 2002).

Principals are the most important people in the district's administrative structure because they work directly with teachers and students. Effective principals can transform a mediocre school into a positive and productive learning environment, but the opposite is also true: An ineffective principal can make a school an unpleasant place in which to work.

■ ■ ■ ■ ■ CHECK YOUR UNDERSTANDING

1.1 Who is legally responsible for governing education in the United States?

1.2 Describe the educational governance structure at the state level.

1.3 Describe the governance structure at the local, district level.

For feedback, go to the appendix, *Check Your Understanding*, located in the back of this text.

SCHOOL FINANCE: HOW ARE SCHOOLS FUNDED?

To begin to understand how school finance affects the lives of teachers, let's return to Carla's work on her school's Elementary Math Steering Committee.

"And based on our analysis of math programs around the country, we believe *this one is best for our children. . . . Any questions?" Carla asks as she concludes her presentation to the school board.*

"Let me make sure that I'm clear about this," one board member responds. *"In addition to the texts themselves, students will need manipulatives. . . . I'm sorry, but I'm not sure exactly what 'manipulatives' are."*

"Manipulatives are concrete objects, such as cubes that could be put in a box to help kids understand the concept of volume, and plastic squares that could be used to illustrate area. The success of this program depends on students seeing math ideas in action."

"Thank you. . . . And teachers will need additional in-service training to bring them up to speed on how to use these new materials. Is that right?"

"Yes. What we've read and heard is that teacher in-service is essential to the success of this program," Carla replies, as her fellow committee members nod in agreement.

"What seems clear to me," the chair of the school board adds, *"is that this program, along with our technology initiative and the changes in our language arts program, is going to need additional funding. We need to make sure that the public understands how and why taxes are going to go up next fall. We've all got a big job ahead of us—selling, no, explaining, why our schools need additional monies."*

Money is important in education. It determines teachers' salaries, professional-development opportunities, and access to resources, such as computers, lab supplies, maps, and a host of other materials. It also influences the quality of schools by allowing districts to do such things as reduce class sizes and recruit and retain qualified teachers (Biddle & Berliner, 2002). From 2003 to 2008, national polls indicated that the general public viewed lack of financial support and funding for education as the biggest problem their local schools face; another major problem was overcrowded schools, an issue closely related to financial support (Bushaw & Gallup, 2008). In this section, we look at where this money comes from and how it influences teachers' lives.

School Funding Sources

Local, state, and federal sources all provide money for education (Brimley & Garfield, 2008). As you can see in Figure 9.3, the state share is nearly half, the local share is more than 40 percent, and both are considerably greater than the federal share, which is less than 10 percent. These facts indicate that the third statement in our *This I Believe* feature, "In the past, the federal government provided the largest source of educational funding," is clearly false, because both state and local shares have been considerably larger.

Figure 9.3 Education Revenues From Local, State, and Federal Sources

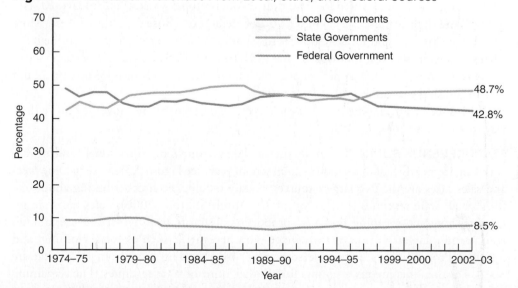

Source: Data from National Center for Education Statistics (2006b).

The share of education funding coming from local, state, and federal sources has changed over time (Brimley & Garfield, 2008). For example, from 1920 to 1980, the federal share increased from virtually nothing to a peak of nearly 10 percent, declining in the 1980s to less than 7 percent before rising to its current level of 8.5 percent. The state and local shares have remained fairly steady, hovering between 42 and 49 percent since 1990. These figures are national averages, and the federal, state, and local proportions can vary significantly from state to state. For example, none of Hawaii's 2002–2003 school budget came from local sources, whereas in Florida, local funds accounted for more than 40 percent of school funding (Brimley & Garfield, 2008).

Shifts in education funding patterns reflect the changing views about education throughout U.S. history. In early America, education was seen as a local responsibility with virtually no involvement by the federal government. In sharp contrast, 20th-century leaders saw a direct connection between education and the country's political and economic well-being. Quality schools and a well-educated workforce became national concerns, and the federal government's role in education increased. Similarly, states began to recognize the importance of education in attracting high-tech industries and high-paying jobs. This insight, plus efforts to equalize funding within states, has led to an increasing state role in educational funding (Biddle & Berliner, 2002).

The educational funding picture changed dramatically in 2009 with the passage of the $787-billion American Recovery and Reinvestment Act, designed to provide an economic stimulus to a faltering U.S. economy (McNeil, 2009). New federal aid to education in that bill totaled $115 billion, with major chunks distributed in the following way:

- State stabilization funds to prevent teacher layoffs and cuts to programs in education ($53.6 billion)
- Additional funds for Title I programs targeting disadvantaged students ($13 billion)
- Increased funding for special education services ($12.2 billion)

In addition, new, one-time funds also targeted specific areas such as Head Start, homeless children, and teacher quality initiatives emphasizing performance pay (D. Hoff, 2009a; McNeil, 2009). However, the long-term availability of many of these federal funds is questionable.

The public is undecided about the relative amounts that local, state, and federal governments should contribute to educational funding. In a 1998 survey, more than 20 percent of those polled favored local funding through property taxes, a third favored state sources, and slightly more than a third favored federal taxes (Rose & Gallup, 1998). More recently, nearly half said local school boards should have the greatest say in influencing what's taught in schools, followed by state (31 percent) and federal (20 percent) levels (Rose & Gallup, 2007). The debate over the role different levels of government should play in funding education is likely to continue.

Let's see how funds are raised at each level of government and how they make their way to your classroom.

STATE REVENUE SOURCES   States are the largest source of educational funding, accounting for nearly half in the 2002–2003 school year (see Figure 9.3). State income taxes and sales taxes are the two largest sources of state income, each contributing about one third of all state revenues (Federation of Tax Administrators, 2006). Sales taxes are regressive, however, meaning they take proportionally more from lower-income families who spend a larger portion of their income on necessities, such as food, clothing, and housing. Progressive states provide some relief by excluding food from items that are taxed. Personal income tax accounts for another third of state revenues. The remaining third comes from other sources such as taxes on liquor and tobacco, oil and mining revenues, and corporate income taxes.

Recently, state lotteries and gambling have become major sources of revenue, but education is often the victim of a zero-sum shell game, in which increased funding from lottery monies is balanced by decreasing monies from other sources, such as sales taxes. In 2005, 42 states had lotteries, but fewer than half allocate profits directly to education, and the percentage of income taxes going to education in these states varies considerably (Brimley & Garfield, 2008; Buchanan, 2007a). Also, states spend around 30 cents of every lottery income dollar on expenses, including advertising and commissions to stores that sell lottery tickets (Stodgill & Nixon, 2007). Research indicates that these gambling ventures generally attract participants who are poor and have had little schooling, and that 10 to 15 percent of players account for 80 percent of lottery sales (Brimley & Garfield, 2008; Stodgill & Nixon, 2007). (Given the terrible odds of winning, some call lotteries "taxes on stupidity.") The long-term viability of gambling revenues for education is uncertain and controversial.

LOCAL FUNDING As we saw in our discussion of school governance, financing education at the local level is the responsibility of local school boards, which is why Carla made her presentation to her local board, and the need for increased funding was one of the implications of her presentation. At the local level, most funding for schools comes from **property taxes**, which are determined by the value of property in the school district (Brimley & Garfield, 2008). Other local revenue sources include income taxes, fees for building permits, traffic fines, and user fees charged to groups that hold meetings in schools. In collecting property taxes, local authorities first assess the value of a property and then tax the owners a small percentage of the property's value (usually less than 1 percent).

Differences in property values among districts affect the quality of life and resources available to teachers as well as students.

Funding education through local property taxes has disadvantages, the most glaring of which is inequities between property resources in different districts (Brimley & Garfield, 2008). Wealthier cities or districts have a higher tax base, so they're able to collect (and spend) more money for their schools. Poorer rural and urban school districts find themselves on the opposite end of this continuum, with a lower tax base, resulting in lower revenues. Property taxes also place an unfair burden on older taxpayers, whose homes may have increased in value while their ability to pay taxes has remained constant or decreased. In addition, many older taxpayers resist these charges because they no longer have children in school and don't see the immediate benefit of increased spending for schools.

The property-tax method of financing schools also has a political disadvantage (Brimley & Garfield, 2008): Unlike sales taxes, which taxpayers pay in small, continual, and almost unnoticed increments, property taxes are more visible targets for taxpayer dissatisfaction. Statements arrive once a year with a comparison to the previous year, and property-tax increases are discussed in public forums whenever school boards ask their taxpayers for increased funding.

Dissatisfaction with this method of funding reached a head in California in 1978 when voters passed an initiative called Proposition 13, which limited property taxes in the state. By the 1990s, 45 other states had passed similar measures (Brimley & Garfield, 2008). The effect on educational funding has been chilling: Schools and school districts have had less to spend and have had to fight harder when requesting new funds from taxpayers.

Property taxes Taxes determined by the value of property in the school district.

FEDERAL FUNDING FOR EDUCATION   The federal government is the third, smallest, and most controversial source of educational funding. As you saw earlier, federal funding for education was virtually nonexistent before 1920 but has increased over time to its present level of about 8.5 percent. Though the amount spent on education has increased to almost $67 billion in fiscal year 2005, the total still accounts for only about 2 percent of all federal expenditures (National Center for Education Statistics, 2005b). Nearly half of federal funds for education are channeled through the U.S. Department of Education, with the next largest proportion—about 20 percent—coming from the Department of Health and Human Services (Sonnenberg, 2004).

Proponents of a greater federal role in education believe that education is essential for the country's continued progress in the 21st century and that the federal government should continue to exert leadership (and provide funds) in this area. Critics warn of increased federal control over what they believe should be a local responsibility (McAndrews, 2006). In addition, political conservatives argue against the expansion of what they consider to be an already bloated federal bureaucracy. For these critics, less is better when it comes to federal funding. In contrast, local funding, they say, makes schools more efficient and responsive to local needs and wishes.

Although the percentage of education funds contributed by the federal government has been small, the impact has been considerable, largely because of the use of **categorical grants**, federal grants targeted for specific groups and designated purposes. Head Start, aimed at preschoolers, and Title I, which benefits economically disadvantaged youth, are examples of categorical aid programs targeting specific needs or populations. Because the funds must be used for specific purposes, categorical grants have strongly influenced local education practices.

During the 1980s, categorical funds were replaced by **block grants**, federal monies provided to states and school districts with few restrictions for use. Begun during the conservative Reagan administration, block grants purposely reduce the federal role in policy making, in essence giving states and districts control over how monies are spent. Proponents contend this makes sense—who knows local needs better than local educators? But critics contend that funds are often misspent or spent in areas where they aren't needed (Brimley & Garfield, 2008).

Educational Revenues: Where Do They Go?

The largest part of states' budget expenditures go to education, with more than a third spent on P–12, and more than 10 percent also going to higher education (McNeil, 2006). In 2007–2008, the 50 states and the District of Columbia spent an average of $9,963 per pupil, but as you see in Table 9.2, spending varied considerably from state to state. The District of Columbia and New Jersey spent the most ($17,449 and $15,374, respectively), and Arizona spent the least ($5,346). The data in Table 9.2 also demonstrate some regional trends. Most of the higher per-pupil expenditures are found in northeastern and upper midwest states, and lower expenditures are found in the South and the West.

It's tempting to conclude that a state's commitment to education can be judged by its per-pupil spending, but some states are wealthier than others, and the number of children per taxpayer varies, so they have a greater capacity to fund education. Funding differences between states are also influenced by the cost of living and the number of

A significant portion of a district's budget goes to transportation, building maintenance, and food services.

Categorical grants Federal grants targeted for specific groups and designated purposes.

Block grants Federal monies provided to states and school districts with few restrictions for use.

Table 9.2   State-by-State Spending per Student

State	Rank	2007–2008 ($)
Alabama	34	8,875
Alaska	19	10,590
Arizona	51	5,346
Arkansas	22	9,591
California	26	9,539
Colorado	29	9,335
Connecticut	7	13,533
Delaware	8	12,977
District of Columbia	1	17,449
Florida	36	8,816
Georgia	23	9,564
Hawaii	14	11,117
Idaho	47	7,305
Illinois	16	10,993
Indiana	28	9,432
Iowa	42	8,432
Kansas	25	9,544
Kentucky	32	9,264
Louisiana	30	9,310
Maine	9	12,802
Maryland	10	11,962
Massachusetts	6	13,768
Michigan	15	11,082
Minnesota	20	10,560
Mississippi	48	7,175
Missouri	41	8,466
Montana	33	9,029
Nebraska	37	8,752
Nevada	49	7,133
New Hampshire	13	11,447
New Jersey	2	15,374
New Mexico	24	9,558
New York	3	15,286
North Carolina	40	8,615
North Dakota	39	8,638
Ohio	35	8,829
Oklahoma	46	7,615
Oregon	27	9,469
Pennsylvania	12	11,659
Rhode Island	11	11,905
South Carolina	38	8,721
South Dakota	43	8,250
Tennessee	44	8,022
Texas	45	7,978
Utah	50	5,734
Vermont	4	14,336
Virginia	17	10,707
Washington	31	9,304
West Virginia	21	10,411
Wisconsin	18	10,643
Wyoming	5	13,967
U.S. and DC Average		9,963

Source: National Education Association (2009). *Rankings and estimates (2007–2008)*. Available at http://www.nea.org/index/html.

children who need to be educated. Utah, for example, which has the second lowest per-student spending in the country ($5,734), also has the highest birth rate in the nation—approximately 1.5 times the national average—so whatever funds are available must be divided among more children.

The effects of funding on excellence in education is controversial, with early research concluding that the amount spent has little or no influence on achievement

Figure 9.4 Educational Expenditures
on Different District Programs

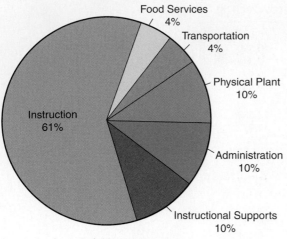

Source: Brimley & Garfield (2008); U.S. Department of Education
(2006c).

(Hanushek, 1996). More recent research, however, found that higher per-pupil expenditures resulted in higher achievement, mainly because of better qualified teachers and smaller class sizes (Krueger & Whitmore, 2002). Increased expenditures seem to have their greatest effect on low-income and minority students.

The relationship between funding and learning isn't simple or precise, however. Achievement tests—the most commonly used measure of student learning—focus on core academic areas, such as reading, math, and science, and not every dollar spent on education goes to teaching these basic subjects. Some monies go to art and music, for example, which are valuable areas of the curriculum, but increased expenditures in these areas won't be directly reflected in higher test scores. Furthermore, as you see in Figure 9.4, only about 61 percent of the money allocated to education is spent on instruction, most of which goes to teacher salaries (U.S. Department of Education, 2006c). The rest is spent on areas that affect achievement only indirectly.

In addition to the more than 60 percent that directly supports instruction, 10 percent of school district funds goes to instructional assistance needs, such as student services, teacher professional advancement, and curriculum development (see Figure 9.4). Another 10 percent goes to administration. Approximately one third of administration funding is spent on the central district office, and two thirds goes to schools, primarily for principal salaries. Maintenance of school buildings and grounds (physical plant) takes up another 10 percent of the budget. Transportation (school buses) and food services (cafeteria lunches) each account for another 4 percent.

To understand the magnitude of transportation expenditures, consider these national figures: In an average school year, 450,000 yellow school buses travel 4 billion—billion, not million!—miles, providing rides to 24 million K–12 students (Brimley & Garfield, 2008). Student activities add 5 million trips. Schools provide transportation to 55 percent of the nation's student population at a cost of $493 per student.

The recent surge in fuel costs has resulted in scheduling changes and cutbacks in bus services for students (Purdom, 2008). A number of smaller, rural districts are experimenting with four-day school weeks, and other districts have changed the requirements for bus services, limiting access to younger students who live more than 2 miles from school. Critics question whether these changes will result in more accidents and deaths from students driving and walking on dangerous streets; currently about 800 students die each year going to and from school (Buchanan, 2007b; Purdom, 2008). Of these, only 20, or about 2 percent, are school bus related, making this one of the safest ways for students to get to school.

Critics often decry the large amount of monies (nearly 40 percent) spent on areas other than academics and have initiated national efforts to mandate that two thirds of education funds go to instruction—teachers and textbooks (D. Hoff, 2005, 2006). School finance experts point out, however, that expenditures for school nurses, school buses, and school lunches, for example, are all part of the total education process, and no research evidence links higher spending on instruction to increases in student achievement (Dounay, 2006). In addition, experts note that the amounts schools spend on administration and maintenance of the physical plant compare favorably with those spent in industry (Brimley & Garfield, 2008). This may be a classic case of micromanaging, in which legislators want to influence education without spending more money.

This section addresses the fourth item on our *This I Believe* feature, "Most of a district's budget goes to funding instruction." This statement is true: The average U.S. district spends more than 60 percent of its budget on instruction.

This I BELIEVE

■ ■ ■ ■ CHECK YOUR UNDERSTANDING

2.1 What are the major sources of educational funding?

2.2 How are educational revenues spent?

For feedback, go to the appendix, *Check Your Understanding*, located in the back of this text.

EMERGING ISSUES IN SCHOOL GOVERNANCE AND FINANCE

As schools confront the challenges of the 21st century, they face a number of issues in the areas of governance and finance. Following are some of the most important:

- Equity in funding, one of the most fundamental issues facing education
- The governance of struggling urban schools
- School choice in the form of charter schools and vouchers

Let's look at these challenges.

Savage Inequalities: The Struggle for Funding Equity

URBAN EDUCATION

Lakesha Lincoln walks into Jackson Middle School among a horde of other students. Jackson is a 72-year-old urban school in a large northeastern city. She doesn't notice that the three of the five lights down the long main hall are out, and that the hall badly needs a paint job.

She walks by the girls' bathroom, where a sign on the door says, "Bathroom out of order. Use the bathroom on the second floor." She decides she'll wait and get permission to go to the bathroom during her first-period class.

She enters her homeroom and sits down. She has barely enough room to squeeze through the rows of desks, because there are 38 students in her homeroom, and the room was built for 25. Discarded paper sits on the floor from yesterday, and the boards haven't been cleaned from the last class of the previous day.

Students are milling around the room as the bell rings, and Mr. Jensen, her homeroom teacher, tries his best to get them to settle down. He is struggling, because he has had no professional training, and he is doing his best to feel his way through his first year of teaching.

Dawn Johnson walks into Forest Park Middle School, which is in the suburbs. It was built in 2001, and it's roomy, well lit, and pleasant. Dawn goes into her homeroom, which is spotless, with ample equipment and materials to support instruction. Her room is comfortable, with plenty of space available for her and 22 classmates.

The last of the students slide into their chairs as the bell rings, and Mrs. August is standing in front of the room ready to begin. She is a 10-year veteran, with a reputation for being demanding but fair. Students agree that they learn a lot from her.

As you saw earlier, research indicates that significant differences in per-pupil expenditures exist, both between and within states (Biddle & Berliner, 2002). Jonathan Kozol (1991) outlines this issue in his influential book, *Savage Inequalities:*

Americans abhor the notion of a social order in which economic privilege and political power are determined by hereditary class. Officially, we have a more enlightened goal in sight: namely, a society in which a family's wealth has no relation to the probability of future educational attainment and the wealth and station it affords. By this

Disparities in property tax revenues can result in dramatic differences in funding for schools that are quite close geographically.

standard, education offered to poor children should be at least as good as that which is provided to the children of the upper-middle class. (p. 207)

This standard of equality is not what Kozol found in his research on school funding. Instead, he found that many urban schools around the country were like Lakesha's—dirty and run down with peeling paint, broken toilets, antiquated or missing textbooks, and teachers who were uncertified or lacked experience, or both. Only miles away, suburban schools such as Forest Park Middle, where Dawn attends, featured new, well-maintained, attractive buildings that were inviting learning environments. And teachers were generally seasoned, knowledgeable professionals. These stark contrasts gave Kozol's book its title.

In 1968, Demetrio Rodriguez, a sheet-metal worker in a poor suburb of San Antonio, Texas, looked at the schools his children were attending, compared them with schools in wealthier districts only 10 miles away, and found similar discouraging contrasts between his children's schools and those of neighboring districts (Sracic, 2006). The primary problem was that property taxes for his district produced only $37 per student compared to $412 per student for the wealthier suburb. These differences aren't unusual: In Texas during the 1980s, for example, the 100 most affluent districts in the state spent an average of $7,233 per student, whereas the poorest 100 averaged $2,978! Faced with these inequities, Mr. Rodriguez sued, contending that his children were being penalized by where they lived (Brimley & Garfield, 2008).

Nationally, wealthy districts spend an average of 23 percent more on their students than do poorer ones (Biddle & Berliner, 2002). Despite efforts to alleviate them, substantial within-state differences continue to exist between districts serving low- and high-income families (Brimley & Garfield, 2008). Similar patterns exist in other states (Kober, 2006).

This section addresses the fifth item in our *This I Believe* feature, "Students in different districts across states are provided with approximately the same amount of money to fund their education." This statement isn't true: Large disparities in the property tax base that provides funds for schools result in widely varying resources for teachers and students.

Legal challenges over funding equity have increased. The battle lines for these cases were drawn in California in 1971, when the California Supreme Court ruled in a 6–1 vote that the use of property taxes to fund education resulted in unconstitutional funding inequities in the state (*Serrano v. Priest*, 1971). To reduce these funding inequities, the state's share of education funding rose from 40 to 70 percent.

The *Serrano v. Priest* lawsuit went all the way to the U.S. Supreme Court. Based on the California decision, many believed that the Supreme Court would find the spending patterns in Texas unconstitutional. However, in a 5–4 vote, it did just the opposite, ruling in 1973 that the U.S. Constitution does not guarantee citizens a right to an education. The Court did point out, however, that funding inequities may violate state constitutions, many of which do guarantee citizens that right.

The Supreme Court ruling on the Rodriguez case sent the issue back to state courts, and many other state suits followed. By 2007, courts had overturned existing systems in eight states and upheld others in nine states, with other cases still pending (Brimley & Garfield, 2008). Differences in state rulings are primarily the result of differences in the wording of state constitutions: Some constitutions are quite specific in guaranteeing "equal education for all," whereas others are vague in specifying that educational opportunity should be "ample" or "efficient." Researchers found that when rulings favored the plaintiffs, inequities were reduced by almost 14 percent. Decreasing or eliminating reliance on the property tax was the primary factor (A. Flanagan & Grissmer, 2002).

Funding inequities are complicated by the fact that not all districts in a state have the same needs (Brimley & Garfield, 2008). Some have a higher proportion of low-income children, nonnative English speakers, or children who need special education services. These students require extra resources. Reformers are calling for funding formulas that go beyond simply equalizing dollars; they want plans that meet the needs of all students (McNeil, 2008b). These proposed reforms are expensive and controversial however, because many parents from wealthier districts object to having their local taxes used to fund distant schools across the state. In addition, the problems involved in quantifying educational needs in terms of dollars and cents are complex (Hanushek, 2006).

One recent change in educational funding attempts to change funding practices within districts rather than between (National Education Association, 2005). The **weighted student formula** allocates resources within a district to schools on a per-school basis according to student needs. Instead of every school in a district getting the same per-pupil amount, the weighted student formula provides more funds to schools that have more special education students or other students requiring additional services. Several U.S. urban school districts—Chicago, Denver, Houston, Los Angeles, and Seattle—have implemented this change. Advocates claim that it's a fairer way of distributing funds and that it decentralizes educational decision making by allowing individual schools to decide how education dollars will be spent. Comprehensive research is still needed to see if this change will work in other, smaller districts where increased funding for some schools could mean decreased, and potentially crippling, funding for others.

The role the federal government should play in reducing or eliminating funding inequities is another issue facing funding reformers. Critics of the current system point out that two thirds of funding differences occur between states rather than within states, and states receiving low levels of educational funding are clustered in the South and Southeast, areas that also have large proportions of poor and minority students. Experts estimate that it would take a minimum of $25 billion to equalize states' expenditures, a daunting figure considering current federal budget deficits (A. Flanagan & Grissmer, 2002).

Urban Takeovers: Alternatives to Local Control

Local control by school boards is the predominant pattern in U.S. education, but what happens when local control doesn't seem to work? Twelve of the largest cities answered this question by authorizing the mayor to take over the running of their city's schools; this occurred in Boston in 1991, in Chicago in 1995, and in New York in 2002 (S. Black, 2008b; Medina, 2009a). The reasons behind mayoral takeovers center on either fiscal mismanagement or academic underachievement of students in the systems. In addition to mayoral takeovers in large urban cities, states have authorized similar moves in smaller districts, removing local school boards and replacing them with a new management team.

Mayors of large cities, seeing education as central to their cities' economic growth, have taken this drastic action in an attempt to turn their educational systems around

URBAN EDUCATION

Weighted student formula
Funding that allocates resources within a district to schools on a per-school basis according to student needs.

(Sack-Min, 2007a). Changes in governance include balancing districts' budgets, raising money through bonds, improving school facilities, and negotiating with unions. Mayors have also experimented with educational reform, expanding choice options through charter schools, creating smaller, thematic high schools, and attempting to tie teacher and principal pay to student achievement (Medina & Gootman, 2008).

One of the more controversial takeovers occurred in Washington, DC, where the mayor's newly appointed superintendent attempted to replace tenure with offers of higher teacher pay (S. Dillon, 2008b). The new superintendent believed that tenure was a major obstacle to removing incompetent teachers and offered significant pay raises (as much as $40,000 per year) for teachers who were willing to forgo tenure. Teachers were offered a choice between the old system with tenure and the new one without, but Washington DC Teachers Union members viewed the proposal with mixed reactions and voted it down, fearing the loss of the political and job protection afforded by tenure.

Experts give takeovers a mixed, but generally positive, report card (S. Dillon, 2008b; Stover, 2008). Schools tend to be run more efficiently, and budgets are balanced. But student achievement, the bottom line for many critics, has shown only modest gains. School district takeovers, as one solution to the problems of failing urban school districts, are probably here to stay. Their success will ultimately be judged by their ability to improve teaching and learning in urban classrooms.

A second type of struggle to wrest control of schools from local school boards occurred at the state level in Maryland (Honawar, 2006). This takeover was precipitated by NCLB, which requires low-performing schools to be restructured after 3 years of subpar performance. The Maryland legislature resisted, claiming that there is little proof that state takeovers actually improve student performance. The U.S. Department of Education to threatened to withhold $171 million in Title I funds if the state didn't restructure the Baltimore schools. Governance battles such as these are likely to increase as more and more schools are found lacking under NCLB guidelines.

School Choice

The freedom to choose is a central American value. Americans can choose where and how they live and what occupation they work in, for example. Shouldn't they also have a choice in the kind of schools their children attend? As presently organized, public-school systems are centralized and bureaucratic, and where students go to school is determined by the neighborhoods they live in. In the name of efficiency, we've created a governance and finance system that begins in state capitals, runs through local district offices, and culminates in schools that are similar in form and function. Walk into most public schools across the country, and you'll see teachers teaching the same content in basically the same way (Cuban, 1993; Goodlad, 1984). Even the boxlike architecture of school buildings is the same everywhere.

Critics decry this uniformity and make several arguments in support of greater variety and choice. For example, we are a nation of 50 states with unique individuals and distinctive subcultures, and our schools ought to reflect this diversity. In addition, experimentation and innovation have been central to our nation's progress, and conformity discourages innovation. From an economic perspective, the present system represents a monopoly that forces parents to send their children to neighborhood public schools (Betts, 2005). Critics believe that alternatives would result in healthy competition, which would ultimately mean better schools. They also argue that the public-school system has become bloated, bureaucratic, and unresponsive to individual citizens' needs. In response to these criticisms, reformers call for school choice.

What does choice mean? At one level, parents already have choices: They can move to neighborhoods served by better schools. The quality of the schools is one of the major features parents consider when choosing a neighborhood (Hassel & Hassel,

2004). If parents don't like the schools in their neighborhood, they can move or send their children to private schools, which 12 percent of parents currently do (Kober, 2006). In addition, through open enrollment and magnet school programs, districts allow parents who believe their local schools are subpar to send their children across town to better schools. Doing so requires greater time and expense, but parents still have choices.

But advocates of choice point out that many poor, minority, and inner-city parents don't have the resources to vote with their wallets or their cars (Goyette, 2008). They can't afford to move to better neighborhoods with better schools, to send their children to private schools, or even to drive across town each day to transport their children to a non-neighborhood public school. In addition, some school districts are so bad, critics contend, that other schools in the district don't really provide viable alternatives. These parents deserve the right to choose, just as much as more wealthy parents do.

But how can parents be provided with options? The concept of school choice has resulted in two educational innovations: charter schools and vouchers.

CHARTER SCHOOLS   **Charter schools** are alternative schools that are independently operated but publicly funded. In many states, parents or others dissatisfied with the local school choices have the right to create their own alternative or specialty schools. Charter schools typically begin when a group—teachers, community members, or a private corporation—develops a plan for a school, including its curriculum, staffing, and budget. This plan, or "charter," must then be accepted by the local school board or state office of education and serves as a contract with the state (Palmer, 2007).

Many school districts already have alternative schools, such as magnet schools with specialized programs and schools designed to meet the needs of students who can't function in regular schools and classrooms, such as young, unwed mothers or children with serious behavior or emotional problems (Jackson, 2007). Charter schools are similar to other alternative schools in that they offer a different curriculum or target special populations; they differ in that they're independently administered public schools and are subject to less regulatory control from a district's central administration (Carnoy, Jacobsen, Mishel, & Rothstein, 2005).

The charter school movement began in Minnesota in 1991, when the legislature approved eight teacher-created and -operated outcome-based schools. (An outcome-based school makes curricular and instructional decisions based on student performance on specified assessments.) Since that time, 39 additional states and the District of Columbia have passed charter school legislation resulting in the creation of more than 4,600 schools with more than 1.3 million students, or about 2 percent of the public school student population (Robelen, 2009b).

The focus of different charter schools varies dramatically, although most attract parents seeking smaller schools and class sizes, better instruction, or alternatives to public-school curricula and environments (Carpenter & Finn, 2006). Many—about one third of all charter schools—are designed by urban community leaders to meet the needs of inner-city youth (West & Manno, 2006), and, nationally, 58 percent of charter students are members of racial or ethnic minorities, compared with 41 percent for regular public schools (Viadero, 2005a). Some, for example, focus on developing students' African heritage through language instruction, literature, and the arts. Others attract parents who want a return to the basics, and still others focus on Hebrew, Arabic, and other languages that parents want to preserve and pass on to their children (Goodnough, 2007; Rimer, 2009).

KIPP Schools.   KIPP—the Knowledge Is Power Program—is a national network of free, open-enrollment charter schools with a stated goal of preparing students in underserved communities for success in college and in life. KIPP schools usually go from fifth to eighth grade, typically with a total of about 300 students. There are currently 66 KIPP

URBAN EDUCATION

Charter schools Alternative schools that are independently operated but publicly funded.

KIPP (Knowledge Is Power Program) A national network of charter schools that stress academics and feature extended school hours and mandatory homework.

schools in 19 states and the District of Columbia serving more than 16,000 students, and the program is looking to expand into early childhood schools (Jacobson, 2009). Almost all KIPP students are from Black or Hispanic families under the poverty line.

KIPP schools significantly increase the length of the school day and the school year, and principals have a great deal of autonomy. For example, school days are $8\frac{1}{2}$ hours long, students attend school on every other Saturday, summer school is required, homework is a must, hard work brings special rewards such as field trips, and principals have the power to hire and fire teachers.

Evidence indicates that KIPP students perform well academically, usually outperforming their peers in other schools. But a study of five KIPP schools in the San Francisco Bay Area indicated that 60 percent of the students who enter the Bay Area KIPP schools in fifth grade leave before the end of eighth grade, and it's consistently the lower performers who leave (San Francisco Schools, 2008). Critics contend many of these low achievers are "pushed out" rather than remediated (Toppo, 2009).

As with many educational reforms, the effectiveness of KIPP schools continues to be debated. And, the schools' policy of lengthening the school day and school year again raises the question of whether time in school should be increased for all students.

Issues of Quality in Charter Schools. Considerable variation exists in the quality of charter schools, and this uneven quality is having a negative effect on the charter school movement (Robelen, 2009b). For example, in Texas—a leader in establishing charter schools—a panel of state lawmakers recommended a moratorium on new charter schools, citing poor student performance, financial troubles, and unexpected closures (Associated Press, 2000). In reviewing existing charter schools, the state education agency gave an "unacceptable" rating to nearly one fourth of the more than 100 charter schools it evaluated (Hendrie, 2002).

Arizona, which has one sixth of the nation's charter schools, and California, another leader in the charter school movement, have had similar problems. Charters in Arizona have been labeled as underperforming at twice the rate of regular public schools (A. Lewis, 2008), and California's Charter School Academy, which operated more than 50 schools, abruptly closed all of its schools, leaving families, teachers, and school officials scrambling (Hutton, 2005). A subsequent state audit found the charter organization had misused state and federal funds and sought the return of more than $20 million from the for-profit management company (Hendrie, 2005b). In 2005, about 65 charter schools in 17 states closed their doors (Robelen, 2006b). One school superintendent in a large urban district estimated that only about 10 to 15 percent of all charter schools are highly effective (E. P. Dannals, personal communication, January 30, 2009).

The problem of quality is partially linked to the large numbers of unlicensed teachers in charter schools. One national study found that more than 4 of 10 charter school teachers lacked appropriate licenses, compared to less than one of 10 in regular public schools, and this figure increased to nearly 6 of 10 in predominantly African American charters (H. Brown, 2003). A major advantage of charter schools—freedom from bureaucratic oversight—is also a major weakness of this reform.

Inadequate resources and facilities are also persistent problems in charter schools (Casey, Andreson, Yelverton, & Wedeen, 2002). Many lack libraries and laboratories and sometimes even basic supplies such as paper and pencils (Carnoy et al., 2005). The arrival of for-profit corporations into the charter school arena, which you see in our *Taking a Stand in an Era of Reform* feature later in the chapter, has exacerbated the problem.

The charter school movement is controversial and highly politicized. Charter advocates generally adhere to a political ideology suggesting that the private sector, such as the business world in our country, is superior to the public sector, in which our public-school system exists. Adherents to this ideology argue that charter schools are superior to regular public schools because they reduce the size of the existing educational bureaucracy and are more consistent with existing business models.

Research, however, doesn't support the assertion that charter schools are superior to regular public schools (Bracey, 2004; Carnoy et al., 2005). In fact, some research has found that in many cases, students in charter schools trail regular public-school students in both reading and math achievement (Dillon, 2009a). With few exceptions, charters are no better than, and are often inferior to, our existing public schools.

The bottom line on charter schools is this: Their designers claimed that they were innovative alternatives to current educational practice and as such would serve as models for public-school reform. Unfortunately, most haven't been innovative alternatives, with instruction basically the same as the schools they were meant to replace; the KIPP schools are a notable exception. In addition, their backers claimed that they would be better than the public schools they replaced; again, this has generally not occurred, with schools such as KIPP being a notable exception. Educators, as well as educational policy makers, need to take a hard, critical, unbiased look at this innovation.

VOUCHERS   Vouchers are a second approach to school choice. A **voucher** is a check or written document that parents can use to purchase educational services. Vouchers are grounded in the belief that parents know what their children need and should be free to purchase the best education wherever they can find it. Some voucher plans give parents the choice of either a public or a private school, whereas others limit the choice to public schools.

Political conservatives often promote vouchers, arguing that public schools are a monopoly and that opening up schools to parental choice allows market forces to improve education. As opposed to schools in immediate neighborhoods, all schools become viable alternatives. Over time, the best schools would attract more students and flourish, whereas weaker schools would be shut down by informed consumers and market forces.

Because of possible disruptive influences on public schools and issues with religious instruction, the voucher movement is highly controversial. Critics, including the National Education Association and the American Federation of Teachers, the two largest professional organizations in education, argue that vouchers increase segregation, split the public along socioeconomic lines, and drain students and resources from already struggling inner-city schools (American Federation of Teachers, 2003; National Education Association, 2002).

Some voucher advocates would also like to use them for religious schools; critics contend that this violates the principle of separation of church and state. In Cleveland and Milwaukee, two cities that have led the country in the voucher movement, religious schools have been the major beneficiaries. For example, in Cleveland, 82 percent of participating schools in a voucher program were religiously affiliated, and 96 percent of participating students attended religious schools (National Association of Elementary School Principals, 2002). Nationally, 76 percent of private schools are religiously affiliated (National Center for Education Statistics, 2008c). Supporters of voucher programs ask why parents should have to pay for a quality education twice—once when they pay public-school taxes and again when they pay tuition at private schools.

In 2002, the U.S. Supreme Court ruled in a 5–4 decision that the voucher program in Cleveland didn't violate separation of church and state (Flanigan, 2003; M. Walsh, 2002a). The idea that voucher funds went to parents rather than directly to religious schools was central to the decision. After the Supreme Court made its decision, the number of applicants for the Cleveland voucher program rose nearly 30 percent, suggesting that more parents are taking advantage of this educational option (Hendrie, 2002). However, a research study conducted by Policy Matters Ohio, a Cleveland-based nonprofit organization, concluded that Cleveland vouchers served more as a subsidy for students already attending private schools than as an "escape hatch" for students eager to leave the public schools.

PEARSON
myeducationlab

To hear a superintendent's perspectives on charter schools, go to the *Assignments and Activities* section of Topic 5: *Governance and Finance* in the MyEducationLab for your course and complete the activity titled *Charter Schools: A Superintendent's Perspective.*

Voucher A check or written document that parents can use to purchase educational services.

Since 1990, three state legislatures have enacted voucher systems: Wisconsin, Ohio, and Florida. However, the Wisconsin and Ohio plans apply only to Milwaukee and Cleveland, respectively, and in 2006, the Florida Supreme Court, in a 5–2 ruling, struck down Florida's voucher system. The court ruled that "the diversion of money not only reduced public funds for a public education but also used public funds to provide an alternative education in private schools that are not subject to the 'uniformity' requirements for public schools" (L. Romano, 2006, p. A05). Legal battles are likely to occur in other states and may prove difficult for voucher advocates because 37 state constitutions currently have language that prohibits state aid to religious schools (Gehring, 2002b).

As with charter schools, the academic benefits of vouchers are unclear. Some research suggests that voucher programs can lead to small achievement gains (Bowman, 2000a, 2000b), but other research indicates no achievement gains (Robelen, 2006c) or gains in some populations (e.g., African American) but not in others (Gewertz, 2003; National Education Association, 2002). A curriculum emphasizing academics, more effective instruction, and greater parental involvement are alternative explanations offered for any gains that exist. Questions about the effects of choice on school diversity are continually raised, as we see later in the chapter.

In general, support for vouchers comes from dissatisfaction with existing public schools, and if public schools improve, public interest in vouchers is likely to wane. In the 2000 election, voters in California and Michigan overwhelmingly (70 percent in California and 69 percent in Michigan) voted against voucher initiatives, which opponents contend sounds a death knell for the movement (M. Walsh, 2000b). But a number of states, including Texas and South Carolina, continue to pursue vouchers despite general public opposition (60%) to the idea (Rose & Gallup, 2007).

State tuition tax-credit plans are a variation on school voucher programs in which parents are given tax credits for money they spend on private-school tuition. Tuition tax credits have emerged in some states as a more politically viable alternative to publicly financed school vouchers (Robelen, 2009a). Research suggests, however, that tuition tax credits primarily benefit wealthy families who are already sending their children to private schools. In Illinois in 2000, for example, tax credits cost the state more than $61 million in lost revenues (Gehring, 2002a). Taxpayers earning more than $80,000 claimed 46 percent of that amount, whereas less than 3 percent went to households making less than $20,000. A similar problem occurred in Arizona (Bracey, 2002), where households earning more than $50,000 received 81 percent of the tax credits as well as 84 percent of the $109 million state revenues spent on tuition tax credits. More equitable ways of distributing the benefits of this form of school choice need to be designed if this reform effort is to grow.

HOMESCHOOLING **Homeschooling**, an educational option in which parents educate their children at home, may be the ultimate form of school choice. Homeschooling has become increasingly popular in recent years, with 2007 estimates of the number of children participating at 1.5 million, accounting for close to three percent of the school-age population, up more than 70 percent from 1999 (Lloyd, 2009).

Parents homeschool their children for a variety of reasons (Lloyd, 2009). Most— nearly 9 of 10—do so because of concerns about the moral climate of existing schools or for religious reasons. Others want a more academic emphasis, or perhaps nontraditional educational approaches. All are seeking an alternative to existing public schools.

State laws regulating homeschooling vary greatly (Fischer, Schimmel, & Stellman, 2006). In most states, parents must demonstrate that their instruction is equivalent to that offered in public schools. Forty-one states don't have any minimum educational qualifications for parents who homeschool their children; eight of the remaining nine states require at least a high school diploma (Zehr, 2004). An increasing number of homeschool parents are turning to cyber-schooling, enrolling their children in online

State tuition tax-credit plans A variation on school voucher programs in which parents are given tax credits for money they spend on private-school tuition.

Homeschooling An educational option in which parents educate their children at home.

The Privatization Issue

One by-product of school choice is privatization. Schools are multibillion-dollar enterprises, and corporations have always looked at education as a possible place to make money. Both textbooks and standardized tests generate billions of dollars for corporations (Cuban, 2004; Molnar, 2005).

Historically, corporate activities in schools have taken three basic forms: 1) selling *to* schools (vending), 2) selling *in* schools (books, computers), and, more recently, 3) selling *of* schools (Molnar, 2005). The move toward school choice has accelerated this last option with privately run, for-profit schools. Modeled after HMOs (health maintenance organizations), EMOs (education maintenance organizations) propose to run and manage either whole districts or specific schools within a district. In addition, the No Child Left Behind legislation, specifying that students in failing schools be provided with supplemental tutoring, has opened the door to a billion-dollar tutoring industry for private corporations (Stover & Hardy, 2008).

Estimates indicate that 70 percent of school districts currently engage in some type of business partnership (L. Alexander & Riley, 2002). At one time, school–business partnerships often consisted of corporations buying a football scoreboard or placing an ad in the school newspaper. More recently, Channel One, a privately run school news/advertising company, offered 10 minutes of news to schools in return for 2 minutes of advertising. Incentives included free satellite disks, a school-wide cable system, and free televisions in all classrooms. In the early 2000s, Channel One reached 12,000 schools and 7 million students, 40 percent of the nation's 12- to 18-year-olds (A. Moore, 2007). This is a huge advertising market.

Certain aspects of school privatization aren't new. Schools have been outsourcing contracts for support services, such as school lunches and transportation, for years. In addition, districts typically hire companies such as IBM and Hewlett-Packard to provide technology support. What is new is the idea of handing over control of a whole school or district to a private corporation.

Corporations such as Edison Schools, Inc., and Sylvan Learning Incorporated are leaders in the school privatization movement. Edison began in 1992 and made its stock public in 1998 with an initial Wall Street offering of $18 per share; optimism soon propelled share prices to $38 (Woodward, 2002). Chris Whittle, its founder and also the creator of Channel One, predicted that by 2020, Edison would run 1 in every 10 schools in the United States, but so far the company has grown slowly, and its stock sank to $2 in 2001. In 2005, Edison ran 136 schools across the country, serving 53,500 students (Reid, 2005). Its most visible challenge came when the School District of Philadelphia, a floundering system suffering from perennial low student achievement, offered Edison a 5-year, $60 million contract to manage 20 of its schools.

Nationwide, the privatization movement has received a big boost from the trend toward school choice, and the number of privately run schools grew rapidly from 285 in 2001 to 417 in 2003 (M. Walsh, 2003a); of these, 74 percent were charter schools. The number of for-profit companies in the educational arena also grew from 21 in 2001 to 47 in 2003.

Technology also plays a key role in the school privatization movement. William Bennett, former secretary of education, founded K12, a virtual school that serves both homeschoolers and charter schools embedded within public school districts (Bracey, 2004). Despite the use of technology, both its curriculum and its instruction appear to be traditional, emphasizing the memorization of facts.

THE ISSUE

As would be expected, private, for-profit schools are highly controversial. Should corporations, whose primary objective is making a profit, be entrusted with the education of children?

Critics make a number of arguments against privatization (Belfield & Levin, 2005; Saltman, 2005). They question the ability of a corporate efficiency model to work in education and assert that corporate strategies will adversely affect both teachers and students. Further, they contend, privatized schools have a dual mission—improving test scores and making a profit—and corporate profits and education don't mix. Attention to the bottom line means that student welfare may be sacrificed to make money. Critics also identify a narrow focus on the basics, as well as neglect of nonnative English speakers and students with special needs as additional problems.

Support for the critics' position can be found in Edison's efforts in Philadelphia, where controversy existed from the beginning. Apparently, the district's call for outside help was based on an evaluation conducted by Edison itself and not sent out for competitive bids (Gewertz, 2002). In essence, the state of Pennsylvania hired Edison to conduct a study, completed in 2 months, for $2.7 million (Bracey, 2002). Not surprisingly, the Edison report concluded that external help should be sought, and the district authorized the creation of 20 Edison charter schools. After less than 1 year of operation, the School District of Philadelphia, citing budget considerations, decided to shift $10 million of the next year's $20 million contract from Edison and other private companies to other reform projects (Gewertz, 2003). One disillusioned parent commented, "I don't consider putting 15,000 students with a company that can't guarantee operations next year reform. It's not just a stock game, this is my child's life" (Saltman, 2005, p. 154).

Teacher morale and lagging student performance in Edison schools have been persistent problems. For example, in an Edison-contracted San Francisco elementary school, approximately half of the teachers left in each of Edison's first 2 years of operation, citing problems with long work hours, a regimented curriculum, and overemphasis on preparing students for tests. There were also claims that students with academic or behavioral difficulties were "counseled out" of the school in hopes of raising test scores (Woodward, 2002). San Francisco canceled its contract with Edison; under a renewed charter contract with the state of California, the Edison school's test scores remained low, ranking last among scores from San Francisco's 75 elementary schools.

Privatization advocates argue that these problems are exceptions, that Edison works in some of the most challenging schools in the country, and that the public shouldn't expect miracles overnight (Chubb, 2007). They also assert that competition from the corporate sector is good because it encourages public schools to reexamine unproductive practices. In addition, advocates claim, the same business efficiencies that have made the United States a world leader can also work in schools, and a focus on performance (as measured by standardized tests) can provide schools with a clear mission to increase student achievement. They also claim that privatization can inject a breath of fresh air into the educational bureaucracy.

Research has found some benefits of privatized schools. They are typically cleaner and more efficiently run than public schools (Reid, 2005). Technology is frequently emphasized, and more attention is given to individualized instruction. However, companies have not provided clear evidence that students learn more in privately run schools, a core assertion of privatization advocates. Some research shows improved achievement, but other research shows either no gain or declines (Campbell, 2007a, 2007b; M. Walsh, 2003b). Unfortunately, the research on achievement gains in privatized schools is murky, clouded by the sponsors—either privatization backers or critics—who seem to produce results that bolster their position.

YOU TAKE A STAND

Now it's your turn to take a position on the issue. Is the privatization of schools by for-profit corporations a positive educational reform or not?

PEARSON myeducationlab To explore both sides of this issue and take a stand, go to the *Book Specific Resources* section in the MyEducationLab for your course, select your text, and then select *Taking a Stand in an Era of Reform* for Chapter 9.

ISSUES IN EDUCATION

Homeschooling provides parents with the opportunity to customize a child's education to a family's specific educational goals.

programs, which provides some measure of control over the curriculum (Huerta, d'Entremont, & Gonzalez, 2006). Approximately half the states require homeschooled students to participate in regular standardized testing. Homeschooled students who take these tests typically do well, scoring, on average, between 15 and 30 percentile points higher than students in public schools (Ray, 2006).

Despite its growing popularity, homeschooling has its critics. The greatest concern centers on the lack of safeguards around the quality of education provided to homeschool children and the possibilities of neglect and even abuse (Gross, 2008). A California court recently jumped into the fray, ruling that homeschooled children must be taught by a credentialed teacher or parents could face possible fines or criminal charges (Terwiller & Toppo, 2008). Advocates, backed by the governor, vow to fight this ruling with new legislation that loosens credentialing requirements.

Other concerns center on whether children schooled at home will learn important social-interaction skills, and whether narrow courses of study will expose children to alternative views and perspectives (Galley, 2003; Reich, 2002). One troubling trend is the tendency of some homeschool learning materials to criticize specific religious beliefs or

School Choice and Cultural Minorities

 School choice is often framed in terms of parental empowerment, or providing parents with educational alternatives. But can the process of school choice result in unintended negative consequences such as increased social and racial segregation, as some critics claim (B. Gill, 2005; Ross, 2005)?

Research from New Zealand, which began experimenting with school choice via a quasi voucher system in 1989, raises some cautionary flags (Fiske & Ladd, 2000). Under choice rules, schools with more student applicants than openings could essentially choose whom they admitted and served. The better schools chose academically motivated students from affluent families, leaving less popular schools with lower-achieving students. Researchers concluded that in New Zealand, "choice and competition are likely to polarize enrollment patterns by race, ethnicity, socioeconomic status, and students' performance" (Fiske & Ladd, 2000, p. 38). These same researchers cautioned against unregulated choice systems that could result in "polarization of enrollment patterns and exacerbation of the problems of non-competitive schools" (Fiske & Ladd, 2000, p. 38). In other words, choice systems have the potential of encouraging social segregation and further damaging already weak inner-city schools.

The same concerns have been raised in the United States: Critics contend that voucher programs and charter schools entice the best students away from poor-performing schools, leaving urban schools, in particular, in even worse shape (Goyette, 2008; Scott, 2005). Further, school choice leads to segregation of students, either by income or by race. One U.S. study supports critics' claims. Researchers found that 70 percent of African American charter school students attend intensely segregated schools, compared with 34 percent of African American students in regular public schools (Frankenberg & Lee, 2003). In virtually every state studied, the average African American charter school student attended a school with a higher percentage of African American students and a lower percentage of White students. But a more recent study found that private, voucher-funded schools in Washington, DC, were less racially homogeneous than their public-school counterparts (Robelen, 2006a).

Research suggests that school choice failed to consider how these options would affect poor and minority households (Goyette, 2008; Lauen, 2007). Wealthier White families, with greater access to information about choice options, are more likely to know about charter and voucher options, and are more able economically and logistically to use them. Lower-SES families and cultural minorities often are unaware of choice options and can't take advantage of them because they lack the resources to transport their children to these sites.

A small town in Arizona, a leader in the charter school movement, illustrates some of the problems associated with school choice (Schnaiberg, 2000). In 1996, two charter schools opened in the small rural school district of Safford, which had approximately 60 percent Anglo and 40 percent Hispanic students. In its first year of enrollment, the Triumphant Learning Center, a back-to-basics school with Christian overtones, enrolled 95 percent Anglo students. Los Milagros, a charter school with Catholic ties, enrolled 75 percent Hispanic students. Although neither school consciously chose to exclude certain types of students, "subtle signals" sent messages to parents. For example, the Triumphant Learning Center emphasized increased parental involvement by encouraging parents to volunteer in the school and by closing their doors every Friday to allow more family time. Poor Hispanic families, in which both parents worked—many holding more than one job—weren't able to participate. In 2000, 53 percent of Los Milagros's students remained Hispanic, and 90 percent of the students in the Triumphant Learning Center were Anglo, but both schools were making efforts to balance their enrollments. Additional research across the country further supports the problem of poor and minority students' access to choice options (C. Baker & Lyon, 2006; Goyette, 2008).

Another area of concern connected with school choice has to do with equal opportunities for students with special needs and how those needs should be funded. In most voucher plans, the voucher amount is equal to the average per-pupil expenditure in the district or state, but the cost for educating children with special needs can be more than twice that amount (National Education Association, 2005). Consequently, students with exceptionalities could find themselves underfunded or even refused admittance by certain schools. This very problem occurred in Massachusetts when for-profit charter schools openly discouraged students with exceptionalities from attending (Zollars, 2000). Only 17 percent of private schools provided special education services (Ferguson, 2002), so the problem of access to choice schools may be particularly acute for students with special needs.

Supporters of school choice programs counter that public schools are already segregated, especially in inner cities, and that choice can actually promote integration. For example, in 1999, 55 percent of all public-school 12th graders attended classes that had either more than 90 percent or fewer than 10 percent minorities (Greene, 2000). In contrast, only 41 percent of students in choice-driven private schools were in similarly segregated classrooms. As we saw with magnet schools in Chapter 6, school choice, when designed strategically, can actually be an integration tool.

The effects of school choice on students from minority groups will remain controversial and are likely to significantly affect education in the future. It's unclear at this time whether these effects will be positive or negative. Ideally, school choice should encourage experimentation and innovation. As with all experiments, mistakes will occur. Whether these mistakes will adversely affect students and the teachers who work with them is an important question.

Diversity in Your Classroom
The controversies surrounding school choice serve as reminders to teachers about their role in helping to achieve equity for all students through quality instruction. A major force behind the choice movement is the perception that schools aren't doing enough to help *all* students learn. Research provides us with some ideas about how to solve this problem. The solution begins with high expectations for all students, which sets the stage for effective instruction, including interactive instruction that is challenging and that provides frequent feedback about learning progress. Effective classrooms with committed teachers would do

much to reduce current calls for alternatives to the classrooms that we now have.

QUESTIONS TO CONSIDER
1. What can teachers do to counteract the negative effects of segregation in their classrooms?
2. Should classroom teachers encourage their students to explore different school choice options?

myeducationlab To respond to these questions online, explore this topic further, and receive feedback, go to the *Book Specific Resources* section in the MyEducationLab for your course, select your text, and then select *Exploring Diversity* for Chapter 9.

entire religions. One study found that some of the more popular religiously oriented homeschool texts described Islam as "a false religion," blamed Hinduism for India's problems, and attributed Africa's problems to the absence of Christian religions (Patterson, 2001/2002).

In addition to controversies about the privatization movement in education, there are concerns about the effects of school choice on cultural minorities. In the *Exploring Diversity* feature on pages 279–280, we analyze some of these issues.

■ ■ ■ ■ CHECK YOUR UNDERSTANDING

3.1 Describe the major issues in school governance and finance.

3.2 What are the major causes of funding inequities in education? What are some proposed solutions to the problem?

3.3 What are the two major forms of school choice? How are they similar and different?

3.4 What is *school privatization*, and what are its pros and cons?

For feedback, go to the appendix, *Check Your Understanding*, located in the back of this text.

In the next section, we invite you to think about governance and finance in terms of your own professional life.

Governance and Finance and Their Effects on Teachers

You've just graduated from a local university with a bachelor's degree, and you're licensed to teach special education. Jobs are plentiful: You've interviewed with three districts, and each has offered you a position.

The first was in a large urban district in the city where you grew up. The interview in the central office went well, and they asked you to interview with a school principal. When you arrived at the school, you were surprised at how run-down the school and the surrounding neighborhoods were. The principal was dedicated and enthusiastic, and when she showed you around the school, you could tell she loved what she did. Her last words to you were, "Think about us. This is a school that needs you, and you can really make a difference here."

Your second interview was in a small rural district near the university you attended. The central office was small; the interview went well, and the assistant superintendent and the head of personnel concluded the interview by walking you down the street to meet the principal you'd be working for. The school was a small, traditional brick building with well-lit halls and high ceilings. Though the pay was not as good as in the urban school, the principal emphasized the opportunities for growth and leadership in a small district like this one. There were only two other full-time special education teachers in the district, and the head of the program would be retiring in a few years.

Your third interview was with a growing suburban district on the edge of a major metropolitan area in your state. The district office was modern and bustling. The head of personnel explained how the district would be hiring 50 new teachers that year and that each would be assigned to a mentor. The school district had the highest tax base in the state, and this was evident in the school you visited: Computers and other forms of technology were everywhere. The pay scale was also the highest in the state.

What would you do in this situation?

9 MEETING YOUR LEARNING OBJECTIVES

1. Describe the major educational governance structures at the state and local levels.

   - The responsibility for governing schools in the United States is given to the states by the Tenth Amendment to the U.S. Constitution. Despite geographic, economic, and political differences among states, the educational governance structure in each is similar.

   - The governor and state legislature in each state are supported by the state board of education, which establishes educational policy for the state. This policy is implemented by the state office of education, which is responsible for teacher licensing, curriculum supervision, approval of school sites and buildings, and collection of statistical data.

   - Local control of education, a uniquely American idea, occurs through individual school districts, which are governed by a local school board and administered by a district superintendent. The superintendent is responsible for overseeing the operations of the individual schools within the district. Principals shape the instructional agenda at the individual school level.

2. Explain the different sources and targets of educational funding.

   • Schools are funded from three sources. Almost half of school funds come from the states, which typically gather funds using state income taxes and special taxes. Local sources provide another more than 40 percent of funding, usually through property taxes. The rest is provided by the federal government.

   • Most education monies go to instructional services, primarily to pay for teacher salaries. The rest is divided about equally among student services, teacher professional development and curriculum development, administration, maintenance of school buildings and grounds, and transportation and food services.

3. Describe major current issues in school governance and finance.

   • Because educational governance is a state responsibility, controversies over inequities in school finance have focused on differences within states. Court cases involving funding inequities have caused states to increase state and decrease local funding. Current approaches to funding equity go beyond absolute dollar amounts to include student and district needs.

   • School choice in the form of charter schools and vouchers provides parents with greater control over their children's education. Charter schools, publicly funded by independent entities, target their efforts on specific educational goals or patrons. Vouchers, essentially tickets for educational services, allow parents to shop around for schools that fit their needs.

   • Privatization, in which corporations contract for certain services within districts and even run specific schools, is a growing but controversial practice. The impact of school choice programs on cultural minorities and integration efforts is still unclear.

IMPORTANT CONCEPTS

block grants (p. 266)
categorical grants (p. 266)
charter schools (p. 273)
homeschooling (p. 276)
KIPP (Knowledge Is Power Program) (p. 273)
local school board (p. 258)
principal (p. 261)

property taxes (p. 265)
school district (p. 257)
state board of education (p. 255)
state office of education (p. 255)
state tuition tax-credit plans (p. 276)
superintendent (p. 260)
voucher (p. 275)
weighted student formula (p. 271)

DISCUSSION QUESTIONS

1. Should legislation be passed to make local school boards mirror the populations they serve? For example, if 25 percent of the population is Hispanic, should one fourth of the school board be Hispanic? What advantages and disadvantages are there to this approach to equitable representation? What other alternatives might be better?

2. Ordinarily, teachers can't be school board members in their own districts because of potential conflicts of interest. Would teachers make good school

board members in districts where they live but don't teach? Should a certain number or percentage of school board positions be reserved for teachers? Why or why not?

3. Should the percentages of male and female principals reflect the gender composition of the teachers at the school level in which the principals work? Why or why not?

4. Should school districts in a state be funded equally? What are the advantages and disadvantages to this approach? Should every school district in the nation receive equal funds? What are the advantages and disadvantages to this approach?

5. Will school choice be a positive or negative development in education? Why?

6. Should vouchers be made available to private religious schools? Why or why not?

PEARSON
myeducationlab

Now go to Topic 5: *Governance and Finance* in the MyEducationLab (www.myeducationlab.com) for your course, where you can:

- Find learning outcomes for *Governance and Finance*, along with the national standards that connect to these outcomes.

- Complete *Assignments and Activities* that can help you more deeply understand the chapter content.

- Apply and practice your understanding of the core teaching skills identified in the chapter with the *Building Teaching Skills and Dispositions* learning units.

- Check your comprehension on the content covered in the chapter by going to the *Study Plan* in the *Book Specific Resources* section for your text. Here you will be able to take a chapter quiz, receive feedback on your answers, and then access *Review, Practice, and Enrichment* activities to enhance your understanding of chapter content.

Develop Your Professional Portfolio

To further apply your understanding of chapter content and address the INTASC standards, go to the *Book Specific Resources* section in the MyEducationLab for your course, select your text, and then select this chapter's *Portfolio Activities*.

"*The main reason I teach is for the students. . . . I teach because I can help people. . . . But I never knew how rewarding, how creative, or important it would be. That's why I teach. I can't imagine any other life.*"

MARY SCHLIEDER,   2008 Teacher of the Year, Nebraska

To view a video of Mary, the 2008 Nebraska Teacher of the Year, go to Topic 4: *Ethical and Legal Issues* in the MyEducationLab for your course and select *Teacher Talk,* then *Mary Schlieder.*

10

School Law: Ethical and Legal Influences on Teaching

CHAPTER OUTLINE

Law, Ethics, and Teacher Professionalism
- Limitations of Laws
- Ethical Dimensions of Teaching

The U.S. Legal System
- Federal Influences
- State and Local Influences
- The Overlapping Legal System

Teachers' Rights and Responsibilities
- Teacher Employment and the Law
- Academic Freedom
- Copyright Laws
- Teacher Liability
- Child Abuse
- Teachers' Private Lives

  Taking a Stand in an Era of Reform: Teacher Tenure

Religion and the Law
- Prayer in Schools
- Religious Clubs and Organizations
- Religion in the Curriculum
- Teaching About Religion in the Schools

Students' Rights and Responsibilities
- Students' Freedom of Speech
- Permissible Search and Seizure
- Student Records and Privacy
- Corporal Punishment
- Students' Rights in Disciplinary Actions
- Students With AIDS

  Exploring Diversity: Integration

LEARNING OBJECTIVES

After you have completed your study of this chapter, you should be able to:

1. **Explain the differences between legal and ethical influences on the teaching profession.** INTASC Standard 9, Teacher Professionalism

2. **Describe how the legal system at the federal, state, and local levels influences education.** INTASC Standard 9, Teacher Professionalism

3. **Explain how factors such as teacher employment, academic freedom, liability, and teachers' personal lives are influenced by the law.** INTASC Standard 9, Teacher Professionalism

4. **Describe the legal implications of religion in the schools.** INTASC Standard 3, Adapting Instruction to Learner Needs

5. **Describe students' legal rights and responsibilities.** INTASC Standard 3, Adapting Instruction to Learner Needs

egal issues may seem unrelated to your life as a beginning teacher and not even very interesting. Imagine, however, that you're a third-grade teacher, and you're called to the main office to talk with a parent. Can you leave your class unsupervised? Or, you're a high school English teacher, and you find a poem that strikes you as a moving commentary on love. Dare you share it with your students without their parents' approval? Or, you're a science teacher, and you find a program on the Internet that you would like to use in your classes. Can you legally download and duplicate the information? As you read the following case studies, think about the different ways that legal issues will influence your life as a teacher.

Jason Taylor is a science teacher in a suburban school in the Pacific Northwest. The town in which he teaches is considering an open-space initiative that will limit urban growth. Environmentalists support the law because they believe it will help to preserve local farms and wildlife habitat; business concerns oppose it because of its potential to curtail economic growth. Jason talks about the initiative in class, explaining how it will help the environment. He mentions that he is head of a local action committee and that interested students can receive extra credit for passing out fliers after school.

Some parents complain to the principal, claiming that school time shouldn't be devoted to political activity. Called in by the principal to discuss the parents' concerns, Jason adamantly argues that he has the right to involve students in local politics, claiming that a part of every course ought to be devoted to civic awareness and action. The principal points out that Jason was hired to teach science, not social studies, and that parents' concerns are important.

Sasha Brown looks at the two folders in front of her and frowns. Her job is to recommend one of two students from her school for a prestigious science and math scholarship to the state university. Although the decision will ultimately be made by a committee, she knows that her recommendation will carry considerable weight because she is chair of the math department.

Brandon, one of the candidates, is a bright, conscientious student who always scores at the top of his class. The son of a local engineer, he has a good grasp of mathematical concepts. Sonia, the other candidate, is not as strong conceptually but often solves problems in creative ways. The fact that she is female is also an issue, because a female hasn't won the award in its 6-year history. In addition, Sasha knows that Sonia comes from a single-parent family and needs the scholarship more than Brandon does.

What would you do in Jason's position? How about Sasha's? What guidelines exist to help you, and how do these dilemmas relate to teacher professionalism? We address these and other questions in this chapter.

Before you begin your study, please respond to the items in the *This I Believe* feature.

LAW, ETHICS, AND TEACHER PROFESSIONALISM

Professionals are responsible for making decisions in ill-defined situations, they have the autonomy to do so, and they use their professional knowledge as a basis for making decisions. Understanding the legal and ethical aspects of their profession is an important part of this knowledge. Research indicates, however, that teachers often lack professional knowledge in these areas, leaving them unprepared to deal with legal and ethical issues when they arise (Schimmel & Militello, 2007). Not surprisingly, students are also often unaware of their constitutional rights and responsibilities (Tonn, 2005a). This chapter examines the law and how it can influence your professional decision making. We begin by putting the legal aspects of teaching into a larger perspective.

For each item, circle the number that best represents your thinking. Use the following scale as a guide.

4 = I strongly believe the statement is true.
3 = I believe the statement is true.
2 = I believe the statement is false.
1 = I strongly believe the statement is false.

1. Teachers have the legal right to determine what is taught in their classroom.

   1   2   3   4

2. Teachers are responsible for the safety of the students in their classrooms.

   1   2   3   4

3. Teachers are held to the same moral standards as other citizens.

   1   2   3   4

4. The law prohibits any form of prayer in the schools.

   1   2   3   4

5. Corporal punishment in schools is prohibited by law.

   1   2   3   4

myeducationlab To download and complete this form, go to the *Book Specific Resources* section in the MyEducationLab for your course, select your text, and then select *This I Believe* for Chapter 10.

This I BELIEVE

Limitations of Laws

You're working in a middle school, and you see a fight between two students on the playground. Does the law address your responsibilities in a situation like this? The answer is yes. You can't ignore the fight, because you're responsible for the safety of the children; in fact, parents have the right to sue a teacher if they can demonstrate that he or she failed to protect students from injury, a problem labeled *negligence*. Should you physically break up the fight, or can you simply report it to the administration? As with many other situations, the law is imprecise, and doesn't specify an exact response.

Laws regulate the rights and responsibilities of teachers, but two limitations affect the extent to which they can guide our professional decisions. First, laws are purposely general, so they can apply to a variety of specific situations. For example, regarding the protection of students from injury, teachers not only have to break up fights on a playground, they also need to supervise chemistry experiments, maintain order at school assemblies, and stop horseplay in locker rooms.

Jason's dilemma is another case. The law generally protects a teacher's freedom of speech, but does it allow him to campaign in his classroom and present issues that may not be part of the assigned curriculum? The answers to these questions are not explicitly described in laws, so professional decision making is necessary.

A second limitation of laws is that they were created in response to problems that existed in the past, so they don't provide specific guidelines for future decisions. New situations often raise new legal questions. For example, what are the rights of students and teachers who have AIDS? (We answer this question later in the chapter.) The use of technology raises additional questions; for example, what kinds of materials can be legally downloaded from the Internet? What are the legal limitations to software use in schools? What can be legally copied? Experts are wrestling with these issues, and preliminary guidelines have appeared, but educators must often make decisions based on their knowledge of

Professional ethics provide broad guidelines for teachers as they make decisions in complex situations.

the law as it exists and their own professional judgment. This again illustrates why professional knowledge is so important.

Ethical Dimensions of Teaching

The law tells teachers what they *can* do (their rights) and what they *must* do (their responsibilities); however, laws don't tell teachers what they *should* do. For information on appropriate conduct, teachers must turn to ethics. *Ethics* is the discipline that examines values and offers principles that can be used to decide whether acts are right or wrong (Gladding, 2007).

Professional ethics are a set of moral standards for acceptable professional behavior. For example, the Hippocratic Oath is a code of ethics that guides the medical profession; in taking the oath, physicians pledge to do their best to benefit their patients, to tell the truth, and to maintain patients' confidences. Other professions have similar ethical codes, which are designed to guide practitioners and protect clients.

You were introduced to the National Education Association's (NEA) code of ethics in Chapter 1 when you studied teacher professionalism (see Figure 1.6). The NEA code provides guidance to teachers in ambiguous professional situations such as those described at the beginning of the chapter.

As with the law, codes of ethics are limited; they provide only general guidelines for professional behavior. To see why, let's look again at Jason's dilemma. Under Principle I of the NEA Code of Ethics, Item 2 states that "the educator . . . shall not unreasonably deny the student access to varying points of view." Has Jason been balanced and fair in presenting both sides of the environmental and political issue? A code of ethics isn't, and never can be, specific enough to provide a definitive answer. Jason must answer the question for himself based on his personal philosophy of education and, within it, his personal code of ethics.

The limitations of the NEA code are also illustrated in Sasha's case. Item 6 of Principle I cautions teachers not to discriminate "on the basis of race, color, creed, [or] sex," but it doesn't tell Sasha which student to choose. Judged strictly on academics, Brandon appears to be the better candidate. If Sasha believes that Sonia is less talented than Brandon, choosing her because she is female would be granting her an unfair advantage. On the other hand, Sasha may believe that Sonia's math talents are different from—but equal to—Brandon's and that it's ethically valid to consider her financial need and the good that might result from giving recognition to a female in a male-dominated area of the curriculum.

In response to these complexities, teachers are often encouraged to "treat all students equally." But even this edict isn't as simple as it appears on the surface. Effective teachers purposely call on shy students to involve them in lessons, sometimes avoid calling on assertive students who tend to dominate discussions, and give students who have difficulty with English more time to answer questions and finish tests. Teachers treat students differently depending on their individual needs; professional ethics direct teachers to treat all students equitably, but not always equally.

These examples illustrate why developing your personal philosophy of education is so important. A philosophy of education provides a framework for thinking about educational issues and guides professional practice. Your personal philosophy will guide you as you make decisions about what's important and what's fair. Because the law and professional codes of ethics can provide only general guidelines, a personal philosophy is essential in helping you make specific decisions each day.

Professional ethics A set of moral standards for acceptable professional behavior.

■ ■ ■ ■ ■ CHECK YOUR UNDERSTANDING

1.1 Explain the differences between legal and ethical influences on the teaching profession.

1.2 What are two limitations of using existing laws as the basis for professional decision making?

For feedback, go to the appendix, *Check Your Understanding*, located in the back of this text.

THE U.S. LEGAL SYSTEM

Having briefly examined ethics and the law, and their limitations, we now look more closely at the legal system in the United States. Laws regulating schools and teachers are part of a larger legal system, which exists at three interconnected levels: federal, state, and local (Underwood & Webb, 2006). This system uses peoples' rights and responsibilities as the basis for defining fairness.

Federal Influences

Through amendments to the Constitution and specific laws enacted by Congress, the federal government plays a central role in defining the rights and responsibilities of teachers and students.

CONSTITUTIONAL AMENDMENTS   Think about the following questions:

- How much freedom do you as a teacher have in selecting topics to teach? Are you limited in what books and articles you can ask your students to read?
- Can you publicly criticize the administrators and school boards you work for?
- How much freedom do students have in running their school newspapers and yearbooks?

The First Amendment to the Constitution guarantees freedom of speech to all citizens of the United States, but where is the line drawn with respect to the preceding questions? You can't have your students read *Playboy* magazine, but how about *Catcher in the Rye*, a classic coming-of-age novel with explicit sexual references? Considering the second and third questions leaves similar uncertainties.

The Fourth Amendment protects citizens from unreasonable searches and seizures. To what extent does this amendment protect teachers and students? For instance:

- Can school officials search students' backpacks and purses when they're on school property?
- Are students' lockers considered personal property, or can they be searched if school officials suspect drugs or weapons are in them?

The Fourth Amendment provides general guidelines about search and seizure but doesn't specifically answer these questions.

The Fourteenth Amendment states, "nor shall any State deprive any person of life, liberty, or property without due process of law." What does "due process" mean in the context of schools? For example:

- Can teachers be fired without a formal hearing?
- Can students be expelled from class without formal proceedings?
- How long can a student be suspended from school, and what kinds of deliberations need to precede such a suspension?

PEARSON
myeducationlab

To learn more about the influence of Constitutional amendments on school law, go to the *Assignments and Activities* section of Topic 4: *Ethical and Legal Issues* in the MyEducationLab for your course and complete the activity titled *Constitutional Amendments and School Law.*

Again, the Constitution provides general guidelines about due process, but specific decisions are left to teachers and other educators.

FEDERAL LAWS   The federal laws passed in Congress also influence education. For example, the Civil Rights Act of 1964 states, "No person in the United States shall on the grounds of race, color, or national origin, be excluded from participation in or be denied the benefits of, or be subjected to discrimination under any program or activity receiving federal financial assistance." This law helped end school segregation in this country. Similarly, Title IX, passed in 1972, prohibits discrimination on the basis of sex and has been instrumental in helping equalize the resources provided for boys' and girls' sports.

State and Local Influences

States influence education by passing laws regulating teachers' qualifications, working conditions, and legal rights. For example, most states require a bachelor's degree to teach, and many are now requiring a major in an academic area.

States also create departments of education with a variety of responsibilities, such as determining the length of the school year and approving textbooks. They also pass laws creating local school districts, which are then legally responsible for the day-to-day functioning of schools.

The Overlapping Legal System

Overlapping levels in the legal system correspond to different responsibilities, but conflicts sometimes occur. When they do, the system attempts to resolve disputes at a lower level before sending them to a higher one. Let's look at two examples.

Brenda Taylor has been hired to teach American history at a rural high school. Three days before the school year begins, her principal informs her that she will be the debate team sponsor. She objects, saying she knows nothing about debate. When the principal insists, she looks into her contract and finds that a description of her duties includes the phrase "and related extracurricular activities." It doesn't mention the debate team. She complains again to the principal, but he is adamant. She writes a letter to the school board, which appoints a grievance committee. The committee rules in the district's favor. Brenda, not willing to back down, hires a lawyer, and her case goes to a state court.

Henry Ipsinger likes his job in a suburban middle school but disagrees with the school's priorities. A strong proponent of middle school philosophy, he believes that middle schools are supposed to be for all kids, not just the academically and athletically talented. He especially objects to his school's participation in Academic Olympics, an interschool academic competition, and the school's emphasis on competitive football and basketball.

Henry isn't afraid to express his opinions, and, to the consternation of his principal, frequently does so at faculty meetings. When his concerns aren't addressed, he takes his complaints to school board meetings. His complaints fall on deaf ears, though they raise a number of eyebrows. He then tries politics, openly backing opposition candidates to the school board. Finally he goes too far: At the end of the school year, he is cited for insubordination, and his contract isn't renewed.

Livid, Henry hires a lawyer, claiming his First Amendment right to freedom of speech has been violated. The case works its way through the court system all the way to the U.S. Supreme Court.

Can teachers be asked to perform duties in addition to their teaching responsibilities? Can their professional opinions cause them to be fired from their jobs? Both of these questions fall into a gray area called *school law* and are addressed by different court systems.

Brenda's and Henry's cases both started at the local level, but Brenda's complaint moved to state courts because her suit involved conditions of employment, which are state responsibilities. Henry's case went to federal courts because freedom of speech is a right guaranteed by the Constitution.

In the next section, we examine teachers' rights and responsibilities, probably the most important dimensions of school law for teachers.

■ ■ ■ ■ CHECK YOUR UNDERSTANDING

2.1 Describe how the legal system at the federal level influences education.

2.2 How do state laws influence education policies and practices?

2.3 What is the educational significance of the overlapping legal system in the United States?

For feedback, go to the appendix, *Check Your Understanding*, located in the back of this text.

TEACHERS' RIGHTS AND RESPONSIBILITIES

As citizens, teachers enjoy the same legal safeguards as all Americans, including freedom of speech and the right to due process. But, because they're professionals entrusted with the care of children, they have responsibilities beyond those of other citizens. These rights and responsibilities exist in six areas, which are outlined in Figure 10.1 and discussed in the sections that follow.

Figure 10.1 Teachers' Rights and Responsibilities

Teacher Employment and the Law

One of the first things you'll think about as you join the teaching profession is how to get and keep a job. Legal guidelines influence the process.

LICENSURE   **Licensure** is the process by which a state evaluates the credentials of prospective teachers to ensure that they have achieved satisfactory levels of teaching competence and are morally fit to work with young people. Every state has licensure requirements, which typically include a bachelor's degree from an accredited college or university with a minimum number of credit hours in specified areas, such as those required for a teaching major or minor.

In addition, prospective teachers are screened for felony arrests or a history of abusing or molesting children. Applicants who fail these screens usually have the right to petition before a state professional practices board that considers individual cases.

Teachers are increasingly being asked to pass competency tests that measure their ability to perform basic skills (reading, writing, and mathematics), their background in an academic area, such as biology, history, or English, and their understanding of learning and teaching. These tests are controversial, but when properly developed and validated, they have been upheld in courts (Fischer, Schimmel, & Stellman, 2006; Underwood & Webb, 2006). Individuals who meet these requirements receive a teaching license that makes them eligible to teach but doesn't ensure employment.

CONTRACTS   A **teaching contract** is a legal employment agreement between a teacher and a local school board. In issuing contracts, school boards must comply with laws that prohibit discrimination on the basis of sex, race, religion, or age. Contracts are legally

Licensure The process by which a state evaluates the credentials of prospective teachers to ensure that they have achieved satisfactory levels of teaching competence and are morally fit to work with young people.

Teaching contract A legal employment agreement between a teacher and a local school board.

binding for both parties. School boards can be sued for breaking one without due cause, and teachers must honor contracts they have signed. Many states permit a teacher's certificate to be revoked for breach of contract, a practice growing more common as the competition for teachers increases (Archer, 2000b).

New teachers should carefully read their contracts and any district policies and procedures manuals covered by the contract. Extracurricular assignments, such as sponsoring school clubs or monitoring sports events, may not be specified in detail in an initial contract but can be required later. This is what happened to Brenda Taylor when her contract said "and related extracurricular activities." Courts have generally upheld districts' rights to require these additional responsibilities, but have also said that a reasonable connection must exist between additional assignments and a teacher's regular classroom duties. So, for example, a speech or English teacher may be required to sponsor a debate club but not have to coach an athletic team if he or she has no corresponding experience.

Collective bargaining between professional organizations and school districts determines teachers' salaries and working conditions.

COLLECTIVE BARGAINING   Many of the details of the contract that you'll sign, such as working conditions, class size, salaries and benefits, and transfer policies, will be determined by collective bargaining agreements between your school district and the local professional organization. Most teachers belong to either the National Education Association or the American Federation of Teachers, and the power of collective bargaining is a major reason they do.

Collective bargaining occurs when a local chapter of a professional organization negotiates with a school district over the rights of the teachers and the conditions of employment. Legally, teachers have a constitutional right to join a professional organization but cannot be forced to do so (Essex, 2006; Fischer et al., 2006). In most states, the law requires the local school board to negotiate with whatever professional organization represents the largest number of teachers in that district. The final agreement applies to all teachers in the district.

If teachers believe that a school district isn't meeting the terms of the contract they signed or believe that they are given unreasonable responsibilities or work conditions, they can file a grievance (Imber & van Geel, 2005). A **grievance** is a formal complaint against an employer alleging unsatisfactory working conditions. When a teacher files a grievance, he or she is usually arguing that a working condition, such as class size or a teaching assignment, violates the teacher's contract. A teacher cannot be dismissed for filing a grievance, and the professional organization that negotiates the contract with the district will usually provide legal counsel.

Teachers also have a limited right to strike in about half of the states. In the others, legislators group teachers with other employees such as police officers and firefighters, believing that the public welfare would suffer from a strike. Because of the variability between states related to strikes and items covered by collective bargaining, beginning teachers should become familiar with the laws governing these issues. Professional organizations in your area are helpful in this regard.

TENURE   **Tenure** is a legal safeguard that provides job security by preventing teacher dismissal without due cause. Tenure is designed to protect teachers from political or personal abuse and to ensure the stability of the teaching force. It's grounded in the principle asserting that teachers should be hired and fired on their professional merits and not because of personal connections or political views. Tenured teachers can be dismissed

Collective bargaining The process that occurs when a local chapter of a professional organization negotiates with a school district over the rights of the teachers and the conditions of employment.

Grievance A formal complaint against an employer alleging unsatisfactory working conditions.

Tenure A legal safeguard that provides job security by preventing teacher dismissal without cause.

only for causes such as incompetence, immoral behavior, insubordination, or unprofessional conduct.

When any of these charges are filed, due process must be observed, and the teacher must be provided with the following:

- A written description of the charges and adequate time to prepare a rebuttal to them
- Access to evidence and the names of witnesses
- A hearing conducted before an impartial decision maker
- The right to representation by legal counsel and the opportunity to introduce evidence and cross-examine witnesses
- A school board decision based on the findings of the hearing
- A written record of the hearing and the right to appeal an adverse decision

These safeguards, guaranteed by the Fourteenth Amendment, provide teachers with the same constitutional protections enjoyed by the population at large.

DISMISSAL   You'll work hard to become licensed and perhaps even harder to get a teaching position. You obviously won't want to lose your job, so it's important to understand your rights in the unlikely event that this occurs.

Most districts require a probationary period before tenure is granted—commonly 3 years. During this time, teachers have a yearly contract and can be dismissed for a variety of reasons, such as believed incompetence, overstaffing, or reduced school enrollments. Although some states require districts to provide a formal hearing on demand when a nontenured teacher is dismissed, this isn't common. Teachers uncertain about their rights during this period should check with their district, state office of education, or professional organization.

Dishonesty on the job application can also result in a new teacher's dismissal. Students close to obtaining their degrees are sometimes offered positions during their internships. They agree but, because of unforeseen circumstances, are unable to graduate or obtain a license. When districts discover the problem, they can either dismiss the teachers or lower their status to substitute teacher, resulting in lower pay and loss of benefits.

Reduction in Force.   Because of declining student numbers, budget cuts, or course or program cancellations, districts are sometimes forced to dismiss teachers. **Reduction in force**, or "riffing," as it's called in industry, is the elimination of teaching positions because of declining student enrollment or school funds. Typically, districts dismiss teachers with the least seniority; in other words, the last in are first out. Fortunately, "riffing" occurs infrequently and, as increasing numbers of students enter the educational system, should be even less common in the future.

Reduction in force can involve both tenured and nontenured teachers and is regulated either by state law or by collective bargaining agreements (Fischer et al., 2006). Teachers faced with this possibility should consult representatives from their local professional organization.

Academic Freedom

Academic freedom refers to the right of teachers to choose both content and teaching methods based on their professional judgment. Although freedom of speech is protected by the First Amendment, professional academic freedom has limits. What are they? Consider these actual cases:

> In an attempt to motivate his students, a teacher organized his classroom around a sports-competition theme called "Learnball." Dividing his students into teams, the teacher instituted a system of rewards that included playing the radio and

Reduction in force The elimination of teaching positions because of declining student enrollment or school funds. Also known as "riffing."

Academic freedom The right of teachers to choose both content and teaching methods based on their professional judgment.

shooting foam basketballs. His principal objected, and when the teacher refused to change his methods, he was fired. He sued to get his job back, claiming his freedom of speech had been violated. (Bradley v. Pittsburgh Board of Education, 1990)

An eleventh-grade English teacher was leading a discussion on taboo words. To illustrate his point, he wrote the four-letter slang word for sexual intercourse on the board. Parents complained and the teacher was dismissed. He sued to get his job back, claiming his freedom of speech had been curtailed. (Mailloux v. Kiley, 1971)

Academic freedom protects teachers' rights to choose both content as well as teaching methods.

Teachers are hired to teach a specific age group or curriculum, such as first grade, middle school science, or high school English. State and district curriculum frameworks exist to guide teachers, and they often identify required textbooks. Within this general framework, teachers are free to teach topics as they see fit. Sometimes these topics and methods are controversial and may result in a teacher being disciplined or dismissed, as in the court cases you just saw.

In resolving disputes about academic freedom, the courts consider the following:

- The teacher's goal in discussing a topic or using a method
- The age of the students involved
- The relevance of the materials to the course
- The quality or general acceptance of the questioned material or methods
- The existence of policies related to the issue

In the case of the teacher using the Learnball format, the courts upheld the district's dismissal. The court based its decision on the fact that this teaching strategy was not widely accepted and that the teacher had been warned repeatedly by the administration to stop using it.

The opposite occurred in the case of the English teacher. The teacher's job was reinstated because the court upheld the importance of two kinds of academic freedom: (1) the "substantive" right to use a teaching method that serves a "demonstrated" purpose and (2) the procedural right not to be discharged for the use of a teaching method not prohibited by clear regulations. The teacher's goal was for his students to understand taboo words and how they influenced literature, a topic that fell under the broad umbrella of the English curriculum. Had this not been the case, or if the teacher had been clearly warned against using this strategy, the outcome would likely have been different.

When considering the discussion of controversial topics or the use of controversial methods, teachers should try to decide whether they fall within the scope of the assigned curriculum. If teachers choose to move forward, they should have clear goals in mind and be able to defend them if objections arise. Academic freedom protects knowledgeable, well-intentioned teachers working within their assigned responsibilities, but the legal process of defending the inclusion of questionable topics can be long and demanding (Zirkel, 2007). If you're uncertain about an issue that might involve academic freedom, you should check with your principal or other school administrator.

Grades and grading are also covered under academic freedom. In general, you are free to assign the grades you deem appropriate, with two caveats. First, your grading system should be consistent with accepted practice in the school and district, and second, you should be able to justify the grade with evidence based on student performance. If these requirements are met, courts rarely intervene in issues involving grading (Zirkel, 2008a).

This section addresses the first item in our *This I Believe* feature, "Teachers have the legal right to determine what is taught in their classrooms." This statement is true: Academic freedom allows teachers to select content for their classrooms if the content is appropriate for their students and teaching assignment.

Copyright Laws

As teachers, we want to share the most current information possible with our students. This can involve copying information from newspapers, magazines, books, and even television programs. Sometimes, however, doing so can violate copyright laws (Underwood & Webb, 2006).

Copyright laws are federal laws designed to protect the intellectual property of authors, which includes printed matter, videos, computer software, and other types of original work. Just as patents protect the intellectual work of inventors, copyright laws protect the work of print writers, filmmakers, software creators, songwriters, and graphic artists. Federal guidelines have been developed to balance the rights of authors with the legitimate needs of teachers and learners.

Fair-use guidelines are policies that specify limitations in the use of copyrighted materials for educational purposes. For example, teachers may make a single copy of a book chapter, newspaper or magazine article, short story, essay, or poem for planning purposes, and they may copy short works (poems that are less than 250 words or prose that is less than 2,500 words) for one-time use in the classroom. However, they may not create class anthologies by copying material from several sources or charge students more than it cost them to copy the materials. In addition, pages from workbooks or other consumable materials may not be copied.

Videotapes and computer software pose unique challenges. They, too, were created by and belong to someone, and fair-use guidelines also apply to them. For example, teachers may record a television program, but they must use it within 10 days. They may show it again for reinforcement but must erase the recording after 45 days. One copy, and no more, of software may be made as a "backup." Materials on the Internet may not be copied unless specific permission is given or unless the document is published by the federal government.

These guidelines restrict teachers, but the restrictions are not usually a major handicap. Teachers should share the principle of fair use with students to help them understand its purpose and the ways that copyright laws help protect people.

Teacher Liability

An elementary teacher on playground duty was mingling with students, watching them as they ran around. After the teacher passed one group of students, a boy picked up and threw a rock that hit another boy in the eye, causing serious injury. The injured boy's parents sued the teacher for negligence. (Fagen v. Summers, 1972)

A teacher was taking a group of first graders on a school-sponsored field trip to the Oregon coast. While some of the students were wading in the water, a big wave rolled in, bringing a big log with it, and one of the children was seriously injured. The parents sued the teacher for negligence. (Morris v. Douglas County School District, 1965)

We don't typically think of schools as dangerous, but large numbers of children in small spaces combined with youthful exuberance and energy can result in falls, scrapes,

Copyright laws Federal laws designed to protect the intellectual property of authors, which includes printed matter, videos, computer software, and various other types of original work.

Fair-use guidelines Policies that specify limitations in the use of copyrighted materials for educational purposes.

and accidents. And, field trips, science labs, woodworking shops, and physical education classes pose special risks.

Teachers are legally responsible for the safety of children under their supervision. The courts employ the principle of **in loco parentis**, which means "in place of the parents," in gauging the limits of teacher responsibility. *In loco parentis* requires teachers to use the same judgment and care as parents in protecting the children under their supervision (Darden, 2007a). **Negligence** is a teacher's or other school employee's failure to exercise sufficient care in protecting students from injury. If negligence occurs, parents may bring a liability suit against a teacher or school district. Liability suits are a major concern of experienced teachers, influencing their day-to-day professional decision making (Public Agenda, 2004).

In attempting to define the limits of teachers' responsibilities in liability cases, the courts consider whether teachers do the following:

- Make a reasonable attempt to anticipate dangerous conditions
- Take proper precautions and establish rules and procedures to prevent injuries
- Warn students of possible dangerous situations
- Provide proper supervision

In applying these principles to the rock-throwing incident, the courts found no direct connection between the teacher's actions and the child's injury. The teacher was properly supervising the children, and events happened so quickly that she was unable to prevent the accident. Had she witnessed, and failed to stop, a similar incident, or had she left the playground for personal reasons, the court's decision would probably have been different.

Field trips pose special safety and legal challenges because of the dangers of transportation and the increased possibility of injury in unfamiliar surroundings. Many school districts ask parents to sign a consent form to inform them of the trip and release school personnel from liability in case of injury. These forms don't do the latter, however; even with signed forms, teachers are still responsible for the safety of the children in their care. The courts ruled in favor of the parents in the Oregon case, because this type of accident is fairly common on beaches along the Oregon coast. The teacher, they ruled, should have anticipated the accident and acted accordingly.

As they supervise, teachers need to consider the ages and developmental levels of students, as well as the type of classroom activity. Young children require more supervision, for example, as do some students with special needs. Science labs, cooking classes, use of certain equipment, and physical education classes pose special safety hazards. Professional organizations, such as the National Science Teachers Association, provide guidelines to help teachers avoid liability-causing situations in their classroom (D. Hoff, 2003), and beginning teachers should be familiar with their guidelines. In addition, teachers should carefully plan ahead, anticipate potential dangers, and teach safety rules and procedures to all students.

In spite of conscientious planning, accidents can and do happen. Beginning teachers should consider the liability insurance offered by professional organizations, which provides legal assistance to members who are sued. In addition, new teachers should check with the districts that employ them for liability coverage. Some type of liability coverage is a good idea for all teachers; for those in riskier areas such as science, vocational education, or sports, it probably is a professional necessity.

This section addresses the second item on our *This I Believe* feature, "Teachers are responsible for the safety of the students in their classrooms." This statement is true. *In loco parentis* suggests that teachers are indeed responsible for the students in their care. Factors such as the age and intelligence of the students, as well as dangers inherent in a particular situation, should guide your actions as you strive to protect the welfare of your students.

In loco parentis A principle meaning "in place of the parents" that requires teachers to use the same judgment and care as parents in protecting the children under their supervision.

Negligence A teacher's or other school employee's failure to exercise sufficient care in protecting students from injury.

Child Abuse

> *Jimmy is a quiet, shy fourth grader. He rarely volunteers in class and seems to withdraw from interactions with the rest of the children. He is underweight, and efforts to sign him up for federally financed lunches have been rebuffed by his parents, who assert they don't need help from anyone.*
>
> *One day you notice a bruise on Jimmy's face. When you talk to him at lunch break, he says he fell while playing, but there aren't any scrapes or abrasions typically associated with a fall. You ask him how things are at home, and his eyes fill with tears. You ask him if he wants to talk about it; he just shakes his head no. When you ask him if someone hit him, he blurts out, "Please don't say anything, or I'll get in trouble."*

What are your responsibilities in this situation? The student begged you to say nothing; do you honor his request? The answer is no. All 50 states and the District of Columbia have laws requiring educators to report suspected child abuse (Fischer et al., 2006). In addition, teachers are protected from legal action if they act in "good faith" and "without malice." Teachers suspecting child abuse should immediately report the matter to school counselors or administrators. Schools generally have an established process for dealing with cases of suspected child abuse, and these guidelines help new teachers understand their role in the process.

Teachers' Private Lives

> *Gary Hansen has lived with the same male roommate for several years. They are often seen shopping together in the local community, and they even attend social events together. Students and other faculty "talk," but Gary ignores suggestions that he's homosexual until the principal calls him into his office, confronts him, and threatens dismissal.*
>
> *Mary Evans has taught in Chicago for more than 8 years and doesn't mind the long commute from the suburbs because it gives her an opportunity to "clear her head." She has been living with her boyfriend for several years, and everything has seemed fine until one day she discovers that she's pregnant. After lengthy discussions with her partner, she decides to keep the baby but not get married. When her pregnancy becomes noticeable, her principal calls her in. She affirms that she isn't married and doesn't intend to be. He asks for her resignation, suggesting she is a poor role model for her students.*

An individual's right to "life, liberty, and the pursuit of happiness" is one of our country's founding principles. What happens, however, when teachers' lifestyles conflict with those of the community where they work? Are teachers' private lives really "private," or can teachers be dismissed for what they do in their free time?

In answering these questions, the courts have relied on a definition of teaching that's broader than classroom instruction. Teachers do more than help students understand English and history, for example: They also serve as role models. As a result, teachers are scrutinized more closely than people in general. Other professionals, such as attorneys or physicians,

Teachers have a right to their own private lives but must meet community standards of acceptable conduct.

might be able to lead lifestyles at odds with community values, but teachers might not. What are teachers' rights with respect to their private lives?

Clear answers in this area don't exist. Morality and what constitutes a good role model are contextual. For example, in the 1800s, women's teaching contracts required them to

- abstain from marriage;
- be home between the hours of 8:00 P.M. and 6:00 A.M. unless attending school functions;
- wear dresses no more than 2 inches above the ankle.

More recently, pregnant teachers were required, even if married, to take a leave of absence once their condition became noticeable. Obviously, views of morality change. As the California Supreme Court noted, "Today's morals may be tomorrow's ancient and absurd customs" (Fischer, Schimmel, & Kelley, 2003, p. 265).

Moral standards also vary among communities: What's acceptable in large cities may not be in the suburbs or rural areas. Cities also provide a measure of anonymity, and notoriety is one criterion courts use to decide whether teachers' private activities damage their credibility as role models. **Notoriety** describes the extent to which a teacher's behavior becomes known and is controversial. For example, many young people are choosing to live together as an alternative to marriage, and this lifestyle is obviously less noticeable in a large city than in smaller communities.

Where does this leave teachers? Generalizations such as "Consider the community in which you live and teach" provide some guidance, as do representative court cases. The law isn't clear and specific, however, with respect to teachers' private behavior.

The issue of homosexuality illustrates how schools can become legal battlegrounds for people's differing beliefs. Some people believe that homosexuality is morally wrong and that people who are homosexual shouldn't be allowed to work with young people; others believe that whether a person is homosexual is irrelevant to schools and teaching. When the issue has gone to courts, they have generally ruled in favor of homosexual teachers. In a landmark California case, a teacher's homosexual relationship was reported to the state board of education, which revoked his license. The board argued that state law required teachers to be models of good conduct, and that homosexual behavior is inconsistent with the moral standards of the people of California (*Morrison v. State Board of Education*, 1969). The California Supreme Court disagreed, concluding that "immoral" was broad enough to be interpreted in a number of ways and stating that no evidence existed indicating that Morrison's behavior adversely affected his teaching effectiveness.

In other cases involving criminal or public sexual behavior, such as soliciting sex in a park, courts have ruled against teachers (Fischer et al., 2006). Notoriety was a key element in these cases.

The case involving the unwed mother further illustrates the murkiness of school law. A case in Nebraska in 1976 resulted in the dismissal of an unwed mother because the school board claimed there was "a rational connection between the plaintiff's pregnancy out of wedlock and the school board's interest in conserving marital values" (*Brown v. Bathhe*, 1976). In other cases, however, courts have ruled in favor of pregnant unwed teachers, including one in Ohio who became pregnant through artificial insemination (Fischer et al., 2006).

Although the law is ambiguous with respect to teachers' private sexual lives, it is clear regarding sexual relations with students (Hendrie, 2003). Teachers are in a position of authority and trust, and any breach of this trust will result in dismissal. When teachers take sexual advantage of their students, they violate both legal and ethical standards.

Other teacher behaviors can also jeopardize their jobs. Drug offenses, excessive drinking, driving under the influence of alcohol, felony arrests, and even a misdemeanor, such as shoplifting, can result in dismissal (Fischer et al., 2006). The message is clear: Teachers are legally and ethically required to be good role models for their students.

Notoriety The extent to which a teacher's behavior becomes known and is controversial.

Teacher Tenure

As you saw earlier in our discussion of teachers' rights and responsibilities, tenure is designed to protect teachers from political or personal abuses and to ensure the stability of the teaching force. But tenure has come under fire by some educational reformers, who believe it's holding back the progress of the teaching profession (Bernstein, 2006). In 1997, lawmakers in Oregon eliminated tenure for teachers, replacing it with 2-year contracts (A. Bradley, 1999). Georgia followed suit in 2000 and attempted to pass legislation that would shorten the amount of time it takes to fire incompetent teachers (J. Reeves, 2004). Talk of similar measures has been heard in other states and districts across the country.

THE ISSUE

Critics of tenure contend that it's outdated and unfair, providing teachers with protections that other professionals don't have. Further, they argue, it's unnecessary, because the existing system provides legal recourse to teachers who believe they have been wrongly dismissed (J. Johnson, 2004).

Most importantly, critics assert, it's virtually impossible to remove a tenured teacher, regardless of performance, which means that tenure protects incompetent teachers. For example, one study of 30 school districts found that only slightly more than one tenth of 1 percent of teachers believed to be incompetent were either dismissed or persuaded to resign (A. Bradley, 1999). Another study, focusing on five urban districts, found that during 1 year only 4 out of a total of 70,000 tenured teachers were formally terminated (Rhee & Levin, 2006). Districts typically respond to the issue by moving incompetent teachers from school to school instead of taking them out of classrooms.

On the other hand, supporters of tenure argue that it was created to protect teachers from political or personal pressure and that it continues to serve that function (Fischer et al., 2006). Teachers who have tenure are more likely to address controversial issues in class without fear of retribution. In addition, tenured teachers are more likely to become politically active, especially in school-related issues such as school board elections and bond issues.

Supporters also contend that teachers need protection from the potential abuse of power that can exist if a principal or other district leader conducts a personal vendetta against a teacher for unprofessional reasons. In addition, during times of teacher shortages, the job security that tenure provides is an incentive for teachers to go into or remain in teaching.

Not surprisingly, administrators and teachers differ dramatically on the issue in polls. For example, 8 of 10 superintendents and 2 of 3 principals believe that good teachers don't have to worry about tenure and think it's hard to justify. On the other hand, nearly 6 of 10 teachers believe that tenure is an important safeguard that protects them from politics, favoritism, and the possibility of losing their jobs to newcomers who could work for less (J. Johnson, 2004).

YOU TAKE A STAND

Now it's your turn to take a position on the issue. Should teacher tenure be abolished or retained?

myeducationlab To explore both sides of this issue and take a stand, go to the *Book Specific Resources* section in the MyEducationLab for your course, select your text, and then select *Taking a Stand in an Era of Reform* for Chapter 10.

ISSUES IN EDUCATION

This section addresses the third item in our *This I Believe* feature, "Teachers are held to the same moral standards as other citizens." This statement isn't true: They are, in fact, held to higher moral standards because they serve as role models for their students.

TEACHERS WITH AIDS   In determining the rights of teachers with AIDS (acquired immune deficiency syndrome) or HIV (human immunodeficiency virus) infections, the courts have generally used nondiscrimination as the legal principle guiding their decisions. The foundation for this principle was established in 1987 in a case involving a Florida teacher with tuberculosis (*School Board of Nassau County, Florida v. Arline*, 1987). The courts' dilemma involved weighing the rights of the individual against the public's concern about the possible spread of disease. The U.S. Supreme Court ruled in favor of the teacher, considering the disease a handicap and protecting the teacher from discrimination because of it.

The Florida decision set a precedent for a California case involving a teacher with AIDS who had been removed from the classroom and reassigned to administrative duties

(*Chalk v. U.S. District Court Cent. Dist. of California*, 1988). The court ruled in favor of the teacher, using medical opinion to argue that the teacher's right to employment outweighed the minor risk of communicating the AIDS virus to children.

Teacher tenure, long considered a teacher right, is becoming a controversial issue nationally. In the box on page 299, we consider the pros and cons of this teacher safeguard.

■ ■ ■ ■ CHECK YOUR UNDERSTANDING

3.1   How are teacher employment issues influenced by the law?

3.2   What is *academic freedom*, and why is it important to teachers?

3.3   How do copyright laws influence teachers' practices?

3.4   What is *teacher liability*, and how does it influence teachers?

3.5   How are teachers' rights regarding their private lives similar to and different from those of the general public?

For feedback, go to the appendix, *Check Your Understanding*, located in the back of this text.

RELIGION AND THE LAW

Religion provides fertile ground for helping us understand how conflicting views of education can result in legal challenges. Religion plays an important role in U.S. citizens' lives: 9 of 10 people claim a preference for some religious group, and nearly 6 of 10 regard their religious beliefs to be very important to them (Rose & Gallup, 2006; Winseman, 2005).

The First Amendment to the Constitution provides for the principle of separation of church and state:

> Congress shall make no law respecting an establishment of religion, or prohibiting the free exercise thereof; or abridging the freedom of speech, or of the press; or the right

Although the Constitution forbids the establishment of any particular religion in schools, a number of complex issues make this a controversial topic.

of the people peaceably to assemble, and to petition the Government for a redress of grievances.

Each of the six clauses of the amendment presents an important legal principle. The amendment begins with the **establishment clause**, the clause that prohibits the establishment of a national religion. The words "or prohibiting the free exercise thereof" is the **free exercise clause**, the clause that prohibits the government from interfering with individuals' rights to hold religious beliefs and freely practice religion. The interpretation of both of these clauses has led to legal battles (Sorenson, 2007).

Because religion is central to people's lives, the issue of religion in schools is legally contentious, and educators are often caught in the crossfire. Important questions that have arisen include the following:

- Are students and teachers allowed to pray in schools?
- Can religion be included in the school curriculum?
- Are religious clubs allowed access to public school facilities?

We answer these questions in the sections that follow.

Prayer in Schools

In the past, prayer and scripture reading were common in many, if not most, schools. In fact, they were required by law in some states. For example, Pennsylvania passed legislation in 1959 that required daily Bible reading in the schools, but exempted children whose parents didn't want them to participate. The law was challenged, and the U.S. Supreme Court ruled that it violated the First Amendment's establishment clause (*Abington School District v. Schempp*, 1963). Nondenominational or generic prayers designed to skirt the issue of promoting a specific religion have also been outlawed. In a New York case, the Supreme Court held that generic prayers violated the establishment clause as well (*Engle v. Vitale*, 1962). Neither schools nor teachers can officially encourage student prayer; prayer is permissible, however, when student initiated and when it doesn't interfere with other students or the functioning of the school (Underwood & Webb, 2006).

The law also forbids the official use of religious symbols in schools. For example, the courts ruled that a 2-by-3-foot portrait of Jesus Christ displayed in the hallway next to the principal's office was unconstitutional (Fischer et al., 2006). Also, the U.S. Supreme Court struck down a Kentucky law requiring that the Ten Commandments be posted in school classrooms (*Stone v. Graham*, 1981).

These cases illustrate a clear legal trend: Officially sanctioned prayer and religious symbols—whether they come from school boards, principals, or teachers—are not allowed in public schools (Sorenson, 2007). They violate the principle of separation of church and state, which was designed to accommodate religious diversity. Students may be Christians, Jews, Muslims, Buddhists, Hindus, or members of other religions. Imposing a particular form of prayer or religion on children in a school can be both illegal and unethical, because it can exclude children on the basis of religion. However, the recent No Child Left Behind (NCLB) Act of 2001 requires each district receiving federal funds to certify that "it has no policy that prevents or otherwise denies participation in constitutionally protected prayer in public schools." So, although schools can't officially promote a particular religion, neither can they prohibit students from privately praying.

Although the courts have been clear about denying prayer as a regular part of schools' opening ceremonies, the issue of prayer at graduation and other school activities is less clear. In a landmark case, a high school principal asked a clergyman to provide the graduation invocation and also suggested the content of the prayer. This was ruled a violation of separation of church and state by the U.S. Supreme Court (*Lee v. Weismann*, 1992). The school's involvement in the prayer was the key point; whether the Court would have

Establishment clause The clause of the First Amendment that prohibits the establishment of a national religion.

Free exercise clause The clause of the First Amendment that prohibits the government from interfering with individuals' rights to hold religious beliefs and freely practice religion.

banned the prayer if it had been initiated by students or parents is uncertain. The Supreme Court also voted 6–3 against student-led prayers at football games in Texas (M. Walsh, 2000a); the Court concluded that students would perceive the pregame prayer as "stamped with the school's seal of approval," thus violating separation of church and state.

In a recent twist on the school prayer issue, several states have instituted mandatory moments of silence in schools (Darden, 2007b). Critics contend these pauses are nothing more than veiled attempts to institute a minute of prayer; advocates say they are designed to help students relax and focus on the day ahead. Courts have used the "Lemon" test to judge the legality of these moments of silence, named after a landmark legal case in this area, *Lemon v. Kurtzman* (1971). In applying the test, the courts ask these questions:

- Is there a secular purpose to the practice?
- Is the primary effect to advance or inhibit religion?
- Does the practice avoid excessive government entanglement in issues of religion?

When applying these criteria to state laws, the courts look to the reasons behind the laws (Darden, 2008a). If the reasons are secular, the laws are allowed to stand; if religious intents are involved, the laws are ruled unconstitutional.

This section addresses the fourth item in our *This I Believe* feature, "The law prohibits any form of prayer in the schools." The law doesn't prohibit prayer in the schools per se. Students can legally pray in school, but neither school officials nor teachers can lead or sanction organized prayer in schools.

This I BELIEVE

Religious Clubs and Organizations

Organized prayer in schools is illegal, but it may be legal for extracurricular religious clubs to meet on school grounds. In one instance, a student in Omaha, Nebraska, requested permission to meet with her Bible study group before school. Officials refused, concerned about the possibility of undesirable groups, such as the Ku Klux Klan, using the case as precedent. The U.S. Supreme Court ruled in the student's favor, stating that schools must allow religious, philosophical, and political groups to use school facilities in the same ways as other extracurricular organizations (*Board of Education of the Westside Community School v. Mergens*, 1990). The fact that the club was not school sponsored or initiated was central to the Court's argument.

A link between church and state may also be permissible in some situations involving religious organizations: For instance, the Supreme Court approved the use of federally funded computers and library books for Catholic schools in Louisiana (M. Walsh, 2000a). The principle of separation of church and state will likely be revisited in future educational court cases.

Religion in the Curriculum

A high school biology teacher prefaces his presentation on evolution with a warning, stating that it is only a "theory" and that many theories have been proven wrong in the past. He encourages students to keep an open mind and offers creationism, or the Biblical version of the origin of the world, as an alternative theory. As part of his presentation, he holds up a pamphlet, published by a religious organization; the pamphlet refutes evolution and argues that creationism provides a more valid explanation. He offers the pamphlets to interested students.

Where does religion fit in the school curriculum? Can a well-intentioned teacher use the classroom to promote his or her religious views? Given court decisions on school prayer, a simplistic answer might be "no" or "never." But considering the enormous influence that religion has had on human history—as evidenced in art and literature—the issue becomes more complex.

Evolution is one point of tension. Concern over this issue dates back to the famous 1925 "Scopes Monkey Trial," in which a high school teacher, John Scopes, was prosecuted for violating a Tennessee state law that made it illegal to teach any theory that denied the divine creation of man as taught in the Bible and to teach, instead, that man is descended from animals. Scopes argued that the law violated his academic freedom, contending that the theory of evolution had scientific merit and should be shared with his high school biology students. Scopes was found guilty of violating the state law and fined $100, but the decision was later reversed on a technicality.

Several states have since attempted to use legislation to resolve the evolution issue. In the 1960s, the Arkansas legislature passed a law banning the teaching of evolution in that state. The U.S. Supreme Court declared the law unconstitutional, because it violated the establishment clause of the First Amendment. In 1982, the Louisiana legislature, trying to create a middle ground, passed a "Balanced Treatment Act," requiring that evolution and creationism be given equal treatment in the curriculum. The U.S. Supreme Court also threw this law out, arguing that instead of being balanced, it was designed to promote a particular religious viewpoint.

In a more recent case involving religion in the public schools, a federal judge in Pennsylvania ruled that intelligent design did not qualify as a scientific theory (Cavanagh, 2006b; Whitson, 2006). *Intelligent design* is the belief that the complexity we see in living things, including humans, is the result of some unnamed guiding force. The Dover, Pennsylvania, school board voted to require that intelligent design be taught as an alternative to evolution. Parents in the district sued, claiming that intelligent design was an attempt to interject religion into the public schools. The judge agreed, concluding, "The overwhelming evidence at trial established that ID [intelligent design] is a religious view, a mere relabeling of creationism, and not a scientific theory" (Cavanagh, 2006b, p. 10). Although the court's ruling has legal standing only in the U.S. District Court for the Middle District of Pennsylvania, legal experts predict that it will carry considerable weight in any future cases involving intelligent design.

The broader issue of religion in the curriculum has also surfaced in several other court cases. In Tennessee, fundamentalist parents objected to including literature such as *The Wizard of Oz*, *Rumpelstiltskin*, and *Macbeth* in the curriculum, arguing that these works exposed children to feminism, witchcraft, pacifism, and vegetarianism. A lower court supported the parents, but a higher federal court reversed the decision, asserting that accommodating every parent's religious claims would "leave public education goals in shreds." It supported the right of districts to use religiously controversial materials if they were useful in achieving important educational goals (*Mozert v. Hawkins County Public Schools*, 1987, 1988). Comparable cases in Alabama (*Smith v. Board of School Commissioners of Mobile County*, 1987) and Illinois (*Fleischfresser v. Directors of School District No. 200*, 1994) resulted in similar outcomes. When schools can show that learning materials have a clear purpose, such as exposing students to time-honored literature, parental objections are usually overridden.

Teaching About Religion in the Schools

Legal controversies have had a dampening effect on teaching about religion in the schools (Hutton, 2008). Here we emphasize the difference between teaching *about different religions* and advocating a particular one. Religion has had an enormous impact on history (e.g., the Crusades, New World exploration) as well as on art and literature. Avoiding the study of religion leaves students in a cultural vacuum that shortchanges their education (Kunzman, 2006).

PEARSON
myeducationlab

To see a video of this controversy in one school district, go to the *Assignments and Activities* section of Topic 4: *Ethical and Legal Issues* in the MyEducationLab for your course and complete the activity titled *Battle Between Faith and Science*.

ISSUES IN EDUCATION

But how can schools teach about religion without provoking religious controversies? The U.S. Department of Education wrestled with this problem and developed the following guidelines (U.S. Department of Education, 1999b):

- Teachers and administrators in public schools should not advocate any religion.
- Public schools should not interfere with or intrude on a student's religious beliefs.
- Public schools may teach about the history of religion, comparative religions, the Bible as literature, and the role of religion in the history of the United States and other countries.

Critics caution that the Bible should not be used as a history textbook, should not be taught exclusively from a Christian perspective, and should not be used to promote the Christian faith or Christian values (Hutton, 2008). To address this issue, the First Amendment Center (1999), a national organization promoting free speech, published the guidelines *The Bible and Public Schools: A First Amendment Guide*. The guidelines, endorsed by the National Education Association, the American Federation of Teachers, and the National School Boards Association, recommend using secondary sources to provide additional scholarly perspectives with respect to the Bible as a historical document. These guidelines seem straightforward, but future legal battles over this emotion-laden issue are likely.

PEARSON
myeducationlab

To learn more about the legal aspects of religion and education, go to the *Assignments and Activities* section of Topic 4: *Ethical and Legal Issues* in the MyEducationLab for your course and complete the activity titled *Religion and the Law*.

CHECK YOUR UNDERSTANDING

4.1 Describe the legal implications of religion in the schools.

4.2 What is the legal status of prayer in schools?

4.3 Can a school allow religious clubs or organizations to meet on school grounds?

4.4 What is the legal status of religion in the curriculum?

For feedback, go to the appendix, *Check Your Understanding*, located in the back of this text.

STUDENTS' RIGHTS AND RESPONSIBILITIES

The law also helps define students' rights and responsibilities, and understanding them can guide you in your work with students. Students' rights and responsibilities fall into six general areas, outlined in Figure 10.2 and discussed in the sections that follow.

Students' Freedom of Speech

URBAN EDUCATION

Many parents in an urban middle school are advocating mandatory school uniforms. They believe that wearing uniforms would reduce classroom management problems, discourage the display of gang colors, and minimize social comparisons between wealthy students and those less fortunate. The school administration supports the proposal.

The student editors of the school newspaper hear of this proposal and conduct a poll of students, which indicates that a majority is opposed to uniforms. The editors want to publish these results along with an editorial arguing for student choice in what to wear. The principal refuses to let them print the article. What are students' rights in this matter?

Figure 10.2 Students' Rights and Responsibilities

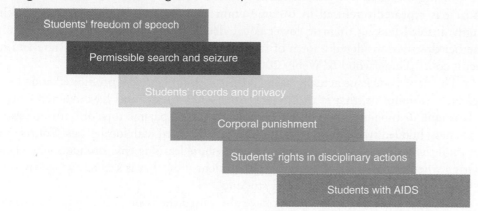

As you've seen throughout this chapter, the First Amendment guarantees citizens freedom of speech, and we want our students to understand and appreciate this right as they prepare to be responsible citizens. Do they retain the right when they enter schools? Yes, but within limits: They have the right to express themselves in schools provided doing so doesn't interfere with learning.

A landmark case in this area occurred in the late 1960s, during the peak of the Vietnam War. As a protest against the war, three high school students wore black armbands to school, despite the school's ban on such protests (*Tinker v. Des Moines Community School District*, 1969). When the students were suspended, they sued the district, arguing that the suspensions violated their freedom of speech. The case went all the way to the U.S. Supreme Court, which ruled in favor of the students. The Court ruled that freedom of speech is a right of all citizens and that students' freedom of expression should not be curtailed if it isn't disruptive and doesn't interfere with the educational mission of the schools (Fossey & Russo, 2008; Mercurio & Morse, 2007).

Students' freedom of speech was tested again in 1986. During a high school assembly held to nominate student government leaders, a student made a speech that contained an explicit metaphor comparing a candidate to a male sex organ. Not surprisingly, students in the audience hooted, made sexual gestures, and became disruptive. The student was reprimanded, and he sued, claiming his freedom of speech had been curtailed. This case also went to the U.S. Supreme Court, which ruled that "schools . . . may determine that the essential lessons of civil, mature conduct cannot be conveyed in a school that tolerates lewd, indecent or offensive speech" (*Bethel School District No. 403 v. Fraser*, 1986). In this instance, the court ruled that the school didn't violate the student's freedom of speech because the speech interfered with learning.

School newspapers pose a special problem with respect to freedom of speech. Court rulings usually reflect the idea that a school newspaper is an integral part of a school's extracurricular activities and should be consistent with the school's goals (Zirkel, 2001/2002). In a pivotal case, students working on a newspaper wanted to print two articles, one detailing the personal stories of three anonymous, pregnant teenage students, and the other dealing with the effects of divorce on children. The principal objected, arguing that the students in the first story might be identified because of details in the articles. The newspaper authors sued, but the U.S. Supreme Court decided that school newspapers could be regulated in cases of "legitimate pedagogical concerns" (*Hazelwood School District v. Kuhlmeier*, 1988).

STUDENT DRESS CODES   Look around you as you go to class and notice the different ways that students dress. How we dress is often an expression of who we are, but is student dress an aspect of free speech covered by the First Amendment? The answer is complex, as you saw in the case involving student protests against the Vietnam War.

Recognizing the complexity of the issue and the need for local norms, the Supreme Court has repeatedly refused to become embroiled in issues such as hair and skirt length, instead leaving them to lower court decisions (LaMorte, 2005). As a result, whether dress is considered a form of student expression depends on the state and its circuit court (Underwood & Webb, 2006).

The dress code issue actually has two sides—clothing that is prohibited and clothing, such as uniforms, that is required (Darden, 2008b). Schools have banned clothes such as tank or tube tops; ripped, baggy, or saggy pants; pajama tops or bottoms; sweat pants; hats; hooded sweatshirts; and athletic wear associated with local gangs. Courts usually ask if the restrictions contribute to positive school learning environments when considering whether they're legal. For example, student dress that is sexually suggestive can be banned because it can distract other students.

Messages and images on T-shirts have also raised the issue of students' freedom of speech (Hendrie, 2005c). In one case, a Virginia middle school banned a T-shirt with a National Rifle Association Shooting Sports Camp logo on the back containing three figures holding or shooting guns. The parents of the student objected, and the courts agreed, saying there was no link between the T-shirt and the district's ability to run safe and manageable schools (Galley, 2004). In a second case, schools banned a student from wearing a T-shirt with the message "Homosexuality is shameful." A federal court upheld the ban, arguing that schools can limit a student's right to free speech when the content of that speech harms other students (Trotter, 2006b). This means that schools can prohibit students from saying things at school that demean students who are members of particular groups, such as gay, Black, Islamic, and Jewish (Mercurio & Morse, 2007). School officials must protect students' freedom of speech but must also protect the rights of others and maintain the efficient operation of their schools.

SCHOOL UNIFORMS   Largely in response to students' wearing gang colors, a growing number of public schools are requiring school uniforms. Proponents claim that gang clothing and designer sports clothes contribute to violence and delinquency. Initial experiments in Baltimore and Long Beach, California, were promising, and a number of districts, including those in New York, Chicago, Miami, and Phoenix, allow schools to require uniforms (Konheim-Kalkstein, 2006).

Proponents of school uniforms also argue that they contribute to improved classroom behavior and respect for teachers, increased school attendance, better academic performance, lower clothing costs, reduced social stratification, and lower rates of crime and violence (Konheim-Kalkstein, 2006). Although uniforms are popular with parents and administrators, critics counter that requiring them violates students' rights, students will find other ways to compete, and uniforms have minimal effect on either behavior or achievement. Instead, they argue, the positive effects are due to greater parental involvement in the school and a visible and public symbol of commitment to school improvement and reform (DeMitchele, 2007).

Currently, half the states have at least one district that requires school uniforms, and the figure is likely to increase in the future (LaMorte, 2005). The courts have generally supported the use of mandatory school uniforms, concluding that they contribute to improved student behavior (Fischer et al., 2006).

What should you strive to teach your students about freedom of speech? You should encourage them to express their opinions, both verbally and in writing, because ideas promote learning and because the process prepares them to take stands and describe their views later in life. But you should also teach them that individual freedoms have limits; for example, they don't have the right to infringe on the rights of others. By encouraging open exchange of ideas while reminding students of their responsibilities to one another, you can create a classroom that becomes a model of democracy. This is a powerful and worthwhile ideal.

Permissible Search and Seizure

The Fourth Amendment to the Constitution protects U.S. citizens from unlawful search and seizure, and warrants are required before a person or that person's property can be searched. How do these protections apply to students? Again, educators face dilemmas. We don't want to run our schools like prisons or teach students that personal privacy is not a right. But because drug and alcohol use and violence on school campuses remain persistent problems, many leaders feel compelled to search students and their property or even use entryway metal detectors and surveillance cameras to maintain safe schools (Warnick, 2007). Where do courts draw the line on the issue?

School officials may search student lockers if they have probable cause to believe they contain something illegal or dangerous.

The issue of unlawful search and seizure surfaced in New Jersey in the 1980s when a teacher discovered two girls smoking cigarettes in a high school restroom. When questioned by the vice principal, one admitted smoking and the other, T.L.O., denied the charge. The vice principal opened T.L.O.'s purse and found both cigarettes and rolling papers, which prompted him to empty the purse where he discovered marijuana, a pipe, empty plastic bags, a number of dollar bills, and a list titled "People who owe me money" (*New Jersey v. T.L.O.*, 1985). T.L.O. confessed that she had been selling marijuana at school and was sentenced to a year's probation by the juvenile court.

T.L.O. appealed the ruling, claiming that she was the victim of an illegal search. The U.S. Supreme Court reviewed the evidence and upheld both the verdict and the legality of the search, concluding that school searches are legal if they target a problem. But schools must have probable cause to conduct the search; that is, they must have a reasonable suspicion that the student being searched deserves the treatment (Zirkel, 2001/2002).

In addition to probable cause, the nature of the search is important: Does it involve passing through a metal detector or opening a school bag, or is it more intrusive? The courts have consistently upheld the legality of metal detectors at school entrances, asserting that such searches are nonintrusive (Fischer et al., 2006). More intrusive strip searches, however, are generally considered illegal. In one case, a high school student was strip-searched after a police dog mistakenly identified her as carrying drugs. (Authorities later found that the dog was drawn to the girl because earlier in the day she had been playing with her dog, which was in heat.) The school district was required to pay damages to the girl's family (*Doe v. Renfrow*, 1980). In a more recent case, high school students were required to strip to their underwear in an attempt to recover missing money ($364) (Hendrie, 2005a). A federal circuit court found the search unconstitutional, concluding that the missing money did not justify the intrusiveness of the search. While condoning searches for probable cause, the courts remain sensitive to the rights of students (Ehlenberger, 2001/2002). School lockers, however, are considered school property and may be searched if reasonable cause, such as suspicion of drug or weapon possession, exists.

The use of urine tests to detect drug use illustrates how legal issues can become convoluted. In one case, the Supreme Court held that random drug testing for student athletes was legal, arguing that the safety of students and the importance of a drug-free school environment outweighed the privacy rights of student athletes who were participating voluntarily (*Board of Education of Independent School District No. 92 of Pottawatomie County v. Earls*, 2002). Despite this ruling, which involved students in voluntary school activities, the courts have been unanimous in prohibiting schoolwide drug testing (Underwood & Webb, 2006).

Student Records and Privacy

Students' records—grades, standardized test scores, teacher comments, and letters of recommendation—can determine whether they are admitted to special programs or colleges of their choice. Records also influence students' ability to get jobs. What legal safeguards guide the creation and use of these records?

In 1974, Congress passed the Family Educational Rights and Privacy Act (FERPA) as an amendment to the Elementary and Secondary Education Act of 1965. Also called the **Buckley Amendment**, FERPA is a federal act that makes school records accessible to students and their parents. Under this act, schools must do the following:

1. Inform parents of their rights regarding their child's records.

2. Provide parents access to their child's records.

3. Maintain procedures that allow parents to challenge and possibly amend information that they believe is inaccurate.

4. Protect parents from disclosure of confidential information to third parties without their consent.

The law doesn't guarantee access to all student records, however. For example, teachers may jot down notes during a busy school day, such as reminders about a student's behavior that will help the teacher decide whether to refer a child for special education testing; these notes can't be made public without the teacher's consent. Also, a teacher's letter of recommendation may remain confidential if students waive their rights to access. To protect teachers in these situations, the Buckley Amendment excludes teachers' private notes, grade books, or correspondence with administrators.

A court case in Oklahoma further defined the types of information protected by the Buckley Amendment (M. Walsh, 2002b). A mother objected to the practice of having her children's papers graded by other students and the results called out in class; she claimed this violated her children's rights to privacy, and a federal circuit court agreed. But in a unanimous decision, the Supreme Court overturned the lower court's decision, concluding that the term *education records* didn't cover student homework or classroom work.

Administrators and teachers have mixed feelings about the Buckley Amendment because of the extra effort and paperwork required to put the procedural safeguards into place and because of potential encroachments into teachers' private records. The law has improved parents' access to information, however, and it has made school officials more sensitive to the importance of confidentiality in dealing with students' and parents' needs for information.

Corporal Punishment

In a Pennsylvania elementary school, a 36-year-old, 6-foot, 210-pound school principal paddled a 45-pound first-grade boy four times during one school day for a total of 60 to 70 swats. After the incident, the boy needed psychological counseling, cried frequently, and had nightmares and trouble sleeping. (Commonwealth of Pennsylvania v. Douglass, 1991)

The Fayette County Board of Education in Tennessee specified in 1994 that any paddles used to discipline students must be

- *Not less than 3/8 inch or more than 1/2 inch thick*
- *Free of splinters*
- *Constructed of quality white ash*

Buckley Amendment A federal law, also called the Family Educational Rights and Privacy Act, that describes who may have access to a student's educational records.

- *Three inches wide (except the handle) and not more than 15 inches long for grades K–5*

- *Three and a half inches wide (except the handle), and not more than 18 inches long for grades 6–12*

Students can receive a maximum of three swats with these district-approved paddles. (R. Johnston, 1994)

Corporal punishment—the use of physical, punitive disciplinary actions to correct student misbehavior—is highly controversial, because of the legal issues involved and the questionable effects of using physical punishment as a disciplinary tool. In a 1977 landmark case, the Supreme Court ruled that corporal punishment isn't a violation of the Eighth Amendment to the Constitution, which prohibits cruel and unusual punishment. The Court further ruled that states may authorize corporal punishment without either prior hearing or prior permission of parents (*Ingraham v. Wright*, 1977). In the 2007 school year, corporal punishment was used with a quarter of a million students, and is much more common in the South and the lower Midwest than in other parts of the country (Ferraro & Weinreich, 2006; Quaid, 2008). As of 2008, it was prohibited in 27 states and the District of Columbia, which means the door is left open for the use of corporal punishment in the remaining 23 states. Research also indicates that where it is legal, corporal punishment is more than twice as likely to be used on Black and Native American students than on those that are White (Quaid, 2008). So where does all this leave prospective teachers?

In states where corporal punishment is permitted, legal guidelines suggest teachers may use corporal punishment under the following conditions:

- The punishment is intended to correct misbehavior.

- Administering the punishment doesn't involve anger or malice.

- The punishment is neither cruel nor excessive and doesn't result in lasting injury.

Teachers considering this disciplinary option should ask themselves several questions:

- Is this the best way to teach students about inappropriate behavior?

- Would other options be more effective in encouraging students to consider their behaviors and the effects of those behaviors on others?

- What does corporal punishment teach children about the use of force to solve problems?

Psychologists disapprove of the use of corporal punishment, both because negative side effects, such as modeled aggression, can occur and because more effective alternatives exist (Berk, 2008). For example, properly administered, detention is an effective form of punishment, and doesn't include negative side effects. Because of both legal and psychological issues, we recommend that you avoid corporal punishment.

This section addresses the fifth item in our *This I Believe* feature, "Corporal punishment in schools is prohibited by law." This statement isn't true. As you saw, the majority of states (27) prohibit the use of corporal punishment, but it is legal in 23 others.

Students' Rights in Disciplinary Actions

Jessie Tynes, a sixth-grade teacher, turns around just in time to see Billy punch Jared.

"Billy, what did I tell you about keeping your hands to yourself?" Jessie demands. "There's no room for this nonsense in our school and our classroom! You're out of this class until I meet with your parents. Come with me to the principal's office where you'll sit until we can solve this problem of keeping your hands to yourself."

Corporal punishment The use of physical, punitive disciplinary actions to correct student misbehavior.

Sean, a high school junior, is walking to his locker when someone reaches in from behind to knock his books on the floor. When he turns around, he sees Dave standing behind him with a smirk on his face. Losing his temper, Sean pushes Dave. A scuffle begins, but it is broken up by Mr. Higgins, the vice principal. Both students receive 10-day suspensions.

How are the two incidents similar and different? Both involve infractions of school rules, but they differ in the severity of the problem and resulting actions. These differences are important when the courts consider due process. The Fourteenth Amendment to the Constitution states that no "state shall deprive any person of life, liberty, or property without due process of law." **Due process** is a key element related to students' rights in disciplinary matters.

Students have a right to an education, and courts specify that limiting this right can occur only when due process is followed. The courts, however, also acknowledge the rights of schools to discipline students in the day-to-day running of schools.

In our first example, suspending Billy is generally considered an internal affair best resolved by his teacher, his parents, and Billy himself. Unless a suspension lasts longer than 10 days or results in expulsion, teachers and administrators are usually free to discipline as they see fit, assuming the punishment is considered fair and equitable. The exact definition of due process varies from state to state, so you need to understand the specifics of the law in your state (Underwood & Webb, 2006).

Actions that lead to suspension, such as the incident between Sean and Dave, entry on a student's record, or permanent expulsion require more formalized safeguards. These include the following:

1. A written notice specifying charges and the time and place of a fair, impartial hearing

2. A description of the procedures to be used, including the nature of evidence and names of witnesses

3. The right of students to legal counsel and to cross-examine and present their own evidence

4. A written or taped record of the proceedings as well as the findings and recommendations

5. The right of appeal

As this list indicates, the procedures involved in long-term (longer than 10 days) suspensions and expulsions are detailed and formal. Because these actions consume considerable amounts of time and energy, schools generally use them only as a last resort.

DISCIPLINARY ACTIONS AND STUDENTS WITH EXCEPTIONALITIES   Students with exceptionalities are provided with additional legal safeguards under the Individuals with Disabilities Education Acts (IDEA) of 1997 and 2004. These laws were passed to ensure students with exceptionalities access to an education while safeguarding the rights of other students (Hardman, Drew, & Egan, 2006; Howard, 2009). IDEA 1997 enabled school administrators to discipline students with disabilities in the same way as students without disabilities but required them to review a change of placement, suspension, or expulsion in excess of 10 days. The purpose of this special review was to determine whether the student's behavior was related to a disability, such as a behavior disorder. If the review determined that the student's behavior wasn't related to the disability, the same disciplinary procedures used with other students could be imposed, but the school must still continue to provide educational services in the alternative placement.

IDEA 2004 revised these discipline procedures to make it easier to remove a student with disabilities under special circumstances, such as bringing a weapon to school; possessing, using, or selling illegal drugs at school; or inflicting serious injury to someone

myeducationlab

Go to the *Building Teaching Skills and Dispositions* section of Topic 4: *Ethical and Legal Issues* in the MyEducationLab for your course and complete the activity titled *Accommodations for Students with Exceptionalities.*

Due process A set of legal guidelines, based on the Fourteenth Amendment to the Constitution, that must be followed to protect individuals from arbitrary or capricious actions by those in authority.

at school. Under these circumstances, school officials can remove a student with disabilities to an interim alternative educational setting for up to 45 school days, regardless of whether the misconduct was related to the child's disability. This provision was designed to ensure the safety of other students and teachers.

Students With AIDS

AIDS became a major health and legal issue in the schools in the 1980s. Previously thought to be limited to sexually active gay men and drug users who shared hypodermic needles, AIDS entered the school-age population through contaminated blood transfusions.

Battle lines were quickly drawn. Concerned parents worried that the AIDS virus would be spread in school through either casual contact or the sometimes rough-and-tumble world of children on playgrounds. Parents of children with AIDS wanted their children to have access to as normal an education as possible. The courts were soon drawn into the fray.

A landmark and precedent-setting case occurred in St. Petersburg, Florida, in 1987 and involved 7-year-old Randy Ray, a hemophiliac infected with the AIDS virus through a blood transfusion. Because of his condition and fears about possible spread of the disease, school officials refused to allow Randy and his two brothers, who also were infected, to attend school. His parents first reacted by moving elsewhere, but when that failed to open school doors, they moved back to St. Petersburg and sued the school district.

A U.S. district court ruled that the boys should be allowed to attend school with special safeguards, including special attention to the potential hazards of blood spills (*Ray v. School District of DeSoto County*, 1987). Subsequent cases involving other students with HIV/AIDS have been similarly resolved, with courts holding that these children are protected by the Individuals with Disabilities Act of 1991 as well as Section 504 of the Rehabilitation Act of 1973, laws that prohibit discrimination against individuals with disabilities. Central to the courts' decisions has been the potential negative effects of exclusion on the social and emotional well-being of the child. The courts have been clear in rejecting exclusion as the automatic solution to the problem of dealing with HIV-infected students and instead have required schools to address the specific risk factors involved in each case.

In this chapter, we've seen that laws are designed not only to protect the rights of individuals but also to further the good of society; eliminating barriers to cultural minorities is a case in point. But federal efforts to eliminate the problem of racial segregation have thrust the U.S. legal system into controversy, as we see in the next section.

■ ■ ■ ■ CHECK YOUR UNDERSTANDING

5.1 What are students' rights with respect to freedom of speech?

5.2 Describe students' rights with respect to permissible search and seizure.

5.3 What is the Buckley Amendment? Why is it important to both schools and teachers?

5.4 Is corporal punishment legal in schools?

5.5 Describe students' rights with respect to disciplinary actions.

5.6 Describe the legal rights of students with AIDS.

For feedback, go to the appendix, *Check Your Understanding*, located in the back of this text.

We know that teacher liability is a scary topic for beginning teachers; it's one that our students always have lots of questions about. In the *Decision Making* feature on page 313, you have an opportunity to weigh in on a case involving teacher liability.

PEARSON
myeducationlab

To see a video of the conflicts over school busing and integration that is highlighted in the *Exploring Diversity* feature on page 312, go to the *Assignments and Activities* section of Topic 4: *Ethical and Legal Issues* in the MyEducationLab for your course and complete the activity titled *School Busing*.

ISSUES IN EDUCATION

Integration

Laws shape our lives and the ways we educate our students. They also shape the ways we approach diversity in our schools. As educators, one of our goals is to teach students to work with and get along with different kinds of people. In addition, we want to ensure that all students have access to a quality education. **Segregation**, or the separation of students on racial or socioeconomic criteria, creates one obstacle to these goals. It's difficult for students to learn to live with different types of students if they can't interact with them in productive ways (Aronson, Wilson, & Akert, 2007). What does the law say about this important education issue?

A historic Supreme Court decision changed the way we approach diversity. Before the momentous *Brown v. Board of Education* decision of 1954, 17 states required segregation in schools and 4 other states allowed it (Underwood & Webb, 2006). The Brown decision ended legal segregation, declaring, "Separate educational facilities are inherently unequal." A long struggle to integrate U.S. schools began with this Supreme Court decision.

Marked by resistance at state and local levels, the struggle hasn't been easy (Pulliam & Van Patten, 2007). School districts dragged their feet, and Congress responded with the Civil Rights Act of 1964, which prohibited discrimination on the basis of race. This legislation employed a carrot and stick approach to integration, providing both funds for desegregation efforts and the power to initiate lawsuits to force integration.

In the 25 years that followed, a tug-of-war ensued between the federal government and state and local

Segregation The separation of students based on racial or socioeconomic criteria.

governments. Mandated busing became the most controversial aspect of this struggle, and was based on the belief that integration was important enough to justify transporting students from their neighborhoods to schools across town. However, parents were upset about both the loss of neighborhood schools and the possibility that their children would be exposed to the drugs, crime, and poverty found in inner-city schools.

Bending to political pressure, federal courts slowly backed away from mandatory busing (Pulliam & Van Patten, 2007). Instead, districts employed a variety of strategies, including magnet schools and transfer programs, to encourage parents to voluntarily send their children to integrated schools.

This approach to integration seemed to work until 2007. In response to parents' objections to busing, school districts in Seattle and Louisville, Kentucky, had designed school desegregation plans based on parental choice. In these plans, more than 90 percent of all students were assigned to their first- or second-choice schools (Wells & Frankenberg, 2007). Some parents objected, however, to the race-based intent of these programs, and the case went all the way to the Supreme Court. The Court ruled that districts cannot take individual students' race into account when assigning them to schools unless the program is specifically designed to remedy the harms of past segregation. Chief Justice Roberts, in defending the 5–4 decision, stated, "The way to stop discrimination on the basis of race is to stop discriminating on the basis of race."

The status of future federal efforts to promote racial integration is unclear. Although the Supreme Court did ban assignment to schools on the basis of race, other districts are successfully de-

signing programs to integrate students on the basis of income or poverty (Kahlenberg, 2006). Because poverty and race frequently occur together (Macionis, 2009), the legal status of these programs is uncertain.

Diversity in Your Classroom

Integration has two goals: to provide all students with access to quality learning environments, and to provide opportunities for people to learn about different cultures and segments of our society.

You can help reach these goals with the decisions you make in your classroom. For example, you can promote a genuine form of integration in your classroom by treating all your students as equitably as possible. This means seating them so they aren't grouped by race or culture, calling on all of them in learning activities, and designing activities and group projects that require students from different racial and ethnic backgrounds to work together. In doing so, students will realize that they're much more alike than they're different, and the barriers that exist among them will gradually break down. In many cases, friendships across racial and cultural lines result from these experiences.

QUESTIONS TO CONSIDER

1. Why is integration important in our society, and why are schools so important in this effort?
2. Why are seemingly simple teacher efforts, such as calling on all students as equitably as possible, effective for promoting integration in classrooms?

myeducationlab To respond to these questions online, explore this topic further, and receive feedback, go to the *Book Specific Resources* section in the MyEducationLab for your course, select your text, and then select *Exploring Diversity* for Chapter 10.

ISSUES IN EDUCATION

Teacher Liability

You are an elementary teacher in a self-contained classroom. You have a class of 29 lively sixth graders, and you've been struggling all year with classroom management. Damien, a larger-than-average boy, seems to resist your efforts at every turn.

You like science and have provided concrete, hands-on science activities whenever you can. You've been debating about a fun activity on chemical changes where students actually test different mystery powders (e.g., sugar, salt, baking soda) with different liquids such as water and vinegar. You decide to go ahead with it and strategically place Damien up toward the front of the room where you can watch him, and have paired him with Katie, one of your more responsible female students. Everything is going well until you go to the back of the room to answer a question and hear a student shriek, "Damien!" As you rush to the front of the room, you see Katie holding her eye, with a mixture of vinegar and baking soda dripping down her cheek. Damien is sitting there with a guilty look on his face. As you rush the crying Katie to the office, you wonder if there isn't something you should have done differently.

What would you do in this situation?

10 MEETING YOUR LEARNING OBJECTIVES

1. Explain the differences between legal and ethical influences on the teaching profession.

   - Both laws and ethical codes provide guidelines as teachers make professional decisions. Laws specify what teachers must and can do. Codes of ethics provide guidelines for what teachers should do as conscientious and caring professionals. Professional organizations such as the National Education Association and American Federation of Teachers publish codes of ethics for teachers.

   - Two major drawbacks to using both laws and ethical codes to guide professional decisions are (1) they are general, lacking in specificity, and (2) they were created to address problems in the past and, consequently, may not be relevant to current issues.

2. Describe how the legal system at the federal, state, and local levels influences teaching.

   - The U.S. legal system is a complex web of interconnected bodies. At the federal level, the U.S. Constitution provides broad guidelines for legal issues, and Congress passes laws that affect education.

   - Most of the direct legal responsibility for running schools belongs to states and local school districts. The U.S. Constitution gives states the legal rights to govern education, and many day-to-day responsibilities are passed on to districts.

   - The overlapping U.S. legal system places the legal responsibility for specific issues or cases at different levels depending on the particular issue involved.

3. Explain how factors such as teacher employment, academic freedom, liability, and teachers' personal lives are influenced by the law.

- Teachers have rights and responsibilities as professional educators. Licensure provides them with the right to teach; a teaching contract specifies the legal conditions for employment. Most new teachers are hired on probationary status. Once granted tenure, teachers cannot be dismissed without due process.

- Teachers' academic freedom is guaranteed by the First Amendment to the Constitution. But in deciding on issues of academic freedom, the courts examine the educational relevance of the content or method involved and the age of the students.

- Copyright laws, designed to protect the property rights of authors, provide restrictions on teachers' use of others' original materials. New questions about fair use are being raised by the increased use of videotape and DVDs and material presented on the Internet.

- Liability poses unique challenges to teachers. The courts hold that teachers act in loco parentis, and when they fail to protect the children under their charge, they can be sued for negligence. When deciding on issues of liability, the courts take into account the age and developmental level of students as well as the kinds of risks involved in an activity.

- Teachers' private lives aren't as private as some would wish. Teachers are expected to be role models to students, so their activities in their hours away from school are often scrutinized and, if illegal, can result in dismissal.

4. Describe the legal implications of religion in the schools.

- Because of differing beliefs about the proper role of religion in education, religion provides a legal battleground in the schools. Organized or school-sponsored prayer is banned in schools, but students' right to pray in school is protected by law.

- Courts have approved religious clubs and organizations and private expressions of student religious beliefs. Religious clubs are provided the same legal safeguards as other extracurricular organizations.

- Although the courts disapprove of religious advocacy, teaching about religion is legal when it can be justified educationally.

5. Describe students' legal rights and responsibilities.

- Many of the same issues of rights involving freedom of speech and due process that affect teachers also pertain to students. Students' right to freedom of speech is protected by the courts, but the expression of free speech must not interfere with the school's or the teacher's instructional agenda.

- Students are protected by the U.S. Constitution from unreasonable search and seizure. Lockers are considered school property, however, and students and their belongings may be searched if school officials have a reasonable suspicion about the possession of drugs or dangerous weapons.

- Students' education records are protected by federal legislation called the Buckley Amendment. The main thrust of this law is to protect the privacy of students' educational records.

- Corporal punishment is legally allowed in a number of states. Those laws contain safeguards against injury and anger or malice.

- Because the courts view attending public schools as a legal right, school officials must conduct student suspension or expulsion from school in a prescribed manner that makes the process transparent to parents or guardians.

- The educational rights of students with AIDS are protected by law. School officials must address specific risk factors to other students when excluding children with AIDS from educational activities.

IMPORTANT CONCEPTS

academic freedom (p. 293)
Buckley Amendment (p. 308)
collective bargaining (p. 292)
copyright laws (p. 295)
corporal punishment (p. 309)
due process (p. 310)
establishment clause (p. 301)
fair-use guidelines (p. 295)
free exercise clause (p. 301)
grievance (p. 292)

in loco parentis (p. 296)
licensure (p. 291)
negligence (p. 296)
notoriety (p. 298)
professional ethics (p. 288)
segregation (p. 312)
reduction in force (p. 293)
teaching contract (p. 291)
tenure (p. 292)

DISCUSSION QUESTIONS

1. What are the advantages and disadvantages of teacher tenure? What arguments might there be for a longer period of probation before granting a teacher tenure? a shorter period? Should teachers be reviewed periodically after tenure is granted?

2. What is the proper role of religion in the schools? In what areas of the curriculum should religion enter? Should teachers reveal their religious beliefs to students? What should a teacher do if a student shares his or her religious beliefs with the class?

3. Touching can be a powerful way of expressing caring or concern. Should teachers touch their students? How and under what circumstances? How might circumstances differ depending on the age and sex of students and the age and sex of the teacher?

4. What place should corporal punishment have in schools? How might the use of corporal punishment be influenced by the following factors: age of student, type of misbehavior, and age and sex of teacher?

5. Should teachers' private lives be placed under greater public examination than the lives of other professionals, such as doctors or lawyers? Why or why not?

Now go to Topic 4: *Ethical and Legal Issues* in the MyEducationLab (www.myeducationlab.com) for your course, where you can:

- Find learning outcomes for *Ethical and Legal Issues,* along with the national standards that connect to these outcomes.
- Complete *Assignments and Activities* that can help you more deeply understand the chapter content.
- Apply and practice your understanding of the core teaching skills identified in the chapter with the *Building Teaching Skills and Dispositions* learning units.
- Check your comprehension on the content covered in the chapter by going to the *Study Plan* in the *Book Specific Resources* section for your text. Here you will be able to take a chapter quiz, receive feedback on your answers, and then access *Review, Practice, and Enrichment* activities to enhance your understanding of chapter content.

Develop Your Professional Portfolio

To further apply your understanding of chapter content and address the INTASC standards, go to the *Book Specific Resources* section in the MyEducationLab for your course, select your text, and then select this chapter's *Portfolio Activities.*

PART 4 Teaching

"I love my classroom; I'm happy in my classroom. Students are funny; they make me laugh. New best practice for teachers: you must laugh with your students at least once a day. Because smiling is contagious, and students will thrive in the positive energy of your classroom."

CHANDRA EMERSON, 2008 Teacher of the Year, Kentucky

To view a video clip of Chandra, the 2008 Kentucky Teacher of the Year, go to Topic 11: *Curriculum* in the MyEducationLab for your course and select *Teacher Talk*, then *Chandra Emerson.*

11

The School Curriculum in an Era of Standards and Accountability

CHAPTER OUTLINE

The Relationship Between Curriculum and Instruction

Components of the Curriculum

- The Explicit Curriculum
- The Implicit Curriculum
- The Null Curriculum
- The Extracurriculum

Forces That Influence the Curriculum

- Standards and Accountability
- The Federal Government
- Textbooks
- Philosophy and Teacher Professionalism

  Taking a Stand in an Era of Reform: The National Curriculum Issue

Controversial Issues in the Curriculum

- 21st Century Skills
- Reading and Math: Back to Basics
- Sex Education
- Moral and Character Education
- Intelligent Design
- Censorship
- Technology and Teaching: The Controversy Over Internet Censorship

  Exploring Diversity: Women and Minorities in the Curriculum

LEARNING OBJECTIVES

After you have completed your study of this chapter, you should be able to:

1. **Describe different definitions of** *curriculum*, **and explain how curriculum and instruction are related.** INTASC Standard 7, Planning for Instruction

2. **Explain how the explicit curriculum, the implicit curriculum, the null curriculum, and the extracurriculum are different.** INTASC Standard 7, Planning for Instruction

3. **Identify different forces that influence the curriculum and explain how each exerts its influence.** INTASC Standard 7, Planning for Instruction

4. **Describe prominent controversial issues in the curriculum.** INTASC Standard 7, Planning for Instruction

In your work as a teacher, you'll be faced with many questions. Three of the most important are: "What should I teach?" "Why am I teaching it?" and "How will I help my students understand it?" These questions are so fundamental that we almost forget that a great deal of thought and decision making (and sometimes controversy) go into answering them. Let's look in on one teacher involved in this process.

It's Saturday afternoon, and Suzanne Brush, a second-grade teacher, is planning for her coming week. She examines her state math standards, and finds the following:

Data Analysis and Probability

Standard 1:
The student understands and uses the tools of data analysis for managing information. (MA.E.1.1)

1. displays solutions to problems by generating, collecting, organizing, and analyzing data using simple graphs and charts. (Florida Department of Education, Sunshine State Standards, Mathematics PreK–2, 2007, p. 2)

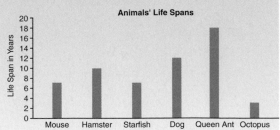

Animals' Life Spans

How much longer is the life of a dog than an octopus?

a. 4 years   c. 9 years
b. 6 years   d. 12 years

Source: Adapted from Florida Comprehensive Assessment Test (2007). *Mathematics Sample Test Book.* Tallahassee: Florida Department of Education.

"Okay, . . . they need to be able to collect data and analyze it using graphs and charts," she thinks.

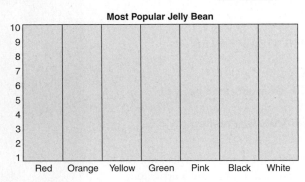

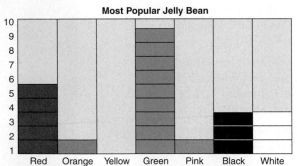

She also goes online and looks at some sample test bar graph from the state high-stakes test to see how her students' understanding of the standard will be measured. She sees the bar graph above.

Based on the standard and the test item, she decides on a motivating activity in which students try different flavors of jelly beans, pick their favorites, and chart their preferences on a bar graph. "I'll do it Monday—it'll be a great way to start the week," she thinks to herself, and she then prepares plastic bags with an assortment of jelly bean flavors in each.

On Monday, she begins, "I'm planning a party for our class, and I want to have some jelly beans for prizes, but I don't know what your favorite flavor is." After several suggestions from students, the class decides to give everyone different flavored jelly beans, have them taste them, and choose their favorite flavor.

Suzanne passes out the plastic bags with jelly beans, the students taste them, and when they're finished, she continues, "We have an empty graph in the front of the room," as she moves to the front and displays the outline of a graph that appears to the upper left.

Suzanne then explains that she has some colored cardboard pieces for the graph that match the colors of the jelly beans. She directs students to come to the front of the room and paste the colored piece that represents their favorite jelly bean on the graph. When the students are done, the graph appears as the one to the left.

Suzanne then reassembles the class and says, "We collected the information and organized it up here on the graph. Now we need to look at it and analyze it."

We'll rejoin Suzanne's lesson later, but for now let's look at her planning. She first made a decision about the general topic she intended to teach and specifically what she wanted students to understand about the topic, and second, she decided how she would help students reach that understanding. The first was a curriculum decision, and the second was a decision about instruction.

We focus on curriculum decisions in this chapter, but before you begin your study, please respond to the items in the *This I Believe* feature on page 321. We address each in the chapter.

THE RELATIONSHIP BETWEEN CURRICULUM AND INSTRUCTION

Educational theorists offer a variety of definitions of *curriculum*, and no single one is generally accepted (Wiles & Bondi, 2007). Some common definitions include the following:

- The subject matter taught to students
- A course of study, or a systematic arrangement of courses
- The planned educational experiences offered by a school
- The process teachers go through in selecting and organizing learning experiences for their students

Also, definitions of *curriculum* and *instruction* often overlap, and in some cases curriculum subsumes instruction. We avoid these issues and define **curriculum** as everything that teachers teach and students learn in schools and define **instruction** as the strategies teachers use to help students reach learning goals in the curriculum. For example, Suzanne wanted her second graders to understand that graphs help us represent information; her learning goal was the result of a curriculum decision. To reach the goal, she had her students sample a variety of jelly beans, pick their favorite flavors, represent their preferences on a large graph, and analyze the information mathematically; the strategy she used to help her students reach the goal reflected a decision about instruction. As an instructional alternative, she could have simply explained why graphs are valuable, modeled the process for creating graphs, given her students some information, and had them graph and analyze it.

■ ■ ■ ■ ■ CHECK YOUR UNDERSTANDING

1.1 What are four definitions of *curriculum*?

1.2 Identify one important difference between the definition of *curriculum* used in this text and the definitions described in item 1.1.

1.3 Explain how curriculum and instruction are related.

For feedback, go to the appendix, *Check Your Understanding*, located in the back of this text.

Curriculum Everything that teachers teach and students learn in schools.

Instruction The strategies teachers use to help students reach learning goals in the curriculum.

COMPONENTS OF THE CURRICULUM

Describing the curriculum as "everything that teachers teach and students learn in schools" makes the concept of *curriculum* very broad. It includes content, such as the geography and climate of a certain region, and academic skills, such as being able to solve math problems. It also includes personal development, social skills, and the attitudes and values that students acquire as part of their day-to-day experiences in school. Experts use four aspects of curriculum to describe how schools help students acquire these different abilities, attitudes, and values (Eisner, 1993):

- The explicit curriculum
- The implicit, or "hidden," curriculum
- The null curriculum
- The extracurriculum

Let's look at them.

The Explicit Curriculum

The **explicit curriculum**, or *formal curriculum*, is the stated curriculum found in textbooks, curriculum guides, and standards, as well as other planned formal educational experiences (Oliva, 2005). It includes everything teachers are expected to teach and students are expected to learn, and what schools are held accountable for. Suzanne's lesson on graphing was part of the explicit curriculum.

The explicit curriculum at the elementary level is quite different from its counterpart in middle, junior high, and high schools. We look at these differences in the next sections.

CURRICULUM IN ELEMENTARY SCHOOLS The elementary curriculum is heavily basic-skills oriented, and each teacher has considerable autonomy in determining how these are taught. To see how this plays out in the classroom, let's look at two elementary

The elementary curriculum is heavily influenced by language arts and reading.

Explicit curriculum (formal curriculum) The stated curriculum found in textbooks, curriculum guides, and standards, as well as other planned formal educational experiences.

teachers' schedules, which you first encountered in Chapter 8. As you recall from that chapter, Sharon is a first-grade teacher, and Susie teaches third grade. Their schedules appear in Table 11.1. Both teachers are responsible for all the content areas, such as language arts, math, and science, and the amount of time they devote to the different areas—a curriculum decision—is a personal one made by each teacher.

Though the specific details of these schedules are different, they reveal two major trends in the elementary curriculum. First, most elementary schools focus heavily on reading, writing, and math. For example, in a 6-hour instructional day (subtracting the time for lunch), Sharon devotes 1 hour and 45 minutes and Susie a minimum of 1 hour and 35 minutes to language arts (including spelling). Both teachers schedule additional time for reading stories.

Second, more time on reading and math means less time for social studies, art, music, and other areas, such as physical education. Also, in spite of the widespread impact of technology on our daily lives, and even though most classrooms have computers in them, little emphasis is placed on computer use and computer skills.

Beginning in the second or third grade, many elementary schools specialize their instruction, assigning one teacher to teach a specific subject. For example, two teachers at

Table 11.1 Two Elementary Schedules			
Sharon's First-Grade Schedule		**Susie's Third-Grade Schedule**	
8:30 AM	School begins	8:30 AM	School begins
8:30–8:45	Morning announcements	8:30–9:15	Independent work (practice previous day's language arts and math)
8:45–10:30	Language arts (including reading and writing)	9:15–10:20	Language arts (including reading and writing)
10:30–11:20	Math		
11:20–11:50	Lunch	10:20–10:45	Snack/independent reading
11:50–12:20	Read story	10:45–11:15	Physical education
12:20–1:15	Center time (practice on language arts and math)	11:15–12:15	Language arts/social studies/science
1:15–1:45	Physical education	12:15–12:45	Lunch
1:45–2:30	Social studies/science	12:45–2:00	Math
2:30–2:45	Class meeting	2:00–2:30	Spelling/catch up on material not covered earlier
2:45–3:00	Call buses/dismissal	2:30–2:45	Read story
		2:45–3:00	Clean up/prepare for dismissal

the same grade level might decide to focus on a different aspect of the morning curriculum: One would teach language arts, including reading, writing, and children's literature, while the other teacher focused on math. In the afternoon, these teachers might also switch science and social studies or music and art. Or, some teachers prefer to keep their own students in the afternoon and teach all these subjects themselves. The advantage of specialization is reduced planning and preparation time; the disadvantages include logistical and coordination problems, as well as not being able to spend time with your own students.

If you observe in elementary classrooms, you'll probably encounter schedules that vary from those in Table 11.1. But even with these differences, you're likely to see primary emphasis placed on reading, writing, and math, and, to some extent, science. We'll see why when we look at forces influencing the curriculum later in the chapter.

CURRICULUM IN MIDDLE SCHOOLS   Middle schools are specifically designed to meet the needs of early adolescents, helping them make the sometimes difficult transition from elementary to high school. The curriculum is organized around specific content areas, and, unlike in elementary schools, the content areas are each allocated the same amount of time (the length of one class period).

The middle school curriculum also focuses on real-life issues that personally concern middle school students, and curriculum developers also strive to make connections among the different content areas (C. Weiss & Kipnes, 2006). Let's look at a team of middle school teachers helping students make these connections.

Carrie Fisher is an eighth-grade American history teacher in an urban middle school. She and her team members have a common planning period each day when the students go to P.E. During this period, they generally discuss the topics they're teaching and the students they share in their classes. The students are heterogeneously grouped and vary widely in ability.

URBAN EDUCATION

To begin today's meeting, Carrie announces, "I'll be starting the Civil War in about 3 weeks. At the end of the unit, each group will have to make a report on some aspect of the war. Is there any way I can connect with what you're doing in the curriculum?"

"I could have them read Crane's The Red Badge of Courage. That's on the district's optional list and really does a good job of communicating the realities of the Civil War," Jim Heath, the language arts teacher, offers.

"That would be great," Carrie replies. "That's just what they need—something to help them understand that history is about real people. How about you, Jacinta? Any links to math?"

"Well, we're just starting to work on different kinds of data such as nominal, ordinal, and interval data. If you can give me some different kinds of data from the Civil War, I can use them to illustrate how different kinds of data provide different kinds of information.

These teachers are working to make the curriculum meaningful for middle-school students by helping them see connections across disciplines. Although these connections are valuable at any level, they are particularly emphasized in elementary and middle schools.

CURRICULUM IN JUNIOR HIGH AND HIGH SCHOOLS   You also saw in Chapter 8 that the organization of junior high schools is similar to that of high schools—hence the name. This organization influences the curriculum. Whereas one team of teachers in middle schools often have the same group of students, as you saw with Carrie and her colleagues, no such coordination exists in the curriculum for junior high and high schools. The curriculum in those schools focuses on separate disciplines and becomes more specialized. Some say it also becomes more fragmented.

Integrated Curriculum.   The emphasis on content in junior and senior high schools has implications for the learning experiences students encounter. For example, a high school student might study geometry from 9:20 to 10:10, English from 10:15 to 11:05, and so on through the rest of the day. Critics argue that compartmentalizing the curriculum in this way detracts from learning, because teaching and learning bear little resemblance to the world outside school. Instead, they argue, schools should offer an **integrated curriculum** (also referred to as an *interdisciplinary curriculum*) in which concepts and skills from various disciplines are combined and related (D. Brown, 2006; K. Wood, 2005). Different forms of integration occur informally in many elementary classrooms. For example, teachers might have students read about a science topic and then have them conduct an experiment, or interview someone who has expertise in the area. As a culminating activity, students write about the topic, thus integrating science with language arts.

In middle and secondary schools, some efforts have been made to formally integrate topics within a content area. For example, in middle schools, students typically take general science in sixth grade, life science in seventh, and physical science in eighth. Some schools integrate these content areas by having students study related topics from earth, life, and physical science in each of the middle school years. For example, using energy as a focal point, students might study the sun as an energy source in earth science, food as a source of energy in life science, and nuclear power in physical science.

An integrated curriculum has the following potential benefits (D. Brown, 2006):

- It increases the relevance of content by making connections among ideas explicit.

- It improves achievement.

- It promotes collaborative planning, which increases communication among teachers.

Even the most ardent proponents acknowledge, however, that the process of integrating curriculum is very demanding and time-consuming, and few teachers have the knowledge of content in different disciplines that is required to create effective integrated units (Nikitina, 2006). Also, in attempts to create links across content areas, teachers are often unable to help students develop a deep understanding of important concepts and bodies of knowledge in individual areas.

Integrated curriculum A form of curriculum in which concepts and skills from various disciplines are combined and related.

Curriculum integration is most popular at the elementary level where a single teacher can relate several topics, and at the middle school level, where teams of teachers periodically meet to interconnect content areas. It's least common at the high school level, where a disciplinary approach to the curriculum is entrenched. The emphasis on standards and accountability that is so prominent in today's schools is likely to reduce the interest on integrating curriculum at all levels, and popular approaches to curriculum development typically don't use it (e.g., Wiggins & McTighe, 2005).

The Implicit Curriculum

A second dimension of the curriculum is the **implicit curriculum**, which includes the unstated and sometimes unintended aspects of the curriculum. It consists of the hidden messages schools and teachers send as children participate in school activities and is heavily influenced by the attitudes and actions of their teachers (Oliva, 2005). Also called the *hidden curriculum* (Feinberg & Soltis, 2004) or the *informal curriculum* (McCaslin & Good, 1996), the implicit curriculum is reflected in the ways teachers present their content, the classroom management routines they establish, the way they treat students and the general climate of the classroom, and the unstated values and priorities that shape the school day. For example, some teachers call only on students with their hands up; shy or reluctant students quickly learn that the way to avoid being called on is to hunker down in their seats and make themselves invisible. Lessons may run more smoothly, but the implicit message is that only "smart" or verbally assertive students should participate in lessons—an unintended consequence of the implicit curriculum.

This I BELIEVE

This section addresses the first item in our *This I Believe* feature, "Teachers' attitudes and values are often reflected in the curriculum." This statement is most definitely true.

> A great deal of learning takes place through the implicit curriculum, and it begins when children are very young. Students, even those of so tender an age, learn early what it takes to "do school." They learn early what a teacher does in a classroom. They learn early how they must behave in order to get on. (Eisner, 2003, p. 648)

As an additional example of how the implicit curriculum influences students, let's return to Suzanne's work with her second graders. Students had represented their jelly bean preferences on the large bar graph at the front of the room, and then Suzanne had reassembled them and said, "We collected the information and organized it up here on the graph. Now we need to look at it and analyze it." We rejoin her class now.

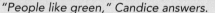

"Tell us what we know by looking at this graph. . . . Candice, what do we know?" she asks, walking toward the middle of the room.

"People like green," Candice answers.

"Candice said most people like the green jelly beans. . . . Candice, how many people like green?"

". . . Nine."

"Nine people like green. . . . And how did you find that out? Can you go up there and show us how you read the graph?"

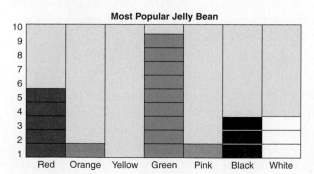

Most Popular Jelly Bean

(bar graph with y-axis labeled 1 through 10; x-axis categories: Red, Orange, Yellow, Green, Pink, Black, White)

Candice goes up to the graph and moves her hand up from the bottom, counting the green pieces as she goes.

Suzanne has students make several more observations of the information on the graph and then says, "Okay, now I'm going to ask you a different kind of question. . . . How many more people liked the green jelly beans than the red?

Implicit curriculum The unstated and sometimes unintended aspects of the curriculum.

> Look up at the graph. Try to find the information, set up the problem, and then we'll see what you come up with. . . . I'm looking for a volunteer to share an answer with us. . . . Dominique?"
>
> "Nine plus 5 is 14," Dominique responds.
>
> "Dominique says 9 plus 5 is 14. Let's test it out." (She asks Dominique to go up to the graph and show the class how she arrived at her answer.) "We want to know the difference. . . . How many more people liked green than red, and you say 14 people, . . . 14 more people liked green. Does that work?"
>
> "I mean 9 take away 5," Dominique says after looking at the graph for a few seconds.
>
> "She got up here and she changed her mind," Suzanne smiles warmly. "Tell them."
>
> "Nine take away 5 is 4."
>
> "Nine take away 5 is 4. So how many more people liked green than red? . . . Carlos?"
>
> "Four."
>
> "Four, good, four," Suzanne again smiles. "The key was you had to find the difference between the two numbers."
>
> Suzanne then has students work at a series of centers, such as graphing the months in which the students' birthdays fall, the most common ways students get to school, and the hair color of each student. After students finish their work, she reviews what they've done and closes the lesson.

What did Suzanne's students learn from this brief episode? The following are likely:

- Math is more than simply memorizing basic facts.
- Making mistakes is a normal part of learning.
- Learning is an active process of applying what we know in our daily lives.

These are powerful messages of the implicit curriculum.

Students learn from the implicit curriculum in many ways. For instance, expert teachers use classroom management to create classroom environments in which experiences make sense to students, and students learn to accept responsibility for their own behavior (Emmer, Evertson, & Worsham, 2009; Evertson, Emmer, & Worsham, 2009). They also learn that all students are welcome and expected to participate and learn. These messages reflect the implicit curriculum and are important parts of students' total learning experiences.

The implicit and the explicit curricula sometimes conflict. For example, research indicates that students who have independent and questioning minds, who are assertive, who challenge authority, and who insist on explanations are sometimes rejected by teachers (Kedar-Voivodas, 1983). This results in a clash between the explicit curriculum, which focuses on learning and mastery of content, and the implicit curriculum, which rewards docile students and conformity. What do students learn when they're expected to listen passively as teachers lecture, or if competition for grades is emphasized? They may learn that "playing the game" and "beating the system" are more important than hard work and mastery of content. These are not messages we want to send.

With awareness, teachers can help ensure that the implicit and the explicit curricula of their classrooms are consistent. Making learning the focal point of your teaching, modeling your own interest in the topics you teach, respecting students, and expecting them to respect you and each other all communicate important, positive values and are part of the implicit curriculum. Some of the most important learning experiences students have in schools are the result of the implicit curriculum.

The Null Curriculum

A third dimension of the curriculum focuses on topics that are ignored or left unexamined. The decisions teachers make about what they won't teach are sometimes as important as what they do teach (Eisner, 1993, 2003). Topics left out of the course of study are referred to as the **null curriculum**. Teachers don't have time to "cover" everything, so they choose topics they consider most important or that they feel most comfortable with. For example, social

Null curriculum Topics left out of the course of study.

studies teachers typically cover the events of the American Civil War, but they're less likely to carefully examine factors such as slavery and racism that converged to trigger the war. These important but controversial cause-and-effect events then become part of the null curriculum.

Teachers demonstrate their professionalism when they think carefully about the topics they choose to emphasize and those they choose to leave out. As with the implicit curriculum, important messages about learning are tacitly communicated through the null curriculum; this addresses the second item in our *This I Believe* feature, "Teachers sometimes influence the curriculum as strongly by what they choose not to teach as by what they choose to teach." This statement is indeed true.

This I BELIEVE

RECESS: THE MISSING FOURTH "R"?   Recess, a topic receiving increased attention today, is thought by many to be a crucial fourth "R," and is considered a prime example of the null curriculum (Parker-Pope, 2009). Estimates are that 30 to 40 percent of elementary classrooms have cut back on or eliminated recess time, and developmental psychologists are worried that young children are missing out on an essential component of the curriculum. Free play during recess can provide students with crucial experiences needed for cognitive, social, and emotional development (Rathunde & Csikszentmihalyi, 2006). In addition, lack of free-play time has been linked to a number of childhood problems, ranging from obesity to anxiety and hyperactivity (Jacobson, 2008). A recent study, involving over 11,000 children, actually linked recess to fewer behavioral problems in the classroom (Samuels, 2009b).

Given these positive benefits, why is recess becoming part of many elementary classrooms' null curriculum? Time, precious time, is the answer, because many teachers and schools are feeling pressures to improve achievement by spending more time on subjects that will be tested on high-stakes tests. Unfortunately, these decisions may be having adverse effects on children's learning and development.

PEARSON
myeducationlab

Go to the *Building Teaching Skills and Dispositions* section of Topic 11: Curriculum, in the MyEducationLab for your course, and complete the activity titled *Identifying Curriculum Types*.

The Extracurriculum

A fourth component of the curriculum, the **extracurriculum**, consists of learning experiences that extend beyond the core of students' formal studies. The extracurriculum includes clubs, sports, school plays, and other activities that don't earn academic credit.

Although outside the explicit curriculum, extracurricular activities provide valuable learning experiences. Research indicates that a well-developed extracurricular program is an integral part of an effective school, and students who participate in extracurricular activities derive the following benefits (Fredericks & Eccles, 2006):

- Higher academic performance and attainment
- Reduced dropout rates
- Lower rates of substance abuse
- Less sexual activity among girls
- Better psychological adjustment, including higher self-esteem and reduced feelings of social isolation
- Reduced rates of delinquent behavior

Extracurricular activities provide valuable learning opportunities for students as well as teachers.

Unfortunately, research also indicates that low-ability students, members of cultural minorities, and at-risk students are less likely to participate in extracurricular activities, which can lead to feelings of alienation toward the school (San Antonio, 2006). Also,

Extracurriculum The part of the curriculum consisting of learning experiences that go beyond the core of students' formal studies.

many low socioeconomic status (SES) high school students are forced to work after school to make ends meet, a practice that not only competes with participation in extracurricular activities, but also can have adverse effects on school success in general (H. Marsh & Kleitman, 2005).

Sports, one form of extracurricular activity, can be an important positive influence on students, especially for members of cultural minorities. Participation in sports can reduce behavior problems and increase positive attitudes toward school (Broh, 2002). Studies of the effects of participation in sports indicate that girls who engage in sports have lower teen pregnancy rates, are less likely to be sexually active, and have fewer sexual partners (A. Feldman & Matjasko, 2005). Experts conclude, "Sports might . . . help girls cut loose from the conventional form of femininity that encourages them to establish self-worth mainly in terms of sexuality and heterosexual appeal" (Sabo, Miller, Farrell, Barnes, & Melnick, 1998, p. 22). All this information relates to the third item in our *This I Believe* feature, "Extracurricular activities, such as clubs and sports, can provide positive outlets for students, but they aren't an essential part of the curriculum." This statement is not true: Extracurricular activities are an essential part of students' total school experience.

Educators wanting to help students develop in healthy ways in this sometimes confusing world might look more closely at extracurricular activities for answers. Experts recommend that schools take a more proactive role in recruiting students for extracurricular activities, by making them aware of the activities available (S. Black, 2002). This is especially important for at-risk students, minorities, and students with exceptionalities, groups that traditionally have been underrepresented in extracurricular activities.

Extracurricular activities also offer beginning teachers opportunities for professional growth. Sponsoring clubs and coaching teams can provide you with a salary supplement, as well as opportunities to interact with your colleagues at a personal level. Working with students in these activities can be emotionally rewarding and can provide you with insights into students' personalities and lives. Both of your authors coached sports and sponsored clubs while teaching in public schools and found the experience time-consuming but rewarding. We were able to get to know students in ways not possible in the regular classroom.

This I BELIEVE

■ ■ ■ ■ CHECK YOUR UNDERSTANDING

2.1 What is the difference between the explicit and the implicit curricula?

2.2 How is the null curriculum different from both the explicit and the implicit curricula?

2.3 Compare the extracurriculum to the other curricula.

For feedback, go to the appendix, *Check Your Understanding*, located in the back of this text.

FORCES THAT INFLUENCE THE CURRICULUM

To this point, we've examined the curriculum as it currently exists in schools. But how did it come to be that way, and what forces are shaping it today? Answers to these questions can be found in society at large, as well as reforms in education (Hewitt, 2006). These forces are outlined in Figure 11.1 and discussed in the sections that follow.

Standards and Accountability

To understand the role of standards and accountability on the curriculum, think again about the emphasis placed on reading, writing, math, and to some extent, science, that we saw in the elementary curriculum. This emphasis is the result of *standards*, statements specifying what students should know and what skills they should have upon completing an area of study, and *accountability*, requiring students to demonstrate understanding of the topics they study as measured by standardized tests. Students are held accountable for their knowledge and skills in reading, writing, and math, and elementary teachers are responsible for their students' performance in these areas. As a result, these are the areas emphasized in the curriculum, and the extent to which science is emphasized will depend on whether it is included on the test; some states include science on their high-stakes tests, whereas others do not. Content areas such as social studies, art, and music are rarely covered on high-stakes tests, so they receive little emphasis in the curriculum.

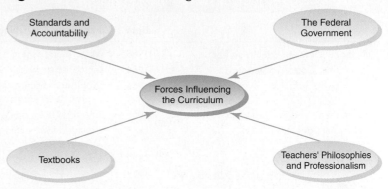

Figure 11.1 Forces Influencing the Curriculum

You also saw the influence of standards and accountability on curriculum decisions illustrated in our opening case study. In planning her lesson, Suzanne first referred to her state's standards, and she even looked for a sample test item to ensure that the way she designed her lesson would be consistent with the standard and the high-stakes test her students would take.

"What gets tested, gets taught" is a common maxim in education today (Cuban, 1996), and some experts suggest that standards are *the* most powerful force influencing the curriculum today (Marzano & Kendall, 2003; Wiggins & McTighe, 2005). Regardless of the state in which you teach, they will be a part of your professional life.

The Federal Government

As you saw in Chapter 6, the framers of the U.S. Constitution granted control of education to the states instead of the federal government. Nevertheless, the federal government has a long and rich history of involvement in education, and this role has increased rather than decreased over time. The No Child Left Behind (NCLB) Act of 2001, a key educational mandate of the George W. Bush administration, is one example of this increased federal role.

The federal government's efforts to influence school curricula dramatically increased in the 1950s when people began to view education as an important vehicle for accomplishing national goals. Table 11.2 outlines some of the major pieces of federal legislation that have influenced not only the curriculum but also other aspects of schools.

As you see from Table 11.2, federal legislation has led to significant changes in U.S. classrooms. The Individuals with Disabilities Education Act (IDEA), federal legislation passed in 1975, requires that students have access to the regular curriculum. One result of this act is the likelihood that you'll have learners with exceptionalities, such as students with learning disabilities, in your classroom. The National Defense Education Act (passed in 1958) resulted in much greater emphasis on math, science, and foreign languages, particularly in high schools. Although this emphasis has varied somewhat over the years, well-qualified math, science, and foreign language teachers continue to be in high demand.

Textbooks

You're a beginning teacher, and you're thinking about what you will teach during the next week. Where will you turn for help? If you're typical, you'll reach for the textbook you're using for the content area you're teaching (Valencia, Place, Martin, & Grossman, 2006).

For better or worse, textbooks are a fact of teaching life. In the United States, districts spend more than $4 billion per year on textbooks. Research indicates that teachers

Table 11.2 The Federal Government's Influence on the Curriculum

Act	Date	Impact on Curriculum
National Defense Education Act	1958	Made math, science, and foreign language high curriculum priorities
Economic Opportunity Act	1964	Increased emphasis on vocational training and teaching marketable skills.
Civil Rights Act	1964	Prohibited discrimination on the basis of race, color, or national origin. Intended to provide all students with equal access to the curriculum.
Elementary and Secondary Education Act	1965	Created Title I, designed to help disadvantaged children acquire basic skills.
Billingual Education Act	1968	Provided for teaching the curriculum in students' native languages as they gradually learned English.
Title IX	1972	Increased girls' participation in physical education and sports.
Individuals with Diabilities Education Act (IDEA)	1975	Increased participation of learners with exceptionalities in the regular curriculum.
Environmental Education Act	1991	Stimulated the modern environmental education movement.
Goals 2000: Educate America Act	1994	Established goals to be met by American education by the year 2000.
No Child Left Behind Act	2001	Requires states to establish standards for what learners should know and be able to do in different subjects and holds them accountable for student performance on tests linked to these standards.

Despite questions about quality, most teachers rely on textbooks for their instruction.

depend heavily on them to select content, sequence topics, and locate instructional activities (Reys, Reys, & Chávez, 2004). In some of your education classes, you may be encouraged to set textbooks aside or at least not depend heavily on them. But research suggests that if you're like other teachers, you probably won't do so (Zahorik, 1991). Other than standards, many experts believe that textbooks are the most powerful influence on teachers' curriculum decisions (C. Marsh & Willis, 2007).

Textbooks can be valuable resources, and we're not suggesting that you abandon them. Instead, we recommend that you use them strategically, de-emphasizing, or even eliminating, some topics and chapters in textbooks while including other valuable topics not in them. The following are reasons for using them selectively:

- *Student needs:* The topics presented in textbooks may not be consistent with the specific needs of your students, school, or district. Following a textbook too closely then fails to meet these needs effectively.

- *Scope:* To appeal to a wide market, textbook publishers include a huge number of topics, more than teachers can possibly teach in the time available. Curriculum experts conclude that texts and curriculum guides often contain twice as much material as is feasible for students to learn. They recommend that teachers select the most important concepts and skills to emphasize and concentrate on the quality of understanding rather than on the quantity of information presented (Marzano, 2003; Patton & Roschelle, 2008).

- *Quality:* Textbooks are sometimes poorly written, lack adequate examples, or even contain errors of fact. One study of history textbooks found "content is thinner and thinner, and what there is, is increasingly deformed by . . . politics" (Sewall, 2000). An analysis of middle school science texts found them to be shallow, superficial, and frequently outdated (Reys et al., 2004). Similar problems have been found in other subject areas (Hecht, 2006; Oakes & Saunders, 2004). Following textbooks too closely can lead to superficial understanding or even faulty ideas that detract from learning.

On the other hand, researchers have found that innovative textbooks and other curriculum materials can be positive catalysts for change, encouraging teachers to rethink what and how they teach (Pittman & Frykholm, 2002). In addition, because of the current emphasis on standards, most publishers now key objectives in their textbooks to state standards, making them useful planning tools.

Philosophy and Teacher Professionalism

The curriculum we create reflects our learning goals. Because time doesn't allow us to teach all goals, teachers have to make decisions about priorities. For instance, of the following goals, which do you consider to be most important?

- To thoroughly understand traditional content, such as important concepts and ideas from literature, science, history, and advanced mathematics

- To develop basic skills, such as the ability to read fluently, write effectively, and complete mathematical tasks

- To develop workplace skills, such as the ability to work with others and solve problems

- To develop learner self-esteem and the motivation to be involved in learning for its own sake

Answers to this question vary. Some educators suggest that the last goal is most important, arguing that intrinsically motivated people will adapt and acquire the skills needed to function effectively in a rapidly changing world. The development of the individual is preeminent in their view. Others favor the third goal, suggesting that society needs people who can solve problems and function well in groups. Still others advocate the first or second goal, asserting that academic skills, knowledge, and understanding are the keys to expertise and the ability to solve today's complex problems.

These arguments are grounded in the different philosophical positions discussed in Chapter 7. Each of these positions has both strengths and weaknesses, as outlined in Table 11.3.

Many of today's curriculum controversies are rooted in these different philosophical positions. For example, reform movements have resulted from widespread complaints

Table 11.3   Philosophical Foundations of Curricula

Basis for Curriculum	Dominant Educational Philosopy	Advantages	Disadvantages
Needs of individuals	Progressivism	• Concern for individuals is placed at the heart of curriculum development. • Learner motivation is promoted.	• Efforts to respond to the special needs of each individual are virtually impossible. • Students may not be the best judges of their long-range needs, opting for shallow learning experiences.
Needs of society	Progressivism Social Reconstructionism	• Students learn to integrate information from a variety of sources. • Curriculum is relevant, contributing to learner motivation.	• Society's needs change rapidly, often making curriculum obsolete. • Learners may be steered into career choices too early, limiting long-range opportunities.
Academic disciplines	Essentialism Perennialism	• Research indicates that expertise and problem-solving ability depend on knowledge (Bruning, Shraw, Norby, & Ronning, 2004). • Schools and teachers are being held accountable, and accountability depends on discipline-based tests.	• Academic disciplines tend to artifically "compartmentalize" what students learn. • Students complain that traditional subjects are irrelevant.

about young people entering the workforce without the basic knowledge and skills needed to function effectively in today's society (Hirsch, 2001). Reformers make essentialist arguments, and we see this essentialist position reflected in a **core curriculum**, a common course of study for all students that emphasizes reading, writing, and math in the elementary curriculum and English, math, and science in high schools.

Although an emphasis on basic skills is currently prominent, the needs of individuals occupy an important place in the curriculum as well. Advocates contend that a major goal of schools should be to give students self-confidence about their ability to learn; critics contend that an emphasis on the development of self-esteem has led to lowered standards and decreased achievement (Schunk, Pintrich, & Meece, 2008). But students can't learn if they dislike themselves and the content they're learning, advocates assert.

One reason you're taking this course is to better understand your crucial role in creating curricula that promote student learning. In Chapter 1, we saw that professionals are people who use their knowledge and understanding to make decisions in complex and ill-defined situations. Nowhere will professionalism be more important than in making curriculum decisions.

Although a number of factors influence what's taught and learned, you, the teacher, are at the center of the process, and each of the elements of professionalism discussed in Chapter 1 comes into play (Remillard, 2005). Professionals frequently make curriculum decisions on their own (autonomy), and these decisions are based on professional knowledge and reflections from their past experiences. They're also made with benefits to students as the primary goal, which is an essential aspect of professional ethics.

We see these elements of professionalism illustrated in Suzanne's work. For example, she used her state's standards as a guide, but the decisions about how to plan and present the content were hers and hers alone. She relied on her professional knowledge when she designed the learning activity to promote her students' involvement and interest. No substitute for this knowledge and professionalism exists.

Middle and secondary teachers, influenced by separate class periods and predetermined time schedules, have only slightly less autonomy. For example, a teacher in beginning algebra might choose to spend a great deal of time on basic skills, solving problems such as $x + 2x + 3x = 24$, or she might choose to emphasize word problems such as the following:

> Greg has some coins in his pocket, Sally has twice as many as Greg, and Juanita has three times as many as Greg. They have 24 coins altogether. How many does each student have?

Again, these are professional decisions based on understanding and knowledge—understanding what students need and how they learn and knowing how to represent a topic so it makes sense to them. For example, one geography teacher might emphasize the influence of geography on culture, whereas another might emphasize climate and physical features, such as mountains, rivers, and plains. Secondary teachers make similar curricular decisions in all content areas every day.

Teachers are essentially "alone" as professionals when they shut their classroom doors. Closing the door is symbolic, representing teachers' professional control over the curriculum and how it's taught.

The information in this section also addresses the fourth item in our *This I Believe* feature, "Because standards and accountability are so important in today's schools, the most important decisions about curriculum and instruction are now out of teachers' hands." This statement isn't true: As you saw earlier in this section, standards present general frameworks for teachers, but the most important decisions about curriculum and instruction remain in their hands.

What does this information mean for you as a teacher? Nowhere in teaching is professionalism more important than in making curriculum decisions (Remillard, 2005;

This I BELIEVE

Core curriculum A common course of study for all students that includes basic skills and knowledge and is supported by essentialist philosophies.

The National Curriculum Issue

The drafters of the U.S. Constitution, in passing the Tenth Amendment, placed curriculum decisions directly in the hands of the states. The principle of state control of curricula has been in place since that time.

Today, this principle is being questioned by some prominent voices who advocate a national curriculum with nationwide standards (D. Hoff, 2009b). And the politics of this controversy have become blurred. Historically, political liberals have advocated a strong federal role in education, whereas conservatives have supported "states'" rights and have advocated a smaller federal presence. However, the NCLB legislation was a massive federal intervention and was promoted and passed by a very conservative Bush administration (R. Gordon, 2006). Though it still left control of the curriculum in states' hands, NCLB exerted a powerful influence on how states implement and test for these standards. For some, a national curriculum with mandated federal testing would be a logical next step.

THE ISSUE

The idea of national standards leading to national standardized tests is highly controversial. Proponents make the following arguments in support of a national curriculum:

- Standards vary significantly from state to state; some states have much lower standards and levels of achievement than others. A national curriculum would create uniform standards for all and help raise achievement for low-SES and cultural minority students in all states (C. Finn & Petrilli, 2009).

- Students in countries such as Germany and Japan, which have national standards and national exams, achieve higher than American students (Kober, 2006).

- A national curriculum would provide stability and coherence. The population in the United States is highly mobile: 20 percent of Americans relocate every year, some urban schools have a 50 percent turnover rate during the school year, and by the end of third grade, 1 in 6 children attends three or more schools (Hartman, 2006). Teachers working with new students from different districts or states often can't tell what they have or haven't already studied.

Opponents of a national curriculum argue that it would create a massive and unwieldy federal bureaucracy, which would also weaken local control and accountability. They also contend that a national curriculum wouldn't be responsive to student diversity and would create more problems for disadvantaged students. Other critics assert that this "either–or" approach—either a nationalized curriculum or the elimination of federal intervention in the curriculum—is invalid, and they further argue that the clash of ideas from different sources makes reforms actually work (Pogrow, 2006).

As a compromise, some experts suggest that the federal government recommend, but not require, exemplary textbooks, because teachers tend to rely on textbooks in making curriculum decisions. For example, several years ago, the U.S. Department of Education published a list of promising and exemplary math texts, most based on NCTM standards (Viadero, 1999).

But even this approach has drawn criticism. One critic, a conservative math professor, commented, "This is an abomination. It [the math curriculum] has no business being debated by the federal government" (Viadero, 1999, p. 14). Similar efforts to influence the reading curriculum have also occurred, with similar controversies (Manzo, 2004, 2006a). Polls indicate that Americans are equally divided about the issue of establishing national standards, which would, in effect, result in a national curriculum (Bushaw & Gallup, 2008).

YOU TAKE A STAND

Now it's your turn to take a position on the issue. Should our country have a national curriculum, or should curriculum decisions be left in the hands of the states?

myeducationlab To explore both sides of this issue and take a stand, go to the *Book Specific Resources* section in the MyEducationLab for your course, select your text, and then select *Taking a Stand in an Era of Reform* for Chapter 11.

ISSUES IN EDUCATION

Thornton, 2005). Professional decision making with respect to the curriculum requires a great deal of knowledge, effort, and energy. Teachers report, however, that the process of personal curriculum construction can be one of the most creative and satisfying aspects of teaching (Clandinin & Connelly, 1996).

As you've seen in this chapter, curriculum exerts a powerful influence on teachers' lives. In *Taking a Stand in an Era of Reform*, above, we examine how the move toward a national curriculum could affect what and how you teach.

■ ■ ■ ■ CHECK YOUR UNDERSTANDING

3.1 Identify four forces that influence the curriculum.

3.2 How does each of the forces in 3.1 exert its influence on the curriculum?

3.3 Why is teacher professionalism so important in making curricular decisions?

For feedback, go to the appendix, *Check Your Understanding*, located in the back of this text.

CONTROVERSIAL ISSUES IN THE CURRICULUM

Should the curriculum center on core knowledge and skills, or should it instead focus on thinking skills needed in the 21st century? We hear a lot today about "back to basics," but what exactly are the basics? What about sex education: Should schools teach it, or should this be handled in the home or church? How about the development of ethics and morals: What should be the role of schools in promoting morality? Should teachers present students with disclaimers in their science curriculum, saying that the theory of evolution is only one explanation of our natural world? And, should teachers be allowed to have students read essentially anything that their professional judgment dictates? Each issue and its impact on the curriculum are controversial, and we examine them in this section. We begin with controversies related to basic knowledge and skills.

21st Century Skills

The 21st Century Skills movement aims to prepare students to thrive in our modern, changing, technological world.

"What do our students need to succeed in our modern technological world?" is a question that educators ask, but they disagree on the answer. Advocates of a curriculum reform movement called *21st Century Skills* recommend a major revamping of our current curriculum offerings to meet this need (Partnership for 21st Century Skills, 2009). The **21st Century Skills** movement promotes global awareness, civic literacy, critical thinking, communication skills, and technology expertise that people need to function effectively in the 21st century. Advocates continue to embrace core content in math, reading, writing, science, and social studies, but they also endorse more emphasis on learning skills, such as problem solving and critical thinking, and life and career skills, such as personal responsibility, initiative, and self-direction. Social and cross-cultural awareness are also important because of our country's rapidly increasing diversity, and technology is a theme for the entire movement. A number of corporations, including Apple, Microsoft, and Intel, support these skills, believing they will make future workers more productive.

Recognizing the magnitude of the task ahead of them, promoters of 21st Century Skills are recommending a multipronged curriculum reform strategy that targets new standards, instruction, assessment, and professional-development opportunities for teachers. Their goal is to reorient the curriculum so that it prepares students for the future.

Critics assert that these skills are nothing more than frills that distract teachers from helping students learn basic skills in reading, writing, and math, and important content in other areas, such as science and social studies, that all students should know (Mathews, 2009). Critics also argue that 21st century skills aren't viable curriculum goals, asserting that the skills can't be taught in the absence of content (Sawchuk, 2009b). The ability to

21st Century Skills A curriculum reform movement that emphasizes skills such as global awareness, civic literacy, critical thinking, communication, and technology expertise, which people need to function effectively in the 21st century.

teach skills, such as critical thinking, problem solving, and communication, outside the context of a content area isn't supported by research on teaching and learning (Eggen & Kauchak, 2010).

Some of the controversies surrounding the 21st Century Skills movement result from philosophical differences about what kind of knowledge is most valuable. As you saw in Chapter 7, essentialists and progressivists disagree about the answers to that question.

The issue of whether emphasis on 21st century skills will distract teachers from helping students develop basic skills in reading and math compounds controversies that already exist in these areas. We examine these controversies in the next section.

Reading and Math: Back to Basics

Basic skills, such as reading and math, are essential for success both in school and in later life. But, educators disagree about the best way to help students acquire these skills. Let's see what all this heat is about.

CONTROVERSIES IN READING   Everyone agrees that helping students learn to read fluently is the goal of reading instruction. But educators disagree about which strategies are most effective for reaching that goal. One camp endorses *whole language* whereas another emphasizes an approach centered on *phonics*. Let's look at their positions.

Whole language is an approach to reading instruction that integrates reading into the total literacy process (i.e., learning to speak, listen, write, and read) (G. Tompkins, 2009). Whole-language classrooms use literature as the foundation of the reading process; books, projects, tapes, and videos are used to discover connections between vocabulary and concepts related to a topic. Whole language has three characteristics:

- It emphasizes language as a communication tool.
- It uses language to think about and describe experiences, linking spoken and written language.
- It connects different content areas by emphasizing language across the curriculum.

Here is how one teacher implements whole language in his classroom.

Sam Taylor's third-grade classroom is a beehive of activity. One corner is decorated with a giant paper spider web with drawings and students' written descriptions comparing spiders' eight legs and insects' six. These came from books and videotapes students had been studying and from a field trip to a park near the school. Students are taking turns reading descriptions of different insects and spiders, matching them to the drawings and checking their answers with a key on the back.

Several students are at their desks, writing about a visit from one of the parents, an amateur entomologist, who had brought a mounted insect collection to class. The rest of the students will later read these descriptions of the visit. In a third corner, students are manipulating multiples of 6 and 8 in math to find patterns, and discussing their thinking and answers with each other.

Sam has the rest of the class in a half circle in front of him. He is reading The Very Quiet Cricket, *by Eric Carle, about a cricket who couldn't find another cricket to talk to among the insects it encountered in a field. When he nears the end, he stops and asks each student to create an ending for the story and to share it with the group. Later in the day, students compare their story endings to the book's.*

Sam capitalized on the first characteristic of whole-language instruction by having students write and having other students read what they wrote. His instruction complemented children's natural tendency to communicate with others. In time, learners see how reading, speaking, and writing are interrelated, and reading becomes an important

Whole language An approach to reading instruction that integrates reading into the total literacy process.

part of the total communication process. He capitalized on the second characteristic by having students write about things they had experienced—insects, the field trip, and the visit from the parent. Third, he emphasized the use of language across the curriculum by using science, for example, as an opportunity to both practice language and study science concepts. Sam capitalized on this dimension by having his students write about insects and discuss their answers in their math activity.

Phonics, by contrast, emphasizes the relationship between letters and the sounds they make, and stresses learning basic letter–sound patterns and rules for sounding out words. For instance, the word *cat* has three sounds—*k, ah*, and *t*. Word sounds are represented by a fixed number of letters or letter combinations, and once students learn them, they can "sound out" new words. However, one-to-one correspondence between letters or letter combinations and sounds doesn't exist, such as the *c* in *cent* and in *cat* and the *ch* in *change, chaos*, and *chiffon*. Nevertheless, a number of rules, such as "When *c* is followed by *a, o*, or *u*, it makes a 'k' sound, and when it's followed by *i, e*, or *y*, it makes an 's' sound," work in enough cases to allow us to use them in sounding out new words. Advocates of phonics argue that these decoding strategies, once learned, allow readers to decipher words automatically, leaving more attention available for comprehension, which is the ultimate goal in reading.

Putting the Reading Debate Into Perspective. The whole-language and the phonics camps are deeply divided, each asserting that their approach is superior. In 1995, California adopted two statutes, called the *ABC Laws*, which require code-based approaches in the schools, because leaders there believed that low reading test scores resulted from reliance on whole-language approaches (Halford, 1997).

What does research suggest? Most reading experts believe that decoding is an essential part of successful reading (Reutzel & Cooter, 2008). But these same experts stress that phonics *alone* isn't effective; additional comprehension strategies are necessary if students are to become skilled readers. This suggests that both camps have valid points—students need decoding skills, but comprehension must also be emphasized. This position makes sense, and it likely explains the problem in California: In focusing solely on meaning, teachers went too far in de-emphasizing decoding skills. On the other hand, exclusive focus on phonics, in the absence of meaning, is equally ineffective. A balanced approach is necessary.

CONTROVERSIES IN MATH   Whereas controversies in reading focus on *how* to teach students to read, controversies in math are broader. Educators disagree about not only how to teach math but also what students should learn.

Historically, math in this country has been taught in a highly proceduralized way (P. Alexander, 2006). For example, students learned to convert fractions to percents by 1) dividing the numerator of the fraction by the denominator, and 2) moving the decimal point two places to the right. So, to convert 3/8 to a percent, we divide 3 by 8 and get .375, and moving the decimal results in 37.5%. Emphasis was on mastery of the procedure and getting the correct answer.

There are two problems with this approach. First, students often perform the operations without understanding them, so they do poorly on tasks requiring transfer to new math problems. Let's see why this might happen. For instance, other than simply accepting it because we're told to do so, why do we place a decimal point after the 3 when we divide it by 8? Also, we're told that 3/8, .375, and 37.5% are equivalent. Three eighths and .375 appear unrelated, and why do we simply move the decimal point two places to the right and then add the percent symbol? Understanding math requires more than the manipulation of symbols. Second, when procedures are emphasized, learners often commit random and chronic errors and fail to question the validity of their answers.

In response to these problems, and with increased understanding of how people learn, reform in the teaching of mathematics has been led by professional organizations, such as the National Council of Teachers of Mathematics, which published standards in 1989 and

Phonics An approach to reading instruction that emphasizes the relationship between letters and the sounds they make and stresses learning basic letter–sound patterns and rules for sounding out words.

revised them in 2000. The *NCTM Standards*, as they're commonly called, contain ambitious goals. At the school and classroom levels, the *NCTM Standards* assert the following:

- Studying mathematics should make sense.
- Math should relate to the real world.
- Mathematics is a problem-solving activity, not the application of rules and procedures.
- Math involves reasoning (with heavy emphasis on estimation) more than memorization.
- Math is communication.

At the same time, the *NCTM Standards* de-emphasize proceduralized aspects of instruction, such as memorizing facts and relationships, using clue words to determine which operation to use, performing paper-and-pencil computations, practicing routine problems and skills out of context, and teaching by telling.

Conservative critics criticize these reform efforts for the following reasons:

- Basic skills are being abandoned at the expense of "fuzzy" mathematics, where estimates replace right answers.
- The reform efforts are one more example of widespread "dumbing down" of the curriculum.
- The "new" math is a misguided attempt to promote self-esteem at the expense of learning. (Van de Walle, Karp, & Williams, 2010)

Let's put the reformers and their critics into perspective. First, children need to know math facts, such $6 + 9 = 15$ and $8 \times 6 = 48$, and most children won't learn the facts as incidental offshoots of problem solving; they need to be practiced to automaticity (Wittwer & Renkl, 2008). Reformers agree, but argue that students spend too much time in drill and seatwork activities, which isn't the best way to produce meaningful learning. Children need to know math facts, but this goal should be balanced with meaningful learning that emphasizes the reasons we perform different math operations. Like reading, an effective math curriculum balances these two approaches—teaching facts and procedures as well as the reasons behind the operations (Cavanagh, 2008b).

PEARSON
myeducationlab

To see how one teacher addresses standards and accountability in her math curriculum, go to the *Assignments and Activities* section of Topic 11: *Curriculum* in the MyEducationLab for your course and complete the activity titled *Elementary Math: Curriculum, Standards, and Accountability.*

Sex Education

Sex education is controversial because people can't agree on where it should occur and what it should look like. In terms of where sex education should occur, some insist that it shouldn't be part of the school curriculum at all, believing that it's the sole or primary responsibility of families or churches. They contend that sex is inextricably connected with personal, moral, and religious values, and the proper place for sex education is the home, where parents can embed it in a larger moral framework.

Proponents of sex education counter with the following statistics:

- In 2001, nearly one half of teens reported being sexually active by the end of high school, and nearly 1 in 10 said they had sex before age 13 (National Campaign to Prevent Teen Pregnancy, 2006).

Sex education, although controversial, has become a common curriculum component in many school districts.

- Almost 13 percent of 10th graders said they had four or more sex partners (Grunbaum et al., 2002).

- The average age of first intercourse dropped from 19 to 15 between 1943 and 1999 (Tonn, 2005b).

- The United States has the highest rate of teenage pregnancy and births in the Western industrialized world (National Campaign to Prevent Teen Pregnancy, 2006).

- Eighty percent of teenagers who become pregnant are unmarried, and most (57 percent) teenage mothers keep their babies (Alan Guttmacher Institute, 2004). These pregnancies take an enormous toll on both the mother and the child.

If parents and churches are responsible for sex education, they're doing a poor job, proponents of sex education contend. They further argue that schools have both a right and a responsibility to ensure that all students have access to information about their developing sexuality, and courts have upheld school districts' rights to offer sex education courses (Fischer, Schimmel, & Stellman, 2006). Parents who object are free to take their children out of the classes or programs.

Further, polls indicate that the majority of parents and the population at large favor some type of sex education. For example, in one poll, 93 percent of high school and 95 percent of middle school parents said they favor sex education and believe that their children should be given information to protect themselves from unplanned pregnancies and sexually transmitted diseases (Kaiser Family Foundation, 2004b). In another, 94 percent of parents said they want schools to address real-life issues, such as pressure to have sex and the emotional consequences of becoming sexually active (T. Hoff, 2002).

Polls also indicate that students feel the same way. In one survey, 17-year-olds expressed a great need for sex education, and they also believed that boys and girls should be taught in nonsegregated groups, men and women should cooperate in leading classes, enrollment in classes should be voluntary, and a variety of viewpoints should be presented (Michener, 2006).

The content of sex education courses is a second controversial issue, and it is highly politicized. Religious conservatives support abstinence-only programs and are strongly opposed to any other form of sex education, including discussion of contraception, arguing that it encourages sexual promiscuity and is fundamentally dangerous to the well-being of our young people and society in general (Dimick & Apple, 2005). The administration of George W. Bush was supportive of conservative groups and promoted abstinence-only programs. For example, the Bush 2006 budget provided more than $200 million to support these programs, an 18.5-percent increase over 2005 (Rocha, 2006). Liberal groups have been equally adamant, arguing that conservatives are doing a disservice to children, including their own (Roffman, 2005). A poll conducted in 2004 indicated that fewer than 1 of 10 parents thought that sexuality education should *not* be taught in schools, and of those, only 15 percent advocated an abstinence-only approach (Kaiser Family Foundation, 2004a).

What does research say? The best available evidence indicates that the most effective programs combine abstinence education and information about birth control and the development of refusal and other communication skills (LaChausse, 2006). Research on abstinence-only programs is mixed at best (M. Young & Penhollow, 2006; Sessions-Stepp, 2007). A recent comprehensive study that tracked teenagers 4 to 6 years after these programs found no differences between students who participated in these programs and those who didn't (Mathematica Policy Research, 2007). In addition, research revealed that teenagers who took virginity pledges had the same number of sexual partners and had sex at around the same age as students who didn't (Samuels, 2009a). Unfortunately, abstinence-pledgers were also less likely to use birth control or condoms when they did have sex. Abstinence-only programs don't seem to be effective in discouraging teenage sexual behavior.

In a review of different sex education programs, C. Everett Koop, the former U.S. surgeon general, concluded that "given that one-half of adolescents in the United States are already sexually active and at risk of unintended pregnancy and STD/HIV infection, it also seems clear that adolescents need accurate information about contraceptive methods so that they can reduce those risks" (quoted in T. Hoff, 2002, p. 61).

Moral and Character Education

Should your job as a teacher be to make students smarter and more knowledgeable, or should it also include making them "better" people? Like sex education, the proper place of values and moral education in the curriculum is also controversial. Although most educators agree that this type of education is needed, they disagree about the form it should take.

One position, called **character education**, suggests that moral values and positive character traits, such as honesty and citizenship, should be emphasized, taught, and rewarded. Proponents believe that right and wrong do exist and that parents and schools have a responsibility to teach students to recognize the difference (Joseph & Efron, 2005). Character education emphasizes the study of values, practicing these values both in school and elsewhere, and rewarding displays of these values when they occur.

Moral education, by contrast, is more value free, emphasizing instead the development of students' moral reasoning. Moral education uses moral dilemmas and classroom discussions to teach problem solving and to bring about changes in the way learners think about moral issues. Critics of character education argue that it indoctrinates rather than educates (Joseph & Efron, 2005); critics of moral education assert that it has a relativistic view of morals, with no right or wrong answers (Wynne, 1997). The strength of character education is its capability to identify and promote core values, such as honesty, caring, and respect for others. Few would argue that these values are unnecessary or inappropriate. Further, research indicates that character education programs are effective for developing both students' social skills and their academic abilities (Viadero, 2003a). However, emphasizing student thinking and decision making is important as well, and this is the focus of the moral education perspective.

For either moral or character education to work, some public consensus must exist about what values are important for students to learn, and polls suggest that this consensus does exist (Bushaw & Gallup, 2008). When asked whether the following values should be taught in public schools, the following percentages of a national sample replied affirmatively: honesty (97 percent), democracy (93 percent), acceptance of people of different races and ethnic backgrounds (93 percent), and caring for friends and family members (90 percent). Fewer people supported the idea of teaching acceptance of people with different sexual orientations, specifically homosexuals or bisexuals (55 percent), and acceptance of the right of a woman to choose an abortion (48 percent). Research indicates, however, that these less popular, more controversial issues receive little or no emphasis in the curriculum (Thornton, 2003).

The classroom environment and the teacher's leadership are more important than the specific approach to developing moral behavior in young people. The teacher sets the moral tone for the classroom, through both words and actions. Core values of honesty and respect for others' rights need to permeate the curriculum. Students must feel that they belong in school, that their teachers are supportive, and that it's safe to offer their views without fear of embarrassment or ridicule (Bryan, 2005; Cohen, 2006). And, other than parents, teachers, through their actions in the classroom, serve as models of moral behavior and are probably the most powerful factor in developing caring and responsible young people (Quick & Normore, 2004).

Character education A curriculum approach to developing student morality that emphasizes teaching and rewarding moral values and positive character traits, such as honesty and citizenship.

Moral education A curricular approach to teaching morality that emphasizes the development of students' moral reasoning.

So, now we have an answer to the fifth item in our *This I Believe* feature, "The major dispute about moral or character education is whether it should be taught in schools." This statement isn't true. Both educators and the general public largely agree that values should be taught in schools; the dispute is about which values and how these values should be taught.

SERVICE LEARNING

Cindy Lloyd's students at Somerset Intermediate School in Westover, Maryland, conducted a grocery drive called Harvest for the Hungry. In addition to collecting and distributing food for the poor, they studied the effects of malnutrition in science. In social studies, they learned about the economics and politics of food distribution. They read novels and poetry about poverty, wrote newspaper articles about their campaign, and toured a food bank. (Adapted from F. Smith, 2006)

Service learning teaches values by actively involving students in community-based service projects.

Service learning is an approach to character education that combines service to the community with content-learning objectives. It blends civic action with academic subjects to provide students with a broader appreciation of the disciplines, while enhancing their sense of civic responsibility (Hart, Donnelly, Youniss, & Atkins, 2007). The rationale is that providing service changes both the provider and the recipient of the service.

Service-learning programs differ in their relative emphasis on the service component versus growth to students, though all service-learning classes have elements of both (Butin, 2003). Examples of service-learning programs that focus on social service include environmental education projects designed to encourage people to recycle, volunteer work in hospitals, and voter education projects aimed at getting people out to vote. Service-learning programs that emphasize student growth include internships and field-based programs that allow students to see academic concepts applied in real-life situations. Because of this emphasis on application, service learning also has motivational benefits. One urban high school student commented,

> Every Wednesday we go out for the entire day and do community service, and it's really made a big difference to me. In our building, we have Early Head Start, where moms drop their babies off, and I go down there and help. That's really made me want to go to school on Wednesdays, getting to loosen up and have a little bit of fun . . . (Cushman, 2006, p. 37)

The popularity of service-learning programs is growing. Between 1984 and 2004, the number of K–12 students involved in service-learning programs rose from 900,000 to more than 10.6 million, and the proportion of high school students participating in service learning grew from 2 to 25 percent during the same time period (F. Smith, 2006).

An important policy question is whether service learning should be voluntary or required. The state of Maryland requires 75 hours of service before high school graduation (F. Smith, 2006). A number of districts in California, Washington, Pennsylvania, and North Carolina have similar requirements (Fischer et al., 2006). Not all parents support these service-learning requirements, however, and some have legally challenged schools that have mandatory service-learning courses. Courts have upheld the legality of these courses, noting that they promote habits of good citizenship and introduce students to the idea of social responsibility.

Service learning An approach to character education that combines service to the community with content-learning objectives.

Intelligent Design

Where did we come from, and how did we get here? These questions have intrigued people since the beginning of time and are central issues in most religions. More directly, what role should schools play in helping students deal with these questions?

Intelligent design is a theory suggesting that certain features of the universe and of living things are so complex that their existence is best explained by an intelligent cause, rather than an undirected process such as natural selection or evolution. Proponents of intelligent design argue that it's a scientific theory that stands on equal footing with, or is superior to, current scientific theories regarding the evolution and origin of life; polls indicate that a significant portion (55 percent) of the public believes in intelligent design and favors its being taught in schools along with evolution (Harris Interactive, Inc., 2005).

Opponents argue that intelligent design is little more than creationism, a religious view suggesting that the universe was created by God as described in the Bible, framed in terms designed to make it appear scientific. And the overwhelming majority of the scientific community views intelligent design as unscientific, pseudoscience, or junk science (Attiel et al., 2006; Bergin, 2006). The U.S. National Academy of Sciences has stated that intelligent design and other claims of supernatural intervention in the origin of life are not science because they can't be tested by experiment, don't generate any predictions, and propose no new hypotheses of their own (Steering Committee on Science and Creationism, 1999).

Intelligent design is intensely controversial and highly politicized, and the issue has even gone to court. In the first direct challenge to a Pennsylvania school district's requirement that science classes teach intelligent design as a viable alternative to evolution, a United States federal court ruled that the requirement was a violation of the establishment clause of the First Amendment to the U.S. Constitution (*Kitzmiller et al. v. Dover Area School District*, 2005).

Controversies over intelligent design are not likely to diminish. For example, in 2009, the controversy reemerged in Texas, as its State Board of Education heard impassioned testimony from scientists and social conservatives on revising the science curriculum (McKinley, 2009). This debate centers on language in the state's curriculum that says students should explore "the strengths and weaknesses" of all theories, including evolution. Critics—essentially the entire scientific community—argue that the phrase "strengths and weaknesses" is a strategy religious conservatives are using to embed creationism in the curriculum. Advocates of the language argue that they are simply fighting for academic freedom and against what they see as fanatical loyalty to Darwin among biologists. Several other states have considered legislation requiring classrooms to be open to discussions about the strengths and weaknesses of evolution (McKinley, 2009).

The issue is broader than language in state standards. For example, business leaders have argued that Texas would have trouble attracting highly educated workers and their families if the state's science programs were seen as a laughingstock among biologists (McKinley, 2009).

You may encounter this issue when you begin teaching, particularly if you're planning to be a science teacher.

Censorship

What do the following books have in common?

Of Mice and Men, by John Steinbeck

The Diary of a Young Girl, by Anne Frank

The Adventures of Huckleberry Finn, by Mark Twain

To Kill a Mockingbird, by Harper Lee

Leaves of Grass, by Walt Whitman

Intelligent design A theory suggesting that certain features of the universe and of living things are so complex that their existence is best explained by an intelligent cause, rather than by an undirected process such as natural selection.

All of these works have, at various times, been targeted to be banned from the public-school curriculum. The language arts area has often been a battleground for curriculum controversy because of the issue of censorship. **Censorship** is the practice of prohibiting objectionable materials, such as certain books used in libraries or in academic classes.

Issues of censorship have existed throughout history and will continue in the foreseeable future. These issues are probably even more prominent and more politicized now with ongoing concerns about the fight against terrorism, moral values, and the rights of gays and lesbians, together with the increased political power of religious conservatives in the United States. In 2005, Oklahoma legislators urged libraries to limit students' access to books with gay themes (Oder, 2005), and librarians in Arkansas were pressured to remove books with similar themes from school libraries (L. Weiss, 2005). In Miami, Florida, the federal courts became embroiled in a censorship battle over a book, *A Visit to Cuba*, that critics believed painted too rosy a picture of communist Cuba (Banning Books in Miami, 2009).

The question of what books and what content students should be allowed, or required, to read in schools remains unanswered. For instance, J. K. Rowling's wildly popular Harry Potter series has raised questions, and more controversial is Phillip Pullman's (2002) *His Dark Materials* trilogy, a series of three novels that are openly anti-Christian in their orientation (Wartofsky, 2001). Defenders of both Rowling and Pullman argue that the books inspire kids to read and involve moral themes, their messages are quite harmless, and censorship is not an appropriate response to controversial literature (Glanzer, 2005). Critics argue that the books send the wrong message to young adults (Glanzer, 2004). The fact that both series are very popular with young people only fuels the controversy.

Censorship also raises questions, with conflicting answers, about other important issues in education. One is parents' control over their children's education. Shouldn't parents have a say in the books their children read? A related question involves professional autonomy: Shouldn't teachers be free to select books that professional judgment tells them are important, if not essential, to student learning and development? In considering these often opposing views, the courts have usually decided against censorship of books, ruling that schools and teachers have a right to expose students to different ideas and points of view through literature (Fischer et al., 2006).

■ ■ TECHNOLOGY AND TEACHING The Controversy Over Internet Censorship

The Internet can be a powerful learning tool, but students' ability to access information from it at the click of a button also raises concerns about the kinds of materials available to children. Internet filtering via software programs can be used to block out entire lists of web pages based on specific, predetermined categories, or people can use certain words to limit access to sites. For example, states typically use filters to prevent students from accessing information in five broad categories: criminal skills, hate speech, drugs, gambling, and sex (Callister & Burbules, 2004).

The United States is not unique in attempting to censor information on the Internet. In 2007, for example, Algeria, China, Egypt, Kazakhstan, Russia, and Thailand all made concerted efforts to censor materials on the Internet, and Australia is planning to spend $82 million on its "cybersafety" plan (Foley, 2008; Global Integrity Commons, 2008).

Several controversies surround this practice. The first is the whole issue of censorship and free speech. Free speech advocates contend that such filtering is unconstitutional, violating students' rights to access to information and free speech.

Also, censorship results in the exclusion of many interesting and educationally defensible sites (Callister & Burbules, 2004). For example, one sex screen banned

Censorship The practice of prohibiting objectionable materials, such as certain books used in libraries or in academic classes.

Women and Minorities in the Curriculum

 The curriculum in U.S. schools has been criticized because, according to critics, it has failed to adequately represent the contributions of women and cultural minorities (Sincero & Woyshner, 2003). For example, until as recently as the 1960s and 1970s, the majority of the works included in junior high and high school literature books were written by White males, such as William Shakespeare, Mark Twain, and Robert Frost, with only a few additional contributions by White women.

Recognition of the historical contributions of minorities was similarly lacking. For example, Dr. Charles Drew (1904–1950), an African American, developed the procedure for separating plasma from whole blood; this was an enormous contribution that unquestionably saved many soldiers' lives in World War II. Dr. Charles Norman (b. 1930), another African American, was the first person to implant an artificial heart in a human. Until recently, most history books ignored contributions such as these.

In response to critics, as well as shifts in our society, this situation has changed. For example, a postage stamp was issued in Drew's honor in 1981, and science fiction writer Isaac Asimov, a friend of Norman's, based his novel *Fantastic Voyage* on work done in Norman's laboratory. History texts have been expanded to include the contributions of women and minorities. Literature books, too, have changed: Many now include works written by members of various cultural minority groups, such as Maya Angelou, Sandra Cisneros, Gary Soto, and Toni Cade Bambara.

The issue is controversial, with critics charging that cultural minorities still remain underrepresented in the curriculum (Banks, 2006). Content focusing primarily on the contributions of men of northern European descent—often derisively described as a "Eurocentric" curriculum—is perceived as out of balance and irrelevant to minorities. For example, a recent analysis of California's social studies standards found that 77 percent of significant contributions mentioned were by Euro-Americans (Sleeter, 2005). Critics argue that because more than a third of our schoolchildren are minorities and because this percentage is increasing, the curriculum should be broadened to better reflect minority members' contributions and presence in our society. In addition, they assert, some time-honored literature, such as Mark Twain's *The Adventures of Huckleberry Finn*, portrays characters in ways that promote racial stereotypes and prejudice.

Some critics argue further that entire curricula should be oriented to specific ethnic groups. For instance, to help African American students understand and appreciate their cultural heritage, proponents of an "Afrocentric" curriculum advocate focusing on the achievements of African cultures, particularly ancient Egypt. Students who study the contributions of people with ethnicity similar to their own will gain in self-esteem, motivation, and learning, they contend. Afrocentric curricula are currently being experimented with in a number of inner-city school districts (Gollnick & Chinn, 2009).

These positions have critics of their own, however. Some educators and social commentators question the accuracy and balance of the content and whether the emphasis on differences leads to racial and ethnic separatism (Coughlin, 1996; Ravitch, 1990). They also argue that schools have already gone too far in emphasizing cultural differences, resulting in the reduction or elimination of studies that focus on some of the great contributions of literature, such as the works of Shakespeare (Hirsch, 1987; Ravitch, 2000). Further, they maintain, we are all Americans, and an overemphasis on diversity has resulted in the failure of students to develop a common cultural heritage and shared national identity (Schlesinger, 1992).

The role of women in the curriculum is also controversial. For example, many feminist groups contend that women continue to be both underrepresented and misrepresented in the curriculum, arguing that students read too many books that portray men as doctors, lawyers, and engineers, and women as nurses, teachers, and secretaries. A recent study of California's history–social science standards found that of the 96 Americans mentioned in the standards, only 18 percent were female (Sleeter, 2005). When this occurs, they assert, girls are sent messages about what are and are not appropriate roles and careers for them (American Association of University Women, 1992).

However, a strong and systematic national effort has been made to address the needs of girls and women in today's schools (Riordan, 2004). Some people contend that the emphasis on girls' needs has gone too far, the argument made in *The War Against Boys*, the provocative book by Christine Hoff Sommers (2000). The debate continues, and the controversy is likely to remain in the future.

Diversity in Your Classroom

A major theme of this chapter has been that teachers, as professionals, exert a powerful influence over the curriculum in their classrooms. Though teachers are expected to help their students reach certain standards, how they do this and the relative emphasis placed on specific standards is up to teachers' professional judgment.

If you are concerned about the coverage of topics regarding women and cultural minorities in the classroom, take a proactive role in reshaping your curriculum. In discussing the Great Depression in United States history, for example, it's relatively easy to include information about how the Depression affected women and minorities. The same is true for most subjects in social studies and literature. In addition, teachers can do much to ensure that the implicit curriculum in their classrooms is

sensitive to gender and culture issues. Some specific ways to do this are found in the questions that follow.

QUESTIONS TO CONSIDER

1. What can teachers do to make sure that their classrooms are free of gender bias?
2. How does the cultural diversity in a class influence the teacher's actions in terms of curriculum? Is the issue of

cultural diversity in the curriculum greater or less for teachers who teach in predominantly White schools?

myeducationlab To respond to these questions online, explore this topic further, and receive feedback, go to the *Book Specific Resources* section in the MyEducationLab for your course, select your text, and then select *Exploring Diversity* for Chapter 11.

---

information on breast cancer, a gambling screen excluded the History of Nevada website, and a screen targeting criminal skills eliminated sites on Marxism and even the Declaration of Independence (presumably because it calls for citizens to violently overthrow their government, if necessary). Critics contend that this indiscriminate screening not only robs students of important information but also may be politically biased, as is the case with Marxism.

Critics of Internet censorship make an additional compelling argument: Censoring the Internet is extremely difficult. When one site is cut off, many more pop up. In spite of concerted efforts by governments around the world, sites are expanding at an accelerating rate, and they're very difficult to control (Global Integrity Commons, 2008).

Censor advocates counter that Internet filtering is no different from selecting curriculum content and textbooks for students based on fundamental principles of good teaching. This comparison with schoolbooks illustrates how challenging and complex Internet filtering can be. Textbook selection is centralized and consequently much easier; school districts and schools are given lists of several textbook series that a state curriculum committee finds acceptable. Internet filtering, by contrast, is aimed at a moving target, because new websites appear daily. For example, one state's system controls access to 100,000 computers used by 900,000 students. The system needs to be updated every night and has blocked access to 7 million web pages (Furlan, 1999).

A third controversy surrounding Internet filtering is the level at which it should occur. Some argue for federal legislation, claiming this is a national problem; others argue for state or district control, pointing out that local agencies are in a better position to decide what's best for the needs of their children. When local control occurs, however, there is the possibility of duplication of effort, with thousands of local districts performing essentially the same function.

There are no easy answers with this issue. In 2000, the U.S. Congress passed the Children's Online Protection Act (COPA), which requires all schools and libraries that receive federal funds for Internet connection to install pornography filters in their systems (M. Walsh & Hendrie, 2003). In 2008, however, COPA was struck down by a circuit court of appeals (*ACLU v. Mukasey*, 2008), and in 2009, the U.S. Supreme Court dismissed a federal government's appeal of the circuit court decision without comment (K. Jones, 2009).

The whole area of Internet access will, in all likelihood, continue to grow in importance as more classrooms use the Internet to access data.

This section focused on controversies in the curriculum. In the *Exploring Diversity* feature on pages 343–344 we examine another controversial issue—the inclusion of women and minorities in the curriculum.

Curriculum Controversies

You're a biology teacher, and you frequently examine topics that illustrate evolution in your classes; your school doesn't have an official policy in place with respect to teaching intelligent design as an alternative to evolution. As a science teacher, your views tend to be aligned with the prevailing views of the scientific community, which is that intelligent design is not a scientific theory and as such isn't an alternative to the theory of evolution. Therefore, in your view, intelligent design should not be taught in science classes.

The day after one of your lessons dealt with evolutionary advances in different organisms, one of your students brings three short articles extolling the virtues of intelligent design to your biology class. He asks to distribute the articles to his classmates and discuss the content in them, because he believes that you are expressing only one view—and a biased view—of the existence of the natural universe.

What would you say to this student regarding his request?

■ ■ ■ ■ CHECK YOUR UNDERSTANDING

4.1 How do issues involving sex education and moral development differ in their influence on the school curriculum?

4.2 Describe the concept of *intelligent design*, and explain how it could influence curriculum decisions.

4.3 How could issues involving censorship influence your curriculum decisions?

For feedback, go to the appendix, *Check Your Understanding*, located in the back of this text.

Each of you, at some time, will confront a curriculum controversy in your teaching. The *Decision Making* feature, above, examines one teacher's experience with this challenge.

11 MEETING YOUR LEARNING OBJECTIVES

1. Describe different definitions of *curriculum*, and explain how curriculum and instruction are related.
   - *Curriculum* is defined in a variety of ways, such as the subject matter taught to students, a systematic arrangement of courses, the planned educational experiences offered by a school, experiences students have in school, and the process teachers go through in selecting and organizing learning experiences for their students.
   - In this chapter, *curriculum* is defined as everything teachers teach and students learn in school, and *instruction* is described as the set of strategies teachers use to help students reach the goals established in the curriculum.

2. Explain how the explicit curriculum, the implicit curriculum, the null curriculum, and the extracurriculum are different.
   - The *explicit curriculum* is the curriculum found in textbooks and other formal educational experiences.

- The *implicit*, or *hidden*, *curriculum* is reflected in the climate of the school and the classroom, along with their unstated values and priorities. It differs from the explicit curriculum in that it isn't specifically prescribed and, in some cases, is out of the teachers' conscious control.

- The *null curriculum* differs from the explicit and the implicit curricula in that they both reflect what is taught, whereas the null curriculum reflects what is not taught.

- The *extracurriculum* includes learning experiences that extend beyond the core of students' formal studies. Participation in extracurricular activities correlates with a number of positive outcomes, including increased achievement and more positive attitudes toward school.

3. Identify different forces that influence the curriculum, and explain how each exerts its influence.

- Standards and accountability, the federal government, textbooks, and a teacher's philosophical views of teaching and learning all influence the curriculum.

- Standards and accountability influence the curriculum because standards specify what students should be learning, and what is tested often becomes what is taught.

- The federal government influences curriculum through its legislative mandates as well as through the programs it supports financially.

- Textbooks influence the curriculum because many teachers use textbooks as a primary source for their curricular decisions about what to teach.

- Teachers' philosophies influence the curriculum because philosophy is grounded in beliefs; professionals teach what they believe is important, and they use approaches they believe are most effective.

4. Describe prominent controversial issues in the curriculum.

- 21st Century Skills, reading, and math, sex education, education in morals and values, intelligent design versus evolution, censorship, and the underrepresentation of women and minorities in the curriculum are controversial issues facing teachers. These issues are likely to remain unresolved in the near future.

- These controversial issues influence the curriculum because they affect what topics are or are not taught and how they are presented to students.

IMPORTANT CONCEPTS

censorship (p. 342)
character education (p. 339)
core curriculum (p. 332)
curriculum (p. 321)
explicit curriculum (p. 322)
extracurriculum (p. 327)
implicit curriculum (p. 325)
instruction (p. 321)

integrated curriculum (p. 324)
intelligent design (p. 341)
moral education (p. 339)
null curriculum (p. 326)
phonics (p. 336)
service learning (p. 340)
21st Century Skills (p. 334)
whole language (p. 335)

DISCUSSION QUESTIONS

1. Which has a greater influence on students' learning, curriculum or instruction? Why do you think so?

2. Think back to your own experiences in schools, and then consider what you've read in this chapter. Which has changed more over time, the curriculum or instruction? Why do you think so?

3. Some critics argue that the implicit curriculum has more impact on students' overall education than does the explicit curriculum. Do you agree or disagree with this argument? Defend your position with a concrete example.

4. During financial crises, some schools have reduced their extracurricular offerings. To what extent does this detract from students' overall education? Defend your position with a concrete example.

5. Which of the factors that influence the curriculum do you believe will most influence your teaching? Why do you think so?

6. Is our current curriculum balanced in attention to the contributions of women and cultural minorities? Why or why not? Should we be doing more in this area? Why or why not?

Now go to Topic 11: *Curriculum* in the MyEducationLab (www.myeducationlab.com) for your course, where you can:

- Find learning outcomes for *Curriculum* along with the national standards that connect to these outcomes.

- Complete *Assignments and Activities* that can help you more deeply understand the chapter content.

- Apply and practice your understanding of the core teaching skills identified in the chapter with the *Building Teaching Skills and Dispositions* learning units.

- Check your comprehension on the content covered in the chapter by going to the *Study Plan* in the *Book Specific Resources* section for your text. Here you will be able to take a chapter quiz, receive feedback on your answers, and then access *Review, Practice, and Enrichment* activities to enhance your understanding of chapter content.

Develop Your Professional Portfolio

To further apply your understanding of chapter content and address the INTASC standards, go to the *Book Specific Resources* section in the MyEducationLab for your course, select your text, and then select this chapter's *Portfolio Activities*.

"When the class is fun and challenging, the students feel a sense of accomplishment, and they leave the room understanding the power of their own minds."

SETH BERG, 2008 Teacher of the Year, Colorado

To view a video clip of Seth, the 2008 Colorado Teacher of the Year, go to Topic 10: *Creating Productive Learning Environments* in the MyEducationLab for your course and select *Teacher Talk*, then *Seth Berg*.

12

Creating Productive Learning Environments: Classroom Management

LEARNING OBJECTIVES

After you have completed your study of this chapter, you should be able to:

1. **Explain how a productive learning environment contributes to learning.** INTASC Standard 5, Classroom Motivation and Management

2. **Describe how effective teachers plan for classroom management.** INTASC Standard 5, Classroom Motivation and Management

3. **Explain how involving parents contributes to a productive learning environment.** INTASC Standard 5, Classroom Motivation and Management

4. **Describe how effective teachers intervene when misbehavior occurs.** INTASC Standard 5, Classroom Motivation and Management

As you look forward to your first classroom, what will be your greatest concern? If you're typical of first-year teachers, the answer is "classroom management." Learning to manage a classroom is the most important and challenging task that new teachers face (Stoughton, 2007). A well-managed classroom is essential for creating a safe and enjoyable environment for both you and your students, as well as for increasing your students' learning and motivation. As you read the following case study, think about what the teacher does to create a productive learning environment in her classroom.

URBAN EDUCATION

Shannon Brinkman, a fifth-grade teacher, is in her third year of work in an urban elementary school in the Southwest. As she anticipates the new school year, she spends several days preparing her room. She tapes posters and pictures on the walls and labels the clock, windows, door, and other common objects with signs in both Spanish and English.

As her students enter her classroom on the first day, she greets them at the door and tells them to find their names on the desks. Shannon has 14 girls and 10 boys in her class, and 8 of them speak Spanish as their first language. As soon as students are settled, she asks them to introduce themselves and describe their families, some of their favorite activities, and anything else they think might be interesting.

After students have introduced themselves, Shannon comments, "We are going to have a great year. I asked you to introduce yourselves because we're all going to work together to help each other learn and grow. Our classroom is like a family, and in families, people help each other. So, that's what we're going to do.

"To be sure we all help each other and learn, we need some guidelines that will make our classroom run as smoothly as possible," she continues, and then asks students to make suggestions that will help them all be comfortable and will keep the classroom safe and orderly. They discuss the suggestions, and Shannon makes notes to be sure she remembers what students have said. After the discussion, she takes a picture of each student with her digital camera.

She prints the pictures of the students that evening, and also creates a poster describing rules and procedures based on their discussion in class. Before school the next morning, she displays the pictures on a bulletin board under a sign that says, "Our class," and also places the rules and procedures where everyone can see.

Her first day has been demanding, but she feels ready to jump into the year.

We return to Shannon's work with her students shortly, but for now, think about two questions: 1) What is a productive learning environment? 2) How can you create this type of environment in your own classroom? We address these questions in this chapter.

Before you begin your study, please respond to the items in the This I Believe feature on the next page. We address each in the chapter.

PRODUCTIVE LEARNING ENVIRONMENTS

At the core of every successful classroom management system is a productive learning environment. A **productive learning environment** is a classroom that is orderly and focused on learning. Students feel physically and emotionally safe, and the daily routines, learning activities, and standards for appropriate behavior are all designed to promote learning. *Orderly* doesn't mean rigid or punitive, however. In productive classrooms, students are well behaved, but the emotional climate is relaxed and inviting. In a productive learning environment, students understand that *learning* is the highest priority, and they are respectful of others and accept responsibility for their actions. Teachers rarely raise their voices, and the focus is on helping everyone learn. Why are classroom environments so important, and how can teachers create them? Research provides some answers.

The Importance of Classroom Management

Classroom management is important to teachers, as well as the general public. For teachers, effective classroom management creates an environment in which they can teach and students can learn. For the public at large, effective classroom management is a clear, visible sign that schools and teachers are in charge and know what they're doing.

Productive learning environments Classrooms that are orderly and focused on learning.

For each item, circle the number that best represents your thinking. Use the following scale as a guide.

4 = I strongly believe the statement is true.
3 = I believe the statement is true.
2 = I believe the statement is false.
1 = I strongly believe the statement is false.

1. The best classroom managers are those who can quickly stop student misbehavior when it occurs.

    1   2   3   4

2. The most effective way to increase how much students learn about a content area, such as math, is to allocate more time to that subject.

    1   2   3   4

3. Caring is important for elementary students, but its importance diminishes as students move into middle and high school.

    1   2   3   4

4. Involving parents in their children's education can actually increase student learning.

    1   2   3   4

5. Teachers are required by law to intervene if students in their classes are involved in a fight or scuffle.

    1   2   3   4

myeducationlab To download and complete this form, go to the *Book Specific Resources* section in the MyEducationLab for your course, select your text, and then select *This I Believe* for Chapter 12.

PROFESSIONAL AND PUBLIC CONCERNS   From the 1960s until 2004, polls identified classroom management as one of teachers' most challenging problems, and from 2004 to the present, it ranked second, behind only school funding, as the most important problem facing schools (Bushaw & Gallup, 2008).

> Classroom management is a topic of enduring concern for teachers, administrators, and the public. Beginning teachers consistently perceive student discipline as their most serious challenge, management problems continue to be a major cause of teacher burnout and job dissatisfaction, and the public repeatedly ranks discipline as the first or second most serious problem facing the schools. (Evertson & Weinstein, 2006, p. 3)

Though the ability to manage classrooms can be challenging, it isn't impossible, and with careful planning and effective instruction, it can be accomplished. Our goal in writing this chapter is to help you acquire the knowledge and skills that will allow you to do so.

INFLUENCE ON STUDENT LEARNING AND MOTIVATION   Learning is the central purpose of schooling, and the primary reason classroom management is so important is that students learn more and are more motivated to learn in well-managed classrooms (Good & Brophy, 2008). For example, students learn more when the environment is comfortable and inviting, so effective teachers strive to create an emotionally safe environment in which students can live and learn (Emmer, Evertson, & Worsham, 2009; Evertson, Emmer, & Worsham, 2009). We emphasize respect and personal responsibility because they promote personal, social, and moral development in our students. We avoid criticizing students because criticism detracts from learning. We create systems of procedures and rules because students learn more in environments that are safe and predictable.

This focus on learning guides our actions as teachers and helps answer this question: Why are productive learning environments so important? They're important because they allow students to learn and teachers to teach.

Goals of Classroom Management

Some of the earliest research on classroom management was done by Jacob Kounin (1970), who helped teachers understand the difference between **classroom management**, comprehensive actions teachers take to create an environment that supports and facilitates academic and social-emotional learning (Evertson & Weinstein, 2006), and **discipline**, teachers' responses to student misbehavior. Kounin found that the key to orderly classrooms is the teacher's ability to *prevent* management problems, rather than handling misbehavior once it occurs. His findings have been consistently corroborated over the years (Evertson & Weinstein, 2006).

This discussion addresses the first item on our *This I Believe* feature, "The best classroom managers are those who can quickly stop student misbehavior when it occurs." This statement isn't true; in fact, experts estimate that anticipation and prevention are 80 percent of an effective classroom management system (Freiberg, 1999a).

Classroom management is more than simply keeping students quiet and in their seats. It is a process that, when effectively done, contributes to learners' academic, personal, and social development. Effective managers have four primary goals:

- Creating a positive classroom climate
- Creating a community of learners
- Developing learner responsibility
- Maximizing opportunities for learning

Let's look at them.

CREATING A POSITIVE CLASSROOM CLIMATE   Students learn more and are happier when the classrooms we create are safe and supportive. A **positive classroom climate** is an environment in which learners feel physically and emotionally safe, personally connected to both their teacher and their peers, and worthy of love and respect (Watson & Battistich, 2006; H. Wilson, Pianta, & Stuhlman, 2007). Physically aggressive acts as well as name-calling, bullying, put-downs, and other forms of hurtful interactions detract from a positive classroom climate and are discouraged.

Shannon promoted a positive classroom climate in several ways. Before the school year began, she created displays and placed pictures on her classroom walls to make her

This I BELIEVE

Classroom management Comprehensive actions teachers take to create an environment that supports and facilitates both academic and social-emotional learning.

Discipline Teachers' responses to student misbehavior.

Positive classroom climate An environment in which learners feel physically and emotionally safe, personally connected to both their teacher and their peers, and worthy of love and respect.

Effective classroom management creates a community of learners in which students learn personal responsibility.

room physically attractive. Because she knew that a number of native Spanish-speaking students were in her class, she labeled objects around the room in both English and Spanish. As students entered the first day, she greeted them at the door, had them introduce themselves, and displayed their pictures on the bulletin board. Each of these actions helped to make her classroom inviting.

CREATING A COMMUNITY OF LEARNERS When the classroom climate is positive, the classroom can become a **learning community**, a place in which the teacher and students work together to help everyone learn (Mason, 2007).

In addition to the trust and the physical and emotional safety essential for a positive classroom climate, learning communities have two important characteristics: 1) inclusiveness and support, and 2) respect for others.

Inclusiveness and Support. In a learning community, promoting learning isn't the teacher's responsibility alone. All students—high and low achievers, members and non-members of cultural minorities, students with and without exceptionalities, boys and girls—participate in learning activities, support each others' learning, and believe all can succeed. Every student believes that he or she belongs in the classroom. Teachers facilitate this process by involving all students in learning activities, calling on all students as equally as possible, and making them believe they belong in and are an important part of the class.

Shannon began this process by having her students offer suggestions for making their classroom a better place to learn. She didn't impose classroom rules on her students; the class collaborated in developing them. Her efforts helped students believe that they have a personal investment in the class and a role in making it a productive place to learn.

Respect for Others. Although trust and emotional safety are essential for a positive classroom climate, respect goes even further. For example, when the teacher speaks, students show respect by listening, and they do the same when a classmate has the floor. When students learn to be respectful, their personal and social development advances, and this development makes classroom management easier.

Young children (and some adults) are egocentric, believing that the whole world revolves around them, and their actions often reflect this belief. Our job as teachers is to help them understand that there are other students in the classroom—people who have feelings and who deserve courtesy and respect. By carefully explaining that classroom rules are designed to protect the rights of students, and that all students have a responsibility to follow them, teachers can make a major contribution to their students' development.

DEVELOPING LEARNER RESPONSIBILITY Another major goal of classroom management is to help students take responsibility for their actions and how they influence others. Teachers do this by developing learner responsibility (Elias & Schwab, 2006; Fletcher & Hoffman, 2006). As learners develop personally and socially, teachers help them understand they are each responsible for creating a productive learning environment. They obey rules because the rules make sense, instead of obeying rules because of the threat of punishment for breaking them. Teachers promote this orientation by explicitly teaching responsibility and emphasizing the reasons for rules and procedures. Students understand that order is important for learning, and they follow rules because they're designed to protect their rights as well as the rights of others.

Developing student responsibility is both sensible and practical. Learners are more likely to obey rules when the rules make sense and when they recognize that rules exist to protect their rights and the rights of others. This responsibility orientation also contributes to ethical thinking and character development (Nucci, 2006). Children don't call their classmates nasty names, for example, because they recognize that name-calling hurts other people's feelings. And, by promoting student responsibility and understanding, teachers actually make their own jobs easier. This takes time, and some classrooms will be more challenging than others, but research indicates that even students who display

Learning community A classroom environment in which the teacher and the students work together to help everyone learn.

aggressiveness and other conduct disorders can be taught to accept responsibility for their own behavior (Singh et al., 2007).

MAXIMIZING TIME AND OPPORTUNITIES FOR LEARNING   Although social-emotional development is an important goal, promoting academic learning is at the core of any effective classroom management system. Academic learning depends on two factors: (1) time available for learning, and (2) the effectiveness of the teacher's instruction. To maximize time for learning, some reformers have suggested lengthening the school year and the school day, and even increasing the amount of time devoted to certain subjects (Gabrieli & Goldstein, 2008). Comparisons with other countries reveal that U.S. students have significantly less instructional time than students in other countries (Gewertz, 2008a). For example, instructional time in Korea totals 1,079 hours per year, versus 799 hours in the United States. But increasing learning by giving students more time isn't as simple as it appears on the surface, because simply allocating more time to a topic may not result in significant increases in learning (Weinstein & Mignano, 2007). The reason for this is significant differences in dimensions of time.

Academic learning time combines student engagement with success to produce learning.

Classroom time exists at four levels:

- Allocated time
- Instructional time
- Engaged time
- Academic learning time

Figure 12.1 Levels of Time

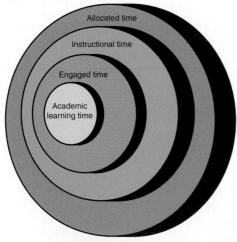

Allocated time The amount of time a teacher designates for a particular content area or topic.

Instructional time The amount left for teaching after teachers have completed routine management and administrative tasks.

These levels can be viewed as the areas of a series of concentric circles, and the correlation with learning becomes stronger as the areas of the circles get smaller. This relationship is illustrated in Figure 12.1 and discussed in the following paragraphs.

Allocated time is the amount of time a teacher designates for a particular content area or topic. For example, teachers in elementary schools typically schedule the majority of their time for reading, language arts, and math, with much less allocated to science, social studies, and other subjects. Although middle, junior high, and high school teachers appear to have less control over time allocations because of their fixed schedules and bells signaling the beginning and end of class periods, all teachers have considerable flexibility. A 10th-grade English teacher, for example, could choose to emphasize writing rather than grammar or literature by simply spending more time on it.

Instructional time is the amount left for teaching after teachers have completed routine management and administrative tasks, such as taking roll, returning papers, and making announcements. Teachers also lose instructional time when they respond to student disruptions and make transitions from one activity to another. Some lost time is out of a teachers' control; one research study found that teachers lost 20 percent of their instructional time to interruptions and delays from outside the classroom (Viadero, 2008c). Unfortunately, teachers are often unaware of the value of the time that they do have, thinking of it instead as something to be filled, used up, or even "killed." For example, compare these two teachers.

Enrico Martinez has a warm-up exercise on the board when his students enter the classroom, and he takes roll and completes routine tasks while they finish it. He then moves immediately to his lesson, and when they're finished, he gives an assignment, and monitors the class while they work on it.

Ted Burroughs takes roll and completes routine tasks while his students talk among themselves. After a few minutes, he begins his lesson and finishes with 10 minutes left in the period, during which he again lets his students talk quietly.

If these differences represent patterns, Ted will lose nearly 40 hours of instructional time over the course of a school year! The obvious result is less student learning.

Now, imagine going into a classroom to observe a teacher. Intuitively, one of the first things you would look for is whether students are paying attention and thinking about the lesson; this describes **engaged time** or time on task, which is the time students spend actively involved in learning activities. Teachers influence their students' engagement by how they teach. Interactive instruction, such as questioning and group work, which place students in active roles, results in higher engagement rates than strategies such as lecture, where students remain essentially passive (Eggen & Kauchak, 2010).

Student frustration also influences engaged time. If work is too difficult for students, they become frustrated, give up, and go off task. *Success* is a key variable in these cases, which leads to the concept of **academic learning time**, the amount of time students are both engaged and successful. When academic learning time is high, both learning and student motivation increase (Brophy, 2004; J. Hughes, Luo, Kwok, & Lloyd, 2008).

As one moves from allocated time to academic learning time, the connection to learning becomes stronger. In classrooms where students are engaged and successful, achievement is high, learners feel a sense of accomplishment, and interest in the topics increases. Unfortunately, a great deal of slippage occurs between allocated and academic learning time; experts estimate that only about 30 percent of the time available for learning actually gets converted into high-quality academic learning time (Weinstein & Mignano, 2007).

Effective classroom management maximizes instructional, engaged, and academic learning time so that the amount allocated to a topic or content area is used as efficiently as possible. Expert teachers are better at this than novices (Bohn, Roehrig, & Pressley, 2004). Less effective teachers waste opportunities for learning and create vacuums where management problems can occur.

Maximizing learning time can also promote responsibility. When students learn that they should begin work as soon as they enter the classroom, teachers don't have to spend time explaining what they're supposed to do and reminding them to get started; they take responsibility for doing it on their own. And, because students act responsibly, more time is available for learning.

This discussion addresses the second item in our *This I Believe* feature, "The most effective way to increase how much students learn about a content area, such as math, is to allocate more time to that subject." This statement isn't true: Although increasing allocated time generally increases learning, the most effective way to increase student learning is for them to participate in learning activities in which they're engaged and successful.

This I BELIEVE

■ ■ ■ ■ ■ CHECK YOUR UNDERSTANDING

1.1 What is a productive learning environment?

1.2 Explain why effective classroom management is so important.

1.3 Describe the goals of classroom management.

For feedback, go to the appendix, *Check Your Understanding*, located in the back of this text.

Engaged time (time on task). The time students spend actively involved in learning activities.

Academic learning time The amount of time students are both engaged and successful.

CREATING PRODUCTIVE LEARNING ENVIRONMENTS

We began the chapter by asking, "What is a productive learning environment?" and "How can you create this type of environment in your classroom?" We answered the first question in the previous section, and now we turn to the second. We begin with teachers.

The Teacher's Role

Teachers are essential for creating productive learning environments; they set the emotional tone for the classroom and create an atmosphere that can be inviting, neutral, or even threatening. (As a student, one of your authors entered his high school biology class and was greeted with, "My name is Isabel Wilharm, and the name means exactly what it says. Step out of line and I *will* harm.") Teachers also create productive learning environments through the learning activities they design, which engage, ignore, or even distance students. During lessons, they interact with students during instruction in ways that motivate, interest, or possibly bore them. Teachers make a difference in how classrooms feel.

Caring, an essential component of a productive learning environment, connects teachers with students on a human level.

CARING: AN ESSENTIAL ELEMENT IN TEACHING Think about some of the best teachers you've had: What comes to mind? If you're typical, the first thing you remember is that you believed they cared about you as a person and were committed to your learning. **Caring** refers to a teacher's investment in the protection and development of the young people in his or her classes, and a caring teacher is at the heart of a productive learning environment (Noddings, 2001; Roeser, Peck, & Nasir, 2006). The importance of caring is captured by one fourth grader's comment: "If a teacher doesn't care about you, it affects your mind. You feel like you're a nobody, and it makes you want to drop out of school" (Noblit, Rogers, & McCadden, 1995, p. 683). Research supports this fourth grader's feelings.

> Students who perceived that teachers cared about them reported positive motivational outcomes such as more prosocial and social responsibility goals, academic effort, and greater internal control beliefs. It appears that students want teachers to care for them both as learners and as people. (Perry, Turner, & Meyer, 2006, p. 341)

Additional research indicates that students are more motivated and learn more in classrooms where they believe their teachers like, understand, and empathize with them (Hallinan, 2008; Stipek, 2006). Students who believe they're welcome and who receive personal support from their teachers also are more interested in their class work and describe it as more important than do students whose teachers are distant. A supportive classroom environment, where each student is valued regardless of academic ability or performance, is essential for both learning and motivation for all students.

This discussion addresses the third item in our *This I Believe* feature, "Caring is important for elementary students, but its importance diminishes as students move into middle and high school." The first part of this statement is true, but the second isn't: A caring teacher is important for students at *all* grade levels, and this importance doesn't diminish as students grow older.

This I BELIEVE

Caring A teacher's investment in the protection and development of the young people in his or her classes.

Communicating Caring.   How do teachers communicate that they care about their students? Some important ways include the following:

* Learning students' names quickly and calling on students by their first name
* Greeting students every day and getting to know them as individuals
* Using effective nonverbal communication such as eye contact and smiling
* Using "we" and "our" in reference to class activities and assignments
* Spending time with students
* Holding students to high standards

The last two items on the list deserve special emphasis. We all have 24 hours in our days—no more, no less—and the way we choose to allocate our time is the truest measure of our priorities. Choosing to spend time with an individual student communicates caring better than any other single factor. Helping students who have problems with an assignment or calling a parent after school hours communicates that teachers care about students and their learning. Spending a moment to ask a question about a baby brother or to compliment a new hairstyle communicates caring about a student as a human being.

The idea that holding students to high standards is an indicator of caring may seem surprising. But as one school motivation expert suggested, teachers demonstrate that they care for students in these ways:

> [N]ot accepting sloppy, thoughtless, or incomplete work, by pressing them to clarify vague comments, by encouraging them not to give up, and by not praising work that does not reflect genuine effort. Ironically, reactions that are often intended to protect students' self-esteem—such as accepting low quality work—convey a lack of interest, patience, or caring. (Stipek, 2002, p. 157)

This view is corroborated by research. When junior high students were asked, "How do you know when a teacher cares about you?" they responded that paying attention to them as human beings was important, but more striking was their belief that teachers who care are committed to their learning and hold them to high standards (B. Wilson & Corbett, 2001).

EFFECTIVE TEACHING   If you observe classrooms in which classroom management doesn't seem to be an issue, one additional factor is apparent: This factor is **effective teaching**, instruction that maximizes learning by actively involving students in meaningful learning activities. It's virtually impossible for teachers to maintain orderly classrooms if instruction is boring or doesn't make sense to students. This relationship is corroborated by research (Kaff, Zabel, & Milham, 2007), and it's true whether you teach elementary, middle, or high school students. As you plan for classroom management, you must simultaneously plan for effective instruction.

Preventing Problems Through Planning

In productive learning environments, management is nearly invisible. The atmosphere is calm but not rigid, movement around the classroom and interaction in lessons are comfortable, and students work quietly. Learning is taking place. Teachers give few directions that focus on behavior, they reprimand students infrequently, and reprimands rarely intrude on learning. How do teachers make this happen?

The cornerstone of an effective management system is a clearly understood and consistently monitored set of rules and procedures that prevent management problems before they occur (Emmer et al., 2009; Evertson et al., 2009). Obviously, some classes are tougher to manage than others, but an orderly classroom is possible in most instances. It doesn't happen by accident, however. It requires careful planning, and beginning teachers often underestimate the amount of time and energy it takes.

Effective teaching Instruction that maximizes learning by actively involving students in meaningful learning activities.

Classroom rules and procedures establish standards for behavior that allow learning to take place.

Procedures The routines students follow in their daily classroom activities.

Rules Guidelines that provide standards for acceptable classroom behavior.

DEVELOPMENTAL DIFFERENCES IN STUDENTS In planning rules and procedures, effective teachers consider the developmental levels of their students. For example, first graders are typically compliant and eager to please their teachers, but they also have short attention spans and tire easily (Evertson et al., 2009). In comparison, middle schoolers often test their developing independence, and they're sometimes rebellious and capricious; they need rules that are clearly stated and administered (Emmer et al., 2009). If you're a first-grade teacher, you will plan differently than if you're a middle school teacher. For first-grade students, you'll need to carefully teach rules and procedures through modeling and examples and systematically reinforce them over time. Middle schoolers understand rules and procedures but need firm and consistent application of them combined with caring and positive expectations for good behavior.

CREATING PROCEDURES AND RULES Keeping students' developmental needs in mind, effective managers then decide about the procedures and rules they will implement in their classroom. **Procedures** are the routines students follow in their daily learning activities, such as how they turn in papers, sharpen pencils, and make transitions from one activity to another. For instance, Shannon's students turn in their papers from the ends of the rows, with each student putting his or her paper on the top of the stack as it moves forward. This allows Shannon to collect the stacks from the first student in each row, and when she returns the papers, she simply gives the stacks to those students, who take their papers and pass the stacks back to the students behind them. Simple procedures such as these both create a sense of order for students and save teachers time and energy.

Effective teachers create procedures for activities such as the following:

- Entering and leaving the classroom
- Handing in and returning papers
- Accessing materials such as scissors and paper
- Sharpening pencils
- Making trips to the bathroom
- Making up work after an absence

After planning and teaching students about procedures, expert teachers have students practice until the procedures become so routine that students follow them virtually without thinking about them.

Rules, such as "Listen when a classmate is talking," are guidelines that provide standards for acceptable classroom behavior, and research confirms their value in creating productive learning environments (Emmer et al., 2009; Evertson et al., 2009). When consistently enforced, clear, reasonable rules not only reduce behavior problems that interfere with learning but also promote a feeling of pride and responsibility in the classroom community. Perhaps surprisingly, students also see the enforcement of rules as evidence of caring: "Students also say that they want teachers to articulate and enforce clear standards of behavior. They view this not just as part of the teacher's job but as evidence that the teacher cares about them" (Brophy, 2004, pp. 29–30).

Examples of rules at different grade levels are found in Table 12.1. Note that some rules occur at all levels, such as students' staying in their seats and waiting for permission to speak. Other rules are specific to a grade level and reflect the developmental needs of students at that level.

Table 12.1 Examples of Classroom Rules

First-Grade Teacher	Seventh-Grade Teacher	Tenth-Grade Teacher
• We raise our hands before speaking. • We leave our seats only when given permission by the teacher. • We stand politely in line at all times. • We keep our hands to ourselves. • We listen when someone else is talking.	• Be in your seat and quiet when the bell rings. • Follow directions the first time they're given. • Bring covered textbooks, notebook, pen, pencils, and planner to class every day. • Raise your hand for permission to speak or to leave your seat. • Keep hands, feet, and objects to yourself. • Leave class only when dismissed by the teacher.	• Do all grooming outside class. • Be in your seat before the bell rings. • Stay in your seat at all times. • Bring all materials daily. This includes your book, notebook, pen/pencil, and paper. • Give your full attention to others in discussions, and wait your turn to speak. • Leave when I dismiss you, not when the bell rings.

Source: Eggen & Kauchak (2007).

Deciding on rules for your classroom is the first step; actually implementing and making them work are next. Following are guidelines for implementing rules:

- State rules positively.
- Emphasize rationales for rules.
- Minimize the number of rules.
- Monitor rules throughout the school year.

These guidelines are designed to help students understand rules and the reasons for them, and this understanding helps students begin to accept responsibility for their own behavior.

Stating rules positively communicates desirable expectations for students. Providing rationales for rules is perhaps the most essential guideline. Students are much more likely to accept responsibility for their own behavior and obey rules when they understand the reasons for them. Keeping the number small helps prevent students from breaking rules simply because they forget. Finally, in spite of teachers' best efforts during planning and the initial teaching of rules, students will need periodic reminders throughout the year.

Go to the *IRIS Center Resources* section of Topic 10: *Creating Productive Learning Environments* in the MyEducationLab for your course to read and analyze the case study titled *Norms and Expectations.*

■ ■ ■ ■ CHECK YOUR UNDERSTANDING

2.1 Describe the personal characteristics of teachers that help create productive learning environments.

2.2 Describe the planning elements that help create productive learning environments.

For feedback, go to the appendix, *Check Your Understanding*, located in the back of this text.

CREATING PRODUCTIVE LEARNING ENVIRONMENTS: INVOLVING PARENTS

Learning is a cooperative venture: Teachers, students, and parents are in it together. Students must be cooperative and motivated to learn if a learning environment is to be productive, and parental support is essential for promoting this cooperation and motivation.

PEARSON
myeducationlab

Go to the *Building Teaching Skills and Dispositions* section of Topic 10: *Creating Productive Learning Enviroments* in the MyEducationLab for your course and complete the activity titled *Parents and Productivity: Overcoming Barriers to Parental Involvement.*

This I BELIEVE

Benefits of Parental Involvement

Students benefit from parental involvement in several ways:

- More positive attitudes and behaviors
- Higher long-term achievement
- Greater willingness to do homework
- Better attendance and graduation rates
- Greater enrollment in postsecondary education (K. Anderson & Minke, 2007; Anfara & Mertens, 2008)

These outcomes result from parents' increased participation in and understanding of school activities, higher expectations for their children's achievement, and teachers' increased understanding of learners' home environments. Deciding how to respond to a student's disruptive behavior is easier, for example, when his teacher knows that his mother or father has lost a job, his parents are going through a divorce, or a family member is ill.

Parent–teacher collaboration can also have long-term benefits for teachers. For example, teachers who encourage parental involvement report more positive feelings about teaching and their school. They also have higher expectations for parents and rate them as being more helpful (Weinstein & Mignano, 2007).

This discussion addresses the fourth item in our *This I Believe* feature, "Involving parents in their children's education can actually increase student learning." This statement is most definitely true: Involving parents in their children's education can have a number of beneficial results, and increased achievement is one of them.

Strategies for Involving Parents

Virtually all schools have formal communication channels, such as open houses (usually occurring within the first 2 weeks of the year, when teachers introduce themselves and describe general guidelines); interim progress reports, which tell parents about their youngsters' achievements at the midpoint of each grading period; parent–teacher conferences; and, of course, report cards. Although these processes are schoolwide and necessary, you can do more, such as the following:

- Send a letter home to parents within the first week of school that expresses positive expectations for students and solicits parents' help. The letter Shannon sent home with her students appears in Figure 12.2. Veteran teachers also include an extra copy of the guidelines for parents' future reference, and send home a follow-up letter to parents who forgot to return the letter the first time.

- Maintain communication by frequently sending home packets of student work, descriptions of new units, and other information about academic work.

- Emphasize students' accomplishments through newsletters, e-mails, or individual notes.

It's important to note that all forms of communication with parents need to be carefully proofread to ensure that they are free of spelling, grammar, and punctuation errors. First impressions are important and lasting: Your communications create perceptions of your competence, and errors detract from your credibility.

One of the most effective ways to involve parents is to call them (Longfellow, 2008). Talking to a parent allows you to be specific in describing a student's needs and gives you a chance to again solicit support. If a student is missing assignments, for example, you can alert the parent, ask for possible causes or explanations, and encourage parents to more closely monitor their child's study habits.

Figure 12.2 Letter to Parents

August 28, 2010

Dear Parents,

I am looking forward to a productive and exciting year, and I am writing this letter to encourage your involvement and support. You always have been, and still are, the most important people in your child's education. We cannot do the job without you.

For us to work together most effectively, some guidelines are necessary. With the students' help, we prepared the ones listed here. Please read this information carefully, and sign where indicated. If you have any questions, please call me at Southside Elementary School (555-5935) or at home (555-8403) in the evenings.

Sincerely,

Shannon Brinkman

Shannon Brinkman

AS A PARENT, I WILL TRY MY BEST TO DO THE FOLLOWING:

1. I will ask my child about school every day (evening meal is a good time). I will ask about what he or she is studying and try to learn about it.
2. I will provide a quiet time and place each evening for homework. I will set an example by also working at that time or reading while my child is working.
3. Instead of asking if homework is finished, I will ask to see it. I will ask my child to explain some of the information to me to check for understanding.

Parent's Signature _____

STUDENT SURVIVAL GUIDELINES

1. I will be in class and seated when the bell rings.
2. I will follow directions the first time they are given.
3. I will bring homework, notebook, paper, and a sharp pencil to class each day.
4. I will raise my hand for permission to speak or leave my seat.
5. I will keep my hands, feet, and objects to myself.

HOMEWORK GUIDELINES

1. Our motto is I WILL ALWAYS TRY. I WILL NEVER GIVE UP.
2. I will complete all assignments. If an assignment is not finished or ready when called for, I understand that I get no credit for it.
3. If I mISS work because of an absence, it is my responsibility to come in before school (8:15–8:45) to make it up.
4. I know that I get one day to make up a quiz or test or turn in my work for each day I'm absent.
5. I understand that extra credit work is not given. If I do all the required work, extra credit isn't necessary.

Student's Signature _____
Please return when signed. Thanks, Shannon

When you talk to parents, make an effort to establish a positive, cooperative tone that lays the foundation for joint efforts. Consider the following:

"Hello, Mrs. Hansen? This is Shannon Brinkman, Jared's teacher."

"Oh, uh, is something wrong?"

"Not at all. I just wanted to call to share with you some information about your son. He's a bright, energetic boy, and I enjoy seeing him in class every day. But he's been having some problems handing in his math homework assignments in my class."

"I didn't know he had math homework. He never brings any home."

"That might be part of the problem. He just might forget that he has any to do. I have a suggestion. Why don't we set up a system that will help him remember? I'll ask the class to write down their math homework in their folders every day. Please ask Jared to share that with you every night, and make sure that it's done. When it's done, why don't you initial it so I know you and he talked? I think that will help a lot. How does that sound?"

> *"Sure. I'll try that."*
>
> *"Good. We don't want him to fall behind. If he has problems with the homework, have him come to my room before or after school, and I'll help him. Is there anything else I can do? . . . If not, I look forward to meeting you soon."*

This conversation was positive, and it created a partnership between home and school. In addition, it created a specific plan of action.

ECONOMIC, CULTURAL, AND LANGUAGE BARRIERS TO COMMUNICATING WITH PARENTS   Economics, culture, and language can all create barriers that limit the involvement of minority and low-SES parents in school activities (J. Lee & Bowen, 2006; Schutz, 2006). Low-SES parents frequently lack resources—such as child care, transportation, Internet access, and even telephones—that allow them to engage in school activities. Multiple jobs often prevent parents from volunteering at school and even helping their children with homework.

Cultural differences can sometimes be misinterpreted (Hu, 2008). Because of their respect for teachers, for example, some Asian and Hispanic parents hesitate to become involved in matters they believe are best handled by the school, but teachers sometimes misinterpret this deference to authority as apathy (Weinstein & Mignano, 2007).

Language can be another barrier: Parents of bilingual students may not speak English, which leaves the child responsible for interpreting communications sent home by teachers. Homework also poses a special problem because parents can't interpret assignments or provide help, and schools sometimes compound the difficulty by using educational jargon when they send letters home.

Home–school partnerships create effective communication channels with parents and promote higher achievement and motivation.

INVOLVING MINORITY PARENTS   Teachers can narrow the home–school gap by offering parents specific strategies for working with their children (Boult, 2006; Cavanagh, 2009). Let's see how one teacher does this:

> *Nancy Collins, a middle school English teacher, has students who speak five native languages in her class. During the first 2 days of school, she prepares a letter to parents, and with the help of her students, translates it into their native languages. The letter begins by describing how pleased she was to have students from varying backgrounds in her class, saying that they enrich all her students' education.*
>
> *She continues with a short list of procedures and encourages the parents to support their children's efforts by*
>
> 1. *asking their children about school each night;*
> 2. *providing a quiet place to study for at least 90 minutes a day;*
> 3. *limiting television until homework is finished;*
> 4. *asking to see samples of their children's work and grades they've received.*
>
> *She tells the students that the school is having an open house and that the class with the highest attendance will win a contest. She concludes the letter by reemphasizing that she is pleased to have so much diversity in her class. She asks parents to sign and return the letter.*
>
> *The day before the open house, Nancy has her students compose a handwritten letter to their parents in their native languages, asking them to attend. Nancy writes "Hoping to see you there" at the bottom of each note and signs it.*

Nancy's letter was effective in three ways. First, writing it in students' native languages communicated sensitivity and caring. Second, the letter included specific suggestions; these are important because they provide parents with concrete ideas for helping their children. Even parents who can't read a homework assignment are more involved if they ask their children to explain their schoolwork. The suggestions also let parents know they're needed. Third, by encouraging parents to attend the school's open house, Nancy increased the likelihood that they would do so. If they did, and the experience was positive, their involvement would likely increase.

■ ■ TECHNOLOGY AND TEACHING Using Technology to Communicate With Parents

Communication is an essential step in home–school cooperation, but parents' and teachers' busy schedules are often obstacles. Technology can help make home–school links more effective (Bitter & Legacy, 2008). Voice mail and e-mail can help overcome these obstacles by creating communication channels between parents who work and teachers who are busy with students all day.

A growing number of teachers use websites that describe current class topics and assignments. In addition, students and parents are now able to monitor missing assignments, performance on tests and current grades via e-mail (Gronke, 2009). Schools also use electronic hotlines to keep parents informed about current events, schedule changes, lunch menus, and bus schedules. However, many parents still prefer traditional information sources such as newsletters and open houses. This may be because some households don't have e-mail, as well as the instinctive desire for the face-to-face contact that exists in open houses.

One innovation uses the Internet to provide parents with real-time images of their children (Kleiman, 2001). Increasing numbers of preschool and day-care programs are installing cameras and Internet systems that provide parents with secure-access websites that can be used to monitor their children during the day.

■ ■ ■ ■ CHECK YOUR UNDERSTANDING

3.1   Explain how involving parents contributes to a productive learning environment.

3.2   What strategies do effective teachers use to communicate with parents?

For feedback, go to the appendix, *Check Your Understanding*, located in the back of this text.

INTERVENING WHEN MISBEHAVIOR OCCURS

Despite the most careful planning, students do misbehave. To see how effective teachers deal with misbehavior, let's revisit Shannon's classroom, where she's involved in a math lesson reviewing decimals and percentages.

"What kind of problem is this, . . . Gabriel?" she asks as she walks down the aisle and points to a problem on the overhead.

". . . It's a percentage problem," Gabriel responds after thinking for a few seconds.

As soon as Shannon walks past him, Kevin sticks his foot across the aisle, tapping Alison on the leg with his shoe while he watches Shannon's back. *"Stop it, Kevin,"* Alison mutters, swiping at him with her hand.

Shannon turns, comes back up the aisle, and continues, *"Good, Gabriel,"* and standing next to Kevin, asks, *"And how do we know it's a percentage problem, . . . Kevin?"* looking directly at him.

URBAN EDUCATION

> *"Uhhh . . . "*
>
> *"What words in the problem give us a clue that it's a percentage problem, Kevin?"*
>
> *". . . 'Which is the better buy?'" Kevin answers, pointing at the sales numbers from the two stores. "We have to figure out which store sale saved us more. That's a percentage problem."*
>
> *"Good," Shannon replies, moving to the overhead and displaying additional word problems involving percentages.*
>
> *"Go ahead and do the first problem," Shannon directs. "Be sure you're able to explain your answer."*
>
> *She watches as students work on the problem and then moves over to Sondra, who has been whispering and passing notes to Nicole across the aisle. "Move up here," she says quietly, nodding to a desk at the front of the room.*
>
> *"What did I do?" Sondra protests.*
>
> *"When we talked about our rules at the beginning of the year, we agreed that it was important to listen when other people are talking and to be quiet when others are working," Shannon whispers.*
>
> *She watches as Sondra changes seats. Then, tapping her knuckle on the overhead, Shannon says, "Okay, let's see how we did on the problem. Explain what you did first, . . . Juanita."*

Shannon's experience illustrates why classroom management can be a vexing problem for teachers. Even when you have planned carefully, disruptions inevitably occur, as you saw in Shannon's lesson. Dealing with off-task or potentially disruptive behavior requires immediate and judicious decision making. If a misbehavior is brief and minor, such as a student asking another student a quick question, it usually can be ignored. But if the behavior has the potential to disrupt the learning activity, you'll need to intervene.

Intervening Effectively

An **intervention** is a teacher action designed to increase desired behaviors or eliminate student misbehavior and inattention. A wide variety of interventions exist, such as praising students for paying attention or working diligently, moving near or calling on inattentive students to bring them back into the lesson, simply telling a student to stop talking, or, in extreme cases, removing a disruptive student from the classroom.

When intervening in the case of misbehavior, you have three goals: 1) stop the misbehavior quickly and simply; 2) maintain the flow of the lesson; and 3) help students learn from the intervention. The following guidelines can help you reach these goals:

- Demonstrate withitness and overlapping
- Preserve student dignity
- Maintain consistency
- Keep communication congruent

Let's look at them.

DEMONSTRATE WITHITNESS AND OVERLAPPING   **Withitness** is a teacher's awareness of what's going on in all parts of the classroom at all times and communicating this awareness to students, and it is an essential component of successful interventions (Kounin, 1970). Expert teachers describe withitness as "having eyes in the back of your head."

Shannon demonstrated withitness in three ways:

- She identified the misbehavior immediately, and quickly responded by moving near Kevin.
- She correctly identified Kevin as the cause of the incident. If, in contrast, she had reprimanded Alison, she would have left students with a sense that she didn't know what was going on.

Intervention A teacher action designed to increase desired behaviors or eliminate student misbehavior and inattention.

Withitness A teacher's awareness of what's going on in all parts of the classroom at all times and communicating this awareness to students.

- She responded to the more serious infraction first. Kevin's poking was more disruptive than Sondra's whispering, so she first called on Kevin, which drew him back into the activity—making further intervention unnecessary—and then she moved over to Sondra to stop her whispering and note passing.

Withitness involves more than dealing with misbehavior after it happens. Teachers who are with-it also watch for initial signs of inattention or confusion; they approach, or call on, inattentive students to bring them back into lessons; and they respond to signs of confusion with questions such as "Some of you look puzzled. Do you want me to rephrase that question?" They are sensitive to students and make adjustments to ensure students are involved and successful.

Notice that Shannon also managed to eliminate Kevin's, Sondra's, and Nicole's misbehavior while maintaining the flow of her lesson. This ability is described as **overlapping**, attending to two issues simultaneously (Kounin, 1970; Wubbels, Brekeimans, den Brok, & van Tartwijk, 2006). Overlapping allows you to maintain the flow of the lesson while stopping the misbehavior, two major goals of interventions.

Research indicates that lack of withitness and overlapping is often a problem for beginning teachers (Wubbels et al., 2006). Teachers have so much to think about that they sometimes simply don't notice misbehavior when it occurs. The best solution to this issue is well-established routines and carefully planned instruction that simplify the amount teachers have to think about.

PRESERVE STUDENT DIGNITY   No one likes to look stupid in front of his or her peers, which makes preserving students' dignity essential for any intervention. As you saw earlier in the chapter, a positive classroom climate is an essential component of a productive learning environment, and the tone of your interactions with students influences both the likelihood of their compliance and the emotional climate in your classroom. Loud public reprimands, criticism, and sarcasm reduce students' sense of safety, create resentment, and detract from a positive classroom climate. When students break rules, simply reminding them of the rule and why it's important, as Shannon did with Sondra, and requiring compliance are as far as a minor incident should go.

MAINTAIN CONSISTENCY   "Be consistent" is recommended so often that it has become a cliché. But the need for consistency is essential for an effective classroom management system. If one student is reprimanded for breaking a rule and another is not, for example, students are unable to make sense of the inconsistency, and they soon learn that the world is an arbitrary and confusing place. They're likely to conclude that the teacher doesn't know what's going on or has "pets," either of which detracts from classroom climate.

Although consistency is important, achieving complete consistency in the real world is virtually impossible; interventions need to be adapted to the student and the context. For example, most classrooms have a rule about speaking only when recognized by the teacher, and as you're monitoring seatwork, one student asks another a question about the assignment and then goes back to work. Failing to remind the student that talking is not allowed during seatwork is technically inconsistent, but an intervention in this case is both unnecessary and counterproductive. On the other hand, a student who repeatedly turns around and whispers becomes a disruption, and intervention is necessary. Students understand the difference, and the "inconsistency" is appropriate and effective.

KEEP COMMUNICATION CONGRUENT   If teachers' communications are going to make sense to students, their verbal and nonverbal behaviors need to be congruent (Doyle, 2006). For example, we've all had the experience of someone talking to us while glancing around the room; even if the person says how glad he or she is to see us, we don't believe it. When verbal and nonverbal behaviors are inconsistent, people attribute more credibility to tone of voice and body language than to spoken words (Aronson, Wilson, & Akert, 2007).

Overlapping A teacher's ability to attend to two issues simultaneously.

Shannon's behavior was congruent. For example, when she moved over to Kevin and called on him, she looked him directly in the eye, and she watched as Sondra changed seats. Her nonverbal behavior communicated that "she meant what she said." If Shannon had glanced over her shoulder at Kevin instead, her communication would have been confusing; her words would have said one thing, but her body language would have said another.

Research supports these contentions. The more eye contact teachers make with their students, for example, the more likely the students are to believe that they're with-it and are in charge of their classes (Wubbels et al., 2006).

Beginning teachers often have difficulty in this area.

> There appeared a distinct difference between beginning and experienced teachers' nonverbal behavior that may be an important cause for the unsatisfying relationships of some beginning teachers with their students. Behaviors that facilitated visual contact (looking to students) and signaling withitness and overlapping were demonstrated by experienced teachers almost twice as much as by student teachers. (Wubbels et al., 2006, p. 1180)

This research suggests that you should be aware of your nonverbal behavior and strive to keep your verbal and nonverbal behavior consistent.

In the *Taking a Stand* feature on the next page, we examine the pros and cons of using punishment as a classroom management tool.

Handling Serious Management Problems: Violence and Aggression

> *Daniel, one of your middle school students, has difficulty maintaining his attention and staying on task. He frequently makes loud and inappropriate comments in class and disrupts learning activities. You warn him, reminding him that being disruptive is unacceptable, and blurting out another comment will result in time-out.*
>
> *Within a minute, Daniel blurts out again. "Please go to the time-out area," you say evenly.*
>
> *"I'm not going, and you can't make me," he says defiantly as he remains seated at his desk.*

How do you react?

> *As you work with a small group of your fourth graders, a scuffle suddenly breaks out between Trey and Neil, who are supposed to be working on a group project together. You look up to the sounds of shouting and see Trey flailing at Neil, who is essentially attempting to fend off Trey's blows. Trey is often verbally aggressive and sometimes threatens other students.*

What do you do?

We have emphasized repeatedly that productive learning environments are safe and inviting. Although incidents of school violence are rare, they do exist, and you should be aware of your professional and legal responsibilities in the unlikely event of an incident of violence in your classroom.

As part of schoolwide safety programs, most schools have created prevention programs, taken security measures, and established detailed procedures to protect students and teachers from violent acts such as those that make national headlines (National Center for Education Statistics, 2005b). When serious problems do arise, teachers are most likely to encounter verbal aggression or student fighting. These incidents are also rare, but teachers need to be prepared for them. Once you know that options are available, you will feel more confident about your ability to deal with these problems.

Handwritten margin notes:
what did you learn?
Thesis: I learned, through the reading, that about different types of punishment and they all have controversial.

What Role Should Punishment Play in Classroom Management?

Did you ever get a speeding ticket? What happened to your subsequent driving behavior—at least for a while? Most of us can attest to the idea that punishment works—at least in the short run. But then what?

Teachers in general, and beginning teachers in particular, worry about whether they will be able to maintain order in their classrooms. Many turn to punishment; but punishment as a major management tool is controversial. Advocates say it's effective and necessary, but critics say it's ineffective and counterproductive. The role of punishment in classroom management, as well as in child raising in general, has been debated for centuries (e.g., "Spare the rod and spoil the child."), and this controversy continues unabated today.

Punishment is the process of decreasing or eliminating undesired behavior through some unpleasant consequence. Punishment can range from a teacher action as simple as saying, "Andrew, stop whispering," to *corporal punishment*, the use of physical, punitive actions, such as paddling students, to eliminate undesirable behavior. Most punishment in the classroom is not corporal, and usually occurs in the form of simple desists, time-out, or detention. **Desists** are verbal or nonverbal communications teachers use to stop a behavior (Kounin, 1970), such as telling a student to stop whispering, or putting fingers to the lips to signal "Shh." **Time-out** involves removing a student from the class and physically isolating him or her in an area away from classmates. *Detention*, most commonly used with older students, is similar to time-out, and involves taking away some of students' free time by keeping them in school either before or after school hours.

THE ISSUE

Punishment *can* be effective in reducing or eliminating unwanted behaviors (How did *your* driving change after receiving a speeding ticket?). Some critics suggest, however, that punishment should never be used in classrooms (e.g., Kohn, 1996), and research indicates that systems based on reinforcing positive behavior are more effective than those using punishment (Alberto & Troutman, 2006). Critics also argue that the use of punishers to maintain an orderly classroom overemphasizes control and obedience instead of emphasizing that students are responsible for their actions—which contributes to personal development (Freiberg, 1999b). Critics further contend that punishing students for simple acts, such as talking without permission, fails to examine possible causes for the behavior, such as ineffective instruction or not understanding why it's important to give everyone a chance to speak. In addition, punishment can have unintended consequences, such as resentment and hostility, and can damage teachers' efforts to create a positive classroom climate.

On the other hand, research indicates that desists, when administered immediately, briefly, and unemotionally, can be effective (Emmer et al., 2009; Evertson et al., 2009). Further, research indicates that time-out is effective for a variety of disruptive behaviors (Alberto & Troutman, 2006), and, although somewhat controversial, detention is widely used and generally viewed as effective (L. Johnson, 2004).

Some forms of punishment are used in virtually all classrooms; veteran teachers believe punishment is acceptable when the severity of the punishment matches the severity of the misbehavior (Cowan & Sheridan, 2003). Additional research suggests that punishment is sometimes necessary; when all punishers are removed, some students become more disruptive (Pfiffner, Rosen, & O'Leary, 1985; Rosen, O'Leary, Joyce, Conway, & Pfiffner, 1984). When paired with explanations about the undesired behavior, punishment can actually be humane because it helps unruly students learn new, more acceptable behaviors quickly (Lerman & Vorndran, 2002).

Handwritten margin notes:
As a child my parents punished us by...
They never did they hit punch...

YOU TAKE A STAND

Now it's your turn to take a position on the issue. What role should punishment play in classroom management?

PEARSON myeducationlab To explore both sides of this issue and take a stand, go to the *Book Specific Resources* section in the MyEducationLab for your course, select your text, and then select *Taking a Stand in an Era of Reform* for Chapter 12.

When students are verbally aggressive, your goal is to keep the problem from escalating. For example, responding to Daniel in a calm and unemotional tone of voice is a first step. Once the student has calmed down, you can send him to a school counselor, ask for additional support, or arrange to talk to him after school. In the case involving fighting, you should follow three steps: (1) stop the incident (if possible), (2) protect the victim, and (3) get help. For instance, a loud noise, such as shouting, clapping, or slamming a chair against the floor will often surprise the students enough so they'll stop. At that point, you can begin to talk to them, check to see if anyone is hurt, and then take the students to the main

Punishment The process of decreasing or eliminating undesired student behavior through some unpleasant consequence.

Desists Verbal or nonverbal communications teachers use to stop a behavior.

Time-out The process of removing a student from the class and physically isolating him or her in an area away from classmates.

This I BELIEVE

office, where help is available. If your interventions don't stop the scuffle, you should immediately rush an uninvolved student to the office for help. Unless you're sure that you can separate the students without danger to yourself, or them, attempting to do so is unwise.

You are legally required to intervene in the case of a fight. If you ignore a fight, even on the playground, parents can sue for negligence on the grounds that you failed to protect a student from injury (Fischer, Schimmel, & Stellman, 2006). However, the law doesn't require you to physically break up the fight; immediately reporting it to administrators is an acceptable form of intervention.

This discussion addresses the fifth item in our *This I Believe* feature, "Teachers are required by law to intervene if students in their classes are involved in a fight or scuffle." This statement is true: To ignore a fight or scuffle could place students' safety in jeopardy and could result in a liability lawsuit.

Breaking up a scuffle is, of course, only a short-term solution. Whenever students are aggressive or violent, experts recommend involving parents and other school personnel (Burstyn & Stevens, 2001). Parents want to be notified immediately if school problems occur. In addition, school counselors, school psychologists, social workers, and principals have all been trained to deal with these problems and can provide advice and assistance. Experienced teachers can also provide a wealth of information about how they've handled similar problems. No teacher should face serious problems of violence or aggression alone. Further, excellent programs are available to teach conflict resolution and to help troubled students (D. Johnson & Johnson, 2006). If teachers can get help when they first suspect a problem, many incidents can be prevented.

To conclude this section, we want to emphasize that classroom violence and aggression, although possible, occur rarely. The vast majority of your management problems will involve issues of cooperation and motivation. Many problems can be prevented, others can be dealt with quickly, and some require individual attention. We have all heard about students carrying guns to school and incidents of assault on teachers. Statistically, however, considering the huge numbers of students who pass through schools each day, these incidents remain very infrequent.

Effective Classroom Management in Urban Classrooms

URBAN EDUCATION

Urban classrooms provide unique challenges to teachers attempting to create productive learning environments. Consider the case of Mary Gregg, a first-grade teacher in an urban school in the San Francisco Bay Area.

> *Mary's classroom is a small portable room with a low ceiling and very loud air fans. The room has one teacher table and six rectangular student tables with six chairs at each. Mary has 32 first graders (14 girls and 18 boys). Twenty-five of the children are children of color; a majority are recent immigrants from Southeast Asia, with some African Americans and Latinos, and seven European Americans. (LePage et al., 2005)*

Research on teaching in urban contexts reveals three themes. First, students in urban environments come from very diverse backgrounds (Macionis & Parillo, 2010). As a result of this diversity, their prior knowledge and experiences vary, and what they view as acceptable patterns of behavior also varies, sometimes dramatically. Second, urban classes are often large; Mary had 32 first graders in a room built for 25. Third, and perhaps most pernicious, negative stereotypes about urban students create the perception that developing a productive learning environment through classroom management is difficult, if not impossible.

Two of the most common stereotypes are "Students can't control themselves" and "Students don't know how to behave because their parents don't care" (R. Goldstein,

2004). In response to these stereotypes, urban teachers often "teach defensively," "choosing methods of presentation and evaluation that simplify content and reduce demands on students in return for classroom order and minimal student compliance on assignments" (LePage et al., 2005, p. 331).

This defensive approach to classroom management and instruction results in lowered expectations and decreased student motivation. Students who aren't motivated to learn are more likely to be disruptive because they don't see the point in what they're being asked to do, a downward spiral of motivation and learning occurs, and management issues become increasingly troublesome.

It doesn't have to be this way. In spite of diversity and large numbers of students in a small classroom, effective urban teachers create active and orderly learning environments. Let's look at Mary Gregg's classroom management during a lesson on buoyancy.

> *Once into the science activity, management appears to be invisible. There is, of course, some splashing and throwing things into the water, but as the lesson progresses, the teacher engages in on-the-spot logistical management decisions. For instance, everyone is supposed to get a chance to go to the table to choose objects to be placed in cups. After choosing the first one to go, Mary sets them to the task. Very quickly, it is the second person's turn and the students do not know how to choose who should get the next turn. At first she says "you choose," then foresees an "It's my turn. No it's my turn" problem and redirects them with a counterclockwise motion to go around the table. (LePage et al., 2005, pp. 328–329)*

This example demonstrates that although challenging, classroom management in an urban environment doesn't have to be overrestrictive or punitive. How is this accomplished? Research suggests four important factors:

- Caring and supportive teachers
- Clear standards for acceptable behavior
- High structure
- Effective instruction

CARING AND SUPPORTIVE TEACHERS   We have emphasized the need for caring and supportive teachers throughout this chapter. Teachers who care are important in all schools but are critical in urban environments. When students perceive their teachers as uncaring, disengagement from school life occurs, and students are much more likely to display disruptive behaviors than their more involved peers (Charles & Senter, 2008).

CLEAR STANDARDS FOR ACCEPTABLE BEHAVIOR   Because they bring diverse experiences to class, urban students' views of acceptable behaviors often vary. As a result, being clear about what behaviors are and are not acceptable is essential in urban classrooms (D. Brown, 2004). As we saw earlier in the chapter, students interpret clear standards of behavior as evidence that the teacher cares about them. One urban student had this to say about clear behavioral expectations:

> She's probably the strictest teacher I've ever had because she doesn't let you slide by if you've made a mistake. She going [sic] to let you know. If you've made a mistake, she's going to let you know it. And, if you're getting bad marks, she's going to let you know it. She's one of my strictest teachers, and that's what makes me think she cares about us the most. (Alder, 2002, pp. 251–252)

The line between clear standards for behavior and an overemphasis on control is not cut-and-dried. One important difference is that in productive urban classrooms, order is created through "the ethical use of power" (Alder, 2002, p. 245). Effective teachers are demanding but also helpful; they model and emphasize personal responsibility, respect,

Classroom Management in Diverse Environments

Learner diversity presents a unique set of challenges for classroom teachers. A long history of research suggests that discrepancies exist in disciplinary referrals and punishment for students who are members of cultural minorities (Gay, 2006). For example, African American boys are referred for behavior problems at a much higher rate than their peers, and they also receive harsher punishments (Skiba, Michael, Nardo, & Peterson, 2002).

Further, research indicates that European American students are disciplined for infractions that could be described as *objective,* such as smoking, leaving school without permission, or profanity. By comparison, African American students are more commonly disciplined for infractions that require a teacher's interpretation, such as disrespect, defiance, or class disruptions. And, subsequent punishments for African American students are more severe (Skiba et al., 2002; Townsend, 2000).

Research suggests that miscommunication often occurs between teachers and students who are members of cultural minorities, because most teachers are White, middle-class females (J. Cooper, 2007).

> Fear may . . . contribute to overreferral [among students of color]. Teachers who are prone to accepting stereotypes of adolescent African American males as

threatening or dangerous may overreact to relatively minor threats to authority, especially if their anxiety is paired with a misunderstanding of cultural norms of interaction. (Skiba et al., 2002, p. 336)

Experts suggest that **culturally responsive classroom management**, which combines cultural knowledge with teachers' awareness of possible personal biases, can help overcome some of these problems. Culturally responsive classroom management has five elements:

- Becoming personally aware of cultural biases
- Understanding students' cultural backgrounds
- Becoming knowledgeable about the sociopolitical and economic contexts of schools
- Creating caring learning environments
- Developing culturally responsive classroom management strategies (Weinstein, Curran, & Tomlinson-Clarke, 2003; Weinstein, Tomlinson-Clarke, & Curran, 2004)

Diversity in Your Classroom

As teachers become more aware of their own possible fears and biases and acquire cultural knowledge about their students' interaction patterns, they often realize that student responses that appear threatening or disrespectful aren't intended that way. Increased awareness and knowledge combined

with culturally responsive classroom management techniques can contribute a great deal toward overcoming the disproportionality in classroom discipline issues (McCurdy, Kunsch, & Reibstein, 2007). These techniques include promoting a positive classroom climate, establishing clear expectations for behavior, carefully teaching rules and procedures, involving students in highly interactive lessons, and providing students with specific and nonjudgmental feedback about their learning progress. As with any set of strategies, these efforts won't solve every problem, but they can contribute to creating a productive learning environment for all your students.

QUESTIONS TO CONSIDER

1. What are two ways to interpret the disparity in disciplinary actions for minority students? How can teachers address these different potential causes?

2. How can teachers learn about their students to minimize the possibility that their disciplinary actions are due to cultural misunderstandings?

myeducationlab To respond to these questions online, explore this topic further, and receive feedback, go to the *Book Specific Resources* section in the MyEducationLab for your course, select your text, and then select *Exploring Diversity* for Chapter 12.

Culturally responsive classroom management Classroom management that combines teachers' awareness of possible personal biases with cultural knowledge.

and cooperation; and they're willing to take the time to ensure that students understand the reasons for rules (Weinstein & Mignano, 2007). Further, in responding to the inevitable incidents of students' failing to bring needed materials to class, talking, or otherwise being disruptive, effective teachers in urban schools enforce rules but provide rationales for them and remind students that completing assigned tasks is essential because it helps develop the skills needed for more advanced work (D. Brown, 2004). In contrast, less effective teachers tend to focus on negative consequences, such as, "If you don't finish this work, you won't pass the class" (Manouchehri, 2004).

Motivation and Management

You're a beginning sixth-grade world history teacher in an urban middle school, and you're having a difficult time maintaining order in your classroom. You're starting a study of factors leading up to World War I, and you explain that one of the factors was increased nationalism—loyalty to a country's language and culture. As you're explaining, some of the students talk openly to

each other, and a few even get out of their seats and sharpen pencils in the middle of your presentation. You point to the rules on the bulletin board, but this seems to work only for a while. You threaten them with referrals and other punishments, which work briefly, but the disruptions soon recur.

Other students seem listless and make no effort to pay attention; several even put their heads down on the desk during the lesson. You try walking around the room as you talk, and you stand near the inattentive students, but

neither strategy works well. So you decide to address the issue directly. You walk up to the front of the room and say in a loud voice, "Class, this content is really important. It will help you understand why we continue to have wars in eastern Europe." As you conclude, you hear a barely audible "Who cares?" from one of the students.

What would you do in this situation, both for the long term and immediately? Why?

HIGH STRUCTURE   Students in urban schools sometimes come from environments where stability and structure may not be a regular part of everyday life, making order, structure, and predictability even more important in urban classrooms (Whitcomb, Borko, & Liston, 2006). Procedures that lead to well-established routines are important, and predictable consequences for behaviors are essential. A predictable environment leads to an atmosphere of order and safety, which is crucial for developing the sense of attachment to school essential for learning and motivation.

EFFECTIVE INSTRUCTION   If students aren't learning and aren't actively involved in classroom life, management problems are inevitable. Classroom management and instruction are interdependent, and, unfortunately, students in urban classrooms are often involved in low-level activities such as listening to lectures and doing seatwork that isn't challenging. This type of instruction contributes to low motivation and disengagement, which further increase the likelihood of management problems.

In the *Exploring Diversity* feature on page 370, we examine the unique challenges of classroom management in classrooms with diverse students.

■ ■ ■ ■ CHECK YOUR UNDERSTANDING

4.1   Describe the characteristics of effective teacher interventions when misbehavior occurs.

4.2   What actions—both short- and long-term—should teachers take when encountering incidents of violence and aggression?

4.3   What makes urban classrooms unique in terms of classroom management?

For feedback, go to the appendix, *Check Your Understanding*, located in the back of this text.

As we've seen, management and motivation go hand in hand. To see how one teacher wrestles with this dual problem, read the *Decision Making* feature on this page.

12 MEETING YOUR LEARNING OBJECTIVES

1. Explain how a productive learning environment contributes to learning.

   - A productive learning environment is orderly and is focused on learning. The emotional climate and all the routines are designed to maximize learning for each student.

   - Classroom management is important because polls indicate that it's a national concern for both teachers and the public at large.

   - Classroom management is also important because research indicates that a strong link exists between orderly classrooms and students' learning and motivation.

   - Effective classroom management creates a positive classroom climate and a community of learners, helps promote the development of learner responsibility, and maximizes time and opportunity for learning.

2. Describe how effective teachers plan for classroom management.

   - Teachers who create productive learning environments care about their students as people and are committed to their learning.

   - Teachers who create productive learning environments teach effectively; they create learning activities in which students are involved in experiences that are meaningful.

   - Planning for classroom management involves considering the developmental characteristics of students, and creating a comprehensive system of procedures and rules.

3. Explain how involving parents contributes to a productive learning environment.

   - Students whose parents are involved in their education have better attitudes toward school, learn more, and are more likely to cooperate in class and do their homework.

   - Teachers who encourage parental involvement also feel more positive about teaching and their school, and they have higher expectations for parents.

   - Teachers can involve parents by sending samples of student work home, emphasizing student accomplishments, and calling parents when necessary.

4. Describe how effective teachers intervene when misbehavior occurs.

   - Effective interventions are designed to stop misbehavior quickly and efficiently, maintain the flow of instruction, and help students learn from the intervention.

   - Teachers who intervene effectively demonstrate withitness, an understanding of what's going on at all times in their classrooms, and overlapping, the ability to deal with two issues at once.

   - Teachers who intervene effectively maintain students' dignity, are consistent in their interventions, and keep their verbal and their nonverbal communication congruent.

   - Serious management problems, although rare, can occur in classrooms, and teachers are required by law to intervene in cases of fighting and scuffling.

   - Effective urban teachers are caring and supportive, establish clear standards for behavior, provide structure in their classrooms, and use effective instruction to complement their classroom management.

IMPORTANT CONCEPTS

academic learning time (p. 355)
allocated time (p. 354)
caring (p. 356)
classroom management (p. 352)
culturally responsive classroom
 management (p. 370)
desist (p. 367)

discipline (p. 352)
effective teaching (p. 357)
engaged time (p. 355)
instructional time (p. 354)
intervention (p. 364)
learning community (p. 353)
overlapping (p. 365)

positive classroom climate (p. 352)
procedures (p. 358)
productive learning environments (p. 350)
punishment (p. 367)
rules (p. 358)
time-out (p. 367)
withitness (p. 364)

DISCUSSION QUESTIONS

1. All teachers agree that it's important to be a good role model. What part does teacher modeling play in an effective classroom management system?

2. How can a teacher tell if students have developed responsibility? How might the definition of responsibility change with grade level? What types of instructional and managerial strategies promote responsibility? What types discourage the development of responsibility?

3. How do the following factors influence the optimal number of procedures in a classroom?

   a. Grade level

   b. Subject matter

   c. Type of student (e.g., high versus low achiever)

   d. Type of instruction (e.g., large group versus small group)

4. What advantages are there to seeking student input on rules? Disadvantages? Is this practice more important with younger or older students? Why?

5. If you were a substitute teacher (or a student teacher) and were going to take over a class mid-year, what kinds of things would you need to know and do in terms of classroom management?

6. How do rules and procedures help develop learner responsibility? What does the teacher need to do to ensure that rules and procedures are an effective tool for developing learner responsibility?

PEARSON myeducationlab

Now go to Topic 10: *Creating Productive Learning Environments in the* MyEducationLab (www.myeducationlab.com) for your course, where you can:

- Find learning outcomes for *Creating Productive Learning Environments* along with the national standards that connect to these outcomes.

- Complete *Assignments and Activities* that can help you more deeply understand the chapter content.

- Apply and practice your understanding of the core teaching skills identified in the chapter with the *Building Teaching Skills and Dispositions* learning units.

- Check your comprehension on the content covered in the chapter by going to the *Study Plan* in the *Book Specific Resources* section for your text. Here you will be able to take a chapter quiz, receive feedback on your answers, and then access *Review, Practice, and Enrichment* activities to enhance your understanding of chapter content.

Develop Your Professional Portfolio

To further apply your understanding of chapter content and address the INTASC standards, go to the *Book Specific Resources* section in the MyEducationLab for your course, select your text, and then select this chapter's *Portfolio Activities*.

"I teach first grade because, to me, there is nothing better than a room full of six- and seven-year-olds who think that everything that you do is amazing, and they think that you are the most magical person in the world. They enter the classroom every day with this incredible amount of curiosity. They energize my spirit. They challenge my thinking. They love me unconditionally. And, I hope I do the same for them."

COURTNEY FOX, 2008 Teacher of the Year, Delaware

To view a video clip of Courtney, the 2008 Delaware Teacher of the Year, go to Topic 12: *Instruction* in the MyEducationLab for your course and select this chapter's *Teacher Talk*, then *Courtney Fox*.

13

Instruction in Today's Schools

CHAPTER OUTLINE

Student Motivation and Effective Teaching
- Motivation and Learning
- Motivation: Increasing Students' Interest

Planning for Effective Teaching
- Select Topics
- Specify Learning Objectives
- Prepare and Organize Learning Activities
- Plan for Assessment
- Ensure Instructional Alignment
- Planning in a Standards-Based Environment

Implementing Instruction: Essential Teaching Skills
- Teacher Characteristics
- Organization
- Focus: Attracting and Maintaining Attention
- Introductory Review
- Questioning
- Feedback
- Application and Closure

   Exploring Diversity: Effective Instruction
   in Urban Classrooms

Instructional Strategies
- Direct Instruction
- Technology and Teaching: Capitalizing on Technology
  in Instruction
- Lecture-Discussion
- Guided Discovery
- Cooperative Learning

   Taking a Stand in an Era of Reform: Paying Students to Learn

LEARNING OBJECTIVES

After you have completed your study of this chapter, you should be able to:

1. **Define *motivation* and identify instructional factors that increase students' motivation.** INTASC Standard 5, Classroom Motivation and Management

2. **Describe basic steps in planning for instruction.** INTASC Standard 7, Planning for Instruction

3. **Describe essential teaching skills, and identify examples in classroom practice.** INTASC Standard 4, Instructional Strategies

4. **Describe instructional strategies, and identify applications of these in learning activities.** INTASC Standard 4, Instructional Strategies

Every beginning teacher wants to be effective, but what does it mean to be effective, and what do teachers do in the classroom that makes them effective? **Effective teaching** maximizes learning for all students, and it is the essence of being a professional. Teaching effectively requires careful planning and complex skills that promote both students' learning and their motivation to learn. We discuss these topics in this chapter. Let's begin by looking at an expert elementary teacher as she plans for her instruction.

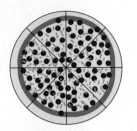

 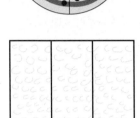

"What are you doing?" Al Barton asks his wife, Shirley, a fourth-grade teacher, on Saturday afternoon as he sees her cutting and drawing on cardboard pieces.

"Working on a unit on equivalent fractions and adding fractions with unlike denominators. . . . Do they look like pizzas and cakes?" she asks, holding up the pieces of cardboard.

"They really do," he smiles, a bit impressed.

"My students had trouble with the equivalency standard on the state test last year, so I'm using more concrete, real-world examples. I want them to understand equivalent fractions, so they'll be able to add fractions with unlike denominators."

"Equivalency standard?"

"Yeah," Shirley says, pointing to a document on her desk. "It says, 'Knows that two numbers in different forms are equivalent or nonequivalent, using whole numbers, decimals, fractions, and mixed numbers.' . . . For instance, 1/3 and 2/6 are equivalent forms of the same fraction."

"I see," Al says, genuinely interested.

"Well, you know how kids are," Shirley continues. "They like to take the easy way out, and they often have misconceptions. . . . Like, this problem," Shirley continues, writing 1/2 + 1/3 on a piece of paper. "What's the answer?"

"Five sixths," Al answers, after a couple seconds.

"Wrong . . . It's two fifths."

Responding to Al's puzzled look, Shirley continues, "The kids see that we're adding, so they just add the top numbers and get 2 and add the bottom numbers and get 5. . . . The answer is five sixths, just as you said, but some of them have misconceptions about adding fractions. So, that's the kind of thing I'm working on."

"Okay," Shirley thinks to herself as Al leaves the room, "I'll use the pizzas for review, and then I'll use the cakes to help them understand equivalent fractions."

She then prepares a worksheet with other geometric figures that students will complete for additional practice on finding equivalent fractions. "If they do okay on the worksheet, I'll give them a quiz Friday, so I can see how well they understand all this," she mumbles out loud. "If they don't do well, I'll give them some more practice."

We examine Shirley's planning further in the sections that follow, but before we do, please respond to the items in the *This I Believe* feature on the next page. We address each in the chapter.

STUDENT MOTIVATION AND EFFECTIVE TEACHING

Think about some of your favorite teachers and classes, and then compare them to teachers and classes that are at the other end of the spectrum. Our students typically use phrases such as "Interesting material," "Tough but worthwhile," "Practical," and "I really got into that content" to describe the classes they enjoyed.

Each of these descriptions relates to your **motivation**, the energizing force behind student learning (Schunk, Pintrich, & Meece, 2008). For example, if you study hard to get high scores on tests, getting high grades motivated your study. On the other hand,

Effective teaching Teaching that maximizes learning for all students.

Motivation The energizing force behind student learning.

you might enjoy reading about history, simply because you're interested in our past and how it influences us today; your interest in history also motivated your studying.

Motivation is often classified into two broad categories. **Extrinsic motivation** is motivation to engage in a behavior to receive some incentive, whereas **intrinsic motivation** is motivation to be involved in an activity for its own sake. When you study to get high test scores, you are extrinsically motivated; because no external incentive exists for reading about history, you are intrinsically motivated.

Intrinsic and extrinsic motivation are not mutually exclusive and can exist at the same time (Schunk et al., 2008). For example, you might study hard both because you want to get a high test score and because you find the content interesting. In this case, you're high in both extrinsic and intrinsic motivation.

Motivation and Learning

Motivation is not only important for current learning; it also sets the stage for future success in school (Eisenman, 2007; Ryan, Ryan, Arbuthnot, & Samuels, 2007). Motivated students

- have more positive attitudes toward school and describe school as more satisfying;
- persist on difficult tasks and cause fewer management problems;
- study and learn information in depth and excel in classroom learning activities (Stipek, 2002).

Not surprisingly, motivation is a powerful factor influencing student achievement, and motivated students are a primary source of job satisfaction for teachers. This is why we introduce our discussion of effective teaching with this topic. It is virtually impossible to teach effectively without considering student motivation. This leads us to what teachers can do to increase their students' motivation.

Extrinsic motivation Motivation to engage in a behavior to receive some incentive.

Intrinsic motivation Motivation to be involved in an activity for its own sake.

Motivating activities pull students into the lesson and actively involve them in learning.

Motivation: Increasing Students' Interest

Effective teachers do a lot of things to motivate students. They get to know their names and treat them as individuals, they create learning activities that students can succeed at, and they grade fairly and reward effort. But most importantly, they create interesting lessons (Anderman & Wolters, 2006).

Teachers increase their students' interest in a lesson in a number of ways (Schraw & Lehman, 2001):

- Attracting and focusing students' attention at the beginning of lessons

- Personalizing content by focusing on real-world applications and linking topics to students' lives

- Promoting high levels of student involvement in learning activities

ATTRACTING AND FOCUSING STUDENTS' ATTENTION   Student attention often wanders during a lesson and frequently isn't focused on the teacher or the content. Effective teachers motivate students by attracting their attention at the beginning of a lesson. For example, an elementary teacher begins her discussion of arthropods by showing students a live lobster. Similarly, Shirley planned to begin her lesson by showing students her cardboard pizzas as an attention getter.

Beginning lessons with attention-grabbing segments both motivates students and increases learning and need not take a lot of extra work. For example, as an introduction to the concept *adverbs*, having a student run across the front of the classroom and then asking his classmates to describe how he moved may take a little extra time or work but can make a significant difference in students' attentiveness. The same is true for most of the topics we teach.

PERSONALIZING CONTENT THROUGH REAL-WORLD APPLICATIONS   Have you ever said to yourself, "I don't get it—it's too abstract; I can't see how all of this applies to me or the real world"? Effective teachers remedy this problem by linking content to students' lives (Brophy, 2008). For example, when students understand that wearing seatbelts in their cars is an application of the *law of inertia*, or that listening politely while a classmate is speaking is an application of *freedom of speech*, part of the First Amendment to the Constitution, their interest in the topics is likely to increase. Effective teachers continually ask themselves, "How can I relate this topic to students' experiences?" Real-world applications make a powerful difference in students' motivation to learn.

Such applications create links to students' personal lives and experiences. Shirley used her pizzas and cakes to illustrate fractions, and the teacher focusing on arthropods had students squeeze their own legs to remind them that our skeletons are inside our bodies, as opposed to arthropods' exoskeletons. As other examples, a language arts teacher puts students' names in examples of well-written paragraphs, and a geography teacher begins a study of landforms by having students describe the area in which they live. Experienced teachers describe personalization as one of the most important ways to promote student interest in learning activities, and its value is confirmed by research (Schraw & Lehman, 2001). As with attention getters, personalizing content need not take a lot of time or effort.

INVOLVING STUDENTS   Involvement, the extent to which students are actively participating in a learning activity, is a third way to increase interest and learning (Lutz, Guthrie & Davis, 2006). Think about your experience with friends at lunch or at a party. When you're talking and actively listening, you pay more attention to the conversation than if you're on its fringes. The same applies in classrooms.

Teachers use two major tools to promote involvement: questioning and group work. We examine questioning in our discussion of essential teaching skills later in the chapter and groupwork in our discussion of different instructional strategies.

This section relates to the first item in our *This I believe* feature, "Some students are more motivated to learn than others, and teachers can do little about those who aren't motivated." This statement isn't true: Some students are indeed more motivated to learn than are others, but teachers can do a great deal to increase motivation in most students.

Being aware of factors that increase students' motivation, you can then consciously plan learning activities to promote your students' motivation. We discuss planning for instruction in the next section of the chapter.

This I BELIEVE

■ ■ ■ ■ CHECK YOUR UNDERSTANDING

1.1   Define *motivation*, and describe the difference between intrinsic and extrinsic motivation.

1.2   Describe the relationship between motivation and student achievement.

1.3   Describe three factors within teachers' control that can increase students' motivation to learn.

For feedback, go to the appendix, *Check Your Understanding*, located in the back of this text.

PLANNING FOR EFFECTIVE TEACHING

Effective teaching doesn't just happen; it needs to be carefully thought about and planned for. As they plan, expert teachers make a series of decisions. For example, Shirley did the following as she planned for her lesson on fractions:

- Selected a topic important for students to study
- Specified learning objectives related to the topics
- Prepared and organized learning activities to help students reach the objectives
- Planned an assessment to determine the extent to which her students reached the objectives
- Ensured that her instruction and assessments were aligned with her learning objectives

These important planning decisions are outlined in Figure 13.1 and discussed in the sections that follow.

Careful planning helps teachers define their goals and ensures that instructional activities are aligned with these goals.

Select Topics

"What's important for students to learn?" is the first essential question teachers ask as they plan (L. Anderson & Krathwohl, 2001). Standards, such as the one Shirley showed Al, as well as textbooks,

Figure 13.1 Planning for Instruction

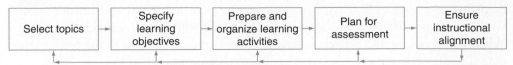

curriculum guides, their personal philosophies, and students' interest in the topic are all sources teachers use to help answer this question.

Your knowledge of content will be particularly important in deciding which topics are important enough to teach, because not enough time exists to teach everything. Effective teachers know their content well enough to target essential topics important for all students to learn.

Specify Learning Objectives

After identifying a topic, teachers answer a second question: What do I want my students to know or be able to do with respect to the topic? The answer to this question is one or more **learning objectives**. Clear learning objectives are essential because they guide the rest of the decisions teachers make during both planning and instruction. Without clear objectives, teachers won't know how to design their learning activities, nor can they create accurate assessments. Objectives also guide teachers as they implement their learning activities. When learning activities are unsuccessful, it can often be traced back to teachers' not being clear about their objectives.

Two of the most popular approaches to writing objectives focus on what students will be able to do after the lesson. One approach was pioneered by Robert Mager (1962) in his highly readable book, *Preparing Instructional Objectives*. Mager recommended that each objective contain a condition, student performance, and criteria for successful completion. If Shirley wrote objectives using Mager's approach, they would appear as you see in Table 13.1.

Norman Gronlund (2004) offered a popular alternative to Mager's approach: He suggested that teachers state a general objective, such as *know, understand*, or *apply*, followed by specific learning outcomes that operationally define what students will be able to do. Table 13.2 includes examples of Shirley's objectives written according to Gronlund's suggestions. Note that in both approaches, the emphasis is on what *students* are learning, not what the teacher is doing. Effective planning begins with a focus on student learning, and teachers then use strategies to promote that learning.

Researchers have developed a classification system to help teachers as they plan their learning activities (L. Anderson & Krathwohl, 2001). A revision of the famous "Bloom's Taxonomy," first published in 1956 (Bloom, Englehart, Furst, Hill, & Krathwohl, 1956), the system uses a matrix with 24 cells that represent the intersection of four types of knowledge with six cognitive processes. The matrix is outlined in Figure 13.2.

Teachers often use the taxonomy to clarify their learning objectives. For instance, Shirley wanted students to "understand equivalent fractions, so they'll be able to add

Learning objectives Statements that specify what students should know or be able to do with respect to a topic or course of study.

Table 13.1	Objectives Using Mager's Approach		
Objective	**Condition**	**Performance**	**Criteria**
Given 3 pairs of fractions, fourth graders will determine whether each pair is equivalent.	Given 3 pairs of fractions	Determine	Each
Given pairs of fractions with unlike denominators, fourth graders will create equivalent fractions for each pair.	Given pairs of fractions with unlike denominators	Create	Each
Given word problems involving adding fractions with unlike denominators, fourth graders will correctly add the fractions in each.	Given word problems with unlike denominators	Add	Each correctly

Table 13.2 Objectives Using Gronlund's Approach

General Objective	Specific Learning Outcome
Understands *equivalent fractions*	1. Identifies pairs of fractions that are and are not equivalent
	2. Creates equivalent fractions
Understands the addition of fractions with unlike denominators	1. Recognizes need for creating equivalent fractions
	2. Performs operations
	3. Solves problems

Source: Gronlund (2004).

fractions with unlike denominators"; this comment described her objectives. *Equivalent fraction* is a concept, so the objective "to understand equivalent fractions" would be written in the cell where *conceptual knowledge* intersects with the cognitive process *understand*. Another objective was for students to be able to add fractions with unlike denominators. Adding fractions involves the application of a procedure, so this objective would go in the cell where *procedural knowledge* intersects with the cognitive process *apply*. Using the taxonomy during planning allows teachers to see what types of knowledge and cognitive processes they're emphasizing in their teaching. It also reminds us that we want our students to do more than just "remember" "factual knowledge," the most basic cell in the taxonomy and the one on which much of schooling focuses. Exposing students to the other forms of knowledge and more advanced cognitive processes is even more important in the 21st century, as student thinking, decision making, and problem solving are increasingly emphasized (van Gelder, 2005).

Prepare and Organize Learning Activities

Once Shirley identified her learning objectives—what she wanted her students to understand and be able to do—she then prepared and organized her learning activities. This process involved two steps: 1) locating high-quality examples or problems to illustrate the topic, and 2) sequencing the examples to be most meaningful to her students.

Figure 13.2 A Taxonomy for Learning, Teaching, and Assessing

The Knowledge Dimension	The Cognitive Process Dimension					
	1. Remember	2. Understand	3. Apply	4. Analyze	5. Evaluate	6. Create
A. Factual knowledge						
B. Conceptual knowledge						
C. Procedural knowledge						
D. Metacognitive knowledge						

Source: From Lorin W. Anderson, et al. *Taxonomy for Learning, Teaching and Assessing: A Revision of Bloom's Taxonomy of Educational Objectives*, Complete Edition, 1/e. Published by Allyn & Bacon/Merrill Education, Boston, MA. Copyright © 2001 by Pearson Education. Reprinted by permission of the publisher.

High-quality examples are representations of content that ideally have all the information in them that students need to learn a topic, and their importance in promoting learning cannot be overstated (Haas, 2005). Teachers' verbal descriptions support and supplement examples, but descriptions alone are usually not adequate for understanding a topic.

Shirley's cardboard "pizzas" and "cakes" were the examples she used to help her students understand equivalent fractions and adding fractions with unlike denominators. For example, she divided her "pizzas" into eight equal parts to illustrate adding fractions where the denominators are the same. She then planned to use her "cakes" to build on this knowledge and to help her students learn how to create equivalent fractions. (We see how Shirley used them in the next section of the chapter when we discuss instruction.)

Shirley's examples were in elementary math, but high-quality examples are important for teaching all topics at all grade levels. For instance, in language arts, teachers often use actual student writing samples to provide concrete examples of good organization, grammar, and punctuation. Science teachers swing cups of water on the ends of strings and use the concept of *inertia* to explain why the water doesn't fly out of the cup. Art teachers use pictures to help students understand concepts such as *perspective* and *shading*, and music teachers use actual music to help students learn ideas such as *melody* and *rhythm*. These topics would be impossible to teach effectively without the use of examples.

Research indicates that effective teachers carefully illustrate their topics with examples, whereas less effective teachers rely solely on verbal explanations to help their students understand an idea (Haas, 2005). High-quality examples are especially valuable for cultural minorities or students who are not native English speakers, because they help accommodate differences in the students' prior knowledge (Echevarria & Graves, 2007).

Plan for Assessment

Effective teachers also plan ahead and consider how they will decide whether students have attained the learning objectives. **Assessment** is the process teachers use to gather information and make decisions about students' learning progress. Effective assessments address two questions: 1) How will I know that my students have reached my learning objectives? 2) How can I use assessment to increase my students' learning?

Shirley considered assessment when she said, "I'll give them a quiz Friday, so I can see how well they understand equivalent fractions and adding fractions with unlike denominators." This helped answer the first question. Her decision, "If they don't do well, I'll give them some more practice," addressed the second. Sample assessment items that Shirley used are illustrated in Figure 13.3.

The results of Shirley's assessment will provide valuable information that she can use to make decisions about further instruction. If students are able to respond correctly to her items, she can move to the next topic; if not, she can provide them with additional practice and examples to increase their understanding.

Research supports the crucial role of assessment in learning:

> Weekly or even more frequent classroom tests provide teachers with information useful in planning their lessons. . . . Frequent tests encourage students to be prepared for classes. Even in themselves, tests can be a powerful source of learning: Regular essays and feedback, for example, help students not only comprehend subject matter but become better writers. (Walberg, 2003, p. 42)

Research also suggests that expert teachers, like Shirley, assess frequently during instruction, using both verbal questions and frequent exercises to provide students and themselves with continual information about learning progress during a lesson (Ciofalo & Wylie, 2006).

Figure 13.3 Sample Assessment Items

Part I

Look at the drawings of pairs of fractions below. Circle the pairs that are equivalent, and explain why they are equivalent in each case.

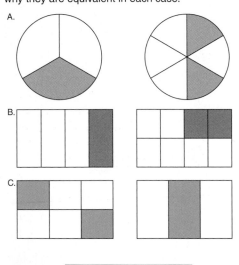

A.

B.

C.

_____

_____

Part II

Add the following fractions.

$\frac{1}{5} + \frac{2}{5} =$ _____ $\frac{2}{7} + \frac{4}{7} =$ _____

$\frac{1}{3} + \frac{1}{2} =$ _____ $\frac{3}{4} + \frac{1}{8} =$ _____

High-quality examples
Representations of content that ideally have all the information in them that students need to learn a topic.

Assessment The process teachers use to gather information and make decisions about students' learning progress.

This section addresses the second item in our *This I Believe* feature, "Because assessing students with quizzes and tests uses instructional time, students who are frequently assessed learn less than those assessed less frequently." The opposite is true: The process of assessment does take time, but it makes a major contribution to learning and is one of the most valuable uses of our instructional time.

Assessment decisions are also essential during planning because they help teachers align their instruction with important standards and objectives. Let's see how teachers do that.

Ensure Instructional Alignment

Thinking about assessment during planning helped Shirley answer an additional question: "How do I know that my instruction and assessments are logically connected to my objectives?" **Instructional alignment** is the match between learning objectives, learning activities, and assessments, and is an essential component of effective instruction (Bransford, Brown, & Cocking, 2000).

> Without this alignment, it is difficult to know what is being learned. Students may be learning valuable information, but one cannot tell unless there is alignment between what they are learning and the assessment of that learning. Similarly, students may be learning things that others don't value unless curricula and assessments are aligned with . . . learning goals. (Bransford et al., 2000, pp. 51–52)

In addition to ensuring that lessons are focused and that they target essential information, instructional alignment helps students identify and understand what's important to learn (Morrison, Kemp, & Ross, 2007). Shirley's objectives, instruction, and assessments were all aligned. Her objectives were for students to understand the concept *equivalent fractions* and to add fractions with unlike denominators; her instruction focused on these objectives, and the sample quiz items in Figure 13.3 directly addressed these objectives.

Alignment isn't as easy as it appears. For instance, if a teacher's objective is for students to be able to write effectively yet learning activities focus on isolated grammar skills, the instruction is out of alignment. It is similarly out of alignment if the objective is for students to apply math concepts to real-world problems but learning activities have students practice computation problems. Instructional alignment encourages teachers to ask, "What does my objective actually mean, and do my learning and assessment activities truly lead to the objective?"

Planning in a Standards-Based Environment

We discuss standards and their impact on teachers in detail in Chapter 14, but we want to briefly address them here because they influence teachers' planning. *Standards* specify what students should know and what skills they should have after completing an area of study. Standards influence the curriculum, or what is taught; the first thing Shirley did in planning her lesson was to refer to her state standards for fourth-grade math.

Standards are essentially statements of learning objectives, but they are written with varying degrees of specificity (Swanson, 2008). So, before you can design learning activities to help students meet a specific standard, you will have to interpret the meaning of that standard (Hamilton, Berends, & Stecher, 2005). See for example, Shirley's standard:

> *Knows that two numbers in different forms are equivalent or nonequivalent, using whole numbers, decimals, fractions, and mixed numbers.*

She interpreted the standard in this way: "For instance, 1/3 and 2/6 are equivalent forms of the same fraction," and she then planned her instruction to help her students understand equivalent fractions. She went further to emphasize adding fractions with unlike

myeducationlab

To view a fifth-grade teacher involving her students in a discussion of the Civil War, go to the *Assignments and Activities* section of Topic 12: *Instruction* in the MyEducationLab for your course and complete the activity titled *Analyzing Instructional Alignment*.

Instructional alignment The match between learning objectives, learning activities, and assessments.

denominators, and her decision to do so illustrates the role of decision making in teacher planning and professionalism.

As Shirley planned, she used a form of **backward design**, an approach to planning in which the teacher first identifies desired learning objectives, then specifies ways to assess whether these objectives are met, and finally establishes learning activities to reach the objectives (Wiggins & McTighe, 2005). This approach to planning often begins with a standard and then works backward to ensure that objectives, assessments, and learning activities are all aligned with standards.

This section addresses the third item in our *This I Believe* feature, "Planning for instruction primarily involves identifying the topics that are important for students to learn." This statement is not true: Though planning involves identifying topics, it is much broader and includes other components to ensure that instructional activities result in student learning.

This I BELIEVE

▪ ▪ ▪ ▪ CHECK YOUR UNDERSTANDING

2.1   Describe the five essential steps in planning for instruction.

2.2   Planning in a standards-based environment involves one additional step beyond the planning steps described in this section of the chapter. What is this additional step?

2.3   Classify the following objectives into one of the cells of the taxonomy table in Figure 13.2 and explain your classification. (1) Students will identify examples of figures of speech such as similes, metaphors, and personifications in written paragraphs. (2) They will write original paragraphs that include those figures of speech.

For feedback, go to the appendix, *Check Your Understanding*, located in the back of this text.

IMPLEMENTING INSTRUCTION: ESSENTIAL TEACHING SKILLS

We've all heard of "basic skills" such as reading, writing, and math (and probably computer literacy as well) that all people need to function effectively in today's world. Similarly, **essential teaching skills** can be considered basic skills for teaching: They are the abilities that all teachers, including those in their first year of teaching, should have in order to help students learn.

Understanding essential teaching skills is important for your development as a teacher because you'll be expected to demonstrate them when you have your own classroom. In addition, they provide you with concrete actions to look for as you go out and observe teachers in classrooms. Derived from a long line of classroom research (Good & Brophy, 2008), these essential teaching skills are outlined in Table 13.3, and discussed and illustrated using Shirley's work with her students in the sections that follow.

Teacher Characteristics

Effective teaching begins with who you are and how you relate to students. The way you think about and treat students sets the stage for other effective teaching actions. In Chapter 12, you saw that caring teachers are essential for creating productive learning environments and effective classroom management, and they are no less so for

Backward design An approach to planning in which the teacher begins with an objective, designs assessments to match the objective, and then creates learning activities to reach the objective.

Essential teaching skills The abilities that all teachers, including those in their first year of teaching, should have in order to help students learn.

Table 13.3 Essential Teaching Skills

Essential Teaching Skill	Description	Purpose in Promoting Learning
Teacher characteristics	Teachers' beliefs and actions that influence the classroom environment	Create a learning environment that promotes student motivation and learning
Organization	Teacher actions that include: 1) starting lessons on time, 2) having materials prepared in advance and ready for use, 3) making smooth transitions from one activity to another, and 4) having well-established routines	Maximizes the amount of time available for instruction
Focus	Concrete objects, pictures, models, and other examples teachers use to illustrate their topics	Attracts and maintain students' attention and provide experiences students use to reach teachers' learning objectives
Introductory review	Introductory activity that summarizes a previous lesson and connects it to the current one	Helps students recall prior knowledge to which new learning can be connected
Questioning	The process of calling on all students in the class, providing cues when students are unable to answer correctly, and giving students adequate time to answer	Promotes the active involvement of students and guide them to teachers' learning objectives
Feedback	The process of providing students with information about their learning progress	Provides students with the information they need to increase their understanding
Closure and application	Summaries at the ends of lessons and practice with the content	Help students develop a deep understanding of the topic

promoting student learning. In addition to caring, these teacher characteristics influence learning:

- Personal teaching efficacy
- Positive expectations
- Modeling and enthusiasm

Let's look at them.

PERSONAL TEACHING EFFICACY   If you really try, will you be able to make a difference in your students' learning? **Personal teaching efficacy** describes teachers' beliefs in their ability to help students learn, regardless of the conditions of the school or students' home lives (Bruning, Shraw, Norby, & Ronning, 2004).

To illustrate this idea, let's look at a brief exchange between Shirley and Jim Fantini, one of her colleagues.

"My students didn't score as well as I would have liked on the math part of the Stanford Achievement Test last year, and I promised myself they were going to do better this year," Shirley comments as she glances through a set of math quizzes.

"But you said your students aren't as sharp this year," Jim responds.

"That doesn't matter. I need to push them harder. I think I can do a better job than I did last year. They're going to be so good at fractions that they'll be able to do the problems in their sleep."

"You never give up, do you?" Jim smiles, shaking his head.

Shirley's comments "I think I can do a better job than I did last year" and "They're going to be so good at fractions . . ." reflect her belief in her ability to help all her students learn. When students aren't learning, high-efficacy teachers don't blame it on lack of intelligence, poor home environments, uncooperative administrators, or some other external cause. Instead, they redouble their efforts. They persevere with low achievers, emphasize praise rather than criticism, and maximize the time available for instruction.

Personal teaching efficacy
Teachers' beliefs in their ability to help students learn, regardless of the conditions of the school or students' home lives.

Low-efficacy teachers, by contrast, spend less time on learning activities, "give up" on low achievers, and are more critical when students fail. Not surprisingly, students taught by high-efficacy teachers learn more than those taught by low-efficacy teachers (Yeh, 2006).

HIGH EXPECTATIONS   It's a fact of classroom life that some students learn quicker and more easily than others. But does this mean that some students can't learn? Effective teachers have faith, not only in their own capabilities but also in their students, holding high expectations for all students. Teacher expectations influence students because of a phenomenon called **self-fulfilling prophecy**, in which students adjust their efforts to meet teacher expectations (Good & Brophy, 2008). When teachers have high expectations for students, effort and learning increase; the opposite is also true.

Research indicates that teachers treat students for whom they have high expectations differently than those for whom they have low expectations. High-expectation students receive differential treatment in the following areas (Good & Brophy, 2008):

- *Questioning:* Teachers call on perceived high achievers more often, they allow these students more time to answer, and they prompt perceived high achievers more often when they can't answer.

- *Teacher effort:* Teachers give perceived high achievers more thorough explanations, their instruction is more enthusiastic, and they require more complete and accurate student answers.

- *Feedback:* Teachers praise perceived high achievers more and criticize them less. They also offer perceived high achievers more complete and lengthier feedback.

- *Emotional support:* Teachers interact more with perceived high achievers, make more eye contact, stand closer, and orient their bodies more directly toward these students.

Students are sensitive to these differences, and even early elementary children are aware of differential treatment (Stipek, 2002). Realizing that these differences influence learning, you should have appropriately high expectations for all your students and strive to treat them as equally as possible.

MODELING AND ENTHUSIASM   Think about times that you've become excited about a topic you were studying. Often, this happened because your teacher was enthusiastic about the topic. Teacher **modeling**, the tendency of people to imitate others' behaviors and attitudes, can have a powerful influence on your students' motivation (Bandura, 2001, 2004). Like all people, students imitate the attitudes and actions of others, and teachers who are enthusiastic about the topics they teach increase the likelihood that students will feel the same way.

Modeling influences students in a variety of ways. For example, imagine how you would feel if one of your instructors said, "I know this stuff is boring, but we have to learn it anyway" compared to "Now this idea is interesting and important; it will help us understand how our students think." Obviously, you're more likely to be interested in the second topic. As another example, if you want your students to be courteous and respectful to you and each other, you need to treat them with courtesy and respect. If you want them to be responsible and conscientious, you need to model these same characteristics by returning their papers promptly, having your instructional materials organized and ready to use, and using your instructional time effectively.

Effective teaching begins with the teacher, and caring, high personal teaching efficacy, positive expectations, and teacher modeling all contribute to effective instruction.

Self-fulfilling prophecy A classroom phenomenon in which student efforts rise or fall to match teacher expectations.

Modeling The tendency of people to imitate others' behaviors and attitudes.

Organization

Have you ever misplaced your keys and spent a frustrating amount of time looking for them? Have you ever said, "I've got to get organized; I can't stand this chaos." Organization not only helps in your personal life but is also essential for effective instruction. To see how, let's join Shirley's class on Monday morning just before math, scheduled each day from 10:00 to 11:00.

> *Shirley walks up and down the aisles, placing sheets of paper on each stu-* *dent's desk as students finish a writing assignment in language arts.*
>
> *At 9:58, she says, "Quickly turn in your writing assignment, and get out your math books." Students stop writing and pass their papers forward, putting their papers on the top of the stack. Shirley puts the papers in a folder and at 10:01 pulls out her cardboard pizzas. "Let's see what we remember about adding fractions. Look at these pizzas. We'll use them to review what we've learned about fractions."*

Shirley scheduled math from 10:00 to 11:00 and announced that it was time for math at 9:58. By 10:01 students had turned in their papers and were ready for math, so she made the transition from language arts to math in 3 minutes. In addition, she had her cardboard pizzas and cakes out where she could easily access them and placed the sheets of paper on students' desks as they turned in their language arts papers. Further, Shirley had taught her students time-saving routines; for instance, they placed their papers on the top of the stacks as they were passed forward, without being reminded to do so.

These examples illustrate **organization**, the set of teacher actions that maximizes the amount of time available for instruction. Teacher actions that promote organization are outlined in Table 13.4.

Less effective teachers spend more time in transitions from one activity to another, so they don't start lessons when they're scheduled; they spend valuable class time accessing materials; and their routines aren't well established. The result is fewer minutes available for instruction and reduced student learning.

Focus: Attracting and Maintaining Attention

In our discussion of motivation, you saw that the ability to attract and maintain students' attention is important for increasing their interest. It's also essential for learning: Students can't learn if they aren't paying attention. Effective teachers plan activities for the beginning of lessons to attract and maintain students' attention.

Shirley's "pizzas" acted as a form of **focus**—concrete objects, pictures, models, materials displayed on the overhead, and even information written on the board that attract and maintain attention during learning activities. High-quality examples, such as those Shirley used in her lesson, are effective forms of focus. Building lessons around examples provides students with experiences that they can use to develop their understanding, so, in addition to helping maintain attention, they also serve as the raw material for constructing ideas.

Table 13.4 Teacher Actions That Promote Organization

Teacher Action	Example
Starting on time	Shirley's students had their math books out and were waiting at 10:01.
Making smooth transitions	Shirley made the transition from language arts to math in 3 minutes.
Preparing materials in advance	Shirley had her cardboard pizzas and cakes easily accessible.
Establishing routines	At Shirley's signal, the students put their papers on the top of the stack without being told specifically to do so.

Organization The set of teacher actions that maximizes the amount of time available for instruction.

Focus Concrete objects, pictures, models, materials displayed on the overhead, and even information written on the board that attract and maintain attention during learning activities.

Introductory Review

Effective teachers not only attract students' attention at the beginning of a lesson, they also link new ideas to content students have already learned. Let's rejoin Shirley's lesson to see how she does this.

"Let's see what we remember about adding fractions," she says, displaying the pizzas as shown on the upper left.

She then removes three pieces from the first and two pieces from the second so they appear as shown on the lower left.

She continues, "What fraction of one whole pizza did we eat?"

After giving students time to think, she asks, "How many pieces of the first pizza did we eat? . . . Devin?"

"Three."

"And how about this pizza? How many pieces did we eat? . . . Kathy?"

"Two."

She then writes 3/8 + 2/8 on the board and, pointing to these numbers, asks, "Why did I write 3/8 here and 2/8 there? . . . Omar?"

"You have eight pieces in each pizza, and you ate three of them in that one," Omar responds, pointing to the one on the left.

"Good," Shirley smiles. "And what about the second one? How many pieces of that pizza did we eat? . . . Selina?"

"Two."

"So what fraction of a total pizza did we eat altogether? . . . Gabriel?"

"Five eighths of a pizza?" Gabriel responds after thinking for a few seconds.

"Good, Gabriel. . . . And, why is it 5/8 . . . Claire?"

"Uhhh . . ."

"How many pieces altogether in each pizza?"

"Eight," Claire answers.

"Good, and how many did we eat, altogether?"

"Five."

"Yes," she smiles at Claire, "so we ate 5/8 of one pizza."

Shirley then writes these additional problems on the board: 3/7 + 4/7 = ?, 2/5 + 1/5 = ?, and 4/8 + 2/8 = ? and reviews them as she did with her pizzas.

"Now remember," she emphasizes, "in each of these problems, the two fractions have the same denominator. . . . Be sure to keep that in mind as we continue our study of fractions.

Shirley's review helped her students activate the prior knowledge needed to understand the content of the current lesson. For example, she reviewed adding fractions with like denominators as preparation for helping them understand equivalent fractions and adding fractions with unlike denominators. Presenting concrete examples, such as the "pizzas," during the review increased its effectiveness by providing additional links to what students already know.

Questioning

Let's return to Shirley's review. A significant aspect of it is that she conducted the entire review with questioning. In the past, teachers simply explained topics and students were expected to listen quietly and then work independently at their desks. But a large body of research suggests that guiding students with questioning is more effective than simply explaining topics to them (Good & Brophy, 2008). Students involved in question-and-answer sessions are more attentive than those who listen passively to teacher explanations, and questioning is the most effective tool teachers have for involving and motivating students.

With respect to questioning, effective and less effective teachers differ in four areas:

- Frequency
- Equitable distribution
- Wait-time
- Prompting

Questioning allows teachers to guide student learning while gauging learning progress.

FREQUENCY   The questions teachers ask during a lesson perform a number of important functions, including actively involving students in the lesson and providing the teacher with valuable information about the lesson's effectiveness. **Questioning frequency** refers to the number of questions a teacher asks during a given period of instructional time. Effective teachers ask many more questions than do less effective teachers, and Shirley's review illustrates this point. She developed her review with questioning, and she directed her questions to a variety of students. This leads us to the concept of *equitable distribution*.

EQUITABLE DISTRIBUTION   Whom should teachers call on when they ask questions? An obvious answer is "students who have their hands up," but this isn't always the best way to involve all students. To examine this question, let's look again at some dialogue from Shirley's review.

Shirley:	*Let's see what we remember about adding fractions. Look at those pizzas. What fraction of one whole pizza did we eat? [After giving students time to think, she continues,] How many pieces of the first pizza did we eat? . . . Devin? [as she displayed the cardboard pizzas]*
Devin:	Three.
Shirley:	And how about this pizza? How many pieces did we eat? . . . Kathy?
Kathy:	Two.
Shirley:	Why did I write 3/8 here and 2/8 there? . . . Omar? [as she pointed to the fractions she had written on the board]
Omar:	You have . . . eight pieces altogether . . . and you ate three of them.
Shirley:	Good. And what about the second one? How many pieces of that pizza did we eat? . . . Selina?
Selina:	Two.
Shirley:	So what fraction of a total pizza did we eat altogether? . . . Gabriel?

In this dialogue, we see that Shirley directed each of her questions to a different student, and in each case, she addressed the student by name. This pattern illustrates **equitable distribution**, the practice of calling on all students—both volunteers and nonvolunteers—as equally as possible (Kerman, 1979). This practice sends an important message to students. By treating students equally, the teacher is communicating:

Questioning frequency The number of questions a teacher asks during a given period of instructional time.

Equitable distribution The practice of calling on all students—both volunteers and nonvolunteers—as equally as possible.

I don't care whether you're a boy or girl, minority or nonminority, high achiever or low achiever, I want you in my classroom, and I want you involved. I believe you're capable of learning, and I will do whatever it takes to ensure that you're successful.

Earlier you saw how important high expectations are for promoting student learning. Nothing communicates high expectations to students better than the practice of equitable distribution. In classrooms where it's practiced, student achievement rises, classroom management problems decrease, and attendance rates go up (Good & Brophy, 2008). Equitable distribution also works at the college level; students who expect to be called on prepare more fully for class, learn more, and are motivated to come to class.

Less effective teachers spend more time lecturing and explaining than do effective teachers, and when they do question, they call on either volunteers or the highest achievers in their classes (S. Jones & Dindia, 2004). Students soon learn that only the "smart ones" participate, and other students soon tune out. Both learning and motivation suffer.

WAIT-TIME   If we want students to think about the questions we ask, we need to give them time to think. To illustrate this idea, let's look again at the dialogue between Shirley and her students. In each case, after asking a question, Shirley paused briefly and gave students a few seconds to think before she called on someone. This period of silence after a question is asked and after a student is called on to answer is called **wait-time**. Giving students a few seconds to think about their answers makes sense, but in most classrooms, wait-times are very short, often 1 second or less (R. Stahl, DeMasi, Gehrke, Guy, & Scown, 2005). Increasing wait-time to 3 to 5 seconds results in higher quality student responses, greater participation from all students, and ultimately increased learning (Rowe, 1986).

PROMPTING   Equitable distribution is fine, you may be thinking, but what do I do if a student is unable to respond? **Prompting**, providing additional questions and cues when students fail to answer correctly, helps not only the stumped student, but also others who may not know the answer. To understand how prompting works, let's look at some additional dialogue from Shirley's lesson.

Shirley:	Why is it [the fraction of the pizza they ate] 5/8? . . . Claire?
Claire:	. . .
Shirley:	How many pieces altogether in each pizza?
Claire:	Eight.
Shirley:	Good, . . . and how many did we eat, altogether?
Claire:	Five.

The value of prompting is well documented by research (Good & Brophy, 2008). As with equitable distribution, it communicates that teachers believe students are capable, and they expect all students to answer successfully.

Less effective teachers tend to turn an unanswered question to another student instead of prompting, asking, for instance, "Can someone help Claire out?" This communicates that the teacher doesn't believe Claire is capable of answering and doesn't expect her to do so—not a message we want to send our students.

This section addresses the fourth item in our *This I Believe* feature, "The most effective teachers in today's schools are those who are best able to clearly explain the content they're teaching their students." In fact, quite the opposite is true: The most effective teachers are those best able to involve their students in lessons through questioning. This doesn't imply that teachers shouldn't be good at explaining; rather, it means that being able to guide students' developing understanding through questions is an important skill that enhances learning.

This I BELIEVE

Wait-time The period of silence after a question is asked and after a student is called on to answer.

Prompting Providing additional questions and cues when students fail to answer correctly.

Feedback

Have you ever been in a class where you handed in assignments and had to wait weeks before they were graded and returned? Or where you had to wait until the midterm exam to find out how you were doing? In both instances, you were left uncertain about your learning progress because of the absence of **feedback**, information about current understanding that can be used to promote new learning.

Teachers provide feedback in a number of ways, including homework assignments, quizzes, and tests, as well as through interactive questioning (Hattie & Timperley, 2007). Shirley did this in her interaction with Claire: She used questioning—and particularly prompting—to provide feedback. Ongoing feedback through questioning is one of the most effective ways teachers have of promoting learning.

Application and Closure

Shirley began her lesson with an effective introductory focus and review, and actively involved students during the lesson. She was well organized, and used questioning to involve students in the lesson. Let's join her lesson once more to see how she develops the lesson and brings it to closure. Notice as you read the case how she continues to use questioning to encourage student involvement.

After completing her review, Shirley continues, "Now, I have a different kind of problem," as she pulls out the two cardboard cakes as shown here.

"I'm eating cake, and I eat this piece," she says, pointing to a third, "and then I eat this piece," she adds, pointing to one of the halves. "How much cake have I eaten?"

Students offer several ideas ranging from 2/3 to 2/5, and Shirley then says, "Take the sheets of paper that I gave you, and fold them like our cakes here."

Shirley helps them fold one of the papers in half and the other into thirds and tells them to shade one section of each as you see to the right.

She continues, "How much cake do we have here? . . . Tim?" [pointing at the paper divided into thirds]

"A third."

"Good," Shirley smiles. "Now, let's all fold our paper this way," and she shows the students how to fold the paper, so it appears as at the bottom right.

"How many pieces do I have now? . . . Karen?"

". . . Six."

"So what portion is now shaded? . . . Jon?"

"Two sixths."

"Good, Jon," and she moves to the board and writes 1/3 = 2/6.

"Now, how do we know that the 1/3 and the 2/6 are equal?"

"It's the same amount of cake," Dan responds.

"Exactly," Shirley smiles. They're called EQUIVALENT FRACTIONS."

Feedback Information about current understanding that can be used to promote new learning.

Shirley then has the students divide the other paper in thirds, so it appears as shown here:

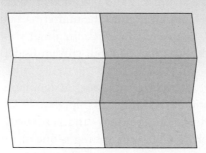

"What do we see here?"

". . . They both have the same number of pieces," Lorraine observes.

"And all the pieces are the same size," Crystal adds.

"I know!" Adam says excitedly. "We've eaten 5/6 of one cake."

"Please explain that for us," Shirley requests.

"It's like the pizza. We have two pieces there, and three pieces there, so it's 5/6 of one cake."

Shirley then models a process for finding equivalent fractions by multiplying the numerator and denominator by the same number, and guides the students through two more problems.

"Now, what have we been doing here? . . . Toni?" Shirley asks.

". . . We're finding equivalent fractions."

"And why do we want to find them? . . . Gary?"

". . . So we can add fractions when the denominators aren't the same."

Shirley praises the class for their good work, gives them a worksheet, and says, "Everyone, let's do the first one on your sheet. What do you get when you add 2/3 and 1/4?"

As students work the problem, Shirley walks up and down the rows to check their progress and offer brief suggestions.

After they have finished the problem, Shirley discusses it, and repeats the process with a second and a third problem. She then has them work independently on additional problems for the remainder of their time in math, and carefully monitors their progress as they work.

Finally, seeing it is 10:59, Shirley says, "It's nearly time for our break. As soon as you've cleaned up around your desks, we'll go."

In this segment of the lesson, Shirley helped students understand the concept *equivalent fraction*, how to add fractions with unlike denominators and then summarized the lesson with closure. **Closure** is a form of review occurring at the end of a lesson that is designed to help students organize what they've learned into a meaningful idea; it pulls the different aspects of the topic together and signals the end of a lesson.

Shirley achieved closure in her lesson in two ways. First, she had students explicitly state the main point of the lesson.

Shirley:	Now, what have we been doing here? . . . Toni?	
Toni:	We're finding equivalent fractions.	
Shirley:	And why do we want to find them? . . . Gary?	
Gary:	So we can add fractions when the denominators are not the same.	

PEARSON
myeducationlab

Go to the *Building Teaching Skills and Dispositions* section of Topic 12: *Instruction* in the MyEducationLab for your course and complete the activity titled *Effective Teaching Methods*.

Closure A form of review occurring at the end of a lesson

Effective teachers also have students apply what they've learned to new situations. Shirley had her students apply their understanding of equivalent fractions and adding fractions with unlike denominators by giving them a worksheet with a series of problems to solve.

As students were working on the problems, Shirley carefully monitored their progress for signs of confusion or off-task behavior. Less effective teachers give students seatwork assignments and then sit at their desks and do work of their own. Teaching is demanding and teachers are very busy, but students need to be carefully monitored to prevent frustration or confusion during their seatwork activities.

The essential teaching skills described in this section are effective in all classrooms. Effective teachers, however, adapt them to meet the specific learning needs of their students. In the next section, we describe how teachers in urban classrooms do this.

Effective Instruction in Urban Classrooms

In our discussions of urban contexts in earlier chapters, several themes emerged. First, urban students are diverse, with backgrounds from a number of countries and cultures (R. Goldstein, 2004). Second, many urban learners struggle in school, and large schools, crowded classrooms, less experienced teachers, and inadequate funding and facilities exacerbate the problem (Armour-Thomas, 2004). These themes have several implications for effective instruction in urban classrooms.

THE NEED FOR EXAMPLES

High-quality examples are important for all learners, but because of the diversity of urban students' prior experiences, they are critical when teaching in urban classrooms. Examples help minimize differences in urban students' backgrounds by providing common experiences for all students. For example, a science teacher explaining the concept of *density* might use the following examples:

- A clear plastic glass filled with cotton that can be compressed to show how density changes when mass doesn't

- Several pieces of screening that are the same size but have different numbers of meshes in them

- Bringing several different-sized groups of students to stand in the same area of the classroom, as shown at the top of the next next columns.

In addition to examples, graphs, models, concrete objects, pictures, and other visuals are especially valuable for English language learners who struggle with both content and language (Echevarria, Powers, & Short, 2006).

Effective teachers in urban classrooms also connect their examples to situations their students can identify with. For example, a world history teacher in an urban high school was discussing the rise of nationalism as an important factor in the events leading up to World War I. The concept was defined in students' textbooks as "a feeling of loyalty and devotion to one's country, language, and culture." This definition is both abstract and distant from the world in which these urban students lived. To personalize the concept and connect it to students' lives, the teacher related nationalism to the rivalries their athletic teams had with other urban high schools in the area, emphasizing both loyalties within their school and competition with other schools. Students started nodding as they began to understand how nationalism could be both a uniting and a divisive force. Urban students, like students in general, sometimes wonder how abstract ideas relate to their lives; making explicit links between new content and their day-to-day experiences increases both motivation and learning (Rosenshine, 2006).

THE NEED FOR INTERACTIVE INSTRUCTION

When working in challenging environments, teachers tend to revert to instructional strategies that afford them the most control. This often results in the use of an inordinate amount of passive learning activities such as lecture and seatwork (Eggen, 1998). One urban high school student complained,

> In my chemistry class, the teacher just keeps going and going and writing on the board. She never stops to ask the class, "Is everyone with me?" She's in her own little world. She never turns around, she just talks to the board, not to us. (Cushman, 2003, p. 8)

Exactly the opposite is needed. "A great deal of classroom research suggests that students need active instruction from their teachers, not solitary work with instructional materials, in order to make good achievement progress" (Brophy, 2004, p. 155).

In a comparison of more and less effective urban elementary teachers, researchers found that less effective teachers interacted with students less than half the time, compared to nearly three fourths of the time for their more effective counterparts (Waxman, Huang, Anderson, & Weinstein, 1997). Interactive teaching is characteristic of good instruction in general; its importance with urban students is crucial.

A common teacher lament is, "I tried calling on students but they either couldn't or wouldn't answer." This is why concrete examples and questioning skills such as prompting are so important. The examples provide a common frame of reference for all students; teacher questions help students use those examples to develop understanding.

Equitable distribution is also essential in urban classrooms. Making equitable distribution the prevailing pattern in your classroom can do more than anything else to communicate your belief that all your students can learn and that you expect them to do so.

THE NEED FOR FEEDBACK AND APPLICATION

Effective teaching also provides urban students opportunities to test their developing ideas and receive feedback. As with high-quality examples and questioning, feedback is even more important when working with urban students. The knowledge urban students develop is likely to vary considerably because their background experiences are so diverse. This means that detailed discussions of assignments, homework, and quiz and test results are essential when working with urban students.

Student success is important in the process (Brophy, 2004). Because urban students often lack a history of successful school experiences, they can quickly become frustrated and give up. Experiencing success is the only long-term solution to this dilemma.

Diversity in Your Classroom

By now you might be saying to yourself, "Wait. Aren't these suggestions just good teaching?" The answer is yes. Effective instructional practices for urban students are not fundamentally different from those for "regular" students. The same essential teaching skills that Shirley Barton used are equally effective with urban students. It is, however, all the more important that teachers apply effective instructional practices conscientiously and thoroughly with urban students.

QUESTIONS TO CONSIDER

1. Active student involvement and teacher–student interaction are two criteria used to evaluate different teaching strategies. How could teaching strategies, such as lecture or cooperative learning/group work, be adapted to promote more teacher–student interaction and encourage more student involvement?

2. A major theme for this chapter is the importance of feedback in effective instruction. Feedback is even more important for urban students, who need regular and continual feedback about their learning progress. Homework provides one effective way to provide both practice and feedback, but can be time and labor intensive. What are different ways that teachers can provide feedback to urban students on their homework, and what are the advantages and disadvantages of each?

myeducationlab To respond to these questions online, explore this topic further, and receive feedback, go to the *Book Specific Resources* section in the MyEducationLab for your course, select your text, and then select *Exploring Diversity* for Chapter 13.

■ ■ ■ ■ CHECK YOUR UNDERSTANDING

3.1 What are the essential teaching skills that all teachers should possess?

3.2 As middle schoolers walk into their geography class, they see a large matrix comparing the climate, geography, and economies of the northern and southern states before the Civil War. As soon as the bell stops ringing, the teacher says, "Write a minimum of two differences each in the geography, climate, and economy columns of the chart." Students begin, and as they're writing the teacher takes roll. Which of the essential teaching skills does this example best illustrate? Explain.

3.3 Shirley used her cardboard "pizzas" in her review and used her "cakes" to introduce the topic of *equivalent fractions*. Which essential teaching skill did the use of these materials best illustrate? Explain.

For feedback, go to the appendix, *Check Your Understanding*, located in the back of this text.

INSTRUCTIONAL STRATEGIES

An important question that all teachers ask is, "What is the best way to teach?" In addition to essential teaching skills, effective teachers also employ a number of alternative teaching strategies in their classrooms. **Instructional strategies** are prescriptive approaches to teaching designed to help students acquire a deep understanding of specific forms of knowledge. In this section, we answer the question by examining four of the most widely used instructional strategies:

- Direct instruction
- Lecture-discussion
- Guided discovery
- Cooperative learning

Direct Instruction

Probably the most widely used instructional strategy in today's classrooms is direct instruction. **Direct instruction** is a teaching strategy designed to teach essential knowledge and skills that are needed for later learning, and its effectiveness is well documented by research (Carnine, Silbert, Kame'enui, Tarver, & Jongjohann, 2006). The reasons for direct instruction's popularity are its straightforward simplicity and its wide applicability. In addition, its use has increased with the current emphasis on testing students for basic skills.

Creating equivalent fractions and adding fractions with both like and unlike denominators, the focus of Shirley's lesson, are examples of skills, as are punctuating in writing, balancing equations in chemistry, and using longitude and latitude to pinpoint locations in geography. Direct instruction

Direct instruction provides students with opportunities to practice new knowledge and skills.

is useful when skills can be broken down into specific steps and is particularly effective in working with low achievers and students with exceptionalities (Turnbull, Turnbull, & Wehmeyer, 2010).

Direct instruction typically occurs in three phases, outlined in Table 13.5 and discussed in the following sections.

Let's see how Shirley used direct instruction to implement each of these phases.

INTRODUCTION AND REVIEW   Shirley introduced her lesson using her cardboard pizzas as examples; their function was to attract students' attention and pull them into

Table 13.5 The Phases of Direct Instruction	
Phase	**Purpose**
Introduction and review: Teachers begin with a review of previous work.	• Attract students' attention. • Access learners' prior knowledge.
Developing understanding: Teachers describe and model the skill or guide students to an understanding of the concept. Teachers use many examples and emphasize high levels of student involvement.	• Develop students' understanding of the concept or skill.
Practice: Students practice the skill or identify additional examples of the concept, and the teacher provides guidance and detailed feedback. During independent practice, students practice on their own.	• Increase students' expertise with the concept or skill, and develop students' understanding to the point that they can identify examples of the concept or perform the skill with little effort.

Instructional strategies
Prescriptive approaches to teaching designed to help students acquire a deep understanding of specific forms of knowledge.

Direct instruction An instructional strategy designed to teach essential knowledge and skills through teacher explanation and modeling followed by student practice and feedback.

the lesson. She then had students add fractions with like denominators. This review served as the springboard for the rest of her lesson.

The value of introduction and review is well established by research. But although its importance seems obvious, the majority of lessons begin with little or no attempt to attract attention or activate relevant prior knowledge (Brophy, 2004).

DEVELOPING UNDERSTANDING   In the developing understanding phase of direct instruction, the teacher helps students acquire a thorough understanding of the skill. It's the most important phase of direct instruction and, ironically, is the one teachers often perform least well (Monte-Sano, 2008). Instead of working to develop student understanding, they often emphasize memorization, fail to ask enough questions, or move too quickly to practice.

Shirley avoided these pitfalls. She began with her "cakes" and involved students by asking a great many questions. She continued providing examples and then modeled the process for finding equivalent fractions by multiplying the numerator and denominator by the same number. She didn't move to the practice phase until she was confident that most of her students understood the process, which is essential for student success during the next phase (Kauchak & Eggen, 2007).

PRACTICE   When students learn a new skill, they need opportunities to practice the skill by applying it to new problems and to receive feedback from the teacher. Once Shirley felt most students understood the concept of *equivalent fractions* and how to create them, she assigned additional problems that required students to find equivalent fractions. As they worked, she carefully monitored their progress and then provided detailed feedback about the first problem before asking students to solve the second. She repeated this process with the second and third problems. Had students struggled, she would have had them solve additional problems under her guidance until she believed they were ready to practice on their own. The goal here is for students' understanding to be developed to the point that they can perform the operation with little conscious effort.

Effective teachers ease the transition into the practice phase through **scaffolding**, instructional assistance that teachers use to assist learners in a task that produces high rates of success (Lutz, Guthrie, & Davis, 2006). Teachers provide scaffolding in a variety of ways, including verbal prompts (e.g., "Don't forget your place values when you subtract."), shorter assignments combined with feedback (e.g., "Do the first three, and we'll check as a class before you do the rest."), and even peer tutoring (e.g., "Check with your partner after you solve the problem and discuss how you each did it."). The purpose of scaffolding is to help students learn by minimizing possibilities for frustration and failure.

Effective teachers also use students themselves to provide practice and feedback during direct instruction. **Peer tutoring** pairs students with classmates as they practice skills to automaticity. **Cross-age tutoring** brings older, more knowledgeable students into classrooms to work with their younger counterparts. In implementing either form of tutoring, training plus carefully planned tutoring materials that guide the process of practice and feedback are essential.

Teachers also frequently assign homework as practice, and when properly used, it can reinforce students' developing understanding and skills (H. Cooper, Robinson, & Patall, 2006). "Properly used" means that teachers assign homework that is an extension of content students have studied and practiced in class; in other words, it's aligned with learning objectives and learning activities (Bransford et al., 2000). Although grading homework can be time-consuming, teachers should have some mechanism for giving students credit and for providing feedback if they are to take it seriously and use it as a learning tool.

PEARSON
myeducationlab

Go to the *IRIS Center Resources* section of Topic 12: *Instruction* in the MyEducationLab for your course and explore the module titled *Providing Instructional Supports: Facilitating Mastery of New Skills*.

Scaffolding Instructional assistance that teachers use to assist learners in a task to produce high rates of success.

Peer tutoring A form of instructional practice in which students work with each other to provide practice and feedback.

Cross-age tutoring Peer tutoring in which older students work with younger ones.

■ ■ TECHNOLOGY AND TEACHING Capitalizing on Technology in Instruction

To be effective, direct instruction needs to include opportunities for students to practice the skills they're learning. But extended practice takes time, and teachers often struggle to provide sufficient opportunities for students to develop the automatic skill levels needed for basic skills. Technology provides one solution to this problem.

Technology can provide an effective way for students to practice skills with immediate feedback.

DRILL AND PRACTICE   Students often use worksheets and flash cards to practice basic skills, such as word recognition and phonetic analysis in reading, and addition and multiplication facts in math. Educators wondered whether computers could be used to provide an improved form of practice. This question led to the development of **drill-and-practice programs**, software designed to provide extensive practice with feedback (Lever-Duffy, McDonald, & Mizell, 2003).

Because students can use drill-and-practice programs on their own, teachers don't have to be directly involved. The programs don't substitute for teachers' expertise, however, and developers assume that students have had previous instruction related to the facts or concepts. For example, when students first learn about multiplication, effective teachers help them understand that 3×4 means 3 sets of 4 items, or 4 sets of 3 items, and they present several concrete examples to illustrate the concept of multiplication. After this initial instruction, teachers can have students use drill-and-practice programs to help them practice until the skill becomes automatic—that is, until they know the facts essentially without having to think about them.

The best drill-and-practice programs are adaptive, matching the demands of the task to a student's ability. For example, in a program designed to improve knowledge of multiplication facts, an adaptive program begins by pretesting to determine what multiplication facts students already know. The program then strategically presents problems to ensure high success rates. When students fail to answer, or answer incorrectly, the program prompts by providing the answer and then retests that fact. The program introduces more difficult problems only when students have reached a certain skill level. Because the ultimate goal is for students to be able to recall math facts automatically, the program shortens the amount of time given to answer as students become more proficient. This also increases motivation by challenging students to become quicker in their responses.

What are the benefits of drill-and-practice programs? First, they provide practice with effective feedback, informing students immediately of what they've mastered and where they need more work. Second, they are often motivating for students turned off by paper-and-pencil exercises (Gee, 2005), and third, they save teachers' time, because they don't have to present information and score students' responses.

Researchers caution, however, that more time on computers does not necessarily equal more learning (Roblyer & Doering, 2010). More important are the quality of the learning experiences and the extent to which they're linked to the teacher's goals.

TUTORIALS   Tutorials provide a second way for teachers to use technology to teach basic skills. A **tutorial** is a software program that delivers an entire integrated instructional sequence similar to a teacher's instruction on the topic. Let's see how Lisa Hoover, a first-grade teacher, uses a tutorial to teach basic skills.

Drill-and-practice programs Software programs designed to provide students with practice and feedback in learning basic skills.

Tutorial A software program that delivers an entire integrated instructional sequence similar to a teacher's instruction on the topic.

Lisa has created a number of learning centers in her classroom where her students work independently. Students can earn "classroom money" for good behavior and finishing assignments and can use the money to purchase prizes from the class store. Students who work in the store as clerks must first complete several of the math units, with the last one focusing on giving change. Lisa's students have widely varying backgrounds, and as a result, she has students who want to take the giving-change unit at different times. In the past, they often had to wait or she had to drop some other activity to teach them the rules for calculating and counting change.

To accommodate their differences in background, she has them work with a computerized tutorial that helps them acquire these skills. The tutorial includes pictures of various coins and presents a number of scenarios that provide students with practice in giving change. Now students can complete the unit anytime they have access to one of the computers in the classroom. In addition, Lisa designs the tutorial so that it will give students a number of problems and ongoing help until they master the information.

Tutorials include specific learning objectives, multiple pathways to them, and quizzes with feedback geared to the objectives. For example, if a teacher's goal is for students to be able to add positive and negative numbers, the tutorial will pretest students and then present instruction with frequent assessment and feedback. When a student answers 2.8 to the problem $-2.3 + .5 = ?$, for instance, the program responds with, "Think about the sign of the numbers and try again." Then, if the student tries again and answers -1.8, the program responds, "Well done, [student's name]. You understand the idea. Now, try this problem." As students' skills improve, they are given increasingly complex problems.

Tutorials can replicate each of the phases of direct instruction, and they have the added advantage of providing the students with ongoing personalized feedback about their progress. The best tutorials include motivational features such as timed tests that provide challenge and lead to automaticity, as well as charts that illustrate increasing skill development.

Tutorials can be linear, but the best are branched, which adapt to learners' responses (Roblyer & Doering, 2010). For example, when a student responds incorrectly to a multiple-choice item, the program explains why that choice isn't correct and repeats the initial instruction.

Effective tutorials are flexible, adaptive, and efficient. For example, Lisa's lesson was available anytime; students didn't have to wait until she had free time to teach them. Also, it provided each student with the right amount of practice needed to master the content, and her students found the pictures and video clips more motivating than traditional worksheets.

Tutorials have been criticized for focusing too much on memorized information instead of challenging students to think and apply understanding (Newby, Stepich, Lehman, & Russell, 2006; Roblyer & Doering, 2010). Although this doesn't have to be the case, finding high-quality tutorial software and effective hypermedia materials is a challenge facing teachers who want to integrate tutorials into their classrooms.

Finally, we want to emphasize that no tutorial, regardless of quality, can replace the skills expert teachers demonstrate with their students. Tutorials support effective instruction; they do not replace it.

Lecture-Discussion

In teaching, we often want to provide our students with the big picture—how important ideas are connected in a cohesive and coherent whole. **Lecture-discussion** is a teaching strategy designed to help students acquire **organized bodies of knowledge**, topics that connect facts, concepts, and principles and make the relationships among them explicit (Eggen & Kauchak, 2006). For example, when students examine relationships among plot, character, and symbolism in a novel such as *Moby Dick* in literature; study land-

Lecture-discussion An instructional strategy designed to teach organized bodies of knowledge through teacher presentations and frequent questioning to monitor learning progress.

Organized bodies of knowledge Topics that connect facts, concepts, and principles and make the relationships among them explicit.

forms, climate, and economy in different regions of the world in geography; or compare parasitic and nonparasitic worms and how differences between them are reflected in their body structures in biology, they are acquiring organized bodies of knowledge.

Teachers have always lectured but, unfortunately, have often done so badly, giving the strategy a bad name. Let's be honest: How many people want to sit through a "lecture"? Lecture-discussions are designed to overcome the weaknesses of traditional lectures, which include the following:

- Lectures place learners in passive roles, so they are ineffective for attracting and maintaining student attention. We have all sat through mind-numbing lectures with the goal of simply getting the time to pass more quickly.

- Lectures involve one-way communication and don't allow teachers to determine whether students are interpreting or learning new information accurately.

- Teachers often present too much information in lectures, so much of it is lost before students can make sense of it.

Lecture-discussions help overcome these problems by interspersing periodic teacher questions into teachers' presentations. Let's see how a 10th-grade American history teacher involves her students in a lecture-discussion lesson.

Diane Anderson is discussing the events leading up to the American Revolutionary War in her American history class. She begins with a review of their previous lesson, and then says, "I want us to understand important events that led up to the Revolutionary War, and to do so we need to back up to the early 1600s. When we're finished, we'll see that there were historical events that made the war inevitable. . . . That's why history is important . . . to see how events that happen at one time affect events even today. . . . For instance, the conflicts between the British and the French in America became so costly for the British that they began policies in the colonies that ultimately led to the Revolution."

She then begins, pointing at a large map, "We know the British established Jamestown in 1607, but at about the same time, a French explorer named Champlain came down the St. Lawrence River and formed Quebec City, here. Over the years, at least 35 of the 50 states were discovered by the French, and they founded several of our bigger cities, such as Detroit, St. Louis, New Orleans, and Des Moines.

"Now, what do you notice about the location of the two groups?"

After thinking a few seconds, Alfredo offers, "The French had a lot of Canada, . . . and it looks like this country, too," pointing to the north and west on the map.

"It looks like the east was . . . British, and the west was French," Troy adds.

"Yes, and remember, this was all happening at about the same time," Diane continues. "Also, the French were more friendly with the American Indians than the British were. Also, the French had what they called a seigniorial system, where the settlers were given land if they would serve in the military. So, . . . what does this suggest about the military power of the French?"

"Probably powerful," Josh suggests. "The people got land if they went in the army."

"And the American Indians probably helped, because they were friendly with the French," Tenisha adds.

"Now, what else do you notice here?" Diane asks, moving her hand back and forth across the width of the map.

"Mountains?" . . . Danielle answers.

"Yes, exactly," Diane smiles. "Why are they important? What do mountains do?"

". . . The British were sort of fenced in, and the French could expand as they pleased."

"Good. Now, the British needed land and wanted to expand. So they headed west over the mountains and guess who they ran into? . . . Sarah?"

"The French?" Sarah responded.

"Right! And conflict broke out. Now, when the French and the British were fighting, why do you suppose the French were initially more successful than the British? . . . Dan?"

> "Well, they had that sig . . . seigniorial system, so they were more eager to fight, because they got land."
>
> "Other thoughts? . . . Bette?"
>
> "I think that the American Indians were part of it. The French got along better with them, so they helped the French."
>
> "Okay, good thinking everyone; now let's think about the British . . . Let's look at some of their advantages." (Adapted from Eggen & Kauchak, 2010)

Let's analyze how Diane used questioning to actively involve her students in the lesson. First, she introduced the topic with a review and attempted to capture students' attention by explaining how events in the past influence the way we live today. Then, she presented information about Jamestown, Quebec, and French settlements in the present-day United States. After this brief introduction, she used questioning to encourage her students to think about the new content. To illustrate, let's look at some of the dialogue from the lesson.

Diane:	Now, what do you notice about the location of the two groups?
Alfredo:	The French had a lot of Canada, . . . and it looks like this country, too [pointing to the north and west on the map].
Troy:	It looks like the east was . . . British, and the west was French.

Diane's questions were intended to actively involve students, check their existing understanding, and help them expand on it. Satisfied with their level of understanding, she returned to presenting information when she said, "Yes, and remember, this was all happening at about the same time." She continued by briefly describing the French seigniorial system and pointing out the friendly relations between the French and the American Indians.

Then she again involved students through questioning.

Diane:	So, . . . what does this suggest about the military power of the French?
Josh:	Probably powerful. The people got land if they went in the army.
Tenisha:	And the American Indians probably helped, because they were friendly with the French.

In this segment, Diane guided students to a deeper understanding of the relationships between different factors, such as the seigniorial system, the partnership between the French and the American Indians, and French military power.

Diane then used the same cycle of information presentation followed by comprehension-checking questions to help students understand the advantages the British had in the conflict. Her goal for the whole lesson was for her students to understand the cause–effect relationships between the French and Indian Wars and the American Revolutionary War—an organized body of knowledge.

The effectiveness of lecture-discussions depends on the frequency and quality of question-driven discussions during the lesson (Wittwer & Renkl, 2008). These discussions allow the teacher to informally assess students' current level of understanding and then guide them to a deeper understanding of the entire body of knowledge. In a traditional lecture, these comprehension checks and the involvement they encourage don't occur, which is the primary reason lecture-discussion is a more effective strategy.

How often should teachers interrupt their presentations to check whether students are understanding? An old rule of thumb is that teachers should limit their talks to the age of their audience; in other words, a first-grade teacher shouldn't talk longer than 6 minutes, but a middle school teacher might go as long as 13 or 14 minutes. Our experience suggests that these limits are overoptimistic, and that students of all ages fade away quicker than their ages would suggest. Keep your presentations short and ask lots of questions—that is the key to successful lecture-discussions.

Guided Discovery

Direct instruction and lecture-discussions are effective, but when overused, can become boring. In addition, they establish the teacher as expert and fail to teach students how to discover new knowledge on their own. Guided discovery is designed to address these problems.

Guided discovery is an instructional strategy that provides students with information and uses teacher guidance to help them process that information into abstractions. When using this strategy, teachers present students with examples, guide them as they attempt to find patterns in the examples, and come to closure when students can describe the idea that the teacher is teaching (Moreno, 2004). It is often contrasted with "pure" or unstructured discovery, where learners identify patterns and relationships without guidance from a teacher. Research indicates that unstructured discovery is less effective than guided approaches because students don't use time efficiently; without help, students often become lost and frustrated, and this confusion can lead to misconceptions (Mayer, 2004). As a result, unstructured discovery is rarely seen in today's classrooms, except in student projects and investigations.

When done well, guided discovery is effective and is supported by research: "Guided discovery may take more or less time than expository instruction, depending on the task, but tends to result in better long-term retention and transfer than expository instruction" (Mayer, 2002, p. 68). When using guided discovery, teachers spend less time explaining and more time asking questions, so students tend to be more cognitively active than they are in more teacher-centered approaches (Moreno & Duran, 2004).

To see guided discovery in action, let's join Lori DuBose, a fifth-grade teacher, as she helps her students understand how *arthropods*, cold-blooded animals with exoskeletons, such as lobsters, crabs, insects, and spiders, are different from human beings.

Lori begins by saying, "OK everyone, reach down and grab your leg. Squeeze it and tell us what you feel. . . . Dorrette?"

Students note that their legs feel soft and warm, and that a bone is inside them. Lori has students explain their observations with questions such as "What do you feel inside your legs?" and "Why do they feel warm?", establishing differences with arthropods, which are cold-blooded and have exoskeletons.

Lori then says, "Look at this," as she pulls a live lobster out of a cooler and has students observe and touch it.

Students squeal "Oooh," "Yuk," and "Gross." Lori settles them down, and then says as she circulates among students, letting them feel the lobster, "Now tell me about this. . . . Sue?"

"It has a shell on it. . . . It feels hard."

"What else? . . . Leroy?"

"It's cold," Leroy replies after placing his palm on the lobster's back.

"Good! "Lori responds as she takes a large beetle out of a plastic bag and begins the same line of questioning as she has been using with the lobster. She also displays a colored transparency of the beetle for the children and tells them to look at the image on the screen when they can't see the actual animal. She then repeats the entire process with a crayfish.

She continues, "Now look at all three of these animals. What is something they all have in common? . . . Sergio?"

". . . They all felt hard."

"And what does that tell us?"

". . . They're skeletons are on the outside!" Sergio responds after thinking for several seconds.

"Well done, Sergio. You've identified one of the important features of these animals. What else did we find was similar about the animals? . . . Judy?"

Guided discovery An instructional strategy designed to teach concepts and other abstractions by presenting students with data and assisting them in finding patterns through teacher questioning.

"They all felt cold."

"Excellent, Judy. How is that different from the way we feel? . . . David?"

"We feel warm. We're warm-blooded!" David concludes excitedly. "These animals are all cold-blooded!"

"Yes, that's outstanding thinking, David," Lori responds with a smile and a wave of her hand.

Lori continues to direct students' analyses of the lobster, beetle, crayfish, and their own bodies, having them identify the jointed legs in each of the animals, and finally having them identify the segmented bodies in each. Let's see how Lori wraps up the lesson.

"Now let's look at the patterns we've found in the animals," Lori directs. *"What do they have in common? . . . Christy?"*

". . . They're all cold-blooded."

"Yes, excellent. That's one common feature of these animals," and with that she writes "cold-blooded" on the chalkboard.

"What else do they have in common? . . . Robert?"

"Skeleton on the outside," Robert replies quickly.

"Good, Robert. That's another important feature," and she writes "outside skeleton" on the board on her list of characteristics.

"Kirsty?"

". . . Their legs are jointed."

"Good! Jason?"

". . . They have segmented bodies."

"Outstanding, everyone! You've identified all the important features of this group of animals. Now does anyone know the name of this animal group?"

After hearing no response Lori says, "We call these animals 'arthropods.' Everybody say that word now."

The students then respond in unison, "ARTHROPODS!"

Lori then quickly erases the board and says, "Now give me a definition of 'arthropods.' I'll let someone volunteer."

With some prompting, they are able to define arthropods as animals that have an outside skeleton, jointed legs, and segmented bodies and are cold-blooded.

Lori extends the lesson by showing the students a clam, a worm, a grasshopper, and even Mrs. Alvarez, their parent volunteer, asking them to tell her if they are arthropods and explain why or why not.

Now, let's look at Lori's lesson in more detail. She began by having students squeeze their legs to determine that their skeletons were inside their bodies and that they were warm-blooded. This was her review, and it helped students contrast these characteristics with those of arthropods.

Lori then provided high-quality examples of arthropods—the lobster, beetle, and crayfish—and she even displayed a large transparency of the beetle in case students couldn't see the actual insect. After displaying each example, Lori actively involved students by asking them to observe and describe each animal, and she then moved the lesson to closure with questions such as, "Now let's look at the patterns we've found in the animals. . . . What do they have in common?"

After identifying common characteristics, Lori identified the animals as arthropods and then had students apply their understanding by having them analyze a clam, a worm, a grasshopper, and Mrs. Alvarez, explaining why each was or wasn't an arthropod.

Notice that in Lori's lesson, as well as in Shirley's and Diane Anderson's, the teachers—although using different strategies—employed the essential teaching skills that you studied in the previous section: They were all enthusiastic and well organized; they began their lessons with a review; they used questioning extensively throughout; and they had a form of clear closure and application. The strategies were different, but they were all supported by the essential teaching skills.

Cooperative Learning

Whole-class, teacher-centered instruction is effective and is widely used in classrooms at all levels. But despite teachers' best efforts, it's often difficult to involve all students in a lesson because of sheer numbers. Cooperative learning addresses this problem by breaking students into smaller groups to work on learning tasks. **Cooperative learning** is a set of instructional strategies used to help learners meet specific learning and social-interaction objectives in structured groups. It has become one of the most popular instructional strategies in schools today; one study found that more than 9 of 10 elementary teachers used some form of cooperative learning in their classrooms (Antil, Jenkins, Wayne, & Vadasy, 1998).

Cooperative-learning activities encourage knowledge construction through social interaction.

Let's begin our discussion of cooperative learning with three short examples, each conducted at a different grade level.

A kindergarten teacher is teaching his students basic shapes. After explaining and illustrating each with cardboard shapes, he divides the class into pairs and asks each group to find examples of circles, squares, and triangles in their own classroom. When the class comes back together, students share their examples.

A middle school math teacher is teaching how to solve word problems involving areas of different geometric shapes. She divides the class into teams of four and asks each team to solve the next few problems. Students in each team take turns explaining their solutions to each other. Later, the teams take turns at the board explaining to the whole class how they solved the different problems.

A senior high English teacher is reviewing literary devices such as simile, metaphor, personification, *and* alliteration. *He assigns a scene from Shakespeare's* Julius Caesar *and asks students in groups of two to identify as many of these devices as they can. The whole class compares their findings after 15 minutes.*

Common to each of these examples is students' working together in small groups toward a specific learning goal.

When implemented effectively, cooperative learning involves all students, which can be difficult in large groups. In whole-class discussions, less confident students may get few chances to participate, so they often drift off. Cooperative learning can also be effective for teaching students social skills such as working collaboratively with others (Payton, Munro, O'Brien, & Weissberg, 2006). By participating in cooperative-learning activities, students learn to understand the perspectives and feelings of others, as well as how to build on the ideas of others in developing their understanding.

Though the specific form varies, most cooperative-learning activities have students work together in groups small enough (typically two to five) so that everyone can

Cooperative learning A set of instructional strategies used to help learners meet specific learning and social interaction objectives in structured groups.

participate in a clearly assigned task (D. Johnson & Johnson, 2006). Effective cooperative-learning tasks also share four other features:

- Learning objectives direct the groups' activities.
- Social interaction is emphasized.
- Students are held individually accountable for their learning.
- Learners depend on one another to reach objectives.

The last characteristic is important because it emphasizes the crucial role that peer cooperation plays in learning (D. Johnson & Johnson, 2006). Accountability is also essential because it keeps students focused on the objectives and reminds them that learning (not visiting) is the major purpose of the activity.

Successful implementation of cooperative-learning activities requires careful teacher thought and planning. We examine factors influencing its success in the following sections.

INTRODUCING COOPERATIVE LEARNING Introducing students to cooperative learning requires careful planning. Poorly organized activities can result in less learning than in whole-group lessons (Brophy, 2006). Suggestions for effectively organizing cooperative learning activities include the following:

- Seat group members together, so they can move back and forth from group work to whole-class activities with little disruption.
- Have learning materials ready for easy distribution to each group.
- Introduce students to cooperative learning with short, simple tasks, and make objectives and directions clear.
- Specify the amount of time students have to accomplish the task (and keep it relatively short).
- Monitor groups while they work.
- Require students to create a product as a result of the cooperative-learning activity (e.g., written answers to specific questions or a completed product).

These suggestions maximize the time available for learning and provide a focal point for students' cooperative-learning efforts.

COOPERATIVE-LEARNING STRATEGIES Different variations of cooperative learning all capitalize on social interaction, but each is designed to accomplish different objectives. Four of the most common are outlined in Table 13.6. Other cooperative-learning strategies exist, and although they differ in specifics, all depend heavily on social interaction for their effectiveness.

Table 13.6 Cooperative Learning Strategies

Strategy	Description	Example
Reciprocal Questioning	Pairs work together to ask and answer questions about a lesson or text.	Teacher provides question stems, such as "Summarize ..." or "Why was ... important?" and students use the stems to create specific questions about the topic.
Scripted Cooperation	Pairs work together to elaborate on each other's thinking.	*Math:* First member of a pair offers a problem solution. The second member then elaborates, and the process is repeated. *Reading:* Pairs read a passage and the first member offers a summary. The second elaborates, and the process continues.
Jigsaw II	Individuals become expert on subsections of a topic and teach it to others in their group.	One student studies the geography of a region; another, the economy; a third, the climate. Each attends "expert" meetings, and the "experts" then teach their content to others in their group.
Student Teams Achievement Divisions (STADs)	Social interaction is used to help students learn facts, concepts, and skills.	The independent-practice phase of direct instruction is replaced with team study, during which team members check and compare their answers. Team study is followed by quizzes, and individual-improvement points lead to team awards.

So, what's the best way to teach? Unfortunately, thousands of studies over years of research have failed to provide a definitive answer. It will be up to you to decide that question for yourself when you have your own classroom. Research *does* tell us that no single instructional strategy is most effective for *all* students or for helping students reach *all* learning objectives (Marzano, 2003). This research indicates that the final item in our *This I Believe* feature, "Rather than exclusively using one particular teaching strategy, effective teachers vary the way they teach," is true. Effective teachers use a variety of instructional strategies to help their students reach different learning objectives (Eggen & Kauchak, 2006).

As we've seen, motivation is an integral part of effective instruction. In the *Taking a Stand in an Era of Reform* box below, we describe a controversial proposal to increase students' motivation: paying them to learn!

This I BELIEVE

Taking a Stand in an Era of Reform

Paying Students to Learn

Did you ever receive money for a good report card? How did it affect your motivation and study habits? We saw earlier that motivation plays a powerful role in influencing student learning. Highly motivated students are a source of pleasure for teachers, and lack of motivation is an ongoing concern.

In response to concerns about learner motivation, and particularly the motivation of students from low-income families, programs around the country reward students for attendance, grades, and learning (Toppo, 2008). The programs vary in their structure. For example, in some, students are awarded McDonald's meals and pizza parties for reading a certain number of books. In others, students are rewarded for high grades; students are assessed every 5 weeks in different subjects and receive $50 for an A, $35 for a B, and even $20 for a C. Students get half the money up front, and receive the remainder when they graduate. A straight-A student could earn up to $4,000 by the end of his or her sophomore year (Sandovi, 2008). Other programs pay students a flat amount, such as $500 for doing well on standardized achievement or AP tests (D. Jones, 2008; Medina, 2007). In some programs, teachers are also rewarded with cash incentives for their students' performance on tests. In most cases, the efforts are funded privately through corporate or philanthropic donors, so state and district money is not being used to pay for the programs.

THE ISSUE

As you might expect, pay-for-learning programs are highly controversial, with opponents presenting a variety of criticisms. Most academicians oppose the programs on theoretical and philosophical grounds and cite research indicating that external incentives, such as money, reduce students' intrinsic motivation (Brophy, 2004). Others argue that schools should be places where learning for its own sake is valued and promoted (Kohn, 1993). Critics also argue that the payouts are nothing more than bribes, and students' efforts will disappear when the bribes are taken away. Other critics are even more blunt, metaphorically comparing them to steroids: They improve short-term performance but cause long-term damage (Toppo, 2008).

Supporters of these incentive programs point out that they're similar to ones that have proven effective in industry (D. Jones, 2008). In addition, they emphasize that the programs are geared primarily toward low-income students who often don't see the value in school work and high grades, because they can't afford to go to college anyway. The possibility of earning money offers at least the opportunity to consider college, which might cause kids to think differently about finishing high school. Further, the money often helps low-income families with finances so parents can spend more time helping their kids with homework and making sure they're prepared for the next day. Finally, supporters argue, many avenues for success exist for bright, hardworking kids, but opportunities for average kids from poor backgrounds are virtually nonexistent. Pay for performance, they argue, could help "level the playing field" (Delp, 2007).

YOU TAKE A STAND

Now it's your turn to take a position on the issue. Is providing students with tangible incentives for learning an effective instructional practice, or does it detract from motivation and, ultimately, learning?

myeducationlab To explore both sides of this issue and take a stand, go to the *Book Specific Resources* section in the MyEducationLab for your course, select your text, and then select *Taking a Stand in an Era of Reform* for Chapter 13.

ISSUES IN EDUCATION

Instructional Strategies

You're a middle school life science teacher beginning a unit on the different body systems, such as the skeletal, the circulatory, the digestive, and the muscular systems. You plan to begin with the skeletal system, and you want your students to understand the relationship between the structures and the functions of the different parts of the skeleton, such as understanding that the skull is essentially solid because it protects the brain, which is the most important organ in the body; the rib cage exists to protect other important organs, such as the heart and lungs; and the leg bones are the size and shape they are because they support the body as we stand and move.

Which instructional strategy would you choose to help you reach your goal? Explain why you would use that strategy.

■ ■ ■ ■ CHECK YOUR UNDERSTANDING

4.1 Describe different instructional strategies, and explain the essential differences in each.

4.2 Which phase of direct instruction is most important for ensuring successful practice? Explain.

4.3 A teacher places her third graders in groups of four and gives each group magnets and a packet containing a dime, a spoon, aluminum foil, a rubber band, a wooden pencil, a paper clip, and nails. She directs the groups to experiment with the magnets and items for 10 minutes, look for patterns, and record these on paper. After the groups have finished, she leads a discussion in which they identify characteristics of materials that are and are not attracted to magnets. The teacher is using which strategy, or strategies, in her learning activity?

For feedback, go to the appendix, *Check Your Understanding*, located in the back of this text.

A major theme of this chapter is that different strategies are designed to meet different teaching goals. The *Decision Making* feature above provides you with firsthand experience in this area.

13 MEETING YOUR LEARNING OBJECTIVES

1. Define *motivation* and identify instructional factors that increase students' motivation.

   • *Motivation* is the energizing force in learning and can have a powerful effect on student success.

   • *Extrinsic motivation* is motivation to engage in an activity to achieve some incentive, whereas *intrinsic motivation* is motivation to engage in a behavior for its own sake.

   • Attracting students' attention, involving students, and helping students apply their understanding to the real world are all factors that can increase motivation to learn.

2. Describe basic steps in planning for instruction.

   - Planning for instruction involves identifying topics, specifying learning objectives, preparing and organizing learning activities, designing assessments, and ensuring that instruction is aligned, that is, making sure that learning activities and assessments are consistent with objectives.

   - Finding or creating high-quality examples or problems is the most important part of preparing and organizing learning activities and is a major reason that specifying clear learning objectives is so important. If objectives are clear, then teachers know what information the examples should contain, and they can then attempt to find or create them.

   - Planning in a standards-based environment often requires teachers to first interpret the standard. Once the standard is clearly understood, the teacher can construct learning objectives and design learning activities.

3. Describe essential teaching skills and identify examples in classroom practice.

   - *Essential teaching skills* are the abilities that all teachers, regardless of topic or grade level, should demonstrate in their teaching.

   - Effective teachers are caring, have high personal efficacy and positive expectations for their students, and communicate their own genuine interest in the topics they teach.

   - Effective teachers are well organized, which means they begin their lessons on time, have their materials prepared and ready, and have efficient, well-established routines in their classrooms.

   - Effective teachers use focus to attract students' attention, involve students through questioning, provide informative feedback, and use reviews to activate students' prior knowledge.

   - Effective teachers help students apply their understanding in new contexts.

4. Describe instructional strategies and identify applications of these in learning activities.

   - Instructional strategies are designed to help students reach specific learning objectives.

   - Teachers who want their students to acquire basic skills, such as adding fractions, would likely use direct instruction.

   - Lecture-discussion is an effective strategy for helping students understand organized bodies of knowledge, such as the relationship between geography and lifestyle in different parts of our country.

   - Guided discovery is an effective strategy for helping students understand concepts and how to form ideas on their own.

   - Cooperative learning can support the other strategies and can be effective for helping students learn social and cooperation skills.

IMPORTANT CONCEPTS

assessment (p. 382)
backward design (p. 384)
closure (p. 392)
cooperative learning (p. 403)
cross-age tutoring (p. 396)

direct instruction (p. 395)
drill-and-practice programs (p. 397)
effective teaching (p. 376)
equitable distribution (p. 389)
essential teaching skills (p. 384)

extrinsic motivation (p. 377)
feedback (p. 391)
focus (p. 387)
guided discovery (p. 401)
high-quality examples (p. 382)
instructional alignment (p. 383)
instructional strategies (p. 395)
intrinsic motivation (p. 377)
learning objectives (p. 380)
lecture-discussion (p. 398)
modeling (p. 386)

motivation (p. 376)
organization (p. 387)
organized bodies of knowledge (p. 398)
peer tutoring (p. 396)
personal teaching efficacy (p. 385)
prompting (p. 390)
questioning frequency (p. 389)
scaffolding (p. 396)
self-fulfilling prophecy (p. 386)
tutorial (p. 397)
wait-time (p. 390)

DISCUSSION QUESTIONS

1. In addition to the motivational strategies discussed in the chapter, how can teachers motivate students during a lesson?

2. Does the importance of motivation vary with grade level? With the ability level of students?

3. Why is the practice of calling on volunteers to answer a question so prevalent? What are its advantages? What are its disadvantages?

4. How does the importance of the following essential teaching skills vary with grade level or content area: focus, questioning, feedback, and review and closure?

5. Many teachers lecture instead of guiding their students to their goals using questioning. Why do you think this is the case? How can teachers avoid this pitfall?

6. Which of the four instructional strategies is easiest to implement? Why? Which is most difficult or challenging?

7. How does the effectiveness of the four instructional strategies vary with grade level? Are some of these more effective or useful for certain content areas? Which, and why?

myeducationlab

Now go to Topic 12: *Instruction* in the MyEducationLab (www.myeducationlab.com) for your course, where you can:

- Find learning outcomes for *Instruction* along with the national standards that connect to these outcomes.

- Complete *Assignments and Activities* that can help you more deeply understand the chapter content.

- Apply and practice your understanding of the core teaching skills identified in the chapter with the *Building Teaching Skills and Dispositions* learning units.

- Check your comprehension on the content covered in the chapter by going to the *Study Plan* in the *Book Specific Resources* section for your text. Here you will be able to take a chapter quiz, receive feedback on your answers, and then access *Review, Practice, and Enrichment* activities to enhance your understanding of chapter content.

Develop Your Professional Portfolio

To further apply your understanding of chapter content and address the INTASC standards, go to the *Book Specific Resources* section in the MyEducationLab for your course, select your text, and then select this chapter's *Portfolio Activities*.

"Even when it all gets hard—and it does—it still is the most rewarding, joyous, and, yes, craziest job on the planet."

KATHLEEN SHEEHY, 2008 Teacher of the Year, District of Columbia

To view a video clip of Kathleen, the 2008 District of Columbia Teacher of the Year, go to Topic 9: *Assessment Statndards and Accountability* in the MyEducationLab for your course and select *Teacher Talk*, then *Kathleen Sheehy*.

14

Assessment, Standards, and Accountability

CHAPTER OUTLINE

The Need for Assessment in an Era of Reform

- Why Is Assessment Important?
- Types of Assessments
- Making Your Assessments Valid and Reliable
- Misconceptions About Assessment
- How Do Teachers Assess?
- Using Assessment to Promote Learning

Grading and Reporting

Exploring Diversity: Effective Assessment Practices With Students From Diverse Backgrounds

- The Teacher's Role in Grading
- Grading and Reporting in Elementary Schools
- Grading and Reporting in Middle and High Schools
- Technology and Teaching: Using Technology in Assessment

Standards, Accountability, and Assessment

- The Standards Movement in Education
- Accountability, Standards, and Assessment

Taking a Stand in an Era of Reform: Does Accountability Through High-Stakes Tests Harm Students?

LEARNING OBJECTIVES

After you have completed your study of this chapter, you should be able to:

1. **Describe the process of assessment, and explain how it promotes student learning.** INTASC Standard 8, Assessment of Student Learning

2. **Explain how grading and reporting relate to the total assessment process.** INTASC Standard 8, Assessment of Student Learning

3. **Define** *standards* **and explain how assessment, standards, and accountability are related.** INTASC Standard 8, Assessment of Student Learning

You're teaching a lesson, and students are involved and paying attention. Everything seems to be going well, and students seem to be "getting it." But are they really, and how can you find out? Keep these questions in mind as you read the following case study.

Jenny Newhall, a fourth-grade teacher, wants her students to understand the principle behind beam balances: that they balance when the weight times the distance on one side of the fulcrum equals the weight times the distance on the other side. She begins by dividing her students into groups of four and giving the groups balances with tiles on them that appear as follows (each of the tiles is the same weight, so the weight will depend on the number of tiles):

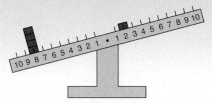

Jenny asks students to figure out different ways to balance the beam, but before adding tiles to the balances, they need to write down possible solutions and explain to their group-mates why they think their solutions will work.

As the class begins to work, Jenny circulates around the room, periodically stopping for a moment to check on the progress of a group, and then moving on to another group.

Students in one of the groups—Molly, Suzanne, Tad, and Drexel—work on the problem, and Suzanne offers the following solution: "There are four on the 8 and one on the 2. I want to put three on the 10 so there will be four on each side," indicating that she believes the beam will balance simply by keeping the number of tiles on each side of the fulcrum equal.

Here's the solution she proposes:

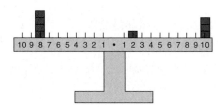

Jenny joins the group as Molly describes her thinking. She agrees that Suzanne's arrangement of tiles will make the beam balance, but offers a different explanation: "I think we should put three on the 10, because four on the 8 is 32 on one side. And since we only have two on the other side, we need to make them equal. So three on the 10 would equal 30, plus 2, and we'd have 32 on both sides."

What should Jenny think about the success of her lesson so far? It would be tempting for her to conclude that students understand the topic, because she observed the other students listening while Molly explained the principle clearly and accurately. Jenny's thinking is likely reinforced by events that follow.

As groups finish their work, Jenny reassembles the class and has Mavrin, who solved the problem correctly, come to the board and explain it, using the sketch you see here, which she has drawn on the board.

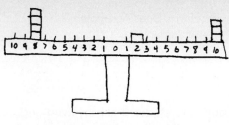

$$8 \times 4 = 32 \qquad (10 \times 3) + 2 = 32$$

Mavrin explains that $8 \times 4 = 32$ on the left side of the fulcrum equals $(10 \times 3) + 2 = 32$ on the right side, referring to the sketch in his explanation. Jenny reviews it, carefully describes the logic of his thinking and concludes by saying, "He has an excellent number sentence here."

Jenny's conclusion that students "get it" makes even more sense now, because she heard both Molly—in the small group—and Mavrin, with the whole class, give accurate

For each item, circle the number that best represents your thinking. Use the following scale as a guide.

4 = I strongly believe the statement is true.
3 = I believe the statement is true.
2 = I believe the statement is false.
1 = I strongly believe the statement is false.

1. Informal assessment is valuable for making decisions related to students' personal and social development, but it is essentially unrelated to instructional decisions.

   1   2   3   4

2. The primary function of the assessment process is to help teachers determine how much students have learned.

   1   2   3   4

3. Time spent on assessment should be kept to a minimum because it uses time that is more effectively spent on instructional activities.

   1   2   3   4

4. Determining students' grades is an important part of the assessment process, and you will be largely on your own in making decisions about students' grades.

   1   2   3   4

5. Because student learning standards are constructed at the state level, they won't have a major impact on your teaching.

   1   2   3   4

myeducationlab To download and complete this form, go to the *Book Specific Resources* section in the MyEducationLab for your course, select your text, and then select *This I Believe* for Chapter 14.

This I BELIEVE!

explanations. And, she reviewed and reinforced Mavrin's explanation herself. There's more to the story, however.

An interviewer from a nearby university is observing the class, and following the lesson, he talks with Suzanne, Molly, Tad, and Drexel about their understanding of beam balances. He gives them the following problem:

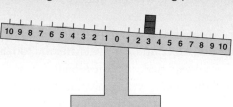

After allowing students some time to think about it, he says, "Suzanne, tell us where you would put tiles to make the beam balance."

Suzanne offers the following solution:

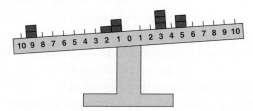

She reasons, "I put two here [indicating that she had added two tiles to the right side of the fulcrum] so that 2 plus 3 equals 5 . . . and 2 plus 1 plus 2 here, so it will be 5" [indicating that she had put five tiles on the left side of the fulcrum]."

It's easy for us all to fall into the trap of concluding that our students understand an idea because we have explained it carefully, or we've heard one or two students respond correctly. But as Suzanne's thinking illustrates, this often isn't the case. In spite of hearing Molly, Mavrin, and Jenny each provide a correct explanation, her original thinking—that the trick to making the beam balance is to keep the numbers of tiles on each side equal—had not changed in the least.

This lesson raises an additional question: How likely is it that Jenny knew that Suzanne retained a misconception about the principle for making beams balance? The answer is that she probably didn't realize that Suzanne (and several others in the class) really didn't understand the topic she was teaching. This leads us to the central role of assessment in teaching—the focus of this chapter. Before you begin your study of the chapter, please respond to the items in the *This I Believe* feature on page 413, designed to examine your current beliefs about assessment.

THE NEED FOR ASSESSMENT IN AN ERA OF REFORM

As you have seen throughout your study of this book, American education is currently in the throes of reform, and assessment of both students and teachers is at the center of this reform movement. Standards and accountability will influence your life as a teacher, and assessment is central to both of these reforms. Unfortunately, research suggests that teachers, both new and experienced, find assessment to be a major challenge (Zientek, 2007).

Why Is Assessment Important?

To begin answering this question, let's consider Jenny's lesson again. The success of her lesson depended on all of her students understanding how balance beams work, but how could Jenny determine whether this is happening? In addition, Suzanne's thinking illustrates another reason why assessing learning progress is so important (and complex): If Jenny didn't assess students' understanding and provide the feedback necessary to change their thinking, Suzanne, and probably several other students, would retain a misconception about the topic, hampering their future understanding of beam balances, problem solving, and math equations.

Assessment is the process teachers use to gather information and make decisions about students' learning and development (McMillan, 2007a; Nitko & Brookhart, 2007). For instance, Jenny, an experienced professional, wasn't fooled into believing that all her students understood the topic based on hearing Molly's and Mavrin's explanations. So, she designed a simple assessment to provide her with information from all her students. Her assessment and one student response are illustrated in Figure 14.1.

We can see from the figure that this student's understanding is still "a work in progress." He was able to determine that the beam would balance in the first problem, but was unable to draw or write a correct solution to the second. His experience wasn't unique: Jenny's assessment revealed that several other students in the class were also still uncertain about solving problems with beam balances. The students' responses to the problems gave her information about their understanding, and, based on that information, she decided to provide students with additional examples and discussion to help them revise their thinking. Gathering the information from all students in a systematic way allowed her to adapt her instruction to their needs and again illustrates why assessment is so important for classroom learning.

This example has important implications for beginning teachers. You will explain topics clearly, and some of your students will seem to "get it," as Molly and Mavrin did

Assessment The process teachers use to gather information and make decisions about students' learning and development.

Figure 14.1 Assessing Understanding of Beam Balances

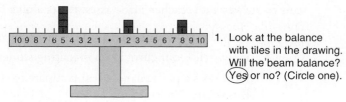

1. Look at the balance
   with tiles in the drawing.
   Will the beam balance?
   Yes or no? (Circle one).

Now, explain why the beam will or will not balance.

It will balance. 2 times 8 is 16, and 2 times 2 is 4 so that's 20. 4 times 5 is 20, so they are the same.

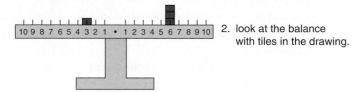

2. look at the balance
   with tiles in the drawing.

Draw more tiles on the drawing so that the beam will be balanced. Then, explain why you placed the tiles where you did.

I want to place more tiles on, so that it will balance. To balance, add 2 tiles to the 6 on the left, so there will be 3 tiles on each side and it will balance.

in Jenny's lesson. But don't be fooled into thinking that *all* your students understand based on your explanation or on the responses of a few. Instead, you'll need to carefully and thoroughly assess your students' understanding, and make assessment an integral part of your teaching process, as Jenny did.

Types of Assessments

Teachers use a variety of assessments in their classrooms. For example, consider the following:

- You likely took the SAT or the ACT during high school, which was used as one criterion in your application to college.
- You watch your students do a seatwork assignment in math, and you see one of them make the same error on three consecutive problems.
- Jenny listened to Molly correctly explain how to make the beam balance.
- You take a multiple-choice quiz in this class.
- A kindergarten teacher watches to see if her students are correctly forming letters in their writing.
- As you go through your teacher preparation program, you create a portfolio of your work.

Each is a form of assessment, but they differ in the kinds of information they provide teachers. We examine these different types of assessments in the sections that follow.

STANDARDIZED AND TEACHER-MADE ASSESSMENTS   The SAT, Scholastic Aptitude Test, and the ACT, American College Testing Assessment, are examples of standardized tests. **Standardized tests** are assessment instruments given to large samples of students—nationwide, in many cases—under uniform conditions and scored and reported according to uniform procedures. We're all familiar with them because we took achievement tests as we moved through elementary school, and the SAT or ACT was a rite of passage from high school to college.

With increased emphasis on accountability, standardized testing has become an even more important part of teachers' and students' lives. For example, you will be expected to prepare your students for the statewide assessment tests that students in all states are now required to take.

Standardized tests Assessment instruments given to large samples of students under uniform conditions and scored and reported according to uniform procedures.

Standardized tests are designed to answer the following questions, which are difficult to answer with teacher-made assessments alone:

- How do the students in my class compare with others across the country?
- How well is our curriculum preparing students for college or future training?
- How does a particular student compare to those of similar ability? (Nitko & Brookhart, 2007).

Teacher-made assessments, in contrast, are created by teachers for the purpose of measuring and promoting students' learning in a particular classroom. The tests and quizzes that you've taken throughout your school careers and performance assessments, such as assessments of class presentations that you've made, are all part of teacher-made assessments.

Each of the types of assessments in the sections that follow are teacher-made; keep that in mind as you study those sections.

INFORMAL ASSESSMENT   Teachers use **informal assessment** to gather information continually as they interact with students in their classrooms. The second and third items in our list of teacher-made assessments—your observing one of your students making a consistent error on math problems and Jenny's listening to Molly correctly explain why the beam would balance—are examples of informal assessments. Neither you nor Jenny planned to gather the information in advance, and you didn't get the same information from each of your students. If one of your students made a consistent error, for instance, that doesn't mean other students made the same error (though it might be likely). Similarly, Molly's correct explanation didn't indicate that all of Jenny's students understood beam balances.

Informal assessments are valuable because they help teachers make the many split-second decisions required every day (P. Black, Harrison, Lee, Marshall, & William, 2004). For example, after seeing a student make the same kind of error on three problems, you might decide to provide extra help so he, and probably other students, could revise their thinking.

These examples also illustrate that assessment is much more than giving tests and quizzes and also focuses on more than just acquiring knowledge. Personal, social, and moral growth are important parts of students' overall development. Virtually all the decisions teachers make in these areas are based on informal assessments, such as observing students on the playground or in class. Deciding to intervene in the case of a group that isn't working well together, concluding that one of your students should be referred for counseling, and asking a student to see you after school because you believe she has a personal problem are all examples of informal assessment and are an important part of your role as a teacher.

This discussion addresses the first item in our *This I Believe* feature, "Informal assessment is valuable for making decisions related to students' personal and social development, but it is essentially unrelated to instructional decisions." This statement isn't true: Informal assessment can be a valuable component of all of these decisions.

FORMAL ASSESSMENT   By contrast, the problems Jenny gave after her lesson and the quizzes that you take in this class are examples of **formal assessments**, assessments designed to systematically gather the same kind of information from every student. The fact that formal assessments systematically gather information from every student is a major advantage, because they provide you with a clearer and more comprehensive picture of the learning that is occurring in your classroom.

Teachers strategically use different types of formal assessments in their classrooms to gather different types of information about learning progress. In addition to traditional tests and quizzes that students take, for example, they also write papers, and instructors evaluate presentations that they make. These are all formal assessments.

This I BELIEVE

Informal assessment The frequent and continual process of gathering information about students' learning and behavior, and making decisions based on that information.

Formal assessment The process of systematically gathering assessment information from every student.

Teachers use three types of formal assessment in their teaching:

- Paper-and-pencil assessments
- Performance assessments
- Portfolio assessments

Paper-and-Pencil Assessments. Paper-and-pencil items are the most common form of assessment in most classrooms. They include the multiple-choice, true-false, matching, completion, and essay items that you've all taken throughout your time in school. They are typically classified as *objective*, because scorers don't have to make decisions about the quality of an answer, or *subjective*, such as essay, because scorer judgment is a factor (Miller, Linn, & Gronlund, 2009).

Performance Assessments. Critics argue that traditional paper-and-pencil assessments, most often in the form of multiple-choice tests, lack validity because they fail to measure important outcomes such as the ability to think critically or to express complex ideas clearly (Corcoran, Dershimer, & Tichenor, 2004; French, 2003). (We examine the concept of *validity* later in the chapter.) In response to these criticisms, the use of **performance assessments**, direct examinations of student performance on tasks relevant to life outside of school, is being emphasized, especially in the language arts (Frey & Schmitt, 2005; Popham, 2005a).

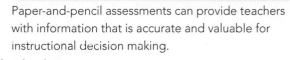

Paper-and-pencil assessments can provide teachers with information that is accurate and valuable for instructional decision making.

Performance assessments take a variety of forms. For example,

A high school English teacher wants her students to be able to write persuasive essays. She shows an example of an exemplary essay and another example of an essay that is flawed. The students discuss the differences between the two, arrive at criteria for high-quality persuasive essays and then write essays of their own. (Stiggins, 2007)

When you make presentations in your classes and your instructors grade them, they are also using a type of performance assessment. When science teachers evaluate students' design of a laboratory experiment, when art teachers observe their students creating a painting, or when kindergarten teachers observe their students forming letters, they also are using performance assessments.

The term *performance assessment* originated in content areas such as science and the performing arts, where students are required to demonstrate an ability in a real-world situation, such as a lab demonstration or recital. Performance assessments have spread to other areas and are quite common in all academic areas.

Portfolio Assessment. **Portfolio assessment** is a third type of formal assessment found in classrooms. A *portfolio* is a collection of student works, such as essays, quizzes, projects, samples of poetry, lab reports, and videotaped performances. Both teachers and students analyze these works using preset criteria to evaluate growth in an area (Popham, 2005a; Stiggins, 2007). The use of portfolios is popular and appears in areas ranging from measuring reading readiness in at-risk children (J. Smith, Brewer, & Heffner, 2003) to assessing biology students' understanding of complex life-forms (Dickson, 2004). As you move through your teacher preparation program, you might be asked to create a portfolio of your work, and you may be beginning the process in this class. And as the use of technology advances, electronic portfolios are becoming increasingly popular (Lambert, DePaepe, & Lambert, 2007).

FORMATIVE AND SUMMATIVE ASSESSMENT Although we often think the purpose of assessment is to assign grades, its most important function is to promote learning (Stiggins, 2007). Teachers often gather assessment information to gauge learning progress but

To look at a report used as an entry in a student's science portfolio, go to the *Assignments and Activities* section of Topic 9: *Assessment, Standards, and Accountability* in the MyEducationLab for your course and complete the activity titled *Portfolio Assessment.*

Performance assessments Direct examinations of student performance on tasks that are relevant to life outside of school.

Portfolio assessment The process of selecting collections of student work that both students and teachers evaluate using preset criteria.

Portfolios provide students with opportunities to view their own growth over time.

don't use it for grading purposes, a process called **formative assessment** (Chappuis & Chappuis, 2007/2008; Guskey, 2007/2008). For example, if you use students' responses to questions during a learning activity as a basis for deciding whether to move forward in the activity, you are involved in formative assessment; you aren't using the information to grade students. Virtually all forms of informal assessment are formative, as are pretests, work samples, and writing assignments that can be rewritten. The primary purpose of formative assessment is to provide students with feedback, which is essential for increasing motivation and achievement (Frey & Schmitt, 2005; Stiggins, 2007). But research suggests that despite its positive effects, teachers don't use formative assessment as much as they should (Frey & Schmitt, 2005).

Summative assessment is the process of assessing learning *after* instruction and using the results for grading decisions. (We discuss grading in detail later in the chapter.) Although used for grading, feedback on summative assessments is also essential, and summative assessments can be effective for promoting learning. In public schools, and particularly in the upper grades, most assessments are used for summative purposes. But both formative and summative assessments can be useful for making instructional decisions and for increasing student motivation to learn.

Making Your Assessments Valid and Reliable

The terms *validity* and *reliability* are often used to describe assessments, and accurate assessments are both valid and reliable. **Validity** refers to the extent to which assessment results are interpreted and used appropriately (Miller et al., 2009). For example, if Jenny interpreted Molly's and Mavrin's explanations as indicating that all students understood her lesson, her conclusion would be invalid, because she didn't have any information about the rest of her students' understanding.

On the other hand, all the students responded to the problem Jenny gave in Figure 14.1, and the student's response we see in the figure demonstrates incomplete understanding. If a number of students responded in a similar way, it would be valid to interpret the results as suggesting that more instruction was needed to clear up the misconceptions. Validity increases when quizzes and tests are aligned with teachers' learning objectives.

To be valid, assessments must be reliable. **Reliability** refers to the consistency of assessment results (Miller et al., 2009). The idea of reliability is intuitively sensible. For instance, if your bathroom scale is reliable and your weight doesn't change, the readings shouldn't vary from one hour or one day to the next. Objective assessment formats, such as multiple choice, are highly reliable, which—in addition to their ease of scoring—is one of the reasons they're commonly used on standardized tests. Unreliable assessments can't be valid because they give inconsistent information.

Validity and reliability can be a problem with informal assessments because teachers' decisions often are influenced by students' physical characteristics (S. Wang, Treat, & Brownell, 2008). For example, good-looking students who have engaging personalities are sometimes awarded higher grades than their less attractive peers (Stehr, 2004). Personalities and looks are irrelevant to how much learners know, so decisions based on them are invalid.

Essay and performance assessments can also be unreliable. We examine this issue in the next section.

Formative assessment The process of using both informal and formal assessments to provide students with feedback about learning progress.

Summative assessment The process of assessing after instruction and using the results for making grading decisions.

Validity The extent to which assessment results are interpreted and used appropriately.

Reliability The consistency of assessment results.

Figure 14.2 Sample Rubric for Paragraph Structure

	Levels of Achievement		
Criteria	1	2	3
Topic Sentence	Not present; reader cannot determine what the paragraph is about	Present but does not give the reader a clear idea of what the paragraph is about	Provides a clearly stated overview of the paragraph
Supporting Sentences	Rambling and unrelated to topic sentence	Provides additional information but not all focused on the topic sentence	Provides supporting detail related to the topic sentence
Summarizing Sentence	Nonexistent or unrelated to the preceding sentences	Relates to topic sentence but doesn't summarize the information in the paragraph	Accurately summarizes information in paragraph and is related to the topic sentence
Overall Score (9 Possible)			

INCREASING RELIABILITY WITH RUBRICS   A **rubric** is a scoring scale that describes criteria for grading; effective teachers use rubrics to help students understand the essential components of successful performance (Andrade, 2007/2008; Stiggins, 2005). Created to help teachers score essays, rubrics are also useful for assessing other performances, such as a student presentation, or products, such as a science lab report.

Figure 14.2 shows a rubric used to assess the quality of paragraphs. In it, you see that the teacher specifies a topic sentence, supporting sentences, and summarizing sentence as criteria for an effective paragraph; these elements appear in a column along the left side of the matrix. The rubric also describes levels of achievement for each criterion, which are then used to make decisions about grading. For example, you might decide that 9 points would be an A, 7–8 points a B, and 5–6 points a C. So to earn an A, a student would have to be at level 3 on all three criteria, and at level 2 on two of the elements and at level 3 on the third to earn a B.

Rubrics are essential for increasing the reliability of assessments that require teacher judgment, such as essays and performance assessments. As a teacher scores students' paragraphs, for example, the descriptions of the dimensions and levels of achievement in Figure 14.2 help maintain consistency in evaluating each student's work. Without the rubric as a guide, the likelihood of inconsistent scoring increases.

Misconceptions About Assessment

Parents, students, and even some teachers have major misconceptions about assessment and its role in the classroom. These misconceptions can have a negative impact on your teaching, so we want to examine them now. They include the following:

- Determining students' grades is the central role of assessment.
- Assessment occurs after a unit of study.
- The assessment process focuses exclusively on students' understanding and skills.
- Assessment exists in the form of paper-and-pencil tests.

Rubric A scoring scale that describes criteria for grading.

DETERMINING GRADES IS THE CENTRAL ROLE OF ASSESSMENT   Even though determining students' grades is an important part of assessment, it's a misconception to conclude that assigning grades is the major reason we assess; on the contrary, assessment is one of the most effective ways teachers have of increasing their students' learning. In fact, experts in the area of assessment created the term "assessment *for* learning" to emphasize the crucial link between assessment and learning (Stiggins, 2007, 2008a). **Assessment *for* learning** makes assessment an integral part of the teaching-learning process by supporting learning through frequent feedback to students about their learning progress. Jenny's assessment items in the chapter-opening case are examples. Responses to them suggested that her students didn't fully understand the principle for making beams balance, so she provided additional instruction, and their understanding was increased. Adapting instruction based on students' responses to assessment is the essence of assessment *for* learning.

This discussion also addresses the second and third items in our *This I Believe* feature, "The primary function of the assessment process is to help teachers determine how much students have learned," and "Time spent on assessment should be kept to a minimum because it uses time that is more effectively spent on instructional activities." Neither of these statements is true: Promoting learning, not giving grades, is the *primary function* of assessment, and time used in assessment is well spent (Stiggins, 2007).

This I BELIEVE

ASSESSMENT OCCURS AFTER A UNIT OF STUDY   The suggestion that assessment occurs *after* a unit of study is a second misconception. Some assessments, such as unit tests, are indeed used after units of study, but assessment is much more than a culminating unit test or chapter quiz. For example, as you saw earlier, informal assessment occurs continually, is an integral part of the teaching-learning process, and is essential for promoting student learning (McMillan, 2007b).

ASSESSMENT FOCUSES EXCLUSIVELY ON STUDENTS' UNDERSTANDING AND SKILLS   Assessing students' understanding and skills is important, but concluding that assessment focuses exclusively on these outcomes is a misconception. Assessment also provides essential information about students' personal and social development. For instance, students' motivation and their ability to pay attention in class, accept responsibility, and interact effectively with their peers strongly influence their learning and development. Students' effort on homework assignments, for example, tells us much more than whether they understand the content: Students who conscientiously do their homework and make an effort to understand it are developing habits that will serve them well throughout life (Anderman & Wolters, 2006). Assessing these different dimensions of development is an important teacher role. Similarly, if a first-grade teacher sees that a student consistently has difficulty maintaining attention, she might decide to initiate a referral that could lead to the student's getting special help. Getting this help early in the child's school experience is important and depends on effective teacher assessments. This is one more example of why assessment is so important to teachers.

ASSESSMENTS ARE PRIMARILY PAPER-AND-PENCIL TESTS   As with the other misconceptions, aspects of this statement are true. Using paper-and-pencil tests is indeed part of the assessment process; however, assessment is much more. It includes informal assessments, such as listening to a 1st grader during oral reading, watching 5th graders interact on the playground, observing junior high students' behavior in group work, and noticing signs that a 10th grader is being harassed by his peers. Each is part of the assessment process, and each provides teachers with valuable information for their decision making.

Assessment *for* learning The use of assessment to support and increase student learning.

How Do Teachers Assess?

The specific ways you assess will be influenced by the grade level at which you teach. Let's look at differences in how elementary teachers assess compared to middle and secondary ones.

ASSESSING LEARNING AND DEVELOPMENT IN ELEMENTARY CLASSROOMS

Elementary classrooms are heavily focused on learning basic skills in language arts and math that will serve as a foundation for students' learning throughout school. Accordingly, elementary teachers use frequent work samples as assessment information to guide their instructional decision making.

Jim Brinson's second graders are working on subtracting one-digit from two-digit numbers with regrouping. He places a series of problems on the chalkboard, and as his students solve them at their desks, Jim circulates around the room.
"Check this one again, Kelly," he says, seeing that Kelly has written

$$\begin{array}{r} 24 \\ -\ 9 \\ \hline 25 \end{array}$$

on her paper.
"I think I'll collect these and grade them," Jim says to himself. After collecting the papers, he scores them and makes notes to himself to do additional work on subtracting with borrowing.

Jim's on-the-spot decisions to formally assess student learning through an actual sample of student work and to provide additional work on subtracting with borrowing are characteristic of elementary teachers, particularly at the primary level. They rely more heavily on performance assessments than on formal tests and quizzes (Popham, 2005a). For example, observing whether a kindergartener can correctly form letters or write numerals is a type of performance assessment (Andrade, Du, & Wang, 2008).

When elementary teachers do give tests, they rarely construct their own items, instead relying on commercially prepared test items, such as those that come with a textbook series. Their assessments also focus on important dimensions of development, such as "works well with others," "accepts responsibility," and "effective communicator"; these characteristics are reflected in report cards at the elementary level, as you see later in the chapter.

ASSESSING LEARNING AND DEVELOPMENT IN MIDDLE-GRADE AND SECONDARY CLASSROOMS

Middle-grade and secondary teachers' assessment practices differ from those of elementary teachers in two ways. First, they depend more on traditional quizzes and tests than on performance measures, and second, they're more likely to prepare their own items instead of relying on published tests. Unfortunately, the items from commercial tests can be ineffective, for the following reasons (Nitko & Brookhart, 2007; Popham, 2007):

- More than three fourths of all items measure recall of factual information, and most of those that require application and analysis are in math and science. In other areas, more than 9 of 10 items are written at the knowledge level.

- Formats such as true-false, matching, and completion are popular because the items seem easy to construct, but they often measure facts. An example is "The two countries that border on Mexico are _____ and _____."

- Very few teacher-made tests use the essay format, though this figure is higher in English classes. This is significant because writing essays requires students to organize and present their thoughts in writing.

- Teachers commonly use test items containing many technical errors.
- Once teachers select items from test banks, they tend to reuse the items without revising them, even if they're ineffective.

Several factors help explain these patterns. First, teachers' jobs are complex and demanding, and secondary teachers respond by simplifying their work; reusing an item is simpler than revising it, for example. Essay items are easy to write but difficult and time-consuming to score; multiple-choice items are just the opposite. The simplest alternatives are the completion and matching formats, which are most popular with teachers, but these items typically measure only recall of information and not higher-level outcomes. Further, knowledge and recall items are easy to construct, score, and defend.

In addition, teachers lack confidence in their ability to write good test items that accurately assess learning (Stiggins, 2008a; Zientek, 2007). Because of inadequate training, teachers frequently have difficulty writing clear and precise test items at a level above knowledge and recall. These findings suggest a need for better quality assessments, particularly items that are unambiguous and that require more of students than the simple recall of factual information.

Having examined teachers' existing assessment patterns, we turn now to characteristics of effective assessments.

Using Assessment to Promote Learning

In less effective classrooms, assessments are given at the end of a unit or course of study to determine the amount that students learned, which is essentially assessment *of* learning. Gathering information for decisions about grading is their primary purpose, and students often don't receive feedback about their performance (Stiggins, 2007, 2008a). Although making decisions about grading is one purpose of assessment, it's only one, and isn't the most important. As you saw earlier, *the primary purpose of assessment is to promote learning and advance development.*

To promote learning and development, your assessments should

- be aligned with standards and your learning objectives;
- measure both students' knowledge and their thinking;
- include detailed feedback;
- avoid social comparisons.

Let's look at these guidelines.

ALIGNMENT WITH STANDARDS AND OBJECTIVES   Instructional alignment is essential for validity; it's impossible for assessments to be valid if they aren't aligned with objectives and learning activities (Miller et al., 2009). In addition, effective teachers align their assessments with standards, increasing the likelihood that their students will perform well on state and national tests.

Jenny's assessments, for example, were aligned. Her learning objective was for students to understand that a beam will balance if the number of tiles times the distance on one side of the fulcrum is equal to the number of tiles times the distance on the other side of the fulcrum. Her assessment measured the extent to which students understood this principle, so it was aligned.

Alignment isn't as easy to achieve as first appears. For example, if a teacher wants students to be able to use figurative language, such as similes and metaphors, in their writing but the assessment has them identify examples of similes and metaphors in sentences, the assessment isn't aligned with the objective; it doesn't measure whether students can actually use figurative language in their writing.

Effective teachers also align their instruction, including their assessments, with state standards. As you will see in the next section, standards play a powerful role in determining both instruction and assessment. Effective teachers realize that they're expected to help students reach these standards, and one way to do this is to align their classroom assessments with assessments students will encounter on state-mandated tests.

ASSESSING STUDENTS' THINKING   Effective assessments focus on both correct answers and students' thinking in arriving at those answers (Burns, 2005). Jenny's assessment measured both. In her first problem (in Figure 14.1), she asked students to determine whether the beam would balance and then asked them to explain why. Her second problem asked them to explain both where they would put tiles to make the beam balance and why they put the tiles where they did. In both cases, the students' explanations provided insights into their thinking.

A primary problem with many objective test formats, such as multiple choice, true-false, and matching, is that they fail to assess students' thinking; a student's answer on a test item often doesn't reflect the thinking that went into the right (or wrong) answer. Effective teachers realize this and thoroughly discuss items that gave students problems. This discussion provides insights into students' thinking, which the teacher can use to clear up problems and misconceptions. It also helps students understand where their thinking went astray and what they need to do to fix the problem.

DETAILED FEEDBACK TO STUDENTS   Of all the factors involved when using assessment to promote learning, providing detailed feedback is arguably the most important (Brookhart, 2008). Some experts suggest that more learning occurs in our discussions of students' responses to assessment items than in the original learning activities themselves, because student interest and motivation are high (Stiggins, 2007, 2008a). For example, after seeing her students' responses to the assessment item in Figure 14.1, Jenny discussed several responses and had students explain their thinking. This process contributed significantly to their understanding.

Detailed feedback to students increases both learning and motivation, and creates a communication link between teachers and students.

AVOIDING SOCIAL COMPARISONS   Finally, effective teachers avoid social comparisons between students, such as listing distributions of scores on the board, making comments about how many students got A's and B's, or any other reference that compares students' performance. Student comparisons on grades and other aspects of assessment can damage motivation for learning, especially with lower ability students (Schunk, Pintrich, & Meese, 2008). Effective teachers encourage students to keep their scores to themselves and emphasize that the purpose of assessment is to promote learning, not see how students perform compared to each other.

Students who consistently score at the top of the class often enjoy social comparisons, of course, but teachers can praise them in private for their good work—which is often even more effective, because it can be personalized and delivered one-on-one.

In summary, when you begin teaching, you should 1) ensure that your assessments are aligned with standards and objectives; 2) assess more than mere recall of factual information and require that students explain their thinking; 3) provide students with detailed feedback on all assessments; and 4) avoid comparisons between students.

To be sure you understand what you've just read, look at the *Check Your Understanding* section that follows. Then, in the *Exploring Diversity* feature box on pages 424–425, we discuss how to adapt these general assessment principles to urban classrooms.

PEARSON
myeducationlab

To view a lesson in which the teacher uses assessment to guide her decision making to increase her students' learning, go to the *Assignments and Activities* section of Topic 9: *Assessment, Standards, and Accountability* in the MyEducationLab for your course and complete the activity titled *Using Assessment in Decision Making.*

CHECK YOUR UNDERSTANDING

1.1 Describe the process of assessment.

1.2 Why is assessment important for promoting student learning?

1.3 What is the difference between informal and formal assessment, and how are validity and reliability related to them?

1.4 What are some common misconceptions about assessment?

For feedback, go to the appendix, *Check Your Understanding*, located in the back of this text.

GRADING AND REPORTING

Have you ever gotten a grade in a course that was lower than you expected? How did you feel? What grade are you getting in this course? Do you feel good about that grade? What is your current GPA? How will it influence job prospects or going on to graduate school?

Grades are important to all students, especially the successful ones. Even students who get low grades are influenced by them. Grades are also important to parents; for

Exploring Diversity

Effective Assessment Practices With Students From Diverse Backgrounds

As you saw in Chapters 3, 4, and 5, learner diversity influences teaching and learning in a number of ways. The process of assessment is one of the most important.

The current reform movement, with its emphasis on standards, has heightened awareness of the pervasive challenges involved in assessing students from diverse backgrounds. The problem is particularly important in urban settings, where diversity is most prevalent (Armour-Thomas, 2004).

Student diversity influences classroom assessment in three ways. First, learners from diverse backgrounds often lack experience with general testing procedures, different test formats, and test-taking strategies. Second, they may not fully un-

URBAN EDUCATION

derstand that assessments promote learning and instead view them as punitive. Third, because most assessments are strongly language based, language may be an obstacle (E. Garcia, 2005).

The following recommendations respond to these issues (Popham, 2005a):

- Create a classroom environment that focuses on learning and reduces the emphasis on grades and grading. Emphasize that assessments promote learning, and thoroughly discuss all assessments after they're given and returned to students.
- Increase the number of assessments, and provide detailed and corrective feedback for all items. Encourage students to ask questions about test items, and when they answer incorrectly, ask them to explain their answers. Emphasize that mistakes are part of learning, and frequently present students with evidence of their learning progress.

- Allow students to drop one or two quizzes per marking period for purposes of grading. This practice reduces test anxiety and communicates to students that you want them to succeed. It also contributes to a positive classroom climate.
- Make provisions for nonnative English speakers by allowing extra time and providing extra help with language aspects of your assessments; such as making translation dictionaries available.
- Ask students to keep all assessment results private, and establish a rule that students may not share their scores and grades with each other. (This is impossible to enforce, but is a symbolic gesture and an attempt to protect students who want to succeed but face peer pressure not to.)

Of these suggestions, feedback and discussion are the most important. Almany, it is the primary way they gauge whether their child is progressing satisfactorily in school (Stiggins, 2008a).

Grades are also important to teachers. Assigning grades can be an especially anxiety-provoking process for beginning teachers, who are used to receiving but not giving grades. For example, we met a first-year teacher who was 6 weeks into his first term before he realized that report card grades were due in 3 weeks. What made the whole situation even more problematic for the teacher was that these grades would be the focal point for his first encounters with parents during parent–teacher conferences.

Giving grades is an important part of your job; when well done, grades provide valuable information about learning progress for both students and their parents. To the extent possible, grades should be an accurate reflection of how much your students have learned; in other words, grades must be valid. An important question all teachers, including those just beginning their careers, should ask themselves is this: "If the grades I've given are ever questioned, can I defend them to students, parents, or administrators?" This suggests that you should have extensive valid and reliable information on which to base your decisions about students' grades. Frequent and thorough assessment is important, and this can take the form of weekly quizzes, systematic recorded observations of students' work using checklists or written notes, and any other reliable data that are used in making grading decisions. Whatever the form, your assessments need to be organized into a comprehensive and understandable grading system; being able to confidently explain and defend your grading system will put your

though important in all environments, they're essential for effective assessment with learners from diverse backgrounds. Students' explanations for their answers often reveal misconceptions, which you can then address. Student feedback can also help identify information in your questions that might be misleading for members of cultural minorities (Popham, 2005a).

Content bias occurs when test items measure content knowledge not specifically targeted by the item. For example, some students may have limited experiences with electric appliances such as an iron or vacuum cleaner, summertime activities such as camping and hiking, musical instruments such as a banjo, or transportation such as cable cars (Cheng, 1987). Assessment items requiring knowledge or experience with these ideas measure both the intended topic and students' general knowledge, which detracts from validity. The only way you can identify potential problems with specific items is to discuss them afterward. Then, you can revise and more

carefully word your assessments to help eliminate bias.

The possibility of assessment bias is even more likely with nonnative English speakers in your classes. Suggestions for supporting these students include the following (Abedi, Hofstetter & Lord, 2004):

- Provide extra time to take tests.
- Allow students to use a translation glossary or dictionary during the test.
- Read directions aloud and allow students to ask questions about any areas of uncertainty.

These adaptations increase validity and also communicate that you want all students to succeed.

Diversity in Your Classroom

Assessment bias is pernicious in two ways: It robs the teacher of valuable information about student learning progress, and it gives students inaccurate information about how they're doing in a class. A first step in reducing assessment bias is to ask ourselves continually whether our assessments are do-

ing what we intended them to do. Low scores on tests and quizzes could mean that students haven't mastered the material, or they could mean that we didn't assess effectively. A second way to reduce assessment bias is to create communication channels that allow teachers to uncover students' thinking as they respond to assessments. A single letter or number on a test item can mean many things; only by talking with students can we understand the thinking that went into a student's response.

QUESTIONS TO CONSIDER

1. How does the problem of assessment bias differ in teacher-made and standardized assessments?
2. How does the problem of assessment bias differ with grade level? with subject area?

myeducationlab) To respond to these questions online, explore this topic further, and receive feedback, go to the *Book Specific Resources* section in the MyEducationLab for your course, select your text, and then select *Exploring Diversity* for Chapter 14.

mind at ease when you complete report cards or anticipate your first parent–teacher conference.

The Teacher's Role in Grading

Grading is the process of condensing large amounts of information into a simple form, usually a letter or number, for ease of communication (Stiggins, 2008a). Teachers have two goals with respect to grading: 1) to create an assessment system that is understandable to students and parents, and 2) to create a system that accurately measures student learning (Brookhart, 2009; Stiggins, 2008a). In doing so, you will need to answer three questions, each designed to ensure that grades accurately reflect how much students have learned:

- How will I balance tests and quizzes with performance assessments?
- How will I count homework?
- How will I report affective dimensions, such as cooperation and effort?

These decisions might seem daunting to a first-year teacher, because you have little experience to fall back on. Knowing that the decisions are yours, however, removes some of the uncertainty. We examine these decisions in the sections that follow as we consider different assessment sources.

PAPER-AND-PENCIL AND PERFORMANCE ASSESSMENTS   For teachers in upper elementary, middle, and high schools, the cornerstones of most grading systems are paper-and-pencil assessments, such as the multiple-choice, true-false, completion, and essay items that you have taken throughout your school careers. Some add tests and quizzes together and count them as a certain percentage of the overall grade; others weigh them differently in assigning grades.

If you're using performance assessments or portfolios as part of your assessment system, you should include them in determining grades; to do otherwise communicates that they are less important than the paper-and-pencil measures you're using. If you rate student performance on the basis of well-defined criteria, scoring will have acceptable reliability, and performance assessments and/or portfolios can then be an integral part of your total assessment system.

HOMEWORK   As you saw in Chapter 13, properly designed homework contributes to learning. For it to be effective, you should collect homework and include it in your grading system (H. Cooper, Robinson, & Patall, 2006; Marzano, 2007). If homework is assigned but you don't collect it and instead have some mechanism for giving students credit for doing it, they won't take it seriously, and it won't be effective for promoting learning.

REPORTING AFFECTIVE DIMENSIONS   In addition to paper-and-pencil assessments, performance measures, and homework, some teachers factor in effort, class participation, and attitude as part of their grading. Assessment experts discourage this practice (Miller et al., 2009): Gathering accurate information about affective variables is difficult, and assessing them is highly subjective. In addition, a high grade based on effort suggests that important content was learned when it may not have been. Factors such as effort and cooperation should be—and usually are—reflected in separate sections of report cards, as you will see in Figures 14.3 and 14.4 in the following sections.

If you teach in an elementary school, your decisions related to paper-and-pencil measures, performance assessments, and affective dimensions will be somewhat different from those in middle or high school. For example, as an elementary teacher, you will likely emphasize performance dimensions, such as "recognizes shapes" and "counts objects" in your assessment system, whereas you will likely place more emphasis on tests and quizzes if you teach in a middle or high school. Let's examine these differences in more detail in terms of the report cards you'll be expected to complete.

Grading and Reporting in Elementary Schools

Earlier you saw that elementary teachers tend to emphasize affective goals, such as "works well with others," "self directed," and "effective communicator," in addition to academic goals, such as students' performance in reading and math. This emphasis is reflected in the report cards students receive and the kinds of assessments elementary teachers make. Figure 14.3 is an example; remember that this is only an example, and report cards will vary from one school district to another. In addition, some districts use the traditional A, B, C, D, F designation for grades, whereas others use a different

Figure 14.3 Elementary School Report Card

Elementary Report Card

Student

Teacher

	Q1	Q2	Q3	Q4
Math				
Number Sense				
Computation				
Data				
Geometry				
Measurement				
Algebra				

	Q1	Q2	Q3	Q4
Reading				
Reading Level				
Reading Strategies				
Fluency				
Comprehension				

	Q1	Q2	Q3	Q4
Writing				
Word Choice & Voice				
Sentence Fluency				
Conventions				
Ideas & Organization				

	Q1	Q2	Q3	Q4
Social Studies				
Applications				
Content				

	Q1	Q2	Q3	Q4
Science				
Life Science				
Physical Science				
Earth Science				
Connections				

	Q1	Q2	Q3	Q4
Health				
Healthy Behavior				
Healthy Influence				

	Q1	Q2	Q3	Q4
Physical Education				
Motor Skills/Knowledge				
Fitness Activity/Knowledge				
Personal & Social Skills				
Music				
Art				

Work Habits	Q1	Q2	Q3	Q4
Quality Worker				
Critical Thinker				
Self Directed				
Effective Communicator				
Responsible				
Collaborative				

Attendance	Q1	Q2	Q3	Q4	YR
Absent	0	0	0	0	0
Dismissed	0	0	0	0	0
Tardy	0	0	0	0	0

Teacher Comments:

has had a good start in first grade. I look forward to meeting with you at conferences.

system, such as E for "exceeds expectations," M for "meets expectations," and PM for "partially meets expectations."

Two aspects of this report care are noteworthy. First, academic areas, such as reading, writing, math, and science, are emphasized: Teachers are asked to evaluate 20 dimensions of academic growth–6 in math, 4 each in reading and writing, 2 in social studies, and 4 in science. Second, teachers are asked to evaluate students' health habits, motor and social skills, and work habits such as "quality worker," "self directed," and "collaborative." This emphasis on specific dimensions of academics as well as affective and developmental areas is typical of elementary school report cards.

For clarity, definitions for different affective dimensions such as work habits are usually printed on the backs of report cards to help parents and caregivers understand what they mean. For example:

- *Quality worker:* Follows directions; completes work and/or homework in a timely manner; meets grade-level expectations for neatness and organization; sets realistic goals to improve work
- *Critical thinker:* Recognizes and is able to ask for help; uses a variety of strategies to solve problems
- *Self directed:* Demonstrates curiosity for learning; takes risks and accepts challenges in learning; completes tasks independently

Assessing the extent to which students meet the criteria for "self directed," for example, can be highly subjective, so, you'll need to carefully document students' performance in these areas. Written notes describing a student's behavior and the context in which the behavior exists, such as independent reading, is one effective form of documentation.

Virtually all of these affective aspects are assessed informally, such as observing students working together in groups. Remembering that you're using informal assessments is important, because—as you saw earlier in the chapter—informal assessments can be unreliable. This suggests that you should make as many observations of individual students as possible before drawing conclusions about social skills, self-regulation, and other nonacademic aspects of students' learning and development.

Grading and Reporting in Middle and High Schools

Teachers in middle and high schools place more emphasis on traditional academic topics, and this emphasis is reflected in their report cards. Figure 14.4 contains an example.

This sample report card reflects emphases typical in high schools. For instance, it includes courses in core subjects such as math, science, English and social studies, which are commonly required in high schools, together with electives. Many electives exist in middle and high schools, such as computer science and band, as you see here, as well as a variety of foreign languages, and these are graded in the same way as required courses.

As is typical for middle and high school report cards, the report card provides columns for grades for each marking period (typically 9 weeks) as well as columns for a final exam grade and a final grade for the course. Affective areas, such as "works well with others," aren't given a grade as they commonly are in elementary schools. However, middle and high school report cards usually have a place for brief comments, such as "Pleasure to have in class," "Puts forth effort," and "Does commendable work," or they have a column where letters designating these comments can be placed, such as you see in the report card in Figure 14.4. These comments are usually independent of students' grades (Miller et al., 2009). The definitions for different grades then typically appear on the back of the report card together with criteria for A, B, C, D, and F, such as A = 94–100, B = 85–93, and so on.

Figure 14.4 High School Report Card

STUDENT NAME		STUDENT NUMBER	QUARTER	GRADE LEVEL	HOMEROOM	REPORT DATE	PROMOTED _____ RETAINED _____	
		O3923448	2	10	204	12/14/10	SSN: 590646060	

PARENT NAME/ADDRESS	SCHOOL/ADDRESS	PRINCIPAL	SCHOOL TELEPHONE
		DR DALTON EPTING	260-3911
	260-MANDARIN HIGH SCHOOL	HOMEROOM TEACHER	GUIDANCE TELEPHONE
	4831 GREENLAND RD	A CANIPE	

COURSE		DISTRICT SCHOOL	PER	GRADES					FINAL		MLST	PERIOD ABSENCES										COMMENTS					EARN CRED	GPA	TEACHER
												1		2		3		4		SUM									
TITLE	NUMBER-SECT			1	2	3	4	SUM	EXAM	AVG		EX	UN	EX	UN	EX	UN	EX	UN	EX	UN	1	2	3	4	SUM			
ALGEBRA II	0108310-002	16-2801	03	A	A				A	A		1	0	2	0												.50	2	G MODRE
COMPU SCI I	0200320-001	16-2801	04	B	B							0	0	2	0													3	M ENG
ENGLISH 10	1001420-002	16-2801	06	B	B							1	0	1	0													3	L FRANZBLAU
AMERICAN HISTORY	1202300-001	16-2801	02	A	A							0	0	0	0													2	J COOKSEY
BAND IV	1302350-003	16-2801	05	A	A							0	0	1	0													2	L PONDER
CHEMISTRY I	2003360-001	16-2801	07	B	B							0	0	3	0													2	E WEISS

Please see reverse side for explanation of grades, attendance, comments and codes

_____
(Parents Signature)
Return to Homeroom Teacher within 3 days.

	1st Quarter				2nd Quarter				3rd Quarter				4th Quarter				Summer				Total			
	Days				Days				Days				Days				Days				Days			
	Enr	Exc	Unx	Tdy	Enr	Exc	Unx	Tdy	Enr	Exc	Unx	Tdy	Enr	Exc	Unr.	Tdy	Enr	Exc	Unr.	Tdy	Enroll	Excuse	Unexcuse	Tardy
	44	0	0	0	45	0	0	1													89	0	0	1

Some of you were on the receiving end of report cards such as this one only a few short years ago, whereas it might have been longer for others. All of you will be on the giving end of this process when you begin your first teaching job, however, and you'll be required to assess your students' academic progress and make decisions about the grades they receive. You will largely be alone in this process, so you should begin thinking about both grading and the entire assessment process now (Reeves, 2008).

One way to begin is to talk to teachers and ask them about their assessment practices when you're out in schools. Questions such as the following can be helpful.

- Does your school use traditional grades, such as A, B, and C? If not, what does it use?
- What do you include in your grading system? Quizzes and tests? Homework? Performance measures? Anything else?
- How often do you give quizzes and tests?
- What, besides grades, do you use to communicate learning progress to parents?
- Does high-stakes testing affect your assessment and grading practices? If so, how?

As you gather information from teachers, you can combine it with what you've studied in this chapter and gradually form your own ideas about assessment in general, and grading in particular. This will help you hit the ground running when you begin your first job.

This section addresses the fourth item in our *This I Believe* feature, "Determining students' grades is an important part of the assessment process, and you will be largely on your own in making decisions about students' grades." This statement is true.

■ ■ TECHNOLOGY AND TEACHING Using Technology in Assessment

Assessing student learning is one of the most important and demanding tasks teachers face, and research confirms that frequent and thorough assessments increase learning (Stiggins, 2007, 2008a). Technology can support this process, serving four important functions, summarized in Table 14.1 and discussed in the sections that follow.

Technology provides teachers with effective tools for assessing student learning.

PLANNING AND CONSTRUCTING TESTS The word processing capabilities of computers provide teachers with effective tools for writing, storing, and revising individual test items, and a number of commercially prepared software programs can assist in this process. These programs can perform the following tasks:

- Develop a test file of multiple-choice, true-false, matching, and short-answer items that can be stored in the system. Within a file, items can be organized by topic, chapter, objective, or difficulty.
- Choose items from the file randomly, selectively, or by categories to generate multiple versions of a test.
- Modify items and integrate them into the test.
- Produce student-ready copies and an answer key.

These software test generators produce a standard layout; they automatically produce alternate forms, which can be helpful for creating makeup tests and preventing cheating; and they can be used to customize commercially prepared test banks that come with textbooks.

Table 14.1	Assessment Functions Supported by Computers
Function	**Examples**
Planning and constructing tests	Preparing objectives
	Writing, editing, and storing items
	Compiling items into tests
	Printing tests
Administering tests	Administering tests online
	Providing feedback
	Analyzing results
Scoring and interpreting tests	Scoring tests
	Summarizing results
	Analyzing items
Maintaining student records	Recording results
	Developing class summaries
	Reporting results to students
	Preparing grade reports

ADMINISTERING TESTS   Computer software now exists that allows teachers to administer tests online (Roblyer & Doering, 2010). This is useful in dealing with students who are absent on the day of the test or in individualized classes where students progress at different rates. These programs can also give students immediate feedback about right and wrong answers and can provide you with specific and updated information about student performance.

Experts believe that online testing will play an increasing role in states' accountability programs in the future (Trotter, 2007). Currently 23 states have either a computerized exam or a pilot project under way to evaluate the effectiveness of computer-based testing. The almost immediate feedback provided to both teachers and students is a strength of these systems. Experts also predict that online technologies will become increasingly important in preparing students for high-stakes tests (Borja, 2003).

Personal response systems, a variation of online testing, allow teachers to gather assessment information during a presentation (Zuger, 2008b). Each student is provided with a handheld infrared transmitter that resembles a TV remote. The teacher asks a question in either multiple-choice or true-false format and asks students to respond. Answers are recorded and analyzed, and the teacher receives immediate feedback in a histogram that shows the number of students who chose each alternative; this allows teachers to address misconceptions immediately. Although most popular at the college level with large lecture classes, this innovation is also finding its way into K–12 classrooms.

SCORING AND INTERPRETING TESTS   Technology can also assist in scoring tests and reporting results, saving time for the teacher and providing students with immediate feedback. For example, a high school teacher with five sections of 30 students taking a 40-item exam faces the daunting task of grading 6,000 individual items! Scoring and analyzing test data, converting scores to grades, and recording the grades can be enormously time-consuming without the help of technology.

A number of software programs are available to machine-score tests. They can do the following:

- Score objective tests and provide descriptive statistics such as mean, median, mode, and range
- Generate a list of items showing difficulty level, the percent of students who selected each response, and the percent of students who didn't respond to an item.
- Sort student responses by score, grade/age, or sex

MAINTAINING STUDENT RECORDS   Technology can also assist with record keeping, and many—if not most—teachers now have access to electronic grading programs and keep their grades in electronic grade books. In addition to saving time and energy, these programs are accurate (assuming the original data are entered accurately) and immediate, which allows teachers to generate grades at the end of a marking period with a few keystrokes. Also, records are available at any time, providing students and their parents with ongoing feedback. Some programs can even print student reports in other languages, such as Spanish (Forcier & Descy, 2005).

■ ■ ■ ■ ■ CHECK YOUR UNDERSTANDING

2.1 How do grading and reporting relate to the total assessment process?

2.2 How do grading and reporting practices in elementary compare to those in middle and secondary schools?

2.3 Explain how grading and reporting practices in elementary, compared to middle and secondary, schools relate to informal and formal assessment.

For feedback, go to the appendix, *Check Your Understanding*, located in the back of this text.

Personal response system A classroom technology that allows teachers to assess students' understanding of content during lessons.

STANDARDS, ACCOUNTABILITY, AND ASSESSMENT

Since the early 1980s, assessment has taken on a broader and more significant role in teaching and learning in our country. This role evolved from concerns about U.S. students' lack of knowledge and skills. For instance, one survey found that more than half of high school students identified Germany, Japan, or Italy, instead of the Soviet Union, as the United States' World War II ally; another indicated that two thirds of high school seniors couldn't explain an old photo of a sign over a theater door reading COLORED ENTRANCE (Bauerlein, 2008). In addition, a survey of 18- to 24-year-olds revealed that 6 of 10 respondents couldn't find Iraq on a map of the Middle East (Manzo, 2006b). Similar concerns have been raised in math and science, where international comparisons indicate that U.S. students lag behind their counterparts in other countries (Gonzales et al., 2004; Lemke et al., 2004). All of this led to the standards movement in education.

The Standards Movement in Education

Standards have been influencing teaching in the United States for a number of years, and their history provides us with insights into their strengths and weaknesses.

A BRIEF HISTORY OF THE STANDARDS MOVEMENT   In response to concerns about students' lack of knowledge and skills, educators established academic **standards**, statements that describe what students should know or be able to do at the end of a period of study (McCombs, 2005). The "standards movement" is commonly traced to the publication of *A Nation at Risk: The Imperative for Educational Reform*, published by the National Commission on Excellence in Education (1983). This document famously stated:

> If an unfriendly foreign power had attempted to impose on America the mediocre educational performance that exists today, we might well have viewed it as an act of war. As it stands, we have allowed this to happen to ourselves. We have even squandered the gains in student achievement made in the wake of the Sputnik challenge. Moreover, we have dismantled essential support systems which helped make those gains possible. We have, in effect, been committing an act of unthinking, unilateral educational disarmament. (National Commission on Excellence in Education, 1983, p. 9)

This report came at a time when other countries, such as Japan, were outcompeting us both industrially and educationally, and it struck a chord with leaders in this country: If we were to compete internationally, we had to have better schools.

Since 1983, public education has been immersed in a wave of efforts to address the concerns raised in *A Nation at Risk*. For example:

- 1989: President George H. W. Bush and the nation's governors held a national education conference to establish six broad goals to address the issues raised in *A Nation at Risk*. Their report emphasized the need to develop student performance standards.

- 1993: The National Council on Education Standards and Testing (NCEST) was established to begin developing bipartisan national standards and testing for K–12 education. This effort to develop standards at the national level was ultimately unsuccessful.

- 1994: President Clinton signed the Goals 2000: Educate America Act, which created a special council to certify national and state content and performance standards as well as state assessments.

Standards Statements that describe what students should know or be able to do at the end of a period of study.

- 1996: A National Education Summit, composed of the governors of more than 40 states and national business leaders, aimed to establish clear standards and subject matter content at the state and local levels.

- 1999: A second summit identified challenges facing U.S. schools in three areas—improving teacher quality, helping all students reach high standards, and strengthening accountability.

- 2000: The federal Elementary and Secondary Education Act (ESEA) was revised and signed into law by President George W. Bush in 2001. Renamed the No Child Left Behind (NCLB) Act, the law asked U.S. schools to describe their success in terms of the extent to which students could meet specified standards.

A desire to improve student learning through standards is the thread that runs through each of these efforts, and since 2000–2001, every state in the nation has developed both standards in different content areas and tests to measure students' attainment of those standards.

STANDARDS IN TODAY'S SCHOOLS   In today's schools, standards have been written for content areas ranging from traditional topics, such as reading, writing, math, and science, to others less prominent, such as the following:

- Physical education
- Fine arts
- Economics
- Agricultural science
- Business education
- Technology applications
- Trade and industrial education
- Spanish language arts and English as a second language

And even this list isn't exhaustive.

Standards are labeled in different ways, such as "Essential Knowledge and Skills" (Texas Education Agency, 2008a), "Learning Standards" (Illinois State Board of Education, 2008a), "Content Standards" (California State Board of Education, 2008a), or "Sunshine State Standards" (Florida Department of Education, 2007). Regardless of the labels, each state's standards describe what students should know or be able to do.

Because space doesn't allow us to list examples from every state, we give representative samples for the sake of illustration. You can easily access every state's standards by going to the following website: http://www.education-world.com/standards/state/index.shtml. Then click on the pull-down menu and select your state.

What do standards from different states look like? The following is an example in fourth-grade math from the state of Texas (Texas Education Agency, 2008b).

(4.2) Number, operation, and quantitative reasoning. The student describes and compares fractional parts of whole objects or sets of objects. The student is expected to:
(A) generate equivalent fractions using concrete objects and pictorial models.

The number (4.2) identifies this as the second standard in the list of fourth-grade standards in math, and the letter (A) represents the first in a list of student expectations. Different states code their standards differently, but all are designed to describe learning and assessment targets for teachers and students.

As another example, the following standard is from the state of Illinois in middle school science (Illinois State Board of Education, 2008a).

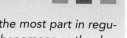

Illinois Science Assessment Framework
Standard 12F—Astronomy (Grade 7)
   12.7.91 Understanding that objects in the solar system are for the most part in regular and predictable motion. Know that those motions explain such phenomena as the day, the year, the phases of the moon, and eclipses.

Although the way the standard is coded is different from what's done in Texas, both describe essential knowledge to be learned and assessed on tests.

As you see from these two examples, standards are stated in different ways and with varying degrees of specificity. Many states' systems of describing standards are quite complex, and understanding and interpreting them can be challenging. For instance, what exactly does "using concrete objects and pictorial models" to generate equivalent fractions mean? And, this is one of the more succinctly written standards. We address this issue in the next section.

Many professional organizations, such as the National Council of Teachers of Mathematics (National Council of Teachers of Mathematics, 2008), the National Council of Teachers of English (International Reading Association & National Council of Teachers of English, 2008), and others that focus on science, social studies, early childhood education, special education, the arts, health education, and bilingual education, also have produced standards. Most of the state standards are grounded in the standards prepared by these organizations.

Next, we discuss ways to help you make standards a meaningful guide in your teaching.

Accountability, Standards, and Assessment

The primary way standards will affect your teaching is through the process of accountability. **Accountability** means that your students will be required to demonstrate that they understand the topics they study, and you will be held responsible for ensuring that your students meet certain standards.

This is where assessment enters the picture. States use assessment to hold students (and their teachers) accountable for meeting prescribed learning standards. In some cases, the assessments are **high-stakes tests**, standardized assessments that states and districts use to determine whether students will advance from one grade to another, graduate from high school, or have access to specific fields of study. For example, if graduating from high school depends on students' performance on the test, the stakes are "high," which is why the tests are described this way. If you recently graduated from high school, you probably took one of these tests yourself. When you teach, you will be on the other side of the fence; you will then be responsible for preparing your students to pass these assessments.

This discussion addresses the fifth item in the *This I Believe* feature, "Because student learning standards are constructed at the state level, they won't have a major impact on your teaching." This statement isn't true: Standards will be an important part of your teaching life throughout your career.

As with standards, state tests have different labels. For example:

Texas Assessment of Knowledge and Skills (TAKS) (Texas Education Agency, 2008c)

Florida Comprehensive Assessment Test (Florida Department of Education, 2008)

California Standards Test (California State Board of Education, 2008b)

Illinois Standards Achievement Test (Illinois State Board of Education, 2008b)

To examine how one school communicates standards to partents, go to the *Assignments and Acitivities* section of Topic 9: *Assessment, Standards, and Accountability* in the MyEducationLab for your course and complete the activity titled *Communicating Standards to Parents.*

This I BELIEVE

Accountability The process of requiring students to demonstrate understanding of the topics they study as measured by standardized tests, as well as holding educators at all levels responsible for students' performance.

High-stakes tests Standardized assessments that states and districts use to determine whether students will advance from one grade to another, graduate from high school, or have access to specific fields of study.

States also vary in the way they administer the tests. For example, the *Texas Assessment of Knowledge and Skills* is given in reading and math at every grade level 3 through 10; science is given in grades 5, 8, and 10; and social studies is given in grades 8 and 10. On the other hand, the *Florida Comprehensive Assessment Test*, which also requires all students in grades 3 through 10 to take the reading and math portions, administers the science portion to students in grades 5, 8, and 11, and social studies is not measured on the exam. When you begin teaching, you need to become fully aware of the testing schedule for your state, because you and your students will be held accountable for their performance on the tests.

To help teachers align their instruction with state standards, sample test items that parallel the items on the standardized assessments, or older versions of the tests themselves, are usually available. Both are linked to specific standards. These sample items and older versions of the tests are useful in two ways. First, as you saw in the preceding section, you must interpret the meaning of the standard, and sample items help you with this process. Second, the sample items guide you as you prepare your students for the tests. The following are sample items that measure the extent to which students have reached standards presented earlier.

For example, a sample test item from the Texas Assessment of Knowledge and Skills designed to measure the extent to which students have reached the fourth-grade math standard shown on page 433 looks like this (Texas Education Agency, 2008c):

23 The model is shaded to represent a fraction.

Which model below shows an equivalent fraction?

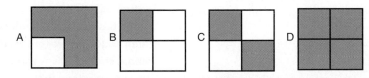

Now look again at the Illinois middle school science standard on page 434 and compare it with a corresponding assessment item from the Illinois Standards Achievement Test linked to that standard (Illinois State Board of Education, 2008c):

12.7.91

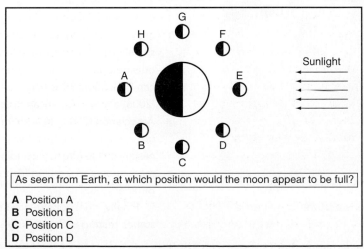

As seen from Earth, at which position would the moon appear to be full?

A Position A
B Position B
C Position C
D Position D

Does Accountability Through High-Stakes Tests Harm Students?

As we've seen, standards, accountability, and high-stakes testing are facts of teaching life. They influence teacher planning, what is taught, how learning is assessed, and consequences for poor performance (Debray, McDermott, & Wohlstetter, 2005). Every state in the nation has created standards in a variety of content areas, and, because of NCLB, schools, districts, and states must report the achievement of different groups of students classified by race, ethnicity, sex, and English proficiency. This requirement has focused attention on the considerable achievement disparities between different groups of students, particularly those who live in poverty and cultural minorities.

Schools are graded—A, B, C, D, and F—depending on how their students perform, and in addition to the stigma that exists for being in a D or F school, sanctions, such as school closings, threaten schools that fail to make adequate yearly progress with any of these student subgroups. The pressure on states, school districts, and particularly on schools and teachers within specific schools is enormous (Christie, 2005).

THE ISSUE

As you might expect, accountability and high-stakes testing are very controversial. Critics argue that they damage both schools and students in several ways (Heilig & Darling-Hammond, 2008; Nichols & Berliner, 2008; Solley, 2007). First, critics assert, faced with pressures to help students achieve in math, reading, and science, teachers de-emphasize other subjects such as social studies, art, music, health, and physical education. This narrowing of the curriculum deprives students of a well-rounded education and also stifles teacher professionalism and creativity because teachers are forced to spend too much time teaching only test content and helping students practice for the tests.

Teachers also report that testing programs have forced them to teach in ways that contradict sound instructional practices. For example, despite knowing that computers can be an effective tool for teaching writing, teachers have abandoned technology because a state writing test is handwritten (Pedulla et al., 2003).

The pressure for students to perform well on the tests can also produce unintended consequences. To avoid test-related sanctions, teachers in states with high-stakes tests frequently request transfers out of grades that are tested. Experts fear that veteran teachers will also transfer out of urban schools where students often underachieve, depriving students of the expert teachers they need (Guarino, Santibañez, & Daley, 2006). In addition, research suggests that high school exit examinations have contributed to the dropout problem, and the adverse effects are greater for low socioeconomic status and cultural minority students (Warren, Jenkins, & Kulick, 2006). In Texas, for example, nearly 1 of every 6 high school seniors in 2007 didn't graduate because of low scores on these tests, including 1 in 4 African American and Hispanic students (Stutz, 2007).

Critics also contend that current tests aren't adequate for crucial decisions about students' lives and that cutoff scores are often arbitrary (Popham, 2004). For example, when the state of Virginia lowered the cutoff score for its test by 1 point, 5,625 failing scores turned into passing scores (Bracey, 2003b). Deciding student grade promotion or graduation on the basis of one score is being increasingly criticized by a number of professional organizations both within and outside education, including the American Educational Research Association (2006) and the American Psychological Association (2006). In addition, other experts warn that high-stakes tests can have negative side effects, including decreased motivation and learning (Amrein & Berliner, 2003).

Finally, questions related to high-stakes testing with minority students

Accountability through high-stakes testing exerts a powerful influence on teachers as well as students.

remain unanswered. One involves test bias and whether existing tests provide an accurate picture of minority achievement and particularly the achievement of students who aren't native English speakers (Abedi, Hofstetter, & Lord, 2004; Popham, 2004).

In summary, critics argue, "The pressure to score well on a single test is so intense that it leads to nefarious practices (cheating on the test, data manipulation), distorts education (narrowing the curriculum, teaching to the test) and demoralizes our educators" (Nichols & Berliner, 2008, p. 672).

But advocates of testing, although conceding that teacher preparation, instructional resources, and the tests themselves need to be improved, argue that these tests are the fairest and most effective means of promoting success for all students (Steches, Hamilton, & Scott-Naflet, 2005). Further, they assert, evidence indicates that educational systems requiring content standards and using tests that thoroughly measure the extent to which the standards are met greatly improve the achievement for all students, including those from disadvantaged backgrounds.

For too long, the poor achievement of our most vulnerable students has been lost in unrepresentative averages. African American, Hispanic, special education, limited English proficient, and many other students were left behind because schools were not held accountable for their individual progress. Now all students count. (U.S. Department of Education, 2004b, p. 18)

Some advocates are even promoting national standards and tests, claiming that those from different states vary too much and result in inequalities between states (Olson, 2005). Hirsch (2000) summarized the testing advocates' position: "They [standards and tests that measure achievement of the standards] are the most promising educational development in half a century" (p. 64).

Public opinion polls don't directly address whether parents believe accountability and high-stakes testing harm students, and poll results present an unclear picture of parents' attitudes toward achievement testing in general. For instance, more than 4 of 10 public school parents believe there is too much emphasis on achievement testing, and only about 1 of 10 say there isn't enough. Another 4 of 10 parents, however, believe that the emphasis on achievement testing is about right (Bushaw & Gallup, 2008). With respect to the issue of narrowing the curriculum, parents' reactions are also mixed. When asked whether reduced emphasis on subjects other than reading and math—because of the reading-math emphasis—was a good or a bad thing, more than half of parents said it would be a good thing. Slightly more than 4 of 10 said it would be a bad thing, with the remainder reporting they didn't know (Bushaw & Gallup, 2008).

YOU TAKE A STAND

Now it's your turn to take a position on the issue. Given the information you've studied here, and any personal experiences you've had with testing, do you believe that accountability and high-stakes testing are beneficial or harmful to students?

myeducationlab To explore both sides of this issue and take a stand, go to the *Book Specific Resources* section in the MyEducationLab for your course, select your text, and then select *Taking a Stand in an Era of Reform* for Chapter 14.

ISSUES IN EDUCATION

These sample standards and items are similar in two ways. First, the items measure more than students' ability to remember factual information, a requirement typical of many, if not most, standards. Each of the sample items go beyond factual knowledge and measure students' understanding of conceptual knowledge (see Figure 13.2). This means that when you align your instruction with standards, you need to teach students to do more than simply memorize information, and you should also develop assessments that do more than measure their knowledge of facts.

Second, the items on the state assessment tests are written in a multiple-choice format, which both increases their reliability and makes them easier to score. The fact that these are multiple-choice items has an important implication for you: You'll need to be sure your students are comfortable with this format. This suggests that some of the teacher-made assessments you create should be in a multiple-choice form to provide students practice responding to this format. It's a demanding process, but one that will help you prepare your students for their assessments and increase the likelihood that their test scores reflect what they actually know.

At this early point in your teacher preparation program, standards, accountability, and high-stakes testing might be somewhat intimidating. But as you spend time on your state's website and get support from your school when you begin your first job, preparing your students for these reforms won't seem so daunting.

Grading and Reporting

You make it a point to assess your students frequently and thoroughly, and you work hard to ensure that your quizzes and tests require more of your students than simple remembering of factual information. You thoroughly discuss each quiz or test after you score and return it.

A parent of one of your students who is barely passing in your class requests a conference with you. In the conference, the parent says that her child thinks your quizzes and tests are unfair. When you ask what she means by unfair, the parent tells you that her child says the items are confusing and tricky. She also says that her child has always been a good student and usually receives A's and B's, but is receiving a C in your class.

How do you respond to this parent?

Standards, accountability, and high-stakes testing, although pervasive across the country, are not without controversy. In *Taking a Stand in an Era of Reform* on pages 436–437, we examine the pros and cons of these reforms.

■ ■ ■ ■ CHECK YOUR UNDERSTANDING

3.1   Define *standards*, and explain why they exist in all states in this country.

3.2   What is *accountability*, and how is it related to standards?

3.3   Describe the relationship between assessment, standards, accountability, and high-stakes tests.

For feedback, go to the appendix, *Check Your Understanding*, located in the back of this text.

Standards and accountability create pressures for both students and teachers. The *Decision Making* feature, above, describes a problem that many teachers encounter when they attempt to address standards in their classrooms.

14 MEETING YOUR LEARNING OBJECTIVES

1.   Describe the process of assessment, and explain how it promotes student learning.

- *Assessment* includes all the processes teachers use to gather information and make decisions about student learning and development.
- Assessment is important because it helps teachers determine how much students are learning and what they can do to increase that learning.
- Different types of assessments include standardized and teacher-made tests, informal and formal assessments, and formative and summative assessment.
- Teachers in elementary schools tend to rely on informal assessments and focus more on nonacademic aspects of schooling than do teachers in middle and secondary schools.
- *Validity* describes the extent to which assessment results are interpreted and used appropriately; *reliability* represents the consistency of assessments.

2. Explain how grading and reporting relate to the total assessment process.

   • Grading and reporting are integral parts of the total assessment process and provide valuable feedback to both students and their parents.

   • Elementary schools tend to focus grades on more nonacademic aspects of students' learning than do middle and secondary schools. Elementary teachers tend to rely on informal assessments in making decisions to a greater extent than do middle and secondary teachers.

   • Technology can be a time-saver as teachers assess their students. Programs are available for storing individual test items, as well as for constructing quizzes and tests. Tests can be administered online, which is a help when students are absent for the test. Machine scoring of objective tests saves teachers large amounts of time and energy. Finally, electronic grade books are a convenient way to store and maintain student records, saving teachers time when report cards are due.

3. Define *standards*, and explain how assessment, standards, and accountability are related.

   • *Standards* describe what students should know or be able to do after a period of study.

   • *Accountability* is the process of requiring that students demonstrate that they understand the topics they study and holding teachers responsible for students' performance.

   • *Assessment* is the process school leaders use to hold students accountable for meeting standards and making teachers responsible for ensuring that students do so.

IMPORTANT CONCEPTS

accountability (p. 434)
assessment (p. 414)
assessment *for* learning (p. 420)
formal assessment (p. 416)
formative assessment (p. 418)
high-stakes tests (p. 434)
informal assessment (p. 416)
performance assessments (p. 417)

personal response system (p. 431)
portfolio assessment (p. 417)
reliability (p. 418)
rubric (p. 419)
standardized tests (p. 415)
standards (p. 432)
summative assessment (p. 418)
validity (p. 418)

DISCUSSION QUESTIONS

1. In comparing elementary, middle, and secondary schools, is assessment more important in one than in the others? Why or why not?

2. Giving assessments and providing detailed feedback can take a considerable amount of class time. Is this time well spent? Why or why not?

3. How does assessment affect students' motivation to learn? Does this change with high- or low-ability students?

4. Many teachers, particularly in the middle and secondary schools, give a weekly quiz, such as an algebra quiz every Friday. Is this effective assessment practice?

5. Has the "standards movement" had a positive or a negative effect on students' learning in this country?

6. What are some of the biggest obstacles to effective assessment?

7. Instead of traditional grades, such as A, B, and C, some schools report student performance with indicators such as "Exceeds expectations," "Meets expectations," "Marginally meets expectations," and "Does not meet expectations." Which of these systems is more effective, or are they equally effective?

8. Some educational leaders advocate abolishing grades. What is your opinion of this suggestion?

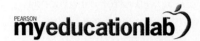

Now go to Topic 9: *Assessment, Standards, and Accountability* in the MyEducationLab (www.myeducationlab.com) for your course, where you can:

- Find learning outcomes for *Assessment, Standards, and Accountability* along with the national standards that connect to these outcomes.

- Complete *Assignments and Activities* that can help you more deeply understand the chapter content.

- Apply and practice your understanding of the core teaching skills identified in the chapter with the *Building Teaching Skills and Dispositions* learning units.

- Check your comprehension on the content covered in the chapter by going to the *Study Plan* in the *Book Specific Resources* section for your text. Here you will be able to take a chapter quiz, receive feedback on your answers, and then access *Review, Practice, and Enrichment* activities to enhance your understanding of chapter content.

Develop Your Professional Portfolio

To further apply your understanding of chapter content and address the INTASC standards, go to the *Book Specific Resources* section in the MyEducationLab for your course, select your text, and then select this chapter's *Portfolio Activities*.

Go to the *Iris Center Resources* section of Topic 10: *Creating Productive Learning Environments* in the MyEducationLab for your course to read and analyze the case study titled *Norms and Expectations*.

Appendix
Check Your Understanding

CHAPTER 1 DO I WANT TO BE A TEACHER?

1.1. What are the major rewards in teaching?

The major rewards in teaching can be divided into two main categories, intrinsic and extrinsic. In terms of intrinsic benefits, emotional rewards such as getting to know students on a personal level and helping young people grow and develop are important, as are the intellectual rewards of learning new content and playing with ideas. Extrinsic rewards include job security, frequent vacations, convenient work schedules, and the relatively high occupational status of teaching.

1.2. What are the major challenges in teaching?

The major challenges in teaching include the complexities of classrooms, which make professional decision making so difficult, and the multiple roles that teachers perform.

The first challenge—the complexity of classrooms—is described by five interrelated characteristics of teaching: It is 1) multidimensional and 2) simultaneous, meaning a number of things are going on in classrooms at the same time; 3) classroom events are pressing, requiring immediate attention from the teacher; 4) classroom events are unpredictable; 5) finally, classrooms are public, making a teacher's decisions visible to students, and even to parents and other professionals.

A second challenge facing teachers is the multiple roles they perform: Teachers are expected to create productive learning environments, work as partners with parents and caregivers, and collaborate with colleagues.

1.3. Identify the four most commonly cited reasons people give for entering teaching.

Results from a national poll, as well as our own informal surveys, indicate that wanting to work with young people and wanting to contribute to society are the two major reasons that people go into teaching. Our results showed that opportunities for personal growth and learning more about a content area were also important.

2.1. What are the essential characteristics of professionalism?

A specialized body of knowledge that sets the professional apart from the lay public is perhaps the most important characteristic of professionalism. Autonomy, which provides the freedom to make important decisions, is a second characteristic. A specialized body of knowledge, together with autonomy, allows the professional to make decisions in ill-defined situations, and reflection helps professionals improve their decisions. Finally, ethical standards provide principles of conduct that guide professionals as they work with students and caregivers.

2.2. What are the primary arguments that teaching is a profession?

Proponents of teaching as a profession point to the growing body of research showing that effective teaching requires several kinds of knowledge and requires an extended period of training for licensure. In addition, teaching professionals engage in continuous decision making in their classrooms and reflect on the effectiveness of these decisions afterward. Teachers also have considerable autonomy in their classrooms and are guided by ethical standards for conduct.

2.3. What are the major arguments that teaching is not a profession?

Critics who claim that teaching isn't a true profession base their claims on two major points. First, they note that teaching often doesn't require rigorous training before licensure. Second, they point out that teacher autonomy is limited by curricular standards and assessment procedures.

2.4. **How do the arguments for and against teacher professionalism balance each other?**

Although the rigor required for teaching isn't as great as for other professions, it is increasing. In addition, although their current autonomy is restricted by standards and testing, teachers still have considerable autonomy in their classrooms. The future of the professionalization movement in teaching will be significantly influenced by current reform efforts.

3.1. **Identify the different dimensions of student diversity. Explain how these dimensions will influence your work as a teacher.**

Culture and ethnicity, language, religion, socioeconomic status, academic ability, physical and emotional maturity, gender, and learner exceptionalities are all sources of diversity. These different dimensions of diversity provide both challenges and opportunities to teachers. Diverse classrooms are more challenging to work in because they increase the number of decisions that teachers have to make. They also provide opportunities for both teacher and student growth. By working with diverse students, teachers learn about themselves and also have opportunities to enrich the lives of their students by helping them understand commonalities and differences in all people.

3.2. **Why is an understanding of different teaching and learning environments important for beginning teachers?**

Each of the different teaching and learning environments offers both opportunities and challenges to beginning teachers. Rural districts are smaller and tend to be more culturally homogeneous. Suburban districts are intermediate in size and tend to be better funded. Urban districts are larger and more culturally diverse. The number of jobs available in urban settings is increasing, and many urban districts target beginning teachers for job offers by offering a number of incentives to work in their classrooms.

4.1. **How is the current reform movement in education changing the teaching profession?**

The current reform movement in education is changing the profession in two major ways. First, reform initiatives that include standards, test-based accountability, and choice are changing teachers' lives. Changes are also occurring in teacher preparation: Teachers are being held to higher academic standards and are having their competency measured through state licensure exams.

4.2. **Describe the major changes in teacher preparation that have resulted from the reform movement in education.**

Major changes in teacher preparation primarily target higher standards for admission and higher academic standards within the programs themselves. Candidates are required to take more rigorous courses both before they enter and within teacher preparation programs. Prospective teachers also face higher licensure requirements for entering the profession, including teacher competency tests. Many teacher preparation programs are being expanded from 4 to 5 years, and experienced teachers are being asked to take more rigorous professional-development courses.

4.3. **What are the major arguments for and against testing teachers?**

Advocates of teacher testing believe this reform provides a valid, reliable, cost-effective, and bias-free method of ensuring that teachers are qualified. Critics believe that these tests aren't valid and don't predict effective teaching in the classroom. In addition, they may be biased against cultural minorities and non-English-speaking candidates.

4.4. **What is the Praxis Series™, and how does praxis relate to the reform movement?**

The Praxis Series™, published by Educational Testing Service, is a comprehensive battery of tests designed to ensure teacher competency. Praxis I measures base skills; Praxis II assesses teachers' knowledge of the content they'll be teaching; Praxis III is designed to assess classroom performance. The Praxis Series is part of a larger reform effort to improve education by improving the quality of teachers.

4.5. **What is the Kentucky Education Reform Act, and how is it similar to and different from No Child Left Behind?**

The Kentucky Education Reform Act was a comprehensive statewide reform effort to improve education by creating state standards and assessment systems and by providing supplementary services for at-risk students. It was similar to No Child Left Behind in attempting comprehensive, system-wide educational reform; it differed from NCLB in that it focused on one state, and provided additional funding to carry out its reform.

CHAPTER 2 DEVELOPING AS A PROFESSIONAL

1.1. Describe the beliefs of beginning teachers.

Beginning teachers are idealistic and believe they will be very effective when they teach. They further believe that they'll be more effective than teachers who are now in the field, and they believe that their confidence in their ability to promote student learning will increase as they gain experience.

Beginning teachers believe that the most effective teachers are those best able to clearly explain the content they teach, and that if they thoroughly understand their content, they will figure out a way to help students learn it.

1.2. How could the beliefs of beginning teachers influence your success in your first years of teaching?

The beliefs of beginning teachers often reveal misconceptions about teaching and learning, and these misconceptions can influence your success as a teacher. For instance, if you retain the belief that the most effective way to help students learn something is to explain it to them, you are likely to be disappointed when you see your students drift off and act bored when you lecture. Similarly, if you believe that you will learn most of what you need to know when you go into classrooms, you are likely to learn less from your university classes than you would if you were more committed to professional growth.

Understanding the beliefs of beginning teachers, and recognizing that they're often misconceptions, will help you better prepare yourself as you anticipate your first teaching position.

1.3. How does teachers' confidence change as they acquire experience?

As beginning teachers acquire experience in their first few years of teaching, their confidence in their ability to help students learn tends to decrease, and they often feel as if "No one prepared me for this." Then, the confidence of successful and less successful teachers diverges dramatically: As successful teachers acquire experience and expertise, their confidence increases, but less successful teachers' confidence continues to decline.

2.1. What are the two primary differences between traditional and alternative licensure?

First, students in traditional licensure programs take professional training courses in education while working toward their bachelor's degree. Alternative licensure students have already earned a bachelor's degree in some field other than education.

Second, traditional licensure candidates get much more professional training in education than do alternative licensure candidates. Typically, alternative licensure candidates take short, intensive training in education, and they're supposed to receive extensive mentoring when they get out on the job. This mentoring is commonly missing, however.

2.2. What are the two most essential factors involved in finding a desirable job?

The two most essential factors involved in finding a desirable job are developing a positive professional reputation and interviewing effectively. If you have developed a positive professional reputation, you'll earn supportive letters of recommendation, which make you more marketable.

Interviewers assess a variety of factors during an interview, such as your professional knowledge, personality, dress, use of language, and enthusiasm for teaching. How you come across in each of these areas will be significant in whether you're offered a job.

2.3. In which areas are teaching jobs most plentiful?

Two categories of plentiful jobs exist. The first is related to content area. For example, jobs are plentiful in areas such as math, science (particularly chemistry and physics), special education, and foreign languages (particularly Spanish).

Many jobs also exist in challenging teaching situations, such as underperforming urban schools with high percentages of minority students and students whose native language isn't English.

3.1. Identify four factors that contribute to a successful first year of teaching.

Organization, classroom management, effective instruction, and knowing your students are four factors that will influence the success of your first year. For this reason, we describe them as "survival skills" for your first year of teaching. Each is important, but classroom management is one of the most essential: More beginning teachers leave the profession because of their inability to manage students than for any other reason.

3.2. What are the characteristics of successful induction programs?

Effective induction programs include systematic efforts designed to assist beginning teachers and to help them link their instruction to state and district standards. They also offer support with everyday problems, encourage teachers to develop a reflective professional attitude, and include professional-development activities designed to increase mentors' effectiveness and provide compensation for mentors. In addition, new teachers in effective induction programs are observed, and are given detailed feedback and support with planning and instruction.

3.3. How are teacher evaluation systems created and used?

Educators base the design of teacher evaluation systems on research and theory that describe connections between teaching and learning. Educators gather and compile findings from a variety of sources and create observation instruments based on research. Administrators or supervising teachers then observe and evaluate teachers using the observation instruments as a guide.

4.1. Describe three career-long professional-development opportunities available to you as a teacher.

Involving yourself in professional organizations, becoming a teacher-leader, and attaining National Board certification are all long-term professional-development opportunities.

4.2. What is INTASC? How has it influenced teacher preparation?

The Interstate New Teacher Assessment and Support Consortium (INTASC) was created in 1987 to help states develop better teachers through coordinated interstate cooperation. It identified core standards for teacher preparation organized around 10 principles; these include knowledge of subject, knowledge of learners and human development, planning and instructional strategies, as well as ways to work with parents and colleagues. These standards have improved the quality of teacher education and brought about greater uniformity in programs across states.

4.3. What are five activities professional organizations support that are designed to improve teaching and schools?

Professional organizations aim to improve teaching and schools by: (1) producing and disseminating professional publications that provide up-to-date research and information on trends in the profession; (2) providing professional-development activities for teachers; (3) holding yearly conferences that present theory and research about recent professional advances; (4) providing resources where teachers can find answers to questions about professional issues and problems; and (5) providing information to politicians and policy makers about important issues facing education.

4.4. What are the two primary assessment processes involved in attaining National Board certification?

The two primary assessment processes involved in acquiring National Board certification are passing a set of exams in a content-area specialty, such as math, science, early childhood, or physical education and health, and submitting evidence of teaching ability, such as videotapes of classroom instruction and a personal portfolio that demonstrates expertise.

CHAPTER 3 CHANGES IN AMERICAN SOCIETY: THEIR INFLUENCES ON TODAY'S STUDENTS

1.1. Describe changes that have occurred in the American family over the last 50 years.

An increasing number of children have parents who are or have been divorced, have single parents, or have both parents working. In addition, an increasing number of families live near or below the poverty level. As a result, parents and other caregivers spend less time with their children than they did 50 years ago.

1.2. Describe the implications of the changes in American families for child care in this country.

In the 1950s, most families (57 percent) had a single breadwinner, and the mother stayed home to care for the children. Currently, only about 25 percent of young children are cared for in the home. This creates a pressing need for quality child care that not only meets children's emotional needs but also prepares them for school.

1.3. Who are latchkey children? What problems do they encounter in their homes?

Latchkey children return home after school to an empty house. They not only have less parental supervision, they also have less access to parental help with homework.

2.1. Define *socioeconomic status*.

Socioeconomic status is a classification system that combines parents' income, occupation, and level of education.

2.2. Explain how different socioeconomic patterns influence school success.

Socioeconomic status influences school success in several ways. First, it influences whether basic needs such as food and shelter are met. It can also influence family stability: Lower-SES families are less likely to provide safe and stable home environments. It also affects the availability of school-related experiences such as travel and going to museums and zoos. Socioeconomic status also influences the amount and kind of adult–child interactions in the home. Finally, SES influences parental attitudes and values about education.

2.3. How does the government define *poverty?* How does poverty influence learning?

The federal government establishes a poverty threshold, the household income level that represents the lowest level of earning needed to meet basic living needs. In 2007, the poverty level for a family of four was $20,065. Poverty influences a family's ability to meet basic needs such as food and shelter as well as educational needs such as books, and the ability to be home to supervise and help with homework.

2.4. How does homelessness influence learning?

Experts estimate that between 500,000 and one million children are homeless at some time during the year. Homeless children suffer from inadequate diets and medical care, frequently come from unstable families, and often don't attend school regularly.

Because their basic needs aren't met, homeless children can't take advantage of learning opportunities in school. In addition, because they don't have a stable home life to return to, they find it difficult to do homework and read at home.

3.1. What changes have occurred in student sexuality over time? What are the implications of these changes for education?

Students are more likely to become sexually active earlier, leading to teenage pregnancies and sexually transmitted diseases. These changes suggest the need for basic sex education that can help students make informed choices.

3.2. Explain the trends in student use of alcohol and other drugs over the last several years, and describe the implications of these changes for education.

Although the use of alcohol, tobacco, marijuana, and cocaine has decreased in recent years, use among students still remains high. This suggests that students need to be educated about the legal, physical, and psychological consequences of using these drugs.

3.3. How has the rate of student obesity changed over the years? How are schools responding to this problem?

The rate of student obesity has tripled since 1980. Schools have attempted to combat this problem by banning the sale of calorie-laden soft drinks in schools. Other issues, such as exercise and healthy diets, still need to be addressed.

3.4. How have crime and violence changed in U.S. schools? What are the implications for education?

The overall rates of crime and violence in schools have decreased in recent years. They still are a reality in many schools, however, and need to be dealt with on multiple levels. At the school level, administrators need to have a comprehensive plan in place for both preventing and addressing crime and violence. Teachers also need to be aware of the possibilities for crime and violence, as well as bullying, in their classrooms and need to know how to deal with them immediately.

4.1. What are the characteristics of at-risk students?

At-risk students often come from unstable families and are often victims of high rates of poverty, violence, and alcohol and drug abuse as well as child abuse. They are often members of cultural minorities, and English may not be spoken at home.

4.2. What unique challenges do urban schools present to at-risk students?

Urban schools present a number of challenges to at-risk students. They tend to exist in high-poverty areas, a factor often associated with lower achievement. They are also funded less well than their suburban counterparts and have fewer experienced teachers. In addition, urban schools are often larger, making it harder for students to establish meaningful interpersonal relationships.

4.3. What can schools and teachers do to help at-risk students achieve success?

Effective schools for at-risk students emphasize a safe and orderly school climate, mastery of essential content, caring and demanding teachers, cooperation, student responsibility and self-regulation, and strong parental involvement.

Effective teachers for at-risk students share many of the characteristics of effective schools. They are caring, have high expectations, and emphasize student responsibility. They also provide instruction that is interactive, with increased structure, support, and feedback.

CHAPTER 4 STUDENT DIVERSITY: CULTURE, LANGUAGE, AND GENDER

1.1. Explain how cultural diversity influences learning.

Cultural diversity influences learning through cultural attitudes, values, and interaction patterns. Some cultural attitudes and values complement classroom learning. For example, some cultures view success in school as an essential component of upward mobility and consequently emphasize the value of schoolwork as well as homework. At other times, cultural values can conflict with school success; this occurs primarily when success in school threatens the loss of the home culture. Language is a prime example here: Sometimes learning English is interpreted as also rejecting the native language.

Not all cultures have the same adult–child interaction patterns. When these interaction patterns are compatible with the rapid question-and-answer style of most classrooms, then learning is facilitated. But when the home interaction patterns differ from those in the classroom, problems can occur. Sensitive teachers are aware of this and both adapt their own interaction patterns and help students change theirs to succeed in the classroom.

1.2. Describe three ways in which effective teachers respond to cultural diversity in their classrooms.

Culturally responsive teaching has three essential components. First, effective teachers accept and value cultural differences and positively communicate this attitude to students. Second, culturally responsive teachers adapt their interaction patterns to students and also teach students about successful classroom interaction practices. Finally, effective teachers build on students' cultural backgrounds, using their neighborhood and home experiences as the foundation for classroom learning.

1.3. Describe the relationship between urban schools and cultural diversity.

Urban schools tend to have greater proportions of cultural minorities than their rural or suburban counterparts. In addition, many of these students don't speak English as their first language, requiring teachers skilled in English as a second language.

2.1. What has been the government's response to language diversity in our nation's schools?

Initially, Congress supported bilingual education with the passage of the Bilingual Education Act of 1968. This was reinforced in 1974 by a U.S. Supreme Court decision requiring districts to address the learning needs of non-English speakers. More recently, both federal and state governments have reversed these trends, emphasizing English-only approaches at the expense of bilingualism.

2.2. What are the primary differences in the two major approaches schools use in working with English language learners?

The two very different approaches to dealing with ELL students differ in the emphasis they place on maintaining the first language. The bilingual approach aims to maintain the native language, using it as the foundation for learning English. A contrasting approach focuses exclusively on learning English. For political and practical reasons, this second approach appears to be currently dominant in the United States.

2.3. What are the major ways that teachers can adapt their instruction to meet the needs of students with varying language backgrounds?

First, teachers should strive to make their classrooms welcoming places where all students feel comfortable. Then they should provide opportunities for students to practice their developing language skills with other students through learner-centered approaches; cooperative learning, peer tutoring, and buddy systems are all effective. Teachers should illustrate their lessons with many examples to provide concrete references for new ideas and vocabulary and frequently check for student understanding. Finally, teachers should be sensitive to embarrassing students whose language skills are still developing.

3.1. Explain how society influences gender differences in our students.

Society influences gender differences between boys and girls primarily through gender-role identity. Every society influences people's perceptions of the proper roles of males and females. Ours does as well, and students come into our classrooms with preconceived notions about how males and females should act, and what careers they should select.

3.2. How should teachers respond to gender differences?

Teachers often treat boys and girls differently based on their own stereotypical views of gender roles. They should be aware of these possibilities and strive to treat boys and girls equally in learning activities. This means that they should call on boys and girls as equally as possible, give them similar amounts of time to answer, ask the same levels of questions, and provide feedback that is similarly detailed.

CHAPTER 5 STUDENT DIVERSITY: DEVELOPMENT, ABILITY, AND EXCEPTIONALITIES

1.1. Describe the major dimensions of development. How are they similar and different?

The three major dimensions of development are *cognitive, moral,* and *personal and social.* They are similar in that they all depend on experiences with parents, teachers, other adults, and peers. In addition, they all change over time, and each influences achievement and satisfaction in school as well as success in later life.

They differ in their specific focus. Cognitive development deals with changes in the way students think about the world; moral development focuses on students' changing conceptions of right and wrong; personal development examines changes in personality and the ability to manage emotions, and social development encompasses changes in the ways students interact with each other.

1.2. How is the thinking of young children different from the thinking of older students?
Young children's thinking tends to be dominated by what they can see, and they focus on the most obvious aspects of objects and events. As children mature, they learn to think logically, and they gradually learn to think abstractly. Students of all ages need concrete experiences, however, to learn and develop fully.

1.3. How is the moral thinking of young children different from that of older students?
Young children tend to think of right or wrong in terms of the consequences of their actions: If they are rewarded, an action is right; if punished, their actions are wrong. As they develop, students begin to understand that conceptions of right and wrong also depend on basic rules and principles, and that the effects of their actions on others are also important.

1.4. What is *social development*, and why is it important for classroom teachers?
Social development refers to the changes that occur in the ways students relate to each other. Students' social development influences success and satisfaction in school as well as their ability to make friends and have meaningful relationships.

2.1. Explain the differences in current definitions of intelligence.
The most widely held definition of intelligence identifies three components: the capacity to acquire knowledge, the ability to think and reason in the abstract, and the ability to solve problems. A differing view of intelligence, based on Howard Gardner's work, suggests that it's composed of eight relatively independent dimensions.

2.2. How do schools respond to differences in ability? What does research suggest about these responses?
Ability grouping is the process of placing students with similar academic abilities in the same learning environments. *Tracking*, popular at the high school level, places students in a series of classes or curricula on the basis of ability and career goals. Although these practices are well intentioned, they have several potential drawbacks, including lowered teacher expectations and poorer instruction for those in lower groups. Experts recommend that teachers minimize the use of ability grouping and constantly be aware of the potential for adverse effects.

2.3. What are *learning styles?* What are the implications of learning styles for teachers?
Learning styles are students' preferred ways of learning, problem solving, or processing information. Learning styles have three implications for teachers. First, to meet students' diverse learning styles, teachers should use a variety of teaching strategies. Second, learning styles remind us that each student is a unique individual. Finally, learning styles suggest the need to make students metacognitively aware of their own learning strengths and weaknesses.

3.1. Explain the legal foundation of special education.
The legal foundation for special education was established in 1975 with the passage of the Individuals with Disabilities Education Act (IDEA), which, combined with later amendments, mandates the following: Students with exceptionalities have access to a free appropriate public education; assessment doesn't discriminate against any students; parents are involved in decisions about their child's educational program; an environment is created that doesn't restrict learning opportunities for students with exceptionalities; and an individualized education program of study is created for each student. Amendments to IDEA extend its provisions to children aged 3 through 5; hold states accountable for locating young children who need special education services; require districts to keep confidential records of each child and to share them with parents on request; require that methods be established to reduce the number of students from culturally and linguistically diverse backgrounds who are inappropriately placed in special education; and specify procedures that allow districts to remove students from the classroom who can potentially injure other students.

3.2. What are the major categories of exceptionalities found in classrooms?
In IDEA, the federal government specifies 13 categories of special education students. More than three fourths of these fall into four categories: learning disabilities, communication disorders, intellectual disabilities, and behavior disorders. Learning disabilities involve difficulties

in acquiring and using listening, speaking, reading, writing, reasoning, or mathematical abilities. Communication disorders interfere with students' abilities to receive and understand information from others and to express their own ideas or questions. Intellectual disabilities include limitations in intellectual functioning, as indicated by difficulties in learning, and problems with adaptive skills, such as communication, self-care, and social interaction. Behavior disorders involve the display of serious and persistent age-inappropriate behaviors that result in social conflict, personal unhappiness, and school failure.

3.3. What roles do classroom teachers play in helping students with exceptionalities succeed in their classrooms?

Classroom teachers perform several important roles in ensuring classroom success for students with exceptionalities. First, they assist in identifying students who need extra help. They also collaborate with other professionals in the creation of an IEP, and then adapt their instruction to meet the specific learning needs of each student. Finally, they are central to monitoring the process and communicating progress to parents, administrators, and special educators.

Though the same basic instructional strategies that work with all students are also effective with students with exceptionalities, teachers also need to provide additional support. This can come from individual help or through peer tutoring. Effective teachers also teach in small steps, provide frequent feedback, model problem-solving steps, provide visual aids and increased time to complete assignments, use technology, and teach students to use strategies.

CHAPTER 6 EDUCATION IN THE UNITED STATES: ITS HISTORICAL ROOTS

1.1. How did the diversity of the original colonies shape the educational system in the United States?

Because of cultural, geographic, economic, and religious differences in the original colonies, it wasn't possible to create a uniform, monolithic school system that would satisfy everyone. This led to regional or state control of education, a system that survives today.

1.2. What role did religion play in colonial schools? What are the implications of this role for contemporary schools?

Religion was often the reason that many colonists came to North America, and it played a central role in colonial life. The colonists therefore included religion as a central part of the school curriculum. The proper role of religion in schools is a contentious issue today because of differing views of the purposes of schools and schooling.

1.3. Explain why the Old Deluder Satan Act of Massachusetts was important for the development of our American educational system.

The Old Deluder Satan Act required every town of 50 or more households to hire a teacher to instruct the children in that town. This provided the legal foundation for public support of education.

2.1. Explain how the early national period influenced education in this country.

The early national period influenced education in this country in three important ways. First, one of the provisions of the First Amendment to the Constitution established the principle of separation of church and state. Second, legislators removed control of education from the federal government and gave it to the states. Third, with the passage of the Land Ordinance of 1785, the federal government established a role for itself in public education. These factors continue to influence today's education.

2.2. What is the Tenth Amendment to the Constitution? Why is it important for education today?

The Tenth Amendment to the Constitution mandated that responsibilities for education not explicitly assigned to the federal government would be the responsibility of each state, which put the responsibility for funding and governing education in the hands of the states. This system of state-controlled education exists today and is unique to the United States.

2.3. What was the historical significance of the Land Ordinance of 1785?

The Land Ordinance was designed to raise money through the sale of land in the territories west of the original colonies that were acquired from Britain at the end of the Revolutionary War. It specified that land was to be divided into townships consisting of 36 one-square-mile sections, with the income from one section reserved for support of public education. In passing the Land Ordinance, legislators established federal funding for public schools and introduced the idea that schools were instruments of national purpose.

3.1. Explain how the common school movement influenced education in our country today.

The common school movement influenced today's education in four important ways. First, it was during that period that states and local governments began directly taxing citizens to support public schools, a process that continues today. Second, states created departments of education and appointed state superintendents of instruction; state departments of education continue to be the institutions that oversee education in the states. Third, educators organized schools by grade level and standardized the curriculum, an organizational structure that remains today. Finally, states improved teacher preparation by creating *normal schools*, schools explicitly developed for the preparation of teachers. Normal schools were important because they addressed the whole issue of teacher quality, which is currently being debated regarding fast-track and alternative certification programs.

3.2. How was the common school movement linked to the growing number of immigrants coming to the United States?

Immigrants brought with them different cultures and languages. Our government needed ways to assimilate them into the increasingly industrialized U.S. economy and to make them productive citizens. Government-supported and -run schools were seen as a way to do this.

3.3. Who was Horace Mann, and what was his contribution to education in the United States?

Horace Mann was an outspoken advocate for universal public education. He was the secretary of the Massachusetts State Board of Education from 1837 to 1848. Because of his influence, Massachusetts doubled state appropriations for education, built 50 new secondary schools, increased teacher salaries by 50 percent, and passed the nation's first compulsory school attendance law in 1852. He was a powerful and effective advocate for public education for everyone.

4.1. Describe the historical roots of contemporary secondary schools.

Contemporary secondary schools can be traced all the way back to the first Latin Grammar school, which was created in 1635 and focused on preparing wealthy males for the ministry or the law. In response to the narrowness of the Latin Grammar schools, *Academies* presented a more practical curriculum; both boys and girls attended, and the precedent for electives in high schools was set. The academies charged tuition, however, so *English Classical Schools*, free secondary schools designed to meet the needs of boys not planning to attend college, were created. They established the precedent of free secondary education for all students. Out of these roots, modern comprehensive high schools gradually evolved, and junior highs and middle schools further evolved as a result of criticisms suggesting that high schools didn't meet the social, emotional, and intellectual needs of young adolescents. Questions about the mission of each of these schools persist today.

4.2. How have the goals of high school education changed over time?

Initially, the predecessors of the contemporary high school were elitist and oriented primarily to preparation for college; institutions such as the Latin grammar school were strictly college preparatory. Later, schools such as Benjamin Franklin's Academy and the English classical school were reoriented to more practical subjects such as bookkeeping and surveying. Initial participation in these schools was still limited to the very wealthy or talented. The idea of a universal high school education didn't really take root until the 1900s.

4.3. How are junior highs and middle schools different from each other?

Junior highs were designed to prepare students for high school. Consequently, they focused primarily on academics and, for the most part, ignored the social and emotional needs of young adolescents. Middle schools evolved out of growing recognition that the developmental needs of early adolescents were unique and were not being met by junior high schools. Middle school adaptations for developing adolescents included a more applied and integrated curriculum, more learner-centered instruction, and classes that allowed teachers and students to interact and get to know each other.

5.1. Identify similarities and differences in minority groups' struggles for educational equality.

Minority groups' struggles for educational equality are similar in that they all were subjected to discrimination at different points in history. Some argue that aspects of discrimination still exist today. They are also similar in that they have become integral parts of American life, but they retain elements of their native cultures, such as holidays, food, and customs.

The groups are different in their histories. First, they came to be in this country for different reasons. For example, Native Americans were here when the first colonists arrived; African Americans were brought over as slaves; and Asian Americans were brought to work on farms and on the transcontinental railroad.

They were also treated differently. For example, attempts were made to assimilate Native Americans into mainstream American society by having them attend boarding schools, adopt the habits of mainstream culture, and reject their native customs and habit. To a certain extent, this was true of Hispanic Americans as well. In contrast, African Americans lived under the policy of *separate but equal* for decades. In practice, however, the policy was *separate but unequal,* because schools African American students attended were virtually always substandard and underfunded.

5.2. How does the concept of *assimilation* relate to Native American boarding schools?

Assimilation is the process of socializing cultural minorities so they adopt the social norms and behaviors of the dominant culture, or Whites. Boarding schools attempted to speed up the process by taking Native American youth away from their families and instructing them in residential facilities. These efforts were mainly ineffective.

5.3. How does "separate but equal" relate to African Americans' educational experience in the United States?

Early attempts to educate African Americans placed them in segregated schools that purported to be separate but equal. Unfortunately, they were separate but unequal in resources and quality.

5.4. How did the process of assimilation relate to Hispanic Americans and their native languages?

In hopes of assimilating Hispanic Americans quickly, schools frequently taught classes in English only, and Spanish was forbidden. This practice not only caused the loss of the first language but also resulted in conflicts between home and school. Bilingual education aimed to retain and build on students' first language skills, but the status of bilingual education is currently in doubt because of restrictive legislation in a number of states.

6.1. How did schools become instruments for national purpose during the modern era?

Schools became instruments for national purpose during the modern era in four important ways: the Cold War, the War on Poverty, the enlistment of schools in competition for economic superiority, and the government's role in equity issues. The federal government significantly increased support for math and science during the Cold War to combat the perceived growing threat of Communism. Education was seen as a tool to eliminate poverty and the economic disparities in our country in the War on Poverty. The government also passed legislation requiring the creation of learning standards in an effort to compete economically with other countries around the world, and it also passed legislation banning discrimination on the basis of culture, race, or sex.

6.2. Identify one way each of the federal government's interventions were similar, and one way they were different.

They were all similar in that they viewed education as a tool for national progress. They were different in their structure. In the Cold War, for example, the government's intervention was primarily the process of providing additional resources, such as funding for the National

Science Foundation. In contrast, with respect to equity issues, the intervention was in the form of legislation requiring the end of discrimination on the basis of race, culture, or sex. The Civil Rights Act and Title IX are examples of this legislation.

6.3. What are magnet schools, and how do they relate to attempts to achieve equality in our schools?

Magnet schools were created as an alternative to forced busing and integration. The goal is to achieve integration by attracting bright students from all cultural groups. The results on magnet schools are mixed. Although they do achieve integration, critics charge that they tend to steal bright minority students from their home schools and that social integration within magnet schools often doesn't occur.

6.4. What is Title IX, and how is it related to the concept of equality?

Title IX was federal legislation enacted in 1972 to eliminate gender bias in the United States. Its most dramatic influence in education has been in the area of sports, where gender-equity advocates have used it to gain equity in facilities and expenditures.

CHAPTER 7 EDUCATIONAL PHILOSOPHY: THE INTELLECTUAL FOUNDATIONS OF AMERICAN EDUCATION

1.1. Define *philosophy* and *normative philosophy*, and explain how they differ from *theory*.

A *theory* is a set of related principles that are based on observations and are used to explain the world. *Philosophy* includes theoretical studies of knowledge, truth, existence, and morality, but goes beyond theories to examine the way the world ought to be, which is called *normative philosophy*.

1.2. To which part of teacher professionalism is philosophy most closely related? Explain.

Philosophy is most closely related to a "specialized body of knowledge." All professions have specialized knowledge, and philosophy is part of this knowledge for professional educators.

1.3. What's the major difference between Allie's and Brad's normative philosophies?

First, Allie believed that essential knowledge exists, as indicated by this comment: "There's real, practical stuff out there that kids need. They have to be good readers, and they need to be able to write, and they need to understand this stuff, the science I'm teaching." She also believed that students must study, practice, and be assessed with respect to that essential knowledge. For her, study, practice, and assessment are the ways teaching and learning "ought to be." Brad, instead, believed that experiences with decision making and problem solving were more nearly the way teaching and learning "ought to be."

2.1. Describe each of the major branches of philosophy.

The four branches of philosophy are *epistemology*, which examines questions about how we come to know the knowledge we acquire; *metaphysics*, which analyzes reality and what is and is not real; *axiology*, which examines matters of right and wrong; and *logic*, which analyzes the process of deriving valid conclusions from basic premises.

2.2. Allie said, "I'm not doing my job if I don't get them to learn as much as possible." This comment best illustrates which branch of philosophy? Explain your answer.

This comment most closely relates to axiology. Allie is saying that it would be unethical if she didn't do her best to help her students learn as much as possible.

2.3. Two teachers are in a discussion, and one says, "Everything we know depends on experience. So, the key is providing lots of experiences in the classroom. If we provide them with enough experiences, they'll learn." To which branch of philosophy is this person's statement most closely related? Explain your answer.

This person's comment most closely relates to epistemology. She is suggesting that the way people come to know what they know is through experiences.

2.4. **"That doesn't quite make sense," a teacher diplomatically comments to a colleague. "You said that your kids are so unmotivated, but last week you said that kids basically want to learn. . . . Those two don't fit." To which of the branches of philosophy is this person's comment most closely related? Explain your answer.**

This person's comment is most closely related to logic. He is saying that the conclusion "Kids aren't motivated" doesn't logically follow from the premise "Kids basically want to learn."

3.1. **Describe the major philosophies of education.**

Perennialism is an educational philosophy grounded in the belief that human nature is constant, and a rigorous intellectual curriculum should exist for all students. Math, science, and literature are important, because they expose students to logical thought and ideas that have endured throughout history.

Essentialism is framed in the belief that a critical core of information exists that all people should possess. Basic skills and academic subjects would make up a curriculum based on essentialist philosophy.

Progressivism suggests that education should focus on real-world problem solving and individual development. Learner-centered curricula would be emphasized in a school grounded in progressivism.

Social reconstructionism contends that schools and teachers should take the lead in creating a better world. It suggests, for example, that issues such as racism, sexism, environmental degradation, and the exploitation of the weak by the powerful are all topics that should be addressed in the school curriculum.

3.2. **Because students must be able to function effectively in, and adapt to, a changing world, a teacher emphasizes the "whole person"—physical, social, emotional, and intellectual—in her students. She stresses and models physical fitness, involves her students in discussions to help them practice social skills and perspective taking, and involves them in problem solving about modern-day topics. To which of the educational philosophies is the teacher's efforts most closely related? Explain.**

This teacher is basing her work on progressivism. Her emphasis on functioning effectively in a changing world illustrates a progressivist approach to education.

3.3. **You visit a school, and you overhear a conversation between two teachers. One says, "I love teaching Shakespeare. His work has been studied for hundreds of years, and it's as timely now as it was then." Which educational philosophy is best illustrated by the teacher's comment? Explain.**

The teacher is expressing views consistent with perennialism. Perennialism emphasizes thought that has endured throughout history, and the study of Shakespeare reflects this emphasis.

3.4. **A teacher who wants her students to examine racism and injustice involves them in a unit on nonviolent noncooperation using a study of Gandhi's struggles against racism in India as an example. She further illustrates the ideas with a study of Martin Luther King Jr.'s nonviolent protests against American racism. To which of the educational philosophies is the teacher's efforts most closely related? Explain.**

This teacher is basing her work on social reconstructionism. Examining issues of injustice and making attempts to eliminate them are consistent with social reconstructionist philosophy, and using Gandhi's and Martin Luther King Jr.'s works as examples to study this issue reflects this orientation.

4.1. **Why is a personal philosophy of education important?**

Forming a personal philosophy of education is important because your philosophy will influence the kinds of content you emphasize in your classes, the instructional decisions you make as a teacher, and the criteria you use to reflect on and analyze your teaching.

A personal philosophy is also important because it will help you explain and defend your educational goals—what you will strive to accomplish in your classroom. Your goals reflect the kind of teacher you want to be, and being able to explain and defend them means that you're knowledgeable and reflective, which are essential characteristics of professionalism.

4.2. What are the three essential steps involved in forming a philosophy of education?

Forming a personal philosophy of education begins with a statement of beliefs about the purpose of schooling and the nature of teaching and learning. The second step involves examining those beliefs to ensure that they're consistent with each other. The third step is actually articulating your philosophy in an internally consistent statement; the statement then gives you a concrete framework that you can use to guide your actions, and because it's tangible, it can be modified when your professional knowledge expands and your beliefs change.

4.3. Look again at Brad's thinking, as indicated by his conversation with Allie. Based on this information, what is his philosophy of education? Explain how his philosophy is based on his beliefs.

Based on his conversation with Allie, Brad's philosophy of education can be described as follows:

School should be preparation for life after students leave the classroom, and the way to best prepare for life is to practice life skills, which are the abilities to make decisions and solve real-world problems instead of focusing on traditional content. For Brad, essential knowledge is the knowledge people need to make decisions and solve problems.

These views are based on the belief that the only way people learn to make decisions and solve problems is to practice both. They're also based on the belief that reality is what people perceive it to be and that it depends on the situation people are in at the time. In this regard, Brad's views are most closely aligned with progressivism.

CHAPTER 8 THE ORGANIZATION OF AMERICAN SCHOOLS

1.1. What are three meanings of the concept *school*?

One definition describes a school as a place where students go to learn and develop; a second describes a school as a physical place—a building or set of buildings. A social institution, an organization with established structures and rules designed to promote certain goals is a third definition and serves as the framework for this chapter.

1.2. What are the major components of a typical school organization?

The components of a typical school are personnel, the physical plant, and the organization of the curriculum. The personnel of a school includes the administrative staff, vice principal, and one or more assistant principals in large schools; support staff, such as clerical workers, receptionists, and custodians; and teachers.

The physical plant often includes several buildings, such as an administrative building, classroom buildings, a cafeteria; and in most middle, junior high, and high schools, sports facilities, such as a gymnasium, football and baseball fields, and perhaps a running track.

The curriculum is designed to teach content that is appropriate for students at different ages, which is the reason that schools are usually organized into elementary, middle or junior high, and high school levels.

1.3. Most school systems are organized into three levels; describe each.

Schools are typically organized into elementary, middle or junior high, and high school levels. Elementary schools usually house students from kindergarten, or pre-K, through the fifth or sixth grade. Middle schools usually involve some combination of fifth through eighth grades, with grades 6–8 being the most common. Junior highs most commonly house some combination of grades 7–9, and high schools typically consist of grades 9–12 or 10–12.

1.4. What are three factors that influence the way schools are organized?

The developmental characteristics of students as well as economics and politics are the three factors that most commonly influence the way schools are organized. Because a typical first grader thinks differently than a typical fifth grader, for example, the curriculum is organized to accommodate those developmental differences.

Economic factors, such as school overcrowding, and political factors, such as high school coaches' wanting potential athletes to be prepared for high school teams, also influence the way schools are organized.

2.1. **What are two ways in which teaching in an elementary school differs from teaching in a middle school, junior high, or high school?**

Elementary teachers are responsible for teaching all the content areas, such as reading, math, science, social studies, art, and music, whereas teachers at the upper levels are responsible for teaching only one area, such as math (or sometimes two, such as a combination of math and science classes). This is one important difference.

In addition, teachers in elementary schools set their own schedule; they decide how many minutes per day they will allocate to each of the content areas. At the upper levels, the time allocated for each class period is preset by schoolwide schedules and bells.

2.2. **What are four differences between effective middle schools and junior highs?**

First, effective middle schools organize teachers and students into interdisciplinary teams, so that all the teachers on a team have the same group of students and instruction emphasizes connections between different curriculum areas. This isn't the case in junior highs. Second, middle schools more strongly emphasize long-term teacher–student relationships, with greater attention to students' emotional development, than do junior highs. Third, teachers in effective middle schools place more emphasis on interactive teaching strategies than do teachers in junior highs. Finally, middle schools eliminate activities in which developmental differences among students become apparent, such as competitive athletics.

2.3. **Describe a comprehensive high school. How does a comprehensive high school differ from a vocational high school?**

A comprehensive high school attempts to meet the needs of all students. This means that it provides offerings for students who are likely to attend college, but at the same time meets the needs of students who will be entering the job market after graduating from high school.

Career technical schools offer a curriculum designed to provide students with education and job skills that will enable them to get a job immediately after graduating from high school.

3.1. **Describe characteristics of an effective school.**

Research indicates that effective schools are optimal in size—neither too small nor too large— have a clear school mission and strong leadership, maintain a solid academic focus, have high collective efficacy, employ interactive instructional strategies, monitor learning progress, have safe and orderly learning environments, and actively involve parents in their children's education.

3.2. **What is the most distinguishing characteristic of effective instruction in effective schools?**

The most distinguishing characteristic of effective instruction is interactive teaching. Instead of lecturing and giving students extensive seatwork, effective teachers design learning activities that actively involve students in the content they're learning.

3.3. **Why is frequent monitoring of student progress essential for an effective school?**

Frequent monitoring of student progress performs several important functions. First, and most important, it tells students whether they're learning important ideas and skills. It also informs teachers of learning gains, allowing them to adjust instruction to meet learning gaps. Finally, it provides helpful information to administrators and parents about children's learning progress.

CHAPTER 9 GOVERNANCE AND FINANCE: REGULATING AND FUNDING SCHOOLS

1.1. **Who is legally responsible for governing education in the United States?**

The Tenth Amendment to the Constitution clearly assigns legal responsibility for education to the 50 states.

1.2. Describe the educational governance structure at the state level.

State governance of education begins with the governor and the legislature. Though they have many other responsibilities, both influence education by focusing attention on educational issues. In addition, state legislatures supply about half of a district's education budget.

The organization directly and legally responsible for governing education is the state board of education. Consisting primarily of noneducators, the state board issues and revokes teaching licenses, establishes the length of the school year, creates standards for the curriculum, and develops and implements a system for gathering educational data.

The state office of education, composed of professional educators, implements education policy on a daily basis. The state office of education is responsible for teacher licensing, curriculum supervision, approval of school sites and buildings, and collection of statistical data.

1.3. Describe the governance structure at the local, district level.

School districts are responsible for the day-to-day functioning of schools. They hire teachers and ensure that students have classrooms and books. They are governed by a local school board, consisting of elected citizens from the community. The school board sets policy; the district superintendent implements that policy. The district office, consisting of educational professionals, orders textbooks and supplies, develops programs of study, administers standardized tests, and evaluates teachers. Finally, the school principal is responsible for governing at the school level. The school principal is key to the quality of education at the school level.

2.1. What are the major sources of educational funding?

The largest percentages (49 and 43 percent, respectively) come from state and local sources. The remaining 8.5 percent comes from the federal government.

Local funding comes primarily from property taxes. State funds for education come from a variety of sources, the two largest being state income taxes and sales taxes. Smaller percentages of state education funds also come from taxes on liquor and tobacco, oil and mining revenues, corporate income taxes, and income from state lotteries and gambling.

2.2. How are educational revenues spent?

The largest percentage of the educational budget (61 percent) goes to instruction, including teacher salaries. Ten percent goes to instructional assistance needs such as student services, teacher professional development, and curriculum development. Another 10 percent goes to administration, at both the district and the school levels. Maintenance of school buildings and grounds takes up another 10 percent. Finally, transportation (school buses) and food services (cafeterias) each account for another 4 percent.

3.1. Describe the major issues in school governance and finance.

Funding inequities in different districts, alternatives to local control, and controversies related to school choice are the three most prominent governance and finance issues in today's schools.

3.2. What are the major causes of funding inequities in education? What are some proposed solutions to the problem?

Funding inequities in education result largely from unequal revenue bases. Within a state, this can result from districts that have differing property values. Because significant portions of educational funding come from property taxes, inequities between districts within a state are common. Between-state differences can also result from differences in states' tax bases. One proposed solution is a greater federal role in equalizing between-state differences. Cost and the issue of increased federal control that might go along with the funding are two obstacles to this proposal.

3.3. What are the two major forms of school choice? How are they similar and different?

The two major forms of school choice are charter schools and vouchers. They are similar in their philosophical underpinnings: Both come from attempts to break up the perceived monopoly that exists in education by providing more alternatives or choices to parents. They differ in how they propose to do this. Vouchers are, in one sense, less radical in that they keep existing educational options as they are and provide parents with tickets or vouchers to shop around and choose an alternative to their neighborhood schools. Charter schools, by contrast, create alternative schools, with self-contained governance and instructional systems.

3.4. What is *school privatization*, and what are its pros and cons?

Privatization involves outsourcing educational services to private companies or corporations. This can involve hiring companies to provide services such as school lunches or transportation, or turning a whole school over to a private business. Advocates of privatization claim that competition from the private sector is good because it will encourage public schools to perform better. They also contend that the efficiencies that work in the business world will produce similar efficiencies in education. Critics point to a narrowed curriculum in privatized schools because of teaching to the test. They also point to the reduced professionalization of teachers that occurs when they're treated like employees rather than knowledgeable professionals.

CHAPTER 10 SCHOOL LAW: ETHICAL AND LEGAL INFLUENCES ON TEACHING

1.1. Explain the differences between legal and ethical influences on the teaching profession.

Laws tell teachers what they *can* do (their rights) as well as what they *must* do (their responsibilities), but they don't tell teachers what they *should* do. This is the role of professional ethics, which provides guidelines for professional conduct.

1.2. What are two limitations of using existing laws as the basis for professional decision making?

One limitation is that laws are left purposely abstract and general so they can apply to a large number of cases. This makes laws vague in terms of specific instances requiring decision making. A second limitation of using laws is that they were created in response to problems that existed in the past and may not provide specific guidelines for future professional decisions.

2.1. Describe how the legal system at the federal level influences education.

Federal laws influence education primarily through three amendments to the Constitution. The First Amendment guarantees all citizens freedom of speech; this amendment forms the basis for academic freedom in the classroom, as well as issues related to students' freedom of speech. The Fourth Amendment protects citizens from unreasonable searches and seizures; this amendment protects students from unwarranted or unreasonable searches while they're on school grounds. The Fourteenth Amendment guarantees due process in issues involving deprivation of life, liberty, or property; this amendment not only protects teachers from dismissal without a formal hearing, it also protects students from expulsion or suspension from school without due process.

2.2. How do state laws influence education policies and practices?

States are legally entrusted with the education of children. States influence education by passing laws regulating teachers' qualifications, working conditions, and legal rights. They also create departments of education, which are given responsibility for formulating educational policies in the state.

2.3. What is the educational significance of the overlapping legal system in the United States?

Because different laws influencing education are created at different levels, legal issues and problems that arise from these different levels need to be resolved at the level at which the law was formed. For example, if a legal dispute involves a teacher's qualifications for being a teacher, this would go to a state court because the laws regulating teacher qualifications are formed at that level.

3.1. How are teacher employment issues influenced by the law?

Teacher employment issues are influenced in several ways by legal considerations. First, licensure is a state responsibility, and rules and regulations passed by each state determine licensure policies and procedures. Local school boards are given the legal responsibility for issuing contracts, which specify the legal conditions for a teacher's employment. Teacher tenure, which is a legal safeguard that provides job security for teachers, is determined at the state level and protects teachers from dismissal without cause. Because of these overlapping spheres of influence, teacher dismissal is a gray area that may be influenced by both state and district legal regulations.

3.2.   What is *academic freedom*, and why is it important to teachers?
Academic freedom, which is based on the First Amendment to the Constitution, protects the right of teachers to choose both content and teaching methods based on their professional judgment. It protects teachers from undue external influences on their classroom instruction.

3.3.   How do copyright laws influence teachers' practices?
Copyright laws are federal laws designed to protect the intellectual property of authors. Fair-use guidelines specify limitations on the number of copies of books that teachers can reproduce for their classrooms. They also place restrictions on the use of videotaped programs and computer software.

3.4.   What is *teacher liability*, and how does it influence teachers?
Teachers are legally responsible for the safety of children under their care. The term *in loco parentis* means that teachers are legally expected to act in the place of parents. Failure to do so can result in negligence and a legal suit involving liability for the teacher.

3.5.   How are teachers' rights regarding their private lives similar to and different from those of the general public?
All citizens of the United States are guaranteed the right to "life, liberty, and the pursuit of happiness." But because teachers, as professionals, are expected to be role models for the children they teach, their rights as private individuals may be curtailed.

4.1.   Describe the legal implications of religion in the schools.
The First Amendment to the Constitution states, "Congress shall make no law respecting an establishment of religion, or prohibiting the free exercise thereof." This law has important implications for teachers. It explicitly forbids the teaching of religion in the schools, and it prohibits the government from interfering with individuals' rights to hold religious beliefs and freely practice religion. It also has implications for prayer and religious clubs in schools, which are addressed in items 4.2, 4.3, and 4.4.

4.2.   What is the legal status of prayer in schools?
Neither schools nor teachers can officially encourage school prayer; however, prayer is permissible when student initiated and when it doesn't interfere with other students or the school. For example, an individual student or students saying grace before lunch in a cafeteria would be permissible under the law.

4.3.   Can a school allow religious clubs or organizations to meet on school grounds?
The U.S. Supreme Court has ruled that if the school doesn't specifically sponsor the religious club or organization, it's legal for it to allow religious, philosophical, and political groups to use school facilities in the same way as other extracurricular organizations.

4.4.   What is the legal status of religion in the curriculum?
Advocacy of religion in the schools is legally forbidden. Teachers may discuss how religion has influenced history or culture, however.

5.1.   What are students' rights with respect to freedom of speech?
The First Amendment to the Constitution guarantees all U.S. citizens freedom of speech. Students in school have this same right, provided that their actions don't interfere with learning. So, for example, students can't get up in a social studies class and make a speech about their political beliefs. This doesn't mean they can't express their beliefs briefly if the context is appropriate, but in exercising free speech, they can't interfere with the teacher's (and the class's) academic agenda.

5.2. Describe students' rights with respect to permissible search and seizure.

If school authorities believe there is probable cause that a student possesses drugs or a dangerous weapon, the school may conduct a nonobtrusive search of the student and his or her possessions (*nonobtrusive* does not include a strip search). School lockers are considered school property and may be searched if reasonable cause of a drug or weapons violation exists.

5.3. What is the Buckley Amendment? Why is it important to both schools and teachers?

The Buckley Amendment protects a family's rights to privacy of school records. It requires schools to: (1) inform parents of their rights regarding their child's records, (2) provide parents access to their child's records, (3) maintain procedures that allow parents to challenge those records, and (4) protect parents from disclosure of confidential information. Because teachers are legal extensions of schools, they are legally bound by the same safeguards.

5.4. Is corporal punishment legal in schools?

Corporal punishment is a state-by-state legal issue. In those states that do allow corporal punishment, it must be administered to correct misbehavior, it can't involve anger or malice, and it can't be cruel or excessive or result in lasting injury.

5.5. Describe students' rights with respect to disciplinary actions.

Students have a right to an education, and this right can be abridged or changed only through due process. If school administrators plan to suspend a student for an extended period of time, they must notify the student in writing of the reasons or charges, share the legal procedures and evidence, guarantee the student access to legal counsel, and record proceedings and findings, and the student must have a right to appeal.

5.6. Describe the legal rights of students with AIDS.

Because they have a right to an education, students with AIDS cannot be automatically excluded from school activities. Schools must address specific risk factors to other students when they change the instructional activities or opportunities for a student with AIDS.

CHAPTER 11 THE SCHOOL CURRICULUM IN AN ERA OF STANDARDS AND ACCOUNTABILITY

1.1. What are four definitions of *curriculum*?

Curriculum has been defined in various ways. For example: the subject matter taught to students; a course of study, or a systematic arrangement of courses; the planned educational experiences offered by a school; and the process teachers go through in selecting and organizing learning experiences for their students.

1.2. Identify one important difference between the definition of *curriculum* used in this text and the definitions described in item 1.1.

The definition used in this text is broader than those in item 1.1. It includes "everything that teachers teach and students learn in schools," which can include attitudes and values students learn that aren't formally taught. In some cases, these attitudes and values are as important for student growth as the "planned educational experiences offered by a school," which is one of the definitions outlined in this section of the chapter.

1.3. Explain how curriculum and instruction are related.

In simple terms, *curriculum* is what teachers teach, and it includes teachers' specific learning goals. The ways teachers help students reach the learning goals constitute *instruction*.

2.1. What is the difference between the explicit and the implicit curricula?

The explicit curriculum is what teachers intentionally teach based on textbooks, curriculum guides, standards, and other sources. In comparison, the implicit curriculum more nearly depends on the school climate and organization and teachers' attitudes and values. As a result, some aspects of the implicit curriculum may be out of the conscious control of the teacher.

2.2. How is the null curriculum different from both the explicit and the implicit curricula?

The explicit and implicit curricula describe what *is* taught, whereas the null curriculum describes what *is not* taught. In particular, the differences between the explicit and the null curricula reflect teachers' views about what is important to study and learn.

2.3. Compare the extracurriculum to the other curricula.

The extracurriculum differs from the explicit curriculum in that the extracurriculum exists outside of students' areas of formal study. It's similar to the implicit curriculum in that important forms of learning result from both, but they are outside the scope of the explicit curriculum. The extracurriculum is different from the null curriculum in that it relates to what is learned (albeit informally learned), whereas the null curriculum relates to what is not learned.

3.1. Identify four forces that influence the curriculum.

The four most important forces that influence curricular decisions are standards and accountability, the federal government, textbooks, and philosophy.

3.2. How does each of the forces in 3.1 exert its influence on the curriculum?

The influence of standards and accountability is illustrated by the fact that many teachers in elementary schools strongly emphasize reading/language arts and math in their teaching because these areas are measured on high-stakes tests.

The federal government's influence is illustrated in legislation such as the Individuals with Disabilities Education Act, which mandates that all students, including those with learning issues, have access to the regular curriculum.

Textbooks influence the curriculum because many teachers tend to teach the topics in their textbooks essentially as they're presented and in the order the textbook presents them.

A school's and teachers' philosophies influence the curriculum through their priorities. For example, Suzanne Brush chose to present her topic in a certain way because of her philosophy with respect to teaching. A teacher with a different philosophy might have chosen a very different approach.

3.3. Why is teacher professionalism so important in making curricular decisions?

Teacher professionalism is essential, because—even though we're living in an era of reform, standards, and accountability—teachers still make most of the decisions that influence what and how students learn. You saw this illustrated in Suzanne's teaching: Although she used the standard and the sample test item as a guide, she made all the decisions about what she would specifically teach, what to emphasize, and how to best present the topic to make it meaningful to the students. This is the case for all teachers. No amount of specifying standards and accountability measures or any other mandates will ever replace the professionalism of the teacher in promoting student learning.

4.1. How do issues involving sex education and moral development differ in their influence on the school curriculum?

Issues involving sex education influence the curriculum primarily in what content should be taught. For example, some argue that students should be exposed only to curriculum that endorses abstinence from sex. Others believe that students should learn about their bodies' reproductive system, and receive information about condoms, the prevention of sexually transmitted disease, and strategies for resisting pressure to have sex.

By comparison, authorities generally agree that ethics and morals should be taught in schools, but they disagree about the approach that educators should take. So, with respect to the development of morals, the issue becomes more one of the approach to instruction than of the content to be taught.

4.2. Describe the concept of *intelligent design*, and explain how it could influence curriculum decisions.

Intelligent design is a theory suggesting that certain features of the universe and of living things are so complex that their existence is best explained by an intelligent cause, rather than an undirected process such as natural selection. Proponents argue that it should be taught in science classes as a viable alternative theory to the theory of evolution. Critics argue that it is not science, and although it may have a place in a social studies or literature class, it does not belong in the science curriculum.

4.3. How could issues involving censorship influence your curriculum decisions?

If certain works of literature are highly controversial, you might choose not to have your students read them, even if you believe that they would contribute to students' learning. You're probably more likely to make a noncontroversial decision when you begin teaching, because you'll be somewhat unsure of yourself. As you gain experience and confidence, you will be more likely to take a more controversial stand.

CHAPTER 12 CREATING PRODUCTIVE LEARNING ENVIRONMENTS: CLASSROOM MANAGEMENT

1.1. What is a productive learning environment?

A productive learning environment is a classroom that is orderly and focused on learning. In productive learning environments, students feel physically and emotionally safe, and the daily routines, learning activities, and standards for appropriate behavior are all designed to promote learning.

1.2. Explain why effective classroom management is so important.

Classroom management is important because, first, it's the primary factor that causes teacher stress and burnout, which can destroy a teacher's career.

Second, classroom management and both learning and motivation are strongly linked. Students are more motivated to learn and learn more in well-managed classrooms.

1.3. Describe the goals of classroom management.

Effective classroom management has four goals: 1) promoting a positive classroom climate, an environment in which learners feel physically and emotionally safe, personally connected to both their teacher and their peers; 2) making the classroom a learning community, a place in which the teacher and all the students work together to help everyone learn; 3) developing student responsibility, where teachers explicitly teach responsibility and emphasize the reasons for rules and procedures, and students obey rules because they understand that order is important for learning and that rules promote that order; and 4) maximizing time available for learning, because the more time productively spent on learning activities, the more students learn.

2.1. Describe the personal characteristics of teachers that help create productive learning environments.

Teachers who create productive learning environments are first and foremost caring people. They care about their students as people, and they are committed to their students' learning. Teachers who create productive learning environments also teach effectively; they actively engage their students in learning activities that are meaningful.

2.2. Describe the planning elements that help create productive learning environments.

Planning that helps create productive learning environments focuses on two aspects of the classroom. First, teachers consider the developmental levels of their students; a first-grade teacher will plan differently than a middle school or high school teacher.

After considering students' developmental level, teachers create a system of procedures and rules that will guide the students' behavior throughout the year.

3.1. Explain how involving parents contributes to a productive learning environment.

Productive learning environments focus on learning. Research indicates that when parents are involved, students are more willing to do homework, their long-term achievement is higher, their attitudes are more positive, and they behave more responsibly. Parental involvement supports the teacher's efforts and contributes to a safe, orderly, learning-focused environment.

3.2. What strategies do effective teachers use to communicate with parents?

Effective teachers use a variety of strategies to communicate with parents. In addition to open houses, interim progress reports, and report cards, effective teachers send letters home, periodically send home packets of student work, and use newsletters, e-mails, and individual notes. In addition, phone calls and home visits are effective.

4.1. Describe the characteristics of effective teacher interventions when misbehavior occurs.

Effective teacher interventions demonstrate withitness and overlapping. *Withitness* means that the teacher is aware of what's going on in all parts of the classroom at all times and communicates that awareness to students. *Overlapping* is the ability to address two issues simultaneously, which is essential in complex classroom settings. Effective interventions also maintain student dignity, are consistent, and ensure that verbal and nonverbal behaviors are congruent.

4.2. What actions—both short- and long-term—should teachers take when encountering incidents of violence and aggression?

Short-term, the teacher should intervene immediately to address the problem; this might consist of a personal intervention, or, if this isn't possible, the teacher should send for help immediately. Long-term, teachers should involve parents and other school personnel in addressing the problems. Parents should be notified and the expertise and guidance of experienced school personnel should be sought.

4.3. What makes urban classrooms unique in terms of classroom management?

First, because urban classrooms tend to be diverse, teachers need to make sure that all students understand classroom rules and procedures and how they contribute to learning. Second, urban classrooms tend to be large, making classroom management more challenging. Third, negative stereotypes often exist about urban students, resulting in teachers' teaching defensively rather than positively.

CHAPTER 13 INSTRUCTION IN TODAY'S SCHOOLS

1.1. Define *motivation*, and describe the difference between *intrinsic* and *extrinsic* motivation.

Motivation is the energizing force behind student learning. *Extrinsic motivation* is motivation to engage in a behavior to receive some incentive, whereas *intrinsic motivation* is motivation to be involved in an activity for its own sake.

1.2. Describe the relationship between motivation and student achievement.

Learner motivation is the primary factor influencing students' achievement and satisfaction with school. In most cases, motivation is a more significant factor than native ability.

1.3. Describe three factors within teachers' control that can increase students' motivation to learn.

Teachers can increase students' motivation to learn by beginning lessons with activities that attract students' attention, promoting high levels of student involvement in learning activities, and helping students apply topics to the real world.

2.1. Describe the five essential steps in planning for instruction.

1. *Select topics* Standards, curriculum guides, textbooks, and the teacher's professional knowledge are sources that help make this decision.

2. *Prepare learning objectives.* Though the format for preparing learning objectives varies, the important aspect of preparing learning objectives is being clear about what you want students to know, understand, or be able to do.

3. *Prepare and organize learning activities.* Preparing and organizing learning activities often begin with finding or creating examples, as Shirley Barton did with her "pizzas" and "cakes."

4. *Prepare assessments.* Assessments that are created during planning instead of after learning activities have been completed help teachers focus their teaching on student learning outcomes.

5. *Ensure instructional alignment. Instructional alignment* means that teachers check that their learning activities and assessments are consistent with their objectives.

2.2. Planning in a standards-based environment involves one additional step beyond the planning steps described in this section of the chapter. What is this additional step?

When teachers' planning involves standards, the first step is to interpret the standard. Descriptions of standards vary; some are very specific, whereas others are quite general. When working with a standard described in general terms, teachers must first decide what the standard means in terms of student learning, then they follow the rest of the planning steps, i.e., plan learning activities and assessments.

2.3. Classify the following objectives into one of the cells of the taxonomy table in Figure 13.2 and explain your classification. (1) Students will identify examples of figures of speech such as similes, metaphors, and personifications in written paragraphs. (2) They will write original paragraphs that include those figures of speech.

Because figures of speech are concepts, and because being able to identify examples of them indicates understanding, the first objective would be classified in the cell where *conceptual knowledge* intersects with *understand*.

Writing paragraphs involves a procedure, and the fact that they must be original involves the cognitive process of creating, so the second objective would be classified in the cell where *procedural knowledge* intersects with *create*.

3.1. What are the essential teaching skills that all teachers should possess?

Essential teaching skills are the skills that all teachers, including those in their first year of teaching, should demonstrate regardless of topic or grade level. They include the personal characteristics of caring, high efficacy, positive expectations, and enthusiasm. Effective teachers are also well organized, and they begin their lessons with reviews, attract and maintain attention, develop their lessons with questioning, provide their students with feedback, and help students apply what they've learned in new contexts.

3.2. As middle schoolers walk into their geography class, they see a large matrix comparing the climate, geography, and economies of the northern and southern states before the Civil War. As soon as the bell stops ringing, the teacher says, "Write a minimum of two differences each in the geography, climate, and economy columns of the chart." Students begin, and as they're writing, the teacher takes roll. Which of the essential teaching skills does this example best illustrate? Explain.

Organization is the essential teaching skill best illustrated in this example. The teacher began the class right on time, and the chart was prepared and waiting when students walked into the room.

3.3. Shirley used her cardboard "pizzas" in her review and used her "cakes" to introduce the topic of *equivalent fractions.* Which essential teaching skill did the use of these materials best illustrate? Explain.

Focus is the essential teaching skill best illustrated by Shirley's use of the "pizzas" and "cakes." Each was an example that Shirley used to attract and maintain students' attention.

4.1. Describe different instructional strategies, and explain the essential differences in each.

Instructional strategies are prescriptive approaches to teaching designed to help students acquire a deep understanding of specific forms of knowledge. They differ in the types of goals they're designed to help students reach. For example, direct instruction is designed to help students develop skills, such as adding fractions; lecture-discussion is designed to help students understand organized bodies of knowledge; and guided discovery is designed to help students understand concepts and other abstractions. Cooperative learning is designed to support each of the other strategies and help students acquire social-interaction skills.

4.2. Which phase of direct instruction is most important for ensuring successful practice? Explain.

The *developing understanding* phase is most important for ensuring student success during practice, and it is in this phase that we see the greatest difference between effective and ineffective teachers. If the developing understanding phase is ineffective, practice can be difficult and confusing. Remember, practice strengthens earlier understanding; it doesn't teach the skill. If teachers have to provide a great deal of explanation during practice, error rates increase and student achievement decreases.

4.3. A teacher places her third graders in groups of four and gives each group magnets and a packet containing a dime, a spoon, aluminum foil, a rubber band, a wooden pencil, a paper clip, and nails. She directs the groups to experiment with the magnets and items for 10 minutes, look for patterns, and record these on paper. After the groups have finished, she leads a discussion in which they identify characteristics of materials that are and are not attracted to magnets. The teacher is using which strategy, or strategies, in her learning activity?

The teacher in this case is using both guided discovery and cooperative learning. She had students work cooperatively to search for patterns in materials that are attracted to magnets, and the teacher then conducted a whole-group discussion and guided students to conclusions about the characteristics of magnetic materials.

CHAPTER 14 ASSESSMENT, STANDARDS, AND ACCOUNTABILITY

1.1. Describe the process of assessment.

Assessment consists of all the processes involved in gathering information and making decisions about students' learning and development. It includes tests and quizzes, observations of student behavior in class and in other school activities, and the decisions that are made based on this information.

1.2. Why is assessment important for promoting student learning?

Assessment is essential because it provides teachers with information about students' learning progress. Without this information, teachers can't make effective decisions that increase students' learning and development.

1.3. What is the difference between informal and formal assessment, and how are validity and reliability related to them?

Informal assessment is the process of continually gathering information about students' learning and behavior and making decisions based on that information. *Formal assessment* is the process of systematically gathering the same kind of information from each student. Both forms of assessment are important, because they provide teachers with information on which their decisions are made. But informal assessments don't provide the same kind of information from each student, so they are often unreliable. As a result, they shouldn't be used as a basis for making decisions about grades, because they wouldn't be valid for this purpose.

1.4. What are some common misconceptions about assessment?

1) *Determining students' grades is the primary purpose of assessment.* Although assessments are used to determine grades, promoting learning is a much more important purpose of assessment. Without assessment, teachers have little basis for making decisions that can increase students' learning. 2) *Assessment occurs after a unit of study.* Some assessments do occur after a unit of study, but assessment should be ongoing; it's an integral part of teaching and learning. 3) *Assessment focuses on students' understanding and skills.* Gathering information about students' understanding and skills is an important part of assessment, but there is more to the assessment process. For instance, gathering information about students' social development and the ability to take responsibility for their own learning is also a component of assessment, and development in these areas is an important part of students' education. 4) *Assessments are primarily paper-and-pencil tests.* In addition to paper-and-pencil tests, perfor-

mance assessments and portfolios as well as observations of students' behavior in both formal and informal settings and making decisions on the basis of those observations are important dimensions of assessment.

2.1. How do grading and reporting relate to the total assessment process?

Grading and reporting are integral parts of the total assessment process. At one level they can be viewed as the culmination of the assessment process, because they reflect teachers' decisions about students' learning progress. For example, an "A" on a report card is intended to communicate that a student's performance in an area of study has been superior during a certain period of time. And, the performance is supposed to suggest that the student's understanding of the topic is broad and deep.

2.2. How do grading and reporting practices in elementary compare to those in middle and secondary schools?

Grading and reporting practices in elementary schools are similar to those in middle and secondary schools, in that grades are supposed to represent specified levels of student performance and learning. They often differ, however, both in emphasis and in how performance is represented. For instance, elementary schools grade and report more developmental, nonacademic aspects of students' learning, such as "works well with others" and "accepts responsibility for learning" than do middle and secondary schools. Middle and secondary schools often report nonacademic information, but it isn't graded as it is in elementary schools.

2.3. Explain how grading and reporting practices in elementary, compared to middle and secondary schools, relate to informal and formal assessment.

As you saw in item 2.2, elementary schools tend to grade and report more nonacademic aspects of students' learning, such as "works well with others." Virtually all of these aspects are assessed informally, meaning they're based on teachers' incidental observations, such as while students work together in group activities. Remembering that conclusions about students' social skills, for example, are based on informal assessments is important for teachers, because informal assessments can be unreliable. This suggests that teachers should be careful to make as many observations of an individual student as possible before drawing conclusions about social skills, self-regulation, and other nonacademic aspects of learning and development.

3.1. Define _standards_, and explain why they exist in all states in this country.

Standards are statements that specify what students should know or be able to do after a period of study. They exist because political and business leaders have expressed concerns about American students' lack of knowledge about their world and poor reading, writing, and math skills. To compete in a global marketplace and in an increasingly technological world, these leaders argue, American students' knowledge and skills need to be increased.

3.2. What is _accountability_, and how is it related to standards?

Accountability is the process of requiring students to demonstrate that they understand the topics they study and making teachers responsible for their students' performance. Standards are attempts to make essential knowledge and skills explicit to both teachers and students.

3.3. Describe the relationship between assessment, standards, accountability, and high-stakes tests.

Assessment is the process that states use for holding students and teachers accountable for meeting standards. These assessments often exist in the form of high-stakes tests. The tests are _high-stakes_ because test results are often used to determine whether students are promoted from one grade level to the next or are allowed to graduate from high school.

References

Abedi, J., Hofstetter, C., & Lord, C. (2004). Assessment accommodations for English language learners: Implications for policy-based empirical research. *Review of Educational Research, 74*(1), 1–28.

Abington School District v. Schempp, 374 U.S. 203 (1963).

Ackerman, P., & Lohman, D. (2006). Individual differences in cognitive function. In P. A. Alexander & P. H. Winne (Eds.), *Handbook of educational psychology* (2nd ed., pp. 139–162). Mahwah, NJ: Erlbaum.

ACLU v. Mukasey. (2008). United States Court of Appeals for the Third District. No. 07-2539.

Adler, M. (1982). *The Paideia proposal: An educational manifesto.* New York: Macmillan.

Adler, M. (1998). *The Paideia proposal: An educational manifesto.* (Reprint.) New York: Simon & Schuster.

Alan Guttmacher Institute. (2004). *Teen pregnancy: Trends and lessons learned.* Retrieved June 13, 2006, from http://www.agi-us.org/pubs/ib_1_02.pdf

Alberto, P., & Troutman, A. (2006). *Applied behavior analysis for teachers* (7th ed.). Upper Saddle River, NJ: Merrill/Pearson.

Alder, N. (2002). Interpretations of the meaning of care: Creating caring relationship in urban middle school classrooms. *Urban Education, 37*(2), 241–266.

Alexander, L., & Riley, R. (2002). A compass in the storm. *Education Week, 22*(6), 36–37, 48.

Alexander, P. (2006). *Psychology in learning and instruction.* Upper Saddle River, NJ: Pearson.

Allen, J. (2007). *Creating a welcoming school: A practical guide to home–school partnerships with diverse families.* New York: Teachers College Press.

Allen, R. (2002). Big schools: The way we are. *Educational Leadership, 59*(5), 36–41.

Allington, R. L., & McGill-Franzen, A. (2003). The impact of summer setback on the reading achievement gap. *Phi Delta Kappan, 85*(1), 68–71.

Alperstein, J. F. (2005, May 16). Commentary on girls, boys, test scores and more. *Teachers College Record.* Retrieved June 21, 2005, from http://tcrecord.org ID Number: 11874.

Altman, L. (2008). *Sex infections found in quarter of teenage girls. New York Times.* Retrieved March 12, 2008, from http://www.nytimes.com/2008/03/12/science/12std.html?_r=1

American Association of University Women. (1992). *How schools shortchange girls.* Annapolis Junction, MD: Author.

American Association of University Women. (1998). *Gender gaps: Where schools still fail our children.* Annapolis Junction, MD: Author.

American Association of University Women. (2001). *Hostile hallways: Bullying, teasing, and sexual harassment in school.* New York: Harris Interactive.

American Association of University Women. (2006). *Drawing the line: Sexual harassment on campus.* New York: Harris Interactive.

American Educational Research Association. (2006). *Standards for educational and psychological testing* (2nd ed.). Retrieved September 6, 2006, from http://www.aera.net

American Federation of Teachers. (2003). *Voucher home page.* Retrieved February 3, 2004, from http://www.aft.org/research/vouchers

American Federation of Teachers. (2006). *About AFT.* Retrieved August 16, 2006, from http://www.aft.org

American Federation of Teachers. (2008). *Survey and analysis of teacher salary trends (2006–2007).* Retrieved January 2009, from http://www.aft.org

American Psychological Association. (2006). *Standards for educational and psychological testing* (2nd ed.). Retrieved September 6, 2006, from http://www.apa.org

Amrein, A., & Berliner, D. (2003). The effects of high-stakes testing on student motivation and learning. *Educational Leadership, 60*(5), 32–38.

Anagnostopoulos, D. (2006). "Real students" and "true demotes": Ending social promotion and the moral ordering of urban high schools. *American Educational Research Journal, 43*(1), 5–42.

Anderman, E., & Midgley, C. (2004). Changes in self-reported academic cheating across the transition from middle school to high school. *Contemporary Educational Psychology, 29,* 499–517.

Anderman, E., & Wolters, C. (2006). Goals, values, and affect: Influences on motivation. In P. Alexander & P. Winne (Eds.), *Handbook of educational psychology* (2nd ed., pp. 369–389). Mahwah, NJ: Erlbaum.

Anderson, J. (1988). *The education of Blacks in the South.* Chapel Hill: University of North Carolina Press.

Anderson, K., & Minke, K. (2007). Parent involvement in education: Toward an understanding of parents' decision making. *Journal of Educational Research, 100*(5), 311–323.

Anderson, L., & Krathwohl, D. (Eds.). (2001). *A taxonomy for learning, teaching, and assessing: A revision of Bloom's taxonomy of educational objectives.* New York: Addison Wesley Longman.

Andersson, U. (2008). Mathematical competencies in children with different types of learning difficulties. *Journal of Educational Psychology, 100*(1), 48–66.

Andrade, H. (2007/2008). Self-assessment through rubrics. *Educational Leadership, 65*(4), 60–63.

Andrade, H., Du, Y., & Wang, X. (2008). Rubric-referenced self-assessment on elementary school students' writing. *Educational Measurement, 27,* 3–13.

Anfara, V., & Mertens, S. (2008). Do single-sex classes and schools make a difference? *Middle School Journal, 40*(2), 52–57.

Antil, L., Jenkins, J., Wayne, S., & Vadasy, P. (1998). Cooperative learning: Prevalence, conceptualizations, and the relation between research and practice. *American Educational Research Journal, 35*(3), 419–454.

Archer, J. (2000a). Competition fierce for minority teachers. *Education Week, 19*(18), 32–33.

Archer, J. (2000b). Teachers warned against teaching contracts. *Education Week, 20*(15), 30.

Archer, J. (2003). Increasing the odds. *Education Week, 22*(17), 52–56.

Archer, J. (2005). Connecticut files court challenge to NCLB. *Education Week, 25*(1), 23, 27.

Archer, J. (2006a). Building capacity. *Supplement to Education Week, 26*(3), S3–S12.

Archer, J. (2006b). The road less traveled. *Education Week, 25*(17), 34–37.

Armour-Thomas, E. (2004). What is the nature of evaluation and assessment in an urban context? In S. R. Steinberg & J. L. Kincheloe (Eds.), *19 Urban questions: Teaching in the city* (pp. 109–118). New York: Peter Lang.

Aronson, E., Wilson, T., & Akert, R. (2007). *Social psychology* (6th ed.). Upper Saddle River, NJ: Pearson.

Associated Press. (2000, December 29). Texas legislative panel calls for charter schools moratorium. *Boston Globe,* p. A13.

Associated Press. (2009). Rigor, rewards, quality: Obama's education aims. *Education Week, 28*(25), 14.

Attiel, A., Sober, S., Numbers, R., Amasino, R., Cox, B., Berceau, B., Powell, T., & Cox, M. (2006). Defending science education against intelligent design: A call to action. *Journal of Clinical Investigation, 116,* 1134–1138.

Baines, L. (2006). Deconstructing teacher certification. *Phi Delta Kappan, 88*(4), 326–329.

Baker, C., & Lyon, J. (2006, July 30). Few poor, minority pupils in charters. *Salt Lake Tribune,* pp. A1, A6–A7.

Baker, D. (2006, July 3). For Navajo, science and tradition intertwine. *Salt Lake Tribune,* pp. D1, D5.

Bali, V., Anagnostopoulos, D., & Roberts, R. (2005). Toward a political explanation of grade retention. *Educational Evaluation and Policy Analysis, 27*(2), 133–155.

Bandura, A. (2001). Social cognitive theory. *Annual Review of Psychology.* Palo Alto, CA: Annual Review.

Bandura, A. (2004, May). *Toward a psychology of human agency.* Paper presented at the meeting of the American Psychological Society, Chicago.

Banks, J. (2006). *Cultural diversity and education* (6th ed.). Boston: Allyn & Bacon.

Banks, J. (2008). *An introduction to multicultural education* (4th ed.). Boston: Allyn & Bacon.

Banning Books in Miami. (2009). *Editorial. New York Times.* Retrieved February 2009 from www.nytimes.com/2009/02/11/opinion/11wed3.html

Bardige, B. (2005). *At a loss for words: How America is failing our children and what we can do about it.* Philadelphia: Temple University Press.

Barnoski, L. (2005). My purpose. *Education Week, 25*(13), 37.

Barone, M. (2000). In plain English: Bilingual education flunks out of schools in California. *U.S. News & World Report, 128*(21), 37.

Barr, R., & Parrett, W. (2001). *Hope fulfilled for at-risk and violent youth* (2nd ed.). Boston: Allyn & Bacon.

Bartell, C. (2005). *Cultivating high-quality teaching through induction and mentoring.* Thousand Oaks, CA: Corwin Press.

Barton, P. (2004). Why does the gap persist? *Educational Leadership, 62*(3), 9–13.

Barton, P. (2006). The dropout problem: Losing ground. *Educational Leadership, 63*(5), 14–18.

Bauerlein, M. (2008). *The dumbest generation: How the digital age stupefies young Americans and jeopardizes our future (or, don't trust anyone under 30).* New York: Tarcher/Penguin.

Bauman, S., & Del Rio, A. (2006). Preservice teachers' responses to bullying scenarios: Comparing physical, verbal, and relational bullying. *Journal of Educational Psychology, 98*(1), 219–231.

Baumrind, D. (1991). The influence of parenting style on adolescent competence and substance use. *Journal of Early Adolescence, 11,* 56–95.

Bazelon, E. (2008). *The next kind of integration.* Retrieved July 21, 2008, from: http://www.nytimes.com/2008/07/20/magazine/20integration-t.html

Belfield, C., & Levin, H. (2005). *The privatization of school choice: Consequences for parents, schools, and public policy.* Boulder, CO: Paradigm.

Benner, A., & Mistry, R. (2007). Congruence of mother and teacher educational expectations and low-income youth's academic competence. *Journal of Educational Psychology, 99*(1), 140–153.

Bennett, C. (2007). *Multicultural education* (6th ed.). Boston: Allyn & Bacon.

Bennett, C., McWhorter, L., & Kuykendall, J. (2006). Will I ever teach? Latino and African American students' perspectives on PRAXIS I. *American Educational Research Journal, 43*(3), 531–575.

Benson, P., Scales, P., Hamilton, S., & Sesma, A. (2006). Positive youth development: Theory, research, and applications. In R. Lerner (Vol. Ed.), *Handbook of child psychology: Vol. 1. Theoretical models of human development* (6th ed., pp. 894–941). Hoboken, NJ: Wiley.

Berger, K. (2007). Update on bullying at school: Science forgotten? *Developmental Review,* 90–126.

Bergin, M. (2006). Junk science. *World Magazine, 21*(8), 317–345.

Berk, L. (2008). *Infants and children* (6th ed.). Boston: Allyn & Bacon.

Berk, L. (2009). *Child development* (8th ed.). Boston: Allyn & Bacon.

Berk, L. (2010). *Development through the lifespan* (5th ed.). Boston: Allyn & Bacon.

Berlin, A. (2008). Social promotion or retention? *Education Week, 28*(9), 28–29.

Berliner, D. (2004). If the underlying premise for No Child Left Behind is false, how can that act solve our problems? In K. Goodman, P. Shannon, Y. Goodman, & R. Rapoport (Eds.), *Saving our schools* (pp. 167–184). Berkeley, CA: RDR Books.

Berliner, D. (2005a). *Our impoverished view of educational reform.* Paper presented at the annual meeting of the American Educational Research Association, Montreal.

Berliner, D. (2005b). The near impossibility of testing for teacher quality. *Journal of Teacher Education, 56*(3), 205–213.

Berninger, V. (2006). A developmental approach to learning disabilities. In K. A. Renninger & I. Sigel (Vol. Eds.), *Handbook of child psychology: Vol. 4. Child psychology in practice* (6th ed., pp. 420–452). Hoboken, NJ: Wiley.

Bernstein, M. (2006). Is tenure an anachronism? *Education Week, 25*(28), 34.

Berry, B., Hoke, M., & Hirsch, E. (2004). The search for highly qualified teachers. *Phi Delta Kappan, 85*(9), 684–689.

Bethel School District No. 403 v. Fraser, 106 S. Ct. 3159 (1986).

Betts, J. (2005). The economic theory of school choice. In J. Betts & T. Loveless (Eds.), *Getting choice right: Ensuring equity and efficiency in education policy* (pp. 14–39). Washington, DC: Brookings Institution Press.

Biddle, B. (2001). Poverty, ethnicity, and achievement in American schools. In B. J. Biddle (Ed.), *Social class, poverty, and education* (pp. 1–30). New York: Routledge Falmer.

Biddle, B., & Berliner, D. (2002). Unequal school: Funding in the United States. *Education Leadership, 59*(8), 48–59.

Billings, L., & Fitzgerald, J. (2002). Dialogic discussion and the Paideia Seminar. *American Educational Research Journal, 39,* 907–942.

Bitter, G., & Legacy, J. (2008). *Using technology in the classroom* (7th ed.). Boston: Allyn & Bacon.

Black, P., Harrison, C., Lee, C., Marshall, B., & William, D. (2004). Working inside the black box: Assessment for learning in the classroom. *Phi Delta Kappan, 86*(1), 9–21.

Black, S. (2002). The well-rounded student. *American School Board Journal, 189*(6), 33–35.

Black, S. (2008a). Switching classes. *American School Board Journal, 195*(10), 47–49.

Black, S. (2008b). The takeover threat. *American School Board Journal, 195*(1), 34–35.

Blair, J. (2000). AFT urges new tests, expanded training for teachers. *Education Week, 19*(32), 11.

Blair, J. (2003). Skirting tradition. *Education Week, 22*(17), 35–38.

Blatchford, P., Bassett, P., & Brown, P. (2005). Teachers' and pupils' behavior in large and small classes: A systematic observation study of pupils aged 10 and 11 years. *Journal of Educational Psychology, 97*(3), 454–467.

Bloom, A. (1987). *The closing of the American mind.* New York: Simon & Schuster.

Bloom, B., Englehart, M., Furst, E., Hill, W., & Krathwohl, O. (1956). *Taxonomy of educational objectives: The classification of educational goals: Handbook 1. The cognitive domain.* White Plains, NY: Longman.

Board of Education of Independent School District No. 92 of Pottawatomie County v. Earls 536 U.S. 822, 1225. Ct. 2559 (2002).

Board of Education of the Westside Community School v. Mergens, 496 U.S. 226 (1990).

Bohman, D. (2006). *School superintendent pay.* Retrieved March 7, 2006, from http://www.tampabays10.com/news. aspx?storyid=25049

Bohn, C., Roehrig, A., & Pressley, M. (2004). The first days of school in the classrooms of two more effective and four less effective primary-grades teachers. *Elementary School Journal, 104*(4), 269–288.

Bolkan, J., Roland, J., & Smith, D. (2006). Designing the new school. *Learning and Leading With Technology, 33*(7), 10–14.

Borja, R. (2003). Prepping for the big test. *Education Week, 22*(35), 23–26.

Borko, H., & Putnam, R. (1996). Learning to teach. In D. Berliner & R. Calfee (Eds.), *Handbook of educational psychology* (pp. 673–708). New York: Simon & Schuster Macmillan.

Borman, G. (2002/2003). How can Title I improve achievement? *Educational Leadership, 60*(4), 49, 53.

Borman, G., & Kimball, S. (2005). Teacher quality and educational inequality: Do teachers with higher standards-based evaluation ratings close student achievement gaps? *The Elementary School Journal, 106*(1), 3–20.

Borman, G., & Overman, L. (2004). Academic resilience in mathematics among poor and minority students. *Elementary School Journal, 104*(3), 177–196.

Botstein, L. (2006). The trouble with high school. *School Administrator, 63*(1), 16–19.

Bottoms, G., Presson, A., & Han, L. (2004). *Research brief: Linking career/technical studies to broader high school reform.* Southern Regional Education Board. Retrieved January 2007 from http://www.sreb.org/programs/hstw/publications/briefs/LinkingCTStudies.asp

Boult, B. (2006). *176 ways to involve parents: Practiced strategies for partnering with families.* Thousand Oaks, CA: Corwin.

Bowman, D. (2000a). Arizona poised to revisit graduation exam. *Education Week, 20*(13), 16, 18.

Bowman, D. (2000b). Charters, vouchers earning mixed report card. *Education Week, 19*(34), 1, 19–21.

Bowman, D. (2000c). White House proposes goals for improving Hispanic education. *Education Week, 19*(41), 9.

Bowman, D. (2004). Spending on anti-smoking education slips. *Education Week, 23*(43), 18–20.

Bracey, G. (2002). The 12th Bracey report on the condition of public education. *Phi Delta Kappan, 84,* 135–150.

Bracey, G. (2003a). Investing in preschool. *American School Board Journal, 90*(1), 32–35.

Bracey, G. (2003b). Not all alike. *Phi Delta Kappan, 84,* 717–718.

Bracey, G. (2004). The 14th Bracey report on the condition of public education. *Phi Delta Kappan, 86*(2), 149–167.

Bracey, G. (2005a). A nation of cheats. *Phi Delta Kappan, 86*(5), 412–413.

Bracey, G. (2005b). And now, the Indian spelling gene. *Phi Delta Kappan, 87*(1), 91–93.

Bracey, G. (2007). The 17th Bracey report on the condition of public education: The first time "Everything changed." *Phi Delta Kappan, 89*(2), 119–136.

Bracey, G. (2008). Public versus private . . . again. *Phi Delta Kappan, 89*(5), 396–397.

Bradley v. Pittsburgh Board of Education, 913 F.2d 1064 (3d Cir. 1990).

Bradley, A. (1999). Confronting a tough issue: Teacher tenure. *Education Week, 18*(17), 48–52.

Bransford, J., Brown, A., & Cocking, R. (Eds.). (2000). *How people learn: Brain, mind, experience, and school.* Washington, DC: National Academy Press.

Bransford, J., Darling-Hammond, L., & LePage, P. (2005). Introduction. In L. Darling-Hammond & J. Bransford (Eds.), *Preparing teachers for a changing world: What teachers should learn and be able to do* (pp. 1–39). San Francisco: Jossey-Bass.

Bransford, J., Derry, S., Berliner, D., Hammerness, K., & Beckett, K. (2005). Theories of learning and their roles in teaching. In L. Darling-Hammond & J. Bransford (Eds.), *Preparing teachers for a changing world: What teachers should learn and be able to do* (pp. 40–87). San Francisco: Jossey-Bass.

Brimley, V., & Garfield, R. (2008). *Financing education* (10th ed.). Boston: Allyn & Bacon.

Broh, B. (2002). Linking extracurricular programming to academic achievement: Who benefits and why? *Sociology of Education, 75,* 69–91.

Brooke, R. (Ed.). (2003). *Rural voices: Place-conscious education and the teaching of writing.* New York: Teachers College Press.

Brookhart, S. (2008). Feedback that fits. *Educational Leadership, 65*(4), 54–59.

Brookhart, S. (2009). *Grading* (2nd ed.). New York: Merrill/Prentice Hall.

Brophy, J. (2004). *Motivating students to learn* (2nd ed.). Boston: McGraw-Hill.

Brophy, J. (2006). Graham Nuttall and social constructivist teaching; Research-based cautions and qualifications. *Teaching and Teacher Education, 22,* 529–537.

Brophy, J. (2008). Developing students' appreciation for what is taught in school. *Educational Psychologist, 43*(3), 132–141.

Brown v. Bathhe, 416 F. Supp. 1194 (D. Neb. 1976).

Brown v. Board of Education of Topeka, 347 U.S. 483 (1954).

Brown, D. (2004). Urban teachers' professed classroom management strategies: Reflections of culturally responsive teaching. *Urban Education, 39*(3), 266–289.

Brown, D. (2006). It's the curriculum, stupid: There's something wrong with it. *Phi Delta Kappan, 87*(10), 777–783.

Brown, H. (2003). Charter schools found lacking resources. *Education Week, 22*(31), 30.

Brown, K., Anfara, V., & Roney, K. (2004). Student achievement in high performing, suburban middle schools and low performing, urban middle schools: Plausible explanations for the differences. *Education and Urban Society, 36*(4), 428–456.

Brown, R., & Evans, W. (2002). Extracurricular activity and ethnicity: Creating greater school connections among diverse student populations. *Urban Education, 37*(1), 41–58.

Brown-Chidsey, R. (2007). No more "Waiting to fail." *Educational Leadership, 65*(2), 40–46.

Bruning, R., Schraw, G., Norby, M., & Ronning, R. (2004). *Cognitive psychology and instruction* (4th ed.). Upper Saddle River, NJ: Prentice Hall.

Bryan, L. (2005). Once upon a time: A Grimm approach to character education. *Journal of Social Studies Research, 29*(1), 3–6.

Buchanan, B. (2007a). Rolling the dice. *American School Board Journal, 194*(5), 25–27.

Buchanan, B. (2007b). The drive to improve safety. *American School Board Journal, 194*(12), 27–29.

Buckley, J., Schneider, M., & Shang, Y. (2005). Fix it and they might stay: School facility quality and teacher retention in Washington, D.C. *Teachers College Record, 107*(5), 1107–1123.

Bullough, R., Jr. (1989). *First-year teacher: A case study.* New York: Teachers College Press.

Bullough, R., Jr. (1999, April). *In praise of children at-risk: Life on the other side of the teacher's desk.* Paper presented at the annual meeting of the American Educational Research Association, Montreal.

Bullough, R., Jr. (2001). *Uncertain lives: Children of promise, teachers of hope.* New York: Teachers College Press.

Bureau of International Information Programs. (2008). Free at last: The U.S. Civil Rights Movement. U.S. Department of State.

Bureau of Labor Statistics. (2009). *Occupational outlook handbook, 2008–2009 edition.* Washington, DC: U.S. Government Printing Office.

Burkam, D., Michaels, D., & Lee, V. (2007). School grade span and kindergarten learning. *Elementary School Journal, 107*(3), 287–304.

Burns, M. (2005). Looking at how students reason. *Educational Leadership, 63*(3), 26–31.

Burris, C., Heubert, J., & Levin, H. (2006). Accelerating mathematics achievement using heterogeneous grouping. *American Educational Research Journal, 43*(1), 105–136.

Burstyn, J., & Stevens, R. (2001). Involving the whole school in violence prevention. In J. Burstyn, G. Bender, R. Casella, H. Gordon, D. Guerra, K. Luschen, R. Stevens, & K. Williams (Eds.), *Preventing violence in schools: A challenge to American democracy* (pp. 139–158). Mahwah, NJ: Erlbaum.

Bushaw, W., & Gallup, A. (2008). The 40th annual Phi Delta Kappa/Gallup poll of the public's attitudes toward the public schools. *Phi Delta Kappan, 90,* 9–20.

Butin, D. (2003). Of what use is it? Multiple conceptualizations of service learning within education. *Teachers College Record, 105*(9), 1674–1692. Retrieved June 2, 2005, from http://www.tcrecord.org ID Number 11561.

Button, H., & Provenzo, E. (1989). *History of education in American culture.* New York: Holt, Rinehart & Winston.

Byrnes, J. (2003). Factors predictive of mathematics achievement in White, Black, and Hispanic 12th graders. *Journal of Educational Psychology, 95,* 316–326.

Caldas, S., & Bankston, C. (2005). *Forced to fail: The paradox of school desegregation.* Westport, CT: Praeger.

California Department of Education (CDE). (2007). *Number of English learners by language.* Retrieved November 2008 from http://dq.cde.ca.gov/dataquest/LEPbyLang1.asp?cChoice=LepbyLang1&cYear=2005-06&cLevel=State&cTopic=LC&myTimeFrame=S&submit1=Submit

California State Board of Education. (2008a). *Content standards.* Retrieved November 1, 2008, from http://www.cde.ca.gov/be/st/ss/

California State Board of Education. (2008b). *2003 – 2007 CST Released Test Questions,* p. 7. Retrieved November 1, 2008, from http://www.cde.ca.gov/ta/tg/sr/documents/rtqgr11ela.pdf

Callister, T., & Burbules, N. (2004). Just give it to me straight: A case against filtering the Internet. *Phi Delta Kappan, 85*(9), 649–655.

Camerino, C. (2003). Pay to play? *Education Week, 22*(23), 32, 34.

Campbell, P. (2007a). Edison is the symptom, NCLB is the disease. *Phi Delta Kappan, 99*(6), 438–443.

Campbell, P. (2007b). High stakes for Edison: A rejoinder to John Chubb. *Phi Delta Kappan, 88*(6), 451–454.

Carnegie Forum on Education and the Economy. (1986). *A nation prepared: Teachers for the 21st century.* Washington, DC: Author. (ERIC Document Reproduction Service No. ED268120)

Carnine, D., Silbert, J., Kame'enui, E., Tarver, S., & Jongjohann, K. (2006). *Teaching struggling and at-risk readers: A direct instruction approach.* Upper Saddle River, NJ: Merrill/Pearson.

Carnoy, M., Jacobsen, R., Mishel, L., & Rothstein, R. (2005). *The charter school dust-up: Examining the evidence on enrollment and achievement.* New York: Teachers College Press.

Carpenter, D., & Finn, C. (2006). *Playing to type.* Washington, DC: Thomas Fordham Foundation. Retrieved June 22, 2006, from www.edexcellence.net

Carr, N. (2003). The toughest job in America. Education vital signs [Supplement.]. *American School Board Journal, 190*(2), 14–19.

Carter, P. (2006). Straddling boundaries: Identity, culture, and school. *Sociology of Education, 79,* 304–328.

Casey, J., Andreson, K., Yelverton, B., & Wedeen, L. (2002). A status report on charter schools in New Mexico. *Phi Delta Kappan, 83,* 518–524.

Casey, M. (2008). *Digging out roots of cheating in high school. New York Times.* Retrieved October 2008 from www.ethicsed.org/programs/integrity-works/pdf/NYTimes_Editorial_2008-10-13.pdf

Cavanagh, S. (2004). Online teacher training courses win converts. *Education Week, 23*(23), 20.

Cavanagh, S. (2006a). Perkins bill is approved by Congress. *Education Week, 25*(44), 1, 27.

Cavanagh, S. (2006b). Possible road map seen in Dover case. *Education Week, 25*(10), 1, 10, 11.

Cavanagh, S. (2008a). American culture seen to thwart girls' math development. *Education Week, 28*(9), 10.

Cavanagh, S. (2008b). Panel calls for systematic basic approach to math. *Education Week, 27*(28), 1, 12.

Cavanagh, S. (2009). Parents schooled in learning how to help with math. *Education Week, 28*(22), 10–11.

Cech, S. (2008a). States' graduation-rate effort inches forward. *Education Week, 27*(45), 8.

Cech, S. (2008b). Testing expert sees "illusions of progress" under NCLB. *Education Week, 28*(6), 8.

Centers for Disease Control and Prevention. (2007). *Youth risk behavior surveillance—United States, 2006.* Retrieved September 2008 from http://www.cdc.gov/HealthyYouth/yrbs/

Centers for Disease Control and Prevention. (2008). *Youth risk behavior surveillance—United States, 2007.* Retrieved July 9, 2008, from http://www.cdc.gov/HealthyYouth/yrbs/

Center on Addiction and Substance Abuse. (2001). *Malignant neglect: Substance abuse and America's schools.* New York: Columbia University

Chalk v. U.S. District Court Cent. Dist. of California, 840 F.2d. 701 (9th Cir. 1988).

Chance, P. (1997). Speaking of differences. *Phi Delta Kappan, 78*(7), 506–507.

Chappuis, S., & Chappuis, J. (2007/2008). The best value in formative assessment. *Educational Leadership, 65*(4), 14–18.

Charles, C., & Senter, G. (2008). *Building classroom discipline* (9th ed.). Boston: Pearson/Allyn & Bacon.

Charner-Laird, M., Watson, D., Szczesuil, S., Kirkpatrick C., & Gordon, P. (2004, April). *Navigating the "Culture Gap": New teachers experience the urban context.* Paper presented at the annual meeting of the American Educational Research Association, San Diego, CA.

Charter Connection. (2006). *Charter school facts.* Center for Education Reform. Retrieved June 22, 2006, from http://edreform.com/charter_schools

Chekles, K. (1997). The first seven . . . and the eighth: A conversation with Howard Gardner. *Educational Leadership, 55*(1), 8–13.

Cheng, L. (1987). *Assessing Asian language performance.* Rockville, MD: Aspen.

Children's Alliance. (2007). *More than 35.5 million Americans go hungry.* Retrieved September 26, 2008, from: http://www.childrensalliance.org/4Download/hunger/Hungry%20in%20Washington%202007.pdf

Chorzempa, B., & Graham, S. (2006). Primary-grade teachers' use of within-class ability grouping in reading. *Journal of Educational Psychology, 98*(3), 529–541.

Christenson, S., & Havsy, L. (2004). Family–school–peer relationships: Significance for social, emotional, and academic learning. In J. Zins, R. Weissberg, M. Wang, & H. Walberg (Eds.), *Building academic success on social and emotional learning* (pp. 59–75). New York: Teachers College Press.

Christie, K. (2005). Providing the facts. *Phi Delta Kappan, 86*(5), 341–342.

Chubb, J. (2007). Confluence is a cure: A reply to "Edison is the symptom, NCLB is the disease." *Phi Delta Kappan, 88*(6), 444–450.

Ciofalo, J., & Wylie, E. (2006, January 10). Using diagnostic classroom assessment: One question at a time. *Teachers College Record.* Retrieved June 20, 2007, from http://www.tcrecord.org/Content.asp.?ContentID=12285

Clandinin, J., & Connelly, M. (1996). Teacher as curriculum maker. In P. Jackson (Ed.), *Handbook of research on curriculum* (pp. 363–401). New York: Macmillan.

Clarke, A. (2006). The nature and substance of cooperating teacher reflection. *Teaching and Teacher Education, 22,* 910–921.

Clement, M. (2008). Improving teacher selection with behavior-based interviewing. *Principal, 87*(3), 44–47.

Cochran-Smith, M. (2005). The new teacher education: For better or for worse? *Educational Researcher, 34*(6), 1–17.

Cohen, J. (2006). Social, emotional, ethical, and academic education: Creating a climate for learning, participation in democracy, and well-being. *Harvard Educational Review, 76*(2), 201–237.

Coleman, J. (2005, November 15). California Latinos to reach parity with Anglos by 2010. *Salt Lake Tribune,* p. C5.

Coleman, J., Campbell, E., Hobson, D., McPortland, J., Mood, A., Weinfield, F., & York, R. (1966). *Equality of educational opportunity.* Washington, DC: U.S. Department of Health, Education and Welfare.

Colgan, C. (2004). The controversy over charter school scores reinforces a partisan split. *The American School Board Journal, 191*(10), 6–8.

Colgan, C. (2005). The new look of school safety. *The American School Board Journal, 192*(3), 11–13.

Comer, J., Joyner, E., & Ben-Avie, M. (Eds.) (2004). *Six pathways to healthy child development and academic success.* Thousand Oaks, CA: Corwin Press.

Commonwealth of Pennsylvania v. Douglass, 588 A.2d 53 (Pa. Super. Ct. 1991).

Compayre, G. (1888). *History of pedagogy* (W. Payne, Trans.). Boston: Heath.

Conant, J. (1959). *The American high school.* New York: McGraw-Hill.

Connelly, F. (Ed.) (2008). *Sage handbook of curriculum and instruction.* Los Angeles: Sage.

Conoley, J., & Goldstein, A. (2004). *School violence intervention: A practical handbook.* New York: Guilford Press.

Conroy, J., Davis, R., & Enslin, P. (2008). Philosophy as a basis for policy and practice: What confidence can we have in philosophical analysis and argument? *Journal of Philosophy of Education, 42,* 165–182.

Cook, G. (2006). What's a teacher worth? Houston joins the push for merit pay. *The American School Board Journal, 193*(3), 4–6.

Cooper, D., & Snell, J. (2003). Bullying—not just a kid thing. *Educational Leadership, 60*(6), 22–25.

Cooper, H., Robinson, J., & Patall, E. (2006). Does homework improve academic achievement? A synthesis of research, 1987–2003. *Review of Educational Research, 76,* 1–62.

Cooper, J. (2007). Strengthening the case of community-based learning in teacher education. *Journal of Teacher Education, 58*(3), 245–255.

Cooperman, S. (2003). A new order of things. *Education Week, 22*(38), 30, 32.

Corcoran, C., Dershimer, E., & Tichenor, M. (2004). A teacher's guide to alternative assessment: Taking the first steps. *The Clearing House, 77*(5), 213–216.

Cornelius, L. (2002, April). *Legal implications of school violence.* Paper presented at the anuual meeting of the American Educational Research Association, New Orleans, LA.

Corporation for Public Broadcasting. (2003). *Connected to the future: A report on children's Internet use from the Corporation for Public Broadcasting.* Retrieved February 2004 from http://www.cpb.org/Ed/resources/connected

Coughlin, E. (1996, February 16). Not out of Africa. *Chronicle of Higher Education,* pp. A6–A7.

Cowan, R., & Sheridan, S. (2003). Investigating the acceptability of behavioral interventions in applied conjoint behavioral consultation: Moving from analog conditions to naturalistic settings. *School Psychology Quarterly, 18,* 1–21.

Crawford, J. (2007). The decline of bilingual education: How to reverse a troubling trend. *International Multilingual Research Journal, 2*(1), 33–37.

Crosnoe, R. (2006, January). The connection between academic failure and adolescent drinking in secondary school. *Sociology of Education, 79,* 44–60.

Cross, T. (2005). *The social and emotional lives of gifted kids: Understanding and guiding their development.* Austin, TX: Prufrock Press.

Cuban, L. (1993). *How teachers taught: Constancy and change in American classrooms: 1890 – 1980* (2nd ed.). New York: Teachers College Press.

Cuban, L. (1996). Curriculum stability and change. In P. Jackson (Ed.), *Handbook of research on curriculum* (pp. 216–247). New York: Macmillan.

Cuban, L. (2003). *Why is it so hard to get good schools?* New York: Teachers College Press.

Cuban, L. (2004). *The blackboard and the bottom line: Why schools can't be businesses.* Cambridge, MA: Harvard University Press.

Cuban, L. (2008). The turnstile superintendency? *Education Week, 28*(1), 26–27.

Cushman, K. (2003). *Fires in the bathroom: Advice for teachers from high school students.* New York: The New Press.

Cushman, K. (2006). Help us care enough to learn. *Educational Leadership, 63*(5), 34–37.

Dalton, B., Sable, J., & Hoffman, L. (2006). *Characteristics of the 100 largest public elementary and secondary school districts in the United States: 2003–2004* (NCES 2006-329). Washington, DC: U.S. Department of Education, National Center for Education Statistics.

Dance, L. J. (2002). *Tough fronts: The impact of street culture on schooling.* New York: Routledge Falmer.

Darden, E. (2007a). A slippery slope. *American School Board Journal, 194*(4), 56–57.

Darden, E. (2007b). Pause and ponder. *American School Board Journal, 195*(5), 48–49.

Darden, E. (2008a). Policy, the law, and you. *American School Board Journal, 195*(4), 54–55.

Darden, E. (2008b). What not to wear. *American School Board Journal, 195*(1), 36–37.

Darling-Hammond, L. (2000). How teacher education matters. *Journal of Teacher Education, 51,* 166–173.

Darling-Hammond, L., & Baratz-Snowdon, J. (Eds.). (2005). *A good teacher in every classroom: Preparing the highly qualified teachers our children deserve.* San Francisco: Jossey-Bass.

Darling-Hammond, L., Berry, B., & Thoreson, A. (2001). Does teacher certification matter? Evaluating the evidence. *Educational Evaluation and Policy Analysis, 23,* 57–77.

Darling-Hammond, L., & Bransford, J. (Eds.). (2005). *Preparing teachers for a changing world: What teachers should learn and be able to do.* San Francisco: Jossey-Bass.

Darling-Hammond, L., Chung, R., & Frelow, F. (2002). Variation in teacher preparation: How well do different pathways prepare teachers to teach? *Journal of Teacher Education, 53,* 286–302.

Darling-Hammond, L., & Hammerness, K. (2005). The design of teacher education programs. In L. Darling-Hammond & J. Bransford (Eds.), *Preparing teachers for a changing world: What teachers should learn and be able to do* (pp. 390–441). San Francisco: Jossey-Bass.

Datnow, A., Hubbard, L., & Conchas, G. (2001). How context mediates policy: The implementation of single gender public schooling in California. *Teachers College Record, 103,* 184–206.

Davis, E., Petish, D., & Smithey, J. (2006). Challenges new science teachers face. *Review of Educational Research, 76*(4), 607–651.

Davis, G., & Rimm, S. (2004). *Education of the gifted and talented* (5th ed.). Boston: Allyn & Bacon.

Davis, M. (2003). Title IX panel deadlocks on critical change. *Education Week, 22*(21), 24–25.

Davis, M. (2006). Drug-free-schools grants targeted by Bush. *Education Week, 25*(25), 21, 23.

Davis, M. (2009). Breaking away from tradition. *Education Week, 28*(26), 8–9.

DeAngelis, T. (2004). Size-based discrimination may be hardest on children. *Monitor on Psychology, 35*(1), 62.

DeBray, E., McDermott, K., & Wohlstetter, P. (2005). Introduction to the special issue on federalism reconsidered: The case of No Child Left Behind Act. *Peabody Journal of Education, 80*(2), 1–18.

Delisle, J. (1984). *Gifted children speak out.* New York: Walker.

Delp, V. (2007). *4 reasons why paying students for good grades might work.* Retrieved January 16, 2009, from http://education.families.com/blog/4-reasons-why-paying-students-for-good-grades-might-work

DeMeulenaere, E. (2001, April). *Constructing reinventions: Black and Latino students negotiating the transformation of their academic identities and school performance.* Paper presented at the annual meeting of the American Educational Research Association, Seattle, WA.

DeMitchele, T. (2007). School uniforms: There is no free lunch. *Teachers College Record.* Retrieved February 13, 2007, from http://www.tcrecord.org

Denig, S. J. (2003, April). *A proposed relationship between multiple intelligences and learning styles.* Paper presented at the annual meeting of the American Educational Research Association, Chicago.

Devlin-Scherer, R., Burroughs, G., Daly, J., & McCarten, W. (2007). The value of the teacher work sample for improving instruction and program. *Action in Teacher Education, 29*(1), 51–60.

Dewey, J. (1902). *The child and the curriculum.* Chicago: University of Chicago Press.

Dewey, J. (1906). *Democracy and education.* New York: Macmillan.

Dewey, J. (1923). *The school and society.* Chicago: University of Chicago Press.

Dewey, J. (1938). *Experience and education.* New York: Macmillan.

Dickinson, G., Holifield, M., Holifield, G., & Creer, D. (2000). Elementary magnet school students' interracial interaction choices. *Journal of Educational Research, 93,* 391–394.

Dickson, S. (2004). Tracking concept mastery using a biology portfolio. *The American Biology Teacher, 66*(9), 628–634.

Dillon, N. (2007a). The merit scale. *American School Board Journal, 195*(4), 28–30.

Dillon, N. (2007b). The trail to progress. *American School Board Journal, 194*(12), 21–24.

Dillon, S. (2006, July 25). Most states fail demands set out in education law. *New York Times,* p. A14.

Dillon, S. (2007, June 18). Long reviled, merit pay gains among teachers. *New York Times.* Retrieved April 2009 from http://www.nytimes.com/2007/06/18/education/18pay.html

Dillon, S. (2008a). *Hard times hitting students and schools. New York Times.* Retrieved September 1, 2008, from http://www.nytimes.com/2008/09/01/education/01school.html?th&emc=th

Dillon, S. (2008b, November 13). School chief takes on tenure, and stirs a fight. *New York Times,* pp. A1, A19.

Dillon, S. (2008c, December 16). Schools chief from Chicago is cabinet pick. *New York Times.* Retrieved February 2, 2009, from http://www.nytimes.com/2008/12/16/us/politics/16educ.html

Dillon, S. (2008d, March 20). States' data obscure how few finish high school. *New York Times.* Retrieved March 2008 from http://www.nytimes.com/2008/03/20/education/20graduation.html

Dillion, S. (2009a, June 22). Education chief to warn advocates that inferior charter schools imperil movement. *New York Times,* p. A10.

Dillon, S. (2009b, April 7). Report envisions shortage of teachers as retirements escalate. *New York Times.* Retrieved April 2009 from http://www.nytimes.com/2009/04/07/education/07teacher.html?em

Dimick, A., & Apple, M. (2005). Texas and the politics of abstinence-only textbooks. *Teachers College Record.* Retrieved June 29, 2005, from http://www.tcrecord.org ID Number 11855.

Doe v. Renfrow, 635 F.2d 582 (7th Cir. 1980).

Doll, B., Zucher, S., & Brehm, K. (2004). *Resilient classrooms: Creating healthy environments for learning.* New York: Guilford Press.

Dounay, J. (2006). Looking back, looking forward. *Phi Delta Kappan, 88*(4), 261–262.

Doyle, D. (1999). De facto national standards. *Education Week, 18*(42), 56, 36.

Doyle, W. (2006). Ecological approaches to classroom management. In C. M. Evertson & C. S. Weinstein (Eds.), *Handbook of classroom management: Research, practice, and contemporary issues* (pp. 97–125). Mahwah, NJ: Erlbaum.

Drevitch, G. (2006). Merit pay: Good for teachers? *Instructor, 115*(5), 21–23.

Dulude-Lay, C. (2000). *The confounding effect of the dimensions of classroom life on the narratives of student teachers.* Unpublished manuscript, University of Utah, Salt Lake City.

Dunn, R., & Dunn, K. (1978). *Teaching students through their individual learning styles.* Reston, VA: Reston Publishing.

Dunn, R., & Dunn, K. (1987). Dispelling outmoded beliefs about student learning. *Educational Leadership, 44*(6), 55–62.

Durst, A. (2005). "The union of intellectual freedom and cooperation": Learning from the University of Chicago's Laboratory School community, 1896–1904. *Teachers College Record, 107*(5), 958–984.

Echevarria, J., & Graves, A. (2007). *Sheltered content instruction* (3rd ed.). Boston: Allyn & Bacon.

Echevarria, J., Powers, K., & Short, D. (2006). School reform and standards-based education: A model for English-language learners. *Journal of Educational Research, 99*(4), 195–211.

Eckholm, E. (2009, March 11). As jobs vanish, motel rooms become home. *New York Times,* pp. A1, A16.

Economic Policy Institute. (2005). *Wage trends.* Retrieved July 14, 2006, from http://www.epinet.org

Education Leaders Council. (2001). *Weekly policy update, October 5, 2001.* Retrieved September 2004 from http://www.educationleaders.org.elc/issues/update/ELC_Weekly_Policy_Update_2001-10-05.pdf

Education Vital Signs. (2005, February). Poverty. *American School Board Journal Supplement,* pp. 22–23.

Education Vital Signs. (2006, February). Student health. *American School Board Journal Supplement,* pp. 12–13.

Educational Testing Service. (2008). *The Praxis Series™: Principles of Learning and Teaching: Grades 7–12 (0524).* Retrieved July 2008 from http://www.ets.org/Media/Tests/PRAXIS/pdf/0524.pdf

Eggen, P. (1998, April). *A comparison of urban middle school teachers' classroom practices and their expressed beliefs about learning and effective instruction.* Paper presented at the annual meeting of the American Educational Research Association, San Diego.

Eggen, P., & Kauchak, D. (2006). *Strategies and models for teachers: Teaching content and thinking skills* (5th ed.). Boston: Allyn & Bacon.

Eggen, P., & Kauchak, D. (2007). *Educational psychology: Windows on classrooms* (7th ed.). Upper Saddle River, NJ: Merrill/Prentice Hall.

Eggen, P., & Kauchak, D. (2010). *Educational psychology: Windows on classrooms* (8th ed.). Upper Saddle River, NJ: Merrill/Prentice Hall.

Ehlenberger, K. (2001/2002). The right to search students. *Educational Leadership, 59*(4), 31–35.

Eide, E. R., & Goldhaber, D. D. (2005). Grade retention: What are the costs and benefits? *Journal of Education Finance, 31*(2), 195–214.

Eisenberg, N., Fabes, R., & Spinrad, T. (2006). Prosocial development. In N. Eisenberg (Vol. Ed.), *Handbook of child psychology: Vol. 3, Social, emotional, and personality development* (6th ed., pp. 646–718). Hoboken, NJ: Wiley.

Eisenman, L. (2007). Self-determination interventions: Building a foundation for school completion. *Remedial and Special Education, 28,* 2–8.

Eisner, E. (1993). *The educational imagination: On the design and evaluation of school programs* (3rd ed.). New York: Macmillan.

Eisner, E. (2003). Questionable assumptions about schooling. *Phi Delta Kappan, 84,* 648–657.

Elias, M., & Schwab, Y. (2006). From compliance to responsibility: Social and emotional learning and classroom management. In C. M. Evertson & C. S. Weinstein (Eds.), *Handbook of classroom management: Research, practice, and contemporary issues* (pp. 309–341). Mahwah, NJ: Erlbaum.

Emmer, E., Evertson, C., & Worsham, M. (2009). *Classroom management for secondary teachers* (8th ed.). Boston: Allyn & Bacon.

Engel, B., & Martin, A. (Eds.). (2005). *Holding values: What we mean by progressive education.* Portsmouth, NH: Heinemann.

Engle v. Vitale, 370 U.S. 421 (1962).

Essex, N. (2006). *A teacher's pocket guide to school law.* Boston: Allyn & Bacon.

Evans, C., Kirby, U., & Fabrigar, L. (2003). Approaches to learning, need for cognition, and strategic flexibility among university students. *The British Journal of Educational Psychology, 73,* 507–528.

Evans, G. W., & English, K. (2002). The environment of poverty: Multiple stressor exposure, psychophysiological stress, and socio-emotional adjustment. *Child Development, 73,* 1238–1248.

Evertson, C., Emmer, E., & Worsham, M. (2009). *Classroom management for elementary teachers* (8th ed.). Boston: Allyn & Bacon.

Evertson, C., & Smithey, M. (2000). Mentoring effects on protégés' classroom practice: An experimental field study. *Journal of Educational Research, 93,* 294–304.

Evertson, C., & Weinstein, C. (2006). Classroom management as a field of inquiry. In C. M. Evertson & C. S. Weinstein (Eds.), *Handbook of classroom management: Research, practice, and contemporary issues* (pp. 3–15). Mahwah, NJ: Erlbaum.

Fagen v. Summers, 498 P.2d 1227 (Wyo. 1972).

Fairchild, T. (2006). Race and class: Separate and not equal. *Education Week, 26*(3), 35, 36.

Faject, W., Bello, M., & Leftwich, S. A. (2005). Pre-service teachers' perceptions in beginning education classes. *Teaching and Teacher Education, 21*(6), 717–727.

Farkas, R. (2003). Effects of traditional versus learning-styles instructional methods on middle school students. *Journal of Educational Research, 97*(1), 42–51.

Fass, S., & Cauthen, K. (2007). *Who are America's poor children? The official story.* New York: Columbus University, Mailman School of Public Health.

Fast, J. (2008) *Ceremonial violence: A psychological explanation of school shootings.* New York: Overlook Press.

Federal Interagency Forum on Child and Family Statistics. (2008). *American's children: Key national indicators of well-being, 2008.* Retrieved September 19, 2008, from http://www.childstats.gov/americaschildren/index.asp

Federation of Tax Administrators. (2006). *State comparisons.* Retrieved March 21, 2006, from http://www.taxadmin.org

Feiman-Nemser, S. (2001). From preparation to practice: Designing a continuum to strengthen and sustain teaching. *Teachers College Record, 103,* 1013–1055.

Feinberg, W., & Soltis, J. (2004). *School and society* (4th ed.). New York: Teachers College Press.

Feldman, A., & Matjasko, J. (2005). The role of school-based extracurricular activities in adolescent development: A comprehensive review and future directions. *Review of Educational Research, 75*(2), 159–210.

Feldman, J., López, L., & Simon, K. (2006). *Choosing small: The essential guide to successful high school conversion.* San Francisco: Jossey-Bass.

Feller, B. (2006, August 17). Support for new high school graduation tests is waning, study says. *Salt Lake Tribune,* p. A4.

Ferguson, J. (2002). Vouchers—an illusion of choice. *American School Board Journal, 189*(1), 42–45, 51.

Ferraro, P., & Weinreich, J. (2006). Protected in the classroom. *American School Board Journal, 193*(11), 40–42.

Ferrero, D. (2005). Does "research based" mean "value neutral"? *Phi Delta Kappan, 86*(6), 425–432.

Fertig, B. (2009). Choosing the direction of New York City Schools. *The New Yorker.* Retrieved February 21, 2009, from http://www.wnyc.org/news/articles/123303

Fine, L. (2002). Writing takes a digital turn for special-needs students. *Education Week, 21*(20), 8.

Finn, C., & Petrilli, M. (2009). Stimulating a race to the top. *Education Week, 28*(24), 31.

Finn, J., Gerber, S., & Boyd-Zaharias, J. (2005). Small classes in the early grades, academic achievement, and graduating from high school. *Journal of Educational Psychology, 97*(2), 214–223.

Finn, K., Willert, H., & Marable, M. (2003). Substance use in schools. *Educational Leadership, 60*(6), 80–85.

First Amendment Center. (1999). *The Bible and public schools: A First Amendment guide.* Nashville, TN: Author. Retrieved February 2004 from http://www.freedomforum.org/publications/first/BibleAndPublicSchools/bibleguide_reprint.pdf

Fischer, L., Schimmel, D., & Kelly, C. (2003). *Teachers and the law* (6th ed.). New York: Longman.

Fischer, L., Schimmel, D., & Stellman, L. (2006). *Teachers and the law* (7th ed.). New York: Longman.

Fisher, D. (2006). Keeping adolescents "alive and kickin' it": Addressing suicide in schools. *Phi Delta Kappan, 87*(10), 784–786.

Fiske, E., & Ladd, H. (2000). A distant laboratory. *Education Week, 19*(56), 38.

Flanagan, A., & Grissmer, D. (2002). The role of federal resources in closing the achievement gap. In J. Chubb & T. Loveless (Eds.), *Bridging the achievement gap* (pp. 199–226). Washington, DC: Brookings Institution Press.

Flanagan, A., & Murray, S. (2004). A decade of reform: The impact of school reform in Kentucky. In J. Yinger (Ed.), *Helping children left behind* (pp. 195–214). Cambridge, MA: MIT Press.

Flanagan, K., & Park, J. (2005). *American Indian and Alaska Native children: Findings from the base year of the early childhood longitudinal study, Birth Cohort (ECLS-B).* Washington, DC: National Center for Education Statistics.

Flanigan, R. (2003). A challenging year for schools. Education Vital Signs [Supplement]. *American School Board Journal, 190*(2), 21–25.

Fleischfresser v. Directors of School District No. 200, 15 F.3d 680 (7th Cir. 1994).

Fleming, W. (2006). Myths and stereotypes about Native Americans. *Phi Delta Kappan, 88*(3), 213–216.

Fletcher, E., & Hoffman, J. (2006). *Guiding children's behavior: Developmental discipline in the classroom.* New York: Teachers College Press.

Florida Department of Education. (2007). *Sunshine state standards.* Retrieved November 1, 2008, from: http://etc.usf.edu/flstandards/sss/index.html

Florida Department of Education. (2008). *Florida Comprehensive Assessment Test.* Retrieved November 1, 2008, from: http://fcat.fldoe.org/fcatsmpl.asp

Foley, M. (2008). *Australia to test web filter to block banned content. New York Times.* Retrieved December 2008 from www.nytimes.com/2008/12/14/world/asia/14australia.html

Fong, T. (2007). *The contemporary Asian American experience: Beyond the model minority* (3rd ed.). Upper Saddle River, NJ: Prentice Hall.

Forcier, R., & Descy, D. (2005). *The computer as an educational tool: Productivity and problem solving* (4th ed.). Upper Saddle River, NJ: Merrill/Prentice Hall.

Fossey, R., & Russo, C. (2008). Teachers' First Amendment rights are shrinking in the wake of a 2006 Supreme Court decision: That can't be good. *Teachers College Record.* Retrieved April 2008 from http://www.tcrecord.org ID Number: 14914.

Fowler, R. C. (2008). The heralded rise and neglected fall of the Massachusetts signing bonus. *Phi Delta Kappan, 89*(5), 380–385.

Francis, B., & Skelton, C. (2005). *Reassessing gender and achievement.* New York: Routledge Falmer.

Frankenberg, E., & Lee, C. (2003). *Charter schools and race: A lost opportunity for integrated education.* Retrieved February 2004 from Harvard University, Civil Rights Project Website: http://www.civilrightsproject.harvard.edu/research/deseg/Charter_Schools03.pdf

Fraser, J. (2006). *Preparing America's teachers: A history.* New York: Teachers College Press.

Fredericks, J. A., & Eccles, J. S. (2006). Is extracurricular participation associated with beneficial outcomes? Concurrent and longitudinal relations. *Developmental Psychology, 42*(4), 698–713.

Freedman, M. (2004). A tale of plagiarism and a new paradigm. *Phi Delta Kappan, 85*(7), 545–548.

Freiberg, J. (1999a). Consistency management and cooperative discipline. In J. Freiberg (Ed.), *Beyond behaviorism: Changing the classroom management paradigm* (pp. 75–97). Boston: Allyn & Bacon.

Freiberg, J. (1999b). Sustaining the paradigm. In J. Freiberg (Ed.), *Beyond behaviorism: Changing the classroom management paradigm* (pp. 164–173). Boston: Allyn & Bacon.

Freire, P. (1989). *Pedagogy of the oppressed.* New York: Continuum Press.

French, D. (2003). A new vision of authentic assessment to overcome the flaws in high-stakes testing. *Middle School Journal, 35*(1), 14–23.

Frey, B., & Schmitt, V. (2005, April). *Teachers' classroom assessment practices.* Paper presented at the annual meeting of the American Educational Research Association, Montreal.

Friedman, T. (2009, April 21). Swimming without a suit *New York. Times,* p. A20.

Friess, S. (2009, April 13). A small Nevada town fears a damaging silence from its school bell soon. *New York Times,* p. A13.

Fulton, B. (2008, March 19). Adolescents dodge the mayhem of junior high. *Salt Lake Tribune,* pp. B1, 2.

Furlan, C. (1999). States tackle Internet-filter rules for schools. *Education Week, 17*(43), 22, 28.

Furlan, C. (2000). Satellite broadcasts seek to enliven study of history. *Education Week, 19*(26), 8.

Gabrieli, C., & Goldstein, W. (2008). *Time to learn: How a new school schedule is making smarter kids, happier parents, and safer neighborhoods.* New York: Wiley.

Galley, M. (2003). Despite concerns, online elementary schools grow. *Education Week, 22*(16), 1, 12.

Galley, M. (2004). Court blocks school ban on weapons images. *Education Week, 23*(16), 6.

Garcia, E. (2005, April). *A test in English is a test of English: Assessment's new role in educational equity.* Paper presented at the annual meeting of the American Educational Research Association, Montreal.

Garcia, R. (2006). Language, culture, and education. In J. Banks, *Cultural diversity and education* (5th ed., pp. 266–291). Boston: Allyn & Bacon.

Gardner, H. (1983). *Frames of mind: The theory of multiple intelligences.* New York: Basic Books.

Gardner, H. (2008). E pluribus . . . a tale of three systems. *Education Week, 27*(34), 40.

Gardner, H., & Hatch, T. (1989). Multiple intelligences go to school. *Educational Researcher, 18*(8), 4–10.

Gardner, H., & Moran, S. (2006). The science of multiple intelligences theory: A response to Lynn Waterhouse. *Educational Psychology, 41*(4), 227–232.

Gay, G. (2005). Politics of multicultural teacher education. *Journal of Teacher Education, 56*(3), 221–228.

Gay, G. (2006). Connections between classroom management and culturally responsive teaching. In C. Evertson & C. Weinstein (Eds.), *Handbook of classroom management: Research, practice, and contemporary issues* (pp. 343–370). Mahwah, NJ: Erlbaum.

Gee, J. (2005). *Learning by design: Games as learning machines.* Retrieved April 23, 2006, from http://labweb.education.wisc.edu/room130/papers.htm

Gehring, J. (2002a). Benefit of Illinois credit misses needy, study says. *Education Week, 22*(8), 11.

Gehring, J. (2002b). Vouchers battles head to state capitols. *Education Week, 21*(42), 1, 24, 25.

Gewertz, C. (2000). Wisconsin study finds benefits in classes of 15 or fewer students. *Education Week, 19*(31), 10.

Gewertz, C. (2002). Edison buffeted by probe, loss of contracts. *Education Week, 22*(1), 3.

Gewertz, C. (2003). Vallas calls for cuts to private companies. *Education Week, 22*(29), 3.

Gewertz, C. (2006a). Groups accuse Fla. districts of harsh discipline approaches. *Education Week, 25*(34), 7.

Gewertz, C. (2006b). H.S. dropouts say lack of motivation top reason to quit. *Education Week, 25*(26), 1, 14.

Gewertz, C. (2006c). Race, gender, and the superintendency. *Education Week, 25*(24), 1, 22, 24.

Gewertz, C. (2008a). Consensus on learning time builds. *Education Week, 28*(5), 14–17.

Gewertz, C. (2008b). Districts see rising numbers of homeless students. *Education Week, 28*(11), 7.

Gibboney, R. (2006). Intelligence by design: Thorndike versus Dewey. *Phi Delta Kappan, 88*(2), 170–172.

Gilbert, L. (2005). What helps beginning teachers? *Educational Leadership, 62*(8), 36–39.

Gill, B. (2005). School choice and integration. In J. Betts & T. Loveless (Eds.), *Getting choice right: Ensuring equity and efficiency in education policy* (pp. 130–145). Washington, DC: Brookings Institution Press.

Gill, S., McLean, M., & Courville, M. (2004). A tale of two professions. *Phi Delta Kappan, 86*(1), 63–64.

Gilman, D., & Kiger, S. (2003). Should we try to keep class sizes small? *Educational Leadership, 60*(7), 80–85.

Gimbel, P. (2008). Helping new teachers reflect. *Principal Leadership (High School ed.), 8*, 6–8.

Ginsberg, A., Shapiro, J., & Brown, S. (2004). *Gender in urban education: Strategies for student achievement.* Portsmouth, NH: Heinemann.

Ginsberg, M. (2007). Lesson at the kitchen table. *Educational Leadership, 64*(6), 56–60.

Ginsberg, M., & Murphy, D. (2002). How walkthroughs open doors. *Educational Leadership, 59*(8), 34–36.

Girard, K. (2005). Lost in translation. *Edutopia, 1*(8), 36–38.

Gladding, M. (2007). *A guide to ethical conduct for the helping professions* (2nd ed.). Upper Saddle River, NJ: Merrill/Prentice Hall.

Glanzer, P. (2004). In defense of Harry . . . but not his defenders: Beyond censorship to justice. *English Journal, 93*(4), 58–63.

Glanzer, P. (2005). Moving beyond censorship: What will educators do if a controversy over "His Dark Materials" erupts? *Phi Delta Kappan, 87*(2), 166–168.

Glasson, T. (2007). The imperial origins of the king's church in early America, 1607–1783. *The William and Mary Quarterly, 64*, 859–861.

Global Integrity Commons. (2008). *Internet censorship: A comparative study.* Accessed January 25, 2009, from http://commons.globalintegrity.org/2008/02/internet-censorship-comparative-study.html

Goddard, R., Hoy, W., & Hoy, A. (2004). Collective efficacy beliefs: Theoretical developments, empirical evidence, and future directions. *Educational Researcher, 33*(3), 3–13.

Goldin, C., & Katz, L. (2008). *The race between education and technology.* Cambridge, MA: Harvard University Press.

Goldstein, D. (2006, May 6). Upset over anthem translation? Change your tune; it's old news. *Salt Lake Tribune,* pp. A1, A4.

Goldstein, R. (2004). Who are our urban students and what makes them so different? In S. R. Steinberg & J. L. Kincheloe (Eds.), *19 urban questions: Teaching in the city* (pp. 41–51). New York: Peter Lang.

Gollnick, D., & Chinn, P. (2009). *Multicultural education in a pluralistic society* (8th ed.). Upper Saddle River, NJ: Merrill/Prentice Hall.

Gonzales, P., Guzman, J. C., Partelow, L., Pahlke, E., Jocelyn, L., Kastberg, D., & Williams, T. (2004). *Highlights from the trends in international mathematics and science study (TIMSS) 2003 (NCES 2005–2005).* U.S. Department of Education. Washington, DC: National Center for Educational Statistics.

Good, T., & Brophy, J. (2008). *Looking in classrooms* (10th ed.). Boston: Allyn & Bacon.

Goodlad, J. (1984). *A place called school.* New York: McGraw-Hill.

Goodnough, A. (2007, August 24). Hebrew charter school spurs Florida church-state dispute. *New York Times,* pp. A1, A17.

Gootman, E. (2007). Taking middle schoolers out of the middle. *New York Times.* Retrieved January 2007 from www.nytimes.com/2007/01/22/education/22middle.html?pagewanted=2&th&emc=th

Gootman, E., & Gebelof, R. (2008, June 19). Poor students lose ground in city's gifted programs. *New York Times,* p. A25.

Gordon, E. (2007). A context for the birth of "The Journal of Negro Education." *The Journal of Negro Education, 76,* 198–203.

Gordon, R. (2006). The federalism debate: Why the idea of national education standards is crossing party lines. *Education Week, 25*(27), 48, 35.

Gordon, R., Della Piana, L., & Keleher, T. (2001). Zero tolerance: A basic racial report card. In W. Ayers, B. Dohrn, & R. Ayers (Eds.), *Zero tolerance* (pp. 165–175). New York: New Press.

Gorski, P. (2008). Peddling poverty for profit: Elements of oppression in Ruby Payne's framework. *Equity & Excellence in Education, 41*(1), 130–148.

Goyette, K. (2008). Race, social background, and school choice options. *Equity & Excellence in Education, 4*(1), 114–129.

Grady, M. (2007, May 7). What districts can do to support high quality education. *Teachers College Record.* Retrieved September 2007 from http://www.tcrecord.org ID#14474.

Grant, L. W. (2006). Persistence and self-efficacy: A key to understanding teacher turnover. *The Delta Kappa Gamma Bulletin, 72*(2), 50–54.

Gratz, D. (2009). Purpose and performance in teacher performance pay. *Education Week, 28*(24), 40.

Graue, E. (2005). Theorizing and describing preservice teachers' image of families and schooling. *Teachers College Record, 107*(1), 157–185.

Green, C., Walker, J., Hoover-Dempsey, K., & Sandler, H. (2007). Parents' motivations for involvement in children's education: An empirical test of a theoretical model of parental involvement. *Journal of Educational Psychology, 99,* 532–544.

Greene, J. (2000). Why school choice can promote integration. *Education Week, 19*(31), 72, 52.

Greene, J. P., & Winters, M. A. (2006). Getting ahead by staying behind: An evaluation of Florida's program to end social promotion. *Education Next, 6*(2), 65–69.

Greifner, L. (2006). National PTA aims to restore time for recess. *Education Week, 25*(28), 12.

Griffith, J. (2002). A multilevel analysis of the relation of school learning and social environments to minority achievement in public elementary schools. *The Elementary School Journal, 102,* 349–366.

Gronke, A. (2009). Plugged-in parents. *Edutopia, 5*(1), 16.

Gronlund, N. (2004). *Writing instructional objectives for teaching and assessment* (7th ed.). Upper Saddle River, NJ: Merrill/Pearson.

Gross, J. (2008). Lack of supervision noted in deaths of homeschooled. *New York Times.* Retrieved January 2008 from www.nytimes.com/2008/01/12/us/12bodies.html

Grunbaum, J., Kann, L., Kinchen, S., Williams, B., Ross, J., Lowry, R., & Kolbe, L. (2002). Youth risk behavior surveillance: United States, 2001. *Morbidity and Mortality Weekly Report, 51* (SS-4), 1–64.

Guarino, C., Santibañez, L., & Daley, G. (2006). Teacher recruitment and retention: A review of the recent empirical literature. *Review of Educational Research, 76*(2), 173–208.

Guglielmi, R. (2008). Native language proficiency, English literacy, academic achievement, and occupational attainment in limited-English-proficient students: A latent growth modeling perspective. *Journal of Educational Psychology, 100*(2), 322–342.

Gurian, M., & Stevens, K. (2007). *The minds of boys: Saving our sons from falling behind in school and life.* San Francisco: Jossey-Bass.

Guskey, T. (2007/2008). The rest of the story. *Educational Leadership, 65*(4), 28–35.

Gutek, G. L. (2005). *Historical and philosophical foundations of education: A biographical introduction.* Upper Saddle River, NJ: Pearson/Prentice Hall.

Guthrie, J., & Schuermann, P. (2008). The question of performance pay. *Education Week, 28*(10), 24–26.

Gutiérrez, R. (2002). Beyond essentialism: The complexity in teaching mathematics to Latino students. *American Educational Research Journal, 39,* 1047–1088.

Haas, M. (2005). Teaching methods for secondary algebra: A meta-analysis of findings. *NASSP Bulletin, 89*(642), 24–46.

Halford, J. (1997). Focusing the debate on student achievement. *Infobrief, 10.* Retrieved July 16, 2009, from http://www.ascd.org/publications/newsletters/infobrief/sept97/num10/toc.aspx

Hall, W. (2008). Baltimore to open schools for grades 6–12. *Education Week, 27*(32), 9.

Hallahan, D., & Kauffman, J. (2009). *Exceptional children* (11th ed.). Needham Heights, MA: Allyn & Bacon.

Hallinan, M. (2008). Teacher influences on students' attachment to school. *Sociology of Education, 81,* 271–283.

Hamilton, L., Berends, M., & Stecher, B. (2005). *Teachers's response to standards-based accountability.* Paper presented at the annual meeting of the American Educational Research Association, Montreal.

Hammack, F. (Ed.). (2004). *The comprehensive high school today.* New York: Teachers College Press.

Hammack, F. (2005). High school reform, again. *Teachers College Record.* Retrieved August 2005 from http://www.tcrecord.org ID Number 11853.

Hammerness, K., Darling-Hammond, L., & Bransford, J. (2005). How teachers learn and develop. In L. Darling-Hammond & J. Bransford (Eds.), *Preparing teachers for a changing world: What teachers should learn and be able to do* (pp. 358–389). San Francisco: Jossey-Bass.

Hansen, D. (Ed.). (2007). *John Dewey and our educational prospect: A critical engagement with Dewey's Democracy and Education.* Albany: State University of New York Press.

Hanushek, E. (1996). A more complete picture of school resource policies. *Review of Educational Research, 66,* 397–410.

Hanushek, E. (Ed.). (2006). *Courting failure: How school finance lawsuits exploit judges' good intentions and harm our children.* Stanford: Hoover Institution Press.

Hardman, M., Drew, C., & Egan, W. (2006). *Human exceptionality: IDEA 2004 update edition* (8th ed.). Boston: Allyn & Bacon.

Hardman, M., Drew, C., & Egan, W. (2008). *Human exceptionality* (9th ed.). Needham Heights, MA: Allyn & Bacon.

Hardy, L. (2005). A place apart: How rural schools are tackling the twin problems of isolation and poverty. *American School Board Journal, 192*(4), 18–23.

Harriet, A. W., & Bradley, K. D. (2003). "You can't say you can't play": Intervening in the process of social exclusion in the kindergarten classroom. *Early Childhood Research Quarterly, 18,* 185–205.

Harris Interactive Inc. (2005). *Nearly two-thirds of U.S. adults believe human beings were created by God.* Retrieved November 8, 2006, from http://www.harrisinteractive.com/harris_poll/index.asp?PID=581

Harris, S., & Lowery, S. (2002). A view from the classroom. *Educational Leadership, 59*(8), 64–65.

Hart, D., Donnelly, T., Youniss, J., & Atkins, R. (2007). High school community service as a predictor of adult voting and volunteering. *American Educational Research Journal, 44*(1), 197–217.

Hartman, C. (2006). Students on the move. *Educational Leadership, 63*(5), 20–24.

Hassel, B., & Hassel, E. (2004). Parents take choice driver's seat, but few have a map. *Education Week, 24*(3), 34, 36.

Hasselbring, T., & Bausch, M. (2005/2006). Assistive technologies for reading. *Educational Leadership, 63*(4), 72–75.

Hattie, J., & Timperley, H. (2007). The power of feedback. *Review of Educational Research, 77*(1), 81–112.

Hazelwood School District v. Kuhlmeier, 484 U.S. 260 (1988).

Hecht, E. (2006). There is no really good definition of mass. *Physics Teacher, 44*(1), 40–45.

Heilig, J., & Darling-Hammond, L. (2008). Students in a high-stakes testing context. *Educational Evaluation and Policy Analysis, 30*(1), 75–110.

Hellmech, N. (2007, March 29). No sugarcoating this: Kids besieged by food ads. *USA Today,* p. 9D.

Hendrie, C. (1999). Harvard study finds increase in segregation. *Education Week, 18*(41), 6.

Hendrie, C. (2002). New scrutiny for sponsors of charters. *Education Week, 22*(12), 1, 18.

Hendrie, C. (2003). States target sexual abuse by educators. *Education Week, 22*(33), 1, 16–18.

Hendrie, C. (2005a). Court: Class strip searches unconstitutional. *Education Week, 24*(3), 3, 22.

Hendrie, C. (2005b). Legislation tightens fiscal oversight of California charters. *Education Week, 25*(7), 18.

Hendrie, C. (2005c). T-shirts on gay issues spur lawsuits. *Education Week, 24*(16), 1, 16.

Henry, G., Gordon, C., & Rickman, D. (2006). Early education policy alternatives: Comparing quality and outcomes of Head Start and state prekindergarten. *Educational Evaluation and Policy Analysis, 28*(1), 77–99.

Herszenhorn, D. (2006, April 19). New York offers housing subsidy as teacher lure. *New York Times,* pp. A1, C15.

Hess, F. (2004a). *School boards at the dawn of the 21st century.* Alexandria, VA: National School Boards Association.

Hess, F. (2004b). The political challenges of charter school regulation. *Phi Delta Kappan, 85*(7), 508–512.

Hess, F., & Squire, J. (2008). From research to policy. *American School Board Journal, 195*(8), 39–41.

Heward, W. (2009). *Exceptional children* (9th ed.). Upper Saddle River, NJ: Merrill/Pearson.

Hewitt, T. (2006). *What we teach and why.* Thousand Oaks, CA: Sage.

Hiebert, J., Gallimore, R., & Stigler, J. (2002). A knowledge base for the teaching profession: What would it look like and how can we get one? *Educational Researcher, 31*(5), 3–15.

Hinkel, E. (2005). *Handbook of research on second language teaching and learning.* Mahwah, NJ: Erlbaum.

Hirsch, E. (1987). *Cultural literacy: What every American needs to know.* Boston: Houghton Mifflin.

Hirsch, E. (2000). The tests we need and why we don't quite have them. *Education Week, 19*(21), 40–41.

Hirsch, E. (2001). Seeking breadth and depth in the curriculum. *Educational Leadership, 59*(2), 22–25.

Hirsch, E. (Ed.). (2005). *What your fourth grader needs to know: Fundamentals of a good fourth-grade education.* New York: Dell.

Hoff, D. (2003). Math education panel issues long-range plan for action. *Education Week, 22*(33), 11.

Hoff, D. (2005). Schools feel pressure of efforts to increase fiscal responsibility. *Education Week, 24*(39), 1, 24.

Hoff, D. (2006). Texas proposes classroom costs per "65 percent" plan. *Education Week, 25*(32), 23, 24.

Hoff, D. (2009a). Local educators prepare to use one-time funds. *Education Week, 28*(22), 1, 14–15.

Hoff, D. (2009b). National standards gain steam. *Education Week, 28*(23), 1, 20–21.

Hoff, T. (2002). A fresh approach to sex education. *American School Board Journal, 189*(11), 60–61, 66.

Holloway, J. (2004). Family literacy. *Education Leadership, 61*(6), 88–89.

Holmes, C. (2006). Low test scores + high retention rates = more dropouts. *Kappa Delta Pi Record, 42*(2), 56–58.

Honawar, V. (2005). Smoking in movies spurs youth to try it, Dartmouth study says. *Education Week, 25*(13), 15.

Honawar, V. (2006). Md. Lawmakers fight school takeover plan. *Education Week, 25*(31), 25, 28.

Honawar, V. (2008). Performance-pay studies show few achievement gains. *Education Week, 27*(27), 7.

Honawar, V. (2009). Teacher gap: Training gets a boost. *Education Week, 28*(17), 28–29.

Honawar, V., & Olson, L. (2008). Advancing pay for performance. *Education Week, 27*(18), 26–31.

Hopkins, J. (2006). All students being equal. *Technology & Learning, 26*(10), 26–28.

Horn, I. (2005). Learning on the job: A situated account of teacher learning in high school mathematics departments. *Cognition and Instruction, 23*(2), 207–236.

Howell, W. (2005). School boards besieged. *Education Week, 24*(26), 44.

Howley, A., Andrianaivo, S., & Perry, J. (2005). The pain outweighs the gain: Why teachers don't want to become principal. *Teachers College Record, 197*(4), 757–782.

Howley, C., & Howley, A. (2004). School size and the influence of socioeconomic status on student achievement: Confronting the threat of size bias in national data sets. *Education Policy Analysis Archives, 12*(52). Retrieved September 26, 2006, from http://epaa.asu.edu/epaa/v12n52/

Hoye, J., & Stern, D. (2008). The career academy story. *Education Week, 28*(3), 24–25.

Hoyt, W. (2005). *An evaluation of the Kentucky Education Reform Act.* Retrieved January 2006 from: http://gatton.uky.edu/cber/downloads/Kentucky_education_reform_act.htm

Hu, W. (2008, November 12). A school district asks: Where are the parents? *New York Times,* p. A25.

Huerta, L., d'Entremont, C., & Gonzalez, M. (2006). Cyber charter schools: Can accountability keep pace with innovation? *Phi Delta Kappan, 88*(1), 23–30.

Hughes, D., Smith, E., Stevenson, H., Rodriguez, J., Johnson, D., & Spicer, P. (2006). Parents' ethnic-racial socialization practices: A review of research and directions for future study. *Developmental Psychology, 42*(5), 747–770.

Hughes, J., Luo, W., Kwok, O., Lloyd, L. (2008). Teacher-student support, effortful engagement, and achievement: A 3-year longitudinal study. *Journal of Educational Psychology, 100*(1), 1–14.

Hulse, C. (2006, May 16). Senate passes a bill that favors English. *New York Times,* p. A19.

Humphrey, D., Wechsler, M., & Hough, H. (2008). Characteristics of effective alternative teacher certification programs. *Teachers College Record, 110*(1), 1–63.

Hunsader, P. (2002). Why boys fail—and what we can do about it. *Principal, 82*(2), 52–54.

Hutton, T. (2005). The charter option: 5 big questions your board should ask before authorizing a charter school. *American School Board Journal, 192*(5), 16–20.

Hutton, T. (2008). Teaching and the Bible. *American School Board Journal, 195*(6), 38–41.

Hyland, N., & Noffke, S. (2005). Understanding diversity through social and community inquiry: An action-research study. *Journal of Teacher Education, 56*(4), 367–381.

Ilg, T., & Massucci, J. (2003). Comprehensive urban high schools: Are there better options for poor and minority children? *Education and Urban Society, 36*(1), 63–78.

Illig, D. (1996). *Reducing class size: A review of the literature and options for consideration.* Sacramento: California Research Bureau.

Illinois State Board of Education. (2008a). *Illinois Science Assessment Framework Standard 12F - Astronomy (Grade 7).* Retrieved November 1, 2008, from http://www.champaignschools.org/index2.php?header=./science/&file=MSCurriculum/astronomy

Illinois State Board of Education. (2008b). *Student assessment.* Retrieved November 1, 2008, from http://www.isbe.state.il.us/assessment/ISAT.htm

Illinois State Board of Education. (2008c). *2008 Science ISAT: Grades 4 and 7,* p. 45. Retrieved November 2008 from http://www.isbe.state.il.us/assessment/pdfs/2008/Science_ISAT.pdf

Imber, M., & van Geel, T. (2005). *A teacher's guide to education law* (3rd ed.). Mahwah, NJ: Erlbaum.

Individuals with Disabilities Education Act of 1997. Pub. L. No. 105–17. C.F.R. 3000 (1997).

Individuals with Disabilities Education Act of 2004. Pub. L. No. 108–446. (2004).

Ingersoll, R., & Smith, T. (2003). The wrong solution to the teacher shortage. *Educational Leadership, 60*(8), 30–33.

Ingersoll, R., & Smith, T. (2004). What are the effects of induction and mentoring on beginning teacher turnover? *American Educational Research Journal, 41*(3), 681–714.

Ingraham v. Wright, 430 U.S. 651 (1977).

INTASC. Interstate New Teacher Assessment and Support Consortium. (1993). *Model standards for beginning teacher licensing and development: A resource for state dialogues.* Washington, DC: Council of Chief State School Officers.

International Reading Association & National Council of Teachers of English. (2008). *Standards for the English language arts.* Retrieved November 2008 from http://www.ncte.org/library/files/Store/Books/Sample/StandardsDoc.pdf

Isaacson, W. (2009). How to raise the standards in America's schools. *Time, 173*(16), 32–37.

Jackson, P. (1968). *Life in classrooms.* New York: Holt, Rinehart & Winston.

Jackson, P. (2007). A choice that works. *American School Board Journal, 194*(12), 34–35.

Jacobsen, D. (2003). *Philosophy in classroom teaching: Bridging the gap* (2nd ed.). Upper Saddle River, NJ: Prentice Hall.

Jacobsen, D., Eggen, P., & Kauchak, D. (2009). *Methods for teaching* (8th ed.). Upper Saddle River, NJ: Merrill/Prentice Hall.

Jacobson, L. (2004). Research updates lives of Perry preschoolers. *Education Week, 24*(4), 6.

Jacobson, L. (2006). Teacher-pay incentives popular but unproven. *Education Week, 26*(5), 1, 20.

Jacobson, L. (2008). Children's lack of playtime seen as troubling health, school issue. *Education Week, 28*(14), 1, 14–15.

Jacobson, L. (2009). KIPP's entry into pre-K world takes some adjustment. *Education Week, 28*(20), 6.

Jimerson, S., Pletcher, S., & Graydon, K. (2006). Beyond grade retention and social promotion: Promoting the social and academic competence of students. *Psychology in the Schools, 43*(1), 85–97.

Johnson, B., & Christensen, L. (2004). *Educational research: Quantitative and qualitative approaches* (2nd ed.) Boston: Allyn & Bacon.

Johnson, D. (2004). Plagiarism-proofing assignments. *Phi Delta Kappan, 85*(7), 549–552.

Johnson, D., & Johnson, R. (2006). *Learning together and alone: Cooperation, competition, and individualization* (8th ed.). Needham Heights, MA: Allyn & Bacon.

Johnson, J. (2004). What school leaders want. *Educational Leadership, 61*(7), 24–27.

Johnson, K. (2008). *On the reservation and off, schools see a changing tide. New York Times.* Retrieved May 25, 2008, from www.nytimes.com/2008/05/25/education/25hardin.html?th&emc=th

Johnson, L. (2004). Down with detention. *Education Week, 24*(14), 39–40.

Johnson, L., Bachman, J., & O'Malley, P. (2001). *Monitoring the future: Questionnaire responses from the nation's high school seniors, 1997.* Ann Arbor, MI: Institute for Social Research.

Johnson, S., & Birkeland, S. (2003, April). *Pursuing a "sense of success": New teachers explain their career decisions.* Paper presented at the annual meeting of the American Educational Research Association, New Orleans, LA.

Johnson, S., & Birkeland, S. (2006). Fast track certification. *Education Week, 25*(23), 48, 37.

Johnson, J. (2004). Authority, inquiry, and education: A response to Dewey's critics. *Educational Studies, 35*(3), 230–247.

Johnston, R. (1994). Policy details who paddles students and with what. *Education Week, 14*(11), 17–18.

Johnson, R., & Viadero, D. (2000). Unmet promise: Raising minority achievement. *Education Week, 19*(27), 1, 18–23.

Jones, D. (2008). *CEOs split on paying for good grades. USA Today.* Retrieved September 2008 from http://www.usatoday.com/money/companies/management/2008-09-10-pay-for-grades_N.htm

Jones, K. (2009). Supreme Court rejects child online protection act. *Information Week.* Retrieved January 28, 2009, from http://www.informationweek.com/blog/main/archives/2009/01/supreme_court_r.html

Jones, S., & Dindia, K. (2004). A meta-analytic perspective on sex equity in the classroom. *Review of Educational Research, 74*(4), 443–471.

Jones, V. F., & Jones, L. S. (2004). *Comprehensive classroom management: Creating communities of support and solving problems* (7th ed.). Boston: Allyn & Bacon.

Joseph, P., & Efron, S. (2005). Seven worlds of moral education. *Phi Delta Kappan, 86*(7), 525–533.

Juvonen, J., Le, V., Kaganoff, T., Augustine, C., & Constant, L. (2004). *Focus on the wonder years: Challenges facing the American middle school.* Santa Monica, CA: RAND Corporation.

Kaff, M., Zabel, R., & Milham, M. (2007). Revisiting cost–benefit relationships of behavior management strategies: What special educators say about usefulness, intensity, and effectiveness. *Preventing School Failure, 51,* 35–45.

Kahlenberg, R. (2006). Integration by income. *American School Board Journal, 193*(4), 51–52.

Kahlenberg, R. (2008). What to do with No Child Left Behind? *Education Week, 28*(8), 40.

Kaiser Family Foundation. (2004a). *Sex education in America: Principals survey.* Retrieved March 20, 2005, from http://www.npr.org/programs/morning

Kaiser Family Foundation. (2004b). *Survey snapshot: The digital divide.* Retrieved June 19, 2006, from www.kff.org

Kamil, M., & Walberg, H. (2005). The scientific teaching of reading. *Education Week, 24*(20), 38, 40.

Karten, T. (2005). *Inclusion strategies that work: Research-based methods for the classroom.* Thousand Oaks, CA: Corwin Press.

Kauchak, D., & Eggen, P. (2007). *Learning and teaching: Research-based methods* (5th ed.). Needham Heights, MA: Allyn & Bacon.

Kaufman, F. (2005). Diabesity. In P. Menzel, *Hungry planet: What the world eats* (pp. 242–243). Napa, CA: Material World Press.

Kedar-Voivodas, G. (1983). The impact of elementary children's school roles and sex roles on teacher attitudes: An interactional analysis. *Review of Educational Research, 20,* 417–462.

Keller, B. (2002). Report urges experimentation with teacher-pay schemes. *Education Week, 21*(39), 11.

Keller, B. (2006). Study for NBPTS raises questions about credential. *Education Week, 25*(37), 1, 16.

Keller, B. (2007). Gone again after five years? Think again. *Education Week, 26*(41), 26–30.

Kellough, R., & Carjuzaa, J. (2009). *Teaching in the middle and secondary schools* (9th ed.). Boston: Allyn & Bacon.

Kennedy, M. (2006). Knowledge and vision in teaching. *Journal of Teacher Education, 57*(3), 205–211.

Kerman, S. (1979). Teacher expectations and student achievement. *Phi Delta Kappan, 60,* 70–72.

Kids Health for Parents. (2006). *About teen suicide.* Retrieved March 21, 2006, from http://www.kidshealth.org/sui_fact.htm

Kincheloe, J. (2004). Why a book on urban education? In S. Steinberg & J. Kincheloe (Eds.), *19 Urban questions: Teaching in the city* (pp. 1–27). New York: Peter Lang.

Kitzmiller et al. v. Dover Area School District, 04cv2688 (U.S. District Court for the Middle District of Pennsylvania, 2005).

Kleiman, C. (2001, October 30). Internet helps parents keep an eye on kids. *Chicago Tribune.* Retrieved May 17, 2005, from http://www.chicagotribune.co

Klein, A. (2009). Budget would boost incentive pay, turnaround aid. *Education Week, 28*(31), 20.

Kliebard, H. (2002). Changing course: American curriculum reform in the 20th century. New York: Teachers College Press.

Kober, N. (2006). *A public education primer: Basic (and sometimes surprising) facts about the U.S. education system.* Washington, DC: Center on Education Policy.

Kohn, A. (1993). *Punished by rewards: The trouble with gold stars, incentive plans, A's, praise, and other bribes.* Boston: Houghton Mifflin.

Kohn, A. (1996). By all available means: Cameron and Pierce's defense of extrinsic motivators. *Review of Educational Research, 66,* 1–4.

Kohn, A. (2000). Burnt at the high stakes. *Journal of Teacher Education, 51*(4), 315–327.

Kohn, A. (2007). Who's cheating whom? *Phi Delta Kappan, 89*(2), 89–97.

Konheim-Kalkstein, Y. (2006). A uniform look. *American School Board Journal, 193*(8), 25–27.

Konstantopoulos, S. (2008). Do small classes reduce the achievement gap between low and high achievers? Evidence from Project STAR. *Elementary School Journal, 108*(4), 275–291.

Kosciw, J., & Diaz, E. (2006). *The 2005 National School Climate Survey: The experience of lesbian, gay, bisexual, and transgender youth in our nation's schools.* New York: Gay, Lesbian and Straight Education Network.

Koth, C., Bradshaw, C., & Leaf, P. (2008). A multilevel study of predictors of student perceptions of school climate: The effect of classroom-level factors. *Journal of Educational Psychology, 100*(1), 96–104.

Kounin, J. (1970). *Discipline and group management in classrooms.* New York: Holt, Rinehart & Winston.

Kozol, J. (1991). *Savage inequalities.* New York: Crown.

Kozol, J. (2005). *The shame of the nation: The restoration of apartheid schooling in America.* New York: Crown.

Kratzig, G., & Arbuthnott, K. (2006). Perceptual learning style and learning proficiency: A test of the hypothesis. *Journal of Educational Psychology, 98*(1), 238–246.

Krauss, S., Brunner, M., Kunter, M., Baumert, J., Blum, W., Neubrand, M., & Jordan, A. (2008). Pedagogical content knowledge and content knowledge of secondary mathematics teachers. *Journal of Educational Psychology, 100*(3), 716–725.

Kristoff, N. (2006, May 14). The model students. *New York Times,* Sect. 4, 13.

Krueger, A., & Whitmore, D. (2002). Would smaller classes help close the Black–White achievement gap? In J. Chubb & T. Loveless (Eds.), *Bridging the achievement gap* (pp. 11–46). Washington, DC: Brookings Institution Press.

Krull, E., Oras, K., & Sisask, S. (2007). Differences in teachers' comments on classroom events as indicators of their professional development. *Teaching and Teacher Education, 23,* 1038–1050.

Kuhn, D. (2007). Is direct instruction the right answer to the right question? *Educational Psychologist, 42,* 109–113.

Kunzman, R. (2006). *Grappling with the good.* Albany: State University of New York Press.

Kyriacou, C., & Kunc, R. (2006). Beginning teachers' expectations of teaching. *Teaching and Teacher Education, 23,* 1246–1257.

Labaree, D. (2004). *The trouble with ed schools.* New Haven, CT: Yale University Press.

Labaree, D. (2005). Life on the margins. *Journal of Teacher Education, 56*(3), 186–191.

LaChausse, R. G. (2006). Evaluation of the positive prevention HIV/STD curriculum. *American Journal of Health Education, 37*(4), 203–209.

Laczko-Kerr, I., & Berliner, D. (2003). In harm's way: How undercertified teachers hurt their students. *Educational Leaderhip, 60*(8), 34–39.

Ladson-Billings, G. (2005). Is the team all right? Diversity and teacher education. *Journal of Teacher Education, 56*(3), 229–234.

Lafee, S. (2005). Another weighty burden. *School Administrator, 62*(9), 10–16.

Lambert, C., DePaepe, J., & Lambert, L. (2007). E-portfolios in action. *Kappa Delta Pi Record, 43,* 76–81.

LaMorte, M. (2005). *School law: Cases and concepts* (8th ed.). Boston: Allyn & Bacon.

Land, D. (2002). Local school boards under review: Their role and effectiveness in relation to students' academic achievement. *Review of Educational Research, 72,* 229–278.

Landry, S., Smith, K., & Swank, P. (2006). Responsive parenting: Establishing early foundations for social, communication, and independent problem-solving skills. *Developmental Psychology, 42*(4), 627–642.

Lashley, C. (2001, April). *Performance-based licensure: Developing support systems for beginning teachers.* Paper presented at the annual meeting of the American Educational Research Association, Seattle, WA.

Lau v. Nichols, 414 U.S. 563 (1974).

Lauen, D. (2007). Contextual explanations of school choice. *Sociology of Education, 80,* 179–209.

Lee v. Weismann, 112 S. Ct. 29649 (1992).

Lee, J., & Bowen, N. (2006). Parent involvement, cultural capital, and the achievement gap among elementary school children. *American Educational Research Journal, 43*(2), 193–218.

Lee, V. (2000). Using hierarchical linear modeling to study social contexts: The case of school effects. *Educational Psychologist, 35,* 125–141.

Lemke, M., Sen A., Pahlke, E., Partelow, L., Miller D., Williams, T., Kastberg, D., & Jocelyn, L. (2004). *International outcomes of learning in mathematics literacy and problem solving: PISA 2003 results from the U.S. perspective (NCES 2005–003).* U.S. Department of Education. Washington, DC: National Center for Education Statistics.

Lemon v. Kurtzman, 403 U.S. 602 (1971).

Leonard, J. (2008). *Culturally specific pedagogy in the mathematics classroom: Strategies for teachers of diverse students.* New York: Routledge.

LePage, P., Darling-Hammond, L., & Akar, H., with Gutierrez, C., Jenkins-Gunn, E., & Rosebrock, K. (2005). Classroom management. In L. Darling-Hammond & J. Bransford (Eds.), *Preparing teachers for a changing world: What teachers should learn and be able to do* (pp. 327–357). San Francisco: Jossey-Bass.

Lerman, D., & Vorndran, C. (2002). On the status of knowledge for using punishment: Implications for treating behavior disorders. *Journal of Applied Behavior Analysis, 35,* 431–464.

Lever-Duffy, J., McDonald, J., & Mizell, A. (2003). *Teaching and learning with technology.* Boston: Allyn & Bacon.

Lew, J. (2006). *Asian Americans in class: Charting the achievement gap among Korean American youth.* New York: Teachers College Press.

Lewin, T. (2006, July 9). At college, women are leaving men in the dust. *New York Times,* pp. A1, A18, A19.

Lewis, A. (2005). More than just cute kids. *Phi Delta Kappan, 87*(3), 179–180.

Lewis, A. (2006). Redefining what high school students learn. *Phi Delta Kappan, 87*(8), 564–565.

Lewis, A. (2008). Learn from education's experience. *Phi Delta Kappan, 90*(4), 235–236.

Lewis, J., DeCamp-Fritson, S., Ramage, J., McFarland, M., & Archwamety, T. (2007). Selecting for ethnically diverse children who may be gifted using Raven's Standard Progressive matrices and Naglieri Nonverbal Abilities test. *Multicultural Education, 15*(1), 38–43.

Lichter, D., & Johnson, K. (2006). Emerging rural settlement patterns and the geographic distribution of America's new immigrants. *Rural Sociology, 71*(1), 109–131.

Liston, D. (2004). The lure of learning in teaching. *Teachers College Record, 106*(3), 459–486.

Liu, X., & Meyer, P. (2005). Teachers' perception of their job: A multilevel analysis of the teacher follow-up survey for 1994–2005. *Teachers College Record, 107*(5), 985–1003.

Lloyd, J. (2009, January 5) Number of home-schooled children on the rise. *USA Today,* p. A1.

Lomawaima, K., & McCarty, T. (2006). *To remain an Indian: Lessons in democracy from a century of Native American education.* New York: Teachers College Press.

Longfellow, C. (2008). Proven tools that work. *American School Board Journal, 195*(12), 25–27.

Los Angeles Board of Education. (2006). *Los Angeles Unified School District R30 language census report, 2005–2006.* Retrieved November 17, 2007, from http://search.lausd.k12.ca.us/cgi-bin/fccgi.exe

Lose, M. (2008). Using response to intervention to support struggling learners. *Principal, 87*(3), 20–23.

Lovelace, M. (2005). Meta-analysis of experimental research based on the Dunn and Dunn Model. *Journal of Educational Research, 98*(3), 176–183.

Luekens, M., Lyter, D., & Fox, E. (2004). Teacher attrition and mobility: Results from the teacher following-up survey. *National Center for Education Statistics Quarterly, 6*(3), 40–46.

Lutz, S., Guthrie, J., & Davis, M. (2006). Scaffolding for engagement in elementary school reading instruction. *Journal of Educational Research, 100*(1), 3–20.

Lynch, R. (2000). High school career and technical education for the first decade of the 21st century. *Journal of Vocational Educational Research, 25*(2). Retrieved September 3, 2006, from http://scholar.lib.vt.edu/ejournals/JVER/v25n2/lynch.html

Macionis, J. (2009). *Society: The basics* (9th ed.). Upper Saddle River, NJ: Prentice Hall.

Macionis, J., & Parillo, V. (2010). *Cities and urban life* (5th ed.). Upper Saddle River, NJ: Merrill/Prentice Hall.

Maeroff, G. (2003). The virtual school house. *Education Week, 22*(24), 40, 28.

Mager, R. (1962). Preparing instructional objectives. Palo Alto, CA: Featon.

Magnet Schools of America. (2006). Retrieved June 2, 2006, from http://www.magnet.ed

Magnuson, K., Meyers, M., Ruhm, C., & Waldfogel, J. (2004). Inequality in preschool education and school readiness. *American Educational Research Journal, 41*(1), 115–157.

Mailloux v. Kiley, 323 F. Supp. 1387 (D. Mass 1971), 448 F.2d 1242 (lst Cir. 1971).

Mandel, S. (2006). What new teachers really need. *Educational Leadership, 63*(6), 66–69.

Manouchehri, A. (2004). Implementing mathematics reform in urban schools: A study of the effect of teachers' motivation style. *Urban Education, 38,* 472–508.

Manzo, K. (2004). Reading programs bear similarities across the states. *Education Week, 23*(21), 1, 13.

Manzo, K. (2006a). Scathing report casts cloud over "Reading First." *Education Week, 26*(6), 1, 24.

Manzo, K. (2006b). Young adults don't think world knowledge is vital. *Education Week, 25*(36), 8.

Manzo, K. (2008). Election renews controversy over social-justice teaching. *Education Week, 28*(22), 1, 12–13.

Margolis, J. (2004). A response to "The National Board Hoax." *Teachers College Record.* Retrieved February 2004 from http://www.tcrecord.org/Collection.asp?CollectionID=72

Marsh, C., & Willis, G. (2007). *Curriculum: Alternative approaches, ongoing issues.* Upper Saddle River, NJ: Merrill/Prentice Hall.

Marsh, H., & Kleitman, S. (2005). Consequences of employment during high school: Character building, subversion of academic goals, or a threshold? *American Educational Research Journal, 42*(2), 331–369.

Marzano, R. (2003). *What works in schools: Translating research into action.* Alexandria VA: Association for Supervision and Curriculum Development.

Marzano, R. (2007). *Classroom assessment and grading that work.* Alexandria VA: Association for Supervision and Curriculum Development.

Marzano, R., & Kendall, J. (2003). *Designing standards-based districts, schools, and classrooms.* Alexandria, VA: Association for Supervision and Curriculum Development.

Marzano, R., Waters, T., & McNulty, N. (2005). *School leadership that works: From research to results.* Alexandria, VA: Association for Supervision and Curriculum Development.

Maslow, A. (1968). *Toward a psychology of being* (2nd ed.). New York: Van Nostrand.

Maslow, A. (1970). *Motivation and personality* (2nd ed.). New York: Harper & Row.

Mason, L. (2007). Introduction: Bridging the cognitive and sociocultural approaches in research on conceptual change: Is it feasible? *Educational Psychologist, 42*(1), 1–8.

Mathematica Policy Research. (2007). *Impact of four abstinence education programs.* Retrieved Sepember 2008 from www.mathematica-mpr.com/abstinencereport.asp

Mathews, J. (2009, January 5). The latest doomed pedagogical fad: 21st century skills. *Washington Post,* p. B02.

Mathis, W. (2005). The cost of implementing the federal No Child Left Behind Act: Different assumptions, different answers. *Peabody Journal of Education, 80*(2), 90–119.

Maughan, A., & Cicchetti, D. (2002). Impact of child maltreatment and interadult violence on children's emotion regulation abilities and socioemotional adjustment. *Child Development, 73,* 1525–1542.

Mawhinney, T., & Sagan, L. (2007). The power of personal relationships. *Phi Delta Kappan, 88*(6), 460–464.

Maxwell, L. (2006). Web systems help schools screen visitors. *Education Week, 25*(32), 5, 16.

Maxwell, L. (2008). Sexual orientation. *Education Week, 28*(8), 5.

Mayer, R. (2002). *The promise of educational psychology: Volume II. Teaching for meaningful learning.* Upper Saddle River, NJ: Merrill/Pearson.

Mayer, R. (2004). Should there be a three-strikes rule against pure discovery learning? *American Psychologist, 59,* 14–19.

McAllister, G., & Irvine, J. (2002). The role of empathy in teaching culturally diverse students: A qualitative study of teachers' beliefs. *Journal of Teacher Education, 53,* 433–443.

McAndrews, L. (2006). *The era of education: The presidents and the schools.* Champaign-Urbana: University of Illinois Press.

McCabe, M. (2006). State of the states. *Education Week, 25*(17), 72–96.

McCardle, P., & Chhabra, V. (2006). Commentary. *Elementary School Journal, 107*(2), 239–248.

McCaslin, M., & Good, T. (1996). The informal curriculum. In D. Berliner & R. Calfee (Eds.), *Handbook of educational psychology* (pp. 622–670). New York: Macmillan.

McCoach, D., O'Connell, A., & Levitt, H. (2006). Ability grouping across kindergarten using an early childhood longitudinal study. *Journal of Educational Research, 99*(6), 339–346.

McCombs, J. (2005, March). *Progress in implementing standards, assessment for highly qualified teacher provisions of NCLB: Initial finding from California, Georgia, and Pennsylvania.* Paper presented at the annual meeting of the American Educational Research Association, Montreal.

McCurdy, B., Kunsch, C., & Reibstein, S. (2007). Secondary prevention in the urban school: Implementing the behavior education program. *Preventing School Failure, 51,* 12–19.

McDermott, J. (1994). Buddhism. *Encarta* [CD-ROM]. Bellevue, WA: Microsoft.

McDevitt, T., & Ormrod, J. (2007). *Child development and education* (3rd ed.). Upper Saddle River, NJ: Merrill/Prentice Hall.

McKinley, J. (2009). In Texas, a line in the curriculum revives evolution debate. *New York Times.* Retrieved January 28, 2009, from http://www.nytimes.com/2009/01/22/education/22texas.html?pagewanted=print

McMahon, R. (2007). *Everybody does it/Academic cheating is at an all-time high. Can anything be done to stop it?* Retrieved February 2009 from www.sfgate.com/cgi-bin/article.cgi?file=/c/a/2007/09/09/CM59RIBI7.DTL

McMillan, J. (2004). *Educational research: Fundamentals for the consumer* (4th ed.). New York: Longman.

McMillan, J. (2007a). *Classroom assessment: Principles and practices for effective standards-based instruction* (4th ed.). Boston: Allyn & Bacon.

McMillan, J. (2007b). *Formative assessment: Theory into practice.* New York: Teachers College Press.

McNeil, M. (2006). States to weight education, fiscal priorities. *Education Week, 26*(16), 18, 21.

McNeil, M. (2008a). Governors face political hurdles in seeking power to appoint chiefs. *Education Week, 27*(20), 1, 20.

McNeil, M. (2008b). Overhaul school finance systems, researchers urge. *Education Week, 28*(11), 10.

McNeil, M. (2009). Rush to pump out stimulus cash highlights disparities in funding. *Education Week, 28*(22), 1, 26–27.

Medina, J. (2007). *Schools plan to pay cash for marks. New York Times.* Retrieved January 17, 2009, from http://www.nytimes.com/2007/06/19/nyregion/19schools.html?_r=1&pagewanted=print

Medina, J. (2009a). *Backers of mayoral school control face resistance. New York Times.* Retrieved February 22, 2009, from http://www.nytimes.com/2009/01/29/education/29learn.html?partner=rss&emc=rss

Medina, J. (2009b, March 11). Boys and girls together, taught separately in public school. *New York Times*, p. A24.

Medina, J., & Gootman, E. (2008, September 2). New campaign under way to keep schools under Bloomberg's thumb. *New York Times*, p. C20.

Meek, C. (2006). From the inside out: A look at testing special education students. *Phi Delta Kappan, 88*(4), 293–297.

Meier, D., & Henderson, B. (2007). *Learning from young children in the classroom: The art and science of teacher research.* New York: Teachers College Press.

Mercurio, M., & Morse, C. (2007). "Tinkering" close to the edge. *Educational Leadership, 64*(6), 52–55.

Merrow, J. (2002). The failure of Head Start. *Education Week, 22*(4), 52, 38.

MetLife Survey of the American Teacher. (2006). *Expectations and experiences.* Retrieved November 2008 from http://www.metlife.com

MetLife. (2009). *Survey of the American teacher: Past, present and future.* Retrieved March 2009 from http://www.metlife.com/assets/cao/contributions/citizenship/teacher-survey-25th-anniv-2008.pdf

Michener, J. (2006). Sex education: A success in our social-studies class. *Clearing House, 79*(5), 210–214.

Michie, G. (2004). *See you when we get there: Teaching for change in urban schools.* New York: Teachers College Press.

Milanowski, A., & Kimball, S. (2005). *The relationship between teacher expertise and student achievement: A synthesis of three years of data.* Paper presented at the annual meeting of the American Educational Research Association, Montreal.

Miller, M., Linn, R., & Gronlund, N. (2009). *Measurement and assessment in teaching* (10th ed.). Upper Saddle River, NJ: Merrill/Pearson.

Mishel, L. (2006). The exaggerated dropout crisis. *Education Week, 25*(26), 40.

Mishel, L., Bernstein, J., & Allegretto, S. (2006). *The state of working Americans, 2004/2005.* Washington, DC: Economic Policy Institute.

Moir, E. (2008/2009). Knowing the drill. *Edutopia, 4*(6), 14.

Molnar, A. (2005). *School commercialism: From democratic ideal to market commodity.* New York: Routledge.

Molnar, A., Percy, S., Smith, P., & Zahorik, J. (1998). *1997–98 results of the Student Achievement Guarantee in Education (SAGE) program.* Milwaukee: University of Wisconsin–Milwaukee.

Monitoring the Future. (2006). *Teen drug use down but progress halts among youngest.* University of Michigan: Michigan Institute for Social Research.

Monke, L. (2005/2006). The overdominance of computers. *Educational Leadership, 63*(4), 20–23.

Monte-Sano, C. (2008). Qualities of historical writing instruction: A comparative case study of two teachers' practices. *American Educational Research Journal, 45*(4), 1045–1079.

Moore, A. (2007). A balancing act. *American School Board Journal, 194*(5), 28–30.

Moore, J. (2007, October). Suicide trends among youths and young adults 10–24 years—United States, 1990–2004. *Youth Today*, p. 29.

Moreno, R. (2004). Decreasing cognitive load for novice students: Effects of explanatory versus corrective feedback in discovery-based multimedia. *Instructional Science, 32*, 99–113.

Moreno, R., & Duran, R. (2004). Do multiple representations need explanations: The role of verbal guidance and individual differences in multimedia mathematics learning. *Journal of Educational Psychology, 96*, 492–503.

Morone, J. A. (2003). *Hellfire nation: The politics of sin in American history.* New Haven, CT: Yale University Press.

Morris v. Douglas County School District No. 9, 403 P.2d 775 (Or. 1965).

Morrison v. State Board of Education, 461 P.2d 375 (Cal. 1969).

Morrison, G., Kemp, J., & Ross, S. (2007). *Designing effective instruction* (5th ed.). Hoboken, NJ: Wiley.

Mosenthal, J., Lipson, M., Torncello, S., Russ, B., & Mekkelsen, J. (2004). Contexts and practices of six schools successful in obtaining reading achievement. *Elementary School Journal, 104*(5), 343–368.

Mozert v. Hawkins County Public Schools, 827 F.2d 1058 (6th Cir. 1987), cert. denied, 108 S. Ct. 1029 (1988).

Mulrine, A. (2002, May 27). Risky business. *U.S. News & World Report*, pp. 42–49.

Muñoz, M., & Portes, P. (2002, April). *Voices from the field: The perceptions of teachers and principals on the class size reduction program in a large urban school district.* Paper presented at the annual meeting of the American Educational Research Association, New Orleans, LA.

Murdock, T. B., & Anderman, E. A. (2006). Motivational perspectives on student cheating: Toward an integrated model of academic dishonesty. *Educational Psychologist, 41*, 129–145.

Murphy, J. (2007). Hey, Ms. A! One student teacher's success story. *Kappa Delta Pi Record, 43*, 52–55.

Murphy, M. (2006). *History and philosophy of education: The voices of educational pioneers.* Upper Saddle River, NJ: Pearson/Prentice Hall.

Murphy, P., DeArmond, M., & Guin, K. (2003). A national crisis or localized problems? Getting perspective on the scope and scale of the teacher shortage. *Education Policy Analysis Archives, 11*(23). Retrieved September 27, 2006, from http://epaa.asu.edu/epaa/v11n23

Murray, F. (1986). *Necessity: The developmental component in reasoning.* Paper presented at the 16th annual meeting, Jean Piaget Society, Philadelphia.

Nathan, J. (2005). Charters "Yes!" Vouchers "No!" *Educational Horizons, 83*(2), 110–124.

National Association of Elementary School Principals. (2002). What you might not know about vouchers. *Education Week, 22*(1), 10.

National Association of Elementary School Principals. (2006). *Principal salaries 2004–2005.* Retrieved February 14, 2006, from http://www.naesp.org

National Association of State Boards of Education. (2007). *State education governance at-a-glance.* Retrieved March 2009 from http://nasbe.org/index.php/file-repository?func=finishdown&id=212

National Board for Professional Teaching Standards. (1994). *What teachers should know and be able to do.* Arlington, VA: Author.

National Board for Professional Teaching Standards. (2002). *What teachers should know and be able to do.* Arlington, VA: Author.

National Board for Professional Teaching Standards. (2006). Retrieved August 16, 2006, from http://www.nbpts.org

National Campaign to Prevent Teen Pregnancy. (2006). *Teen pregnancy—so what?* Retrieved July 31, 2006, from http://www.teenpregnancy.org/whycare/sowhat.asp

National Center for Education Information. (2000). *Alternative teacher certification: A state by state analysis.* Washington, DC: Author.

National Center for Education Statistics. (2002). *Digest of education statistics.* Washington, DC: U.S. Department of Education.

National Center for Education Statistics. (2005a). *Digest of education statistics, 2005.* Retrieved November 2008 from http://www.nces.ed.gov/programs/digest/d05/tables/dt05_053.asp

National Center for Education Statistics. (2005b). *Federal expenditures for education.* Washington, DC: Author. Retrieved July 1, 2006, from http://nces.ed.gov/ubs2005/2005074.pdf

National Center for Education Statistics. (2005c). *Indicators of school crime and safety: 2005.* Retrieved July 27, 2006, from http://nces.ed.gov/programs/crimeindicators/index.asp?

National Center for Education Statistics. (2005d). *Public school enrollments.* Washington, DC: U.S. Government Printing Office.

National Center for Education Statistics. (2005e). *The condition of education 2005.* Washington, DC: U.S. Department of Education.

National Center for Education Statistics. (2006a). *Internet access in U.S. public schools and classrooms: 1994–2003.* Retrieved January 3, 2006, from http://nces.ed.gov

National Center for Education Statistics. (2006b). *The condition of education 2006.* Washington, DC: U.S. Department of Education.

National Center for Education Statistics. (2007a). The *condition of education 2007.* Washington, DC: Author. Retrieved July 21, 2007, from http://nces.ed.gov/pubs2007/2007064.pdf

National Center for Education Statistics. (2007b). *Crime, violence, discipline, and safety in U.S. public schools: Findings from the School Survey on Crime & Safety: 2005–2006.* Retrieved October 4, 2007, from: http://nces.ed.gov/pubsearch/pubsinfo.asp?pubid=2007361

National Center for Education Statistics. (2008a). *Participation in education: Elementary and secondary education, Indicator 3 (2004).* Washington, DC: Author.

National Center for Education Statistics. (2008b). *Projection of education statistics to 2017* (36th ed.). Washington, DC: Author.

National Center for Education Statistics. (2008c). *The condition of education 2008.* Washington, DC: U.S. Department of Education.

National Commission on Excellence in Education. (1983). *A nation at risk: The imperative for educational reform.* Washington, DC: U.S. Government Printing Office.

National Council of Teachers of Mathematics. (2008). *Math standards.* Retrieved November 2008 from http://www.nctm.org/standards/

National Education Association. (1975). *Code of ethics of the education profession, NEA Representative Assembly.* Washington, DC: Author. Retrieved March 2009 from http://www.nea.org/home/30442.htm

National Education Association. (2002). *Status of the American public school teacher, 1999–2000.* Washington, DC: Author.

National Education Association. (2005). *Weighted student formula (WSF).* Washington, DC: Author. Retrieved January 30, 2006, from http://www.nea.org/index.html

National Education Association. (2006a). *Rankings and estimates.* Retrieved January 30, 2006, from http://www.nea.org/index.html

National Education Association. (2006b). *Status of the American public school teacher, 2003–2004.* Retrieved August 16, 2006, from http://www.nea.org

National Education Association. (2009). *Rankings and estimates (2007–2008).* Retrieved July 9, 2009, from http://www.nea.org/index.html

National Federation of State High School Associations. (2008). *2007–2008 high school athletics participation survey.* Retrieved September 2008 from http://www.nfhs.org/core/contentmanager/uploads/2007-08%20Participation%20Survey.pdf

National Law Center on Homelessness and Poverty. (2006). Retrieved June 1, 2006, from http://www.nlchp.org

Neville, K., Sherman, R., & Cohen, C. (2005). *Preparing and training professionals: Comparing education to six other fields.* New York: The Finance Project.

New Jersey v. T.L.O., 105 S. Ct. 733 (1985).

New York State School Board Association. (2006). *Board members top 3 concerns: Academics, academics, academics.* Retrieved February 1, 2006, from http://222.nyssba.org

Newby, T., Stepich, D., Lehman, J., & Russell, J. (2006). *Instructional technology and teaching and learning* (3rd ed.). Upper Saddle River, NJ: Merrill/Prentice Hall.

Newman, J. (2006). *America's teachers* (5th ed.). Boston: Allyn & Bacon.

Newman, R. (2008). Adaptive and nonadaptive help seeking with peer harassment: An integrative perspective of coping and self-regulation. *Educational Psychologist, 43*(1), 1–15.

Ng, J., & Thomas, K. (2007). Cultivating the cream of the crop: A case study of urban teachers from an alternative teacher education program. *Action in Teacher Education, 29*(1), 3–13.

Ngo, B., & Lee, S. (2007). Complicating the image of model minority success: A review of southeast Asian American education. *Review of Educational Research, 77*(4), 415–453.

Nichols, S., & Berliner, D. (2005). *The inevitable corruption of indicators and educators through high-stakes testing.* Tempe, AZ: Education Policy Studies Laboratory.

Nichols, S., & Berliner, D. (2008) Why has high-stakes testing so easily slipped into contemporary American life? *Phi Delta Kappan, 89,* 672–676.

Nieto, S. (2004). *Affirming diversity* (4th ed.). New York: Longman.

Nikitina, S. (2006). Three strategies for interdisciplinary teaching: contextualizing, conceptualizing, and problem-centering. *Journal of Curriculum Studies, 38*(3), 251–271.

Nitko, A., & Brookhart, S. (2007). *Educational assessment of students* (5th ed.). Upper Saddle River, NJ: Merrill/Pearson.

Noblit, G., Rogers, D., & McCadden, B. (1995). In the meantime: The possibilities of caring. *Phi Delta Kappan, 76,* 680–685.

Noddings, N. (2001). The caring teacher. In V. Richardson (Ed.), *Handbook of research on teaching* (4th ed., pp. 99–105). Washington, DC: American Educational Research Association.

Noguera, P. (2003). The trouble with black boys: The role and influence of environmental and cultural factors on the academic performance of African American males. *Urban Education, 38*(4), 431–459.

Norris, N. (2004). *The promise and failure of progressive education.* Landham, MD: Scarecrow Press.

Nucci, L. (2006). Classroom management for moral and social development. In C. Evertson & C. Weinstein (Eds.), *Handbook of classroom management: Research, practice, and contemporary issues* (pp. 711–731). Mahwah, NJ: Erlbaum.

Null, J. (2007). William C. Bagley and the founding of essentialism: An untold story in American educational history. *Teachers College Record, 109*(4), 1013–1055.

Oakes, J. (2005). *Keeping track: How schools structure inequality* (2nd ed.). New Haven, CT: Yale University Press.

Oakes, J. (2008). Keeping track: Structuring equality and inequality in an era of accountability. *Teachers College Record, 110*(3), 700–712.

Oakes, J., & Saunders, M. (2004). Education's most basic tools: Access to textbooks and instructional materials in California's public schools. *Teachers College Record, 106*(10), 1967–1988.

Oakes, J., & Wells, A. S. (2002). Detracking for high student achievement. In L. Abbeduto (Ed.), *Taking sides: Clashing views and controversial issues in educational psychology* (2nd ed., pp. 26–30). Guilford, CT: McGraw-Hill Duskin.

O'Conner, C., & Fernandez, S. (2006). Race, class, and disproportionality: Reevaluating the relationship between poverty and special education placement. *Educational Researcher, 35*(6), 6–11.

Odden, A. (2003). Leveraging teacher pay. *Education Week, 22*(43), 64.

Odden, A., Borman, G. D., & Fermanich, M. (2004). Assessing teacher, classroom, and school effects, including fiscal effects. *Peabody Journal of Education, 79*(4), 4–32.

Oder, N. (2005). Oklahoma legislators urge limits on kid's books with gay themes. *Library Journal, 130*(11), 16–17.

OELA (Office of English Language Acquisition). (2004). *National clearinghouse for language acquisition and language instruction programs.* Retrieved March 2, 2006, from www.ncela.gwu.edu/languages

Ogbu, J. (1999). Beyond language: Ebonics, proper English, and identity in a Black-American speech community. *American Educational Research Journal, 36,* 147–184.

Ogbu, J. (2003). *Black American students in an affluent suburb: A study of academic disengagement.* Mahwah, NJ: Erlbaum.

Ogbu, J., & Simons, H. (1998). Voluntary and involuntary minorities: A cultural-ecological theory of school performance with some implications for education. *Anthropology & Education Quarterly, 29*(2), 155–188.

Oliva, P. (2005). *Developing the curriculum* (6th ed.). Boston: Allyn & Bacon.

Olson, L. (2003). The great divide. *Education Week, 22*(17), 9–20.

Olson, L. (2005). Nationwide standards eyed anew. *Education Week, 25*(14), 1, 24.

Olson, L. (2006a). A decade of effort. *Education Week, 25*(17), 8–16.

Olson, L. (2006b). The down staircase. *Education Week, 25*(41S), 5, 6, 10, 11.

Olson, L. (2008). Human resources a weak spot. *Education Week, 27*(18), 12–19.

Orfield, G., & Lee, C. (2004). *Brown at 50: King's dream or Plessy's nightmare?* Available at www.civilrightsproject.harvard.edu/research/reseg04/brown50.pdf

Ormrod, J. (2006). *Educational psychology: Developing learners* (5th ed). Upper Saddle River, NJ: Merrill/Prentice Hall.

Ormrod, J. (2008). *Educational psychology: Developing learners* (6th ed). Upper Saddle River, NJ: Merrill/Prentice Hall.

Orr, A. (2009). Homework and diapers: How adults can help students juggle pregnancy, parenthood, and school. *Edutopia, 5*(1), 18–20.

Ortiz, F. (2004). Essential learning conditions for California youth: Educational facilities. *Teachers College Record, 106*(10), 2015–2031.

Ozmon, H., & Craver, S. (2007). *Philosophical foundations of education* (8th ed.). Upper Saddle River, NJ: Pearson.

Padilla, A. (2006). Second language learning: Issues in research and teaching. In P. Alexander & P. Winne (Eds.), *Handbook of educational psychology* (2nd ed., pp. 571–592). Mahwah, NJ: Erlbaum.

Palmer, L. (2007). The potential of "alternative" charter school authorizers. *Phi Delta Kappan, 89*(4), 304–309.

Park, S., Oliver, J. S., Johnson, T., Graham, P., & Oppong, N. (2007). Colleagues' roles in the professional development of teachers: Results from a research study of National Board certification. *Teaching and Teacher Education, 23,* 368–389.

Parker-Pope, T. (2008). *Hint of hope as child obesity rate hits plateau. New York Times.* Retrieved May 28, 2008, from http://www.nytimes.com/2008/05/28/health/research/28obesity.html

Parker-Pope, T. (2009). The 3 R's? A fourth is crucial, too: Recess. *New York Times,.* Retrieved February 24, 2009, from http://www.nytimes.com/2009/02/24/health/24well.html?th&emc=th

Partnership for 21st Century Skills. (2009). *Overview.* Retrieved April 2009 from http://www.21stcenturyskills.org

Patterson, F. (2001/2002). Teaching religious intolerance. *Rethinking Schools, 16*(2), 6, 7.

Patton, C., & Roschelle, J. (2008). Why the best math curriculum won't be a textbook. *Education Week, 27*(36), 32, 24–25.

Payne, R. (2005). *A framework for understanding poverty.* Highland, TX: Aha! Process Press.

Payton, J., Munro, S., O'Brien, M., & Weissberg, R. (2006). Common ground. *Edutopia, 2*(6), 53–55.

Pecheone, R. L., & Chung, R. R. (2006). Evidence in teacher education: The performance assessment for California teachers. *Journal of Teacher Education, 57*(1), 22–36.

Pedulla, J., Abrams, L., Madaus, G., Russell, M., Ramos, M., & Miao, J. (2003). *Perceived effects of state-mandated testing programs on teaching and learning: Findings from a national survey of teachers.* Boston: Boston College.

Peevely, G., Hedges, L., & Nye, B. A. (2005). The relationship of class size effects and teacher salary. *Journal of Education Finance, 31*(1), 101–109.

Peregoy, S., & Boyle, O. (2008). *Reading, writing, and learning in ESL* (5th ed.). New York: Longman.

Perkins-Gough, D. (2005a). Fixing high schools. *Educational Leadership, 62*(8), 88–89.

Perkins-Gough, D. (2005b). The perils of high school exit exams. *Educational Leadership, 63*(3), 90–91.

Perry, N., Turner, J., & Meyer, D. (2006). Classrooms as contexts for motivating learning. In P. Alexander & P. Winne (Eds.), *Handbook of educational psychology* (2nd ed., pp. 327–348). Mahwah, NJ: Erlbaum.

Petroska, J., Lindle, J., & Pankratz, R. (2000). *Executive summary: 2000 Review of research on the Kentucky Education Reform Act.* Retrieved February 17, 2004, from http://www.kier.org/2000Research.html

Pew Hispanic Foundation. (2003). *Latinos in higher education: Many enroll, too few graduate.* Retrieved April 27, 2004, from http://www.pewhispanic.org/site/docs/pdf

Pfiffner, L., Rosen, L., & O'Leary, S. (1985). The efficacy of an all-positive approach to classroom management. *Journal of Applied Behavior Analysis, 18,* 257–261.

Piaget, J. (1952). *Origins of intelligence in children.* New York: International Universities Press.

Piaget, J. (1965). *The moral judgment of the child.* New York: Free Press. (Original work published 1932).

Piaget, J. (1970). *The science of education and the psychology of the child.* New York: Orion Press.

Pittman, M., & Frykholm, J. (2002). *Turning points: Curriculum materials as catalysts for change.* Paper presented at the annual meeting of the American Educational Research Association, Seattle, WA.

Pitts, L. (2008). Which books would Palin want to ban? Detroit Free Press. Retrieved November 16, 2008, from http://freep.com/apps/pbcs.dll/article?AID=/20080923/OPINION01/809230333/0/NEWS15

Pogrow, S. (2006). The Bermuda Triangle of American education: Pure traditionalism, pure progressivism, and good intentions. *Phi Delta Kappan, 88*(2), 142–150.

Pomerantz, E., Moorman, E., & Litwack, S. (2007). The how, whom and why of parents' involvement in children's academic lives: More is not always better. *Review of Educational Research, 77*(3), 373–403.

Popham, W. (2004). *America's failing schools: How parents and teachers can cope with No Child Left Behind.* New York: Routledge Falmer.

Popham, W. (2005a). *Classroom assessment: What teachers need to know* (4th ed.). Boston: Pearson.

Popham, W. (2005b). NAEP: Gold standard or fool's gold? *Educational Leadership, 68*(8), 79–81.

Popham, W. (2007). Who should make the test? *Educational Leadership, 65*(1), 80–82.

Pressley, M., Raphael, L., & Gallagher, J. G. (2004). Providence-St. Mel School: How a school that works for African American students works. *Journal of Educational Psychology, 96*(2), 216–235.

Proefriedt, W. (1999). Sorry, John. I'm not who you thought I was. *Education Week, 29*(15), 28, 30.

Public Agenda. (2002). *Sizing things up: What parents, teachers and students think about large and small high schools.* Retrieved June 15, 2004, from http://www.publicagenda.org/research/research_reports_details.cfm?list=21

Public Agenda. (2003). *Stand by me: What teachers really think about unions, merit pay, and other professional matters.* Retrieved May 15, 2006, from http://www.publicagenda.org/specials/standbyme

Public Agenda. (2004). *Teaching interrupted.* Retrieved June 12, 2004, from http://www.publicagenda.org

Pulliam, J., & Van Patten, J. (2007). *History of education in America* (9th ed.). Columbus, OH: Merrill.

Pullman, P. (2002). *His dark materials* (trilogy). New York: Knopf.

Purdom, G. (2008, July 10). Schools cutting bus service because of fuel prices. *USA Today,* p. 3A.

Putnam, R., & Borko, H. (2000). What do new views of knowledge and thinking have to say about research on teacher learning? *Educational Researcher, 29*(1), 4–15.

Qin, D. (2006). "Our child doesn't talk to us anymore": Alienation in immigrant Chinese families. *Anthropology and Education Quarterly, 37*(2), 162–179.

Quaid, L. (2008, August 20). Study: Minority students more likely to be paddled. *Salt Lake Tribune,* p. A8.

Quick, P., & Normore, A. (2004). Moral leadership in the 21st century: Everyone is watching—especially the students. *Educational Forum, 68*(4), 336–347.

Quinlan, T. (2004). Speech recognition technology and students with writing difficulties: Improving fluency. *Journal of Educational Psychology, 96*(2), 337–346.

Rainwater, L., & Smeedings, T. (2003). *Poor kids in a rich country.* New York: Russell Sage Foundation.

Ramirez, A. (2001). How merit pay undermines education. *Educational Leadership, 58*(5), 16–20.

Raskauskas, J., & Stoltz, A. (2007). Involvement in traditional and electronic bullying among adolescents. *Developmental Psychology, 43*(3), 564–575.

Raths, J., & Lynman, F. (2003). Summative evaluation of student teachers. *Journal of Teacher Education, 54,* 206–216.

Rathunde, K., & Csikszentmihalyi, M. (2006). The developing person: An experiential perspective. In R. Lerner (Ed.), *Handbook of child psychology* (6th ed., pp. 465–515). New York: Wiley.

Ravitch, D. (1990, October 24). Multiculturalism yes, particularism, no. *Chronicle of Higher Education,* p. A44.

Ravitch, D. (2000). *Left back: A century of failed school reforms.* New York: Simon & Schuster.

Ravitch, D. (2006). National standards. *Education Week, 25*(17), 54–58.

Ray v. School District of DeSoto County, 666 F. Supp. 1524, (M.D. Fla. 1987).

Ray, R. (2006). *Research facts on homeschooling.* National Home Education Research Institute. Retrieved February 2009 from http://www.nheri.org/content/view/199

Ready, D., & Lee, V. (2008). Choice, equity, and the schools-within-schools reform. *Teachers College Record, 110*(9). Retrieved April 2008 from http://www.tcrecord.org ID Number: 15178.

Recruiting New Teachers. (2006). *Teacher shortage areas.* Retrieved July 3, 2006, from http://www.recruitingteachers.org/channels/clearinghouse

Reese, W. (2005). *America's public schools: From the common school to No Child Left Behind.* Baltimore: Johns Hopkins University Press.

Reeves, D. (2008). Effective grading. *Educational Leadership, 65*(5), 88–89.

Reeves, E., & Bylund, R. (2005). Are rural schools inferior to urban schools? A multi-year analysis of school accountability trends in Kentucky. *Rural Sociology, 70*(3), 360–386.

Reeves, J. (2004, January, 20). Riley proposal would eliminate tenure panel [Electronic version]. *The Decatur Daily News.*

Reich, R. (2002). The civic perils of home schooling. *Educational Leadership, 59*(7), 56–59.

Reid, K. (2005). Sharing the load. *Education Week, 25*(12), 27–30.

Reis, S., Colbert, R., & Hébert, T. (2005). Understanding resilience in diverse, talented students in an urban high school. *Roeper Review, 27*(2), 110–120.

Remillard, J. (2005). Examining key concepts in research on teachers' use of mathematics curricula. *Review of Educational Research, 75*(2), 211–246.

Reutzel, D., & Cooter, R. (2008). *Teaching children to read: The teacher makes the difference* (5th ed.). Upper Saddle River, NJ: Merrill/Pearson.

Reyes, A. (2006). *Discipline, achievement, and race: Is zero tolerance the answer?* New York: Rowman & Littlefield.

Reys, B., Reys, R., & Chávez, O. (2004). Why mathematics textbooks matter. *Educational Leadership, 62*(5), 61–66.

Rhee, M., & Levin, J. (2006). Staffing urban schools. *Education Week, 25*(16), 52, 30.

Richard, A. (2004). W. Va. eyes softer stand on school mergers. *Education Week, 23*(21), 16, 20.

Richard, A. (2005). Fla. board seeks social-promotion ban in all grades. *Education Week, 24*(20), 22, 27.

Richardson, J., & Newby, T. (2005, April). *The role of students' cognitive engagement in online learning.* Paper presented at the annual meeting of the American Educational Research Association, Montreal.

Richardson, P., & Watt, H. (2005). "I've decided to become a teacher": Influences on career change. *Teaching and Teacher Education, 21,* 475–489.

Richardson, V. (2003, April). *Preservice teachers' beliefs.* Paper presented at the annual meeting of the American Educational Research Association, Chicago.

Rimer, S. (2009). *Immigrants see charter schools as a haven. New York Times.* Retrieved January 2009 from http://www.nytimes.com/2009/01/10/education/10charter.html?partner=rss

Riordan, C. (2004). *Equality and achievement: An introduction to the sociology of education* (2nd ed.). Upper Saddle River, NJ: Merrill/Prentice Hall.

Robelen, E. (2006a). D.C. schools that take vouchers found to be less racially isolated. *Education Week, 25*(20), 13.

Robelen, E. (2006b). Disputes over charter closures winding up in court. *Education Week, 25*(16), 1, 11.

Robelen, E. (2006c). No test-score edge for Cleveland voucher students. *Education Week, 25*(24), 18.

Robelen, E. (2009a). Growth of "neovouchers" sparks debate over policies. *Education Week, 28*(16), 18–19.

Robelen, E. (2009b). Quality seen as job one for charters. *Education Week, 28*(22), 1, 16.

Roberts, S. (2007). In name count, Garcias are catching up to Joneses. *New York Times.* Retrieved November 17, 2007, from http://www.nytimes.com/2007/22/17/us/17surnames.html?th&emc=th

Roberts, W. (2006). *Bullying from both sides.* Thousand Oaks, CA: Corwin Press.

Roblyer, M., & Doering, A. (2010). *Integrating educational technology into teaching* (5th ed.). Upper Saddle River, NJ: Merrill/Prentice Hall.

Rocha, A. (2006, March 1). The sex education controversy. *The Palo Alto Weekly: Online Edition.* Retrieved June 13, 2006, from http://www.paloaltoonline.com/weekly/story.php?story_id=461

Roeser, R., Peck, S., & Nasir, N. (2006). Self and identity processes in school motivation, learning and achievement. In P. Alexander &

P. Winne (Eds.), *Handbook of educational psychology* (2nd ed., pp. 391–424). Mahwah, NJ: Erlbaum.

Roffman, D. M. (2005). Lakoff for sexuality educators: The power and magic of "framing." *SIECUS Report, 33*(4), 20–25.

Rogers, C. (1967). Learning to be free. In C. Rogers & B. Stevens (Eds.), *The problem of being human.* Lafayette, CA: Real People Press.

Rogers, J., & Oakes, J. (2005). John Dewey speaks to Brown: Research, democratic social movement strategies, and the struggle for education on equal terms. *Teachers College Record, 107*(9), 2178–2203.

Romano, L. (2006, January 6). Fla. voucher system struck down: Court's ruling could affect programs in other states. *Washington Post,* p. A05. Retrieved April 23, 2006, from http://www.washingtonpost.com/wp-dyn/content/article/2006/01/05/AR2006010501983.html

Romano, M. (2006). "Bumpy moments" in teaching: Reflections from practicing teachers. *Teaching and Teacher Education, 22,* 973–985.

Romboy, D., & Kinkead, L. (2005, April 14). Surviving in America. *Deseret Morning News, 155*(303), pp. 1, 11, 12.

Rose, L., & Gallup, A. (1998). The 30th annual Phi Delta Kappa/Gallup Poll of the public's attitudes toward the public schools. *Phi Delta Kappan, 80,* 41–56.

Rose, L., & Gallup, A. (2006). The 38th annual Phi Delta Kappa/Gallup poll of the public's attitudes toward the public schools. *Phi Delta Kappan, 88*(1), 51–53.

Rose, L., & Gallup, A. (2007). The 39th annual Phi Delta Kappa/Gallup poll of the public's attitudes toward the public schools. *Phi Delta Kappan, 89,* 33–48.

Rosen, L., O'Leary, S., Joyce, S., Conway, G., & Pfiffner, L. (1984). The importance of prudent negative consequences for maintaining the appropriate behavior of hyperactive students. *Journal of Abnormal Child Psychology, 12,* 581–604.

Rosenshine, B. (2006). The struggles of the lower-scoring students. *Teaching and Teacher Education, 22,* 555–562.

Ross, K. (2005). Charter schools and integration: The experience in Michigan. In J. Betts & T. Loveless (Eds.), *Getting choice right: Ensuring equity and efficiency in education policy* (pp. 146–175). Washington, DC: Brookings Institution Press.

Rother, C. (2005). Teachers talk tech. *Technological Horizons in Education, 33*(3), 34–36.

Rothman, R. (1997). KERA: A tale of one school. *Phi Delta Kappan, 79,* 272–275.

Rothstein, R. (2004a). *Class and schools: Using social, economic, and educational reform to close the black–white achievement gap.* New York: Teachers College Press.

Rothstein, R. (2004b). The achievement gap. *Educational Leadership, 62*(3), 40–43.

Rowe, M. (1986). Wait-time: Slowing down may be a way of speeding up. *Journal of Teacher Education, 37*(1), 43–50.

Rubenstein, G. (2007). Head of class: Home room. *Edutopia, 3*(1), 17.

Rubin, K., Bukowski, W., & Parker, J. (2006). Peer interactions, relationships, and groups. In N. Eisenberg (Vol. Ed.), *Handbook of child psychology: Vol. 3. Social, emotional, and personality development* (6th ed., pp. 571–645). Hoboken, NJ: Wiley.

Rubinson, F. (2004). Urban dropouts: Why so many and what can be done? In S. R. Steinberg & J. L. Kincheloe (Eds.), *19 Urban questions: Teaching in the city* (pp. 53–67). New York: Peter Lang.

Rutter, M., Maughan, B., Mortimore, P., Ouston, J., & Smith, A. (1979). *Fifteen thousand hours: Secondary schools and their effects on children*. Cambridge, MA: Harvard University Press.

Ryan, K., Ryan, A., Arbuthnot, K., & Samuels, M. (2007). Students' motivation for standardized math exams. *Educational Researcher, 36*(1), 5–13.

Sabo, D., Miller, K., Farrell, M., Barnes, G., & Melnick, M. (1998). The women's sports foundation report: Sport and teen pregnancy. *Volleyball, 26*(3), 20–23.

Sack-Min, J. (2007a). The issues of IDEA. *American School Board Journal, 194*(3), 20–25.

Sack-Min, J. (2007b). The new breed: Today's big-city mayors eye takeovers as an opportunity to produce results. *American School Board Journal, 194*(11), 35–37.

Saha, L., & Biddle, B. (2006). The innovative principal: Research in action. *Principal, 85*(5), 28–31.

Saltman, M. (2005). *The Edison schools: Corporate schooling and the assault on public education*. New York: Routledge/Falmer.

Samuels, C. (2006a). Flexibility detailed for testing students with disabilities. *Education Week, 25*(16), 20.

Samuels, C. (2006b). Stricter school soda limits offered. *Education Week, 25*(36), 1, 18.

Samuels, C. (2008). "Response to intervention" sparks interest, questions. *Education Week, 27*(20), 1, 13.

Samuels, C. (2009a). Abstinence education. *Education Week, 28*(16), 5.

Samuels, C. (2009b). Recess and behavior. *Education Week, 28*(20), 4.

Samuels, C. (2009c). "What works" guide gives RTI thumbs up on reading. *Education Week, 28*(23), 7.

San Antonio, D. (2006). Broadening the world of early adolescents. *Educational Leadership, 63*(7), 8–13.

San Francisco Schools. (2008). *Study: Local KIPP schools lose 60% of their students*. San Francisco: Author. Retrieved February 22, 2008, from http://www.sfschools.org/2008/09/study-local-kipp-schools-lose-60-of.html

Sandham, J. (2000). Home sweet school. *Education Week, 19*(20), 24–29.

Sandovi, C. (2008). *Earn an A? Here's $50. (Eke out a C? That's still good for $20.) A Chicago Public Schools pilot program will pay up to 5,000 freshmen for good grades. Is that a smart idea? Chicago Tribune*. Retrieved January 16, 2009, from http://archives.chicagotribune.com/2008/sep/11/local/chi-money-for-grades-11-sep11

Sapon-Shevin, M. (2007). *Widening the circle: The power of inclusive classrooms*. Boston: Beacon Press.

Sawchuk, S. (2008). Study details barriers to career-changers going into teaching. *Education Week, 28*(4), 10–11.

Sawchuk, S. (2009a). "21st Century Skills" focus shifts W. Va. teachers' role. *Education Week, 28*(16), 1, 12.

Sawchuk, S. (2009b). Backers of "21st Century Skills" take flak. *Education Week, 28*(23), 1, 14.

Sawchuk, S. (2009c). Stimulus bill spurs focus on teachers. *Education Week, 28*(24), 1, 18.

Sawchuk, S. (2009d). Teacher training goes in virtual directions. *Education Week, 28*(26), 22–25.

Schemo, D. (2006). Federal rules back single-sex public education. *New York Times*. Retrieved March 2009 from www.nytimes.com/2006/10/25/education/25gender.html?pagewanted=1&ei=50887en=70f2ee029e27c6c3&ex=1319428800&partner=rssnyt&emc=rss

Schibsted, E. (2006). Fighting for fitness. *Edutopia, 1*(9), 30–37.

Schiever, S., & Maker, C. J. (2003). New directions in enrichment and acceleration. In N. Colangelo & G. Davis (Eds.), *Handbook of gifted education* (3rd ed., pp. 163–173). Boston: Allyn & Bacon.

Schimmel, D., & Militello, M. (2007). Legal literacy for teachers: A neglected responsibility. *Harvard Educational Review, 77*(3), 257–284.

Schlesinger, A. (1992). *The disuniting of America: Reflections on a multicultural society*. New York: Norton.

Schnaiberg, L. (2000). Charter schools: Choice, diversity may be at odds. *Education Week, 19*(35), 1, 18–20.

School Board of Nassau County, Florida v. Arline, 480 U.S. 273 (1987).

Schraw, G., & Lehman, S. (2001). Situational interest: A review of the literature and directions for future research. *Educational Psychology Review, 13*(1), 23–52.

Schrimpf, C. (2006). This is me. In E. Keefe, V. Moore, & F. Duff (Eds.), *Listening to the experts* (pp. 87–90). Baltimore, MD: Paul H. Brookes.

Schulz, L., & Bonawitz, E. (2007). Serious fun: Preschoolers engage in more exploratory play when evidence is confounded. *Developmental Psychology, 43*(4), 1034–1050.

Schunk, D. (2004). *Learning theories: An educational perspective* (4th ed.). Upper Saddle River, NJ: Merrill/Prentice Hall.

Schunk, D., Pintrich, P., & Meece, J. (2008). *Motivation in education: Theory, research, and applications* (3rd ed.). Upper Saddle River, NJ: Merrill/Pearson.

Schutz, A. (2006). Home is a prison in the global city: The tragic failure of school-based community engagement strategies. *Review of Educational Research, 76*(4), 691–743.

Scott, J. (2005). *School choice and diversity: What the evidence says*. New York: Teachers College Press.

Sears, J. (1993). Responding to the sexual diversity of faculty and students: Sexual praxis and the critically reflective administrator. In C. Capper (Ed.), *Educational administration in a pluralistic society*. Albany, NY: SUNY Press.

Seider, S. (2009). An MI odyssey. *Edutopia, 5*(2), 26–29.

Sergiovanni, T. (2009a). *Educational governance and administration* (6th ed.). Boston: Allyn & Bacon.

Sergiovanni, T. (2009b). *Principalship: The reflective practitioner perspective* (6th ed.). Boston: Allyn & Bacon.

Sessions-Stepp, L. (2007). Study casts doubt on abstinence-only programs. *The Washington Post*. Retrieved January 28, 2009, from http://www.washingtonpost.com/wp-dyn/content/article/2007/04/13/AR2007041301003.html

Sewall, G. (2000). History 2000: Why the older textbooks may be better than the new. *Education Week, 19*(38), 36, 52.

Shakeshaft, C., Mandel, L., Johnson, Y., Sawyer, J., Hergenrother, M., & Barber, E. (1997). Boys call me cow. *Educational Leadership, 55*(2), 22–25.

Shapka, J., & Keating, D. (2003). Effects of a girls-only curriculum during adolescence: Performance, persistence, and engagement in mathematics and science. *American Educational Research Journal, 40*(4), 929–960.

Sheldon, S. (2007). Improving student attendance with school, family, and community partnerships. *Journal of Educational Research, 199*(5), 267–275.

Shepard, L., & Smith, M. (1990). Synthesis of research on grade retention. *Educational Leadership, 47*(8), 84–88.

Silver-Pacuilla, H., & Fleischman, S. (2006). Technology to help struggling students. *Educational Leadership, 63*(5), 84–85.

Simonson, M., Smaldino, S., Albright, M., & Zavacek, S. (2009). *Teaching and learning at a distance* (4th ed.). Upper Saddle River, NJ: Pearson.

Sincero, P., & Woyshner, C. (2003). Writing women into the curriculum. *Social Education, 67,* 218–225.

Singh, N., Lancioni, G., Joy, S., Winton, A., Sabaawi, M., Wahler, R., & Singh, J. (2007). Adolescents with conduct disorder can be mindful of their aggressive behavior. *Journal of Emotional and Behavioral Disorders, 15,* 56–63.

Siris, K., & Osterman, K. (2004). Interrupting the cycle of bullying and victimization in the elementary classroom. *Phi Delta Kappan, 86*(4), 288–291.

Skiba, R., Michael, R., Nardo, A., & Peterson, R. (2002). The color of discipline: Sources of racial and gender disproportionality in school punishment. *The Urban Review, 34,* 317–342.

Skiba, R., & Peterson, R. (1999). The dark side of zero tolerance. *Phi Delta Kappan, 80,* 372–376, 381–382.

Slavin, R. (2009). *Educational psychology* (9th ed.). Boston: Allyn & Bacon.

Slavin, R., & Cheung, A. (2004). *Effective reading programs for English language learners: A best-evidence synthesis.* Baltimore: Center for Research on the Education of Students Placed At Risk, Johns Hopkins University. Retrieved April 23, 2006, from www.csos.jhu.edu/crespar/techReports/Report66.pdf

Slavin, R., & Cheung, A. (2005). A synthesis of research on language of reading instruction for English language learners. *Review of Educational Research, 75*(2), 247–284.

Sleeter, C. (2005). *Un-standardizing curriculum: Multicultural teaching in the standards-based classroom.* New York: Teachers College Press.

Smart, C. (2008, November 20). Wasatch school district may realign schools. *Salt Lake Tribune,* p. B3.

Smith v. Board of School Commissioners of Mobile County, 827 F.2d 684 (llth Cir., 1987).

Smith, F. (2005). Intensive care. *Edutopia, 1*(9), 47–49.

Smith, F. (2006). Learning by giving. *Edutopia, 2*(1), 54–57.

Smith, J., Brewer, D., & Heffner, T. (2003). Using portfolio assessments with young children who are at risk for school failure. *Preventing School Failure, 48*(1), 38–40.

Smith, P., Molnar, A., & Zahorik, J. (2003). Class-size reduction: A fresh look at the data. *Educational Leadership, 61*(1), 72–74.

Smith, T., Desimone, L., & Ueno, K. (2005). "Highly qualified" to do what? The relationship between NCLB teacher quality mandates and the use of reform-oriented instruction in middle school mathematics. *Educational Evaluation and Policy Analysis, 27*(1), 75–109.

Smith, T., Polloway, E., Patton, J., & Dowdy, C. (2004). *Teaching students with special needs in inclusive settings* (4th ed.). Boston: Allyn & Bacon.

Snider, J. (2006). The superintendent as scapegoat. *Education Week, 25*(18), 40, 31.

Soenens, B., Vansteenkiste, M., Lens, W., Luyckx, K., Goossens, L., Beyers, W., & Ryan, R. (2007). Conceptualizing parental autonomy support: Adolescent perceptions of promotion of independence versus promotion of volitional functioning. *Developmental Psychology, 43*(1), 633–646.

Solley, B. (2007). On standardized testing. *Childhood Education, 84,* 31–37.

Sommers, C. (2000). *The war against boys: How misguided feminism is harming our young men.* New York: Simon & Schuster.

Sommers, C. (2008). The case against Title-Nining the sciences. *Teachers College Record.* Retrieved October 1, 2008, from http://www.tcrecord.org

Sonnenberg, W. (2004). Federal support for education: Fiscal years 1980 to 2003. *National Center for Education Statistics: Education Statistics Quarterly, 6*(3), 65–68.

Sorenson, R. (2007). Bible board. *American School Board Journal, 194*(5), 32–34.

Speer, N. (2008). Connecting beliefs and practice: A fine-grained analysis of a college mathematics teacher's collections of beliefs and their relationship to his instructional practices. *Cognition and Instruction, 26,* 218–267.

Spring, J. (2005). *The American School 1642–2004* (6th ed.). Boston: McGraw-Hill.

Spring, J. (2006). *American education* (12th ed.). Boston: McGraw-Hill.

Sracic, P. (2006). *San Antonio v. Rodriguez and the pursuit of equal education: The debate over discrimination and school funding.* Lawrence: University Press of Kansas.

Stabiner, K. (2003, January 12). Where the girls aren't. *New York Times.* Retrieved April 2005 from http://www.nytimes.com/2003/01/12/education/where-the-girls-aren-t.html

Stahl, R., DeMasi, K., Gehrke, R., Guy, C., & Scown, J. (2005, April). *Perceptions, conceptions and misconceptions of wait time and wait time behaviors among pre-service and in-service teachers.* Paper presented at the annual meeting of the American Educational Research Association, Montreal.

Stahl, S. (1999). Different strokes for different folks? A critique of learning styles. *American Educator, 23,* 27–31.

Stahl, S. (2002). Different strokes for different folks? In L. Abbeduto (Ed.), *Taking sides: Clashing on controversial issues in educational psychology* (pp. 98–107). Guilford, CT: McGraw-Hill/Duskin.

Standen, A. (2007). Gender matters: Educators battle over single-sex schools. *Edutopia, 3*(1), 46–49.

Starnes, B. (2006). What we don't know *can* hurt them: White teachers, Indian children. *Phi Delta Kappan, 87*(5), 384–392.

Steches, B., Hamilton, L., & Scott-Naflet, S. (2005, April). *Introduction to first-year findings: Implementing standards-based accountability (ISBA) project.* Paper presented at the annual meeting of the American Educational Research Association, Montreal.

Steele, C., Spencer, S., & Aronson, J. (2002). Contending with group image: The psychology of stereotype and social identity threat. In M. Zanna (Ed.), *Advances in experimental social psychology* (Vol. 34, pp. 379–440). San Diego: Academic Press.

Steering Committee on Science and Creationism. (1999). *Science and creationism: A view from the National Academy of Sciences* (2nd ed.). Washington, DC: National Academies Press.

Stehr, M. (2004). Study credits attractive people with longer life. *Daily Nebraskan.* Retrieved March 2009 from http://www.pbs.org/weta/washingtonweek/voices/200412/1206nat1.html

Sternberg, R. (2007). Who are bright children? The cultural context of being and acting intelligent. *Educational Researcher, 36*(3), 148–155.

Stiggins, R. (2005). *Student-centered classroom assessment* (4th ed.). Upper Saddle River, NJ: Merrill/Pearson.

Stiggins, R. (2007). Assessment through the student's eyes. *Educational Leadership, 64*(8), 22–26.

Stiggins, R. (2008a). *An introduction to student-involved assessment for learning.* Upper Saddle River, NJ: Pearson.

Stiggins, R. (2008b). *Student-involved assessment for learning* (5th ed.). Upper Saddle River, NJ: Merrill/Pearson.

Stigler, J., Gonzales, P., Kawanaka, T., Knoll, T., & Serrano, A. (1999). *The TIMSS videotape classroom study: Methods and finding from an exploratory research project on eighth-grade mathematics instruction in Germany, Japan, and the United States* (NCES 990074). Washington, DC: U.S. Department of Education, National Center for Educational Statistics.

Stipek, D. (2002). *Motivation to learn* (4th ed.). Boston: Allyn & Bacon.

Stipek, D. (2006). Relationships matter. *Educational Leadership, 64*(1), 46–49.

Stobbe, M. (2007, December 4). Studies suggest online harassment of children is on the rise. *Salt Lake Tribune,* p. E4.

Stodgill, R., & Nixon, R. (2007). For schools, lottery payoffs fall short of promises. *New York Times.* Retrieved October 2007 from www.nytimes.com/2007/10/07/business/07lotto.html

Stone v. Graham, 449 U.S. 39 (1981)

Stoughton, E. (2007). "How will I get them to behave?": Pre service teachers reflect on classroom management. *Teaching and Teacher Education, 23,* 1024–1037.

Stover, D. (2008). Take it to the limit. *American School Board Journal, 194*(11), 33–34.

Stover, D., & Hardy, L. (2008). As tutoring becomes a billion-dollar industry, are you doing what it takes to make a difference for your students? *American School Board Journal, 195*(2), 15–19.

Strickland, B. & Turnbull, A. (1990). *Developing and implementing Individualized Education Programs* (3rd ed.). Upper Saddle River, NJ: Merrill/Prentice Hall.

Strong, J., & Hindman, J. (2003). Hiring the best teachers. *Educational Leadership, 60*(8), 48–52.

Stutz, T. (2007, May 12). 16% fail TAKS graduation test. *Dallas Morning News.* Retrieved December 2008 from http://www.dallasnews.com/sharedcontent/dws/news/texassouthwest/stories/051207dntextaksfails.5c9ba6b1.html

Swaim, S. (2004). Strength in the middle. *Education Week, 23*(32), 32.

Swanson, C. (2004). *The real truth about low graduation rates: An evidence-based commentary.* Washington, DC: Urban Institute. Retrieved March 30, 2006, from http://www.urban.org

Swanson, C. (2006a). Bigger district size gives superintendents earnings edge. *Education Week, 25*(43), 18–19.

Swanson, C. (2006b). Tracking U.S. trends. *Education Week, Technology Counts, 25*(35), 50–55.

Swanson, C. (2008). Grading the states. *Education Week, 27*(18), 36–38.

Swarns, R. (2008). *U.S. reports drop in homeless population. New York Times.* Retrieved July 30, 2008, from http://www.nytimes.com/2008/07/30/us/30homeless.html

Swidler, S. (2004). *Naturally small.* Greenwich, CT: Information Age.

Sykes, S. (2006, July 31). College recruitment efforts will raise tuition. *Salt Lake Tribune,* p. B5.

Szczesiul, S. (2004, April). *Urban definitions, urban differentials: Implications for how new teachers locate the urban school problem.* Paper presented at the annual meeting of the American Educational Research Association, San Diego, CA.

Tallent-Runnels, M., Thomas, J., Lan, W., Cooper, S., Ahern, T., Shaw, S., & Liu, X. (2006). Teaching courses online: A review of the research. *Review of Educational Research, 76*(1), 93–135.

Tanner, D., & Tanner, L. (2007). *Curriculum development: Theory into practice.* (4th ed.). Upper Saddle River, NJ: Pearson.

Tanner, L. (2008, July 7). Cholesterol drugs OK'd for patients 8 and under. *Salt Lake Tribune,* p. A1.

Tanner, L. (2009, April 7). Among 4-year-olds, 1 in 5 obese. *Salt Lake Tribune,* p. A7.

Taylor, B., Pressley, M., & Pearson, P. (2002). Research-supported characteristics of teachers and schools that promote reading achievement. In B. Taylor & D. Pearson (Eds.), *Teaching reading: Effective schools, accomplished teachers* (pp. 361–374). Mahwah, NJ: Erlbaum.

Terwiller, H., & Toppo, G. (2008, March 10). Home schooling takes a hit. *USA Today,* p. 5D.

Texas Education Agency. (2008a). *Texas essential knowledge and skills.* Retrieved November 1, 2008, from: http://www.tea.state.tx.us/teks/

Texas Education Agency. (2008b). *Chapter 111. Texas essential knowledge and skills for mathematics: Subchapter A. Elementary.* Retrieved November 2008 from http://www.tea.state.tx.us/rules/tac/chapter111/ch111a.html

Texas Education Agency. (2008c). *Texas Assessment of Knowledge and Skills (TAKS) - Spring 2006.* Retrieved November 2008 from http://scotthochberg.com/files/taas/math4.pdf

Thiers, N. (2006). Do single-sex classes raise academic achievement? *Educational Leadership, 63*(7), 70.

Thirunarayanan, M. (2004). National Board certification for teachers: A billion dollar hoax. *Teachers College Record.* Retrieved May 24, 2005, from http://www.tcrecord.org

Thornton, S. (2003). Silence on gays and lesbians in social studies curriculum. *Social Education, 67,* 226–230.

Thornton, S. (2005). *Teaching social studies that matters: Curriculum for active learning.* New York: Teachers College Press.

Tinker v. Des Moines Community School District, 393 U.S. 503 (1969).

Tomasello, M. (2006). Acquiring linguistic constructions. In D. Kuhn & R. Siegler (Vol. Eds.), *Handbook of child psychology: Vol. 2. Cognition, perception, and language* (6th ed., pp. 255–298). Hoboken, NJ: Wiley.

Tomlinson, C. (2006). *Fulfilling the promise of the differentiated classroom: Strategies and tools for responsive teaching.* Alexandria, VA: Association for Supervision and Curriculum Development.

Tompkins, G. (2009). *Literacy for the 21st century: A balanced approach* (5th ed.). Upper Saddle River, NJ: Merrill/Prentice Hall.

Tompkins, R. (2008). Rural schools: Growing, diverse, and . . . complicated. *Education Week, 27*(19), 24–25.

Tong, F., Lara-Alecio, R., Irby, B., Mathes, P., & Kwok, O. (2008). Accelerating early academic oral English development in transitional bilingual and structured English immersion programs. *American Educational Research Journal, 45*(4), 1011–1044.

Tonn, J. (2005a). First amendment attitudes found troubling. *Education Week, 24*(21), 6.

Tonn, J. (2005b). Sexual behavior. *Education Week, 25*(9), 15.

Toppo, G. (2008). Good grades pay off literally. *USA Today.* Retrieved January 17, 2009, from http://www.usatoday.com/news/education/2008-01-27-grades_N.htm

Toppo, G. (2009, February 12). KIPP proves powerful point. *USA Today*, p. 6D.

Townsend, B. L. (2000). The disproportionate discipline of African American learners: Reducing school suspension and expulsions. *Exceptional Children, 66,* 381–391.

Trotter, A. (2006a). Minorities still face digital divide. *Education Week, 26*(3), 14.

Trotter, A. (2006b). U.S. court backs school's decision to bar student's anti-gay T-shirt. *Education Week, 25*(34), 9.

Trotter, A., (2007, June 2.). Online testing demands careful planning. *Education Week: Digital Directions*, pp. 20–21.

Turiel, E. (2006). The development of morality. In N. Eisenberg (Vol. Ed.), *Handbook of child psychology: Vol. 3. Social, emotional, and personality development* (6th ed., pp. 789–857). Hoboken, NJ: Wiley.

Turnbull, A., Turnbull, R., &. Wehmeyer, M. (2010). *Exceptional lives: Special education in today's schools* (6th ed.). Upper Saddle River, NJ: Merrill/Pearson.

Tyack, D. (2003). *Seeking common ground: Public schools in a diverse society.* Cambridge, MA: Harvard University Press.

Tyson, H. (1999). A load off the teachers' backs: Coordinated school health programs. *Phi Delta Kappan, 80*(5), K1–K8.

Ubben, G., Hughes, L., & Norris, C. (2006). *The principal: Creative leadership for excellences in schools* (6th ed.). Boston: Allyn & Bacon.

Underwood, J., & Webb, L. (2006). *School law for teachers.* Upper Saddle River, NJ: Pearson.

U.S. Bureau of Census. (2003). *Statistical abstract of the United States* (123rd ed.). Washington, DC: U.S. Government Printing Office.

U.S. Bureau of Census. (2004). *The foreign-born population in the United States: 2003.* Washington, DC: U.S. Government Printing Office.

U.S. Bureau of Census. (2005). *Income, poverty, and health insurance coverage in the United States, 2004.* Washington, DC: U.S. Government Printing Office.

U.S. Bureau of Census. (2006a). *Effects of government taxes and transfers on income and poverty: 2004.* Washington, DC: U.S. Government Printing Office.

U.S. Bureau of Census. (2006b). *Statistical Abstract of the United States: 2006* (126th ed.). Washington, DC: U.S. Government Printing Office.

U.S. Bureau of Census. (2007a). *American community survey (online).* Retrieved September 19, 2008, from http://www.census.gov/acs/www/Products/index.html

U.S. Bureau of Census. (2007b). *Income, earnings, and poverty estimates released in American Fact Finder, 8/28/07.* Retrieved December 19, 2007, from http://factfinder.census.gov/home/saff/main.html?_lang=en

U.S. Bureau of Indian Affairs. (1974). Government schools for Indians (1881). In S. Cohen (Ed.), *Education in the United States: A documentary history* (Vol. 3, pp. 1734–1756). New York: Random House.

U.S. Department of Education. (1995). *Digest of education statistics, 1994.* Washington, DC: U.S. Government Printing Office.

U.S. Department of Education. (1999a). *Digest of education statistics, 1998.* Washington, DC: U.S. Government Printing Office.

U.S. Department of Education. (1999b). *Teachers' guide to religion in the public schools.* Washington, DC: Author.

U.S. Department of Education. (2003a). *Digest of education statistics, 2002.* Washington, DC: U.S. Government Printing Office.

U.S. Department of Education. (2003b). Title I—Improving the academic achievement of the disadvantaged. *Federal Register, 68*(236). Washington, DC: U.S. Government Printing Office.

U.S. Department of Education. (2004a). Individuals with Disabilities Education Act (IDEA) data (Table AA3). Washington, DC: Author. Retrieved August 23, 2005, from http://www.ideadata.org/PartBdata.asp

U.S. Department of Education. (2004b). *Twenty-sixth annual report to Congress on the implementation of the Individuals With Disabilities Education Act.* Washington, DC: U.S. Government Printing Office.

U.S. Department of Education. (2005a). *Education for homeless children and youth.* Washington, DC: U.S. Government Printing Office. Retrieved July 12, 2006, from www.ed.gov//programs/homeless/index.html

U.S. Department of Education. (2005b). *The condition of education in 2005 in brief.* Washington DC: National Center for Education Statistics.

U.S. Department of Education. (2006a). *Fact sheet on Title I.* Retrieved August 15, 2006, from http://www.ed.gov/title1

U.S. Department of Education. (2006b). *Magnet schools assistance program.* Retrieved June 13, 2006, from http://www.ed.gov/programs/magnet

U.S. Department of Education. (2006c). *Statistics of state school systems: Revenues and expenditures to public elementary and secondary education, 2001–2002.* Washington, DC: National Center for Education Statistics.

U.S. Department of Education. (2008a). *Common core of data.* Washington, DC: Author.

U.S. Department of Education. (2008b). *Digest of education statistics, 2007.* Washington, DC: Author.

U.S. Department of Health and Human Services. (2006). *AIDS info.* Retrieved July 31, 2006, from http://www.aidsinfo.nih.gov/

U.S. Department of Health and Human Services. (2007). *The 2007 HHS poverty guidelines—One version of the U.S. Federal Poverty Measure (2007).* Retrieved July 9, 2008, from http://aspe.hhs.gov/poverty/07poverty.shtml

U.S. English. (2008). *Official English.* Retrieved March 2008 from http://www.us-english.org

U.S. Government Accounting Office. (2006). *No Child Left Behind Act: Additional assistance and research on effective strategies would help small rural districts.* Washington, DC: U.S. Government Printing Office.

U.S. Government Printing Office. (1975). *Historical statistics of the United States: Colonial times to 1970* (Vol. I). Washington, DC: Author.

Valencia, S., Place, N., Martin, S., & Grossman P. (2006). Curriculum materials for elementary reading: Shackles and scaffolds for four beginning teachers. *Elementary School Journal, 107*(1), 93–120.

Van de Walle, J., Karp, K., & Williams, M. (2010). *Elementary and middle school mathematics: Teaching developmentally* (7th ed.). Boston: Pearson.

van den Berg, R. (2002). Teachers' meanings regarding educational practice. *Review of Educational Research, 72,* 577–625.

van Gelder, T. (2005). Teaching critical thinking: Some lessons from cognitive science. *College Teaching, 53,* 41–46.

Van Horn, R. (2008). *Bridging the chasm between research and practice: A guide to major educational research.* Lanham, MD: Rowman & Littlefield Education.

Vander Ark, T. (2002). It's all about size. *American School Board Journal, 89*(20), 34–35.

Vander Ark, T. (2003). America's high school crisis: Policy reforms that will make a difference. *Education Week, 22*(29), 52, 41.

Vaughn, S., & Bos, C. (2006). *Strategies for teaching students with learning and behavior problems* (6th ed.). Boston: Allyn & Bacon.

Vaughn, S., Bos, C., Candace, S., & Schumm, J. (2006). *Teaching exceptional, diverse, and at-risk students in the general education classroom* (3rd ed.). Boston: Allyn & Bacon.

Vergon, C. (2001, April). *The exclusion of students of color from elementary and secondary schools: A national dilemma and some research-based suggestions for its resolution.* Paper presented at the annual meeting of the American Educational Research Association, Seattle, WA.

Viadero, D. (1996). Middle school gains over 25 years chronicled. *Education Week 16*(8), 7.

Viadero, D. (1999). Education Department is set to release its list of recommended math programs. *Education Week, 19*(6), 1, 14.

Viadero, D. (2000). Lags in minority achievement defy traditional explanations. *Education Week, 19*(28), 1, 18–19, 21.

Viadero, D. (2003a). Staying power. *Education Week, 22*(39), 24–27.

Viadero, D. (2003b). Two studies highlight links between violence, bullying by students. *Education Week, 22*(36), 6.

Viadero, D. (2005a). Key data on charter achievement missing as policy questions mount. *Education Week, 25*(13), 6.

Viadero, D. (2005b). Smoking-prevention programs in schools found ineffective for teens. *Education Week, 24*(26), 6.

Viadero, D. (2006). Rose reports influence felt 40 years later. *Education Week, 25*(41), 1, 21–24.

Viadero, D. (2008a). Career academies found to pay off in higher earnings. *Education Week, 27*(43), 10.

Viadero, D. (2008b). Evidence for moving to K–8 model not airtight. *Education Week, 27*(19), 1, 12.

Viadero, D. (2008c). Research yields clues on the effects of extra time for learning. *Education Week, 28*(5), 16, 17.

Viadero, D. (2008d). Social development. *Education Week, 28*(15), 5.

Viadero, D. (2009a). Book probes scoring gaps tied to race. *Education Week, 28*(20), 1, 10, 11.

Viadero, D. (2009b). Delving deep: Research hones focus on ELLs. *Education Week, 28*(17), 22–25.

Viadero, D., & Honawar, V. (2008). Credential of NBPT has impact. *Education Week, 27*(42), 1, 16.

Virtual High School. (2009). *About us.* Retrieved March 2009 from http://www.govhs.org/website.nsf

Votruba-Drzal, E. (2006). Economic disparities in middle childhood development: Does income matter? *Developmental Psychology, 42*(6), 1154–1167.

Wadsworth, D. (2001). Why new teachers choose to teach. *Educational Leadership, 58*(8), 24–28.

Wainer, H., & Zwerling, H. (2006). Evidence that smaller schools do not improve student achievement. *Phi Delta Kappan, 88*(4), 300–303.

Walberg, H. (2003). Accountability helps students at risk. *Education Week, 22*(33), 42, 44.

Walsh, B. (2008). Dying for a drink. *Time, 172*(24), 46–49.

Walsh, M. (2000a). Church–state rulings cut both ways. *Education Week, 19*(42), 1, 40–41.

Walsh, M. (2000b). Voucher initiatives defeated in Calif., Mich. *Education Week, 19*(11), 14, 18.

Walsh, M. (2002a). Charting the new landscape of school choice. *Education Week, 21*(42), 1, 18–21.

Walsh, M. (2002b). Peer grading passes muster, justices agree. *Education Week, 21*(24), 1, 28, 29.

Walsh, M. (2003a). Private management of schools. *Education Week, 22*(29), 17.

Walsh, M. (2003b). Reports paint opposite pictures of Edison achievement. *Education Week, 22*(25), 5.

Walsh, M., & Hendrie, C. (2003). High court upholds law on Internet filtering in libraries. *Education Week, 24*(42), 24.

Wang, J., & Odell, S. (2002). Mentored learning to teach according to standards-based reform: A critical review. *Review of Educational Research, 72,* 481–546.

Wang, S., Treat, T., & Brownell, K. (2008). Cognitive processing about classroom-relevant contexts: Teachers' attention to and utilization of girls' body size, ethnicity, attractiveness and facial affect. *Journal of Educational Psychology, 100*(2), 473–489.

Ware, H., & Kitsantas, A. (2007). Teacher and collective efficacy beliefs as predictors of professional commitment. *Journal of Educational Research, 100*(5), 303–310.

Warner, J. (2009). Dude, you've got problems. *New York Times.* Retrieved April 2009 from http://warner.blogs.nytimes.com/2009/04/16/who-are-you-calling-gay/?em

Warnick, B. (2007). Surveillance cameras in schools: An ethical analysis. *Harvard Educational Review, 77*(3), 317–343.

Warren, J., Jenkins, K., & Kulick, R. (2006). High school exit examinations and state-level completion and GED rates, 1975 through 2002. *Educational Evaluation and Policy Analysis, 28*(2), 131–152.

Wartofsky, A. (2001, February 19). The last word: Philip Pullman's trilogy for young adults ends with God's death and remarkably few critics. *Washington Post,* p. C–1.

Waterhouse, L. (2006). Multiple intelligences, the Mozart effect, and emotional intelligence: A critical review. *Educational Psychologist, 41*(4), 217–225.

Watkins, W. (2001). *The White architects of Black education: Ideology and power in America, 1860–1954.* New York: Teachers College Press.

Watson, M., & Battistich, V. (2006). Building and sustaining caring communities. In C. M. Evertson & C. S. Weinstein (Eds.), *Handbook of classroom management: Research, practice, and contemporary issues* (pp. 253–279). Mahwah, NJ: Erlbaum.

Watt, H., & Richardson, P. (2007). Motivational factors influencing teaching as a career choice: Development and validation of the FIT-choice scale. *Journal of Experimental Education, 75*(3), 167–202.

Waxman, H., Huang, S., Anderson, L., & Weinstein, T. (1997). Classroom process differences in inner-city elementary schools. *Journal of Educational Research, 91*(1), 49–59.

Wechsler, D. (2003). *Wechsler Intelligence Scale for Children* (4th ed.). San Antonio, TX: Psychological Corporation.

Weiner, L. (2006). *Urban teaching: The essentials.* New York: Teachers College Press.

Weinstein, C. (2007). *Middle and secondary classroom management* (3rd ed.). Boston: McGraw-Hill.

Weinstein, C., Curran, M., & Tomlinson-Clarke, S. (2003). Culturally responsive classroom management: Awareness into action. *Theory Into Practice, 42,* 269–276.

Weinstein, C., & Mignano, A., Jr. (2007). *Elementary classroom management: Lessons from research and practice* (4th ed.). New York: McGraw-Hill.

Weinstein, C., Tomlinson-Clarke, S., & Curran, M. (2004). Toward a conception of culturally responsive classroom management. *Journal of Teacher Education, 55,* 25–38.

Weiss, C., & Kipnes, L. (2006). Reexamining middle school effects: A comparison of middle grades students in middle schools and K–8 schools. *American Journal of Education, 112,* 239–272.

Weiss, L. (2005). Book battle in Fayetteville, AR, rages on. *School Library Journal, 51*(11), 20.

Weiss, S., DeFalco, A. A., & Weiss, E. M. (2005). Progressive = permissive? Not according to John Dewey . . . Subjects matter! *Essays in Education, 14,* 1–21.

Wells, A., & Frankenberg, E. (2007). The public schools and the challenge of the Supreme Court's integration decision. *Phi Delta Kappan, 89*(3), 178–188.

Wessel, K. (2005). Campus leaders: Why this gender discrepancy? *Lessons, 7*(1), 16–19.

West, M., & Manno, B. (2006). The elephant in the reform room. *Education Week, 25*(34), 44, 36.

Whalen, S. (2002). *The Polk Bros. Foundation's Full-Service Schools-Initiative: Synopsis of evaluation findings.* Retrieved June 1, 2006, from http://www.polkbrosfdn.org/full_service_schools_initiative.htm

Whitcomb, J., Borko, H., & Liston, D. (2006). Living in the tension—living with the heat. *Journal of Teacher Education, 57*(5), 447–453.

Whitcomb, J., Borko, H., & Liston, D. (2007). Stranger than fiction: Arthur Levine's *Educating School Teachers*—The basis for a proposal. *Journal of Teacher Education, 58*(3), 195–201.

Whitson, J. (2006, January 4). *The Dover (PA) evolution case: A true win for education? Teachers College Record.* Retrieved January 18, 2006, from http://www.tcrecord.org ID Number 12271.

Wiersma, W., & Jurs, S. (2005). *Research methods in education: An introduction* (8th ed.). Needham Heights, MA: Allyn & Bacon.

Wiggins, G., & McTighe, J. (2005). *Understanding by design* (2nd ed.). Upper Saddle River, NJ: Pearson.

Wiles, J., & Bondi, J. (2007). *Curriculum development: A guide to practice* (7th ed.). Upper Saddle River, NJ: Pearson.

Will KERA come to PA? (2003). *Education Advocate, 4*(3), 1–2. Retrieved August 14, 2005, from http://www.ceopa.org/documents/Page1–4_001.pdf

Willard, N. (2006). *Cyberbullying and cyberthreats: Responding to the challenge of online social cruelty, threats and distress.* Eugene, OR: Center for Safe and Responsible Internet Use.

Williams, J. (2003). Why great teachers stay. *Educational Leadership, 60*(8), 71–75.

Williams, J. (2007). Revolution from the faculty lounge: The emergence of teacher-led schools and cooperatives. *Phi Delta Kappan, 89*(3), 210–216.

Wilson, B., & Corbett, H. (2001). *Listening to urban kids: School reform and the teachers they want.* Albany: State University of New York Press.

Wilson, H., Pianta, R., & Stuhlman, M. (2007). Typical classroom experiences in first grade: The role of classroom climate and functional risk in the development of social competencies. *Elementary School Journal, 108*(2), 81–96.

Wilson, S., & Youngs, S. (2005). Research on accountability processes in teacher education. In M. Cochran-Smith & K. Zeichner, *Studying teacher education: The report of the AREA panel on research and teacher education* (pp. 591–644). Mahwah, NJ: Erlbaum.

Winitzky, N. (1994). Multicultural and mainstreamed classrooms. In R. Arends (Ed.), *Learning to teach* (3rd ed., pp. 132–170). New York: McGraw-Hill.

Winograd, K. (1998). Rethinking theory after practice: Education professor as elementary teacher. *Journal of Teacher Education, 49,* 296–303.

Winseman, A. (2005). *Religion in America: Who has none?* Retrieved November 2006 from http://www.galluppoll.com/content/?ci=20329&pg=1

Wittwer, J., & Renkl, A. (2008). Why instructional explanations often do not work: A framework for understanding the effectiveness of instructional explanations. *Educational Psychologist, 43*(1), 49–64.

Wolf, R. (2007, August 29). Poverty drops as nation's median income climbs. *USA Today,* p. 7A.

Wong, H., Britton, T., & Ganser, T. (2005). What the world can teach us about new teacher induction. *Phi Delta Kappan, 86*(5), 379–384.

Wood, K. (2005). *Interdisciplinary instruction* (3rd ed.). Upper Saddle River, NJ: Pearson.

Wood, M. (2005). *High school counselors say they lack skills to assist gay, lesbian students.* Retrieved July 14, 2006, from www.bsu.edu/news

Woodward, T. (2002, June 20). *Edison's failing grade. Corporate Watch.* Retrieved November 23, 2005, from http://www.corpwatch.org/issues/PID.jsp?articleid=2688

World of Sports Science. (2008). *Title IX and United States female sports participation.* Retrieved September 17, 2008, from http://www.faqs.org/sports-science/Sp-Tw/Title-IX-and-United-States-Female-Sports-Participation.html

Wubbels, T., Brekeimans, M., den Brok, P., & van Tartwijk, J. (2006). An interpersonal perspective on classroom management in secondary classrooms in the Netherlands. In C. M. Evertson & C. S. Weinstein (Eds.), *Handbook of classroom management: Research, practice, and contemporary issues* (pp. 1161–1191). Mahwah, NJ: Erlbaum.

Wynne, E. (1997, March). *Moral education and character education: A comparison/contrast.* Paper presented at the annual meeting of the American Educational Research Association, Chicago.

Wyse, A., Keesler, V., & Schneider, B. (2008). Assessing the effects of small school size on mathematics achievement: A propensity score-matching approach. *Teachers College Record, 110*(9). Retrieved April 2008 from http://www.tcrecord.org ID Number: 15175.

Yan, W., & Gong, Y. (2003, April). *Who selects teaching as a career? An analysis of Hispanic American high school students' career aspiration of teaching.* Paper presented at the annual meeting of the American Educational Research Association, Chicago.

Yates, G. (2000). Applying learning style research in the classroom. Some cautions and the way ahead. In R. Riding & R. Rayner (Eds.), *International perspectives on individual differences. Vol. 1: Cognitive styles* (pp. 347–364). Stamford, CT: Ablex.

Yecke, C. (2006). Mayhem in the middle. *Education Week, 25*(21), 44.

Yeh, Y. (2006). The interactive effects of personal traits and guided practices on preservice teachers' changes in personal teaching efficacy. *British Journal of Educational Technology, 37,* 513–526.

Young, M., & Penhollow, T. (2006). The impact of abstinence education: What does the research say? *American Journal of Health Education, 37*(4), 194–202.

Young, M., & Scribner, J. (1997, March). *The synergy of parental involvement and student engagement at the secondary level: Relationships of consequence in Mexican-American communities.* Paper presented at the annual meeting of the American Educational Research Association, Chicago.

Younger, M., & Warrington, M. (2006). Would Harry and Hermione have done better in single-sex classes? A review of single-sex teaching in coeducational secondary schools in the United Kingdom. *American Educational Research Journal, 43*(4), 579–620.

Zahorik, J. (1991). Teaching style and textbooks. *Teaching and Teacher Education, 7,* 185–196.

Zehr, M. (2002). Voters courted in two states on bilingual ed. *Education Week, 22*(2), 1, 22.

Zehr, M. (2004). Va. plan would ease standards for home school parents. *Education Week, 23*(34), 26.

Zehr, M. (2008). Native American history, culture gaining traction in state curricula. *Education Week, 28*(11), 1, 12.

Zehr, M. (2009). NYC test sizes up ELLs with little formal schooling. *Education Week, 28*(23), 13.

Zeichner, K. (2007). Accumulating knowledge across self-studies in teacher education. *Journal of Teacher Education, 58*(1), 36–46.

Zeldin, A., & Pajares, F. (2000). Against the odds: Self efficacy beliefs of women in mathematical, scientific, and technological careers. *American Educational Research Journal, 37,* 215–246.

Zhao, Y. (2002). Wave of pupils lacking English strains school. *New York Times.* Retrieved March 2005 from http://www.nytimes.com/2002/08/05/education/05ESL.html

Zientek, L. (2007). Preparing high-quality teachers: Views from the classroom. *American Educational Research Journal, 44*(4), 959–1001.

Zigler, E. (2009). A new Title I. *Education Week, 28*(20), 34, 26.

Zins, J., Bloodworth, M., Weissberg, R., & Walberg, H. (2004). The scientific base linking social and emotional learning to school success. In J. Zins, R. Weissberg, M. Wang, & H. Walberg (Eds.), *Building academic success on social and emotional learning* (pp. 3–22). New York: Teachers College Press.

Zirkel, P. (2001/2002). Decisions that have shaped U.S. education. *Educational Leadership, 59*(4), 6–12.

Zirkel, P. (2007). Weird science? *Phi Delta Kappan, 88*(5), 414–416.

Zirkel, P. (2008a). Much ado about a C? *Phi Delta Kappan, 89*(4), 310–318.

Zirkel, P. (2008b). Unfunded mandate? *Phi Delta Kappan, 90*(2), 701–703.

Zollars, N. (2000). Schools need rules when it comes to students with disabilities. *Education Week, 19*(25), 1, 46, 48.

Zuger, S. (2008a). Build better e portfolios. *Tech and Learning, 29*(1), 46–47.

Zuger, S. (2008b). Interactive math classroom adds up to success. *Tech and Learning, 29*(3), 14.

Zweirs, J. (2007). *Building academic language: Essential practice for content classrooms.* San Francisco: Jossey-Bass.

Glossary

A

Ability grouping. The practice of placing students of similar abilities into groups, and matching instruction to the needs of each group.

Academic freedom. The right of teachers to choose both content and teaching methods based on their professional judgment.

Academic learning time. The amount of time students are both engaged and successful.

Academy. An early secondary school that focused on the practical needs of colonial America as a growing nation.

Acceleration. A gifted and talented program that keeps the regular curriculum but allows students to move through it more quickly.

Accountability. The process of requiring students to demonstrate mastery of the topics they study as measured by standardized tests, as well as holding educators at all levels responsible for students' performance.

Action research. A form of applied research designed to answer a specific school- or classroom-related question.

Adequate Yearly Progress (AYP). A provision of No Child Left Behind that requires students to demonstrate progress in statewide tests toward meeting state standards.

Administrators. People responsible for the day-to-day operation of a school.

Advanced placement classes. Courses taken in high school that allow students to earn college credit, making college less time-consuming and expensive.

Allocated time. The amount of time a teacher designates for a particular content area or topic.

Alternative licensure. A shorter route to licensure for those who already possess a bachelor's degree.

American Federation of Teachers (AFT). The nation's second largest teacher professional organization, founded in 1916 and affiliated with the AFL-CIO, a major national labor union.

Assessment. The process teachers use to gather information and make decisions about students' learning and development.

Assessment *for* learning. The use of assessment to support and increase student learning.

Assimilation. A process of socializing people so that they adopt dominant social norms and patterns of behavior.

Assistive technology. A set of adaptive tools that support students with disabilities in learning activities and daily life tasks.

At-risk students. Students in danger of failing to complete their education with the skills necessary to survive in modern society.

Autonomous morality. A stage of moral reasoning in which children develop rational ideas of fairness and see justice as a reciprocal process of treating others as they would want to be treated.

Autonomy. The capacity to control one's own professional life.

Axiology. The branch of philosophy that considers values and ethics.

B

Backward design. An approach to planning that begins with an objective, designs assessments to match the objective, and then creates learning activities to reach the objective.

Behaviorism. A view of learning suggesting that people respond primarily to influences in their environments.

Between-class ability grouping. Dividing all students in a given grade into high, medium, and low groups.

Bilingual maintenance language programs. Language programs that place the greatest emphasis on using and sustaining the first language.

Block grants. Federal monies provided to states and school districts with few restrictions for use.

Block scheduling. A high school scheduling option in which classes are longer but meet less frequently.

Buckley Amendment. A federal law, also called the Family Educational Rights and Privacy Act, that describes who may have access to a student's educational records.

Bullying. A systematic or repetitious abuse of power between students.

C

Career academy. An alternative to large, comprehensive high schools that places students in small, vocationally oriented learning communities.

Career ladder system. A professional-development system that provides teachers with opportunities to assume different leadership responsibilities in a school or district.

Career technical schools. Schools designed to provide students with education and job skills that will enable them to get a job immediately after high school.

Caring. A teacher's investment in the protection and development of the young people in his or her classes.

Categorical grants. Federal funds targeted for specific groups and designated purposes.

Censorship. The practice of prohibiting objectionable materials, such as certain books used in libraries or in academic classes.

Certification. Special recognition by a professional organization indicating that a person has met certain rigorous requirements specified by the organization.

Character education. A curriculum approach to developing student morality that emphasizes teaching and rewarding moral values and positive character traits, such as honesty and citizenship.

Charter schools. Alternative schools that are independently operated but publicly funded.

Classroom management. Comprehensive actions teachers take to create an environment that supports and facilitates both academic and social-emotional learning.

Closure. A form of review occurring at the end of a lesson.

Cognitive development. Changes in students' thinking as they mature and acquire experiences.

Cognitive psychology. A view of learners that suggests that they are thinking beings who are mentally active as they gather information, organize it to make sense of it, and store it in memory for future use.

Collaboration. Joint communication and decision making among educational professionals to create an optimal learning environment for students with exceptionalities.

Collective bargaining. The process that occurs when a local chapter of a professional organization negotiates with a school district over the rights of the teachers and the conditions of employment.

Common school movement. A historical attempt in the 1800s to make education available to all children in the United States.

Compensatory education programs. Government attempts to create more equal educational opportunities for disadvantaged youth.

Comprehensive high school. A secondary school that attempts to meet the needs of all students by housing them together and providing curricular options (e.g., vocational or college-preparatory programs) geared toward a variety of student ability levels and interests.

Constructivism. A view of learning that suggests that to make sense of their experiences, students construct their own understanding of the topics they study instead of having that understanding transmitted to them by someone else.

Cooperative learning. A set of instructional strategies used to help learners meet specific learning and social-interaction objectives in structured groups.

Copyright laws. Federal laws designed to protect the intellectual property of authors, including printed matter, videos, computer software, and various other types of original work.

Core curriculum. A common course of study for all students that includes basic skills and knowledge and is supported by essentialist philosophies.

Corporal punishment. The use of physical, punitive disciplinary actions to correct student misbehavior.

Credentials file. A collection of important personal documents teachers submit when they apply for teaching positions.

Cross-age tutoring. Peer tutoring in which older students work with younger ones.

Cultural diversity. The different cultures encountered in classrooms and how these cultural differences influence learning.

Culturally responsive classroom management. Classroom management that combines teachers' awareness of possible personal biases with knowledge of students' cultures.

Culturally responsive teaching. Instruction that acknowledges and accommodates cultural diversity.

Culture. The knowledge, attitudes, values, customs, and behavior patterns that characterize a social group.

Curriculum. Everything that teachers teach and students learn in schools. Also may include unintended outcomes from school experiences.

Cyber-bullying. The use of electronic media to harass or intimidate other students.

D

Decision making. Problem solving in ill-defined situations, based on professional knowledge.

De jure **segregation.** Segregation resulting from laws, such as those existing in many states that created schools that were supposedly "separate but equal."

De facto **segregation.** Segregation resulting from individuals' private choices, primarily from housing, or where people live.

Desists. Verbal or nonverbal communications teachers use to stop a behavior.

Development. The physical, intellectual, moral, emotional, and social changes that occur in students as a result of their maturation and experience.

Developmental programs. Programs that accommodate differences in children's development by allowing them to acquire skills and abilities at their own pace through direct experiences.

Digital portfolio. A collection of materials contained in an electronic file that makes the information accessible to potential viewers.

Direct instruction. An instructional strategy designed to teach essential knowledge and skills through teacher explanation and modeling followed by student practice and feedback.

Disabilities. Functional limitations or an inability to perform a certain act, such as hear or walk.

Discipline. Teachers' responses to student misbehavior.

Discrepancy model of identification. One method of identifying students with exceptionalities that focuses on differences between classroom performance and tests, achievement and intelligence tests, or subtests within tests.

Distance education. Organized instructional programs in which teachers and learners, though physically separated, are connected over the Internet.

Drill-and-practice programs. Software designed to provide students with extensive practice with feedback in learning basic skills.

Due process. A set of legal guidelines, based on the Fourteenth Amendment to the Constitution, that must be followed to protect individuals from arbitrary or capricious actions by those in authority.

E

Early childhood education. A general term encompassing a range of educational programs for young children, including infant intervention and enrichment programs, nursery schools, public and private prekindergartens and kindergartens, and federally funded Head Start programs.

Effective school. A school in which learning for all students is maximized.

Effective teaching. Instruction that maximizes learning by actively involving students in meaningful learning activities.

Engaged time. The time students spend actively involved in learning activities. Also called *time on task*.

English as a second language (ESL) programs. Language programs emphasizing rapid transition to English through content-area instruction that provides additional assistance for ELL students.

English classical school. A free secondary school designed to meet the needs of boys not planning to attend college.

English language learners (ELLs). Students whose first language isn't English and who need help in learning to speak, read, and write in English.

Enrichment. A gifted and talented program that provides richer and more varied content through strategies that supplement usual grade-level work.

Epistemology. The branch of philosophy that examines questions of how we come to know what we know.

Equitable distribution. The practice of calling on all students—both volunteers and nonvolunteers—as equally as possible.

Essential teaching skills. Abilities that all teachers, including those in their first year, should have in order to help students learn.

Essentialism. An educational philosophy suggesting that a critical core of knowledge and skills exists that all people should possess.

Establishment clause. The clause of the First Amendment that prohibits the establishment of a national religion.

Ethics. Sets of moral standards for acceptable professional behavior.

Ethnicity. A person's ancestry; the way individuals identify themselves with the nation they or their ancestors came from.

Explicit curriculum. The stated curriculum found in textbooks, curriculum guides, and standards, as well as other planned formal educational experiences.

External morality. A stage of moral reasoning in which children view rules as fixed, permanent, and enforced by authority figures.

Extracurriculum. The part of the curriculum consisting of learning experiences that go beyond the core of students' formal studies.

Extrinsic motivation. Motivation to engage in a behavior to receive some incentive.

Extrinsic rewards. Rewards that come from outside, such as job security and vacations.

F

Fair-use guidelines. Policies that specify limitations in the use of copyrighted materials for educational purposes.

Feedback. Information about existing student understanding used to enhance future learning.

Focus. Concrete objects, pictures, models, materials displayed on the overhead, and information written on the board that attract and maintain attention during learning activities.

Formal assessment. The process of systematically gathering assessment information from every student.

Formative assessment. The process of using both informal and formal assessments to provide students with feedback about learning progress.

Formative evaluation. The process of gathering information and providing feedback that teachers can use to improve their practice.

Free exercise clause. The clause of the First Amendment that prohibits the government from interfering with individuals' rights to hold religious beliefs and freely practice religion.

Full-service schools. Schools that serve as family resource centers to provide a range of social and health services.

G

Gender bias. Discrimination based on gender that limits the growth possibilities of either boys or girls.

Gender-role identity. Differences in expectations and beliefs about appropriate roles and behaviors of the two sexes.

Gifted and talented. Students at the upper end of the ability continuum who need special services to reach their full potential.

Grade retention. The practice of requiring students to repeat a grade if they don't meet certain criteria.

Grievance. A formal complaint against an employer alleging unsatisfactory working conditions.

Guided discovery. An instructional strategy designed to teach concepts and other abstractions by presenting students with data and assisting them in finding patterns through teacher questioning.

H

Head Start. A federal compensatory education program designed to help 3- to 5-year-old disadvantaged children enter school ready to learn.

High collective efficacy. The belief by teachers that their school can make a difference in students' lives.

High-quality examples. Representations of content that ideally have all the information students need in order to learn a topic.

High-stakes tests. Standardized assessments that states and districts use to determine whether students will advance from one grade to another, graduate from high school, or have access to specific fields of study.

Homeschooling. An educational option in which parents educate their children at home.

Humanistic psychology. A psychological view that emphasizes the "whole person's development," including physical, social, emotional, thinking, and aesthetic dimensions.

I

Immersion programs. Language programs that emphasize rapid transition to English by exclusive use of the English language.

Implicit curriculum. The unstated and sometimes unintended aspects of the curriculum.

In loco parentis. A principle meaning "in place of the parents" that requires teachers to use the same judgment and care as parents in protecting the children under their supervision.

Inclusion. A comprehensive approach to educating students with exceptionalities that includes a systematic and coordinated web of services.

Individualized education program (IEP). An individually prescribed instructional plan collaboratively devised by special education and general education teachers, resource professionals, and parents (and sometimes the student).

Individualized family service plan (IFSP). A comprehensive service plan, similar to an IEP, that targets the families of young children (birth to 2 years) who are developmentally delayed.

Induction programs. Professional experiences for beginning teachers that provide assistance to ease the transition into teaching.

Informal assessment. The frequent and continual process of gathering information about students' learning and behavior, and making decisions based on that information.

Instruction. The strategies teachers use to help students reach learning goals in the curriculum.

Instructional alignment. The match between learning objectives, learning activities, and assessments.

Instructional strategies. Prescriptive approaches to teaching designed to help students acquire a deep understanding of specific forms of knowledge.

Instructional time. The amount of time left for teaching after routine management and administrative tasks are completed.

Integrated curriculum. A form of curriculum in which concepts and skills from various disciplines are combined and related.

Intelligence. The capacity to acquire and use knowledge, solve problems, and reason in the abstract.

Intelligent design. A theory suggesting that certain features of the universe and of living things are so complex that their existence is best explained by an intelligent cause, rather than by an undirected process such as natural selection.

Intervention. A teacher action designed to increase desired behaviors or eliminate student misbehavior and inattention.

Intrinsic motivation. Motivation to be involved in an activity for its own sake.

Intrinsic rewards. Rewards that come from within oneself and are personally satisfying for emotional or intellectual reasons.

J

Junior high schools. Schools designed for early adolescents that are similar in form and focus to high schools.

K

KIPP (Knowledge Is Power Program). A national network of charter schools that target at-risk students and that stress academics and feature extended school hours and mandatory homework.

L

Latchkey children. Children who go home to empty houses after school and who are left alone until parents arrive home from work.

Latin grammar school. An early college-preparatory school designed to help boys prepare for the ministry or, later, for a career in law.

Learning community. A classroom environment in which the teacher and students work together to help everyone learn.

Learning objectives. Statements that specify what students should know or be able to do with respect to a topic or course of study.

Learning styles. Students' personal approaches to learning, problem solving, and processing information.

Lecture-discussion. An instructional strategy designed to teach organized bodies of knowledge through teacher presentations and frequent questioning to monitor learning progress.

Licensure. The process by which a state evaluates the credentials of prospective teachers to ensure that they have achieved satisfactory levels of teaching competence and are morally fit to work with youth.

Local school board. A group of elected lay citizens responsible for setting policies that determine how a school district operates.

Logic. The branch of philosophy that examines the processes of deriving valid conclusions from basic principles.

Looping. The practice of keeping a teacher with one group of students for more than a year.

Lower class. The socioeconomic level composed of people who typically make less than $25,000 per year, have a high school education or less, and work in low-paying, entry-level jobs.

M

Magnet schools. Public schools that provide innovative or specialized programs and accept enrollment from students in all parts of a district.

Mainstreaming. The practice of moving students with exceptionalities from segregated settings into regular education classrooms.

Mentors. Experienced teachers who provide guidance and support for beginning teachers.

Merit pay. A supplement to a teacher's base salary used to reward exemplary performance.

Metacognition. Students' awareness of the ways they learn most effectively and their ability to control these factors.

Metaphysics (ontology). The branch of philosophy that considers what we know.

Middle class. Socioeconomic level composed of managers, administrators, and white-collar workers who perform nonmanual work.

Middle schools. Special schools targeting grades 6–8 and designed to meet the unique social, emotional, and intellectual needs of early adolescents.

Modeling. The tendency of people to imitate others' behaviors and attitudes.

Montessori method. An approach to early childhood education that emphasizes individual exploration and initiative through learning centers.

Moral development. Students' conceptions of right and wrong that change with experience and maturity.

Moral education. A curricular approach to teaching morality that emphasizes the development of students' moral reasoning.

Motivation. The energizing force behind student learning.

Multicultural education. A general term that describes a variety of strategies schools use to accommodate cultural differences in teaching and learning.

Multiple intelligences. A theory that suggests that overall intelligence is composed of eight relatively independent dimensions.

N

National Board for Professional Teaching Standards (NBPTS). A professional board that sets voluntary standards for experienced teachers to recognize those who possess extensive professional knowledge.

National Education Association (NEA). The nation's oldest and largest teacher professional organization, founded in 1857.

Negligence. A teacher's or other school employee's failure to exercise sufficient care in protecting students from injury.

No Child Left Behind. A 2001 reauthorization of the Elementary and Secondary Education Act that mandates state-level testing in reading and math for grades 3–8, and holds individual schools accountable for student achievement in these areas.

Normal schools. Two-year postsecondary institutions developed in the early 1800s to prepare prospective elementary teachers.

Normative philosophy. A description of the way professionals ought to practice.

Notoriety. The extent to which a teacher's behavior becomes known and controversial.

Null curriculum. Topics left out of the course of study.

O

Old Deluder Satan Act. A landmark piece of legislation designed to create scripture-literate citizens who would thwart Satan's trickery.

Organization. The set of teacher actions that maximizes the amount of time available for instruction.

Organized bodies of knowledge. Topics that connect facts, concepts, generalizations, and principles, and make the relationships among them explicit.

Overlapping. A teacher's ability to attend to two issues simultaneously.

P

Parenting style. General patterns of interacting with and disciplining children.

Pedagogical content knowledge. A part of teachers' professional knowledge that includes the ability to represent abstract concepts in ways that students understand.

Peer tutoring. A form of instructional practice in which students work with each other to provide practice and feedback.

Perennialism. An educational philosophy suggesting that nature—including human nature—is constant and that schools should teach classic knowledge.

Performance assessments. Direct examinations of student performance on tasks that are relevant to life outside of school.

Personal development. Changes in one's personality and the ability to manage one's feelings.

Personal response system. A classroom technology that allows teachers to assess students' understanding of content during lessons.

Personal teaching efficacy. Teachers' beliefs in their ability to help students learn, regardless of the conditions of the school or students' home lives.

Philosophy. The study of theories of knowledge, truth, existence, and morality.

Philosophy of education. A framework for thinking about educational issues, and a guide for professional practice.

Phonics. An approach to reading instruction that emphasizes the relationship between letters and the sounds they make and stresses learning basic letter–sound patterns and rules for sounding out words.

Piaget's Cognitive Developmental Theory. A theory that describes how student thinking about the world changes over time and how experiences contribute to development.

Portfolio assessment. The process of selecting collections of student work that both students and teachers evaluate using preset criteria.

Positive classroom climate. An environment in which learners feel physically and emotionally safe, personally connected to both their teacher and their peers, and worthy of love and respect.

Poverty thresholds. Household income levels that represent the lowest earnings needed to meet basic living needs.

Principal. The person who has the ultimate administrative responsibility for a school's operation.

Procedures. Management routines students follow in their daily learning activities.

Productive learning environment. A classroom that is orderly and that focuses on learning.

Professional ethics. A set of moral standards for acceptable professional behavior.

Professional portfolio. A collection of materials representative of one's work that provides a concrete and effective way to document competence and qualifications.

Professionalism. Characteristic of an occupation having a specialized body of knowledge with emphasis on autonomy, decision making, reflection, and ethical standards for conduct.

Progressivism. An educational philosophy emphasizing curricula that focus on real-world problem solving and individual development.

Prompting. Providing additional questions and cues when students fail to answer correctly.

Property taxes. Taxes determined by the value of property in a school district.

Punishment. The process of decreasing or eliminating undesired student behavior through some unpleasant consequence.

Q

Questioning frequency. The number of questions a teacher asks during a given period of instructional time.

R

Reduction in force. The elimination of teaching positions because of declining student enrollment or school funds. Also known as "riffing."

Reflection. The act of thinking about and analyzing one's actions.

Reforms. Suggested changes in teaching and teacher preparation intended to increase student learning.

Reliability. The consistency of assessment results.

Response to intervention model of identification (RTI). A method of identifying a learning disability that focuses on the specific classroom instructional adaptations teachers use and their success.

Resilient students. At-risk students who have been able to rise above adverse conditions to succeed in school and in other aspects of life.

Résumé. A document that provides a clear and concise overview of a person's job qualifications and work experience.

Rubric. A scoring scale that describes criteria for grading.

Rules. Guidelines that provide standards for acceptable classroom behavior.

S

Scaffolding. Instructional assistance on a task that teachers provide learners to produce high rates of success.

School district. An administrative unit within a state, defined by geographical boundaries, and legally responsible for the public education of children within those boundaries.

Schools within schools. Smaller learning communities within larger schools where both teachers and students feel more comfortable.

Segregation. The separation of students based on racial or socioeconomic criteria.

Self-fulfilling prophecy. A classroom phenomenon in which student efforts rise or fall to match teacher expectations.

Separate but equal. A policy of segregating minorities in education, transportation, housing, and other areas of public life if opportunities and facilities were considered equal to those of nonminorities. In education, the policy was evidenced by separate schools with different curricula, teaching methods, teachers, and resources.

Service learning. An approach to character education that combines service to the community with content-learning objectives.

Sexual harassment. Unwanted and/or unwelcome sexually oriented behavior that interferes with a student's sense of well-being.

Single-sex classes and schools. Classes and schools where boys and girls are segregated for part or all of the day.

Social development. Changes over time in the ways we relate to others.

Social institution. An organization with established structures and rules designed to promote certain goals.

Social reconstructionism. An educational philosophy suggesting that schools, teachers, and students should lead in alleviating social inequities in our society.

Socioeconomic status (SES). The combination of family income, parents' occupations, and level of parental education.

Special education. Instruction designed to meet the unique needs of students with exceptionalities.

Standardized tests. Assessment instruments given to large samples of students under uniform conditions and scored and reported according to uniform procedures.

Standards. Statements specifying what students should know or be able to do upon completing an area of study.

State board of education. The legal governing body that exercises general control and supervision of the schools in a state.

State office of education. Office responsible for implementing education policy within a state on a day-to-day basis.

State tuition tax-credit plans. A variation on school voucher programs in which parents are given tax credits for money they spend on private-school tuition.

Stereotype. A rigid, simplistic caricature of a particular group of people.

Students with exceptionalities. Learners who need special help and resources to reach their full potential.

Summative assessment. The process of assessing after instruction and using the results for making grading decisions.

Summative evaluation. The process of gathering information about a teacher's competence, usually for the purpose of making decisions about retention and promotion. Can also apply to students' academic progress.

Superintendent. The school district's head administrative officer who, along with his or her staff, is responsible for implementing policy in the district's schools.

T

Teach for America. An alternative licensure program that enables recent college graduates without state licensure to teach in hard-to-staff schools following a short period of training and supervision.

Teacher–student ratio. A measure of class size found by dividing the average number of students in classes by the number of classroom teachers.

Teaching contract. A legal employment agreement between a teacher and a local school board.

Tenure. A legal safeguard that provides job security by preventing teacher dismissal without cause.

Theory. A set of related principles that are based on observation and are used to explain the world around us.

Title I. A federal compensatory education program that funds supplemental education services for low-income students in elementary and secondary schools.

Tracking. Placing students in a series of different classes or curricula on the basis of ability and career goals.

Time-out. The process of removing a student from the class and physically isolating him or her in an area away from classmates.

Transition programs. Language programs that maintain the first language until students acquire sufficient English to succeed in English-only classrooms.

Tutorial. A software program that delivers an entire integrated instructional sequence similar to a teacher's instruction on the topic.

21st Century Skills. A curriculum reform movement that emphasizes the development of students' technological, analytical, and communication skills, which are needed to function effectively in the 21st century.

U

Underclass. People with low incomes who continually struggle with economic problems.

Upper class. The socioeconomic class composed of highly educated (usually a college degree), highly paid (usually above $170,000) professionals who make up about 5 percent of the population.

V

Validity. The extent to which assessment results are interpreted and used appropriately.

Virtual schools. Schools offering comprehensive K–12 courses that connect teachers and students over the Internet.

Voucher. A check or written document that parents can use to purchase educational services.

W

Wait-time. The period of silence after a question is asked and after a student is called on to answer.

War on Poverty. A general term for federal programs designed to eradicate poverty during the 1960s.

Weighted student formula. Funding that allocates resources within a district to schools on a per-school basis according to student needs.

Whole language. An approach to reading instruction that integrates reading into the total literacy process.

Within-class ability grouping. Dividing students in one classroom into ability groups.

Withitness. A teacher's awareness of what is going on in all parts of the classroom at all times and the communication of this awareness to students, both verbally and nonverbally.

Working class (also called *lower middle class*). The socioeconomic level composed of blue-color workers who perform manual labor.

Z

Zero-tolerance policies. Policies that call for students to receive automatic suspensions or expulsions as punishment for certain offenses, primarily those involving weapons, threats, or drugs.

Name Index

Abedi, J., 181, 425, 437
Ackerman, P., 139
Adler, M., 202
Akert, R., 312, 365
Alan Guttmacher Institute, 80, 338
Alberto, P., 367
Albright, M., 240
Alder, N., 93, 369
Alexander, L., 277
Alexander, P., 336
Allegretto, S., 74
Allen, J., 12
Allen, R., 242
Allington, R. L., 77
Alperstein, J. F., 116
Altman, L., 81
American Association of Unversity Women,
    82, 116–117, 343
American Educational Research
    Association, 436
American Federation of Teachers, 8, 9, 57,
    74, 275
American Psychological
    Association, 436
Amrein, A., 226, 436
Anagnostopoulos, D., 137
Anderman, E., 130, 378, 420
Anderman, E. A., 200
Anderson, J., 179
Anderson, K., 360
Anderson, L., 379, 380, 393
Anderson, L. W., 381
Andrade, H., 419, 421
Andreson, K., 274
Andrianaivo, S., 261
Anfara, V., 78, 118, 119, 360
Antil, L., 403
Apple, M., 338
Arbuthnot, K., 377
Arbuthnott, K., 142
Archer, J., 28, 38, 48, 93, 247, 257, 292
Archwamety, T., 149
Armour-Thomas, E., 22, 393, 424
Aronson, E., 312, 365
Aronson, J., 181
Atkins, R., 340
Attiel, A., 341
Augustine, C., 237

Bachman, J., 83
Bahrenburg, D., 222
Baines, L., 38
Baker, C., 279
Baker, D., 109
Bali, V., 137
Bandura, A., 386
Banks, J., 104, 106, 180, 181, 211, 343

Bankston, C., 182
Baratz-Snowdon, J., 36, 47, 227
Bardige, B., 78
Barnes, G., 328
Barnoski, L., 95
Barone, M., 114
Barr, R., 70, 94
Bartell, C., 52
Barton, P., 48, 78, 79, 91, 92
Bassett, P., 248
Battistich, V., 12, 352
Bauerlein, M., 212, 432
Bauman, S., 86, 87
Baumrind, D., 133
Bausch, M., 153
Bazelon, E., 75
Beckett, K., 36, 206
Belfield, C., 277
Bello, M., 36
Ben-Avie, M., 93, 184
Benner, A., 78
Bennett, C., 26, 111
Benson, P., 133
Berends, M., 383
Berg, S., 348
Berger, K., 86
Bergin, M., 341
Berk, L., 72, 77, 78, 81, 83, 88, 116, 133,
    137, 229, 232, 235, 237, 309
Berlin, A., 237
Berliner, D., 26, 36, 38, 56, 73, 171, 185,
    206, 213, 226, 254, 263, 264, 269, 270,
    436, 437
Bernstein, M., 299
Berry, B., 17
Berstein, J., 74
Betts, J., 272
Biddle, B., 75, 171, 226, 254, 263, 264,
    269, 270
Billings, L., 202
Birkeland, S., 38, 50
Bitter, G., 363
Black, P., 416
Black, S., 233, 237, 271, 328
Blair, J., 38, 62, 93
Blatchford, P., 248
Bloodworth, M., 131
Bloom, B., 380
Bohman, D., 261
Bohn, C., 355
Bolkan, J., 228
Bonawitz, E., 232
Bondi, J., 235, 320
Borja, R., 431
Borko, H., 14, 19, 34, 371
Borman, G., 53, 94, 95, 184, 187
Borman, G. D., 53

Bos, C., 141, 151, 152, 153
Botstein, L., 239
Bottoms, G., 239
Boult, B., 362
Bowen, N., 362
Bowman, D., 83, 180, 276
Boyd-Zaharias, J., 243
Boyle, O., 113, 114
Bracey, G., 47, 72, 91, 106, 183, 200, 232,
    275, 276, 277, 436
Bradley, A., 299
Bradley, K. D., 135
Bradshaw, C., 246
Bransford, J., 15, 16, 19, 34, 36, 56, 79,
    171, 206, 227, 383, 396
Brehm, K., 92
Brekeimans, M., 365
Brewer, D., 417
Brimley, V., 21, 75, 167, 254, 257, 258,
    263, 264, 265, 266, 268, 270, 271
Britton, T., 52
Broh, B., 328
Brooke, R., 21
Brookhart, S., 414, 416, 421, 423, 426
Brophy, J., 26, 50, 51, 95, 136, 141, 142,
    143, 151, 175, 229, 245, 351, 355, 358,
    378, 384, 386, 389, 390, 393, 394, 396,
    404, 405
Brown, A., 383
Brown, D., 324, 369, 370
Brown, H., 274
Brown, K., 78
Brown, P., 248
Brown, R., 92
Brown, S., 118
Brown-Chidsey, R., 150
Brownell, K., 418
Bruning, R., 212, 244, 331, 385
Bryan, L., 339
Buchanan, B., 265, 268
Buckley, J., 46
Bukowski, W., 133
Bullough, J., Jr., 7, 71, 75, 77, 85
Burbules, N., 342
Bureau of International Information
    Programs, 178
Burkam, D., 230
Burns, M., 423
Burris, C., 141
Burroughs, G., 40
Burstyn, J., 368
Bushaw, W., 26, 54, 89, 200, 263, 333, 339,
    351, 437
Butin, D., 340
Button, H., 178
Bylund, R., 21
Byrnes, J., 247

Subject Index

Knowledge Covered in the PRAXIS™ Principles of Learning and Teaching Tests	Chapter Topic Aligned with Knowledge Covered in the PRAXIS™ Principles of Learning and Teaching Tests
B. Planning instruction	**Ch. 13** Planning for effective teaching Ensuring instructional alignment **Ch. 14** Planning and constructing tests Alignment with standards and objectives
C. Assessment strategies	**Ch. 8** Frequent monitoring of student progress **Ch. 11** Standards and accountability **Ch. 13** Planning for assessment **Ch. 14** Assessment in an era of reform Grading and reporting Standards, accountability, and assessment

III. TEACHER PROFESSIONALISM (APPROXIMATELY 22% OF TOTAL TEST)

A. The reflective practitioner	**Ch. 1** Characteristics of professionalism Emphasis on decision making and reflection **Ch. 2** Induction and mentoring programs Teacher evaluation INTASC: A beginning point for teacher development Membership in professional organizations Becoming a teacher-leader National Board for Professional Teaching Standards **Each Chapter** Decision making: Defining yourself as a professional
B. The larger community	**Ch. 1** Working with parents and other caregivers Collaborating with colleagues **Ch. 2** Membership in professional organizations Becoming a teacher-leader **Ch. 3** It takes a village: The community-based approach to working with at-risk children **Ch. 8** Strong parental involvement **Ch. 12** Benefits of parental involvement Strategies for involving parents Using technology to communicate with parents

IV. COMMUNICATION TECHNIQUES (APPROXIMATELY 11% OF THE TEST)

A. Effective verbal and nonverbal communication	**Ch. 1** Creating productive learning environments Collaborative colleague **Ch. 3** Effective teachers for at-risk students **Ch. 4** Accommodating cultural interaction patterns **Ch. 5** Instructional responses to learning styles **Ch. 12** Using technology to communicate with parents **Ch. 13** High expectations Modeling and enthusiasm Questioning **Ch. 14** Grading and reporting
B. Cultural and gender differences in communication	**Ch. 3** Effective teachers for at-risk students **Ch. 4** Culturally responsive teaching Language diversity in the classroom Gender and classrooms **Ch. 5** Learning styles: Implications for teachers Students with exceptionalities: Implications for teachers **Ch. 12** Strategies for involving parents **Ch. 13** Questioning Effective instruction in urban classrooms
C. Stimulating discussion and responses in the classroom	**Ch. 1** Creating productive learning environments **Ch. 3** Effective teachers for at-risk students **Ch. 4** Culturally responsive teaching **Ch. 5** Instructional responses to learning styles **Ch. 12** Questioning Lecture discussions Cooperative learning Guided discovery

Principle	Description of Teacher Performance	Chapter and Topic
1. Knowledge of subject	The teacher understands the central concepts, tools of inquiry, and structures of the discipline(s) he or she teaches and can create learning experiences that make these aspects of subject matter meaningful for students.	Ch. 2 The INTASC Standards Ch. 7 Philosophies of education Ch. 11 The explicit curriculum Ch. 12 Classroom management Ch. 13 Planning for effective teaching Planning for assessment Instructional strategies
2. Learning and human development	The teacher understands how children learn and develop, and can provide learning opportunities that support their intellectual, social and personal development.	Ch. 1 Creating productive learning environments Ch. 5 Developmental differences in the classroom Ch. 8 Early childhood programs, elementary schools, junior highs, and middle schools, and high schools What is an effective school? Ch. 11 Curriculum in the elementary schools Curriculum in middle schools Curriculum in junior high and high schools Ch. 12 Developmental differences in students Ch. 13 Student motivation and effective teaching Instructional strategies
3. Adapting instruction	The teacher understands how students differ in their approaches to learning and creates instructional opportunities that are adapted to diverse learners.	Ch. 3 Changes in American families The influence of socioeconomic factors on students Changes in our students At-risk students Ch. 4 Cultural diversity Language diversity Gender Learning styles Ch. 5 Developmental differences in the classroom Differences in ability Learners with exceptionalities Technology and Teaching: Employing technology to support learners with disabilities **Each Chapter** Exploring Diversity
4. Strategies	The teacher understands and uses a variety of instructional strategies to encourage students' development of critical thinking, problem solving, and performance skills.	Ch. 3 Effective teachers for at-risk students Ch. 4 Culturally responsive teaching Language diversity in the classroom Gender and classrooms Ch. 5 Learning styles: Implications for teachers Students with exceptionalities: Implications for teachers Ch. 13 Specify learning objectives Questioning Direct instruction Lecture discussions Cooperative learning Guided discovery Capitalizing on technology in instruction
5. Motivation and management	The teacher uses an understanding of individual and group motivation and behavior to create a learning environment that encourages positive social interaction, active engagement in learning, and self-motivation.	Ch. 1 Creating productive learning environments Ch. 3 Effective teachers for at-risk students Ch. 4 Culturally responsive teaching Language diversity in the classroom Gender and classrooms Ch. 5 Learning styles: Implications for teachers Students with exceptionalities: Implications for teachers Ch. 8 High collective efficacy Interactive instruction Safe and orderly environment

Principle	Description of Teacher Performance	Chapter and Topic
5. Motivation and management (continued)		**Ch. 12** Caring Creating communities of learners Creating a positive classroom climate **Ch. 13** Student motivation and effective teaching Personal teaching efficacy Positive teacher expectations Modeling and enthusiasm Questioning Effective feedback
6. Communication skills	The teacher uses knowledge of effective verbal, nonverbal, and media communication techniques to foster active inquiry, collaboration, and supportive interaction in the classroom.	**Ch. 1** Working with parents and other caregivers Collaborating with colleagues **Ch. 3** Effective teachers for at-risk students **Ch. 4** Accommodating cultural interaction patterns **Ch. 5** Learning styles **Ch. 12** Creating communities of learners Creating a positive classroom climate Using technology to communicate with parents **Ch. 13** Positive teacher expectations Questioning
7. Planning	The teacher plans instruction based upon knowledge of subject matter, students, the community, and curriculum goals.	**Ch. 1** Creating productive learning environments Teaching in an era of reform **Ch. 3** Effective teachers for at-risk students **Ch. 4** Culturally responsive teaching Language diversity in the classroom Gender and classrooms **Ch. 5** Learning styles: Implications for teachers Students with exceptionalities: Implications for teachers **Ch. 11** Standards and accountability **Ch. 13** Planning for effective teaching Specifying learning objectives Ensuring instructional alignment
8. Assessment	The teacher understands and uses formal and informal assessment strategies to evaluate and ensure the continuous intellectual, social and physical development of the learner.	**Ch. 8** Frequent monitoring of student progress **Ch. 11** Standards and accountability **Ch. 13** Feedback **Ch. 14** The need for assessment in an era of reform
9. Commitment	The teacher is a reflective practitioner who continually evaluates the effects of his/her choices and actions on others (students, parents, and other professionals in the learning community) and who actively seeks out opportunities to grow professionally.	**Ch. 1** Characteristics of professionalism Emphasis on decision making and reflection **Ch. 2** INTASC: A beginning point for teacher development Induction and mentoring programs Teacher evaluation Membership in professional organizations Becoming a teacher-leader National Board for Professional Teaching Standards **Each Chapter** Decision making: Defining yourself as a professional
10. Partnership	The teacher fosters relationships with school colleagues, parents, and agencies in the larger community to support students' learning and well-being.	**Ch. 1** Working with parents and other caregivers Collaborating with colleagues **Ch. 2** Membership in professional organizations Becoming a teacher-leader **Ch. 3** It takes a village: The community based approach to working with at-risk children **Ch. 8** Strong parental involvement **Ch. 12** Benefits of parental involvement Strategies for involving parents Using technology to communicate with parents